THE ROUTLEDGE COMPANION
TO POSTMODERNISM

What does 'postmodernism' mean? Why is it so important? Now in its second edition, thoroughly revised, updated and expanded with new material, *The Routledge Companion to Postmodernism* combines a series of in-depth background chapters with a body of A to Z entries to create an authoritative yet readable guide to the complex world of postmodernism. Following full-length articles on postmodernism and philosophy, politics, feminism, religion, post-colonialism, lifestyles, television, and other postmodern essentials, readers will find a wide range of alphabetically organized entries on the people, terms and theories connected with postmodernism. Students interested in any aspect of postmodernist thought will find this an indispensable resource.

Stuart Sim is Professor of Critical Theory at the University of Sunderland. His work has been translated into nine languages, and he is a Fellow of the English Association. Publications include *Post-Marxism: An Intellectual History* (2000) and *Fundamentalist World: The New Dark Age of Dogma* (2004).

You may also be interested in the following Routledge Student Reference titles:

Cultural Theory: The Key Concepts
Edited by Andrew Edgar and Peter Sedgwick

Cultural Theory: The Key Thinkers
Andrew Edgar and Peter Sedgwick

Communication, Cultural and Media Studies: The Key Concepts, 3rd edn
John Hartley

The Concise Encyclopedia of Western Philosophy and Philosophers, 3rd edn
Edited by J. O. Urmson and Jonathan Rée

Contemporary British Novelists
Nick Rennison

Fifty Key Contemporary Thinkers
John Lechte

The Routledge Companion to Feminism and Postfeminism
Edited by Sarah Gamble

Post-Colonial Studies: The Key Concepts
Bill Ashcroft, Gareth Griffiths and Helen Tiffin

Semiotics: The Basics
Daniel Chandler

THE ROUTLEDGE COMPANION TO POSTMODERNISM

Second edition

Edited by
Stuart Sim

Routledge
Taylor & Francis Group

LONDON AND NEW YORK

First published in the United Kingdom 1998 by Icon Books Ltd
as *The Icon Critical Dictionary of Postmodern Thought*

First published in the United States of America 1999 by Routledge
as *The Routledge Critical Dictionary of Postmodern Thought*

Reissued 2001 by Routledge
as *The Routledge Companion to Postmodernism*

Second edition published 2005
by Routledge
2 Park Square, Milton Park, Abingdon, Oxon OX14 4RN

Simultaneously published in the USA and Canada
by Routledge
270 Madison Ave, New York, NY 10016

Routledge is an imprint of the Taylor & Francis Group

© 1998, 2001, 2005 Stuart Sim

Typeset in Times New Roman by
BOOK NOW Ltd
Printed and bound in Great Britain by
MPG Books Ltd, Bodmin

British Library Cataloguing in Publication Data
A catalogue record for this book is available from the British Library

Library of Congress Cataloging in Publication Data
The Routledge companion to postmodernism / edited by Stuart Sim.— 2nd ed.
p. cm. — (The Routledge companions)
Rev. ed. of: Routledge critical dictionary of postmodern thought. 1999.
Includes bibliographical references and index.
1. Postmodernism. I. Sim, Stuart. II. Routledge critical dictionary of postmodern thought.
III. Series.
B831.2.R68 2004
149'.97—dc22   2004009640

ISBN 0–415–33358–X (hbk)
ISBN 0–415–33359–8 (pbk)

CONTENTS

PREFACE TO THE SECOND EDITION

FROM THE MODERN TO THE POSTMODERN

It is a cliché by now to say that we live in a postmodern world, and indeed 'postmodern' has become one of the most used, and abused, words in the language. Yet it is striking that few people can say with any sense of assurance what that term 'postmodern' actually means or involves. Some theorists have suggested that it is as much a mood or attitude of mind as anything else, but they do seem to be agreed that it is widely in evidence. *The Routledge Companion to Postmodernism* is designed to outline what the phenomenon is, and where to find it.

In a general sense, postmodernism is to be regarded as a rejection of many, if not most, of the cultural certainties on which life in the West has been structured over the past couple of centuries. It has called into question our commitment to cultural 'progress' (that national economies must continue to grow, that the quality of life must keep improving indefinitely, etc.), as well as the political systems that have underpinned this belief. Postmodernists often refer to the 'Enlightenment project', meaning the liberal humanist ideology that has come to dominate Western culture since the eighteenth century: an ideology that has striven to bring about the emancipation of mankind from economic want and political oppression. In the view of postmodernists this project, laudable though it may have been at one time, has in its turn come to oppress humankind, and to force it into certain set ways of thought and action not always in its best interests. It is therefore to be resisted, and postmodernists are invariably critical of universalizing theories ('grand narratives' or 'metanarratives' as they have been dubbed by the philosopher Jean-François Lyotard), as well as being anti-authoritarian in their outlook. To move from the modern to the postmodern is to embrace scepticism about what our culture stands for and strives for.

Since the first edition of this work was published in 1998, the cultural context in which postmodernism operates has changed quite dramatically. The events of 9/11 demonstrate that grand narratives can reinvent themselves, and the grand narrative of religious fundamentalism is now an acknowledged threat to global peace. One could argue that this is a phenomenon which undermines many of the claims of postmodernism, revealing these to be over-optimistic as to the extent of the cultural change that has occurred in recent times; equally, one could see it as evidence of why we need postmodernism to combat this essentially regressive tendency. The remainder of this introduction will look at postmodernism in a wider historical context, including recent challenges to its ethos, to argue that what postmodernism represents is still valuable and that it is more than just a brief historical episode of late twentieth-century culture that has now exhausted its cultural role. The postmodern is still with us: a positive aspect of our culture that deserves our support. We set out, therefore, to define and defend the postmodern.

A BRIEF HISTORY OF A CONCEPT

The first recorded use of the word 'postmodern' is back in the 1870s, and although it proceeds to crop up periodically over the next few decades, sometimes with positive, sometimes with negative connotations, it is only in the latter half of the twentieth century that it comes to take on the precise meaning of a reaction against modernism and modernity. We can run through some of those usages briefly to see how the concept achieves its current form.

In the 1870s the English painter John Watkins Chapman suggested that any art that went beyond Impressionism, the revolutionary new art style of the period, would be definable as 'postmodern painting'. By 1917 'postmodern' was the term chosen by the author Rudolf Pannwitz to describe the new form of militaristic and anti-humanist culture developing in a Europe ravaged by war. In the 1920s and 1930s the term had more positive overtones in the work of the American theologian Bernard Iddings Bell, for whom a postmodernist was someone who had turned his back on the secular modern world and embraced religious faith instead. A postmodernist was, in Bell's words, 'intellectually humble and spiritually hungry'. Bell is certainly anti-modernist, but not in the sense of the postmodernists of our own day. The eminent historian Arnold Toynbee returned to the pessimistic application, when in *A Study of History* he spoke of the period from 1875 onwards as the 'post-Modern Age of Western history'; an age marked by cultural decline as evidenced in its two 'world' wars. A postmodern world was an altogether less secure and inviting place to live in than the modern one (1475–1875) it had replaced. Eventually, 'postmodern' begins to take on the meaning of 'ultra-modern', with the architectural theorist Joseph Hudnut deploying it in that fashion to describe the new prefabricated buildings being produced in the aftermath of the Second World War. Hudnut's postmodern man was unsentimental, and looked to science to improve the quality of his life.

It has proved to be in the field of architecture that postmodernism has taken root as a conceptual term. The architectural theorist Charles Jencks has done more than anyone to popularise postmodernism as a theoretical concept, particularly in the series of editions of his best-known book *The Language of Postmodern Architecture* (first edition, 1977). Jencks was highly critical of modern architecture, which he thought had lost touch with the general public. It was the so-called 'International Style', with its severe tower blocks constructed of concrete and glass, all straight lines and lacking in ornamentation, with which Jencks took issue. As the name indicated, this had come to dominate architectural practice worldwide, with nearly all large cities featuring at least some buildings in that style. Jencks famously claimed that when one of the most representative examples of the style, the award-winning Pruitt-Igoe housing complex in St Louis, Missouri, was demolished in 1972, modern architecture died. Pruitt-Igoe had proved a failure, declining into a vandalized shell of its former self in barely twenty years. For Jencks, that was a deeply symbolic history, the clear message being that the public had rejected the modernist creed encoded in a scheme like Pruitt-Igoe. Henceforth, architects were warned to come up with buildings in which the public would feel comfortable rather than alienated; in other words, buildings that could be described as 'double coded': able to appeal to both professional architects and the general public. The trend towards eclecticism in architecture, with old and new styles being freely mixed, was given its greatest boost by Jencks, and its products can now be found in most major cities (ironically enough, it has the makings of a new 'International Style' in this respect, if a less programmatic one than the previous).

Although architecture is arguably the area in which postmodernism first became a cause as such, the reaction to modernity and modernism has been widespread, expressing itself in a variety of ways. An ecology movement developed over the later twentieth century, concerned at the effect of technological progress on the environment. 'Green' political parties were formed in many Western European countries in consequence. Creative artists began to rebel against the strictures of the modernist style, which demanded, for example, abstraction in art and dissonant non-tonal composition in music. Many creative artists reverted to older styles that audiences felt more comfortable with, rather as Charles Jencks was calling on architects to do in their field. Philosophers and cultural theorists reacted against theories such as structuralism, which reduced the world to a series of interlinked systems with their own internal dynamic, or 'deep structure'. The workings of the entire world could be mapped out in terms of these deep structures, which dictated how all systems operated. One unfortunate consequence of the theory was that it seemed to deny the existence of free will; as Roland Barthes famously remarked of language, it spoke through human beings, suggesting that we were no more than channels for the actions of mysterious external forces. Structuralism's dominance in mid-century intellectual enquiry (particularly in France) led to a reaction, collectively called poststructuralism, which increasingly came to challenge the assumptions on which structuralist analysis rested. Whereas structuralists emphasized similarity and interconnectedness, poststructuralists emphasised difference and open-endedness. Structuralism was a universalizing theory, poststructuralists spent their time demonstrating how such theories must always fail: the battle lines were drawn.

For our purposes here, postmodernism will be taken to encompass figures and debates within poststructuralism as well. Poststructuralism is a term that refers to a wide range of responses to the structuralist paradigm – responses such as the philosophically oriented 'deconstruction' of Jacques Derrida, the various 'archaeological' and 'genealogical' enquiries into cultural history of Michel Foucault, and the 'difference feminism' of such theorists as Luce Irigaray.

Poststructuralism has been an influential part of the cultural scene since the 1960s, but nowadays it can be seen to be part of a more general reaction to authoritarian ideologies and political systems that we define as postmodernism. We might say that postmodernism subsumes poststructuralism, and we shall proceed on that basis in this volume.

FROM POSTMODERNISM TO REACTION

Postmodernism is therefore a principled reaction to modernism and modernity and what are regarded as their social and political failings, but since this book was first published it has become apparent that there can be large-scale reactions in turn against the postmodern ethos. Religious fundamentalism is only the most obvious example of a grand narrative reasserting itself in the face of what it considers to be unacceptable cultural trends, this time the drift towards moral relativism. A host of other grand narratives can also be instanced as in a process of reassertion: market fundamentalism, eco-fundamentalism, various kinds of political and nationalistic fundamentalism, to name the most prominent. I talk about these and others in my book *Fundamentalist World: The New Dark Age of Dogma* (2004), but it is worth running through some of them briefly here to discover what they can tell us about the current state of postmodernism as a cultural movement.

Postmodern theorists like to claim that we have crossed a watershed into a new world order where institutional authority no longer commands automatic respect, but it is clear that not just modernity but pre-modernity is fighting back and that grand narratives can still speak meaningfully to large sections of the world's population. Islamic fundamentalism is a very significant global force, seemingly able to claim the support, whether tacit or overt, of a majority of Muslim communities in its struggle against Western cultural imperialism. Several Islamic states, or significant areas of these states, have reverted in recent years to shariah law, where the Q'ran is used as the foundation for the legal and political systems. Adherence to shariah law turns nation-states into theocracies, in which religious doctrine controls all aspects of human existence. Grand narrative in such cases is embraced with an enthusiasm which the postmodernist will find deeply disturbing. Institutional authority is once again accepted unquestioningly, obeyed blindly, and allowed to direct the individual's life in the name of a larger cause. Faith, rather than reason or scepticism, becomes the basis of the cultural process. In its more extreme form – as with the Taliban regime in Afghanistan – Islamic fundamentalism is effectively a return to a pre-modern society, where almost all the modern world is rejected (with the significant exception of its weaponry).

Christian fundamentalism has been no less active of late, as witness the infiltration of the Republican Party in America by the Christian Right. Activists have led campaigns at local, state, and national level to curb liberalizing legislation in areas such as sexual behaviour and abortion. Any move towards cultural relativism is bitterly opposed: conformity not difference is the ideal sought. Christian fundamentalism also has interesting, and more than somewhat bizarre, links with Zionist fundamentalism, since its theories of the Millennium demand a strong Jewish presence in the Holy Land (as was), in order for their conversion to be achieved – the conversion of the Jews being one of the critical signs of the imminence of the Second Coming. Zionist fundamentalists are happy to go along with this notion, as it fits in with their own desire to recreate Israel as it was in biblical times, the land of God's 'chosen people' (Palestinians excluded, of course). The close political links between America and Israel owe at least something to the successful lobbying by the Christian Right amongst high-ranking Republican politicians. The grand narrative of the Bible is held to provide all the information we need for the unfolding of human history. Cultural relativism is nowhere to be found on the agenda.

In the economic realm market fundamentalism is the current paradigm, and to its adherents it is a matter of blind faith, too. The term 'market fundamentalism' was coined by the international financier George Soros to describe the unrestricted, unregulated laissez-faire capitalism favoured by the International Monetary Fund (IMF) and the World Bank. These institutions tend to impose this model on failing economies around the globe, sometimes, as in the case of Argentina, with quite disastrous results. Market fundamentalism demands the dismantling of the state sector (encouraging privatization programmes for all state-owned industries), low interest rates, and an open market for capital. When Argentina followed such prescriptions, as directed, it led to the collapse of the currency and banking system; but to the IMF and the World Bank the needs of the market came first. Once more, faith was to be placed in the grand narrative at the expense of its impact on individuals. The market was to be regarded as an authority which could not be called into question.

Political and nationalistic fundamentalism put their trust in grand narratives, of the political system or national identity, that assume an aura of total authority. For thinkers like Francis Fukuyama, Western liberal democracy is the only acceptable political system: the system which has unequivocally established its superiority over all others. We have reached the 'end of history', and it will only be a matter of time before everyone conforms to the Western model. Even more insidiously, the Western states at the forefront of this cultural trend often espouse a nationalism which seeks to keep the relevant national identity as pure as possible and immigration from other poorer parts of the world at a minimum. Dissenting views are not tolerated, and indeed intolerance is a general feature of grand narratives. Postmodernism, with its commitment to dissent, pluralism, cultural difference, and scepticism towards authority, finds itself in direct conflict with such systems, which substitute the authoritarian collective will for the individual. When eco-fundamentalists blow up ski resorts because of the threat they pose to local wildlife, or when pro-life advocates bomb abortion clinics, they do so in the name of grand narratives which are taken to represent universal truths overriding all opposition. In today's world, postmodernism confronts an array of such narratives, modern and pre-modern, that refuse to accept any challenge to their authority. The postmodern commitments just mentioned have a definite political edge.

DEFINING AND DEFENDING THE POSTMODERN

Postmodernism remains a notoriously diffuse cultural movement, but it does mean something – and does stand for something. This volume will show what that meaning is, in all its breadth and variety, and why so many thinkers and creative artists consider it to be worth defending. If the cultural context has altered in the past six years, the need to argue the case for the postmodern has not.

STRUCTURE AND SCOPE OF THE VOLUME

Dictionaries aim to provide reference information, and *The Routledge Companion to Postmodernism* comprises a critical dictionary of postmodern thought that is more ambitious than a standard reference dictionary. It is divided into two parts: (I) Essays, and (II) Names and terms. Part I consists of fifteen extended essays (3,000–5,000 words) tracing both the sources and the impact of postmodern thought, and includes such topics as 'Postmodernism and philosophy', 'Postmodernism and politics', 'Postmodernism and feminism', and 'Postmodernism and science and technology', as well as a series of essays dealing with postmodernism and the arts (architecture, literature, film, music, etc.). The concluding essay, 'Postmodernism, modernity and the tradition of dissent', draws together the various strands of criticism of postmodernism, in order to demonstrate just how controversial the movement has turned out to be, and how much opposition it has managed to arouse even in such a relatively short time. Collectively these essays establish the breadth of postmodern thought that has transformed the cultural landscape of the late twentieth and early twenty-first century.

In Part II, the reader will find brief portraits of the leading theorists and creative artists who go to make up the postmodern world and its debates (well over one hundred figures listed), including influential voices from the past whose work either has been reappropriated by postmodernism, or has in some significant way informed its debates. It is difficult to engage with postmodernism without also engaging with, for example, the work of Marx, Kant or Nietzsche. Though brief, the portraits are pithy and informative, presenting the most relevant details of each figure's career and ideas, and placing him or her in the development of the postmodern movement. Alongside the portraits are short definitions of the key terms associated with postmodern thought. The object of the book is to provide accessible material on what can appear to be a forbiddingly complex and disparate area of discourse: a guide to 'who's who' and 'what's what' in postmodernism.

HOW TO USE THIS VOLUME

To facilitate cross-reference, all the entries in Part II (both names and terms) are picked out in bold when they appear elsewhere, and a comprehensive index is also provided to enable readers to follow up the various appearances of specific names and terms over the course of the volume as a whole, should they so wish. If, for example, you consult the entry on postmodernism, you will encounter the name of the philosopher Jean-François Lyotard, who features in an entry of his own. This entry makes it clear that Lyotard is one of the key figures in the development of postmodern philosophy, which leads you towards the opening essay 'Postmodernism and philosophy'. Throughout that essay various other names will appear, picked out in bold type, such as Gilles **Deleuze**, Jacques **Derrida** and Michel **Foucault**. Their entries in turn will deal with concepts and theories (again in bold), such as **desiring-machines**, **deconstruction** and **genealogy**, which can then be followed up for more detail; as can other names mentioned in the course of these same entries (Félix **Guattari**, Roland **Barthes**, etc.). The index will provide yet more references to consult on any of the entries above.

The two sections of the *Companion* are designed to interact, allowing more or less detailed information to be accessed, depending on the reader's requirements. You may merely want to refresh your memory as to the definition of a term, or brush up on the work of a particular thinker, or go into more depth in, say, philosophy. Alternatively, you may simply wish to range around the various networks of information the book offers, in order to build up your own particular picture of what postmodernism involves; dictionaries provide just that creative possibility for each individual reader, and the choice is yours.

CONTRIBUTORS

The contributors to this volume are drawn from both academic and professional life, and are acknowledged experts in their particular fields. Their collective aim has been to map the postmodern such that its richness, diversity and cultural significance can be appreciated by the general reader. Initials are given to identify A–Z entry writers. The contributors are, in alphabetical order:

Pamela Sue Anderson (Regents' Park College, Oxford) [PSA]
Adrian Baker [AB]
Eleanor Byrne (Manchester Metropolitan University)
Peter Dempsey (University of Sunderland) [PD]
Brian Dillon (University of Kent) [BD]
Sara Dodd (Open University) [SD]
Antony Easthope (late Manchester Metropolitan University) [AE]

Sarah Gamble (University of Northumbria) [SG]
Iain Hamilton Grant (University of the West of England) [IHG]
Sean Griffiths [SGr]
Valerie Hill (University of Coventry)
Stephanie Hodgson-Wright (University of Huddersfield) [SH-W]
Sam Jacob [SJ]
Barry Lewis (University of Sunderland) [BL]
Karin Littau (University of Essex) [KL]
Anthony McGowan [AM]
Diane Morgan (University College Northampton)
Marc O'Day (University College, Suffolk)
Elisa Oliver [EO]
Danielle Ramsay (University of Sunderland) [DR]
Derek B. Scott (University of Salford)
Stuart Sim (University of Sunderland) [SS]
Lloyd Spencer (Trinity and All Saints, Leeds) [LS]
John Storey (University of Sunderland) [JS]
John Strachan (University of Sunderland) [JStr]
Sue Thornham (University of Sussex) [ST]
Colin Trodd (University of Manchester) [CT]
David Walker (University of Northumbria) [DW]
Nigel Watson (University of Sunderland) [NW]
Alison Younger (University of Sunderland) [AY]

Part I
POSTMODERNISM:
ITS HISTORY AND
CULTURAL CONTEXT

1

POSTMODERNISM AND PHILOSOPHY

STUART SIM

Philosophy, particularly the recent French philosophical tradition, has been both a prime site for debate about **postmodernism** and a source of many of the theories of what constitutes postmodernism. Probably the leading figure to be cited is Jean-François **Lyotard**, whose book *The Postmodern Condition: A Report on Knowledge* (1979) is widely considered to be the most powerful theoretical expression of postmodernism. Lyotard's plea that we should reject the '**grand narratives**' (that is, universal theories) of Western culture because they have now lost all their credibility, sums up the ethos of postmodernism, with its disdain for authority in all its many guises. There is no longer any point in engaging with, for example, **Marxism**, the argument goes; rather, we should ignore it as an irrelevance to our lives. Postmodern philosophy provides us with the arguments and techniques to make that gesture of dissent, as well as with the means to make value judgements in the absence of such overall authorities.

One of the best ways of describing postmodernism as a philosophical movement would be as a form of scepticism – scepticism about authority, received wisdom, cultural and political norms, etc. – and that puts it into a long-running tradition in Western thought that stretches back to classical Greek philosophy. Scepticism is an essentially negative form of philosophy, which sets out to undermine other philosophical theories claiming to be in possession of ultimate truth, or of criteria for determining what counts as ultimate truth. The technical term to describe such a style of philosophy is '**anti-foundational**'. Anti-foundationalists dispute the validity of the foundations of **discourse**, asking such questions as 'What guarantees the truth of your foundation (that is, starting point)?' Postmodernism has drawn heavily on the example set by anti-foundationalist philosophers, perhaps most notably the iconoclastic nineteenth-century German philosopher Friedrich **Nietzsche**, whose call for a 'revaluation of all values' constitutes something of a battle-cry for the movement.

Before considering postmodernism's sceptical credentials in greater detail, however, it would be helpful to say what, and who, can be regarded as falling under the heading of postmodern philosophy. It will be understood here to mean not just the inclusion of such avowedly postmodernist thinkers as Lyotard, but also the various discourses, such as **deconstruction**, that go under the name of **poststructuralism**. Poststructuralism's rejection of the **structuralist** tradition of thought is yet another gesture of scepticism towards received authority, and can be treated as part of the postmodern intellectual landscape. Although postmodern philosophy is a somewhat disparate area, we can note certain recurrent features, such as that gesture of scepticism, an anti-foundational bias, and an almost reflex dislike of authority, that make it reasonable to discuss it as a recognizable style of philosophy in its own right.

Poststructuralism is a broad cultural movement spanning various intellectual disciplines that has involved a rejection not just of structuralism and its methods, but also the ideological assumptions that lie behind them. It is to be regarded as both a philosophical and a political movement therefore, as is postmodernism in general. Poststructuralism called into question the cultural certainties that structuralism had been felt to embody: certainties such as the belief that the world was intrinsically knowable, and that structuralism gave us a method-ological key to unlock the various systems that made up that world. Structuralism takes its cue from the linguistic theories of the Swiss linguist Ferdinand de Saussure, who revolutionized the study of linguistics in his posthumously published *Course in General Linguistics* (1916). Saussure's major point about language is that it was above all a system: a system with rules and regulations (or internal grammar) that governed how the various elements of language interacted. Language was made up of **signs**, and signs consisted of two parts, a signifier (word) and a signified (concept), which combined, in an act of mental understanding, to form the sign. Although there was no necessary connection between a word and the object it named (they were 'arbitrary', as Saussure admitted), the force of convention ensured that they did not change at anyone's whim. There was at the very least a *relative* stability to language and the produc-tion of meaning, and language was to be viewed as a system of signs which induced a predictable response on the part of the linguistic community.

The linguistic model set up by Saussure formed the basis of structuralist analysis, which applied it to systems in general, making the assumption that every system had an internal grammar that governed its operations. The point of structuralist analysis was to uncover that grammar, whether the system in question was tribal myth, the advertising industry, or the world of literature or fashion. Ultimately, what poststructuralists object to is the overall tidiness of the structuralist enterprise, where there are no loose ends and everything falls neatly into place. Thus for a thinker like Claude **Lévi-Strauss**, or the early Roland **Barthes**, every detail of a **narrative** was significant in terms of the structure of the final product (there being no random elements), and narratives fell into specific genres, of which particular instances – say, a given tribal myth – were merely variations on a central theme. From such a perspective one system (or narrative) comes to seem much like any other, and the analysis of its grammar turns into a fairly predictable exercise, almost as if one knew beforehand what one was going to find. One could even argue, and poststructuralists did, that the analytical tech-niques being used by the structuralist *determined* the results. What structuralism seems to allow little scope for is chance, creativity or the unexpected. For a poststructuralist these are much more important than all the similarities between systems, and there is what amounts to a commitment to locating, and dwelling on, dissimilarity, difference and the unpredictability of analysis among post-structuralist thinkers.

Jacques **Derrida's deconstruction** became one of the most powerful expressions of the poststructuralist ethos. Deconstruction was directed against the system-building side of structuralism, and took issue with the idea that all phenomena were reducible to the workings of systems, with its implication that we could come to have total control over our environment. Derrida was concerned to demonstrate the instability of language, and indeed of systems in general. Signs were not such predictable entities in his view, and there was never any perfect conjunction of signifier and signified to guarantee unproblematical communication. Some 'slippage' of meaning always occurred. For one thing, words always contained echoes and traces of other words, with their sound quality, for example, invariably putting one in mind of a range of similar-sounding words. Derrida provided evidence of this slippage in action by means of a concept called '**différance**', a neologism derived from the French word *différence* (meaning both difference and deferral). One could not detect which of the two words was intended in speech (they are pronounced the same), only in writing. To Derrida, what was revealed at this point was the inherent indeterminacy of meaning. Linguistic meaning was an unstable phenomenon: at all times, and all places, différance applied. (It is worth noting that Derrida denies that différance is a concept; for him it is merely the identification of a process embedded within language itself.) The fondness for pun and word-play within deconstructive writing – a recurrent feature of all its major practitioners – has as its goal the illustration of language's instability, as well as its endlessly creative capacity to generate new and unexpected meanings.

Meaning is therefore a fleeting phenomenon that evaporates almost as soon as it occurs in spoken or written language (or keeps transforming itself into new meanings), rather than something fixed that holds over time for a series of different audiences. Derrida contends that all Western philosophy is based on the premise that the full meaning of a word is 'present' in the speaker's mind, such that it can be transmitted, without any significant slippage, to the listener. This belief is what he calls the '**metaphysics of presence**', and for Derrida it is an illusion: différance always intrudes into communication to prevent the establishment of 'presence', or completeness, of meaning. The emphasis on difference, and on what fails to conform to the norm or to system-building, that we find in deconstruction is very characteristic of the postmodern philosophical ethos.

Michel **Foucault** is another thinker who turned against the system-building and difference-excluding tendencies of structuralist thought. Once again, it is the fact of difference that is emphasized. In Foucault's case, there is a particular interest in marginalized groups whose difference keeps them excluded from political **power**; groups such as the mentally ill, prisoners and homosexuals. Post-Renaissance culture has been committed to the marginalization, even demonization, of difference, by its setting of norms of behaviour. Foucault has written a series of case studies describing how these norms were implemented in seventeenth- and eighteenth-century Western Europe, such that a whole new range of regimented institutions – insane asylums, prisons, hospitals – came into being in order to deal with the 'different'. For Foucault these institutions are expressions of political power, and of the way that a dominant faction in society can impose its will on others.

To demonstrate how sexual difference had been demonized in **modern** society, Foucault turned back to classical times in his three-volume study *The History of Sexuality* (1976–84) to investigate how homosexuality functioned in Greek and Roman culture. Greek society was more tolerant of sexual difference than our own, although no less moral in its outlook. In Foucault's parlance, it had a different discourse of sexuality in which no one practice was privileged over others, but homosexuality and heterosexuality flourished side by side. Foucault contrasted this unfavourably to modern times, when heterosexuality was turned into a norm from which all other forms of sexual expression were treated as deviations. This insistence on the norm at the expense of the different is all part of the authoritarianism that thinkers like Foucault associate with modern culture.

Gilles **Deleuze** and Félix **Guattari**'s *Anti-Oedipus* (1972) represented yet another poststructuralist attack on authoritarianism; in this case the authoritarianism embedded within psychoanalytic theory, which, through the mechanism of theories like the **Oedipus** complex, seeks to control the free expression of human **desire**. For Deleuze and Guattari individuals are '**desiring-machines**', who lack the sense of unity we generally associate with individual identity, but who find the opportunity to express their desire being curbed by the socio-political authorities (with fascism as the most potent example of how the process works). Psychoanalysis becomes for Deleuze and Guattari a symbol of how desire is suppressed, and in opposition to it they posit '**schizoanalysis**', based on the experience of the schizophrenic – who in their scheme becomes some kind of ideal model of human behaviour. The political dimension to poststructuralist thought, often somewhat hidden under cloudy metaphysical discussions in deconstruction, is unmistakably foregrounded here.

Difference feminism can also be included under the heading of poststructuralism, in that it queries the supposed rigidity of gender categories. The argument is that gender identity, particularly female, is not fixed, but is instead a fluid process that cannot be reduced to any essence or norm of behaviour (in this instance a patriarchally derived norm of behaviour). Theorists such as Luce **Irigaray** have used this form of argument to challenge the assumptions of patriarchy, in particular the assumption of specifically male and female gender traits that lead to gender stereotypes that our society still largely adheres to, and uses as a basis for the suppression of women.

The most influential voice of postmodern philosophy is Jean-François Lyotard, and there is a consistent thread of anti-authoritarianism running through his philosophical writings that we can now recognize as quintessentially postmodern. In his early career Lyotard can be described as a Marxist. He was a member of the group Socialisme ou Barbarie (Socialism or Barbarism), who were dedicated to subjecting Marxist theory to a searching critique from the inside, and he acted as the spokesperson on Algeria for the group's newspaper. Lyotard's writings on the Algerian war of liberation in the 1950s and 1960s reveal someone who is far from being an orthodox Marxist, and more than willing to call Marxist principles into question. The major objection he registers is that Algeria was being treated by the Communist Party hierarchy as a classic case of proletarian revolution, when in reality it was a peasant society where Marxism had little practical value.

After the break-up of Socialisme ou Barbarie in the 1960s, Lyotard self-consciously distanced himself from his Marxist past. Like many French intellectuals of his generation he was disenchanted by the pro-establishment position adopted by the French Communist Party in the 1968 Paris *événements*, and in works such as ***Libidinal Economy*** (1974) he vented the frustration he felt by then towards official Marxism. *Libidinal Economy* claimed that Marxism was unable to encompass the various libidinal drives that all individuals experienced, since these drives lay beyond any theory's control (the argument is similar to the one expressed in *Anti-Oedipus*). What was precisely wrong with Marxism was that it tried to suppress these energies, and in so doing revealed its latent authoritarianism. Behind the book's vicious attack on Marxism lay a belief on Lyotard's part that neither human nature nor historical process was as predictable, and therefore controllable, as Marxist theory insisted. Lyotard asked us to accept that libidinal energy (something like the complex of subconscious drives identified by **Freud**) demolished any claim that Marxism may have had to be able to direct events. The book can be seen as the beginning of the critique of 'grand narrative' that was to lie at the heart of Lyotard's most successful and influential work, *The Postmodern Condition*.

The Postmodern Condition argues that knowledge is now the world's most significant commodity, and that it may well become a source of conflict between nations (science writers have speculated that future generations of super-computers, or 'artilects', could have such an effect). Whoever controls knowledge, Lyotard insists, now exerts political control, and he is keen to ensure that the dissemination of knowledge is kept as open as possible. His alternative to the centralized political control of knowledge is to make all data banks accessible to the general public. Knowledge is seen to be communicated by means of narrative, and Lyotard is critical of what he calls grand narratives: theories that claim to be able to explain everything, and to resist any attempt to change their form (or 'narrative'). Marxism, for example, has its own particular narrative of world history which it feels is true and thus beyond any criticism or need of revision. It is not a narrative to be reinterpreted constantly in the light of changing cultural events, but an impregnable theory that holds over time and whose authority must never be doubted. To Lyotard, such an attitude is authoritarian, and he celebrates '**little narrative**' (*petit récit*) in its stead. Little narratives are put together on a tactical basis by small groups of individuals to achieve some particular objective (such as the 'little narrative' combination of students and workers in the 1968 *événements*, calling for government reforms), and do not pretend to have the answers to all society's problems: ideally, they last only as long as is necessary to achieve their short-term goals. Lyotard considers that little narratives are the most inventive way of disseminating, and creating, knowledge, and that they help to break down the monopoly traditionally exercised by grand narratives. In science, for example, they are now to be regarded as the primary means of enquiry. '**Postmodern science**', Lyotard informs us, is a search for paradoxes, instabilities and the unknown, rather than an attempt to construct yet another grand narrative that would apply over the entire scientific community.

Lyotard's objective is to demolish the authority wielded by grand narrative, which he takes to be repressive of individual creativity. 'We no longer have recourse to the grand narratives', he declares; that is, we can no longer rely on them to guide our action, either at the public or private level. We are not to fight the grand narratives but simply to stop believing in them; in which case they will be assumed to wither away. Although this is a somewhat idealistic view of the political process, something like this withering away did occur a few years after the publication of *The Postmodern Condition*, when Eastern European communism collapsed – largely without any violent clashes with the political authorities. In postmodern terms of reference, the populace stopped believing in the prevailing ideology, which then ceased to have any authority to enforce its will.

One of the problems we are left with when we dispense with grand narratives, or central authorities of any kind, is how to construct value judgements that others will accept as just and reasonable. Lyotard confronts this problem in *Just Gaming* (1979) when he argues that it is still possible to make value judgements, even if we have no grand narrative to back us up, on a 'case-by-case' basis (a form of pragmatism he adapts from Aristotle's political and ethical writings). Operating in a case-by-case manner, where one is admitting the absence of any absolute criteria, is the condition Lyotard refers to as '**paganism**', and it becomes an ideal of how we ought to proceed in a postmodern world. There never will be such absolute criteria, or foundations of belief, to guide us; but that need not, Lyotard insists, entail a collapse into social disorder, as critics from the grand narrative side are wont to suggest it will. Lyotard is espousing anti-foundationalism: a rejection of the idea that there are foundations to our systems of thought, or belief, that lie beyond question, and that are necessary to the business of making value judgements. Postmodernist philosophy has proved to be resolutely anti-foundational in outlook, and unwilling to accept that this renders it dysfunctional in any way as philosophy.

Lyotard's later philosophy is very much concerned with what he calls the '**event**', the concept of the '**differend**' and the **sublime**. The event is for Lyotard an occurrence that dramatically alters the way we view the world, and casts all our ideological assumptions into doubt in the process. Auschwitz is one such event, the *événements* another. The former in particular cannot be explained away by the application of grand narrative theory; in fact, it represents the point at which grand narrative theorizing breaks down. As for the latter, it is an explosion of libidinal energy which the system cannot deal with either. To acknowledge that there are events which cannot be forecast or encompassed within any neat universal theory is to acknowledge not just the limitations of grand narrative but also the essential openness of the future. This openness becomes an article of faith to postmodernists: the future must not be considered as determined in advance such that all human effort is rendered meaningless.

Differends are conflicts of interest between parties which cannot be resolved, but must be acknowledged and kept in view at all times (see particularly *The Differend* (1983)). Each party inhabits what Lyotard calls a different 'phrase regime' whose objectives are **incommensurable** with the other, and neither of which has any ethical right to make the other conform to its wishes. What tends to happen in practice, particularly political practice, is that one party to the dispute enforces its view on the other, 'resolving' the dispute to its own advantage. In Lyotard's terms of reference, one phrase regime exerts dominance over another – a classic instance of authoritarianism in action. As an example of this in the everyday world, Lyotard cites the case of an exploited employee who cannot gain any redress for her exploitation if she brings an action against her employer, since the court that hears her plea is set up on the principle that such exploitation is legal. The employer's phrase regime is excluding the other from having a proper voice. It is the business of philosophers to help such suppressed phrase regimes find their voice, this being what Lyotard describes as a 'philosophical politics'. Philosophical politics – the search for new, counter-cultural, phrase regimes – can be considered the highest expression of postmodern philosophy.

Lyotard develops an obsession with the sublime, which comes to represent for him the fatal flaw in any totalizing philosophy. Immanuel **Kant** had wrestled with the notion of the sublime in his *Critique of Practical Reason* (1788), since it appeared to create a gap in his theory of knowledge. This theory required our concepts and our sense experience of the world to conform to each other. When we turned to the sublime, however, we were confronted with something infinite and absolute; that is, with the inconceivable, and thus a challenge to our claims to knowledge. While Kant was dismayed by this finding, Lyotard appropriated it for the cause of the postmodern as proof that no philosophical theory could provide a total picture of existence. The sublime always lay beyond our powers to represent or explain, and in consequence acquired immense symbolic importance for postmodern thought. All attempts to construct a grand narrative would be undermined by the fact of the sublime.

Towards the end of his career Lyotard is very much concerned with the way the forces of 'techno-science' (for which we can read the multinationals) are attempting to hijack the course of human history, by preparing for the end of life on Earth. Lyotard argues that techno-scientists are gradually eradicating humankind from the picture, by developing increasingly sophisticated computer technology with the ability to reproduce itself and to continue existing somewhere else in the universe when the Earth dies (an event some 4.5 billion years or so down the line). Techno-science's ultimate goal, Lyotard warns us in *The Inhuman* (1988), is to make thought possible without a body, and this represents a threat to humanity and its values that should be strongly resisted, being 'inhuman' in spirit. What techno-science wants is to reduce humanity to its assumed essence, that is, thought, and then to render this compliant in computer program form. Given thought without a body there are no longer events or differends to worry about of course, nor the openness of the future that postmodernists so prize. It is another case of excluding the different and the unpredictable in order to exert control. What gets left out of the equation is the individual as well as the little narrative, neither of which has any place in the authoritarian scheme of things – and to wish to dehumanize humankind by reducing it to thought-process alone is an ultimate act of authoritarianism to Lyotard. Resistance at little narrative level becomes an ethical act on behalf of the cause of difference; and it is difference that must be protected at all costs in the postmodern world.

Jean **Baudrillard**'s work is another important expression of postmodern philosophy. He too came to be very critical of Marxism and structuralism, eventually rejecting the notion that there were hidden structures behind all phenomena which it was the analyst's task to identify and explain. Baudrillard contended instead that the postmodern world was a world of **simulacra**, where we could no longer differentiate between reality and **simulation**. Simulacra represented nothing but themselves: there was no other reality to which they referred. In consequence, Baudrillard could claim that Disneyland and television now constituted America's reality, and, even more provocatively, that the Gulf War of 1991 did not happen, but was merely a simulation (along the lines of a video game, it would seem). Not surprisingly, this was a view that attracted a great deal of criticism for its apparent cynicism and lack of sensitivity to the human dimension involved.

Another argument of Baudrillard's that has inspired considerable controversy is that systems no longer need to be opposed, and that they can instead be 'seduced' – by which he means beguiled into submission (see particularly *Seduction* (1979)). Feminists have been extremely critical of what to them is the implicit sexism of the notion of seduction, and have accused Baudrillard of reinforcing sexual stereotypes by its use. While acknowledging the force of the feminist rejoinder, one might also regard seduction as yet another character-istically postmodern attempt to undermine systems by locating their weak spots. Postmodern philosophy in general sees no need for outright confrontation with systems of power, being more concerned to demonstrate how such systems (Marxism and communism being outstanding examples) can be made to implode.

The reaction against doctrinaire Marxism in the work of thinkers like Lyotard and Baudrillard is part of yet another cultural trend that is now known as **post-Marxism**. Post-Marxism has become an important theoretical position, and includes not just figures who wish to reject their Marxist beliefs – Lyotard and

Baudrillard, for example – but also those who want to revise Marxism in terms of new theoretical and cultural developments. Ernesto **Laclau** and Chantal **Mouffe** gave voice to the latter constituency when they published their controversial book *Hegemony and Socialist Strategy* in 1985. In this study they argued that Marxism ought to be aligning itself with the various new social movements that had been springing up (feminism, the **Greens**, ethnic and sexual minorities, for example); in other words, for Marxism to embrace political **pluralism** and drop its pretensions to be a body of received truth. Marxism also needed to take account of the various new theories that had been coming into prominence – theories such as deconstruction or postmodernism. Once again we can observe the characteristic postmodern distrust of grand narratives and their dogmatism coming to the fore. What is felt to be wrong with Marxism is that it has failed to move with the times, and to realize how various (or 'plural') society has become. Marxism was instead stuck at the level of trying to impose its theories on others, on the grounds that it alone possessed the truth. Viewed from this perspective, Marxism is an authoritarian theory. Laclau and Mouffe, on the other hand, are putting the case for a more 'open' Marxism, able to adapt to changing cultural circumstances – and to attract new audiences in the process. Predictably enough, the Marxist establishment has been dismissive of Laclau and Mouffe's claims that Marxism requires drastic revision, or that it should aspire towards pluralism, holding on instead to Marxism's supposed truth and universality of application.

It is this distrust of grand theory, and its authoritarian bias, that can be considered the distinguishing feature of postmodern philosophy, which maintains a libertarian attitude throughout its various expressions. In the Anglo-American philosophical world, we can find such views being espoused by the American pragmatist philosopher Richard **Rorty**, a well-known champion of the recent **continental philosophical** tradition. Rorty also has no time for grand theory, and, in prototypically pragmatist fashion, is less concerned with whether theories are true or false than whether they are useful and interesting. Philosophy, for Rorty, is no more than a form of conversation, and his own preference when it comes to identifying a source of ideas to guide our behaviour is for other subjects such as literature. Rorty's turn to '**post-philosophy**', as it has been called, is characteristically postmodern in its rejection of the standard narrative associated with the Western philosophical tradition. Yet another authority is unceremoniously consigned to the historical dustbin.

Not everyone has been happy with postmodernism's frequent recourse to the historical dustbin. The American critic Fredric **Jameson** has dubbed postmodern theory 'the cultural logic of late capitalism', regarding it as being, unwittingly or otherwise, in collusion with the powers-that-be in helping to maintain the political status quo. Postmodernists have consistently criticized the left's belief in the efficacy of ideological confrontation, and for a Marxist like Jameson that has the effect of serving the cause of the right, which has a vested interest in promoting apathy about the political process. Terry **Eagleton** has taken a similar view to Jameson, constantly drawing attention to the ideological implications of adopting the postmodern line, which he treats as inimical to socialist ideals. Christopher **Norris** has been harshly critical of Baudrillard's work, in particular what he feels is his flippant attitude towards the Gulf War. Baudrillard's denial of that war's reality is symbolic of postmodernism's emptiness as a cultural theory for Norris, and he cannot accept his apparent insensitivity to political turmoil and human suffering. Jürgen **Habermas** is another to find postmodernism ideologically suspect, and has taken issue with Lyotard's philosophy on this ground. (For more on the topic of postmodernism's critics, see 'Postmodernism, modernity and the tradition of dissent', pp. 143–52).

Overall, postmodern philosophy is to be defined as an updated version of scepticism, more concerned with destabilizing other theories and their pretensions to truth than with setting up a positive theory of its own; although of course to be sceptical of the theoretical claims of others is to have a definite programme of one's own, if only by default. Postmodern philosophy, therefore, is a deployment of philosophy to undermine the authoritarian imperatives in our culture, at both the theoretical and the political level. Whether such a trend will command interest for very much longer it is difficult to say. To some extent postmodernism has become its own grand narrative (there is a definite postmodernist line to most philosophical issues), and therefore vulnerable to attack in its turn. It is also possible to argue that postmodern philosophers have overstated the decline of grand narratives, and one highly pertinent objection to Lyotard's dismissal of their continuing significance has been that **religious fundamentalism** (a grand narrative if ever there was one) has manifestly been on the increase in recent decades. The growth of Islamic fundamentalism in particular seems to challenge the validity of Lyotard's judgement on this score, given that it now controls the political life of an increasing number of countries in the Middle East and Asia, making it a critical influence on the global political scene. Post-9/11 we must assume that postmodernism is in open conflict with fundamentalist trends in our world (we can include **market fundamentalism** in the equation as well).

Lyotard himself takes a cyclical view of cultural history, in which postmodernism and modernism succeed each other over time in unending sequence. Thus there have been postmodernisms in the past (figures like Rabelais or Laurence Sterne qualifying as postmoderns for Lyotard), and there will be both modernisms and postmodernisms again in the future. It is just possible to argue that we are already into a **post-postmodernist** world, in which different cultural preoccupations (such as the reconstruction of grand narratives) are making their presence felt. Scepticism has tended to go in and out of fashion over the course of philosophical history, and it may well be that the current round has served its usual purpose in drawing attention to the weaknesses of certain philosophical positions, and that a less negatively oriented philosophical programme can take its place for the immediate future. Watch this space: but be vigilant, also, for any drift back into intellectual authoritarianism.

2

POSTMODERNISM AND POLITICS

IAIN HAMILTON GRANT

Ever since **postmodernism** hit the cultural news-stand, it has been incessantly interrogated as to its politics. With its 'anything goes' pluralism and its delirious celebration of **difference**; with reality, according to Jean **Baudrillard** – to many, the 'high priest of postmodernism' – 'no longer what it used to be', what grounds remain for a politics necessary to counter the widespread and manifest injustices that remain in our postmodern world? Surely any prospect of tackling endemic racism, the horrors of the military–industrial–entertainment complex, the invasion of Iraq, religious and political persecution or Chinese tanks crushing the bodies of protesting students, is given up in advance by any movement that, like postmodernism, renounces the **modern** ideals of universal freedom, equality and rights, without proposing any alternatives?

In many ways 'postmodern politics' is a problem peculiar to the history of postmodernism in the English-speaking world, where the term first arose in the world of art and architecture. Once postmodernism had reached a certain critical mass, it became irresistible to academic interests, and the path that it then took shifted from the arts to politics and philosophy, from which something known loosely as 'postmodern theory' began to emerge. The various elements from which theoretical postmodernism emerged were almost exclusively, however, fragments of French philosophy. It is to some extent a consequence of this speculation or free trade in theories divorced from their historical, political and philosophical contexts that the question of postmodern politics has appeared to be so open and, therefore, to host an apparently endless range of debates.

Two questions may therefore be asked. First, what impact has postmodernism had on politics in what Richard **Rorty** calls the North Atlantic bourgeois community, and second, what are the politics that inform the philosophy imported from France to this community in the guise of postmodern theory? The answers to both of these questions are linked through one of the very few **continental philosophers** to have directly addressed postmodernism. Jean-François **Lyotard**'s *The Postmodern Condition* (1979) crops up in virtually every discussion of every aspect of these debates, so that his self-confessed extreme simplifications have assumed a definitive character with regard to postmodernism. With this text comes an entire history and an entire politics – one that is generally replicated in all the European theorists who supply the resources for postmodern theory.

Before addressing this history directly, however, it is necessary, given the enormous credibility attaching to Lyotard's text, to consider some of its main points alongside critical reactions to them. While this may seem to over-restrict the full range of contributions to the theme of postmodern politics, it will get us to the core of many of the key debates in this area. Among the 'extreme simplifications' *The Postmodern Condition* announces, the one that has had perhaps the greatest impact concerns the status of what Lyotard calls '**meta-**' or '**grand narratives**'. While grand narratives such as the **Enlightenment** narrative of infinite progress in knowledge and liberty, or the **Marxist** narrative of the progressive emancipation of labouring humanity from the shackles imposed upon it by industrial capitalism, have played a crucial role in anchoring knowledge and politics in modernity, **postmodernity** has entailed a crisis of confidence in them. One reason for this crisis is the rise of critical philosophy, begun, ironically, with the Enlightenment. While **Kant**, who initiated critical philosophy at the end of the eighteenth century, had intended it to supply human reason with the means for self-government, rather than relying on some divine arbiter or other unknowable phenomena, reason was to subject itself to criticism in order to know itself and its limits. By the end of the nineteenth century, however, criticism was being directed at the hard-won gains of the Enlightenment itself with **Nietzsche** proclaiming that God is dead, and that truth, morality and knowledge itself were mere illusions. Marx had also chipped away at the Enlightenment edifice, arguing that its politics had concentrated on ideals of progress at the expense of real progress in matters of human freedom, and that this idealism, rather than being a mistake, was a complex reflection of the ideals of the ruling classes. Meanwhile, Marxism has not yet brought about the freedom it promised, but has instead produced a series of anomalies, such as the crushing of popular protest against Soviet rule in Budapest in 1956 and the bloody terrors of Stalin's gulags.

Progressive conflict between the narratives has therefore weakened them all, so that, at the beginning of the twenty-first century, there seem to be no candidates to take over from them in tying all our knowledge and our actions to some coherent historical plan. All that is left is a field where the fragments left over from these grand narratives compete with one another and with new rivals. This field, however, is governed by a new alliance between technology and capitalism, constituting what some theorists have dubbed '**post-industrial** society'. But what big story does capitalism have to tell? Whereas it used to tell the Enlightenment tale of increasing liberty being best guaranteed by a free market capitalism that maximizes choice and minimizes state intervention in the lives and careers of individuals, under alliance with technology, the efficiency gains of, for example, computing fall into line with the drive to profit, so that 'minimum in, maximum out' becomes the only rule governing commercial, social and political concerns alike. Moreover, as a rule, it is its own justification: when profit is made and efficiency gained, the rule is justified, short-circuiting any appeal to larger-scale **narratives** to '**legitimate**' it. Indeed, the other side of this coin is that governments and other regulatory bodies are misled if they suppose they can control, by the imposition of political ends, the 'free' movements of capital across national boundaries. Governments and their economic policies no longer tell stories that affect the real movements of money: consider the recent problems of Argentina.

While 'late capitalism', to use political theorist Ernest Mandel's phrase, popularized by Fredric **Jameson**, is a major player in postmodern or post-industrial societies, as noted by many critics and theorists, its presence in Lyotard's text is often overlooked. As we shall see later in this essay, it points to a very different evolutionary path for postmodernism than is often assumed by the celebrants of postmodern **difference**: the postmodern condition is a historical tale of the survival-of-the-fittest narrative. To return then to the matter of narrative, with capitalism ultimately triumphant in the conflict of the narratives, no single story is left to hold things together; as many stories are told as there are groups to tell them. None, however, has any cultural, historical, philosophical or political priority over any other. It is in this field that, by common consent, postmodern politics finds itself: where there was unity, so the story goes, now there are only differences. Where the political will of a people, a nation or a culture used to be harnessed to long-term general goals, now fragmented groups engage in short-term struggles. The spread of identity politics over the last few decades is testimony to this, with its emphasis on ethnicity, class, gender and sexuality replacing political credo.

Adherents of this state of affairs suggest that the celebration of the differences between such groups and identities allows for a politics to develop that no longer needs, as did ideals of the 'general will' of the people, or the political ideal of cultural revolution, to subjugate its members' interests to an orthodoxy. Instead, micro-political alliances may unpredictably emerge that remain attentive to the differences between their constituent groups. Marxists, feminists, **Greens** and gays may thus find themselves in a loose coalition concerning one issue, but may equally find themselves at odds over another. Moreover, with the revolution off the agenda for the foreseeable future, direct action and issues-based politics assume a more urgent and realistic significance. Detractors, however, point to two main defects in such a view of the postmodern political condition. The first is, how can a culture organize itself around this liberal-pluralist, 'anything goes' ideology without the political muscle to back it up against those who, quite simply, are too different from ourselves, and who view Western liberalism in general, and the North Atlantic bourgeois community in particular, as pathologically weak and misguided? Consider, for example, the various **fundamentalisms** at work in the contemporary world. How does the North Atlantic bourgeois community respond when its basic rights are infringed, as happened when an ayatollah issued a fatwa against an author for blasphemy? If that community follows its liberal-democratic principles and continues to celebrate difference, how can it object to the death sentence? Such scenarios call for a basic commitment to enforcing certain laws and rights against those who are so different as to deny the value of difference. Second, by concentrating all its attention on 'micro-political' issues, or on short-term single-issue politics, the very real large-scale political structures that govern our everyday lives are disregarded and left uncontested to the enemy, which simply translates into covert support for, or actual complicity with, the status quo.

15

Meanwhile, of course, the champions of difference can point to a past riven with intolerance and the suppression of the majority of the world's population by a tiny minority of white, male, North Atlantic, well-educated and economically powerful individuals. Rather than celebrating difference, this regime has enacted a huge programme of colonization, political disenfranchisement and outright suppression. A postmodern world of differences opens up possibilities for the oppressed to find a voice with which to struggle against their oppression. Here, however, another aspect of postmodernism comes to the fore. Just as the Nation, the People or the Party are condemned for their totalizing aspirations, so too the ideal of a coherent and integrated self, such as promised by psychoanalysis, falls under suspicion. Once again, this is a problem that was initially opened up by Kant, who introduced an unbridgeable gulf between the knowable self and the knowing self, a gulf that was only provisionally held together by our ability to use the word 'I'. Nietzsche, seizing on the grammatical core of the Kantian **subject**, set about criticizing the belief in a coherent and integrated self as a product of a misplaced faith in grammar. **Freud** put paid to this idea by drawing attention to conflicts between aspects of the self, and located diverse parts of our 'psychical personalities', the unconscious bulk of which remains permanently inaccessible to us. Finally canonized in postmodernism as multiple or schizophrenic selves, postmodern difference seems to give with one hand what it takes with the other: for difference to offer any liberatory potential, the corrosion of the self must come to an end so that there is some identity that can serve as the basis of an identity politics. Such dilemmas are keenly felt and hotly debated in many fields, notably feminism. On the one hand, postmodern feminists like Judith **Butler** argue that there is no core identity, no essential self, nor any essentialist category 'woman' that would serve to unify the aims of a political mass movement. Instead, the self and its gender are realized only as performances. Others, however, argue for the maintenance of the essentialist category 'woman', since without it what purpose could feminism conceivably serve? If we let go of the essential reality of women's oppression, we simultaneously take leave of our responsibilities to real women, making 'feminism' merely an academic ploy.

Apart from feminism's problematic alliance with postmodern theory, how do the main protagonists in the debates about postmodern politics line up? To develop this snapshot of the postmodern condition, I will continue to focus on positions that engage with Lyotard's version of postmodernism, since it has been one of the most influential and since a great deal more has, of course, been said about the themes of this essay than could be treated within it. As already noted, postmodernism came of intellectual age in the English-speaking world in the early 1980s. Hal Foster's collection *Postmodern Culture* (1985) marks this transition well. Originally titled *The Anti Aesthetic* (1983), the retitling of this collection of essays by academic heavyweights such as Jürgen **Habermas**, Edward **Said**, Fredric **Jameson** and Jean Baudrillard clearly signals postmodernism's shift away from the art world towards broader issues. The early forays of two contributors in particular into this new territory have continued to focus debates ever since.

Habermas's essay in *Postmodern Culture*, 'Modernity – An Incomplete Project', clearly signals his rejection of 'postmodernism'. If, according to Lyotard and other recent French philosophers, whom Habermas will later collectively call the 'young conservatives', none of modernity's narratives of emancipation and progress have borne fruit, this does not mean that they never will, but rather that they have *not yet* fully developed. Diagnosing the problem faced in late modernity as what he calls the 'fragmentation of the lifeworld' by the evolution, during modernity, of an increasing abstraction and specialization in the fields of knowledge (science), practical life (politics) and artistic practices, Habermas proposes to reinvigorate the Enlightenment project that directed all progress to the ideal benefit of the human race as a whole. Therefore, exponents of these rarefied practices ought to justify their abstractions to the lifeworld.

The means by which Habermas envisages this happening are found in the principles that govern communicative action: insofar as I speak to you, I give tacit assent to your speaking to me in return. Moreover, since speech replaces and modifies direct action (I do not just go ahead and change the world without asking), I also implicitly agree to be bound to seek agreement with you, rather than riding roughshod over your views. In other words, the aim of all rational communication is to reach agreement on what should be done. By not observing the rules implicit in all communicative action, I forfeit any right to engage in dialogue. Postmodernism, by insisting that this project is at an end, is simply not playing the game. That narratives are discredited and fragmented is no reason to assume that they need always be so. This merely poses us a problem that we must direct our efforts towards resolving.

Moreover, Lyotard, whose book *The Postmodern Condition* appeared in 1979 (Habermas's essay was first delivered in 1981), in relating a grand narrative about the end of grand narratives exposes a central contradiction in his account of postmodernism: if there is no longer any belief in grand narratives, then what grounds could there be for accepting Lyotard's own account? If we do accept this account, therefore, then paradoxically it must be wrong about the status of grand narratives. Moreover, in offering it, Lyotard must himself believe that it must have some credibility, so that even Lyotard himself believes his account to be false.

Of course, in making these criticisms, Habermas effectively discredits Lyotard's extended analysis of *how it is* that this situation has indeed come about. We will return later to the roots of Lyotard's diagnosis of the condition of narrative under victorious capitalism. If Lyotard does not believe in the collapse of grand narratives, then, Habermas clearly does – certainly as regards Lyotard's narrative, at any rate! To the postmoderns, Habermas has too ideal a sense of what actually happens in communication: inevitably interested parties set agendas, so that agreement must be won even by threat and coercion: that is, by the exercise of power.

Habermas's own suggestions for healing the splits in the everyday lifeworld in which we all live and act are riven with effects of **power** to which they remain blind: either agree or shut up. To the postmoderns, this merely emphasizes the illegitimacy of consensus as an ideal outcome, since it is won at the cost of suppressing dissent. The solution offered by Lyotard is therefore not to suppress, but rather to emphasize and even experimentally to aggravate dissensus. Rather than accept norms and rules imposed top-down by circumstance or project, open-ended experimentation will create new rules from the ground up. (As we shall see in 'Postmodernism and science and technology' (pp. 58–70), the scientific overtones in the language of experiment are crucial to understanding aspects of postmodernism that are often overlooked.)

While Habermas, following in the footsteps and the professorial chair of the **Frankfurt School** of Social Research, retains some of his forebears' commitment to the Marxist project along with his version of Kant's enlightened democracy, there are many other strands of the Marxist reaction to postmodernism. Ranging from Félix **Guattari**'s neo-communist outright dismissal of postmodernism as 'no philosophy at all . . . just something in the air' like a fragrance or a flu virus, to Chantal **Mouffe** and Ernesto **Laclau**'s **post-Marxist** hybrid of Marxism and postmodernism Marxist analyses have had, perhaps, the most to lose from the demise of the grand narrative of emancipated human labour and the postmodern disregard of large-scale political phenomena, such as the economy or the revolution. It is at least curious, then, that the renowned Marxist critic and theorist Fredric Jameson seems so positive about it. Even more paradoxically, his contribution to Foster's collection and his *Postmodernism, or, the Cultural Logic of Late Capitalism* (1991) – along with Laclau and Mouffe's *Hegemony and Socialist Strategy* (1985), one of the most cited Marxist addresses to post-modernism – seems to buck the trend represented by Foster's collection to have moved postmodernism from aesthetics to philosophy and politics, insofar as they resolutely remain within the realm of the aesthetic. This paradox is only apparent, however.

The title of Jameson's book, which refers to postmodernism as the cultural logic of late capitalism, repeats the orthodox Marxist distinction between the economic base of society and the cultural superstructure that reflects the conditions of this base. Art and philosophy are among the superstructural phenomena of a society, so that, as Marx put it regarding philosophy, 'the ruling ideas in a society are simply the ideas of the ruling class'. By insisting that postmodernism has its roots in cultural phenomena, or, in other words, that it is located within this superstructural field, Jameson's book is a contribution to a long-running debate regarding the extent to which art and philosophy are to be regarded as simple expressions of fundamental economic shifts in society's base. A 'postmodern politics' would therefore be a misnomer, but the politics of postmodern culture can be revealed through the analysis of postmodern theoretical, philosophical and cultural artefacts. Rather than simply adopting the well-used strategy of criticizing it for its politics, Jameson is determined to gamble that, by conducting such analyses, postmodernism may be susceptible to treatment by Marxist theory, and to find a place within the persistence of the Marxist dialectic. Against Lyotard, then, Jameson argues that incredulity in grand narratives is not a final position on postmodernism, but rather that this incredulity has its roots within economic phenomena. One of the themes to which Jameson constantly returns is therefore the prevailing nostalgia for the exuberant confidence and economic security of North American society in the 1950s evident in so much contemporary film and literature. It is the collapse of this economic utopia under the regimen of late capitalism, then, that lies at the root of the distrust of large-scale political narratives and provokes what Daniel **Bell** called, in 1960, 'the end of ideology', finding expression in so much contemporary philosophy and theory, so that postmodernism's vaunted theories of fragmentation turn out to be expressions of this, or analyses of these expressions.

Jameson does not, however, think that Marxism can survive these economic and cultural shifts without adapting its own theory to the new structures of the economic base effected by what sociologists such as Alain Touraine have referred to as 'post-industrial society'. The analysis of postmodern culture will therefore have lessons for Marxism as well as postmodern political theorizing; for one thing, the strict separation of base and superstructure must be modified to take account of the dialectical effects on the base of cultural phenomena. After all, the idea that we can gain direct and unmediated access to economic reality by somehow sidestepping all theory and philosophy seems as untenable as the worst excesses of a 'just the facts, ma'am' scientism.

One of the holes in Jameson's book, which he explicitly and regretfully notes, is the absence of any discussion of recent cyberpunk fiction. As cyberpunk author Bruce Sterling notes, writing science fiction in today's technologically sophisticated world faces a new challenge: the readers of such works have themselves, owing to an ever-increasing rate of technological change, grown up in a science fictional world. Now, disregarding for the moment the problems this presents to science-fiction writers and readers, cyberpunk fiction none the less reveals a concern with the singular phenomenon of runaway technological development. This, nevertheless, is one of the concerns that animates Lyotard's report on the postmodern condition. While the ins and outs of this development will be further discussed in 'Postmodernism and science and technology', it is important to note the extent to which Lyotard's account is an extension of the Marxist emphasis on the means of production to an analysis of changes in this sphere within post-industrial or computerized societies. That technology does not figure largely in Jameson's account demonstrates the possibility that the restriction of postmodernism to the field of culture and aesthetics is shaky, a shakiness compounded by his insistence that Lyotard's experimentalism is solely an advocacy of the avant-garde practices enshrined in aesthetic modernism.

To develop this point, however, it is finally necessary to return to what this essay promised at the start: the political roots of Lyotard's postmodernism. Far from being particular to Lyotard, however, the French philosophies that have been imported into the English-speaking world to form that hybrid creature, postmodern theory, have all been shaped, to varying degrees, by these same political histories and events. To understand why this is so, it is necessary to bear in mind the intellectual climate of post-war France. Between the two world wars, the names on everybody's contents pages were dominated by the 'three Hs': **Hegel**, **Husserl** and **Heidegger**. After the war, Sartre, whose existentialist philosophy was the culminating French expression of this holy trinity, began to attempt to move towards an accommodation with Marxism, finally declaring the latter to be the 'inescapable horizon of all thought in the twentieth century'. This reflected the rise to intellectual prominence of the so-called 'masters of suspicion': Marx, Nietzsche and Freud. One reason for this, apart from much cultural soul-searching following the ghastly spectacle of France's collaboration with the Nazis under the reviled Vichy regime, were the Paris lectures of Alexandre Kojève on Hegel's philosophy. Kojève's lectures, which brought a particularly Marxist slant to the reading of Hegel, had a defining influence on the entire generation of thinkers who were to rise to the dizzy heights of canonization as 'postmoderns'. Marxism, then, became that narrative against which the **legitimacy** of all others must be measured. In consequence, it is for the collapse of this narrative in particular that we must account in order to understand the passage from a Paris saturated with Marxism to its collapse in postmodernism.

The *événements* in Paris of May 1968 saw students and workers barricading the streets of a modern, first-world economic power to such an extent that the government was on the brink of being overthrown. When the unions, the parties, the intellectuals and the good men of the left condemned the popular insurrection in the streets of Paris in May 1968, Marxism's promise of a revolutionary future redeemed from capitalist exploitation, and hence its legitimacy among the intellectual left in general, evaporated. Lyotard, for instance, scandalized by the French Communist Party's condemnation of the occupation of the Nanterre campus of the University of Paris by the radical student group led by Daniel Cohn-Bendit, the 22nd March Movement (commemorating the arrest of the student leaders of an anti-Vietnam protest organization), supported them against the Party, the unions, the press, the university authorities, the government and, ultimately, against the violent suppression of their occupation when Nanterre was stormed by the French riot police in early May. When the students reacted by taking to the streets in the company of the workers who, rejecting government pay policy, had staged a massively successful general strike, the failure of the Party and the unions to support the revolution, and their complicity with the state in helping to put it down in the name of a return to 'popular government', clearly demonstrated the left's betrayal of its revolutionary promise and its function as an organ of statist control. It is for this reason that Lyotard continued into the 1980s to regard May 1968 as a razor's edge severing the atrophied Marxist **metanarrative** from postmodernity. Hence, also, one of the slogans daubed on the walls of Paris during the *événements*: 'Comrades, humanity will never be happy until the last capitalist is hung on the guts of the last bureaucrat.'

Such a view had been vigorously championed by the **Situationist** International (SI), whose pamphlet of 1966, 'On the poverty of student life', written in collaboration with Strasbourg student activists enraged by the university's role as a training ground for the managers of the 'spectacle', forced the state to arrest, try and condemn the students – and to recognize the threat posed to the everyday banality of life under capitalism by the SI. The Situationists themselves made much of their role in the *événements,* commenting that their strategies had been implemented as if taken from a Situationist textbook; even taking to the streets was a strategy the Situationists called 'drifting', a means of reappropriating the urban environment for the imagination: 'Beneath the paving stones, the beach!' Not only do elements of Situationist vocabularies and analyses find their way into Lyotard's texts from the late 1960s and early 1970s, it was also from this background that Jean Baudrillard's thesis of a society of simulated **desire** emerged, taking its cue from Guy **Debord**'s *The Society of the Spectacle* (1967), with its theses concerning the management and production of desire through what remained, in de Gaulle's France, a state-run media. Whereas, however, the crux of Debord's analysis was that, under spectacular society, we either acquiesce as passive consumers of the spectacle of our own, alienated lives or, overthrowing the spectacle and its apparatus, we become active producers of revolution; for Baudrillard, a revolution against the spectacle can only take the form of a spectacle, since if it did not, it literally could not take place, and would not register within spectacular society.

The immediacy of the revolution for which the Situationists agitated, while it found equally immediate expression in the streets of Paris, ran directly counter both to the Marxian ideal of revolution as an organic development from capital itself, and to its Trotskyite variant, for which the proletariat had to be helped to see how unfortunate and miserable they were by an intellectual and political vanguard. Neither war nor economic hardship had produced a revolution; but the stifling banality of the affluent society had. The failures of both these programmes to deliver the revolution, and the increasing bureaucratization of international Marxism, had already prompted a large-scale re-evaluation of Marxism by groups such as Socialisme ou Barbarie (Socialism or Barbarism), to which both Debord and Lyotard belonged. Between 1956 and 1964, Lyotard, a tutor in Algeria at the time, contributed analyses of the popular struggle for Algerian independence and the lessons for Marxism it contained. The group's basic thesis was that the bureaucratization of international communism revealed the extent to which it had become an organ of bureaucratic capitalism. After the group began itself to become rigid and doctrinaire, Lyotard left to join 'Workers' Power', where he remained until 1966, at which point, disillusioned, he became active in the emergent student politics and eventually joined the 22nd March Movement.

Although often enough at odds with each other, the Situationists, Socialisme ou Barbarie and the enraged students all shared the conviction that Marxism no longer held the blueprints of the revolution. In other words, Marxism was already a thing of the past, for Lyotard, by the time of the *événements.* What then prompted him to claim so decisive a position, vis-à-vis Marxism, for these events?

Surely Marxism was already at an end? Not so. While the immediate revolution of May 1968 demonstrated the unviability of Marxism as a political programme, the collapse of the Marxist grand narrative, that was to reach its culminating *synthesis* in the great proletarian revolution arising out of capitalism itself, does not entail the rejection of Marxist *analysis*, merely a reorientation of its questions and a re-evaluation of its aims such as Lyotard had already been engaged in since 1956. Thus, if we look at the core questions asked in *The Postmodern Condition* – What form does capital take in postmodern society? How do the means of production in postmodernism differ from previous social formations? What form must a politics capable of responding to this situation take? – more rather than less continuity is revealed between the basic political orientation of Lyotard's thought on either side of the 'razor's edge' of May 1968.

What form, then, does postmodern capitalism take? As noted earlier, one crucial element of postmodern societies is the new alliance forged between capitalism and technology. It is this that provides the material basis for Lyotard's argument that capitalism emerges victorious from the conflict of the narratives: profit no longer need be legitimated by reference to a grand narrative of progressive realization of individual liberty through the market, since it is justified immediately by sharing its sole criterion of success with a technology that has become the means of production of knowledge, information and power. Thus the means of production that secure power in postmodern societies are informational rather than industrial. Every time a computer maximizes the output of information from the minimum of input, on every occasion when time or labour are saved by the implementation of a technology, capitalism immediately wins again. We cannot argue with capitalism, since within it there is no longer any role left for discursive reason. Nor does capitalism require propaganda: a self-confessed enemy of the state as much as of socialism, capital acts without loyalties, in accordance with its one rule of maximizing efficiency. The high ground of macro-political reality is not therefore merely 'left to the enemy', as so many critics of postmodern politics have suggested; rather, the postmodern condition results directly from these new social structures. What form, then, should a postmodern politics take? Lyotard's advocacy of experimentation, mentioned earlier, must be applied to the context of the material organization of postmodern societies. Such a situation requires experimentation not only at the aesthetic level, as Jameson argues Lyotard's experimentalism reduces to, nor solely at the level of narrative: it requires that the media of techno-capital in which knowledge, power and information are stored, be the object themselves of radical experimentation.

This, then, is the history of the postmodern condition: on the one hand, a history of the evolution of capitalism into techno-capital, on the other, a history of the demise of the Marxist grand narrative and a response to the void left by this most accomplished of critical repertoires. The free trade in theory characteristic of postmodernism in the English-speaking world has, generally speaking, sacrificed the political history of the French philosophy of postmodernism to a kind of short-term expediency, paradoxically derived in large part from theses propounded in such works. The rush for the new at the expense of its historical embeddedness remains, however, something of an experiment in forms of knowledge and political action, and the incursions made by postmodernism into fields such as law, political theory and feminism clearly demonstrate the stakes of this experiment: if theory is regarded as a kit to be assembled, not in accordance with some scholarly sense of its history, but variously according to the demands of the task at hand, then withdrawing it from the sterile catacombs of scholarly debate may yet have pragmatic benefit. Of course, ignorance of history, as is often remarked, condemns the ignorant to repeat it, but it is in the nature of an experiment to have an unknown outcome. Besides, if the tools of the past – Marxism, the Enlightenment project, market liberalism and so on – have been tried and found wanting, then experiment is demanded. As Lyotard says, the 'post' of 'postmodernism' does not signal that it comes at the end, but at the beginning of modernity. What new modernity might yet dawn from postmodern politics?

3

POSTMODERNISM AND FEMINISM

SUE THORNHAM

POLITICS AND THEORY

Feminism is above all a politics, aimed at changing existing **power** relations between women and men. Its starting point, as Maggie Humm points out, is 'the understanding that, in all societies which divide the sexes into different cultural, economic or political spheres, women are less valued than men' (*Feminisms: A Reader* (1992)). As a social or political movement, its theoretical developments have been bound up with demands for political change. The emergence of 'second-wave' feminism, the term now usually used to describe the post-1968 Women's Liberation Movement, was marked by new political groupings and campaigns, organized around abortion legislation, demands for legal and financial equality, and against pornography and sexual violence against women. But it was also marked by the publication of ambitious theoretical works such as Kate Millett's *Sexual Politics* and Shulamith Firestone's *The Dialectic of Sex* (both 1970). Both works offered themselves as texts of revolution. Firestone insisted that what she called the 'pioneer Western feminist movement' of the nineteenth and early twentieth centuries should be seen as merely the first onslaught of 'the most important revolution in history'. Millett heralded the emergence of 'a second wave of the sexual revolution'. Both sought to reclaim a feminist history; both identified feminism as theoretical standpoint with the women's movement as political practice.

For feminism, politics and theory are interdependent. But as the books by Firestone and Millett make clear, feminist politics have engaged as much with issues of culture and **representation** as in campaigns for social and economic change. Feminist theorists from Mary Wollstonecraft (1759–97) onwards have seen cultural constructions of femininity as a primary source of women's oppression. Women, writes Wollstonecraft, have been reduced to 'insignificant objects of desire'; the category 'woman' is constructed in opposition to that of 'human'. From its beginnings, feminism has seen 'ideas, language and image as crucial in shaping women's (and men's) lives' (Annette Kuhn, *The Power of the Image* (1985)). It has been concerned both to analyse and intervene in the construction of knowledge, meaning and representations. It has also been concerned with the struggle to find a voice through which such knowledges might be expressed. For the development of an autonomous female **subject**, capable of speaking in her own voice within a culture which has persistently reduced her to the status of object, is also part of feminism's project. As Rosalind Delmar

24

describes it, feminism has sought to transform women's position from that of object of knowledge to knowing subject, from the state of subjection to subjecthood.

AN ENLIGHTENMENT NARRATIVE?

All of this would seem to place feminism as an offshoot of the 'emancipatory **metanarratives**' of **Enlightenment modernism**, and this is indeed where many feminist theorists would position themselves. If, as Lyotard suggests, two major forms of '**legitimation narrative**' have been used to justify the Enlightenment quest for knowledge and the importance of scientific research, both find their echo in feminist theory. The first, the 'narrative of emancipation', in which knowledge is sought as a means to liberation, finds a clear echo in the concept of 'women's liberation'. As Sabina Lovibond writes, 'it is difficult to see how one could count oneself a feminist and remain indifferent to the modernist promise of social reconstruction' (in T. Docherty, *Postmodernism: A Reader* (1985)). But **Lyotard**'s second legitimation narrative, that of the speculative mind, in which knowledge is sought for its own sake, also finds its feminist echo – in the practice of 'consciousness raising'. Through consciousness raising, insight into the operations of male power (a feminist 'enlightenment') is achieved through communal self-analysis. The result is liberation from internalized patriarchal assumptions and ways of understanding (a patriarchal 'false consciousness'). Like **Marxism**, therefore, feminism's initial project ties the theoretical analysis of oppression to a narrative of emancipation through social transformation.

Early feminism, then, had as its aim women's equality, through admission to those spheres from which they had been excluded, and this included the spheres of rational thought and intellectual discourse. If women have been excluded from political theory, Marxism, philosophy, psychoanalysis and other dominant theoretical discourses, then women's inclusion could expand and perhaps transform those discourses, while at the same time their insights might be used to illuminate women's experience. Much feminist theory of the 1960s and early 1970s, therefore, set out to expand and transform existing theoretical models. But there are a number of problems with this approach. In the first place, it became clear that to expand such models to include women simply would not work, for women's exclusion is not an accidental omission but a fundamental structuring principle of all patriarchal thought. As Simone de Beauvoir pointed out in 1949, woman in Western thought has represented the **Other** that can confirm man's identity as Self, as rational thinking being. The concept of Self, she writes, can be produced only in opposition to that of not-self, so that the 'category of the *Other* is as primordial as consciousness itself'. To constitute himself as Subject, man has constructed woman as Other: 'she is the incidental, the inessential as opposed to the essential. He is the Subject, he is the Absolute – she is the Other' (*The Second Sex*).

Second, even if women could be included within these discourses, it would be

25

in terms only of *sameness* not **difference**: that is, within frameworks which could discuss women only in terms of a common, male-referenced humanity (what Luce **Irigaray** calls the 'hom(m)osexual economy' of men) not specifically as women. As subjects of these knowledges, therefore – that is, as thinkers and writers – women could occupy only a range of pre-given positions. They could speak only from within a masculine logic, as surrogate men. Indeed, it became increasingly clear that the 'universal subject' of Enlightenment modernism, far from being ungendered and 'transcendent', was not only gendered but very specific: a Western, bourgeois, white and heterosexual man.

Once this theoretical step is taken, a further step is inevitable: if feminists seek to construct a universal 'essential' woman as subject and/or object of their own thought, then that figure will be as partial, as historically contingent and as exclusionary as her male counterpart. Given her origins, she will simply be a Western, bourgeois, white and heterosexual woman. Feminist theory cannot both claim that knowledge and the self are constituted within history and culture and that feminist theory speaks on behalf of a universalized 'woman'. Rather, it must embrace differences between women and accept a position of partial knowledge(s). And once it occupies this position, feminist thought begins to move away from its Enlightenment origins, and to have much in common with postmodernist theory.

FEMINISM AND POSTMODERNISM

Craig Owens (in H. Foster, ed., *Postmodern Culture* (1985)), suggests a number of points of convergence between the two. Both feminism and **postmodernism** argue that the '**grand**' or 'master' **narratives** of the Enlightenment have lost their **legitimating** power. Not only, they would both suggest, have claims put forward as universally applicable in fact proved to be valid only for men of a particular culture, class and race; the ideals which have underpinned these claims – of 'objectivity', 'reason' and the autonomous self – have been equally partial and contingent. Both argue that Western **representations** – whether in art or in theory – are the product of access not to Truth but to power. Women, as Owens points out, have been represented in countless images (and metaphors) throughout Western culture, often as a symbol of something else – Nature, Truth, the **Sublime**, Sex – but have rarely seen their own representations accorded legitimacy. The representational systems of the West have, he argues, admitted only 'one vision – that of the constitutive male subject'. Both present a critique of **binarism** – that is, thinking by means of oppositions – in which one term of the opposition must always be devalued. We have seen in the discussion of de Beauvoir's work how fundamental this critique has been to feminist thought. Both, instead, insist on 'difference and **incommensurability**'. Finally, both seek to heal the breach between theory and practice, between the subject of theory/ knowledge and its object. Women, of course, are both the subjects and the objects of feminist theory, and women's sense of self, it has been argued, is far more 'relational' than that of men (see Nancy Chodorow, *The Reproduction of Mothering* (1978), and Carol Gilligan, *In a Different Voice* (1983)).

In place of an essential, universal man or woman, both feminism and post-modernism offer, in Jane Flax's words, 'a profound skepticism regarding universal (or universalizing) claims about the existence, nature and powers of reason, progress, science, language and the subject/self' ('Gender as a Social Problem' (1986)). Yet the alliance thus formed is an uneasy one. Feminism, as I have indicated, is itself a 'narrative of emancipation', and its political claims are made on behalf of a social group, women, who are seen to have an underlying community of interest, and of an embodied female subject whose identity and experiences (or 'truth-in-experience') are necessarily different from those of men. If we replace the concept of 'woman' by that of 'myriads of women living in elaborate historical complexes of class, race and culture' (H. Crowley and S. Himmelweit, eds, *Knowing Women* (1992)), as some theorists propose – if, in other words, we remove gender (or sexual difference) as a central organizing principle – how can a feminist political practice be any longer possible? If sexual difference becomes only *one* term of difference, and one which is not funda-mentally constitutive of our identity, then how can it be privileged? Surely to privilege is to create, in Christine Di Stefano's words, 'just another . . . totalizing fiction' which should be **deconstructed** and opposed in the name of difference (*Feminism/Postmodernism*).

In throwing in its lot with postmodernism, then, might not feminism be colluding in its own eradication, accepting the demise of 'metanarratives of emancipation' at a point when women's own emancipation is far from complete? Feminists are understandably divided as to the answer to this question. Some, like Sabina Lovibond, insist that feminism must not be seduced by the attractions of postmodernism, for if feminism disowns 'the impulse to "enlighten"' it loses the possibility of all political and social action. Others take a very different line, arguing that the critiques of Enlightenment beliefs which feminist theory has mounted must place it as 'a type of postmodern philosophy'. Jane Flax, for example, argues that feminist theories, 'like other forms of postmodernism, should encourage us to tolerate and interpret ambivalence, ambiguity, and multiplicity as well as to expose the roots of our needs for imposing order and structure no matter how arbitrary and oppressive these needs may be' (*Feminism/Postmodernism*). In this argument, postmodernism becomes a sort of therapeutic corrective to feminism's universalizing tendency. In similar vein, Nancy Fraser and Linda Nicholson, whilst rejecting the philosophical pessimism of Lyotard, wish to adopt his critique of metanarratives for a feminist social criticism. Such a feminist theory, they argue, would eschew the analysis of grand causes of women's oppression, focusing instead on its historically and culturally specific manifestations. It would also replace unitary conceptions of 'woman' and female identity with '**plural** and complexly structured conceptions of social identity, treating gender as one relevant strand among others, attending also to class, race, ethnicity, age, and sexual orientation'. In a thoroughly feminizing metaphor, they conclude that such a theory 'would look more like a tapestry composed of threads of many different hues than one woven in a single color' (*Feminism/ Postmodernism*).

This move towards a radical **anti-essentialism** finds perhaps its most powerful voice in the work of Judith **Butler**. Butler goes much further than Flax, or Fraser and Nicholson, in arguing that the very category of gender is a 'regulatory fiction' which functions to enforce compulsory heterosexuality (everyone is *either* male or female; opposites complement/attract). For Butler, gender is 'a kind of impersonation and approximation . . . but . . . a *kind of imitation for which there is no original*'. The appearance of 'naturalness' which accompanies heterosexual gender identity is simply the effect of repeated imitative performance. What is being imitated, however, is 'a phantasmatic ideal of heterosexual identity'. There is no essence of heterosexual masculinity or femininity which precedes our performance of these roles; we construct the ideal of that essence through our performances (D. Fuss, ed., *Inside/Out* (1991)). And we construct it in the service of a regulatory heterosexual binarism. Gender, like other categories of knowledge, is the product not of Truth but of power expressed through **discourse**. Moreover, as a copy of a fantasized ideal, heterosexuality always fails to approximate its ideal. It is thus doomed to a kind of compulsive repetition, always threatened by failure and always liable to disruption from that which is excluded in the performance. Gender, in this view, is a performance which constructs what it claims to explain. Rather than persisting in clinging to it as an explanatory category, therefore, feminists should celebrate its dissolution into 'convergences of gender identity and all manner of gender dissonance' (Butler, *Feminism/ Postmodernism)*. Its abandonment promises the possibility of new and complex subject-positions and of 'coalitional politics which do not assume in advance what the content of "women" will be' (Butler, *Gender Trouble* (1990)).

Other feminists, however, whilst not wishing to return to a unitary concept of 'woman', are far more sceptical about the transformative possibilities of a feminism which embraces postmodernism. These theorists point to a number of major problems in this projected alliance. At the heart of all of these is the issue of power. Postmodernism, unlike feminism, as Linda Hutcheon reminds us, is not a politics: it has no strategies of resistance and is not concerned with social and political change. A postmodernist feminism, in which sexual difference is no longer seen as a fundamental organizing category, but is replaced by the concept of multiple and shifting differences, threatens to make a feminist politics impossible. Such a politics must assume women to be a specific – and a specifically oppressed – constituency. If we turn, for example, to the political strategy proposed by Judith Butler, we find this problem. Butler proposes a strategy of 'gender parody', in which gender is self-consciously and parodically performed, in a masquerade which subverts because it draws attention to the non-identity of gender and sexuality, to the multiple sexualities which can be written on our bodies. This is, as Tania Modleski points out in *Feminism Without Women* (1991), an 'extremely individualistic solution to the problem of women's oppression'. It is also one which is imbued with the political ambiguities of postmodernism. Parody, after all, depends on the stability of that which it imitates for its critical force. It oscillates, as Butler herself concedes, between complicity and critique. It is difficult, therefore, to see the 'new configuration of politics' advocated by Butler as extending beyond a repeated movement to displacement and excess and into strategies for social change.

Such concerns are even more evident when we consider how easily this emphasis on self-conscious parody and play can be co-opted for a notion of '**post-feminism**'. Originating as a term in popular journalism of the 1980s, post-feminism was seen as heralding a release from the narrow preoccupations of feminism, in a celebration of difference, personal liberation and play, performed primarily through processes of consumption. In recent years it has been taken more seriously, proposed as both a continuation and a critique of 'second-wave' feminism, incorporating feminism's goal of equality whilst embracing the pluralism and diversity characteristic of postmodernism Most of all, however, it has embraced postmodernism's political ambivalence. When popular television series like *Buffy the Vampire Slayer* (1997–2003), or *Sex and the City* (1998–2004) are described as post-feminist, for example, what is being referred to is their privileging of style and a notion of gender masquerade, but without any clear critical or subversive intent.

A NEW MASTER NARRATIVE?

Feminists, then, have criticized postmodernism's indifference to issues of power and politics. As Meaghan Morris points out, the contemporary crisis in modernism's 'legitimation narratives' diagnosed by theorists of the postmodern will not necessarily benefit women, their designation as '*master* narratives' notwithstanding. It might just as well mean the collapse of arguments for any kind of political intervention – since there are no longer grounds for deciding where, when or as whom to intervene. As Donna Haraway put it in *Simians, Cyborgs, and Women* (1991),

> We unmasked the doctrines of objectivity because they threatened our budding sense of collective historical subjectivity and agency and our 'embodied' accounts of the truth, and we ended up with one more excuse for not learning any post-Newtonian physics and one more reason to drop the old feminist self-help practices of repairing our own cars. They're just texts anyway, so let the boys have them back.

With no arguments for change, power is once again ceded to the powerful.

This last point takes us on to a further argument: that postmodernism may not simply be indifferent to questions of power. It may be in the process of constituting itself as the new 'master' discourse. Craig Owen's concern at the absence of feminist voices within postmodernism, for example, offers to reinscribe feminism as 'an *instance* of postmodern thought'. Postmodernism, that is, constitutes itself – where it considers feminism at all – as the *inclusive* category, of which feminism is merely one example. In so doing, it can be argued, it simultaneously moves to erase the specificity of the feminist critique and, in a repeat of modernism's self-constitution, to silence the voices of women.

That postmodernism has sought to deal with the feminist critique by offering itself as a 'framing discourse' for feminism is a point made by a number of feminist theorists. They have pointed to the fact that postmodernism's debate with – or deconstruction of – modernism has been conducted pretty well exclusively within and by the same constituency as before: white, privileged men of the industrialized West. It is a constituency which, having already had its Enlightenment, is now happy to subject that legacy to critical scrutiny. In this debate the contribution of feminism, whilst acknowledged to be a key factor in the destabilizing of modernism's concept of a universal 'subject', is of necessity (re)marginalized. The central protagonists are once again to be found elsewhere. Nancy Hartsock articulates feminist suspicions of this move. 'Why is it,' she asks, 'that just at the moment when so many of us who have been silenced begin to demand the right to name ourselves, to act as subjects rather than objects of history, that just then the concept of subjecthood becomes problematic?' (*Feminism/Postmodernism*). It is no accident, she argues, that at the moment when those who have been excluded begin both to theorize and to demand political change, there emerges uncertainty about whether the world *can* be theorized and about whether progress is possible or even, as a 'totalizing' ideal, desirable. For Hartsock, the intellectual moves of postmodernism constitute merely the latest accent of the voice of the 'master discourse', as it attempts to deal with the social changes and theoretical challenges of the late twentieth century.

Two further feminist suspicions are worth enumerating here. They concern the way in which postmodern 'gender-scepticism' permits an easy slide into what Susan Bordo calls the 'fantasy of *becoming* multiplicity – the dream of endless multiple embodiments, allowing one to dance from place to place and self to self' (*Feminism/Postmodernism*). This has two aspects. The first is that being *everywhere* is pretty much the same as being nowhere; in other words, postmodernism offers to its male theorists simply another version of the disembodied detachment which characterized the Enlightenment speaking position. For postmodernist feminists to seek to occupy this position is to risk their own obliteration as distinctive voices. As Tania Modleski argues, only those who have a sense of identity can play at not having it. The kind of disembodied, anti-essentialist feminism which is produced from postmodernism's embrace is, she argues, at best a luxury open only to the most privileged of women. At worst, it is to collude in the masculine disavowal of female embodiment.

The second aspect of postmodernism's 'fantasy of becoming' which is worth noting is its tendency to become a fantasy of woman, even of 'becoming woman'. If, as Craig Owens suggests, the mission of modernity's narratives was to transform

30

the world into a representation, with man as its subject and woman its represented object, then postmodernism's narratives exhibit little change. For Baudrillard in particular, the feminine is a constant metaphor for the post-modern. It is woman's lack of subjectivity, her position outside truth or meaning, her conflation of authenticity and artifice, that for Baudrillard constitute the horror and seduction of the postmodern. But, as Alice Jardine points out, this use of femininity to represent the unrepresentable is yet another appropriation. The 'discourse of woman' is in reality the discourse of male philosophy. In this way, as Tania Modleski puts it, 'male power . . . works to efface female subjectivity by occupying the site of femininity'. Women, as embodied subjects, are erased.

'STANDPOINT' THEORIES

How, then, can feminist theory both hold on to a belief in 'woman' *and* respect cultural diversity and difference? Can we both accept the plurality and multiplicity of women's discourse and insist on the centrality of sexual difference in the construction of subjectivity? Attempts to answer this question – to, in Alice Jardine's words, 'dive into the wreck' of Western culture rather than simply pushing it aside – have produced some of the most exciting feminist thinking over the past decade. One possible answer is provided by what have been termed feminist 'standpoint' theorists. Borrowing from Marxism, these thinkers argue that the subjugated or marginalized not only produce different knowledges from those in positions of privilege; they also produce less distorted, less rationalizing, less falsely universalizing accounts. Nancy Hartsock, for example, argues that 'out of this concrete multiplicity [we must] build an account of the world as seen from the margins, an account which can expose the falseness of the view from the top and can transform the margins as well as the center' (*Feminism/Postmodern-ism*). The task, she suggests, is to develop an account of the world which treats these alternative perspectives not – as they are seen from the centre – as subjugated or disruptive knowledges, but instead as primary and as capable of constituting a different world. This is an approach also embraced by black feminists like Patricia Hill Collins, who argues for what she terms a black women's or Afrocentric feminist epistemology. Like other subordinate groups, argues Collins, African-American women have not only developed distinctive interpretations of their own oppression, but have done so by constructing alternative forms of knowledge. The specific forms of black women's economic and political oppression and the nature of their collective resistance to this oppression mean, she argues, that African-American women, as a group, experi-ence a different world from those who are not black and female. The specificity of this experience in turn produces a distinctive black feminist *consciousness*, and a distinctive black feminist intellectual tradition. These 'engaged visions', in Hartsock's terms, can then produce the grounds for the recognition of common-alities, and 'the tools to begin to construct an account of the world sensitive to the realities of race and gender as well as class' (*Feminism/Postmodernism*).

There are problems, however, with this rather literal interpretation of what a 'politics of location' (Adrienne Rich, *Blood, Bread and Poetry* (1986)) might mean. It can become over-simplified and reductive (*this* set of experiences inevitably produces *that* mode of consciousness). It is difficult to know which set of experiences is constitutive of a particular group and mode of knowledge production. It places an emphasis on experience which should perhaps more properly be placed on particular ways of *interpreting* that experience. Finally, the appeal to a commonality of experience can elide both differences between and differences within women. Collins's work, for example, persistently assumes that all black women are American, insisting that '[l]iving life as an African American woman is a necessary prerequisite for producing black feminist thought' (in B. Guy-Sheftall, ed., *Words of Fire* (1995)), and that all African-American women share a common position. On the other hand, once we allow for the multiplicity of positionings within every 'standpoint', the concept of a common-ality of experience within oppressed groups – and hence a distinctive standpoint – can become lost.

SITUATED KNOWLEDGE AND POLITICAL FICTIONS

The concept of 'situated knowledges' developed by theorists like Rosi Braidotti and Donna Haraway is a more complex answer to the question of how, in Braidotti's words, to 'figure out how to respect cultural diversity without falling into relativism or political despair' (*Nomadic Subjects* (1994)). The 'situatedness' envisaged here, however, is no simple affair. It is in the first place a position which insists on the embodied and therefore sexually differentiated nature of the female subject. But embodiment does not, in this context, mean 'essentialism', where essentialism is defined as implying a fixed and monolithic essence to female identity which is beyond historical and cultural change. The embodied female subject envisaged here is, on the contrary, a '**nomadic**' subject, to use Braidotti's terminology. That is, she is 'the site of multiple, complex, and potentially contradictory sets of experiences, defined by overlapping variables such as class, race, age, lifestyle, sexual preference, and others'. Haraway goes further: in the contemporary high-tech world, feminist embodiment is about 'nodes in fields, inflections in orientations, and responsibility for difference in material **semiotic** fields of meaning' (*Simians, Cyborgs, and Women* (1991)). What both thinkers are trying to do in these rather complex formulations is to insist both that the female subject is embodied – that women's knowledge and thought cannot be separated from their lived experience – and that this insistence does not mean that feminism cannot recognize the differences both between women and within each woman. Within all of us, argues Braidotti, there is an interplay of differing levels of experience, so that our identities, whilst situated, are not fixed but 'nomadic'. It is such situated knowledges – 'partial, locatable, critical knowledges' – that permit both a new definition of objectivity (objectivity as partial, situated knowledge) and the possibility of new political coalitions.

But this still leaves the difficulty of how, in Braidotti's words, to 'connect the "differences within" each woman to a political practice that requires mediation of the "differences among" women'. For it is difficult – to say the least – to see how women could unite around the formulations quoted above. In answer, both Braidotti and Haraway offer 'political fictions' (Braidotti) or 'foundational myths' (Haraway) as a way of framing understanding. These 'politically informed images' (Braidotti), or 'figure[s] of hope and desire' (Patricia Clough, *Feminist Thought* (1994)), are offered as a means of empowering both a shared sense of identity and the struggle against oppression. Political fictions, argues Braidotti, may be more effective at this moment than theoretical systems. Braidotti's image is the figure of the nomad, who is neither exile (homeless and rootless) nor migrant (displaced and suspended between the old and the new). Instead, 'situated' but mobile, the nomad employs a critical consciousness to cultivate 'the art of disloyalty to civilization', thus resisting incorporation by the host culture. Haraway's 'political fiction' is more challenging. It is the figure of the **cyborg**, a hybrid of body and machine, a 'kind of disassembled and reassembled, post-modern collective and personal self' (in *Feminism/Postmodernism*). As hybrid figure, the cyborg blurs the categories of human and machine, and with it those other Western dualisms: self/Other, mind/body, nature/culture, male/female, civilized/primitive, reality/appearance, whole/part, agent/resource, maker/made, active/passive, right/wrong, truth/illusion, total/partial, God/man. It is embodied but not unified, and being a figure of blurred boundaries and regeneration rather than (re)birth, it cannot be explained by reference to conventional narratives of identity. It is locally specific but globally connected: Haraway reminds us that 'networking' is a feminist practice as well as a multinational corporate strategy: a way of surviving 'in diaspora' (*Feminism/Postmodernism*).

It can be objected that theorists like Braidotti and Haraway are trying to have it both ways: to be both situated and multiple, within and outside postmodernism. They can also be accused of replacing a narrative of liberation directed at change in the real world with a utopian fantasy, whose notions of 'embodiment' and 'situatedness' are slippery in the extreme. Susan Bordo, for example, criticizing Haraway's image of the cyborg, protests:

> What sort of body is it that is free to change its shape and location at will, that can become anyone and travel anywhere? If the body is a metaphor for our locatedness in space and time and thus for the finitude of human perception and knowledge, then the postmodern body is no body at all.
>
> (in *Feminism/Postmodernism*)

For Bordo, this kind of response to what Sandra Harding (in *Knowing Women*) calls the contemporary 'instabilities' of feminism's analytical categories will leave feminist thought 'cut . . . off from the source of feminism's transformative possibilities' (*Feminism/Postmodernism*). A similar charge is made by Tania Modleski (*Feminism Without Women*), who argues that it will leave us with a 'feminism without women'. Nevertheless, the dilemma which all these theorists articulate is the same: in Modleski's words, how to 'hold on to the category of woman while recognizing ourselves to be in the *process* (an unending one) of *defining* and *constructing the category*'. Since it is, as Donna Haraway comments, 'hard to climb when you are holding on to both sides of a pole, simultaneously or alternately' (*Simians, Cyborgs, and Women*), the various 'political fictions' offered by feminist theorists can be seen as a way of finding new terms in which to theorize a way forward. For the danger they recognize is also the same: that male postmodern theory will simply repeat the gesture of its modernist predecessors in appropriating 'femininity' as one of its multiple possible positions, at the same time as it erases and silences the work and lives of women. The task which is being addressed is, in the words of Meaghan Morris (*The Pirate's Fiancée* (1988)), 'to use feminist work to frame discussions of postmodernism, and not the other way around'.

4

POSTMODERNISM AND LIFESTYLES

NIGEL WATSON

It was during the late 1980s and early 1990s that **postmodernism** and its linkage to our everyday lifestyles first moved from the academic literature and into popular consciousness. At this time, the *Independent on Sunday* newspaper asked the question: 'Why is Fergie [Sarah Ferguson, the Duchess of York] like Batman, Ross Perot [a former presidential candidate in the US elections], Vimto, a Mazda and the new MI6 building?' The answer they gave was because all of these people and products had been labelled postmodern, they were all said to share a self-consciousness about the past and they all only fully made sense if an ironic attitude of playfulness was acknowledged. The film *Batman*, for example, played upon references from comic books, while the Mazda MX5 was a contemporary recreation of the English sports car of the 1960s. This feature of postmodern styling and design has become best known as **retro** and a glance through catalogues of consumer goods will demonstrate the extent to which this trend has become part of everyday life, with telephones, radios, bathroom fittings and furniture all drawing upon our desire to recreate the mood of an imagined past.

The public images of Fergie and Ross Perot made sense by referring to the past rather than the future: Fergie because she drew upon a former age of royal decadence and Ross Perot because he appealed to the so-called lost values of a former America. The former Conservative prime minister, John Major, attempted a similar appeal in the UK by evoking an England of warm beer, cricket on village greens and spinsters cycling to church on balmy summer evenings. It has also been suggested that Ross Perot represented another feature of the postmodern in that he was a single-issue politician without roots in the traditions of party. The same was said of Sir James Goldsmith's Referendum Party in the 1997 UK general election which had only one policy and which claimed that it would dissolve itself if its aim was achieved.

Postmodern politics are said to revolve around particular campaigning issues in which previously disparate groups coalesce and then dissolve again. This is exemplified by the so-called rainbow coalition of the 1980s and by the protests and campaigns against live animal exports in which elderly Tory women, liberal academics and New Age travellers united against the injustice of sending animals to their deaths thousands of miles away within the confined conditions of an animal transporter. At root this aspect of the postmodern condition is related to the dissolution of traditional class and status groupings. Values and allegiances are now transitional and no longer centred in the old alliances of production-based relationships and class-based political parties. Retro styling and the dissolution of tradition are only some of the features which characterize post-modernism and more of these will be explored later in this essay.

In the same article the *Independent on Sunday* went on to ask a number of celebrities if they could define the exact nature of postmodernism. Most were sceptical or dismissive, though some did attempt an answer. The Head of BBC Music and Arts said: 'Post modernism is a rather glib way of saying flexibility; of saying that hierarchies aren't what they used to be, that you can mix and match different hierarchies of culture.' He was a brave man, because one of the most quoted writers on postmodernism and culture – Jean **Baudrillard** – refused the invitation and replied in this way: 'I cannot explain and I will not explain. Post modernism for me is nothing. I do not worry about this term. I am very exhausted with this post modernism. All that I will say is that the post modern is maybe postmodern.'

In the early part of the twenty-first century there is still some confusion and controversy surrounding the concept, and for some philosophers, like Christopher **Norris**, the term is little more than a lazy way of collecting together some of the features of contemporary culture and combining them with partly digested aspects of continental thought. It is, they argue, only a transitory and relatively insignificant phase in our understanding of contemporary experience. Postmodernism is probably backgrounded more now than in the 1990s; however, it cannot be denied that the concept has had a major impact across a range of areas of thought ranging from geography to literary theory to cinema to architecture, and that for many writers it has provided a satisfactory way of explaining the significant changes in the nature of social experience over the past fifty years or so. This essay considers these changes in relation to consumer culture and in particular will reflect upon contemporary social identity. I try to answer the question whether the basis of everyday life can be said to have changed sufficiently to justify the claims of some writers that we are living in a new era or epoch – an era that can be called '**postmodernity**'.

POSTMODERNISM, IDENTITY AND LIFESTYLE

Although, for some, postmodernism remains a confused and vacuous term, it has been in use for long enough to have achieved at least a basic consistency of definition. Most commentators agree that there is a cluster of features which characterize contemporary culture and which when taken together can be called postmodern. Perhaps the most important of these for the purposes of this section is the suggestion that our experiences are now rooted in the processes of consumption rather than production. This can perhaps be illustrated by thinking of those regions of the UK which were once dominated by heavy industry. For most people in these largely working-class areas the future was one defined by a relationship with work and with, for example, the production of coal, or ships or cotton. The people were miners, shipbuilders, or mill workers and the basis of social life was for these men and women their relationship with the process of production. Their personal, collective and cultural identities were rooted in the locality around the workplace and in the values of the industry for which they worked.

The past forty years have seen a radical shift in the nature of this relationship. The land which used to house the factories and mines has now been developed for out-of-town shopping areas such as the MetroCentre in Gateshead or Meadowhall in Sheffield, while the land by the rivers has been turned over to leisure marinas, theme parks and heritage museums. In fact the heritage museum, such as the one at Beamish in the north-east of England, epitomizes the postmodern process whereby a past is nostalgically recreated as a form of substitute reality. Ex-miners are employed to inform the rest of us about mining in a time in which they did not live, while the need for 'real' mining has disappeared. We pay our money and are entertained by consuming second-hand experiences which once formed the basis of everyday life. To a significant extent we have become tourists in our own cultures. Sunday no longer means a trip to church or chapel, but rather a visit to the cathedrals of consumerism. Shopping malls have become major sites of leisure activity; the pilgrimage is enough even without the act of buying.

We no longer conform to the traditions of the old occupational cultures and instead we choose a lifestyle. This term, not in itself a new one, was taken by the advertising and designer culture of the 1980s to stand for the individuality and self-expression that were the cornerstone of the free market revolution of that decade. The era of mass consumption, with its emphasis on conformity and similarity, has been replaced by an apparently endless choice and variety of consumer goods aimed at specific market segments. While it is important to remember that some people in developed societies and many throughout the world are excluded from this process, it is equally important to understand that the construction of identity through the acquisition of consumer goods is a voluntary one. Those of us who participate are not just fashion victims, we actively wish to join in and actively **desire** the opportunities for self-expression and display which are provided by the choices of the shopping malls. It is true that we may be targeted as part of grey power, owners of a pink pound or subscribers to consumption smoothing, but we like to identify with the style that best represents the way that we wish to be seen. **Power** has now come to be seen as the capacity to spend in order to find expression for an aspirational lifestyle.

Perhaps one of the most noticeable areas of growth in consumer markets has been in men's fashion and lifestyle accessories. The male body has been increasingly used in advertising, not simply in a functional capacity, as it would have been in the 1950s, but in a decorative one as well. Men are no longer just portrayed as the expert advisers to women on technical matters such as the choice of washing machine; they are also at the aspirational heart of advertising style. Older as well as young men now articulate their identity through a conscious and selective process of consumption involving clothes, hairstyles and body decoration. A casual glance at any newsagent's shelves shows a wide range of fashion and image magazines as well as those devoted to the latest electronic gadgets. Men are the focus of a shifting process of consumerization in which image overrides utility. This has developed through constructions like the 'new man' of the 1980s and 'lads' of the 1990s, leading to versions of male identity linked to self-conscious, playful and sexualized processes, unimaginable in the decades to which John Major so nostalgically referred.

The body is also a focus for identity construction in a more permanent and serious way. The opportunity for changing the shape and structure of our physical bodies through cosmetic surgery is widely advertised in fashion and style magazines. Noses can be reshaped, wrinkles removed, faces lifted, fat siphoned and breasts reduced or augmented. The body itself can be seen as a consumer commodity, and this is a process available and promoted to both men and women. In a competitive world it is not enough to be ordinary and we are all encouraged to approach more nearly the ideal of youthful bodily perfection in order to give ourselves added market value. We may even soon be able to design our children to correspond with our aspirations and pay a surrogate mother to grow the child in order to avoid disruption of career and lifestyle.

A massive, worldwide industry has developed devoted to assisting us in our responsibilities to maintain our bodies. The healthiness of the body has become associated with its appearance, and it is possible to buy into a bewildering array of products and services that trade upon the importance of the cultural values of youth and beauty. In this context youth and beauty are aligned with slenderness, muscularity and physical fitness, one extremity of which is represented by the increasing popularity of bodybuilding for both men and women. The corollary of this is that the ageing body has become a source of anxiety, and the non-exercised and overweight body a source of shame and ridicule. Although we are surrounded by health-promoting messages which encourage us to exercise and to eat the 'right' foods, the drive for us to achieve fitness is related as much to the desire for surface attractiveness as it is to the protective dimensions of health promotion.

It is not a coincidence that management of our lifestyles is at the heart of the health-promotion process. We are encouraged to believe that our leisure time should be devoted to activities which will enhance our potential for healthy longevity. It is as important to be able to demonstrate and display an association with the correct attitude as it is actually to participate. Owning a mountain bike and Lycra shorts immediately confers the desired surface appearance, provided of course those unsightly bulges can be hidden. Similarly, eating low-fat foods and the other acceptable commodities comprising a healthy diet gives an assurance of risk reduction and adequate body maintenance even if they are consumed in addition to, rather than instead of, proscribed foodstuffs. It is often the case that an emphasis on body maintenance is combined with the celebration of excess and indulgence. Postmodern fragmentation extends into dietary habits in which contradictory messages can be believed and simultaneously followed.

It can seem as if the efforts of the advertising industry are directed entirely towards the generation of false needs within us all, but one of the great strengths of the process of consumerism is that it is able to harness and direct our genuine needs, even if the goods and services on offer more often than not leave us frustrated and unfulfilled. Humankind has almost certainly always desired better health, greater beauty, sexual fulfilment and longer life. The issue is, however, whether these are now sought at the expense of other more substantial aspects of life. It is also important to reflect what happens to the excluded in a world devoted to valuing the surface appearance. This will be returned to in the conclusion.

A FEW NECESSARY THEORETICAL POINTS

One of the features that emerges from the above discussion is that post-modernism emphasizes the importance of style and appearance over content. The construction of a personal lifestyle through the consumption of desirable consumer services has little to do with the usefulness of the goods and much to do with image and the way that they appear to others. This argument has also been applied to entertainment and to the arts. Many commentators have observed that the distinction between high art and popular culture has been lost because of the uncertainty which now surrounds establishing unequivocal criteria for judging the value of cultural forms. This is a difficult point, but essentially from a postmodern perspective it is not possible to assert that Shakespeare is better than *EastEnders* or *Coronation Street*. Certainly there are writers for whom this would be an absurd statement because they continue to believe in the traditional standards by which literary merit is judged, and who would counter any assault on these standards with bitter and hostile academic debate.

There is an important link here with one of the fundamental characteristics of most postmodern thought. The key thinkers have all identified a common theme in the scepticism of the twentieth century towards the once great certainties of history and society. We no longer unquestioningly accept the universal claims to knowledge and truth of the great stories which have organized our culture. These include religion, the progress of **modernism**, the progress of science, and absolute political theories like **Marxism**.

It is not always easy to grasp the significance of these abstract ideas for everyday life, but what is really in question is whether it is any longer possible to agree on absolute truth. We often hear on the television and radio about a break-down in society because of the decline in shared values. Politicians of the main parties in the UK speak of the need to re-establish a common core of beliefs in order to bring society back together. From a postmodern perspective this does not make sense because the politicians are basing their claims on a mistaken belief in universal truths, or **metanarratives**, as postmodern thinkers would say. The supremacy of Western thinking has been challenged throughout the twentieth century and especially with the decline of colonial empires. The explicit assumption that their cultures and ideas represented the progress of civilization is one that we no longer accept. It is now much more commonplace to assume that we cannot say that one society or culture is better than another one.

Postmodern thinkers also point to the fragmentation of experience and a compression of time and space as defining features of the late twentieth century. It is now accepted that changes in the structure of multinational companies have led to the globalization of production. Cars, for example, may now be assembled in the UK using parts that have been manufactured at factories throughout the world. Communication and transport systems have developed to allow links between countries to occur with great rapidity. European financial institutions are able to transmit their data electronically to be processed overnight on the Indian subcontinent, ready for return for business the next day. The **Internet** allows us to view from home, and in real time, events on the other side of the world. When we telephone to a call centre, it may be located anywhere in the world. Whereas forty years ago the family holiday might have been spent in Blackpool or Bournemouth, it is now unremarkable to travel to Florida, the Caribbean or the Far East. It is quite possible for the more adventurous to explore the Himalayas or the Arctic. A visit to any supermarket provides the opportunity to purchase food from every culture on the globe and which was growing on the other side of the world perhaps only two days previously. The average high street in the UK contains restaurants and takeaways offering cuisine from every continent. All of these practical changes in our opportunities to experience the world mean that our conscious appreciation of time and of physical space is compressed when compared with even the middle of the twentieth century. In the next section we will look at the implications of these ideas for our experience of leisure and entertainment, but before doing so we need briefly to consider the ideas of one particular theorist of the postmodern – Jean Baudrillard.

Baudrillard is associated, perhaps more than any other writer, with the cultural implications of postmodernism. His early writings provide a neo-Marxist critique of consumption in capitalist societies. However, he later comes to criticize any theories, like psychoanalysis, Marxism or **structuralism**, which depend upon looking beneath the surface appearance to an underlying truth or essence. Baudrillard is strongly influenced by a tradition in French philosophy called **semiology**. This leads him to look at the way that we understand signs and symbols in our culture, semiology being the science of **sign** systems which includes language, as well as visual and social codes.

The basis of this tradition is that we make sense of the world around us by associating signs and symbols with objects or ideas which are called referents. Baudrillard has outlined four stages in the way that the signs relate to their referents and he has called this relationship **simulation**. It is possible to illustrate this in relation to the creation of images. While in medieval times the image was simply a direct reflection of reality, in the Renaissance period images were the individual and creative work of a single artist. The sign was emancipated and open to artistic interpretation; most importantly, it was unique and could not be reproduced in the same form: there is only one 'Mona Lisa'. He then points to the Industrial Revolution and the emergence of processes of production which allow for the manufacture of endless copies of the same artefact. In terms of images the camera provides the best example of this. There is no original of a photographic image, although it refers to an external reality. Finally he suggests that, with the start of postmodernism, we have entered the era of **hyperreality** in which the signs stand only for themselves. Signs are the reality, and the imaginary and the real have become confused. This can be illustrated in relation to the imagery of the pop video in which time and place are hard to identify and in which a blend of styles and references mix together, teasing, but not depending upon our knowledge of previous artists. These brief and fast edited videos can then be watched in no particular order on digital music channels. Playful references to earlier musical styles are at the core of successful bands, whilst others blend an eclectic mix of cultural and musical styles including Asian, European and Afro-Caribbean. Similarly, in our pursuit of a healthy identity, the fitness bike or the home rowing machine have come to have a place of their own. Such aids depend upon our understanding of the real processes of rowing or cycling, but their usage has evolved into independent activities with a reality of their own. At the core of this series of observations is a central tenet of postmodern thinking: images and cultural artefacts no longer refer to a single reality, but have instead become realities in their own right.

POSTMODERNISM, CITIES AND LEISURE

It was mentioned earlier that another of the features of postmodern analysis is the claim that there has been a breakdown in the distinction between elite art and popular culture. This is not a new observation and over sixty years ago the mass culture critics expressed concern that high culture would be undermined because of the commercial exploitation of mass taste. The major difference, though, between these early writers and the contemporary postmodern critics is that the latter are celebrating these developments. One of the central claims made by writers who are optimistic about postmodern changes is that the process is democratizing and potentially classless, and this is an issue that will form the basis of the concluding section. However, we are now going to look at the impact of postmodern change upon leisure and the urban spaces in which we live and work.

The starting point for much of the debate about postmodern issues in the twentieth century has been architecture. It has even been suggested that the transition from the modern to the era of the postmodern can be specified as 3.32 p.m. on 15 July 1972. This is the time when a prize-winning example of modern housing – the Pruitt-Igoe housing development in St Louis – was blown up because it was considered unsuitable for human habitation even by those on a low income. Modern architecture was characterized by the principles of architects such as Le Corbusier who was at his most influential in the 1920s, though his ideas are typified by the high-rise flats which came to dominate our cities in the 1960s.

The modernist architects – like modernist writers and painters in their respective fields – rejected all previous forms and insisted that both traditional and classical forms of architecture should be replaced by buildings based upon rational and universal principles. In practice this meant an emphasis on plain functional design, usually in concrete and glass. The building was decontextualized and universalized. The hearts of cities were flattened, to be replaced all over the world by buildings which looked the same. This was the metanarrative of modernism.

In contrast postmodern buildings and cityscapes are characterized by a sensitivity to context and self-conscious playfulness in which different styles and references to different historical periods are mixed together in an **ironic** and eclectic way. There is a characteristic focus on appearance over substance and purpose. It contains a deliberate mixing of vernacular and classical features as part of the process whereby popular and elite culture are given equal value. In many of our cities the cobbled streets ripped up in the 1960s are being replaced and embellished with fibreglass reproduction gas lamps, in an attempt to evoke the past.

In a related sense the Metro Centre in Gateshead (north-east England) has shopping areas that are themed to provide us with a pastiche experience. In the Mediterranean village it is possible to eat pasta in an Italian trattoria or calamares in a tapas bar on opposite sides of the mall with twinkling light bulbs designed to remind us of those longed-for sultry summer nights. If you are overcome by these feelings then travel agents are handily placed to complete the experience. Just around the corner we can enter a Dickensian world of cobbles, street-lamps and small-pane-windowed shops where we can eat cream teas or buy humbugs. Many writers, including Baudrillard, have pointed to theme parks, and especially Disneyland, as examples of postmodern entertainment space. However, we have to travel to them. In the themed shopping mall we have the playful creation of alternative realities brought to us as part of an everyday experience of shopping.

A unique feature of the twentieth century has been the expansion and proliferation of electronic means of communication which fill our world with a confusion of images and sounds unimaginable a hundred years ago. The very existence of so much competing information means that our attention span is shortened and that the potential for a continuous thoughtful **narrative** is undermined. Instead we mix and match styles and genres, creating an eclectic mix of short-lived experiences. This is exemplified by the increasing numbers of television channels across the world, all of which can be surfed by using the remote handset. The television becomes like a magazine in which we flick from page to page, mostly just looking at the pictures, sometimes taking in sections but rarely completing a programme or article from end to end.

This dimension of discontinuity is even more marked in the development of digital storage media such as the i-pod, the DVD or the CD-ROM. While it is possible to disrupt the linear flow of television, the programmes are nevertheless made to be watched from beginning to end. Even the video recorder only provides a faster way of shifting the time experience, which nevertheless remains essentially linear. CD-ROM-based reference materials like Encarta or Cine-mania allow us to make a potentially infinite series of connections, creating our own sequences and patterns without the constraints of pre-given stories or argument. This is a truly postmodern experience in which time and content are separated and narrative is controlled by the viewer and is always in the present. Similarly the i-pod allows for the reorganization of a music playlist into a personal order.

There have been a number of recent examples of television programmes which have been said to reflect postmodern culture. One of the most often quoted examples of postmodern TV and cinema is *Twin Peaks*. Like many of David **Lynch's** films for the cinema, this was characterized by disruptions of temporal and spatial relationships and by elements of parody and pastiche. *Twin Peaks* was notable for the fact that the entire series centres on a murder which occurred before the action began. It is referred to and elements of it are glimpsed in flashback, but the murder itself is never depicted. Lynch chose instead to make a film for cinema which disclosed the events upon which the television series was based, but only after the series had finished its run. It is a matter of controversy as to whether this film had a life of its own, or whether it depended for its sense and coherence upon knowledge of the television series. Certainly the sense of the television programmes was richest if the constant references to other television styles and series were appreciated. It has even been said that the programmes were as much about television as a medium as they were about the storyline, exemplifying the postmodern emphasis on surface and play.

It would be possible to give many other examples of the extent to which the characteristics of the postmodern can be seen in cinema, television and adver-tising. The films of Quentin **Tarantino**, especially *Pulp Fiction*, and numerous television campaigns all contain the elements which have been discussed so far in this chapter. It is clear that there has been a major shift in the field of repre-sentation and in the way that signs and symbols are presented to us. In essence it is no longer possible to be naive in our understanding of culture. It is characterized more often than not by a knowing irony which clearly marks out the difference between the modern and the postmodern.

CONCLUSION

In summary, this essay has examined two central and related themes. First, the extent to which our activities as consumers define our identities in the contemporary world and, second, the impact of the postmodern upon our day-to-day lives. In particular the discussion has identified a shift from substance to style and has suggested that the certainties and the metanarratives of the modern era are no longer sustainable. If, as has been said, in the postmodern world the basic dictum is: 'I shop therefore I am', we need to reflect on the question of what happens to those who cannot shop and are therefore excluded from the basis of social identity. This is of particular importance as the old principles of the welfare state are challenged by new values of consumerism. In this new world, pensions, healthcare, and social support shift from the responsibility of the state to the responsibility of the individual. From a materialist perspective our capacity to consume these services constructs more than identity; it affects the physical basis of day-to-day life.

Critics of the postmodern perspective have pointed out that it can lead to an unprincipled emphasis upon personal and individual gratification at the expense of our responsibilities to others. For some writers this represents the capitalist market economy taken to its logical conclusion. For others, postmodern ideas are democratic, and it is argued that the dissolution of old class barriers and the strongholds of elite culture give all of us greater opportunities for full social participation.

I will finish with a quotation from the sociologist Zygmunt Bauman. In his recent writing he has explored the tension between acknowledging the reality of postmodern change and recognizing that it has led to the exclusion of many from a full and active part in society. This extract is taken from his book *Freedom* (1988).

> For most members of contemporary society, individual freedom, if it is available, comes in the form of consumer freedom, with all of its agreeable and less palatable attributes. Once consumer freedom has taken care of individual concerns, or social integration and systematic reproduction (and consumer freedom does take care of all three), the coercive pressure of political bureaucracy may be relieved, the past political explosiveness of ideas and cultural practices defused and a plurality of lifestyles, politics, moral or aesthetic views may develop undisturbed. The paradox is of course, that such freedom of expression in no way subjects the system or its political organization to control by those whose lives it determines. Consumer and expressive freedoms are not interfered with politically, so long as they remain politically ineffective.

5

POSTMODERNISM AND RELIGION

PAMELA SUE ANDERSON

Postmodernism does not have one simple definition in any field of study or practice. Its definitions continue to vary with the subject matter, or academic discipline, as well as with time and place; and often its definition varies within any one discipline. The field of religion is no exception. To understand this field, it is useful to assume at the outset that postmodernism is characterized by the loss of the **modern** belief in (i) the moral progress of humankind in history, (ii) a conception of reason as ushering in universal agreement, or certainty, and (iii) a **grand narrative** account of being created human (assuming human sameness, not **differences**). This threefold loss has had a decisive impact upon twenty-first-century religion. In the extreme case, postmodernism undermines the very essence, or any definition, of religion as literally *religio*: bond.

The postmodern displacement of belief undermines religion understood in an epistemological sense: that is, religion as a body of commonly held beliefs binds believers together, and insofar as these beliefs can be rationally justified as true, they establish a foundation for knowledge. Knowledge as justified true belief is, more or less, the epistemological focus of modern Western philosophy. Postmodernism tends to shift the focus of religion away from the epistemology of belief. Certain postmodern philosophers of religion energetically urge practitioners to move 'beyond belief' (see Ellen Armour, in John Caputo, ed., *The Religious* (2001); and Amy Hollywood, in Pamela Sue Anderson and Beverley Clack, eds, *Feminist Philosophy of Religion* (2004)).

Is religion a matter of belief? Or is seeking to justify religious belief a modern and Western distortion of the lived experiences of religious communities? The postmodern move beyond belief is re-enforced by a **postcolonial** insistence that the focus in this field of study should be world religions, not religion in the singular. It becomes clear that 'postmodernism and/in religions' refers to an ambivalent and uncertain relationship.

A straightforward account of the relationship between postmodernism and religion – as two Western conceptions – has been one of direct opposition and discontinuity. Whereas postmodernism undermines biological, cognitive and moral certainties, religions rest on them. An author of popular books on contemporary philosophy of religion and ethics confirms this for Christianity:

> With the advent of Christianity, God was seen as providing . . . a fixed point of meaning, truth and value in an unstable world. Postmodernism denies that there are any such rocks of certainty. It calls to human beings in the raging sea to

abandon the search for rocks, to 'go with the flow' and simply to seek to understand where they are.

(Peter Vardy, *Being Human* (2003))

I would neither accept nor reject this account as a correct picture of Christianity and postmodernism. This Western picture may be true for a certain conception of religion, especially a **fundamentalist** view of religious belief. Yet, **ironically**, the contemporary popularity of fundamentalism, despite more mystical practices, infiltrates not just Christianity and Islam, but Orthodox Judaism and the Oriental religions.

It has been argued that fundamentalism in world religions has taken on Westernized forms, especially when resisting a rational quest for knowledge. Religious fundamentalism appears to be an offshoot of postmodernism itself; fundamentalists who seek an unequivocal foundation for their beliefs tend to build their certainties point by point in a dependent, but oppositional relationship to postmodern uncertainties. Despite the ease with which an author could map out an oppositional relationship between postmodernism and fundamentalist religions in terms of arguments for and against specific uncertainties, a straightforward separation of the two should be resisted. Arguably, the worst extreme of fundamentalism – notably the religious believer who justifies terrorist tactics globally – is one of the defining features of the contemporary world.

Another issue related to the opposition between postmodernism and religious fundamentalism is moral relativism. That is, the flip side of asserting the absolute values of any fundamentalist position is a relativist account explaining the co-existence of opposing values. Relativism is also raised in the context of conceiving religion in terms of local narratives and practices, whether sustained by universal claims or not. The nature and dangers of this relativism is addressed elsewhere as one of the earliest indications of postmodernism (as in Ernest Gellner, *Postmodernism, Reason and Relativism* (1992), and Vardy, *Being Human*).

The global increase in fundamentalist religions runs parallel to a more widespread, postmodern celebration of differences of – in this case, religious – perspectives. The religions of the world reflect academic shifts in thinking about belief as well as technological, economic and other cultural transformations. Religions at the beginning of the twenty-first century are inevitably, if at times unwittingly, influenced by certain general characteristics of postmodernism: its fluidity, diversity, uncertainty and, ultimately, its lack of concern with (e.g. belief in) truth.

It is crucial to postmodernism and religion that Christianity is no longer the central or privileged focus. Postmodernism has shifted both academic and popular concern to world religions. Nevertheless, it is still common for Westerners to think of other religions in terms derived from their own values and concepts within a Christian tradition. So the implicit Westernized Christian values and concepts in the study of religions have to be uncovered. It has already been suggested that belief as an epistemological term is a primary example of a modern – arguably, Western – imposition on the study of religions. For another example, the label 'Judaeo-Christian' has come to seem an unwelcome imposition of Christianity as the rightful completion of Jewish tradition.

The academic discipline of theology as a systematic study of the traditions and subject matter of the Christian religion faces the uncertainties of its own future. One threat is that theology will be marginalized, and ultimately replaced, by the more wide-ranging (or inclusive) categories of religious studies and world religions. This changing scene gives evidence of the disruption of university departments of theology and of religion by the fluidity of postmodern thinking. The twofold phenomenon of change and of resistance to innovation in the study of religions is an indication of the contemporary process constituting the postmodern transformation of religion, its definition and discipline.

One increasingly popular postmodern contention is that the philosophy of religion should no longer be the study and justification of belief in a personal God (i.e. theism), but the critical engagement with religious 'practice' (see, for example, Pierre Bourdieu, *Outline of a Theory of Practice* (1977)). Here the postmodern critic claims that philosophy's obsessive concern with justification is a product of modern philosophy's privileging of reason. Reason's role in the justification of theistic beliefs, reason's neutrality and universality are brought into question. Not only does the postmodern critic claim that belief is a Western abstraction, reason as a faculty of the human mind, not the body, is also criticized for being a particular Western, male construction. In the extreme case, postmodernism subverts modern philosophy of religion by engaging in **genealogical** studies of ritual action and bodily practices. Ritual action becomes the crucial form of signification, instead of philosophical analysis of concepts. The postmodern critique of analytical reason poses a particular challenge to modern philosophy, as well as the equation of religion with belief. If successful, this critique would be a first step towards opening up the field of religion to issues of gender, sexuality, class, race and bodily practices.

To grasp the diverse aspects of the impact of postmodernism on Christian theology, it helps to consider David Brown's *Tradition and Imagination: Revelation and Change* (1999). Brown observes that 'Christian theology has conventionally sought to provide . . . an overarching narrative, and indeed the term "systematic theology" is often interpreted to mean just that, the attempt to systematize all of reality under a single Christian frame of reference.' An overarching narrative is precisely the target of the postmodern critic Jean-François **Lyotard**. Lyotard's account of the postmodern 'incredulity toward metanarratives' seems to force the conventional conception (as in Brown above) of Christian theology into a defensive position, if not to undermine it completely. Yet Brown maintains that the matter is not so simple, and he documents five different theological uses of postmodernism. I will not explore each of these. But one of the uses is especially worth exploring in this context: rather than opposing postmodernism, certain 'Radical Orthodox' theologians, such as John Milbank, embrace it as a critique of a particular secular framework, that of so-called 'universal reason'.

The Radical Orthodox conception of postmodern theology is a response to the incredulity toward the master narrative of **Enlightenment** philosophy; and in particular, toward the optimistic view of historical progress, secular reason and 'man's' ability to find truth without God. So, unlike the earlier opposition between postmodernism and fundamentalist religions, the Radical Orthodox theology seeks to create an alternative framework, which would be genuinely universal, since it would be based upon the truth of Christianity under which all of reality fits (see John Milbank, Catherine Pickstock and Graham Ward, eds, *Radical Orthodoxy: A New Theology* (1999)).

It might be possible to imagine that Radical Orthodoxy demonstrates that theology is more compatible with postmodern philosophy than with modern epistemology. For Radical Orthodoxy, the postmodern claim to dethrone human reason opens the way to the faith of Christianity. Modern scepticism, for such theologians, rendered the faith which has characterized Christianity obsolete, while scepticism also made it impossible to demonstrate the certainty of God's nature and existence. Postmodern fluidity and uncertainty could seem preferable to the fixed certainties (for example, moral progress in history, God's creation of human identity, the truth of reason) characterizing modern philosophy. However, not all philosophers or theologians are persuaded that this is a positive move. Brown himself points to the postmodern irony at the heart of the Radical Orthodox reconception of Christian theology as the new – truthful – master narrative. The decisive problem with the claim that this master narrative is universal remains that not everyone – not even every theist or Christian – would accept Radical Orthodox theology as a true account of reality, and, in particular, as an account of human and divine relations. Brown finds a similar problem with other exclusive master narratives, such as Alvin Plantinga's warrant theory of belief, produced and advocated for contemporary philosophy of religion.

Plantinga raises a general epistemological question: is Christian belief acceptable for intelligent people living in a postmodern world? He answers by arguing that Christian beliefs are warranted to the extent that they are formed by properly functioning cognitive faculties. Plantinga's argument is that humans not only have natural cognitive faculties such as perception, memory and reasoning that allow them to know things, but we also have a natural cognitive faculty that enables us to form basic beliefs about God. Plantinga advocates his Reformed epistemology to demonstrate that *warrant* distinguishes knowledge from true belief. But, problematically, he assumes that a notion of sin derived from the theology of John Calvin applies to believers and non-believers: that this natural cognitive faculty can be dulled or damaged by sin. Plantinga's universal master narrative also assumes that those without Christian beliefs, or certainty, need to have faith 'repair' the damaged faculty, in order to have warranted Christian belief (see Alvin Plantinga, *Warranted Christian Belief* (2000)).

In the end, although Radical Orthodoxy and Reformed epistemology offer their respective master narratives as positive postmodern alternatives to either Enlightenment or fundamentalist forms of religion, there are serious worries with these alternatives. The ambivalence between Enlightenment and post-modern conceptions of religion worries certain feminist philosophers of religion, especially when it comes to questions of women's identity, rationality and autonomy (see, for example, Pamela Sue Anderson, *A Feminist Philosophy of Religion* (1998)). Does postmodernism not run the risk of undermining the many positive advances made for women in religion by the Enlightenment? Women may be loath to give up certain modern values. Steps taken as part of the Enlightenment in the eighteenth and nineteenth centuries to enable and protect women's self-identities as autonomous rational and moral agents within human communities remain hugely valuable and significant for overcoming various forms of oppression, including sexual, racial, social, material and economic oppression. The worry is that the creation of a postmodern Christian **narrative** (whether Radical Orthodoxy or Reformed epistemology) becomes essentially a return to pre-modern conceptions of religion, which were not only dogmatic, but oppressive to women and all those on the margins of socially and economically privileged theological circles. The choice of dogmatism rather than scepticism is not necessarily an attractive or forward-looking alternative to religion. Rather than being more inclusive the conceptions of religion at the heart of master narra-tive forms of postmodernism exclude all but certain practitioners of Christianity. A similar ambivalence toward postmodernism characterizes feminist debates more widely, in the context of **cultural studies** and other critical social theories (see 'Postmodernism and feminism', pp. 24–34).

Further responses to postmodernism draw upon yet other aspects in the field of religion. One other major response to the postmodern threefold loss of belief focuses upon religious experience understood as essentially outside the limits of possible knowledge. Here the terms employed are compatible with the Enlightenment philosophy of **Kant**; postmodern religion becomes an exercise in finding new possibilities in experiencing the impossible. That is, Kant moves modern philosophy to the limits of human knowledge, and this postmodern response runs with the idea that religion lies outside the possible, outside of language, in the realm of mystery and 'gift'. Postmodern discussions of gift seek to demonstrate the way in which the instability of this concept results in experiencing the impossible: that is, as soon as a donor gives someone a gift the recipient is put into debt; this adds to the donor, not to the recipient; but this is exactly the opposite of what the gift is supposed to do. Jacques **Derrida** and Jean-Luc Marion present a fascinating, give-and-take interchange on the gift in John D. Caputo and Michael J. Scanlon, eds, *God, The Gift and Postmodernism* (1999). Caputo brings together such postmodern thinkers elucidating the desire to experience the impossible, or to recognize the inscrutable, as the defining element of postmodernism for a new, more inclusive – however mystical – conception of religion.

Lyotard is also picked up here to support the **desire** and possibility of experiencing the impossible in terms of the Kantian **sublime**. The sublime is an experience of the absolute greatness which cannot be capped by reason, understanding or imagination (see Lyotard, *Lessons on the Analytic of the Sublime* (1994)). But, crucially, for Lyotard the sublime also always constitutes a barrier to any search for totality. Postmodernism as conceived by Lyotard himself is a movement against all totalizing accounts of ultimate reality. So any form of religion which seeks or offers a totalizing project is doomed to failure. Nevertheless, postmodern forms of religion shaped by the sublime, its greatness and inexpressibility could (possibly) avoid the problems with limiting religion to the realm of the possible. It is hoped by advocates of this mystically inclined, postmodern religion that these post-Kantian moves may equally avoid the problem of conceiving God, or the divine, in anthropomorphic or gynaecological terms, each of which are exclusive of an opposite sex. Hence it is not surprising that some feminist theologians and philosophers of religion have found this mystical alternative attractive for religion. Yet there remains the danger of illusion and mystification – dangers which the modern conception of religion aimed to avoid.

In conclusion, postmodernism and/in religion(s) is a topic that opens up a whole array of significant questions for the religious believer and for students of religions. Is religion as fundamentalism too fixed as a subject? This would seem to assert certainties for a global world, which can never maintain such forms of security. What would happen to religion if its focus turned to ritual action as forms of signification? Modern philosophy's focus on the justification of theistic belief may be undermined by the postmodern focus on bodily practice and ritual action. Yet the definition and value of religion would remain indefinite: only as stable as the practice defining each action, only as strong as the **power** shaping each ritual and only as fixed as the gender of each construction. Is religion as a new master narrative compatible with the postmodern critique of the **metanarrative** of secular reason? This seems at first glance (only) to offer an alternative, which successfully replaces modern scepticism concerning religious belief. This leaves unresolved the problem that not everyone assents to the universal narrative; to say that this failure to assent to what is universal results from sin seems an inadequate response. Finally, is religion in a postmodern world bound to seek experience of the impossible opened up by the fluidity and uncertainty in the gaps of reason, understanding and imagination? An answer to this question suggests a focus on the post-Kantian sublime as the heart of religion. For some postmodern philosophers, inexpressible greatness gives a sense of the divine not available to modernity. Yet a problem arises concerning the precise content of this religion, which tends to suffer a loss of particularity and certainty concerning human embodiment and difference. Ultimately, it would seem that in a postmodern world 'religion' always remains in an unstable tension with the recognition of multiple concrete material and social differences.

6

POSTMODERNISM AND THE
POSTCOLONIAL WORLD

ELEANOR BYRNE

If the interest in **postmodernism** is limited to a celebration of the fragmentation of the '**grand narratives**' of post-**enlightenment** rationalism then, for all its intellectual excitement, it remains a profoundly parochial enterprise. The wider significance of the postmodern condition lies in the awareness that the epistem-ological 'limits' of those ethnocentric ideas are also the enunciative boundaries of a range of other dissonant even dissident histories and voices – women, the colonized, minority groups, the bearers of policed sexualities.

(Homi K. **Bhabha**, *The Location of Culture* (1994))

In recent years some of the most interesting interventions in discussions of **postmodernity** have come from a number of critics working on the borders of **postcolonial** and postmodern theory. In his above comment, in the introduction to his influential work *The Location of Culture*, the critic Homi K. Bhabha predominantly associated with postcolonial theory attempts to relocate the significance of postmodernism and the postmodern condition. He suggests that an effective understanding of the much fêted crisis of 'grand narratives' outlined by Jean-François **Lyotard** in his early work, *The Postmodern Condition* (1979), involves a recognition that these seemingly overarching explanatory narratives might be ethnocentrically limited. That is to say, they are revealed as kinds of belief systems and **narratives** that are attached to particular cultural histories of communities, cultures and elites. He further suggests that even critics and theorists who enthusiastically theorize postmodernism might be guilty of a similar ethnocentrism, not recognizing that one of the critical forces that has destabilized so-called grand narratives is the impact of a range of dissident and dissonant voices, hailing from a range of minority positions. He locates them at the limits, a presence at the boundary, following Martin **Heidegger**'s comments in his essay 'Building, Dwelling, Thinking' (in *Poetry, Language, Thought* (1971)) that the border is not only the limit or the end of a particular thing, but the place where the presencing of something else begins. For Bhabha this might be a useful formulation for the way in which minority voices could be envisaged.

Bhabha is clearly suggesting here that rather than seeing the experience of the postmodern condition as exclusively located in and experienced by the inhabi-tants of the so-called first world, that is to say largely Western or Westernized industrialized and capitalist countries or regions, the concerns of postmodernism might usefully be thought through the experiences of colonialism and post-colonial negotiations and struggles. In fact in another essay in the same collection 'The Postcolonial and the Postmodern' he goes further:

> My growing conviction has been that the encounters and negotiations of differential meanings and values within 'colonial' textuality, its governmental discourses and cultural practices, have anticipated, *avant la lettre*, many of the problematics of signification and judgement that have become current in contemporary theory – **aporia**, ambivalence, indeterminacy, the question of discursive closure, the threat to agency, the status of intentionality, the challenge to 'totalizing' concepts, to name but a few.
>
> (*The Location of Culture* (1994))

Bhabha suggests that what are commonly viewed as characteristically postmodern concerns might easily be found in the context of colonial and anti-colonial narratives and histories from the postcolonial world. His proposals are based around the peculiar narratives and identities that colonialism produces both for colonizer and colonized. The experiences of both conditions are arguably highly differentiated and diverse depending upon the cultures involved, whether the colonies are settler or non-settler, and change historically through different periods of colonization. However, Bhabha's broad observations of the contradictions of colonial narratives; as a civilizing mission enforced by armed brutality; as a product of 'democratic' government which refuses to allow colonial democracy; as a system which asks its subjects to imitate or mimic its imposed culture, but never allows full membership of that culture – 'almost the same but not white' – suggest that the totalizing 'grand narratives' of colonialism are perpetually in a state of crisis.

Ranajit Guha's writings on colonial power relations in India are suggestively illustrative of Bhabha's model:

> The colonial state in South Asia was very unlike and indeed fundamentally different from the metropolitan bourgeois state which had sired it. The difference consisted in the fact that the metropolitan state was **hegemonic** in character with its claim to dominance based on a power relation in which the moment of persuasion outweighed that of coercion, whereas the colonial state was non-hegemonic with persuasion outweighed by coercion in its structure of dominance.
>
> (*Dominance Without Hegemony* (1997))

Coming from a rather different angle, but equally concerned with the relationship between postmodernism and the postcolonial world, the **Marxist** critic Aijaz Ahmad is concerned in his book *In Theory* (1992) with the ways in which the category of third world is understood, and looks at both its origins and its provenance. Ahmad discusses the problems he finds in the work of a major theorist of postmodernism, Frederic **Jameson**, in his essay 'Third World Literature in the Age of Multinational Capitalism' (*Social Text* (1986)). Ahmad is concerned that Jameson sees all 'third-world' literature as having a single objective: that of producing 'national allegories'. He is disturbed that he as an Indian Marxist who also writes poetry in Urdu has in fact been '**Othered**' by a critic he has profoundly identified with and felt common cause with. He suggests that one of the causes for Jameson's homogenization and categorization of 'third-world literature' in this way is the mode in which he understands the term itself.

> I find it significant that First and Second Worlds are defined in terms of their production systems (capitalism and socialism respectively), whereas the third category – the Third World – is defined purely in terms of an 'experience' of externally inserted phenomena. That which is constitutive of human history itself is present in the first two cases, absent in the third.
>
> (*In Theory* (1992))

Ahmad is sceptical about the various characterizations of the third world as either the reborn 'Orient' politically armed with a new confident nationalism, challenging Western imperialism and imperialist Bolshevism, as the critic Edward **Said** had suggested in his seminal **text** *Orientalism* (1979), or as a militarily non-aligned configuration of largely postcolonial nations that would be a force for peace. Ahmad questions how the third world is understood in such a formulation, if it is understood to be neither capitalist nor socialist. He offers the example of contemporary India as a case that disturbs a homogenized view of the nations supposed to make up the third world and suggests that both India's industrialization and the growth of its multinational corporations bear comparison with the first world, and notes that its 'unbroken parliamentary rule of the bourgeoisie since Independence in 1947', is 'a record quite comparable to the length of Italy's modern record of unbroken bourgeois-democratic governance' (*In Theory*).

Ahmad's point is to unsettle any complacent labelling, and also to destabilize what he sees as a **binary opposition** created in Jameson's construction of a capitalist first world and 'a presumably pre- or non-capitalist Third World' (*In Theory*). Significantly he also turns the terms of the investigation on their heads, asking when the first world became the first. At the end of his discussion of Jameson he comments:

> Even if I were to accept Jameson's division of the globe into three worlds, I would still have to insist . . . that there is right here, within the belly of the First World's global postmodernism, a veritable Third World, perhaps two or three of them.
>
> (*In Theory*)

It is not entirely clear here whether Ahmad sees this 'third world' as participating in or distinct from the experience of postmodernism in the first world. He is certainly far more cautious than Bhabha about the figuring of minority experiences as postmodern. He comments scathingly on Bhabha's proposition that minority perspectives in dialogue with **poststructuralist** theory might effectively intervene in **discourses** of **modernity**:

> Bhabha of course, lives in those material conditions of postmodernity which presume the benefits of modernity as the very ground from which judgements on that past of this post- may be delivered. In other words it takes a very modern, very affluent, very uprooted kind of intellectual to debunk . . . the idea of progress . . . Those who live with the consequences of that long past good and bad, and in places where a majority of the population has been denied access to such benefits of modernity as hospitals or better health insurance or even basic literacy; can hardly afford the terms of such thought.

(In Theory)

Ahmad shares this scepticism about the possible convergence of post-modernism and postcolonial critical approaches with a number of important critics associated with postcolonial theory. In his review of Ian Adam and Helen Tiffin's *Past the Last Post: Theorizing Post-Colonialism and Post-Modernism* (1990), Roger Berger cites **Marxist** postcolonial critic Benita Parry with approval. For Benita Parry postcolonial and postmodern methodologies should be recognized as distinct and unlikely to sustain a useful critical dialogue. A postcolonial approach, she suggests, should be understood as one which under-stands that cultural meanings are always finally political meanings, and that texts are 'inseparable from the conditions of their production and reception in history'. Postmodernism, Berger claims, wants to 'expand the territorial claims of the discursive infinitely, and therefore privilege textual stratagems as in and of themselves the location of gathering points for solidarity' (Berger, *Postmodern Culture* (1992)).

Berger's comments in his review of *Past the Last Post* point to a tendency within the featured debates on the relationship between postmodernism and postcolonialism to polarize around questions of textuality. Berger's particular re-use of Stuart Hall's formulation certainly does this when he characterizes a postmodern concern with textuality as operating in a neo-colonial mode; 'territorial expansion' suggests that postmodernism should be understood as complicit with late capitalism in the West and enacts a kind of 'western textual imperialism' (Berger).

This is a critical paradigm through which a binary opposition is reinforced between a postmodern focus on 'text' and a postcolonial 'experience', but it does have some serious shortcomings. Berger comments that there is 'a fundamental incompatibility of post-modernist textuality and the lived realities of the post-colonial (or really neo-colonial) experience' (Berger). Inevitably such a characterization of both camps is far too sweeping. Whilst this approach seeks to align postmodernism with Western experiences and preoccupations, the erection of a binary between 'text' and 'experience' also risks performing a neo-colonial gesture where the colonial subject represents a 'good object' for colonial or neo-colonial knowledge and the 'truth' of colonized experiences enables the self-knowledge of the colonizer. It is arguably precisely this model that structured the Victorians' display of the possessions of indigenous peoples of the British Empire as artefacts in their museums.

This problematic had been discussed almost ten years earlier by one of the foremost and influential postcolonial critics, Gayatri Chakravorty Spivak in an interview in 1984 for the UK Channel 4 *Voices* series, *Knowledge in Crisis* (published as 'The Post-modern Condition: The End of Politics?', in S. Harasym, ed., *The Postcolonial Critics: Interviews, Strategies, Dialogues* (1990)). Being asked to account for a poststructuralist assault on 'grands récits' (grand narratives) by Geoffrey Hawthorn, Spivak gives an answer that resonates with both postcolonial and postmodern concerns:

> I think of it myself as a radical acceptance of vulnerability. The grands récits are grand narratives and the narrative has an end in view. It is a programme which tells how social justice is to be achieved. And I think that the post-structuralists, if I understood them right, imagine again and again that when a narrative is constructed, something is left out. When an end is defined, other ends are rejected, and one might not know what those ends are. So I think what they are asking about is over and over again, What is it that is left out? Can we know what is left out?
>
> (*The Post-Colonial Critic*)

Spivak's description would seem to open both fields very productively onto one another. Further, she outlines comprehensively how a poststructuralist interest in 'text' should not be read as supporting a binary division between narrative and experience which goes almost uninterrogated in the *Past the Last Post* collection.

> Text in the way in which certainly Derrida and Lyotard understand it is not at all the verbal text. There are two ways once again perhaps of looking at this problem. When they read actual verbal objects that are political philosophy, philosophy of history or whatever, they like to show that those things are also produced in language – because there is a tendency to forget that they're produced in language. There you may say that the text is understood verbally. But when they talk about there is nothing but text, etc., they are talking about a network, a weave – you can put names on it – politico-psycho-sexual-socio, you name it . . . The moment you name it there's a network that's broader than that. And to an extent that notion that we are effects within a much larger text/tissue/weave of which the ends are not accessible to us is very different from saying that everything is language.
>
> (*The Post-Colonial Critic*)

It is perhaps the work of Jacques Derrida that has been most frequently cited as proving problematic to certain postcolonial perspectives because of a perceived difference between poststructuralist questionings of foundational concepts in 'Western' philosophy and what is sometimes seen as an investment in some of those foundational concepts by some postcolonial critics. Primarily such polarization centres around questions of identity, where the 'decentring' of identity and the rejection of stable subjectivity are perceived to be a Western luxury contrasted to a need to adopt what Spivak calls 'strategic essentialism' on the part of those struggling against colonial and neo-colonial forces. Such a strategy might involve uniting around particular categories of identity, ethnicity, gender or class positions. In recent years, however, a number of critics working in the postcolonial field have offered compelling arguments for a reconsideration of Derrida's work from postcolonial perspectives, as being, to use the overused term 'always already' postcolonial.

In his essay '**Deconstruction** and the Postcolonial' (in Nicholas Royle, ed., *Deconstructions: A User's Guide* (2000)), Robert Young reflects upon his own changing apprehensions of the ways in which the emergence of poststructuralist modes of thinking needs to be rethought. His comments come from his opening remarks in his influential work *White Mythologies: Writing History and the West* (1990):

> If so-called 'so-called poststructuralism' is the product of a single historical moment, then that moment is probably not May 1968 but rather the Algerian War of Independence – no doubt itself both a symptom and a product. In this respect it is significant that Sartre, Althusser, Derrida and Lyotard, among others, were all either born in Algeria or personally involved with the events of the war.

Young argues there has been a characterization of poststructuralism (and we might usefully read postmodernism here too) as entirely in and of the West. He takes Aijaz Ahmad to task for assuming that 'anything that has come to be regarded as being of intellectual or political significance in the West could have nothing to do with the (so-called) third world' ('Deconstruction and the Postcolonial'). He continues,

> Those who reject contemporary postcolonial theory in the name of the 'third world' on the grounds of it being Western, however are negating the very input of the third world, starting with Derrida, disavowing therefore the very non-European work which their critique professes to advocate at the moment when they espouse it.
>
> ('Deconstruction and the Postcolonial')

Young argues that the references to this elsewhere, the decentred Algerian identity, have always been detectable in Derrida's work, but that in recent years he has increasingly come to be explicit about what he terms his Franco-Maghrebian identity. In *The Monolingualism of the Other or the Prosthesis of Origin* (1998) Derrida reflects on this trajectory in his thinking:

> Certainly, everything that has, say interested me for a long time – on account of writing, the **trace**, the deconstruction of phallogocentrism and the Western metaphysics . . . all of that could not proceed from the strange reference to an 'elsewhere' of which the place and the language were unknown and prohibited even to myself, as if I were trying to translate into the only language and the only

French Western culture that I have at my disposal, the culture into which I was thrown at birth, a possibility that is inaccessible to myself.

Thus the two terms being discussed here, postmodernism and postcolonialism, find themselves intimately linked, co-dependent, rather than exploitative of one another. Interestingly, Derrida's own short article 'Et Cetera . . .' in the collection *Deconstructions: A User's Guide* would just as readily apply to this volume, where the key term (in the latter case deconstruction and in this case postmodernism) is paired with a wide spectrum of topics. He comments on the ways in which the pairing-up process depends upon the third term, the 'and', that appears insignificant but must produce a set of categorizations and orderings that actually contributes in delineating what can be added together, thought together or understood as belonging to the same series. That is to say that the 'and' can be seen as bringing two terms together, linking them in some way, but also asserting the lack of homogeneity between the two; otherwise there is no need for the 'and' in the first place. As we have already seen, some discussions of the postcolonial and the postmodern polarize around 'experience' and theory or text and reality. However, we might see in Derrida's intervention a truly postcolonial mode of addressing the imperative in this volume, this companion to postmodernism, to bring the categories of postmodernism and the postcolonial world into play. He comments on the diverse provenance of 'and': 'scansion, spacing, quasi-punctuation, respiration, exclamative opening, neutral addition, linking or following on, disjunction or simple scansion, upping the ante, objection, concession, etc.'

Putting this kind of pressure on the third word, which we might have risked assuming had really only a subdued role in relation to the other two terms, opens up vastly different ways of reading. Consider: postmodernism 'therefore' the postcolonial world, postmodernism 'what's more' the postcolonial world, postmodernism 'against' the postcolonial world. Rather than seeing this as a retreat into textuality it might be critical that we are able to view with extreme caution our own investment in models of categorizing and knowing, surely an important strategy for any postcolonial activist and/or critic.

7

POSTMODERNISM AND SCIENCE
AND TECHNOLOGY

IAIN HAMILTON GRANT

Of all the worlds in which we might expect to discover signs of **postmodern** life, those of science and technology seem the least probable. Even those feedlines from science into culture that seem the most suited to **postmodernity**'s climate, such as the renowned uncertainties of **quantum** physics, stem not from **narratives**, but from nature. If postmodernism is simply, as Fredric **Jameson** has it, a cultural affair, then the sciences, reading only the book of nature, are surely unaffected by any postmodern 'loss of reality' – they never lost their way in the dead ends and labyrinths of the library of Babel. With postmodernism insisting, with **Heidegger**, that 'where word breaks off, no thing may be' – that beyond **signs** independent of speakers, beyond **text**, narrative or **discourse**, there is nothing – it remains difficult to consider tectonic plate movements and earthquakes as self-contained texts or discourses. So, with postmodern narrative in ruins, still reeling under the gravity of its collapse, could science simply step in to show, with mathematical precision, why stories have never been a substitute for formulae and experiment in the matter of the real? Nature, as Francis Bacon put it at the dawn of **modern** science, does not yield her secrets to the incantations of the poets or the bookish disputations of philosophers; the experimental sciences must *force* them from her. Moreover, with the postmodern 'empire of **signs**' leaving reality the victim of a crime so perfect, as Jean **Baudrillard** says, that even its corpse has disappeared, science and technology step onto the scene: what if this crime were a sideshow, and the real is elsewhere?

With all these grounds for scepticism concerning the very idea of '**postmodern science**', it is surprising to find so much of science currently under the glare of postmodern scrutiny. Three aspects of science have in particular been singled out for postmodern interrogation: first, the study of science as a postmodern phenomenon; second, how postmodernism and science are negotiated within the scientific community; and finally, theories of postmodern science itself. Moreover, as will become increasingly apparent, technology, on which modern science has become almost entirely dependent, is also a crucial factor in this equation. Without compasses, printing presses, microscopes, computers and particle accelerators, whole chapters in the book of nature would remain illegible, or unwritten. Technology not only therefore emerges as what permits the study of nature – the 'racks' upon which Nature is laid to enable her secrets, in Francis Bacon's gruesome phrase, to be forced from her; the changing forms and functions of technology in the postmodern world have become inseparable from even the forms contemporary science takes, prompting some historians to consider *Technological Innovation as an Evolutionary Process* (John M. Ziman (2000)), and some scientists to leave organic life behind for the *Sciences of the Artificial* (Herbert Simon (1996)) – **artificial intelligence** and **artificial life**. With these sciences, we are never far from science fictions, on the one hand, or from postmodern **simulation**, on the other. Given this unexpected convergence between the natural and the human sciences, technology, **ironically**, emerges as a vital component driving and shaping postmodern culture itself.

First, then, to the study of science as a postmodern phenomenon. Ever since Thomas **Kuhn**'s *The Structure of Scientific Revolutions* (1962), the world of the natural sciences has been opened up to study through the lenses of the social sciences. Arguing that the history of the sciences shows a discontinuous series of breaks with, and radical departures from, past sciences (called '**paradigm shifts**' – a term that has enjoyed a certain celebrity in postmodern circles), rather than a progressive, linear accumulation of scientific knowledge, Kuhn effectively demystified science as the 'disinterested search for facts', and showed how scientific agendas were set by faculty squabbles, funding pressures and peer groups as much as by theoretical problems and experimental results. Science may or may not have been the study of nature, but it now became a culture to be studied like any other.

Of course, Kuhn's portrait of science-as-culture did not go unchallenged. Outraged scientists and philosophers lined up to knock holes in his theses. Some challenged the culturalist implications of Kuhn's ideas, insisting that just because science is inevitably practised within a culture, it would be absurd to say that this was all there was to it. Apart from this cultural dimension, there was also the thorny problem of nature itself, to which science had so successfully devoted its productive career. While from the armchair or the questionnaire science may look Kuhnian, laboratory work offered a very different, hands-on experience. Science could, therefore, be studied as a culture, but science would continue to study nature, regardless. Out of these disputes in the Anglo-American academy there emerged what came to be known as science studies. In the UK, for instance, groups devoted to the sociological study of science formed in the universities of Edinburgh and Bath, while in the mid-1970s the journal *Radical Science* began publication. These groups tended to examine the history and sociology of specific scientific and technological programmes, such as the development of missile-guidance systems or the politics of IQ testing, asking questions concerning the funding, ideology, and politics of scientific knowledge. With scientific knowledge enjoying high status, and science studies being broadly **Marxist** in orientation, emphasis began to be placed on the role played by science in the social construction of broader questions. For example, while it is perhaps difficult to see 'life' as studied by biochemists as having any great social consequences, issues surrounding abortion make permanent appeal to scientific 'facts' about the age at which a foetus may be regarded as independently sentient, effectively defining the field in which these issues are contested and the roles of the contestants within it. Not only does the 'finished' science – science as a body of facts – therefore have enormous social implications, but so too does science in action, leading sociologists of science to consider 'laboratory life' (what do scientists actually do?) as centred around both the practical (which groups, in what circumstances and by what means, made what 'discovery'?) and ideological (how are class and gender positions implicated in scientific practice? What role does science play in constructing cultures?) construction of fact. If the first response to Kuhn had therefore been to 'naturalize' science, the second concentrated on science as a 'socialized' *power*, and set about exposing its class and gender biases.

Feminist science studies, indeed, have yielded some of the most pertinent work from the perspective of postmodernism, science and technology. The medicalization of childbirth, for example, provides an early example of the way in which medical science (obstetrics) and hospital technology (bed, stirrups, forceps) position women in childbirth as passive bodies on which medicine acts. Childbirth is therefore no longer exclusively a female act; women require medical intervention to deliver a child, and so must submit to the medical regime as the dominant or active partner in the act of childbirth. Issues such as the gender composition (how many doctors are women?) and distribution (how many nurses are men?) of the medical workforce begin to abut onto the complicity between medicine's **representations** of women and social representations of women: women are passive, while science and men are active, even in childbirth. The study of these situations is therefore crucial to understanding the relationship between science and the dominant social conceptions of femininity, as well as the social roles of women.

Such concerns eventually led to the question 'Whose science, whose knowledge?' What if science was not simply statistically male (dependent upon the proportions of men to women working in the field) but also *epistemologically* male: does the way in which scientific knowledge is produced reflect, far from the universal truths of nature, merely the results of a partial and therefore historically and culturally male experience of it? Francis Bacon's already-cited call to 'place Nature on the rack in order to force her to yield her secrets', clearly distributing gender roles to nature as a passive, scientific object and science as an active, knowing, male **subject**, seems to provide a vindication of this critical strand. Following many studies of science and its impact on the lives and social roles of real women alongside its role in the social construction of femininity, feminist science studies, in the work of Sandra Harding, Ludmilla Jordanova and Donna **Haraway**, began to move to what became recognizably postmodern science studies.

Suddenly, from being a practice and a body of unimpeachable fact inaccessible to study by the social sciences or by cultural criticism, science became first a socialized, ideological phenomenon susceptible to historical and sociological scrutiny and, second, a 'text', composed of representations that, regardless of their factual status, formed one set in a broader network of representations and

discourses that themselves construct dominant images and concepts of women, animals and machines. It was insufficient to target local instances of the economic or lived reality of scientific intervention; rather, the discourses and representations produced by science, and even the discourses of science itself that perpetuate its immense power and prestige, must come under scrutiny. If this power was produced in a discourse of which the appeal to 'nature' or 'reality' was a component, critical science studies could not stop at demonstrating that nature is otherwise than science represents it.

The discourses that granted science its power and prestige had also to be challenged at the level of discourse itself. Not only therefore could scientific discourse be **deconstructed** to reveal its internal inconsistencies, other discourses could also be produced in which this challenge could be most powerfully mounted. Just as for early feminist studies in literary representations of women the twin images of the goddess on a pedestal, or the disease-ridden, whorish and inscrutable *femme fatale* bent on the destruction of men, created the social reality according to which women were classified, so too, for postmodern, feminist science studies, the myth is indissociable from the reality of science. Thus Haraway, building on Bruno **Latour**'s 'actor-network theory' in a famous essay entitled 'A Manifesto for **Cyborgs**', concluded that, always the passive objects to active, scientific subjects, animals, machines and women formed an unstable network of unrealized alliances between both human and non-human actors.

Rather than stopping her critical labour at the very point of exposing the ideological, fictional and mythic structures inhabiting an allegedly purified scientific discourse (although this is precisely what she does in her epic study of the development of primatology in *Primate Visions* (1989)), Haraway accepted that science-as-mythology was a major component of its real situation and that science fiction formed a core resource for its expansion. Memorably noting, therefore, that 'fact' is simply the past tense of 'fiction', both deriving from the verb 'to make' or 'to fabricate', Haraway puts a slice of **cyberpunk** politics into the cybernetic ideal of biology and technology united under a single scientific paradigm. Accordingly, from the social and natural phenomena 'subjugated' by scientific mythology, she produces a '**hybrid**', cybernetic mythology where 'nature' is a trickster, a wily coyote, and where women and machines fuse, feminizing the cybernetic ideal from within the discourses of science themselves, while simultaneously refusing the feminist critique of technology that reduces it to a 'male thing'. Thus Haraway concludes the cyborg manifesto with the dazzling line, 'I would rather be a cyborg than a goddess'.

Bizarre mixtures and cultural affinities aside, it may seem that the cyborg remains only an image: a cybernetic Minerva sprung fully formed from the head of a dreaming Zeus. Surely inventing such figures cannot of itself have any effects beyond the marginal realm of science-fiction fandom? As a 'non-human actor', however, a cyborg cannot merely be reduced to image; science and technology, indeed, are increasingly augmenting naturally occurring non-humans with artificial tones: nanomachines, robots, clones. While the postmodern reflex may be to ask in turn, 'Ah, but nothing, not even science, can escape this realm of signs. All cultural struggles are fought out there, in a world that is inescapably narrated rather than "natural", and science is a part of culture, after all', Haraway remains wary of claims to 'nature' being reducible to 'narrative', or science to signs. Rather, it is important to Haraway, and other postmodern science students, not to operate such a reduction, but rather to consider 'hybrids' as the points of connection between scientific, cultural and political issues without annexing reality to discourse. The hybrid and the network in which it is a node have become the crucial conceptual means of organizing science studies in postmodernity. Rather than '*either* narrative *or* nature; *either* real *or* simulated', postmodern science studies such as Haraway, Michel Serres or Bruno Latour are engaged in emphasize a 'hybrid' and inclusive approach to the networks of events, problems, inventions, technologies, fictions, simulations and ideas that most adequately characterize the social role of science. Both the 'naturalizing' bent of early science studies and the 'narrativizing' bent of the more recent, deconstructive approaches, present bad, one-dimensional images of science. Haraway's cyborg therefore both combines the hybrid 'nature-culture' of the scientifically, technologically and critically sophisticated world, and the rise of 'non-human actors' within it.

The concepts of the hybrid and the network lend themselves to the post-modern imagination, not least because hybrid entities form an increasing element of contemporary *life*, in both the physical and the cultural sense. The human genome (part computer program, part chemical catalogue, all human) and cloning technologies; genetically modified plant and insect species; the rise of socio-biology and evolutionary psychology; the entire continuum of modified ecologies stretching from global warming and decreasing biodiversity to drawing-board protocols for terraforming (that is, engineering the atmospheres of currently uninhabitable planets) and the conservative idea of a genetic database; microchip palliatives for physiological incapacities and the re-engineering and patenting of organic forms as commercial entities: history has never witnessed such hybridizations as are now reported on a daily basis. Just as the mutability of bodies has *physically* eliminated the idea of biological essences, so culturally, without core identities or essences sustaining 'the self', we postmoderns are hybrids of cultural influences, racial and sexual identities, histories and memories both real (my memories) and artificial (my memories of that movie). Further, **Deleuze** and **Guattari**'s idea of two types of organizational structure, the one vertical, independent, top-down and 'arborescent' or 'tree-like', and the other horizontal, multiply connected, bottom-up and '**rhizomatic**', easily blends an apt image of postmodern conceptual relations where connections spread and multiply rather than being constrained by imposed and inflexible hierarchies, with methodologies being adopted in mathematics, physics and artificial intelligence research (in many ways, this coincidence of nature and culture is one of the most fascinating aspects of Deleuze and Guattari's work). Going further still, and prompting the question 'Science fiction or social fact?', networks, according to Jean-François **Lyotard**, have even become one of the most important, even definitive, non-human actors in the production of the postmodern world, even suggesting that the 'post' of 'postmodernism' refers not to coming after **modernism**, but to the 'posts' at which subjects and objects are connected in computerized societies.

While we can now see how easily science studies becomes susceptible to 'postmodernization', it remains doubtful how far science itself could be regarded as postmodern. There are, perhaps, two ways of thinking about postmodern science. First, science displays some of the features commonly associated with postmodernism; and, second, there is science that *calls itself* postmodern. Much recent science invites description as 'postmodern' and, in *The Postmodern Condition*, Lyotard even canonizes René **Thom** and Benoit **Mandelbrot** as practitioners of postmodern science. Thom, in particular, seems to be postmodern in his 'hybrid' researches into mathematics, science, anthropology and **semiotics**. We know we are on postmodern tracks when we read that 'scientists are sorcerers'! Mandelbrot's **fractals**, meanwhile, have become the icon of chaos that seems so aptly to sum up the endless fragmentations of postmodernity, with mathematics, since the mid-nineteenth century, dumping the strategy of approximating the ideal and unchanging forms of a Euclidean world for a geometry of endless change and differentiation. If under Mandelbrot, *geo-metry* goes back to the Earth, then it is only to prove that the Earth, once thought flat (pre-modern), then spherical (modern), is now fractal and infinite, thus demonstrably postmodern. It is not postmodern, however, because there is the possibility that this may be 'the truth' (although this is itself paradoxical); it is by virtue of the intensely paradoxical idea of a 'postmodern nature' as described by fractal geometries, along with the generalized pursuit of paradox by **complexity**, **chaos** or **catastrophe theory**, that its aims can be considered postmodern.

Even among scientists, however, there are advocates of a postmodern turn. Although Lyotard had coined the term in 1979, 'postmodern science' in this more 'hardline' context first appeared in the subtitle of cosmologist Stephen Toulmin's *The Return to Cosmology* (1982). What Toulmin refers to is, however, less recognizably postmodern than the work of Mandelbrot and Thom mentioned above. As we have already seen in our discussion of Haraway, modern science, its practitioners and its philosophers, had drawn a picture of the world subjugated to active subjects in pursuit of the knowledge of essentially passive objects. Moreover, nature was to be opened violently to the scientists' penetrating gaze, as can be seen from all the narratives of scientific heroism filling the pages of popular accounts of great scientific discoveries. Modern science, then, 'objectifies' nature, regarding it as something to be turned at will to the purposes of active subjects. With this bipolar split, science posed itself the insoluble problem of bridging the gulf between the subject's alleged knowledge and the actual constitution of the object in itself.

While such a characterization may seem excessively abstract and metaphysical, it comes into focus when we consider the debates about objectivity surrounding, for example, primatological field studies. Following Jane Goodall's well-publicized excursions into the field to study the great primates, a scandal broke out when it was revealed that she had solved the problem of making 'first contact' with a group of chimpanzees by laying out food for them. This, detractors argued, contaminated the evidence of her study since she had contaminated the habitat and intervened in an unacceptably overt manner to alter the conditions under which the chimps related to her, thus raising doubts as to the subsequent character of their behaviour, and in consequence invalidating Goodall's findings.

Others have, of course, confronted this problem. The philosopher Willard van Orman Quine posited the following situation, which he called 'radical translation': suppose you were an anthropologist visiting a hitherto undiscovered culture. You want to understand their language, but since it has never been heard beyond that culture, you have nothing to go on. How do you set about assembling a dictionary? The anthropologist must, Quine responded, assume that the members of the visited culture organized their linguistic world no differently from the way we do ours. As a result of this assumption, which came to be known as the 'principle of interpretive charity', objectivity becomes meaningless. The culture under study is less an object than a group of subjects whose actions must be understood through the anthropologist's hands-on intervention. But what grounds do we have, other than sheer pragmatism, for making Quine's 'charitable' assumptions? The anthropologist Claude **Lévi-Strauss**, for example, perpetually asked how, when studying other cultures, it was possible to avoid contaminating the specimen with imported prejudices specific to the scientist's culture. Even the presence of the scientist significantly alters the situation, introducing **differences** where there were none, and forcing the culture to confront, and thus to renegotiate its relations to, a new outsider. Lévi-Strauss's solution was not to try to minimize contact or disguise his presence, nor to assume that the differences were negligible, but to attempt to be absorbed into that other culture: to become, as he expressed it, 'the language spoken by its myths'. Even the physical sciences face this problem: insofar, for example, as subatomic particles are to become available to observation, they must be 'produced' in a particle accelerator; to what extent, then, does the physicist observe natural or artificial phenomena? Just as there are those who argue the objectivist case that such particles could not be produced for observation if the situation in which they were so produced did not correspond in essential respects to the natural situation, so too there are 'instrumentalists', such as Ian Hacking, who insist that science is engaged in the manufacture and observation of artefacts that, as hybrid products of observation technologies and nature, could not otherwise be available.

If these scenarios problematize objectivity from an abstract point of view, primatologist Dian Fossey, following in Goodall's footsteps, brings the problem into a starkly moral focus. Fossey's objectivity was so shrouded in doubt that stories began to circulate about 'unnatural relationships' she may have been having with a gorilla. Things were exacerbated when hunters trapped and beheaded her favourite gorilla, prompting her to track the hunters in turn, only to become their next victim. In such circumstances, the question seems to be less one of how to maintain the proper scientific objectivity and detachment, than how pathological such detachment would be. Postmodern science, according to Toulmin, has learnt this lesson: nature is not an object – something that stands against us that we must subdue in order to know. Instead, postmodern science becomes part of 'man's new dialogue with nature', as complexity theorists Ilya Prigogine and Isabelle Stengers put it (*Order Out of Chaos* (1984)). After centuries of subjecting her to torture, the knowing subject decides nature is better conceived as a conversation partner. Like Richard **Rorty**'s ongoing 'North-Atlantic bourgeois conversation', postmodern science has discovered that, even without the purist, modern order of truth and objectivity, 'it's good to talk'.

The hermeneutic overtones in this version of postmodern science mark it out, however, as less postmodern than many a philosopher or **critical theorist** would recognize. Paradoxically, such postmodern science seems merely to have learnt the lessons of Martin Heidegger's hermeneutic critique of the 'essence of modern science', over-polarized between maniacally mathematizing subjects and indifferent, inactive objects, and insufficiently attentive to the being of nature, to how nature *is*. Modern science, Heidegger argued, has imposed an image upon nature that, rather than revealing or 'dis-covering' it, covered it over again, so that the 'age of the world-picture' dominates all the procedures and dis-coveries of modern science. Heidegger, however, while no modernist, is perhaps better characterized as anti- rather than post-modern. And, similarly, the 'discursive' turn to include nature as a partner in dialogue parallels Jürgen **Habermas**'s advocacy of the 'unfinished project of modernity' against a postmodernist renunciation of its ideals.

Once again, however, Heidegger's 'world-picture' brings us back to the issue of whether science studies nature or representations, substance or signs. Surprisingly, perhaps, it is along the lines of signs, representations and simulation that much of what is more recognizably postmodern in the sciences is currently leading. The sciences of the artificial have in effect mounted a two-pronged attack on modern science with its predilection for nature over representations, on the one hand, and analysis over synthesis, on the other. On the one hand, artificial intelligence (AI) research has become less concerned with programming the functions of understanding into a machine than with *simulating* intelligence. Thus the 'Turing test' for machine intelligence, named after its inventor, Alan Turing, placed a person into a divided room and asked them, by means of a typewriter, to engage the subject on the other side of the divider in conversation. The machine passed its intelligence test if the person was fooled into thinking that the machine was another person. Here the nature or essence of human intelligence is less important than its appearance: seeming or behaving intelligently is sufficient. As Lyotard says of postmodern knowledge in general, the goal is no longer truth but performance: we do not need to know what intelligence really is, just how to simulate it. Of course, AI therefore provokes questions which, ironically, have resulted in machines modelling human intelligence, rather than humans providing the 'program' for machine intelligence. Moreover, the manner in which machines 'learn' in contemporary AI research is, in Deleuze and Guattari's terms, more 'rhizomatic' than 'arborescent': learning makes connections between things rather than mining a thing for as much information about it as possible. In AI, this approach is therefore called 'connectionism', and the hardware that learns through such means is called a 'neural net', eradicating the difference between real and artificial neurones. Rather than the image of arborescent supercomputers such as HAL 9000 from the film *2001: A Space Odyssey*, which must be programmed with intelligence before carrying out intelligent functions, neural nets form rhizomatic networks of computers that interact with each other and, through this interaction, resolve random input into emergent patterns (see **complexity theory** and **fuzzy logic** in Part II), thus actually learning. The 'cybernetic brains' of 1950s science fiction became, in the last years of the twentieth century, intelligent simulations of intelligence.

Perhaps the most obviously postmodern of all the sciences, however, is that of artificial life (Alife), otherwise known as 'synthetic biology'. Artificial life dispenses with nature altogether, studying instead the actions and simulated evolutions of pixel-creatures in computer environments. Surely, at last, science is studying signs and representations rather than nature? Once again, however, the difference between the real and the artificial is what is eradicated. Thus evolutionary biologist and Alife researcher Thomas S. Ray twists this paradoxical science still further, stating, at this new discipline's fourth international conference in 1994, that the life processes studied in Alife are not themselves artificial but natural; the resultant life-forms merely 'live' in an artificial environment. Thus Alife naturalizes the artificial, making **simulacra** of life indistinguishable from their real-life counterparts. In a sense, Ray and other Alife researchers are quite right: what current definition of life – self-moving, feeding and excreting, growing and reproducing – can rule these artificial aliens out of the natural world of evolutionary biology, even if the life in question is silicon- rather than carbon-based? Synthetic biology, in the words of one of its avatars, is not so much the study of life as it is, but life as it could be.

If Alife represents a simulationist extreme of postmodern science, at the other, realist, extreme, the sciences in postmodernity make an important contribution to the rethinking of cultural phenomena in general. This was already explicit in Lyotard's *Postmodern Condition*, although it is often overlooked: grand narratives do not collapse due to the withering effects of the progressive nihilism Nietzsche forecast, or merely because this is something 'in the air', but because of the *effects of computerization*. Computer-mediated communications replace language as the vehicle of reason with information measured according to its effects. In other words, the postmodern condition is effected by a technology that harnesses language for quantitative evaluation, so that it is no longer determined by universal ideals (truth, the just society, freedom, etc.), but rather by local imperatives ('re: figures – my desk, tomorrow'; divert resources from failing department, progress this project, etc.), subject only to the law of increased efficiency.

On the one hand, narratives, representations, metaphors; on the other, science, technology, determinisms; Lyotard's account gives equal weight to both poles of the postmodern condition. Ultimately, however, although he insists that the goals of postmodern epistemologies and sciences are species of 'local determinisms', his characterization of the condition as a whole is premised on the technological seizure of the means of communication. While technology does not do this in a vacuum, but acquires agency by the social premium placed by capitalism – or more precisely capitalist techno-science – on a performative efficiency that elevates information exchange above all other uses of language, the determination of language by technologically achievable imperatives (instant response, minimal transfer time between information and execution, everyone at their 'post', and so on) becomes a *universal determination of the social bond*; and it is this that finally puts paid to the great stories that sustained the modernist ideal of the rational co-determination of social goals by free participants. Although, therefore, the postmodern condition may appear to be – and has all too often been interpreted simply as – nothing but a play of discourses, a matter of narratives only, Lyotard's thesis is ultimately that technology has become finally determinant. This sits ill at ease with the 'something in the air' notion that postmodernity consists in what Baudrillard has called the 'perfect crime': the death of the real can neither be confirmed nor denied since the corpse has disappeared.

The antithesis between this 'realist' understanding of postmodernity and the more common account given of it, satirized by the **Sokal** affair (when the physicist Alan Sokal had a spoof article, 'Transgressing the Boundaries: Towards a Transformative Hermeneutics of Quantum Gravity' accepted by the American academic journal *Social Text* (1996)), as open-ended and non-foundational discursive power play (reality does not determine the fittest narrative, but is instead fixed by the dominant narratives, which therefore lack firm foundations, so that they are susceptible of deconstruction, reversal, and replacement), is brought into sharp focus by a realism underlying the 'postmodern' sciences. Mandelbrot, for example, celebrated by Lyotard as an exemplar of postmodern science, insists on the paradoxically infinite measurements demanded by the *actual* coastline of Britain on the basis of the return of 'geo-metry' to the measurement of the real Earth. Thom, similarly disposed to paradox in his modelling of unpredictable changes of state – catastrophes – in a system, is driven to this by a realist conception of mathematics in the morphology of living systems, following his mentor D'Arcy Thomson.

Nor is this thesis proposed by Lyotard alone. The 1977 winner of the Nobel prize for chemistry Ilya Prigogine wrote in 1979, with chemist and philosopher Isabelle Stengers, of a 'new alliance' between the physical and the human sciences. The new alliance was premised on the discovery that time was not simply an abstract frame of reference, as Henri Bergson had complained against

Einstein's conception of it when they debated the issue in Paris in 1922; nor was it, as Einstein in turn complained of Bergson's notion of it, merely a 'philosopher's time': rather, Prigogine's discovery of *nonlinear* processes in the natural world established that time was integral to physical processes where there emerges 'order out of chaos', as the edited English language version of 1985 was titled. Significantly, one of the elements cut from the English edition was the author's discussion of Deleuze's work as an important contribution to rethinking nonlinear processes. At the very moment, then, when the humanities were reeling under postmodernism's revelation that 'reality' was a matter of social or discursive construction, and that therefore 'scientific discourse' could be attacked for its 'unfounded' attempts to state the truth about nature, the sciences were promoting a critique of the conceptual conservatism of the sciences and a new realism therefore concerning not just the scientific, but also the philosophical, engagement with the world, its history, its ideas and its physics. Offering a non-reductive approach to scientific theory, the nonlinear physics Prigogine and Stengers promote has been embraced by both commentators on postmodern thought such as Brian Massumi and Ira Livingstone, and by those who embrace what such commentators would likely call 'scientism': the uncritical adoption of the explanatory goals and methods of the physical by the social and human sciences. Nonlinearity has not only, that is, been borrowed as a metaphor or narrative device, but has also been embraced as enabling an account of sociological and cultural processes by the same theories that are employed by the physical sciences. Whether overcome or repaired, the gulf between the physical sciences and the humanities, formalized by Wilhelm Dilthey in the mid-nineteenth century, lies at the core of the issues foregrounded under the rubric of postmodernism and science. Precisely where **Foucault** famously sees only epistemic discontinuities, breaks, and ruptures in scientific practice and theory, the sciences invent the basis of a new continuity.

This situation, however, has also led some who might be expected to have the most to gain from the postmodern turn to signs and constructions to reject it altogether. Thus sociologist of science Bruno Latour, on whose ideas Haraway, for example, has extensively drawn, rejects the ideological criticism of science as practised by many of the originators of his field of study, but also, in response to the question of postmodernism, insists 'we have never been modern'. In place of the simple segregation of the human world of thought and language from the physical one of things, Latour proposes the non-modern interconnection of concept and chemical, meaning and matter. In place of a world that restricts the capacity for action to rational beings, Latour draws our attention to the effects on that world of non-human agents. For example, viruses are discursively constructed, certainly (HIV as 'God's plague upon the sinner'; the immune system which HIV attacks as marking the limits of personal identity), but this is not all there is to them. They are also particular protein codes that can be isolated in laboratories, that have their own inscrutable genetic history, that have undeniably physical effects, and that spontaneously mutate and threaten populations.

Similarly, technology is not simply an inert tool enabling human intervention in and control over the physical and social world; rather, it becomes an agent embroiled alongside human components in systems whose effects are greater than their constituents.

Perhaps the most powerful examples of such networks are provided by the emergent field of biotechnology: the ongoing genetic modification of natural organisms is neither natural nor discursive alone, although it combines both into a series of technologies with the aim of creating new specifications for natural objects. Such objects are not metaphorically, but literally hybridized, and not only in the specifically biological sense of the term: the effects of biotechnological networks can neither be contained under traditional scientific paradigms, nor under traditionally humanistic ones, since politics, economics and commerce are inextricably tied up with the particular functions newly engineered into real organisms. In place, therefore, of the sciences' rejection of the social, and of humanists' rejection of the physical, Latour's 'non-modernism' proposes a 'new constitution' that combines both the physical and the discursive, mountains, madness and machines, GM crops, global commerce, Frankenstein's monster and ecological politics as irreducible elements of one reality.

In one sense, then, the conjunction of postmodernism, technology and science yields new critical methods for the humanities' scrutiny of the sciences; in another, it occasions attempts to establish conceptual frameworks for a new connectivity between physical and discursive objects. While these are perennial concerns, and not specific to postmodernity alone, Lyotard, for example, argues precisely that postmodernity is what it is by virtue of the technological transformation of the paradigmatically humanist medium of language in general, subjecting it not merely to philosophical, literary and cultural study, but to engineering and physics. The net effect of this, Lyotard argues, is to spawn an urgent experimentation in modes of linguistic intervention, artistic practices and scientific theorizing alike. Concerning this latter, we have seen that there is experimentation aplenty, theoretical and practical. Unlike previous attempts to introduce theories stemming from the physical sciences into the social sciences – such as, for example, Auguste Comte's positivism, or Herbert Spencer's social Darwinism – the attempts of the last thirty years or so do not seek simply to explain social and cultural phenomena in terms of physics, but rather pursue a larger philosophical agenda. Thus we find scientific theorists such as Roland Omnès arguing that the best guide to the overwhelmingly complicated ontology of quantum physics is not to be found amongst the back-catalogue of scientific heroism, nor in systematizing the current state of research, nor even from the sterile epistemological debates of the philosophy of science. Rather, Omnès' *Quantum Philosophy* (2002) claims, Heidegger's prolonged interrogations of Being, and the third-century neoplatonist philosopher Plotinus' complex meditations on the relation between language, logic, and nature, will serve better to explicate the relations between *logos* and reality involved in the quantum world. The agenda is quite simply a new metaphysics.

Three figures dominate postmodern science: the hybrid, the network and non-linearity. If the wave of experimentation affecting the arts, humanities and the sciences is what defines the postmodern condition, its outcome hinges on the simple antithesis brought to light by considering the interconnections between science, technology and postmodernism: are hybridity, networks and nonlinearity *simply* figures, metaphors or 'manners of speaking', or are they the non-reductive articulators of a new metaphysical realism?

8

POSTMODERNISM AND ARCHITECTURE

DIANE MORGAN

Whilst motoring across the Californian desert, a young woman encounters a young male student who had been engaged in the militant activities of May '68. He is later shot by the police. Thanks to this encounter, her eyes are opened to the capitalist materialism surrounding her; the prevalence of consumer culture; social inequality and the shady dealings of big business. She arrives at her destination in the middle of the desert, and enters her boss's house – a splendid **modernist** oasis, consisting of a cantilevered steel frame with strip windows, which perches on the edge of an arid rocky outcrop. She can now see through its refined design to its impure preconditions: its slick form, cleverly unobtrusive, as it parasitically clings to the natural surroundings, sums up the exploitation rife in society at large. She exchanges knowing looks with the native American servants in the house and appears to sense what natural values might be as she gives herself up to a water-fall in the grounds of the house. For her boss, by contrast, value is not something intrinsic in things or people but rather a product of commercial speculation. He reminds his business contact, hesitant about signing a deal with him for the development of a shoreside site, that 'the price of anything is neither high nor low except in relation to its potential use'. Value is only to be assessed in terms of what can be extracted financially. Water is not to be treasured for its natural properties but for the business opportunities it opens up: in this case, the construction of a marina, pier and airstrip and perhaps hotel complexes so as to turn the place into a marketable resort. Having understood the full significance of the house and its residents, the woman imagines it being blown up, being dramatically ripped apart by an explosive rejection. As the highly aesthetic modernist house bursts into flames, it is followed up by further iconoclastic demonstrations: fridges, clothes, all sorts of commodities are blasted into the air. These emblems of a materialistic culture epitomize a society gone astray: an instrumentalized world which 1960s youth refuses in the name of fundamental rights and natural values.

The film I have just described is Antonioni's *Zabriskie Point* (1969) and it provides a good starting point for a discussion of **postmodern** architecture. In this film, modernist architecture is no longer associated with the innovations of the avant-garde – as it was in the 1920s and 1930s – but with the establishment, the well-heeled, the older generation. Its pure, transparent style, the regime of living it offers to its residents, is equated with the arrogance of wealth and power. The sweeping away of its traces in the film marks the possibility of a radically new departure which is also a return to, or retrieval of, all too neglected values. This

71

reinscription of the past conjoined with an enthusiasm for the variety of the contemporary could serve as a positive definition of postmodernism as understood by Charles **Jencks**, its most vocal of exponents on things architectural.

Jencks suggests that postmodern architecture at once continues the traditions of modernism and transcends them – his term for this process is '**double coding**'. Anxious to defend postmodernism against allegations that it is just an irresponsible free-for-all, whose lack of political commitment plays straight into the hands of those who want to maintain the status quo at any price, Jencks stakes out nobler aims. Postmodernism, he claims in *What is Post-modernism?* (1986), aims at a realization of 'the great promise of a **plural** culture with its many freedoms'. Whereas modernism was a 'univalent formal system' which suffocated dissenting voices in an attempt to impose general principles of minimalist taste, Jencks associates postmodern architecture with eclecticism and openness. For us to understand the stakes of this debate between postmodernist and modernist architecture, it is necessary to trace the latter's passage from the exciting and dynamic world of Bauhaus and Le Corbusier in the earlier twentieth century through to the 1960s and 1970s where what used to be the avant-garde is now perceived as the enemy of change.

One of the most telling images of a modernist architect is given to us by Ayn Rand. In her best-selling novel, *The Fountainhead* (1943), the uncompromising architect Howard Roark declares: 'I set my own standards. I inherit nothing. I stand at the end of no tradition. I may, perhaps, stand at the beginning of one.' Here, modernist architecture is represented by one who is unwilling to adapt his projects to the tastes of his public. Ahead of his time, he will not pander to the retrograde mass demands for mock-classical buildings with their tacked-on pilasters, scrolls and leaves. His constructions are absolute in their demand for recognition: harsh, rigid glass skyscrapers and standardized mass housing which does away with individualized nooks and crannies, the idiosyncrasies of clutter, in the name of purity and clarity. Democracy, the negotiation of **differences**, is regarded by him as a levelling of genial creativity.

In *The Decorative Art of Today* (1925) Le Corbusier also announces a rejection of past standards. He kicks away the props and supports of conventional taste, castigating old-fashioned, artisanal values as redundant in the age of the machine aesthetic: 'Hand-made work. The cult of failures. The apologia for daubing. The relaxed hour of the inexact. The triumph of the limp ego. The jubilation of the free will, the respect for the as-for-me. The suppression of control.' Handed-down assumptions must be put to the test, not just absorbed unquestioningly. The architect is a virile superman, an affirmative nihilist boldly overturning today's conventional values in an attempt to think and construct the future. In *Towards a New Architecture* (1923) he explains that 'culture is the final outcome of an effort of selection. Selection means to put to one side, to prune, clean up, to bring out the naked and clear essential'.

This tough selection process, this jettisoning of all that is presumed to be superfluous, weak and impure in the name of discipline and hygiene, coupled with Le Corbusier's personal admiration for technocrats and strong, if not totalitarian states, brings together most of the worrying aspects of modernist architecture. A movement which started off with utopian visions of serving the masses, introducing standardization so as to set higher standards of living for all – not just the already privileged – seems to end up dictating to those same masses.

The same disquieting tendency can be detected with the Bauhaus. As essays by Grete Lihotsky and Bruno Taut included in *The Weimar Republic Sourcebook* (A. Kaes *et al.*, eds (1995)) made clear, this highly influential school of thought and practice saw in mass mechanical reproduction a solution to social injustice and gender inequality. Cheaply manufactured mass housing, rationalized into compact housing units, would not only reduce the difference between rich and poor by setting minimal standards for all, but would also emancipate the woman from household slavery by systematizing the 'best and simplest way' to keep the house in running order. Such Taylorist efficiency would mean that household chores would become so self-evident and easy to accomplish that even husbands and children could contribute to 'making the beds, cleaning the washstand, etc as necessary'! The final result would mean that the woman would save time and be freed up for other activities – intellectual pursuits or leisure activities as she wished.

This liberating aspect of Bauhaus's ethos has to be read alongside the other, more sinister, side of systematized rationalization. Consider this extract from Rudolf Arnheim's 'The Bauhaus in Dessau' (in *Sourcebook*):

> In a room hung with diagonal curtains, in which a sofa sits obliquely to the corner and ten different, fully loaded little tables are set up every which way, there is hardly any reason why a new floor lamp should be placed here rather than there. But the position of everything in a Bauhaus room can be decided with nearly lawlike precision. One will soon learn to understand theoretically that it is not a question here of subjective taste, but that such feelings are a very secure and generally valid psychological phenomenon that leads to very similar results from different people. That is why one can speak even in the case of such problems as those of 'objectively determined solutions'.

Here more manipulative overtones creep in. Instead of standardization promoting individuation, a general programmatization of taste is fantasized. In a Bauhaus flat there would only be one destination for your newly acquired lamp. Your flat would be designed in such a way that that particular item would belong to it *there* as if it were conforming to some ineluctable natural law. Emancipation tips over into dictatorial prescription; egalitarian standardization becomes totalitarian uniformity; the iconoclastic break with the past cashes out as a smashing of people's sense of place and rootedness; a disrespect for the all too human fondness for familiar localities.

For Jencks, the alienation felt by residents forced to fit into idealistic, over-zealous modernist building schemes marks the failure of that movement (and the beginning of a more modest, *post*modernist reorientation). He describes how grand 'utopian' housing schemes gradually fell into disrepair, being progressively vandalized as the inhabitants tried to register their sense of despair at being abandoned to soulless, concrete jungles. In *The Language of Post-modern Architecture* (1975) he writes:

> Modern architecture died in St Louis, Missouri on July 15, 1972 at 3.32pm (or thereabouts) when the infamous Pruitt-Igoe scheme, or rather several of its slab blocks, were given the final *coup de grâce* by dynamite . . . Pruitt-Igoe was constructed according to the most progressive ideals of CIAM and it won an award from the American Institute of Architects when it was designed in 1951. It consisted of elegant slab blocks fourteen storeys high with rational 'streets in the air' (which were safe from cars but as it turned out, not safe from crime); 'sun, space and greenery', which Le Corbusier called the 'three essential joys of urbanism' (instead of conventional streets, gardens and semi-private space, which he banished). It had a separation of pedestrian and vehicular traffic, the provision of play space, and local amenities such as laundries, crèches and gossip centres – all rational substitutes for traditional patterns. Moreover, its Purist style, its clean, salubrious hospital metaphor, was meant to instill, by good example, corresponding virtues in the inhabitants.

Modernist architecture is regarded as having brutalized people in its attempt to rationalize, to impose a strict and systematic order on, their ways of living. Unfortunately for the idealist, humans are not entirely rational, ordered or disciplined. Their tastes are variable and mostly non-justifiable, and they are prone to fits of folly. For these reasons postmodern architecture, with its proclivity for crazy pastiche, its wacky blending of styles, its disrespect for monastic regularity and tolerance for historical referentiality is deemed more human than the rigours of modernist purism. As Jencks explains in *What is Post-modernism?* (1986) modernist architects were characteristically unsympathetic to human foibles: 'Ornament, polychromy, metaphor, humour, symbolism and convention were put on the Index and all forms of decoration and historical reference were declared taboo.'

Postmodern architecture is also more cautious about the uses technology can be put to and more sceptical about the merits of industrialization. Whereas mechanization was jubilantly celebrated by the modernists for its exactitude – see Le Corbusier's tirade against imperfect artisanal goods, cited above – its ability to dispel the stuffy **aura** of the past and to launch a fresh, disenchanted modern world, postmodernists are less optimistic. The world post-Auschwitz, post-Hiroshima, knows too much about the terrors of abstraction and instrumentalization. A dislocated, disembodied relation to the world results in people becoming figures to be 'processed' or materials to be 'recycled'. (Alain Resnais' documentary film, *Night and Fog* (1956), on the Nazi concentration camps, contains some of the most graphic evidence of the results of such abstraction. People are reduced to spare parts – divided up, sorted into piles: hair for stuffing cushions, skin for soap and lampshades.) Science should not be allowed to 'progress' according to its own self-generating laws, without due concern to its long-term impact on the world and its inhabitants. As a consequence, Jencks wants to suggest that postmodernist architecture draws on some of the ethical and ecological lessons the past has inadvertently taught us. As in *Zabriskie Point,* Jencks suggests that once having rejected the arrogant assumptions of the modernist elite, one rediscovers the rights of the environment:

> Perhaps in the future with the environmental crises and the increasing **globalization** of the economy, communications and virtually every specialization, we will be encouraged – even forced – to emphasise the things which interact, the connections between a growing economy, an ideology of constant change and waste. They who don't realize the world is a whole are doomed to pollute it.
>
> (*What is Post-modernism?* (1986))

Reacting against the modernist disdain for personalized space and thereby reconsidering the artisanal respect for the local and the traditional, postmodern architecture reinscribes place whilst meeting the challenge of present-day globalization. It is this double articulation, the negotiation of place and that which threatens to erode it, the placelessness of global communication networks, which is a central concern for postmodern architects.

As architecture is the most down-to-earth art form, the most fixed in space, it has an intimate relation to questions of **presence**, origin, rootedness and dwelling. All these concepts have taken a battering from postmodern thought. The virtual world of the **Internet** is one development which poses a serious challenge to architects used to concretizing projects in the here and now. If liberation is now to be equated with exhilarating surfing forays on the Net, which seems to promise another, virtual world, not tied down to earthly restrictions or prejudices, how is the architect supposed to carry on constructing the future? As we have seen, in the past the architect felt it was incumbent on him, as heroic demiurge, to take upon his shoulders the burden of responsibility for building the right, improving context for society. In the postmodern world, the restrictions of a particular place appear to have been circumvented. One might not have or know any neighbours, but instead be in regular, even intimate, contact with people all over the globe whom one has never met *as such*, according to traditional notions of encounter.

Faced with such developments in information technology, there can be no nostalgic return to an antiquated idea of place, despite the lamentable attempts of architects such as Quinlan Terry to return to a bygone age. Indeed any such hankering after precise geographical fixity and any such celebration of rooted, supposedly unproblematic identity is regarded as reactionary by this ever emerging mobile global culture which espouses decontextualized **hybridity** and the intersplicing of cultural differences. Architectural theorists have reacted to such challenges to their profession in different ways.

Kenneth **Frampton**, who is no friend of Jencks and his version of postmodernism – indeed he dismisses it as mere 'entertainment' – nevertheless agrees that the modernist project is at an end and that what comes after is to be radically rethought. In his 'Towards a Critical Regionalism' (H. Foster, ed., *Postmodern Culture* (1985)), he accepts the fact that modernization can no longer be celebrated, as it was by his modernist predecessors, as the key to progress. Such a blind faith in the power of technology, as well as a nostalgic return to a pre-industrial past, cannot be sustained. Frampton at once recognizes the dangers inherent in an avant-garde movement which has an overbearing sense of its own importance and truth, yet he is not prepared to lapse into apolitical quietism. He is still searching for a critical purchase on society and advocates that this stance is best achieved by an 'arrière-garde', not tempted by the **grand narratives** of modernism, which is still invested in resisting dominant forms of ideology.

Frampton's form of postmodernism focuses on architecture which can mediate between the 'ubiquitous placelessness of our modern environment' and a particular site. His stance can best be understood by juxtaposing him with what he is reacting against: consider this ecstatic celebration of the American city – that antithesis of the well-integrated environment, that enemy of the urban project – by the guru of postmodern euphoria, Jean **Baudrillard** in *America* (1986):

> No, architecture should not be humanized. Anti-architecture, the true sort (not the kind you find in Arcosanti, Arizona, which gathers together all the 'soft' technologies in the heart of the desert), the wild inhuman type that is beyond the measure of man was made here – made itself here – in New York, without consider-ations of setting, well-being, or ideal ecology. It opted for hard technologies, exaggerated all dimensions, gambled on heaven and hell . . . Eco-architecture, eco-society . . . this is the gentle hell of the Roman Empire in decline.

Baudrillard disdains a 'soft' consideration for human scale and local setting. Postmodernism, with its exciting new technologies, is not to be shackled by the dead weight of the human with his pedestrian concerns. Instead he extols the intricacies of the freeways and that antithesis of the European urban experience, Los Angeles:

> No elevator or subway in Los Angeles. No verticality or underground, no intimacy or collectivity, no streets or facades, no centre or monuments: a fantastic space, a spectral and discontinuous succession of all the various functions, of all signs with no hierarchical ordering – an extravaganza of indifference, extravaganza of undifferentiated surfaces – the power of pure, open space, the kind you find in the deserts.

Frampton exactly pitches himself against this uncritical acceptance of the decline of the urban project. He seeks to puncture this rhetoric of **simulation** and the **hyperreal** with buildings which, interacting with the singularity of their sites, resonate with a certain 'density' of experience. Subverting the otherwise unquestioned superiority of the eye over the remaining senses, Frampton calls on architecture to appeal to the tactile: 'The tactile resilience of the place-form and the capacity of the body to read the environment in terms other than those of sight alone suggest a potential strategy for resisting the domination of universal technology' ('Towards a Critical Regionalism'). Touch, smell, the 'whole range of complementary sensory perceptions which are registered by the labile body' are evoked by Frampton as a way of reinscribing the human into an *experience* of place. Rejecting apocalyptic cries by the likes of Stelarc – see 'Towards the Post-human', *Architectural Design* (1995) – announcing the obsolescence of the body in this '**post-human**' age, Frampton sees his variety of postmodernism as permitting the resurgence of what Jean-François **Lyotard** would call '**little narratives**' or 'local **legitimacies**'.

Another theorist who, like Frampton, takes a stand against the prevailing placelessness of postmodernist architecture, is **Fredric Jameson**. In 'Postmodernism and Consumer Society' (in H. Foster, ed., *Postmodern Culture* (1985)), he too recognizes the ossifying institutionalization of modernism against which postmodernism reacts. He is also trying to reinvent artistic experimentation – a sign of oppositional, critical art which rudely disrupts conventionalized ways of seeing – whilst not falling into the trap of modernism, which all too quickly became equated with elitism because of its uncompromising difficulty. For Jameson, the summation of postmodern despair, the total abandonment of any attempt to contribute positively to the urban environment, is encapsulated by the Bonaventura Hotel in Los Angeles. This building frustrates the experience of place. Whereas the nineteenth-century city, the home of the **nomadic** *flâneur*, provided a forum for enriching, if brief, encounters, this hotel pre-empts exploration. It discourages independent mobility, obliging the unsuspecting visitors passively to give themselves up to its 'transportation machines' which conduct them from one isolated point to another. Instead of the rich 'density of objecthood' sought by Frampton, this hotel thins out space by disallowing any appreciation of volume. No general impression of the building can be snatched, no transitory vantage point can be seized from which to gather some sense of place. However, this is not to say that, by contrast, modernist space provided the visitor with static, solid viewing platforms with nicely set up perspectival privileges from which to dominate the surroundings. Far from it: the modernists delighted in spaces which were dynamic, even vertiginous, but which could be *experienced* as such. Indeed Sigfried Giedion's book *Buildings in France: Building in Iron, Building in Ferro-Concrete* (1928) is packed full of exhilarating descriptions of buildings such as the Eiffel Tower and the Transporter Bridge in Marseilles, the precursors of modernist architecture, which orchestrate dizzy and destabilizing – yet enriching – experiences of space. By contrast, it is the paucity of the 'postmodern' experience which is lamented by Jameson. (Or to reframe this debate yet further using Walter **Benjamin's** distinctions in 'Experience and Poverty' (1933), one could contrast the stark, 'barbaric poverty' of modernist architecture, which violently breaks with the past in order to begin afresh, with the opulent paucity of postmodernism which marks a compromise with the status quo.) The Bonaventura Hotel, with its opaque reflecting surfaces, is therefore seen to be repelling the fractured city outside, refusing any communication with it, and thereby to have self-destructively turned in on itself. It cannot generate any meaning from within itself and the result is a 'milling confusion'.

Jencks begs to differ from critics such as Jameson. In *What is Post-modernism?* he reads postmodernism not as a destructive emptying out of, or as a sceptical rejection of, value, but rather as a paradoxical 'embracing of absolute relativism, or fragmental holism', a challenge to attempts to categorize postmodernism as any one thing. Robert **Venturi**, the other architectural theorist most associated with the fate of postmodernism, also equates it with a medley of different styles and approaches:

> Architects can no longer afford to be intimidated by the puritanically moral language of orthodox Modern architecture. I like elements which are hybrid rather than 'pure', compromising rather than 'clean', distorted rather than 'straight-forward', ambiguous rather than 'articulated', perverse as well as impersonal, boring as well as 'interesting'.... I'm for messy vitality over obvious unity. I include the non sequitur and proclaim the duality.
>
> (*Complexity and Contradiction in Architecture* (1968))

Mocking the rigid and minimalist purity of modernist architects such as Mies van der Rohe, who had proclaimed earlier on in the century that 'less is more' – Venturi saucily retorts 'less is a bore' – he celebrates the 'messy vitality' of places like Las Vegas. The casinos, diners, hotels and bars of Las Vegas are often mainly composed of enormous signs designed to catch the eye of touring motorists prowling The Strip for somewhere ostentatiously to squander their money. As Venturi remarks in *Learning from Las Vegas* (1972): 'The sign is more important than the architecture . . . The sign at the front is a vulgar extravaganza, the building at the back, a modest necessity.' The signs are not just words but pictures, shapes and figures illustrating the enticing nature of the place: one of Venturi's examples is: 'a duck store in the shape of a duck, called "The Long Island Duckling"'. Venturi goes on to explain how Las Vegas would be blasphemous for modernist architects who strictly adhere to the biblical injunction against 'graven images' in the name of pure spatial expression:

> During the last 40 years, theorists of Modernist architecture . . . have focused on space as the essential ingredient that separates architecture from painting, sculpture and literature. Their definitions glory in the uniqueness of the medium; although sculpture and painting may sometimes be allowed spatial characteristics, sculptural or pictorial architecture is unacceptable – because Space is sacred.
>
> (*Learning from Las Vegas* (1972))

The example Venturi uses to illustrate his argument is a most convincing one: Mies van der Rohe's German Pavilion in Barcelona, described by Henry-Russell

Hitchcock in *The International Style* (1966) as 'perhaps the supreme example of architectural design of the decade of the twenties'. Mies' 'universal grammar of steel I-beams' filled in with glass and brick is interrupted, but by no means disrupted, by the inclusion of a single statue, the Kolbe sculpture of a naked woman. As Venturi points out: 'Objects of art were used to reinforce architectural space at the expense of their own content. The Kolbe in the Barcelona Pavilion was a foil to the directed spaces: The Message was mainly architectural.' Rather like the Bauhaus lamp mentioned above, the Kolbe statue is fitted into an overall design, not for its own sake but as the ornament which is required to adorn the building at that point, in that previously determined and circumscribed place. Far from producing a dissonant note which upsets the harmony of the building, the statue actually effaces itself, symbolically communicating nothing boldly. By contrast, by celebrating the garish language of signs, Venturi is praising the merits of 'an architecture of bold communication' over 'one of subtle expression'. However, the question can be raised: how boldly can one communicate if the vehicle one is using is one that consists of pastiche, play, incongruity, eclecticism and 'disjunctive variety'?

Returning to our initial point of departure: can we be so certain about the statement being made at the end of Antonioni's film, *Zabriskie Point* when the modernist house is blasted away? In the film there is a shift which can be registered between the dynamiting of the house and the ensuing images of exploding consumer items. The house itself is an example of the work of an architect such as Frank Lloyd Wright. He was hardly a purist, producing a textualized form of modernism, which made great use of building materials such as timber and stone. These blended gracefully into the natural surroundings in an eco-friendly sort of way. When the scene changes to the consumer items, the colours become artificially pastel and the music surges, underscoring the release of tension as these symbols of materialist culture are jubilantly jettisoned. Whereas the woman appeared hesitant about doing away with the villa, the other objects are relinquished without delay. Is the woman actually rejecting modernism and embracing what comes after – that is, postmodernism? She is presumably putting into practice her newly found radical politics. Can this be equated with the postmodernist theories of Jencks and Venturi who have no scores to settle with capitalism and consumer culture? Indeed, the former goes so far as to declare that today's society showers us with a superabundance of choice; according to him we are overwhelmed with an *'embarras de richesses'* and bathed in an atmosphere of 'widespread pluralism'. However, Jencks then adds: 'With no recognized authority and centre of power many professional groups (and even whole countries) feel victimized by a world culture and marketplace that jumps, sporadically, in different directions.'

Indeed, these 'groups' and 'even countries' who anxiously sit at the margins of an unpredictably expanding and contracting postmodern universe – suffering as they do from 'mild paranoia' – just cannot see the pleasures Jencks is trying to point out to them. They see mockery written into Ricardo **Bofill**'s pastiche classical 'Versailles for the masses', his 'Espaces d'Abraxas' housing project at Marne la Vallée which was damningly described by Martin Filler in *The Times Literary Supplement* ('Building in the Past Tense', 24 March, 1989) as 'lifeless monumentality of crushing inhumanity'. Equally, Venturi's assumption that Americans especially 'feel uncomfortable sitting in a square: they should be working at the office or home or with the family looking at television' could be deemed by them to be a gross generalization which leads to a regrettable neglect of public space and to a failure to foster civic identity. Maybe the postmodernist architectural theorists who would have most in common with the woman's reluctant destruction of the utopian modernist project turned elitist, and her unhesitating blasting of the symbols of consumer culture, would be Jameson and Frampton. At least they are still holding on to the notion of postmodern critique which is also a postmodern counter-culture. However, to cite Jameson's concluding words, this idea might have to remain elusive. It does not give us much solid to build on:

> We have seen that there is a way in which postmodernism replicates or reproduces – reinforces – the logic of consumer capitalism; the more significant question is whether there is also a way in which it resists that logic. But that is a question we must leave open.
>
> ('Postmodernism and Consumer Society')

In more recent years, debates in architecture have moved away from the issue of the modernist/postmodernist divide. Indeed, the particular 'debate' outlined above, which was such a key one for understanding the topic of postmodernism as a whole in the 1980s/1990s, is now largely only of contextual interest within a history of architectural theory. It was itself followed by a '**deconstructionist**' phase, during which architects such as Peter **Eisenman** interrogated the 'metaphysics of architecture', the grounding principles informing building per se, including the very concept of dwelling, and produced heavily theorized accompanying documents which drew explicitly on the work of Jacques **Derrida**. Such experiments were, to begin with, eagerly watched and analysed by philosophers who regarded them as possible sites of collaboration between the praxis of architecture and the often abstract world of philosophy. The latest trend, which also reflects shifts in philosophical currency, is that of 'non-standard architecture': this title was adopted for the 2004 Pompidou Centre exhibition which displayed the work of architects who recurrently cite the philosophical texts of Gilles **Deleuze** in order to explain their exploration of 'self-organizing' topological forms, the products of sophisticated computer programs and new building materials, which are seen as transforming – rather than just deforming *à la* deconstructionists – structure.

However, perhaps ultimately more lasting and interesting architectural works have been produced by collaborative teams of architects and engineers which straddle the divide between 'modernism' and 'postmodernism', or rather which draw on those aspects of modernism which had been elided in the false polarity set up between modernism and the reaction against it (the 'post') that was supposed to have followed its demise. Some of the most successful recent projects – gauged in terms of their appreciation not only by the profession itself but also by the general public – such as Frank Gehry's Bilbao Guggenheim Museum, Herzog & de Meuron's London Tate Modern or Calatrava's Alamillo Bridge in Seville – are not to be characterized as 'anti-modernist'. Unlike postmodern architecture, they are not refusing and reacting against a homogenized concept of what modernism is, or, even worse, 'was'. Instead they draw on different strands of what is even now an eclectic and ever-changing 'tradition', or *traditions*, which continue to incorporate new building materials, such as free-form cable nets and PVC-coated Terylene, in order to develop further techniques such as tensile structures, which can themselves be dated back as far as the first Bedouin tents and the first sails used by Mediterranean mariners.

Rather than Venturi's 'postmodern' response, 'less is a bore', to Mies van der Rohe's 'less is more', maybe of more long-term interest will be Buckminster Fuller's economical – and therefore *ecological* – 'more for less'. The prolific Buckminster Fuller, whose life itself spanned the supposed divide between modernism/postmodernism, active as he was designing and writing from the 1930s to his death in 1983, continues to provide impetus not only to engineers and architects using the principle he coined, 'tensegrity', to build light-weight structures which use discontinuous compression and continuous tension to maintain themselves, but also to cultural theorists interested in synergy and intentional communities, and to biologists such as Donald Ingber researching cell structure, which uses tensegrity as its primary organizing tool – to name but a few domains which have been and continue to be influenced by Fuller's holistic vision. Rather than, for instance, trying to compose architecture out of bits, compiling buildings out of an amalgam of different styles and traditions as did postmodernism, or breaking it down into its component parts as did deconstructionism, Fuller advocated a thinking of the whole – not only of a whole building, not only of a whole way of life but of Life itself – which is more than a sum of its parts. It is at this far more ambitious level, which supersedes the rather academic flavour of the 'postmodern debate' in architecture, that an engagement with globalization, both critical and affirmative, might begin.

9

POSTMODERNISM AND ART

COLIN TRODD

In his seminal essay 'Three American Painters: Kenneth Noland, Jules Olitski, Frank Stella' (*Three American Painters* (1965)), Michael Fried claimed that the self-critical nature of **modernist** painting was an expression of an ethical need to embody the 'denseness, structure and complexity of moral experience'. However, the 'continuous intellectual and moral alertness' of modernism is subject to the tyrannical interests of mass culture, which would reduce it to a condition of cultural and cognitive thralldom. Fried's essay exemplifies a key claim of modernist criticism: that the modernist artist digs deep into the materiality of his medium to find the forms that might advance debates and practices concerning public culture, or, if that heroic aspiration fails, to secure, by the disciplinary procedures of self-denial, an artistic identity resistant to the manipulating effects of popular culture. In the works of Noland, Olistki and Stella, then, could be discovered a critical unity of intention and practice, a concern with the 'plight' of visual experience in an age of mass-produced pictorial forms, the collective need to eliminate combinations of matter or signs of solid substance, and the consequent affirmation of the nature of the canvas as material object rather than a space of and for illusion.

Emerging as a critical tool describing the characteristics of 'new' art in the late 1960s, **postmodernist** criticism was accompanied by a rethinking of the modernist canon itself. The rediscovery of dada, surrealism and Marcel **Duchamp**'s ready-made sculptures were instrumental in the re-evaluation of Fried's developmental model of modernist practice, which had been produced in terms of the necessary eviction of ordinary experience from the realm of visual aesthetics. Fried's claims, developing the ideas of Roger Fry and Clement Greenberg, entailed the mobilization of an artistic 'bloodline' for the preservation of the autonomy of art from the debasing image culture of industrial capitalism. In this context, 'abstract art' operates as a shifting network of practices designed to block the commodification of visual culture: it constitutes a synthesis of core values that function to guarantee the integrity of communication as a cultural-ethical act; it comes into being to oppose the threatening forces of social reality. This approach was rejected by a number of young American artists such as Andy Warhol and James Rosenquist, both of whom became prominent in the early 1960s.

FORMATIONS OF POSTMODERN ART

Warhol and Rosenquist were neo-Duchampian in the sense that they identified the nirvanic nothingness of consumer culture with the compulsive nature of the human condition, and their work, fusing glamour and hollowness, **simulation** and mass production, disrupts the stable pictorial or physical order of late modernist art through the generation of a paradoxical realm of spectral physicality and an erotic space of ubiquitous but inaccessible **desire**. This disordering of the modernist object suggested that the 'denseness, structure and complexity of moral experience' could be explored through the rearticulation of the common materials of social life as entities hovering between documentary fact and symbolic expression.

Elsewhere in the late 1960s and early 1970s, we see the emergence of an art concerned with producing a commentary on the modernist interest in the process of **representation**. In the work of Gerhard **Richter**, for instance, the presence of material things expresses social and psychic blockage: the manifestation of blurred, grainy and ghostly objects renders uncanny the experience of the relation between space and matter. Indeed, by blurring the grounds between painting and photography, Richter's so-called 'photo-paintings' should be seen as self-conscious meditations on the claims of naturalistic representation and not evidence of a desire to 'return' to realism. His objects, forms and bodies are isolated and haunted, or becoming washed out by the processes of representation. From 'portraits', such as *Uncle Rudi* (1965), to the series of 'history paintings' concerned with the demise of the Baader-Meinhof gang entitled *18 October 1977* (1988), Richter confronts his spectators with a pictorial realm where the sensation of equivocation or loss becomes the official language of public experience. From the smiling figure of a wartime officer of the German Wehrmacht to the frozen profile of the dead Ulrike Meinhof in *Dead* (1988), Richter makes history unreadable by asserting that its visible facts lack legibility. What is being lost in this world is the idea that meaning can be fully determined, experienced or represented.

Where Richter associates the 'denseness, structure and complexity' of public experience with the impenetrable nature of the matter of historical evidence, it is the inarticulateness of ordinary experience – its definition as something disruptive of the systematizing imperatives of high modernism – that is a marked feature of those many forms of cultural expression of what has come to be called postmodernism. Since the late 1970s, postmodernist art has been a complex of stylistic and critical concerns rather than a coherent movement. At different moments critics discovered its characteristics in the violated and forlorn inscriptions of historical memory in Anselm **Kiefer**'s paintings of diseased myth; in the representation of the real as the accumulation of contradictory mechanisms and spectacles trapped in the abundant and redundant surfaces of David Salle's polysemic paintings; in the endless circuits, grids and reproductive systems of Peter **Halley**'s 'Neo-Geo' abstract simulations; and in the Walter

Benjamin-inspired photomontages of Barbara Kruger, where representation incorporates fragments of advertizing and consumer culture into itself in order to display (or embody) the irreconcilable forces bearing down on social experience. In addition, we should notice the association of postmodernism with a wide range of feminist artist-writers including Mary Kelly, Martha Rosler and Louise Lawler, all of whom argue for the interrogation of models of social experience as the ground from which contemporary art practice might dismantle the apparently 'universalist' claims of high modernism as a form of cultural politics. Elsewhere the kitsch sacramentalism of **Gilbert and George** is emblematic of a neo-rhetorical definition of the function of art, but here it becomes aligned with the actualization of ludic and libidinal forces, which act as surrogates for the performance of legible public rituals.

What these practices share in common is a fascination with the multiple conditions in which common experience enters into the realm of the aesthetic and disrupts the hierarchical and classificatory procedures of modernism. Thus, in the work of Young British Artists (YBAs) of the 1990s – Damien **Hirst**, Gary Hume, Tracey Emin, Marcus Harvey, Richard Patterson and Jake and Dinos Chapman – the materials of art are scooped and scraped from the viscous, inchoate and disorderly material conditions of life (and death). If these multiple postmodernisms have enabled artists to attack the allegedly mandarin nature of modernism, reorient artistic practice and enlarge the productive range of 'visual culture', is it possible, one might ask, to see in these new 'energies' some attempt to grapple with the social landscape of **postmodernity**? And, if this is so, does artistic postmodernism comment upon the new economies of labour, leisure and consumption? Can it have anything to say about a social realm characterized in terms of the deregulation of financial markets and the consequent mobility of capital, the inexorable growth of privatization, the internationalization of the division of labour, the introduction of 'flexible' manufacturing systems, the development of specialized product cultures and the ubiquity of 'customized' advertizing campaigns? If it is possible to refer to different models of post-modernism, is it sensible to make the distinction between a postmodernism that seeks to *resist* postmodernity and a postmodernism that *embraces* it? Is it worth distinguishing between an oppositional postmodernism and an eclectic post-modernism? And, if we can make such a division, does it enable us to refer to 'good' and 'bad' forms of artistic practice?

The starting point for such issues is the critical landscape in which modernism was discussed in the late 1970s and 1980s. In essence, most of the advanced debates about modernism were structured through accounts of the veracity of modernist criticism. Here the writings of Clement Greenberg were crucial. Greenberg was the great mandarin of modernism throughout the 1950s and 1960s. 'Avant-Garde and Kitsch' and 'Modernist Painting' (1939, 1961; in John O'Brian, ed., *Clement Greenberg; The Collected Essays and Criticism*, vols 1 and 3 (1986, 1989)) provided a critical template for the evaluation of modernism. In the first essay Greenberg argues that avant-garde art, the distillation of Western culture, fights to preserve its purity from the seductive but banal charms of kitsch culture and what he calls the 'Alexandrianism' (stultification) of academic culture. It does this in two ways: it operates as a process of auto-critique; and it is a model for the elimination of 'external' effects and forces. To be avant-garde is to embrace ceaseless change *and* to struggle to realize a condition of changeless aesthetic purity, which announces itself in the self-perfecting perfection of pristine abstraction. However, by the late 1970s and early 1980s, many artists and critics identified the social landscape of kitsch in terms of an oceanic plenitude of choice and pleasure, a constantly mobile realm of energies that seemed much more vivid and vital than the 'Alexandrianism' of late modernism itself. For the American artists David Salle, Jeff **Koons** and Haim Steinbach, confrontation with kitsch culture was a necessary precondition for the rearticulation of an avant-garde culture devoted to variation rather than uniformity.

By probing and testing the Greenbergian model of modernism, postmodernist artists and critics contested the established cultural orthodoxy and developed a number of different critical strategies. Throughout the late 1970s and 1980s these 'engagements' made it possible to claim that postmodernism was iconoclastic, progressive and demotic. The most important of these practices comprised: the presentation of a variety of text-based processes as radical examinations of the institutional machinery of the art world; the definition of the artist as the conduit for the dissemination of an impure but healing art; and the identification of **appropriation art** as a way of trumping the idea of the unity and uniqueness of the individual cultural artefact.

What were the motivations behind these three developments? First, the site-specific works of the Belgian Marcel Broodthaers and the German Hans Haacke were made with the intention of revealing the framing devices used by museums and art galleries. Second, the new figuration of the German painter Anselm Kiefer, in its identification of the picture-plane as a violent space where the signs of history are compressed and contorted, questioned modernism's residual commitment to the idea of beauty as truth. Third, in its most vivid form, that of the New York 'Neo-Geo' or simulationist artist Peter Halley, the appropriation of modernist 'icons', such as Piet Mondrian and Barnett Newman, provided a context for an examination of the relationship between modernism and the social, cultural and economic institutions of the modern capitalist state.

As these moves are interrelated – the first deals with the idea of the governmental agencies of art, the second is concerned with the communicative and expressive qualities of painting, and the third addresses the flow of **power** within a 'globalized' economy – the rest of this essay outlines three case studies drawn from each of these practices.

EXPERIENCING POSTMODERN ART

The first of our case studies involves the subject of **installation art**, which in the 'designs' of Broodthaers and Haacke questioned the belief in the purity and

85

self-defining nature of the modernist art object. Broodthaers' work, which developed a new intensity after the events of 1968, attempted to circumvent the intellectual division of labour that sustains and reinforces the authority of art galleries. Identifying himself with an imaginary museum – the Musée d'Art Moderne – he wrote accounts of his art from the position of the curatorial and cultural establishment. By conflating the realms of creativity and criticism he could make art 'speak' against the institutional languages which framed it. In this sense his denial of the division of labour established by the museum also challenged the articulation of cultural authority in cognate institutions.

For Haacke, it is not only the art object but the management and organization of the social networks of culture that are of importance; and, like Broodthaers, he sets out to interrogate the institutions of modern art. By producing works that focus on the relationship between the art gallery and the corporations which sponsor them, he wants to examine the way in which business legitimizes itself through cultural patronage. He asks: what purpose does art serve in modern society and what interests are masked by corporate patronage? Two examples of this process are germane. In 1971 the Guggenheim Museum cancelled Haacke's exhibition because the artist declined an offer to remove a couple of controversial pieces that dealt with the practices of some of its trustees. Entitled *Real Time Social Systems*, these works comprised diagrams, maps and photographs which constituted a visual 'plan' of the interplay between economic power and cultural identity. The 'plan' detailed how slum landlords transformed themselves into respectable figures by buying into the realm of culture. Examining the flow of capital from 'private' to 'public' spaces, the work addressed the relationship between the accumulation of different forms of authority, status, prestige, power and property.

Three years later Haacke was invited to exhibit at the Wallraf-Richartz Museum in Cologne. Once again, in drawing attention to the management of culture within capitalist society, his work met with suppression by the cultural managers of this institution. On this occasion Haacke's installation art involved the production of a detailed history of Manet's *Bunch of Asparagus*, which the museum had recently acquired from a local industrialist. This history took the form of inverting the relationship between the object and its elucidation: the 'art' comprised a series of wall panels, each one of which traced the history of the ownership of the Manet. These biographical vignettes concluded with an account of Hermann J. Abs, trustee of the museum and former owner of the painting. The museum required Haacke to remove this work because his final wall panel drew attention to Abs' relationship with the industrial and economic policies of the Third Reich.

Acting as the mediator between installation art and our second case study, the so-called postmodernist '**trans-avant-garde**', we find the anarcho-spiritual performance art of Joseph **Beuys**. For Beuys, art is the sensuous domain that reveals the aesthetic nature of the material world. The Beuysian pursuit of the mystic union of self and nature is a noticeable feature of the work of his most celebrated student, Anselm Kiefer. Kiefer, echoing Beuys, is always in the process of declaring the redemptive quality of his art. Where Beuys' oracular rhetoric conflates a mystical version of dada and the theatrical nature of performance art, Kiefer's art returns to German Romanticism in order to confront its disturbing legacy. Like his teacher, Kiefer identifies the power of art as a form of magical fertility; the surfaces of his paintings are mobile forests of marks, wounds and growths. These skeins of paint – drifting, dripping and forming **nomadic** traces across the canvas – are forever entangled with new surfaces, new spaces and new morphologies. Evidently Kiefer identifies the authority of painting with its capacity to translate **narrative** into the transfiguring intensity of his materials. In such a scenario painting becomes a form of incantation and enchantment: it will raise the darkness of Teutonic mythology in order to face its primitivism and irrationality.

This turning away from the 'universalism' of high modernism is characteristic of the other main figures associated with this mode of postmodernism. The belief that the return to painting involves a refiguring of the mythologies of national culture can be seen in the work of Kiefer's compatriots Markus Lupertz and Georg Baselitz, both of whom invoke Germanic culture in their work. Although they resist Beuys' sibylline utterances on the nature of art, they, like Kiefer, transform his 'postmodernism of immediacy' from the theatrical forms of 'body art' into a violent, dynamic expressionistic style that hovers between the mythic and the autobiographical.

The idea that the mystical totality of art forms a separate magical kingdom is also expressed by the Italian wing of this 'trans-avant-garde', where Francesco Clemente and Sandro Chia led the return to the conventional media of oil painting and fresco. For the Italian critic Achille Bonito Oliva, the leading champion of this votive style, it is by rejecting the uniformity of modernism that this 'nomadic' art propagates versions of 'desire' that direct their energies against the repressive forces of 'the Law'. This reintroduction of 'painting into art', a process which includes descriptive and decorative elements, enables Oliva to claim that Clemente and Chia are at once radical *and* traditional. According to Oliva, their work 'intentionally lacks character, does not hold heroic attitudes and does not recall exemplary situations'. Thus the virtuous humbleness of this 'weak' art is established by the **hybrid** nature of its 'healing' powers and in the metamorphic character of its creators.

These twin claims – that the artist is a spiritual healer who performs or projects those forms of sensuous experience that invoke a universal condition of expressive truth, or that art is the embodiment of the pathos of all life processes – are firmly rejected by the figures associated with appropriation art, the third of our case studies, and the one I want to examine in most detail.

Instead of relying on practices that are supposed to merge the artist with the artwork, a marked characteristic of the romanticized mythology of the 'trans-avant-garde', Sherie Levine, Cindy **Sherman**, Peter Halley, Haim Steinbach and Jeff Koons, all of whom came to prominence in the late 1970s and early 1980s, produce work that resists the idea of an unmediated individual authority and artistic creativity.

Levine and Sherman emerged in 1977 when their simulatory art was identified as a breakthrough in the formation of postmodernist aesthetics. Douglas Crimp, the recently appointed managing editor of *October*, the most important journal concerned with reframing art theory through the use of **poststructuralist** ideas, contrived a show entitled 'Pictures', which was held at Artists' Space in Lower Manhattan, the self-styled 'alternative gallery'. This event was to be seminal because Crimp's catalogue essay, republished in expanded form in *October* in 1979, argued that the figures he had picked for this event subscribed to the notion that our experience of reality is organized and determined by the systems and processes in which it is reproduced, restaged and simulated. Thus, he claimed, 'to an ever greater extent our experience is governed by pictures, pictures in newspapers and magazines, on television and in the cinema. Next to these pictures, first-hand experience begins to retreat, to seem more and more trivial.' For Crimp, the paradoxical power of Levine and Sherman resided in a capacity to assert that their work *lacked* all creative authority; as machines of nothingness their photographs, denuded of substantive content, were postmodernist because they confirmed the mythological status of '**authorship**'.

Sherman's *Untitled Film Still No. 21* is a classic example of her early technique. The female figure (it is Sherman herself), photographed in black and white, appears to be involved in some form of homage to the pictorial language of depersonalization, in that Sherman's identity disappears into filmic representation of anxiety or alienation. Meaning is generic rather than specific in an image where ordinary or common experience becomes rhetorical performance rather than real action. This sense of proliferating obscurity is intensified by three factors: the framing of a figure caught from an odd, almost elliptical, angle, which suggests the operation of mechanical vision rather than human sight; the capacity of the work to encourage and block our expectation that this inexplicable fragment of experience should be part of a repeated structure in which a story of some kind is formed, developed and rationalized; and the anonymous but symbolic naming of the work, which encourages the belief that its meaning is determined by the place it occupies in a wider structure of connected artworks.

Sherman's denial of the referential nature of the photographic image is continued by Sherie Levine. In her appropriation of canonical images by Edward Weston and Walker Evans, we see the conflation of the idea of simulation and gender politics. It is certainly the case that these images declare that art is forever implicated in the process of representation; that the burden of all art is its inescapable attachment to tradition and custom; and that it is somehow radical to criticize those conventions that claim to represent external reality. Here photography does not provide a window looking out into the world: it is a mirroring process that reflects its own normalized codes and techniques for recording, framing and organizing the world. This interest in the 'fictive' quality of originality was continued in her 1984 show at the Nature Morte Gallery in New

York, which comprised copies of drawings by Schiele and Malevich, the irreconcilable 'bodily' and 'metaphysical' wings of early modernism.

A similar fascination with the nature of representation is a marked feature of Peter Halley's work. Deploying cells and conduits within a grid-like geometric field, his art is informed by his reading of **Foucault** and **Baudrillard**. For Levine and Sherman, working through the photographic medium, representation never refers back to some pristine state of being in nature; compositions are imprisoned by those inherited codes that shape, pattern and frame them; images are entangled within visual systems from which it is impossible to escape; photographic works are copies of copies. To this interest in representation-as-repetition, Halley, the main painter and theorist in this group, brings his concern with the relationship between representation and power. Looking at modernism is to see models, networks, movements – the flows of matter and energy. Thus Stella's aluminium 'grid' paintings of the late 1950s, generally regarded as the zenith of late modernism, are made to reveal and express the physical and spatial logic of the massive interstate highways that traverse America.

Halley concentrates on the idea of geometry in order to ask: why does modern society associate it with freedom, light, reason and truth? In 'Notes on Painting' (*Collected Essays* (1987)), he identifies abstraction as a form of confinement: non-representational art, hollowed out of its utopian rhetoric, is assimilated into the visual languages of multinational corporations. The modernist artefact has become part of the logic of late monopoly capitalism: in its geometrical and grid-like forms Halley discovers social, governmental and financial networks. Modernism's search for absolute visual purity is no longer 'innocent': instead of its association with idealist aesthetics, Halley connects it with the imprisoning spaces of consumer capitalism. Thus he claims that his paintings 'are a critique of idealist modernism. In the "colour field" is placed the jail. The misty space of Rothko is walled up.'

Far from being a process of social enlightenment, geometry is, in fact, an instrument of social control. Therefore he links the geometric sign to what he sees as the dominant image of surveillance: the grid. He writes: 'On the grid, there are no monuments. Only the grid itself is a monument to its own endless circulatory nature . . . On the grid there is only the presentness of unending movement, the abstract flow of goods, capital and information.' Public space has been hollowed out and private space has collapsed into a zone of endless, empty consumption.

It is in this context that we should approach a painting such as *Day Glo Prison* (1982). Deliberately disorienting, it seems to combine elements of kitsch and abstraction, i.e. junk culture and high modernism. We note both the garish, electric light colour *and* the rigour of geometric modernism. This is a weird mutation or **hybrid**: it is as if the colour scheme of suburbia has entered the 'pure' space of modern art. By appropriating the day-glo colour scheme of Stella's work from the early 1960s, he affirms that such apparently pure art is an echo of the social furniture of **post-industrial** life. By including Roll-a-tex, a mock stucco, to 'adorn' the square figure that commands the image, colour becomes coloration: it is that which is produced and reproduced by instruments and that which registers the nature of its own reproduction. Colour does not 'refer' to nature but to Roll-a-tex. Common experience invades the sanctified realm of abstraction to declare that it is itself a prison (or zoo) in which the residual forms of everyday (consumer) life are trapped or suspended.

The presentation of postmodern art as something locked into networks of leisure and consumption is continued in the work of Haim Steinbach and Jeff Koons. If Halley sees the geometric sign as the essence of modernity, both these artists are fascinated with the world of shopping. They replicate the objects of consumption as the banal and enigmatic facts of social experience. In the case of Steinbach, shopping becomes a form of urban exploration in which commodities function as souvenirs: the act of consumption is entangled in a phantastic process of nostalgia for the return of an experience that has never been known.

This simulated art takes as its reference point that most contemporary of environments: the shopping mall. A place of motion, expansion and shrinkage, the shopping mall organizes space as a flow system in which histories, cultures, styles, identities and experiences are knitted together in 'unique' configurations. Reproducing shopping as a leisure 'experience' through the articulation of 'themed' zones, the shopping mall blends the 'ordinary' and the 'exotic', making consumption into something 'exciting'. Here shopping becomes the dream of escape, the transformation of consumption into holiday time. Shopping, we might say, contains and re-creates the world: it is a simulation of tourism in which the shopper is an entrepreneur of (touristic) sensation.

Steinbach, who, in a 1986 panel discussion which included Halley and Koons, opined 'in a sense the media have been turning us into tourists and voyeurs outside our own experience . . . in my case I spend a lot of time shopping', creates objects and micro-environments. Or, more accurately, he manages the sensibilities with which products are associated. Placed on Formica shelves resembling plinths, his vacant or empty product-works suggest the 'denseness, structure and complexity' of a world in which manufacturing gives way to consumption, and industrial work is replaced by a form of capitalist pastoralism. It is the production of pleasure that governs Steinbach's vision of the organization of the business-life of consumption.

The product-works produced by Steinbach examine how 'empty' commodities become icons of sensibility, objects of steady-state desire. His achievement is to connect two realities: the shopping mall and the home; and to express the way in which the experience of both is built around a comforting, homely, tranquillizing banality. If objects of consumption, the commodities we buy, have become the modern equivalents of primitive totems, this may be because in our world shopping is a kind a religion: a desire for physical or social apotheosis in which the subject achieves a condition of purity to which common experience *aspires*. Steinbach displays and critiques this imaginary order of things by drawing attention to the machinery of solidity and signification. The 'substance' of his product-works is their inescapable emptiness. They form meaningless sequences of forms, which cannot be redemptive precisely because the logic of consumerism is based on the idea of the endless production-line nature of consumption.

In Britain a self-consciously whimsical or quirky attitude to appropriation is found in the work of Tony Cragg, Bill Woodrow and Edward Allington, all of whom make reference to forms of mass production, although the allusions to the world of commerce and kitsch tend to be 'poetical' rather than 'political'. Elsewhere the camp, sentimental militarism of Gilbert and George assimilates the iconic powers of medieval art and Soviet Socialist Realism, generating tableaux devoted to and obsessed by masculinity, fecundity, authority and death. In such appropriated iconography, which composes the world as a series of pictograms or isotypes, we find the pomp/banality of regimented glamour in which bodies and objects are at once physical facts and abstract ideas. Appropriation of a different kind is found in the work of Damien Hirst. From his dead cows and sheep, with their associations with Rembrandt's *The Flayed Ox*, to his 'dot' paintings, which allude to Phillip Taaffe's simulation of Op Art during the 'golden age' of New York simulationism in the 1980s, Hirst's work has acknowledged the endless entangling of 'high' and 'low' subjects in the history of post-Renaissance European art.

POSTMODERNISM AND THE REPRODUCTION OF MODERNITY

At the beginning of this essay I asked: is there anything of value to be gained by coupling the culture of postmodernism with social postmodernity? Well, if there are no simple alignments between the processes of cultural heterogeneity and social fragmentation – alignments that enable us to distinguish between 'good' and 'bad' art – we can at least conclude our investigation by confirming that some forms of contemporary practice establish more interesting and more critical dialogues with modernism and the social landscape of late monopoly capitalism than others. Thus, in the case of the American sculptor Richard Serra we find works concerned with those public spaces that 'shopping mall' postmodernism declares to have vanished into the simulated spaces of replication and miniaturization. The sheer physicality of Serra's sculptures, which tend to inhabit the open-air urban environment, encourage spectators to reflect upon the nature of the lived experience of built space. That the nature of this art could be something other than a polite disagreement with postmodernist consumer culture can be seen in the controversy surrounding his *Tilted Arc*, which was destroyed after its removal from New York's Federal Plaza in 1989.

In its combination of brute matter and indomitable form *Tilted Arc* resisted the idea that public art should decorate, adorn or aestheticize public space. There was nothing about *Tilted Arc* to suggest it was implicated in the rhetoric of 'urban renewal'; nothing that resembled the bovine pastoralism of much contemporary public art. This object was in no sense charming or convivial. Indeed, its capacity to block any real sense of spatial orientation required its audience to address its physicality or bulky ugliness. To be sure, the work denied its public the opportunity to scan or survey the immediate environment. To this should be added the ghostly nature of the thing: here the matter of industrial engineering returned to a de-industrialized governmental, financial and consumer sector of the city, bringing with it the buried history of industry. This registration of the uncanny was compounded by the dimensions of a work that suggested both vertigo and claustrophobia: here was an object whose presence was both ubiquitous and elusive; at once inviting the individual to 'merge' with its form and resisting the idea of physical absorption.

It was the unhomely nature of *Tilted Arc* – an ability to resist urban assimilation by registering the inescapable strangeness of urban space – that brings this postmodernist work back to one of the central themes of literary and philosophical modernity: that consciousness is marked by its sense of transcendental homelessness. In the writings of Schlegel, Baudelaire, Kierkegaard, Benjamin, Kafka, **Adorno** and **Heidegger** we find the idea that being is a form of alienation: that life is a form of exile or the registration of an inescapable and catastrophic loss. It is, then, the simultaneous strength and weakness of art that it is generated from this experience of estrangement from the world. From this paradoxical nature, combining both utopian hope for a better world and melancholic recognition of separation from this immediate world, the most intractable or commanding works of art establish their sensuous and critical properties. In an age where museums and art galleries begin to resemble shopping malls by processing and marketing consumption and leisure as 'experiences', perhaps it is in those forms of art that reach for the utopian through the melancholic that deserve our greatest attention. Is it possible, therefore, to draw some form of **ironic** comfort from the fact that the new 'de-industrialized' postmodern classes, with their bases in the media, advertising, financial services, marketing, merchandizing, leisure and retailing, were the very groups whose campaign resulted in the destruction of *Tilted Arc*? If so, we are obliged to resist the apocalyptic or iconoclastic rhetoric of those forms of postmodernism that tell us we are condemned to a simulated world, and insist that the most controversial forms of contemporary art continue to engage with the most compelling themes of modernism itself.

10

POSTMODERNISM AND CINEMA

VAL HILL

Postmodern cinema has been conventionally described in terms of its bright surfaces, **intertextuality**, knowingness, referentiality, and nostalgia for past forms, genres and styles. All of this is true, and those markers have now crystallized into unstoppable, or rather unendable, commodities. The 'endless circulation of commodities and desire' is perfectly exemplified in contemporary cinema. We see the film at the cinema, or rather the multiplex. We watch on VHS (less), on DVD (more), on our screens, digital, plasma, hung on the wall, in our 'home cinema'. The major Hollywood product, the blockbuster, is continually revised, re-edited, re-packaged. Often, within a series of films, it is not just the narratives that connect from film to film, but products that are outside of mainstream cinematic distribution. If you own, or are aware of, all possible objects tied to a particular title, then you will be able to make connections to find out more about characters, flesh out obscure bits of plot, have even more 'stuff' to put on your website or say to your friends. We can watch, hire and buy prequels, sequels, soundtracks, video games, box sets, directors' cuts, producers' cuts. We can play arcade games, buy merchandise, go to conventions. We, the consumers, never have the finished product; there is always another one, always another version.

Raiding the cinematic archive is yet another way in which what used to circulate outside of the **text** is raised to the level of the commodity, and becomes part of what we consume rather than part of what we produce. Quentin **Tarantino** is probably the most famous exponent of this tendency. His films are full of chat, anecdotes about aspects of popular culture, music, films, TV shows, actors, actresses. In *Pulp Fiction* (1994), at the end Jules (Samuel L. Jackson) is forced to open his case by Pumpkin/Ringo (Tim Roth). The audience is never allowed to see what is inside the case; all we see is a golden glow reflected on the lid. The dialogue is not helpful either: 'Is that what I think it is?' 'Yes.' 'It's beautiful.' For those with sufficient cultural capital this moment, this object, invokes at least three other movies and the myth of Pandora's box: *Repo Man* (1984), *Raiders of the Lost Ark* (1981), and what has been called the last *film noir*, *Kiss Me Deadly* (1955), where the case contains the 'Big Whatsit', the Bomb (nuclear not terrorist) and the film ends with the end of the world.

The film *Predator 2* (1990) contains a smaller but efficient moment when the head of the Alien from the *Alien* series may be observed as one of the trophies on the wall in the Predator's spacecraft, reminding us, at the time of the film release, of an already existing arcade game and pointing forward to a film which is about to be released, as well as constructing a galaxy that contains both species. The series of objects that form the *Matrix* commodity are worth noting. At the time of writing there are three films available on DVD, with extensive add-ons, commentaries, etc., especially around what became known as 'bullet time'. Indeed, *Matrix Revisited* (2001) describes itself as 'A mind-expanding look at "The Matrix" from conception to phenomenon', and promises that 'It will make you dream in bullet time'. There is also available a set of short animation films, in the style of Japanese anime. The short films tell you more about the storylines and characters in the three feature films. There is also a game called 'Enter the Matrix', where you may 'battle alongside the original motion picture cast', as well as a soundtrack CD, comics and many other bits of merchandise. What all these objects provide, apart from the obvious pleasures of consumption, is more detail about what emerges as a kind of meta-story. It is more than any or even all of the films.

There are other implications and manifestations of this postmodern knowing-ness, **irony**, pastiche and blank parody, catalogued by Fredric **Jameson** in 'Postmodernism, or, The Cultural Logic of Late Capitalism' (*New Left Review* (1984)) as filling the textual space of cinema. In the first of the *Scream* (1996) series there is a sequence where the kids are sitting around drinking beer and watching *Halloween* (1978). Suddenly one of the characters pauses the movie and delivers what amounts to a lecture on the conventions of slasher films:

> That's why she [Jamie Lee Curtis] outsmarted the killer in the long chase scene at the end. Only virgins can do that. Don't you know the rules? There are certain rules that one must abide by in order to successfully survive a horror movie. For instance, number one, you can never have sex. Big no-no. Big no-no. Sex equals death. Okay, number two, you can never drink or do drugs. The sin factor. It's a sin, it's an extension of number one. And number three, never, ever, ever, under any circumstances say, 'I'll be right back', because you won't be back.

On the DVD for *Scary Movie* (2000) you can read 'Scary Movie: Guide for the Culturally Challenged Pop Up'. This includes explanations of cultural references and inside jokes, which, as the name suggests, pop up as you are watching the film. So the commodity sucks up our chatter, our pleasures, our knowledge, and makes them part of itself. We are faced with the commodification of everything, from the unconscious to outer space. So what do we do, as audience, as academics? What is left for us to say if it is all on the disc or in the text?

The development of special effects, which have now almost become 'ordinary effects', is another great marker of the films of this period; a powerful part of the marketing and the 'bonus' material on offer on DVDs. Special effects are, however, also a determinant of the content and structure of the product itself. The work of the **narrative** is slowed and halted by major set pieces. Indeed the narrative almost becomes a blockage to the 'true' celebration of the specificity of cinema itself. The 'cinema of attractions', the 'cinema of affect', can almost be read as the logical consequence of **globalization** and postmodernism. The narrative of history and the specificity of social and cultural referents are lost in the shock to the senses that constitutes so much of postmodern cinema.

In the wake of these changes, postmodern film theory has celebrated the vivid intensity of the surface and the multivocal readings that postmodern cinema allows. The question needs to be asked concerning what (under)pins the text and if the position of the reader is as 'free' as has been claimed by the theorists of relativism. It is proposed that the thematic concerns produced within post-modern cinema reveal a very particular set of values. The scenarios found in many postmodern films express a number of repetitions, particularly around the issues of sexuality and ethnicity, that makes the notion of free-floating signification problematic. Why, in the light of a reflexive critical sophistication towards the strictures of the text, do audience, director, and critic continue to collude, most often pleasurably, in the maintenance of narrative structures which repetitively replay the gains and losses of '**difference**', albeit in new and mutated forms? The human body, always marked by difference, under the sign of post-modernism also holds the play, struggles and contradictions of difference. Under the **sign** of postmodernism the intensification of the signifiers of difference ('more human than human') spreads itself over the majority of Hollywood productions, especially the well-funded, globally targeted blockbuster.

However, it might be useful to think of many Hollywood movies made between 1984 (the date of publication of the Jameson essay) and 2004 as fitting into one of two categories: 'critical' and 'uncritical' postmodernism. The phrase 'critical dystopia' has been used as a way of talking about films such as *Terminator* (1984), that use the future and the trappings of science fiction to critique the present and speculate about the impact of the present on the future. By extension many films of the 1980s and 1990s, and the new millennium, can be seen to use the formal and aesthetic properties of postmodernism in a way which appears to accept the analysis made by Jameson. Perversely, the same can also be said of films which might be labelled as uncritical postmodernism. The tick boxes for pastiche, blank parody, depthlessness, the decay of meaning, the end of history can all be checked in relation to films as different as *Back to the Future* (1985, 1989, 1990) (all of them), *Blue Velvet* (1986), *Mulholland Drive* (2001), *Kill Bill* (2003), and *Charlie's Angels Full Throttle* (2003). Many of these films work on the pleasure of recognition, and sometimes just the sheer pleasure of the experience of the cinematic; you do not have to ask what it means in the case of *Mulholland Drive*; you just let the cleverness and beauty of the surface wash over you.

The endlessly circulating commodity of postmodern cinema contains signifying systems that carry with them both the values of capitalism and the contradictory signs of the struggle produced within it. This means that the stories of postmodern cinema are particular stories that work through very particular themes. Now this can be said of any period of history or culture, which is precisely why it must be said about postmodern cinema. The postmodern cinematic market-place is dominated by American products. This domination has consequences both for the form of the American film, and for other national, local and independent cinemas which tend to be absorbed, ignored or marginalized. At the same time, the American film is required to reduce its own cultural specificity in order to satisfy the demand to be 'global'. So, while the forms, codes, conventions and narrative structure possess a strong resemblance to that of the mass-produced cinema of **modernity**, the need for globalization produces both an intensification of its formal specificities and an allowed and necessary address to difference. 'Difference' is being doubly stressed here, to refer both to the organization of sexual and ethnic difference within the structure of the text and to the visibility of those representations of difference within the play of the text. Difference is allowed, celebrated and commodified. The cultural politics of difference becomes the cultural commodity of difference. Postmodern cinema celebrates, at surface level, its own exchange and use value. We are told how it was made, how much it cost and what it is about. This is especially true for what, in a sense, is a paradigmatic instance of postmodern cinema, the action film. In the action film the history and conventions of many Hollywood genres – the western, the thriller, the horror film, the war film, the romance and the family drama – are distilled and intensified to produce a commodity that contains all of the pleasure, all of the pain, and works in as many markets as possible – while never quite giving up on American values. I would argue that these 'intensifications' fit with the observations made by Jameson and **Baudrillard** in terms of the intensity of the surface of the postmodern film. They also produce the critical emphasis on the reflexive nature of the postmodern text. The film and its audience 'know their own histories'. The pleasure of the text spills over into the audience's knowledge of other films, other performances, other musics: the referent becomes part of the treasure house of signifiers that constitute popular culture.

Some theorists, like Baudrillard, extend this line of argument to conclude that the social world 'outside' of popular culture has 'gone away'; cinema can now only refer to other signifiers of popular culture. Postmodern theory speaks of the end of history, the loss of the referent, the impossibility of critical distance and the celebration of 'new-found' difference. However, if you add the first three of these to the last one, then you are forced to ask: 'What is difference?' Without history, without reference to the social, without some sense of distance (what one might call an ethics or politics) the notion of difference itself is placed under question. It is this tension between the desire to celebrate difference within the commodity form and, at the same time, the need to construct a commodity world without history or social referent or contradiction, that lets loose the kinds of difference that emerge in postmodern cinema. The weakening of the **grand narratives** (**Lyotard**) releases difference from the tidy shackles of modernism – this does not, however, just mean that previously subjugated others are released into a different, more intense visibility. Indeed 'old' **binaries** themselves mutate towards a more exaggerated, almost parodic, existence or are displaced through the production of new forms of **Otherness**. Gender attributes wander across the old binary divide: Linda Hamilton in *Terminator 2* (1991) can have muscles, and we can all derive voyeuristic pleasure from Brad Pitt's butt in *Thelma and Louise* (1991). Difference itself becomes a crucial organizer and signifier within the texts of postmodern cinema.

The strong, not to say hysterical, version of masculinity, as played out by Stallone in the action movie, embodies a desire for a fixed relation to the symbolic: the world where the law still operates, made less possible by the weakening of the grand narratives that also kept difference in place. *First Blood* (1982) could be argued to be a film in which the weight of historical trauma is borne by the body of Stallone – a new and shocking male body soon to be commodified and multiplied in the forms of Schwarzenegger, Van Damme, and others. The desire to win a war that had already been lost can itself be seen as a form of nostalgia for a present that never was. Although these bodies are on one level superhuman, too much, hysterical, they are also suffering, immolated bodies – almost to the point of death. We have become used to suffering male bodies in film genres dependent on male–male relationships, but in the post-Rambo action movies, the 'buddy' is absent, and it is not homosexuality that is defended against, but psychosis. Indeed it has been argued that if postmodernism does involve a theoretical retreat from the problem of **power** relations within capitalism, then there has to be a displacement of that antagonism onto other markers of difference, which come to bear an intolerable burden of suffering and other forms of surplus investment held in the signifiers of liberal humanism.

The contradiction within postmodern cinema's celebration of difference can be seen in the way that contradictions emerge within particular narratives. In *Predator 2* (1990) Danny Glover moves from the place of 'black sidekick who usually dies first' to that of black hero who survives. At the same time as Glover's textual liberation from stereotype, however, the Predator is constructed as an other that carries signifiers of a more familiar representation of blackness – its 'hair' resembling dreadlocks. His figure is that of a hunter or warrior. He is seen as tribal, even within the context of high-tech space flight and weaponry. In the *Alien* 'quadrilogy' (1979, 1986, 1992, 1997) Ripley's (Sigourney Weaver) progress is significant. She moves from apparently single woman to good mother, to sacrificing mother carrying an alien child/queen, to child-sacrificing half-human half-alien mother. All of the *Alien* films use the discourse of difference to carry the narrative, although the absent cause is clearly capital, present in the film in the form of the Company.

Blade Runner (1982) presents the transmutation of difference and Otherness in a more complex way, setting humans against **cyborgs**. One can read the film as if the cyborg other reproduces humanity at the point at which the human race is losing its humanity. However, the emergence of the cyborg, the unhuman, can be read differently. Cinema and other popular cultural forms of the 1980s and 1990s contain either the fantasy of 'leaving the meat' (body) or the transformation of the body into something more, something different (*The Fly* (1986), *Nightbreed* (1990), *Lawnmower Man* (1992)). The disappearance of the human race is on the agenda in the 1990s – and maybe we should argue that this is nothing more than a coding of the imagined disappearance of white dominance. The union of Rachel and Deckard at the end of *Blade Runner* speaks of an escape from the misery of the human condition into a fantasy rural idyll (in the originally released cut of the film). The twist in the tale – the possibility that they are both cyborg, and the certainty that at least one is (something not seen before as anything other than a threat) – reveals the depths of contemporary anxiety about the future of the human.

However, just as the word 'human' may be standing in for the word 'white' in relation to *Blade Runner*, so the word human, and the anxiety and pain that surrounds it, may also stand in for the masculine. The 'cost' of the gains of women in the world, or some parts of it, and the qualification of those gains, may be registered on the bodies of the female corpses that insistently haunt the screens of postmodern cinema. In the failure of the text satisfactorily to 'put things back together' in the face of the commodification of difference she/it becomes the currency through which to repay an impossible debt. In *Basic Instinct* (1992) we are 'allowed' to see a strong beautiful woman, Sharon Stone, maybe get away with murder. She is bisexual: getting both the men and women she wants. However, in order for her to achieve her end, Michael Douglas and the ice-pick under the bed, the text produces corpses – most notably those of her girlfriend Roxy, a strongly if conventionally represented lipstick lesbian with a taste for voyeurism, and a female psychiatrist previously 'contaminated' by Stone's seduction. (This also shows that the free play of difference is not that free.)

Silence of the Lambs (1991) reproduces the same pattern. The wonderful Jodie Foster, lesbian icon, wins out, but at the same time the text produces a trail of flayed female corpses. *Blue Velvet* (1986) shows us the **abjected**, less than perfect body of Isabella Rossellini; *Rising Sun* (1993) contains the digitally encoded and replayed sexual murder of an unnamed woman. *Twin Peaks* (1990) and *Murder One* (1999) show us twin female corpses wrapped in plastic. A woman's corpse sutures the narrative, producing a double emptying of the female body, a double death; the weight of sexual difference is removed from the body and it becomes a thing, both a blockage and a suture – it makes sense of the narrative and compensates for a femininity 'out of place', while making no sense itself. It is as if it emerges in the real outside of signification.

In the first two decades after the publication of Jameson's 1984 essay the shifts and changes in the fabric of the world have been held cinematically in two ways. There has always been a strand of critical postmodernism. Films such as *Blade Runner, Terminator, Alien* and *Brazil* (1984) and more recently *Fight Club* (1999) and *The Matrix* films (1999, 2003, 2003) show an anxiety concerning both the present and the future constructed out of the visual detritus of the past and the signifiers of historical trauma. For example, the scenes of the future catastrophe in *Terminator* could be argued to be drawing their signifiers from the Holocaust, Hiroshima or Cambodia after Pol Pot's Year Zero. Against these run uncritical postmodernism – *Star Wars* (1977), *Back to the Future, Scream, Scary Movie, Down with Love* (2003), *Charlie's Angels Full Throttle, The Fifth Element* (1997).

These films conform to conventional American values, and celebrate past genres and past conventions with often crystalline perfection but with no comment. These are the blank parodies that Jameson refers to.

Reservoir Dogs (1992) is probably both one of the most extreme examples of uncritical postmodernism, and also a film in which the agenda of capital, its strains and contradictions, are worked out most tellingly in the speech and on the bodies of men. All others (almost) are held at the level of speech. The 'Dogs' worry around the signifiers of woman, black people, Jews and homosexuals. There is a resonance here between the hystericized bodies of men and the hystericized speech of men in this film and others directed by Tarantino and Scorsese. This speech is predicated on anxiety. So although we are presented with what is almost a cloning of a certain kind of white heterosexual masculinity as a defence against the postmodern condition, and given the abundant fetishistic pleasures of the visual and aural surfaces of the film as it attempts to defend against any suggestion of crisis, the particularities of the speech of the 'Dogs' says something else: 'What do women want?' (this was of course Freud's great question). 'Are they virgins or whores? Do they earn too much or too little? In the case of black women, are they strong or subservient to their men?' The sexuality of black men and women carries with it the intensity we have spoken of earlier; but it is actually the sexuality of black men that is the real problem for the 'Dogs', especially when combined with the 'threat' of homosexuality. The difficulty of a film full of men – a subject already well documented in modernist film theory – is displaced and projected into the **discourses** of homophobia and racism. What the narrative finally produces is their deaths; the real conditions of existence return revealing a white heterosexual masculinity in crisis.

Postmodern cinema as a useful, strong category is now shadowed by other signifiers. The words 'global' and 'imperial' might apply more usefully to the Hollywood product. Elsewhere other cinemas respond to both the invitation of the global market and the changing circumstances of world politics and history. The question of how we make films and how we understand films after 9/11, during the war against terror, is answered very differently by different nations, directors and industries. Hollywood's response is complex, and has nothing to do with temporal logic. The figures of Ripley and Clarice Starling fall and dissolve, to reveal, after the fact, the masculine figure that held the trauma, the horror – that of the serial killer. Over the time before 9/11 he had held sway over the imagination of the West in the form of Hannibal Lecter: urbane, cultured, deadly. Over time other manifestations of the serial killer have become more and more anonymous, invisible: named after any unidentified male corpse as in *Seven* (1995), disappearing altogether as in *The Minus Man* (1999). In *American Psycho* (2000) the subjectivity of the killer, the carefully constructed persona, dissolves in the gaze from the obscene objects of his own fantasy. One of the great cinematic villains of this period, Keyser Soze (*The Usual Suspects* (1995)), walks away, disappears, having constructed himself from random images, words and things that surrounded him in the police station. It is Soze who provides the link between the increasingly anonymous serial killers and Hollywood's, the West's, new villain, who, having had a past is now hesitating on the edge of **representation** (in both the film world and the 'real' world, given the elusiveness of Bin Laden and other 'usual suspects'), due to the events of 9/11 and the subsequent War against Terror: the terrorist.

The past five years has also seen the production of several high-profile war films, some dealing with long-past wars, and some with more recent conflicts in Bosnia and Africa. One of these films, Kathryn Bigelow's *K19: The Widow Maker* (2002), can almost be read as a film nostalgic for the kind of hero/warrior/man who would have survived if the Soviet Union had not 'gone wrong'. An anthem for a lost masculinity.

This last comment is a perfect way to introduce *Fight Club*. David Fincher's film starts from inside the body; it has been described as a sort of interior action movie: from the brain we travel to the bomb. We have arrived at the end, at the moment before the bang, the moment before corporate America goes up in flames in a series of images that are hard to bear after 9/11. This is maybe the same choice we confront at the end of *The Matrix* (1999), but the journey is held in a different set of signifiers. The other obvious similarity is the position of the hero, or one of them, Jack (Edward Norton). Jack works as a risk assessor: what costs less – to recall a car with a fault and thus save lives or pay the insurance? Like Neo, he works in an office, but he has another life as a hacker. He is Ikea Man. He is Life Style. Given that this film is another post-, post-politics, he has no union struggles. He does have a relationship, of sorts, in that instead of looking at pornography in the toilet, he looks at the Ikea catalogue. He travels extensively, but everything is always the same. No enjoyment of the **bricolage** of postmodern life for him. The hotels are the same, the planes are the same, the food is the same – until one day he meets Tyler Durden (Brad Pitt). Durden's life is totally different: he does mundane jobs, but he subverts them. He pees in the soup, he splices pornographic stills into family films, he makes incredibly expensive soap out of liposuction detritus. He is beautiful and fearless even with a broken nose and blood streaming down his face. He lives in a derelict house on top of a toxic dump in the wonderfully named Paper Street. Durden is anti-style, anti-consumer, anti-capital: he is everything Jack is not. Together, after Tyler has blown up Jack's apartment, they form Fight Club, and then Project Mayhem – and finally with the aid of their own warriors they blow up the skyscrapers that house everybody's credit records. The aim is to cause chaos, to go back to a financial year zero, and presumably start the revolution.

What has not been mentioned so far is the existence of Marla, who wanders between Jack and Tyler, significantly ending up with Jack after Tyler has been abolished, both watching the explosions passively, while holding hands. Again, post-politics, the film has found a way of dealing with class struggle. By holding the struggle mostly in the figures of these two men the film stays safe and nothing is mysterious – except for Jack who has to expel the destructive, revolutionary figure of Tyler Durden. We are deprived of the vision of Ikea Man becoming the One. Once again the narrative produces its couple, although Tyler's existence is marked 'outside' of the text in the form of interference with what appears to be the standard FBI warning, and a 'cock shot' cut in during the credits.

So the argument has gone that not only is postmodernism no guarantee of the loosening of the reins of difference, in the end, but also that in 2004 it is masculinity that is carrying the weight of the contradictions of the contemporary event. Women do not seem very visible or very important at the moment, unless it is as the ultimate fetish figures of Lara Croft or Charlie's Angels. When we first saw the images of 9/11 many people said that it looked like a movie that we were all in some way familiar with. I would like to suggest that over time the images and sounds of 9/11 expose the specificity of cinematic construction, and even the work of sexual and ethnic difference. The films become less than those images. However, in the West, masculinity is the discourse that holds the anxiety, the trauma of the contemporary, unlike in the 1980s. Even the efficient figure of the serial killer drops away. What could be interpreted as part of an imperial or colonial fantasy in *Independence Day* (1996) or *The Siege* (1998) returns in the real – thrust there by the Twin Towers falling. What the falling of the towers seemed to deny was the possibility of representing anything, of telling any story. Retrospectively, many American movies speak to the **event**, but to speak beyond the event or even of the event is much more difficult. After the debate concerning whether or not images of the Twin Towers should be removed from existing films and TV programmes, a few directors have kept them in the history of New York, and allowed their absence to be part of the landscape. The figuration of the contemporary crisis seems best held in the stories that won Oscars in 2004, such as *The Lord of the Rings* cycle (2001, 2002, 2003). In the latter the world (of the Shires) is saved, a world that is an idealized vision of rural England: saved by the sacrifices of millions and the labours of princes and hobbits. The postmodern version of capitalism sets up an inclusive circuit, and maybe, in the West at least, forecloses for the moment on the idea of any kind of revolutionary or radical art. 'Everything is a copy of a copy of a copy.' Cinema doubles this capture, this inclusion, because of its temporal and spatial specificities and because of its dependence on and imbrication in language and narrative. Jameson sees postmodernity as impossible to map or represent in any way that is adequate. What we are presented with are mythic versions of the past, or the setting up of new mythical spaces and narratives held (mostly) in the actions of men. Jameson's call for maps is really a call for the (re-)emergence of class consciousness within that form of popular culture known as postmodernism.

Finally, in *11.09.01* (2003) there has been an attempt to document responses to 9/11. It is a production in which eleven film makers make short films lasting 11 minutes 9 seconds and one frame. Sean Penn is the American contributor. His film is a little narrative involving the veteran Hollywood actor Ernest Borgnine. He plays an old man whose wife has died, but who still performs the melancholic chore of putting her clothes out every morning and generally behaving as if she were still alive. His only regret is that she loved plants, but in the darkness of their apartment they would never grow. A brilliant light suddenly fills the apartment, the Twin Towers have fallen, and the plants flourish. The Twin Towers are represented as a **presence** and absence of light. It is an odd little film, but what film could anyone make of this event at the moment?

11

POSTMODERNISM AND TELEVISION

MARC O'DAY

Despite occasional claims that we have entered the post-television age, television in the digital era remains a postmodern medium par excellence. Whether we are discussing **postmodernism**, postmodernization, **postmodernity** or just the postmodern in general, contemporary television offers us lively examples of the ideas and trends invoked by these terms. Many of the buzz words which have charged postmodern debates – **simulation**, **hyperreality**, fragmentation, heterogeneity, **intertextuality** and pastiche to name but a few – are ready-made for application to TV; indeed, several of them were stimulated by facets of TV in the first place. Television's continued rapid evolution within increasingly multimedia-based and globally oriented conglomerates exemplifies the socioeconomic processes of postmodernization, while the fractured, conflicting ideologies of programmes on burgeoning numbers of TV channels, cross-promoting to **dot.com** sites and merchandizing tie-ins, fluidly incarnate the experience of postmodernity. Particular channels or programmes, from MTV, *Miami Vice* and *Twin Peaks* to *The Simpsons*, *24* and *CSI: Crime Scene Investigation,* also provide us with some of the best formal examples of postmodernism in any medium. At the same time, not all television is postmodern and postmodern perspectives provide only one set of approaches, albeit compelling ones, to understanding television.

POSTMODERN TELEVISION, HYPERREALITY AND CONSUMERISM

Jean **Baudrillard**, in *Simulations* (1983), uses the terms 'simulation' and 'hyperreality' to describe the 'mediatization' of reality in contemporary society. He rarely mentions television by name but his speculations make most sense in the context of TV viewing. He argues that with the massive increase in **signs** and images circulating in media-saturated societies, the distinction between objects and their representations disappeared. We are, he alleges, living in a world of 'simulation', where media-generated images function independently of any reality external to them. Signs and meanings float in a self-referential 'hyper-reality' – an excessive reality and also one literally 'hyped' by advertisers and others.

Baudrillard overstates his case, yet there are increasingly numerous examples where the 'reality' of television problematizes or even replaces everyday reality. The canonical instance was Baudrillard's claim that the 1991 Gulf War did not take place except as a simulation. At one level this was absurd and offensive; at another, for the vast majority of people the war, like much of the wall-to-wall breaking news and current affairs coverage of CNN and its rivals, was only experienced as a media event. The same is true both of the 2003 Gulf War and the most iconic international news event of recent years, the airliner hijacks which led to the destruction of the two World Trade Center towers in 2001 (now remembered as a spectacular image and simply known as '9/11').

Soap operas have long encouraged an enjoyable confusion between actors and the characters they play, but the distinction between media and everyday reality has been pushed to new levels of intertextual sophistication within the burgeoning genre of 'reality television'. Premised on access to apparently unscripted interactions of 'ordinary' people, reality TV shows range from docusoaps (with titles like *Airport*, *Holiday Rep* or *Vets in Practice*) to competitive game show formats (*Survivor*, *Temptation Island*, *Wife Swap* and the huge international success *Big Brother*). Such shows deliberately play with the boundaries of ordinariness and celebrity, allowing people we have never heard of to enter, however temporarily, the vastly expanded arena of contemporary celebrity culture. More generally, television has arguably contributed to a mutation in everyday perception, insofar as our view of the world is increasingly mediated by the vast mental image bank we each store in our minds. Thus, when I visit the Eiffel Tower in Paris or the Statue of Liberty in New York, I have already 'visited' them in **representation** – in *Holiday* or one of its many magazine show equivalents – and may even be disappointed if they do not live up to the idealized TV images. More radically still, there is a sense in which we may even at times process the meanings of our own lives through the grids of established televisual codes and conventions. We may begin to understand our own personal and family relationships in terms of soap opera, or our safety (or lack of it) in the community in terms of crime shows.

Allied to the postmodern claim that 'TV is the world' is neo-**Marxist** Fredric **Jameson**'s proposal that postmodernism is 'the cultural logic of late capitalism'. For Jameson television functions as the social glue in increasingly subcultural and privatized consumer cultures. The growth of consumer societies, first in the United States and then in Europe and elsewhere, was fuelled by the simultaneous expansion of media, especially television, which promoted the desirability of commodities and reproduced a consumerist ideology. In his classic *Postmodernism, or, The Cultural Logic of Late Capitalism* (1991), Jameson shows how the aesthetic forms and techniques of the avant-garde and **modernism** have been placed at the service of consumerism in postmodern aesthetics. Thus the emphasis on style, novelty and innovation which motivated the avant-garde were co-opted into the packaging and marketing of everyday commodities, while the history of art became a vast cultural repertoire to be raided by advertisers looking for a new 'take' on a product. The promotion of 'lifestyle' options in which the imaginary, symbolic and associational qualities – the sign values – of homes, cars, clothes, cosmetics or food and drink are more important than their physical uses – their traditional use values – has become, for Jameson, the real business of television and other media.

Again this case is over-generalized but there is no doubt that television is fundamental to consumer culture. To counter the ability of digital video and DVD recorders such as TiVo and Replay TV to omit advertisements or fast forward through them, virtual digital advertising is now increasingly used to promote brands within programmes: for instance, in sporting events where logos appear superimposed on the pitch. Product placement within shows has also become far more sophisticated and programme sponsorship is the norm. The prodigious growth of lifestyle channels and programming, memorably dubbed by Rachel Moseley as the 'makeover takeover', has seen shows about transforming your self, life, cuisine, home or garden migrate from the daytime schedules into prime time ('Makeover-Takeover on British Television', *Screen*, 41:3 (2000)). In the United Kingdom, for instance, popular shows such as *What Not to Wear*, *Changing Rooms*, *Home Front* and *Ground Force* have recently been supplemented by property shows on moving (*Location, Location, Location*), moving up the market (*Property Ladder*) and building your dream home (*Grand Designs*). At the same time, interactive and digital services enable us to buy in services such as films and one-off sports events, order pizza while watching our favourite show, vote people out of reality TV shows or gamble on winners and losers (on, as I write, 2004's *I'm a Celebrity, Get Me Out of Here*), visit a show's website and purchase merchandise relating to it (for example, the conspicuously consumerist *Sex and the City*), or just shop. These trends continue to develop within the heterogeneous environment of the postmodernized TV and new media industries, whose audiences understand and enjoy the intertextuality, recycling and self-conscious play which permeate postmodern TV and media.

POSTMODERNIZATION, INDUSTRY AND AUDIENCE

In the 1960s, Marshall **McLuhan** characterized post-war media society as an 'electronic global village'. Changes in the structure of the television industry over the past twenty years or so, along with the arrival of other information technologies and the increasing convergence between media, have confirmed the relevance of this prophetic label. Ien Ang, in *Living Room Wars: Rethinking Media Audiences for a Postmodern World* (1996), remarks on these changes: 'Television itself has undergone massive postmodernization – manifested in a complex range of developments such as pluralization, diversification, commercialization, commodification, internationalization, decentralization – throwing established **paradigms** of how it operates in culture and society into disarray.' It may not be strictly necessary to describe these changes as 'postmodernization'; nevertheless, they are arguably homologous with changes in other spheres which frequently attract the label postmodern.

Since the early 1980s, there has been a diversification and a fragmentation in the technologies by which television is transmitted. Broadcast television has been supplemented and challenged by the arrival of satellite, cable, digital and interactive TV and the **Internet**. The diffusion of these technologies has been encouraged by 'deregulation', which has seen market forces become increasingly prevalent. In the United States, for instance, the network TV system dominated by the giants ABC, CBS and NBC has been transformed by large numbers of more specialized and local channels. In Europe, the traditional public-service broadcasting systems have been forced to adapt in response to competition from commercial subscription satellite, cable and digital channels. At the same time, the extended reach of these technologies has opened up large areas of the world to penetration by international and multinational media conglomerates. Post-modernization aspires to a genuinely global reach (and, alongside this, somewhat paradoxically, an increased local reach). Together, these changes have led to a volatile, competitive market which typifies the postmodern processes of so-called 'disorganized capitalism'. In fact, it is anything but disorganized; it is, however, relatively fluid, flexible and fast-changing.

What are the implications of this for the television audience? In the post-modern era producers, while they remain obsessed with success and delivering the desired audience to sponsors and advertisers, recognize the need to build 'coalition audiences' from diverse constituencies, which may differ by gender, class, race, region or lifestyle and may be mobilized to watch a programme for a variety of reasons. At the same time, it has become increasingly important to try to direct user flows between television and other ancillary and digital media, especially dot.com sites which operate alongside TV shows in a variety of relationships. Niche marketing across new media is increasingly the name of the game as audiences become ever more fragmented and heterogeneous and ever less governed by channel or schedule loyalties. In the case of pay-per-view TV, for instance, used in particular for boxing and other sporting events, audiences continue to be built on a one-off basis, while the possibilities of digital convergence were powerfully suggested by the interacting plots and characters of NBC's late 1990s *Homicide: Life on the Streets* and the website 'Homicide: The Second Shift'.

Researchers, for their part, have continued to move away from the traditional audience models employed within the sociology of mass communications. The effects model conceptualized the audience as passive, and has come to be seen as an offshoot of earlier, modernist ambitions to deploy television as an instrument of social management. The uses and gratifications model, although it posited an active individual viewer, was also instrumental in its understanding of the TV–viewer relation, and lacked any real social context which could account for ways in which TV is embedded in the culture of everyday life. In place of these models, the trend since the 1970s has been towards ethnographic and other studies of variable audiences engaged in watching television in various contradictory ways, making active choices concerning what they watch and when, in particular view-ing contexts. Here the emphasis is on the diversity and situatedness of viewing practices, very much in line with the postmodern turn towards **difference** and micro-politics of all kinds.

The shorthand term for this trend, 'the active audience', may seem to empower the audience too much. The best research in this area, however, by David Morley, Ien Ang, Henry Jenkins and Maria Gillespie among others, is well aware of the dangers inherent in constructing a transgressive, pleasure-seeking viewer completely free to 'graze' the galaxy of sumptuous signifiers which is postmodern television and the worldwide web. Choices, providing we can pay, may appear to be widening but they are still the choices that the fashion system of postmodern consumer culture makes available to us. In this sense, it might be argued that not watching TV, not consuming the media, is the more genuinely transgressive act.

Since hardly anyone, however, does not watch at least *some* television, we can ask what the postmodern viewer is up to today. It is easy to produce an identikit postmodern hedonist: the archetypal decentred subject with a maximum attention span of three minutes. Living in a world of schizophrenically fragmented instants, he cruises the surfeit of channels available to him, **zapping** his remote control and hopping between channels and programmes unconnected by time, space or genre. He is unconcerned with **narrative**, coherence or rational understanding; rather, he constructs a largely random bricolage out of bits and pieces of television, which he connects with only in a bored and distracted fashion. He is the viewer figured in a cryptic and almost science-fictional way by Baudrillard in his essay 'The Ecstasy of Communication' (in H. Foster, ed., *Postmodern Culture* (1985)), who is merely an extension of small-screen technology: 'With the television image – the television being the ultimate and perfect object for this new era – our own body and the whole surrounding universe become a control screen.'

Over against this in many ways nonsensical model, we can posit an alternative postmodern viewer (though no less an identikit, if truth be told). She is aware of the choices that the new TV technologies offer, and how much they cost. She knows what kind of programmes she likes, and why. She is happy watching television in different environments (home, bar, shopping mall) with various social groups (alone, partner, children, whole family, best friend, group of friends, strangers) and with varying degrees of attention (from 'literary mode' – serious, attentive, diligent, analytic, watching from beginning to end in the right order – through to 'video mode' – playful or distracted, hopping, pausing, replaying, sampling, indulging, ignoring). She integrates television into her everyday life, taking full advantage of the postmodernization of TV while being able to switch deftly between postmodern and other modes of viewing.

One more point about both of these viewers. As more and more people become adept multitaskers in the new media environment, they are combining and switching easily between media. Though still in front of iconic small screens, a lot of the time they are not watching broadcast or narrowcast TV at all. Still using the TV set, in conjunction with the VCR or DVD they may be time-shifting, watching material recorded off-air to their individually tailored menus or pre-recorded material not available on television; or they may be visiting related dot.com sites, playing video games, or using their mobile phone video or Internet facilities.

POSTMODERN PROGRAMMES

Within the specificities of TV as a medium combining image and sound and transmitted twenty-four hours a day, many of the postmodern formal features of particular channels or programmes closely resemble those in other arts and media: thus postmodern TV is characterized by a high degree of excess, fragmentation, heterogeneity, **hybridization**, aestheticization, stylization, intertextuality, recycling, **bricolage**, self-referentiality, parody and pastiche. Postmodern programmes are often ontologically unstable, playfully foregrounding production contexts and environments (never doing this in the sober and revelatory fashion of the modernist text), shifting between realistic and fantasy worlds without comment, blurring the boundaries between fact and fiction or past, present and future, and casually using computer graphics and special effects to create, warp or wipe out televisual worlds. It is television which in many respects assumes a sophisticated and playful audience with a highly developed media literacy: an audience, in short, who have been watching lots of television all their lives, and for whom TV is culture which is (second) nature.

The initial 1980s accounts of postmodern TV were dominated by 'M's: MTV, *Miami Vice* and *Moonlighting*. In one of the earliest book-length studies of postmodern television, E. Ann Kaplan argued, in *Rocking Around the Clock: Music Television, Postmodernism, and Consumer Culture* (1987), that MTV was emblematic of the emergence of specialist genre or theme-based channels – which have since expanded into the fields of sport, films, science fiction and fantasy, comedy, drama, lifestyle and shopping, children's TV and so on – in postmodern consumer culture. It typified the increasing fragmentation and specialization of postmodern TV, initially showing pop videos, with their glamorous, eroticized and youth-oriented images, non-stop. Theoretically, viewers could spend their whole lives watching it. MTV has since gone from strength to strength, diversifying into (at present) four channels, and its success has spawned a number of competing music channels which are integral to today's global celebrity-based consumer culture.

Lawrence Grossberg, in 'The In-Difference of Television' (*Screen*, 28 (1987)), addressed postmodern aesthetics when he berated the American cop show *Miami Vice* for its stylization and empty intertextuality: '*Miami Vice* . . . is all on the surface. And the surface is nothing but a collection of quotations from our own collective historical debris, a mobile game of Trivia . . . The narrative is less important than the images.' The show's pop video aspects have since passed into the mainstream, not least in the pneumatic erotics of the massively popular *Baywatch*. Twenty or so years later, the arrival of *CSI: Crime Scene Investigation* and its spin-off series *CSI: Miami* (which takes us back to Miami's capitalist and gangster gloss) returned us to the same debates with their shimmering and frankly beautiful images of stunning detectives (male and female) investigating hideous and often sexual crimes to the sounds of entrancing popular music.

The playful, pastiche-y ambience of the comedy crime series *Moonlighting*, which paired Cybill Shepherd and Bruce Willis as private detectives engaging in war-of-the-sexes screwball banter as they lightheartedly pursued capering criminals, was also much discussed by TV critics. Partly working in *The Avengers* tradition, it was itself a powerful influence on *The X Files*, which in turn partly enabled the fantasy 'action babe' cycle from the mid-1990s, including *Buffy: The Vampire Slayer*, *Xena: Warrior Princess*, *Dark Angel* and *Charmed*. All these shows combined fantastic spectacle with a knowing recycling of plots and fragments from the media past. More generally, in programmes which are not necessarily formally postmodern, hybridization between 'masculine' and 'feminine' genres has been a feature of TV series from *Cagney and Lacey* to *The Bill*, as well as lifestyle television, where men are increasingly featured and addressed alongside women.

Since the 1990s, the intertextuality, recycling and self-referentiality of the postmodern form have also passed into the TV mainstream. At a fundamental level, the expanding number of TV channels has created an ever-increasing demand for programming of all kinds. One effect of this is that much more of television's past is on TV *now*, albeit often watched by relatively small audiences. This in turn has partly underpinned the self-referentiality of much television made today. It is only exaggerating slightly to claim that the entire popular cultural archive of the last forty years and beyond is now available to raid and recycle. While there are endless shows which literally recycle the mediated past (*The 100 Greatest Advertisements*, *I Love the Seventies*) many comedy, drama, music, chat, news and current affairs shows, for instance, literally or parodically reuse bits and pieces of past film and television within their formats. In terms of comedy, for instance, think of Victoria Wood, *The Comic Strip Presents*, *French and Saunders*, *The Day Today*, *Brass Eye*, *Knowing Me, Knowing You with Alan Partridge* and *Ali G* to name but a few.

In the early 1990s, the most canonical postmodern TV series to date, *Twin Peaks,* typified postmodern genre-mixing to achieve 'multi-accentuality'. Marketed both as auteur-based 'quality television' masterminded by oddball movie director David **Lynch** and as touching genre soap opera, it moved between the classic detective investigation, science fiction/horror and melodrama/soap in a fashion designed to appeal to both **ironic** postmodern and straightforward emotion-oriented sensibilities. If it was hard to know how to take it this was precisely the point. It set the trend for maverick 'quality' TV series, from *Ali McBeal* to *The Sopranos* and *Six Feet Under*, whose eccentricities have a broad niche appeal but which are designed above all to pull in high income and therefore desirable viewers.

Television comes and goes, so let us close with two current postmodern favourites (in the first version of this essay these were *Ren and Stimpy* and *Fantasy Football League*). One is the thriller *24*, which has so far run for two series, and is dependent on reversing the phenomena of time-space compression and fragmentation which typify postmodernity. Each series has taken the form of twenty-four hour-long episodes (though they are only 48 minutes when you allow for advertising) which operate in 'real time' to narrate agent Jack Bauer's attempt to save the President of the United States (series 1) and thwart a terrorist nuclear bomb (series 2). The series have been much praised for their creation of traditional suspense and drama. The other is undoubtedly the most hallowed series of the last few years, *The Simpsons*, an animated situation comedy featuring an all-American working-class family whose adventures are at once absolutely quotidian and absolutely fantastic. The show's ability to work with contemporary topical agendas and the popular cultural archive, as well as its inclusion of innumerable guest star appearances, at present seem to have marked it out as the masterpiece of its moment, and it has also achieved the production longevity which means it will be showing on TV screens (or watched on tape or DVD or your personal computer) for the foreseeable future. The Simpsons also demonstrate that many of our greatest cultural icons in the postmodern era are not real people.

However, as I mentioned at the outset, we should not assume that all TV is postmodern. Much programming and viewing is reassuringly traditional. Call me old-fashioned, but I for one still regularly sit and watch the conventional realist narratives of *Coronation Street* and *EastEnders* pretty much from beginning to end, with little or no zapping or hopping (though I do some timeshifting now and again).

12

POSTMODERNISM AND FICTION

BARRY LEWIS

From the vantage point of the new millennium, it is clear that the dominant mode of literature in the second half of the twentieth century was **postmodernist** writing. The fiction later to be classified under this rubric emerged at around the time of the erection of the Berlin Wall in the early 1960s. By 1989, with the Wall demolished and the Cold War almost over, postmodernism had established itself as the dominant **paradigm** for the culture. After this point, the concept saturated the media and academia to such an extent that the term has become problematic as an explanatory force. Evidence for the exponential interest in the idea of **postmodernity** can be gleaned from information available on the Amazon.com website, one of the most comprehensive listings of books that are currently available or out of print. According to this source, approximately 95 per cent of titles containing the words 'postmodern' or 'postmodernism' were published after 1989.

The Berlin Wall, like postmodernism itself, is now dispersed everywhere. A 1999 article in *Time* magazine revealed that sections of the ugly, graffitied concrete divide between West and East Berlin can be found in such diverse places as the CIA headquarters in Langley, Washington; newspaper offices in Buenos Aires; a Las Vegas urinal; and as part of the Microsoft Art Collection in Redmond, Washington. Similarly, the word 'postmodern' now crops up in the most diverse of contexts. It can apply to anything from the porridge of mythologies and magic in the Harry Potter novels by J. K. Rowling to the work of virtually any writer from an ethnic minority, deemed to be postmodern by virtue of their **hybrid** status in a displaced, **globalized** society.

It would seem, then, that the epistemic break that occurred around 1990 concerns two understandings of the concept of postmodernism in relation to literature. Before that date, it referred to an overlapping set of characteristics that applied to a particular set of writers, bound together by their agonistic relation to modernism. Particularly contested were the totalizing tendencies of the great modernists such as Proust, Joyce and Woolf, and the distinctions they made between low and high culture. After that date, the term mushroomed into the widest of catch-alls.

Several commentators intuited that the literature of exhaustion (John **Barth's** phrase for the last-gasp attempt of the novel to achieve pre-eminence in the electronic global village) itself became exhausted around 1990. De Villo Sloan, in his essay 'The Decline of American Postmodernism' (1987), wrote: 'Post-modernism as a literary movement . . . is now in its final phase of decadence'.

Malcolm Bradbury and Richard Ruland, in their sweeping survey *From Puritanism to Postmodernism* (1991), asserted: 'Postmodernism now looks like a stylistic phase that ran from the 1960s to the 1980s.' If we take these statements seriously, it follows that a large proportion of writing published after 1990 which is dubbed 'postmodernist' is really '**post-postmodernist**', or 'post-pomo' for short. It is the **texts** published between 1960 and 1990 that are more precisely to be regarded as postmodernist.

Bradbury did much to chart the territory and promulgate the perception of the writing between 1960 and 1990 as a self-contained period. He admitted that the problems of mapping contemporary literature are considerable, and that its diversity presents problems for the would-be cartographer. Postmodernism is, of course, only part of the total landscape, but like a mountain range it looms over everything else, and plodding over its peaks and valleys is no easy task. Luckily other intrepid guides have explored its contours and reliefs. The most useful textbooks are Patricia Waugh's *Metafiction* (1984), Larry McCaffery's *Postmodern Fiction* (1986), Brian McHale's *Postmodernist Fiction* (1987) and Mark Currie's *Postmodern Narrative Theory* (1998).

Postmodernist fiction is/was an international phenomenon, with major representatives from all over the world: Günter Grass and Peter Handke (Germany); Georges Perec and Monique Wittig (France); Umberto **Eco** and Italo **Calvino** (Italy); Angela **Carter** and Salman **Rushdie** (Britain); Stanislaw Lem (Poland); Milan Kundera (former Czechoslovakia); Mario Vargos Llosa (Peru); Gabriel Garcia Márquez (Colombia); J. M. Coetzee (South Africa); and Peter Carey (Australia). Yet, despite this cosmopolitanism, Malcolm Bradbury quipped that 'When something called postmodernism came along everyone thought it was American – even though its writers had names like Borges, Nabokov, Calvino and Eco.' This is because the number of Stateside writers who published postmodernist fiction was large. Here are twenty names usually included in such lists: Walter Abish, Kathy **Acker**, Paul **Auster**, John Barth, Donald **Barthelme**, Richard Brautigan, William Burroughs, Robert **Coover**, Don **DeLillo**, E. L. Doctorow, Raymond **Federman**, William Gass, Steve Katz, Jerzy Kosinski, Joseph McElroy, Thomas **Pynchon**, Ishmael **Reed**, Gilbert Sorrentino, Ronald **Sukenick**, Kurt **Vonnegut**. A similar list for the post-1990 or post-pomo generation would probably include: Sherman Alexie, Mark Amerika, T. Coraghessan Boyle, Douglas **Coupland**, Ricardo Cortez Cruz, Mark Z. Danielewski, William **Gibson**, Lyn Hejinian, Harold Jaffe, Maxine Hong Kingston, Jonathan Lethem, Mark Leyner, Richard Powers, Joanna Russ, Joanna Scott, Leslie Marmon Silko, Lynne Tillman, Gerald Vizenor, William T. Vollman, David Foster Wallace. Raymond Federman states in 'Self-Reflexive Fiction' (1988) that 'it cannot be said that these [postmodernist] writers . . . formed a unified movement for which a coherent theory could be formulated'. It is difficult to disagree with this, as the novels and short stories of both sets of authors vary a great deal. However, the first group have more of a common end and means than the second. They exaggerate certain techniques previously associated with the modernists in order to signal their perception that cultural values have shifted.

Some of the dominant features of their postmodernist fiction include: temporal disorder; the erosion of the sense of time; a pervasive and pointless use of pastiche; a foregrounding of words as fragmenting material **signs**: the loose association of ideas; paranoia; and vicious circles, or a loss of distinction between logically separate levels of **discourse**. Traits such as these are encountered time and time again in the bare, bewildering landscapes of the original post-modernists. John W. Aldridge puts it like this in *The American Novel and the Way We Live Now* (1983):

> In the fiction of [postmodernist writers] . . . virtually everything and everyone exists in such a radical state of distortion and aberration that there is no way of determining from which conditions in the real world they have been derived or from what standard of sanity they may be said to depart. The conventions of verisimilitude and sanity have been nullified. Characters inhabit a dimension of structureless being in which their behaviour becomes inexplicably arbitrary and unjudgeable because the fiction itself stands as a metaphor of a derangement that is seemingly without provocation and beyond measurement.

Although Aldridge's statement could also be applied to the post-pomo writers who appeared after 1990, it should be noted that their use of these techniques is routine and no longer radical, and the experimentation of their predecessors is now deeply absorbed into the mainstream. The following brief survey will therefore concentrate on the characteristic derangements of the writers who belong to the pre-1990 dispensation. It will also focus primarily on the novel. Postmodernism has, of course, infiltrated all literary forms. The paradoxes and perplexities of John **Ashbery** and Susan Howe, and the word games of the Language poets such as Ron Silliman and Bob Perelman, are well documented. In drama, David Mamet, Caryl Churchill, Sam Shepherd and Tony Kushner exhibit a postmodern sensibility. Yet it is within the genre of the novel that postmodernism has had the most impact. For this reason, I will focus on post-modernist fiction, although it is possible to find many of the features it discerns in other types of contemporary writing.

TEMPORAL DISORDER

Postmodernism, according to Linda Hutcheon in *A Poetics of Postmodernism: History, Theory, Fiction* (1988), is a 'contradictory enterprise: its art forms . . . use and abuse, install and then destabilize convention . . . [in] their critical or ironic re-reading of the art of the past'. She argues further that postmodernist writing is best represented by those works of 'historiographic **metafiction**' which self-consciously distort history. This can be accomplished by several means, as Brian McHale notes in the study mentioned earlier: apocryphal history, anachronism, or the blending of history and fantasy.

Apocryphal history involves bogus accounts of famous events. Thomas Pynchon's *Mason & Dixon* (1997), for instance, implies that its two eponymous heroes were aware that their famous line, dividing Maryland from Pennsylvania, would eventually lead to civil war. Anachronism disrupts temporal order by flaunting glaring inconsistencies of detail or setting. In *Flight to Canada* (1976) by Ishmael Reed, Abraham Lincoln uses a telephone, and his assassination is reported on television. Tom Crick, a schoolteacher in Graham Swift's *Waterland* (1983), blurs history and fantasy by combining his account of the French Revolution with personal reminiscences and unsubstantiated anecdotes about his own family history.

Postmodernist fiction does not just disrupt the past, but corrupts the present too. It disorders the linear coherence of **narrative** by warping the sense of significant time, *kairos,* or the dull passing of ordinary time, *chronos. Kairos* is strongly associated with those modernist novels which are disposed around moments of epiphany and disclosure, such as James Joyce's *A Portrait of the Artist as a Young Man* (1916). Postmodernist novels such as *Gerald's Party* (1986) by Robert Coover chuckle at such solemnities. The sheer abundance of incidents that occur over one night (several murders and beatings, the torture of Gerald's wife by the police, and the arrival of an entire theatre group) distends time beyond recognition. Realist writing specializes in *chronos*, or common-or-garden clock time, and this too is ridiculed in some postmodernist texts. Nicholson **Baker**'s *The Mezzanine* (1989), for instance, comprises a series of extended meditations on why the central character's shoelace snapped during one particular lunchtime.

Postmodernist writing is full of these kinds of temporal disorder. Its disruptions of time anticipate a world that was soon to be 24/7. Warhol's prediction that in the future everybody would be famous for fifteen minutes was mistaken: fifteen seconds is nearer the mark.

PASTICHE

The Italian word *pasticcio* means 'A medley of various ingredients: a hotchpotch, a farrago, jumble' (OED), and is the etymological root of the word 'pastiche'. Pastiching an individual writer is rather like creating an anagram, not of letters, but of the components of a style. Pastiche is therefore a kind of permutation, a shuffling of generic and grammatical tics.

The mere presence of pastiche in postmodernist writing is not in itself unique. The infancy of the novel form itself was marked by a succession of parodies, from Samuel Richardson to Laurence Sterne. Yet, as John Barth points out in his essay 'The Literature of Exhaustion' ([1967], in M. Bradbury, ed., *The Novel Today* (1977)) and its sequel 'The Literature of Replenishment' (*Atlantic Monthly*, 245 (1980)), there is certainly something peculiar and distinctive about the mania for impersonation between 1960 and 1990. However, by the year 2000 pastiche began to look nostalgically authentic when pitted against the widespread plagiarism and piracy made possible by the **dot.com Internet** explosion.

Barth's earlier essay epitomizes a mood in the late 1960s, when critics such as Susan Sontag were busy greatly exaggerating rumours about the death of the novel. The traditional devices of fiction seemed clapped out, unable to capture the complexities of the electronic age. At first it was thought that Barth, by stressing the exhaustion of both realism and modernism, had not only joined the novel's funeral procession, but was volunteering to be chief pall-bearer. However, the critics overlooked his claim (reasserted in the later essay) that the corpse could be revivified by stitching together the amputated limbs and digits in new permutations: by pastiche, in other words.

Pastiche, then, arose from the frustration that everything has been done before. As Fredric **Jameson** notes in 'Postmodernism and Consumer Society' (in H. Foster, ed., *Postmodern Culture* (1983)), 'the writers and artists of the present day will no longer be able to invent new styles and worlds . . . only a limited number of combinations are possible; the most unique ones have been thought of already'. So instead of honing an unmistakable signature like D. H. Lawrence or Gertrude Stein, postmodernist writers tended to pluck existing styles higgledy-piggledy from the reservoir of literary history, and match them with little tact.

This explains why many novels between 1960 and 1990 borrow the clothes of different forms (for example: the Western, the sci-fi yarn and the detective tale). The impulse behind this cross-dressing is more spasmodic than parodic. These genres provide ready-made forms, ideal for postmodernist miscegenation. The Western, as Philip French observes, is 'a hungry cuckoo of a genre . . . ready to seize anything that's in the air from juvenile delinquency to ecology'. It is already a bastardized form. Examples of the postmodern Western include *The Hawkline Monster* (1974) by Richard Brautigan, *Yellow Back Radio Broke-Down* (1969) by Ishmael Reed, and *The Place of Dead Roads* (1983) by William Burroughs. Science fiction was another popular source for postmodernist pastiche. Some critics claimed it to be the natural companion to postmodernist writing, because of their shared ontological occupations. (See especially *Solaris* (1961) by Stanislaw Lem, *Cosmicomics* (1965) by Italo Calvino, and *Slaughterhouse-Five* (1969) by Kurt Vonnegut.) Lastly, the detective genre was another candidate for the post of true companion of postmodernism. The pursuit of clues appealed to the postmodernist writer because it so closely parallels the hunt for textual meaning by the reader. The most popular postmodernist detective fictions are *The Name of the Rose* (1984) by Umberto Eco, *The New York Trilogy* (1987) by Paul Auster, and *Hawksmoor* (1985) by Peter **Ackroyd**. Two decades on, these books have assumed the status of classics, slightly quaint in their self-conscious fusions. To the post-pomo generation, and writers of recent American crime fiction such as James Ellroy and Kinky **Friedman**, genre-blending is a sine qua non.

FRAGMENTATION

John Hawkes once divulged that when he began to write he assumed that 'the true enemies of the novel were plot, character, setting and theme'. Certainly many

authors did their best after the 1960s to sledgehammer these four literary cornerstones into oblivion. Either plot is pounded into small slabs of event and circumstance, characters disintegrate into a bundle of twitching desires, settings dwindle to little more than transitory backdrops, or themes become so attenuated that it is often comically inaccurate to say that certain novels are 'about' such-and-such.

'Too many times', as Jonathan Baumbach observes in a short story in *The Return of Service* (1979), 'you read a story nowadays and it's not a story at all, not in the traditional sense.' The postmodernist writer distrusted the wholeness and completion associated with traditional stories, and preferred to deal with other ways of structuring narrative. One alternative was the multiple ending, which resists closure by offering numerous possible outcomes for a plot. *The French Lieutenant's Woman* (1969) by John Fowles is the classic instance of this. The novel concerns the love of respectable amateur naturalist Charles Smithson (engaged to the daughter of a wealthy trader) for Sarah Woodruff, an outcast rumoured to have been scandalously involved with a French lieutenant. Although the book is set in Lyme Regis in 1867, and follows several love story conventions, it is far from being a regular historical romance.

Fowles disrupts the narrative by parading his familiarity with **Marx**, Darwin and others. He directly addresses the reader, and even steps into the story himself at one stage as a character. The multiple endings are a part of these guerrilla tactics. Fowles refuses to choose between two competing dénouements: one in which Charles and Sarah are reunited after a stormy affair, and the other in which they are kept irrevocably apart. He therefore introduces an uncertainty principle into the book. He even dallies with a third possibility of leaving Charles on the train, searching for Sarah in the capital: 'But the conventions of Victorian fiction allow, allowed no place for the open, the inconclusive.'

Another means of allowing space for the open and inconclusive was to break up the text into short fragments or sections, separated by space, titles, numbers or symbols. The novels and short stories of Richard Brautigan and Donald Barthelme are full of such fragments. Some authors went even further and fragmented the very fabric of the text with illustrations, typography, or mixed media. As Raymond Federman puts it in the introduction to *Surfiction: Fiction Now . . . and Tomorrow* (1975): 'In those spaces where there is nothing to write, the fiction writer can, at any time, introduce material (quotations, pictures, diagrams, charts, designs, pieces of other discourses, etc.) totally unrelated to the story.'

Willie Masters' Lonesome Wife (1967) by William Gass does just about all these things in its sixty-odd pages, and is a postmodernist text par excellence. The pages themselves come in four different colours: jotter blue, khaki green, strawberry red and glossy white. The nude woman lounging full-frontal on the title-page is Babs. She is a frustrated spouse who figuratively embodies the language/lovemaking equation examined by Gass. The layout is so eccentric it might have been designed by Marshall **McLuhan** on mescaline. Multiple typefaces (bold, italic), fonts (Gothic, script), characters (musical symbols, accents), and miscellaneous arrangements (columns, footnotes) jostle for air alongside some visual jokes (coffee-cup stains, huge asterisk). In a review, Ronald Sukenick called it 'a cloudburst of fragmented events'.

With works such as these by Fowles, Brautigan, Barthelme and Gass it is difficult not to be reminded of the famous epigraph to E. M. Forster's *Howards End* (1910): 'Live in fragments no longer. Only connect.' We can counterpoint this with an utterance by a character in Barthelme's 'See the Moon?' from *Unspeakable Practices. Unnatural Acts* (1968): 'Fragments are the only forms I trust.' These two statements evince a crucial difference between modernism and postmodernism. The Forster phrase could almost be modernism's motto, as it points to the need to find new forms of continuity in the absence of the old linear plots. Conversely, Barthelme's gem hints at postmodernist fiction's wariness of wholeness. Yet in the age of **hypertext** and the instant sound bite, even fragments appear to be suspiciously holistic.

LOOSENESS OF ASSOCIATION

Another means by which many postmodernist writers disrupted the smooth production and reception of texts was by welcoming chance into the compositional process. The infamous *The Unfortunates* (1969) by B. S. Johnson, for instance, is a novel-in-a-box which instructs the reader to riffle several loose-leaf chapters into any order. Only the first and last chapter are denominated, otherwise the sections can be freely mixed. The point of this contrived format is not just to perform a cold, technical experiment. Rather, Johnson wishes to recreate the unique disposition of his thoughts on a particular Saturday afternoon, when reporting a football match in Nottingham for the *Observer*. It was the first time he had returned to the city since the death of his friend, Tony. The peculiar form of the novel mirrors his churning feelings. So, **ironically**, the loose leaves of *The Unfortunates* are not intended to be random at all, but strive to render the workings of the mind more naturally.

William Burroughs also forayed frequently into serendipity. The arrangement of the twenty-two individual sections of *Naked Lunch* (1959) was regulated solely by the adventitious order in which they happened to be sent to the publishers. Indeed, the untidiness of the room in which the manuscript was assembled sometimes disturbed the sequence of pages. Small wonder that Burroughs confessed that 'You can cut into *Naked Lunch* at any intersection point'. Burroughs wields chance less randomly in three novels from the 1960s which are often grouped together as a trilogy: *Nova Express* (1964), *The Soft Machine* (1968) and *The Ticket That Exploded* (1967). These books make methodical use of the cut-up.

The cut-up is the brainchild of the artist Tristan Tzara, who envisaged it as a verbal equivalent to the cubist and Dadaist collages in the visual arts. Further extensions of the idea can be traced through the poetry of T. S. Eliot and Ezra

Pound, and the newspaper pastiches of John Dos Passos. The cut-up involves placing excised sentences from a range of texts into a hat or other container, shaking them, then matching together the scraps of paper which are picked out at random. This rigmarole has prompted sceptical critics to make unflattering comparisons between Burroughs and monkeys with typewriters.

Another chance technique favoured by Burroughs was the fold-in, in which a page of text is folded vertically, and then aligned with another page until the two halves match. Just as the cut-up allowed writing to mimic cinematic montage, the fold-in gave Burroughs the option of repeating passages in a specifically musical way. For example, if page 1 is folded in with page 100 to form a composite page 10, phrases can flash forwards and back like the anticipation and recapitulation of motifs in a symphony.

The fold-in, like the cut-up, strained to evade the manacles of ordinary fiction. Burroughs' spirit of chance-taking was decidedly congenial to the postmodernist writer. In this respect he is rather like the musician John **Cage**, who opened up tremendous ground for exploration by later composers, although his experiments with dice and the *I-Ching* proved to be unrepeatable. Nevertheless, as Julian Cowley noted in an essay on Ronald Sukenick (1987), in both music and writing 'Readiness to ride with the random may be regarded as a characteristically postmodern attitude.' Indeed, at the beginning of the twenty-first century, it is now wholly subsumed into the everyday splice-and-mix culture.

PARANOIA

Paranoia, or the threat of total engulfment by somebody else's system, is keenly felt by many of the dramatis personae of postmodernist fictions between 1960 and 1990. It is tempting to speculate that this began as an indirect mimetic representation of the climate of fear and suspicion that prevailed throughout the Cold War, although following 9/11 conspiracy theory is simply a modus vivendi for the majority. The protagonists of postmodernist fiction often suffer from what Tony Tanner calls in *City of Words* (1971) a 'dread that someone else is patterning your life, that there are all sorts of invisible plots afoot to rob you of your autonomy of thought and action, that conditioning is ubiquitous'.

Postmodernist writing reflected paranoid anxieties in many ways, including: the distrust of fixity, of being circumscribed to any one particular place or identity, the conviction that society is conspiring against the individual, and the multiplication of self-made plots to counter the scheming of others. These different responses are immanent in three distinct areas of reference associated with the word 'plot'. The first meaning is that of a piece of ground of small or moderate size sequestered for some special purpose, such as a plot for growing vegetables or building a house. A stationary space, that is to say, intimidating to the postmodern hero. Randle McMurphy in Ken Kesey's *One Flew Over the Cuckoo's Nest* (1962), Yossarian in Joseph Heller's *Catch-22* (1962) and Billy Pilgrim in Kurt Vonnegut's *Slaughterhouse-Five* (1969) are each confined to their own 'plots' in this sense by the authorities. McMurphy is committed to a mental hospital, Yossarian is conscripted to the air force, and Billy Pilgrim is interned in a German prisoner-of-war camp. A vindictive bureaucracy controls these mavericks by medication, red tape or the force of arms.

In each instance the imprisoning of the individual by outside powers propagates a panic of identity. So McMurphy's protests that he is sane prove his insanity. Pilgrim's belief that he is the subject of an experiment is belied by the offhand way his German captors treat him. To compensate for the hopelessness of their predicaments, these paranoids long for a state of complete fluidity and openness. However, their impulse towards freedom is tainted both by their terror of the actual open road and their cynicism about possible escape. McMurphy, Yossarian and Pilgrim are simultaneously safe and insecure in their 'plots' of the Oregon Asylum, the Pianosa air-force base, and the Dresden slaughterhouse.

A second meaning of 'plot' is that of a secret plan or conspiracy to accomplish a criminal or illegal purpose. The protagonist of the postmodernist novel sometimes suspects that he or she is trapped at the centre of an intrigue, often with some justification. McMurphy is right to be afraid of Nurse Ratched and the Combine, who eventually force him to undergo shock treatment and an unwarranted lobotomy. Yossarian's parachute is stolen by Milo Minderbinder and replaced by a useless M & M Enterprises voucher. General Peckham sends Yossarian's squadron out on dangerous bombing missions simply to obtain decent aerial photographs for the magazines back home. Nately's whore stabs Yossarian, in the belief that he killed her lover. In *Slaughterhouse-Five*, Billy Pilgrim also correctly perceives that others wish to control his welfare. His daughter commits him to a mental institution and Paul Lazarro later kills him as a revenge for allegedly allowing Roland Weary to die.

There is but a small step from these private apprehensions to a more distressing speculation. Perhaps the whole of society is a plot against the citizen. What if all the major events of history are really side-shows orchestrated by unseen ringmasters for hidden motives? This is known as paranoid history. Thomas Pynchon is enthralled by the topic. Stencil in *V.* (1963), Oedipa Maas in *The Crying of Lot 49* (1966), Slothrop in *Gravity's Rainbow* (1973), Prairie in *Vineland* (1990), and the protagonists of *Mason & Dixon* (1997): each stumble upon subterranean schemes and cabals which threaten the rights of the individual. As Pynchon remarks in *Gravity's Rainbow,* their multiplying anxieties are triggered by 'nothing less than the onset, the leading edge, of the discovery that everything is connected, everything in the Creation'. These days, thanks to the world wide web, everything *is* connected to everything – at least, digitally.

The third, more mundane, meaning of plot is, of course, that of a plan of a literary work. In an interview, John Barth called this 'the incremental perturbation of an unstable homeostatic system and its **catastrophic** restoration to a complexified equilibrium'. This humorous definition suggests that a plot has a particular shape: somebody is challenged, certain obstacles are overcome, and a new state of affairs is reached. Plot is shape, and shape is control. Postmodernist writers proliferated plot, as if to prove through zealous mastery that they were free of the straitjackets of control by outside forces. The best of these maximalist works are *Foucault's Pendulum* (1988) by Umberto Eco, *Life: A User's Manual* (1978) by Georges Perec and *Letters* (1979) by Barth himself.

VICIOUS CIRCLES

Vicious circles arise in postmodernist fiction when both text and world are permeable, to the extent that we cannot separate one from the other. The literal and the metaphorical merge when the following occur: short circuits (when the author steps into the text) and double binds (when real-life historical figures appear in fictions).

The short circuits which plagued postmodernist fiction rarely occur in other forms of fiction. In realist literature, for example, there is an unbroken flow of narrative 'electricity' between text and world. The author never appears directly in his or her fictions, other than as a voice that indirectly guides the reader towards a 'correct' interpretation of the novel's themes. Conversely, much modernist fiction is motivated by the desire to expunge the author from the text altogether. Think of James Joyce's image of the artist standing behind the work, paring his fingernails. This again ensures that there is little chance of confusing the world inside the text with the world outside the text. In the postmodernist novel and short story, however, such confusion was rampant. Text and world fused when the author appeared in his or her own fiction. The best examples of this occur in Ronald Sukenick's *The Death of the Novel and Other Stories* (1969) and *Out* (1973), and Raymond Federman's *Double or Nothing* (1971) and *Take It or Leave It* (1976).

The double bind is a concept elaborated by Gregory Bateson and others to explain an inability to distinguish between different levels of discourse. When a parent chastises a child, for instance, they may undermine the punishment by smiling as they smack. If these kinds of contradictory messages are repeated obsessively, it may lead to the child's breakdown. The boundaries separating the literal and the metaphorical will never fully form, and any moves to resolve matters result only in further entanglement. It is well known that schizophrenics often confuse fact and fantasy in their delusions. The patient who thinks he is Jesus Christ manifests a typical symptom of the illness.

The equivalent of the double bind occurred in postmodernist fiction when historical characters appeared in a patent fiction. We are used to the idea of the historical novel, which shows famous people from the past acting in ways consistent with the verifiable public record. A common alternative was to sketch in the 'dark areas' of somebody's life, and again care is usually taken not to contradict substantially what we already know about them. In postmodernist writing, however, such contradictions were actively sought. So in Max Apple's *The Propheteers* (1987). the motel mogul Howard Johnson plots against Walt Disney. In Guy Davenport's 'Christ Preaching at the Henley Regatta' (1981),

Bertie Wooster and Mallarmé stand on the banks watching the boat race. In E. L. Doctorow's *Ragtime* (1975), **Freud** and Jung go through the Tunnel of Love together at Coney Island.

To compare such distortions with the derangements of insanity, as I have done, is apt. Some major **poststructuralist** thinkers enlist ideas connected with schizophrenia in their diagnoses of postmodern society. Jean-François **Lyotard**, for instance, employs the metaphors of fragmentation in *The Postmodern Condition* (1979) to convey the splintering of knowledge into a plethora of **incommensurate** discourses. Gilles **Deleuze** and Félix **Guattari** speak of 'schizoanalysis' in *Anti-Oedipus* (1977). Lastly, Fredric Jameson's full-length study *Postmodernism, or, The Cultural Logic of Late Capitalism* (1991) employs schizophrenia as an analogy for the collapse of traditional socio-economic structures. This recurrent linking of mental illness, the fractures of late capitalist society and the linguistic experiments of the postmodernists is not accidental. Temporal disorder, involuntary impersonation of other voices (or pastiche), fragmentation, looseness of association, paranoia and the creation of vicious circles are all symptoms of the language disorders of postmodernist fiction. Whether or not these tropes are adequate to describe the unruliness of the post-pomo writers, too, is open to debate.

13

POSTMODERNISM AND MUSIC

DEREK B. SCOTT

Postmodernism began to have an impact upon music and musicology in the 1980s when it became evident that a **paradigmatic shift** in thought was needed in order to find answers to the theoretical impasse that had been reached in several areas.

First, the idea that a mass audience did no more than passively consume the products of a culture industry had become discredited. Yet tacit acceptance of this idea explains why, for instance, the legendary jazz saxophonist Charlie Parker did not appear in the *New Oxford History of Music* and the rock guitarist Jimi Hendrix was absent from 1980 edition of *The New Grove Dictionary of Music and Musicians*. Anyone caring to peruse the index of the *Oxford History* will indeed find Parker listed, but this is the American organist and composer Horatio Parker (1863–1919). Giving priority to the latter makes a clear statement of value: Horatio is of greater musical importance than Charlie. Today, it is evident that classical music is as involved in the marketplace as pop and jazz (conductors and singers can become superstars, and even a 'serious' composer like Górecki has appeared in record charts). Moreover, the serious vs. light opposition that kept mass culture theory going is also found repeated in jazz and rock – for example, 'real' jazz vs. commercial dance band; 'authentic' rock vs. superficial pop.

Second, the musical genealogical tree had needed surgery too often: lines connecting composers and charting musical developments and influences, had been redrawn too many times. One has only to consider the major reassessment of Monteverdi and Berlioz in the 1960s. The linear paradigm works to include and to exclude: those who do not obviously connect are out (for example, Kurt Weill and Benjamin Britten). The related issue of the evolution of musical style was now questioned: if atonality was presented as an inevitable stylistic evolution, then clearly Duke Ellington was a musical dinosaur.

Third, the neglect of the social significance of music had become more apparent, especially the way cultural context often determines the legitimacy of styles of playing and singing, and changing social factors alter our response to existing works. Would we any more wish to hear John Lee Hooker attempting Puccini's *Nessun Dorma* than Luciano Pavarotti singing Chicago bar blues?

Fourth, the impact of technology had to be considered, especially the effects that sampling and remixing had on the concept of the composer as originating mind.

Furthermore, students who had grown up during the 'rock revolution' were inclined to see the **modernist** inclinations of university departments of music as the new orthodoxy. Perhaps more disturbing still was that it became common for a composition tutor to find students earnestly composing a type of music that they would never dream of actually going to a concert hall to hear. Other factors bearing upon the present situation were the rise of period instrument performances, making old music seem new (and arguably a replacement for the new), and crossovers between 'classical' and 'popular' idioms by increasing numbers of performers and composers.

Consequently, the time was ripe for postmodernism to offer a new theoretical perspective. Its impact is discussed below under a number of headings; these are not to be taken, however, as representing a particular hierarchical order.

'ART FOR ART'S SAKE' CHALLENGED

Postmodernism ousted notions of universalism, internationalism and 'art for art's sake', and replaced them with concerns for the values of specific cultures and their differences. 'Art for art's sake', a nineteenth-century doctrine born of distaste for industrialization, had proved to be an insuperable obstacle to the production of music that satisfied widespread social needs. Indeed, by the time Debussy was composing, the elitist attitude that 'art' is of no use to 'the masses' was common. However, by the 1980s there was a growing interest in uncovering the complicity between art and entertainment rather than drawing a contrast between these two terms. Among the middle classes and the 'educated' – and among 'serious' musicians – attention drifted away from high culture to popular culture. It was no longer pressing to debate whether Boulez, **Cage** or Tippett represented the 'way ahead' for high culture since, to echo a well-known song, those taking the high road had been overtaken by those taking the low road. Moreover, since the 1960s there had been a remarkable similarity in marketing techniques used for the classical repertoire and for pop music.

The opposition art vs. entertainment is an assumption of mass culture theory and may be regarded as an ethical rather than an aesthetic opposition. To choose examples from the careers of major figures in the classical canon, one can show that Mozart abandoned a flute concerto in mid-composition because a commissioner failed to pay up; the same composer was persuaded by a concert promoter to change a movement of his Paris Symphony; and it was a publisher who persuaded Beethoven to replace the finale of his late String Quartet in B flat with something more conventional. Today, Michael **Nyman** does not feel associations with businesses compromise his artistic integrity: *MGV* was commissioned to mark the opening of the Paris to Lille high-speed rail link, and car manufacturer Mazda UK Ltd commissioned a concerto in 1997.

THE COLLAPSE OF HIGH AND LOW: CROSSOVERS AND NEW GENRES

The amount of 'crossover' between 'serious' and 'popular' culture has been increasing since the late 1950s. This differs from the co-opting of jazz by the French avant-garde in the 1920s and 1930s. In that case, the jazz elements were used to shock a bourgeois concert audience. The attempts of earlier avant-garde movements to place art in the service of social change had by then been abandoned. Jazz itself took over that political role in 1940s Britain, when revivalist bands played at socialist rallies and accompanied the Aldermaston marches of the Campaign for Nuclear Disarmament.

The widening influence of pop music was heard in the soundtracks of films: in the 1940s Flash Gordon conquered the universe to the strains of Liszt, whereas in the 1980s his crusading was accompanied by the rock band Queen. In the 1980s performance artist Laurie **Anderson** had a remarkable crossover hit with 'O Superman'. In recent years, the violinist Nigel Kennedy has tried his hand at rock, while blues guitarist Eric Clapton has performed an electric guitar concerto. The Kronos String Quartet has an arrangement of Jimi Hendrix's 'Purple Haze' in its repertoire. Opera singers of the calibre of Kiri Te Kanawa, Placido Domingo and Bryn Terfel have ventured into the popular arena.

Some works now cannot easily be categorized: for example, Philip **Glass**'s Low Symphony and Heroes Symphony (both based on albums produced in the 1970s by David Bowie and Brian Eno); *The Juliet Letters* by Elvis Costello and the Brodsky Quartet; Karl Jenkins' *Adiemus* project; and the peculiar mixture of medievalism and jazz in the albums *Officium* by Jan Garbarek and the Hilliard Ensemble, and *Terror and Magnificence* by John Harle. It has been claimed that shared features in the music of **minimalism** and pop (allowing the Orb to borrow from Steve **Reich**) are of negligible import compared to the very different ways in which minimalism is disseminated, presented and promoted, which all serve to maintain a high/low divide. Yet, there is growing evidence of omnivorous appetites on the part of listeners that clouds the issue. Taste categories in music are no longer looking as stable as they were twenty years ago. Besides, music of postmodernist character does not have to be consumed in an identical way by all.

Pop music has developed features of its own that have been greeted as postmodernist (see 'Postmodernism and popular culture', pp. 133–42). Music videos, MTV, sampling and the phenomenon of 'world music' have received a lot of attention from postmodernist theorists. The influence of high cultural styles on popular music needs to be carefully evaluated since in some cases, such as the 'progressive' rock of the early 1970s, it may indicate modernist aspirations rather than a postmodernist play of styles.

THE END OF 'GRAND NARRATIVES'

Modernists have continually seen works as 'pointing forwards' to others, thus reinforcing a sense of self-determining progress in the arts. But can Wagner's *Tristan und Isolde* really be said to point forward to the sudden and rapid developments of 1908–9, such as Strauss's *Elektra* and Schoenberg's *Erwartung*? If a fifty-year gap is possible, why not concede a three-hundred-year gap and allow the idea that Gesualdo's colourful treatment of harmony pointed forward to Debussy? A major problem for 'linear modernism' is that, while Beethoven and Wagner appear to follow an evolutionary 'progress' in their own music, many otherwise impeccable modernists, like Debussy and Schoenberg, do not. What is more, modernist composers are not even reliable in their tastes: Debussy admired Gounod and Richard Strauss but not Schoenberg; Stravinsky admired Weber and Tchaikovsky but loathed Wagner.

The dominant **grand narrative** for musical modernism was that of the evolution and dissolution of tonality (major and minor keys). Schoenberg claimed that atonal music grew out of necessity, yet this necessity was itself born of a set of particular cultural assumptions. A belief in the historical necessity of atonality led to the neglect of many areas of twentieth-century music history, such as the importance of Vienna to Hollywood (Korngold) or of Puccini to 'The Generation of the 1880s' in Italy. Worst of all, perhaps, was the almost complete disregard of jazz.

The BBC's thinking has for a long time been informed by modernist **metanarratives**: the corporation's admiration for 'forward-looking' composers, and of 'progressive' music is part of the left luggage from the years when Sir William Glock controlled the Third Programme's output, but remains dispiriting for anyone who rejects that theoretical paradigm. Nyman feels that the musical establishment has given him the cold shoulder, as evidenced by the neglect of his music by BBC Radio 3 and his lack of Proms commissions. It is erroneous to believe that an 'adventurous' style requires greater compositional skill than a 'simple and direct' style; such a position serves only to offer a facile proof, for example, that Birtwistle must be better than Pärt. As a criterion of musical value, the important thing is the relationship of style and idea.

SOCIO-CULTURAL CONTEXT REPLACES AUTONOMY

The modernist interpretation of music history emphasized formal and technical values, novelty and compositional 'coups'. The stress was on the composition in itself and its place in an autonomous musical process. A well-known example of how Mozart's life and music may be interpreted through this reading of history is offered by Peter Shaffer's *Amadeus*, in which art is seen as a reflection of life (a corruption of the distinction between Romantic self-expression and the Baroque 'Doctrine of Affections' that codified musical devices in terms of the emotions they evoked); art is perfection, the artist is a visionary (Salieri cannot understand Mozart's unique vision in the 'confutatis' of his *Requiem*), and social and political issues are cast aside (Mozart, a member, it seems, of the republican Illuminati, says he is 'not interested in politics', and *The Magic Flute* with its Masonic messages is described as a vaudeville). It is all too easy when constructing the history of a cultural practice to assume one is dealing with facts and not interpretation.

Raymond Williams has pointed out how lines are drawn to link together ancestors within a cultural tradition. However, with the passage of time some lines become weaker, some are erased and new ones are drawn in. At the beginning of the twentieth century, the reputations of Gounod, Spohr and Borodin were high, but are no longer so. Since the 1960s, lines from Josquin and from Monteverdi have been strengthened, and in the 1970s eclectic modernists like Ives and Varèse were brought in from the margins following the failure of attempts to establish a common practice in total serialism (an attempt to impose order on length and loudness of notes as well as on their pitches). This enabled the USA to take its place in the history of modernism, since a line drawn from Varèse to Cowell to Cage could illustrate a progressively radical exploration of sound colours.

The linear paradigm works to create canonic figures and marginalize others. Canons imply an autonomous cultural development, and those who fail to participate in that particular development, or who seek alternatives, are marginalized, as were Korngold and Eisler for rejecting modernism. The linear paradigm is a means of defending a single authentic culture, but that requires a common practice and modernism failed to establish one.

Aesthetics cannot be easily divorced from social significance. Can anyone listen to those old recordings of castrati who survived into the twentieth century with an aesthetic sensibility unmoved by the knowledge that these singers were mutilated as children? Social factors affect our response to music in a variety of ways. For example, French concern at the lack of an operatic tradition, which led to the unearthing of Rameau's *Hippolyte et Aricie* early in the twentieth century, developed in the context of nationalism following a political defeat. Changing social factors affect our response to works which may have previously provoked quite different reactions: *Così fan tutte* is not the same after the cultural impact of the women's movement of the 1970s, and *Peter Grimes* has become problematic due to the greater awareness of child abuse that developed in the 1980s (we are no longer so ready to accept Grimes as a tortured idealist).

THE END OF THE 'INTERNATIONAL STYLE'

The belief in a universal aesthetic, that 'art music' transcends social and cultural context, lay behind the internationalist aspirations of modernism. Having developed his atonal style, Schoenberg gave voice to his conviction in 1910 that in ten years time every talented composer would be writing that way. Modernism was never internationalist in a **pluralist** sense, but in the sense of a *single* culture with *universal* values. Composers of different nationalities and different musical traditions were shown to be moving towards the same end, usually that of embracing twelve-note music.

The ambitions of modernist music towards internationalism have been overtaken by pop, which has already become a more widely accepted international style. The social history of our times is inseparable from pop music so that, measured in terms of social significance, the twelve-bar blues may be said to have been of greater importance to twentieth-century music than the twelve-note row. Today, after all the efforts expended by ethno-musicologists, it is difficult to avoid the conclusion that music is no more international than other forms of cultural expression.

RELATIVISM REPLACES UNIVERSALISM

Modernism, an attempt to defend one universalist culture, was often forced to attack regionalism as parochialism, nationalism as chauvinism, and popular music as entertainment not art. The postmodern alternative is to accept that we are living in an age of **cultural relativism**. Cultural relativism, a perspective taken from anthropology, has been the key to socio-musicological interpretation since the 1980s. The argument that cultural values could be historically located was already familiar and was expanded by the recognition that significance could also be socially located. The last idea fuelled the main argument against mass culture theory: that meaning could be made in the act of consumption, rather than consumption being simply passive.

STYLES AS DISCURSIVE CODES

Contrary to Stravinsky's opinion that expressive devices are established by convention within an autonomous musical practice, they are established as conventions through social practice and can be related to social changes. Musical meanings are not labels arbitrarily thrust upon abstract sounds; these sounds and their meanings originate in a social process and achieve their significance within a particular social context. Musical signifiers develop in tandem with society. The opening of Vivian Ellis's *Coronation Scot* uses no musical technique or dissonant vocabulary which would have surprised Beethoven, yet it is meaningless unless one is familiar with the sound of a steam train pulling away. The piece could not have been written before the advent of the steam locomotive. Indeed, what would boogie-woogie piano or much of the characteristic style of blues harmonica have been without trains?

Schoenberg's free atonal period can be related to the new science of psychoanalysis and **Freudian** investigations into the inner reaches of the human psyche. Expressionist artists envied the supposed power of music to express the composer's internal life. Just as the modernist painter Kandinsky spoke of 'inner necessity', Schoenberg placed his trust in 'unconscious logic'; yet, if atonality was historically inevitable, this trust was as much a corollary as a catalyst to his adopting a new musical language. Even so, it would appear odd that the development of an extreme chromatic language should coincide merely by chance with an expressionist interest in extreme emotional states.

At the same time, it is important to recognize that style codes have developed from the solidification of conventions and that these involve technical features as well as socially constituted meanings. Although style codes may be subject to further development and change, that cannot be achieved by rupturing, negating or contradicting their most important and defining attributes. The music-historical problem for jazz has been its resistance to assimilation into the Western 'art music' tradition because of fundamental aesthetic conflicts. The criteria for determining what is a beautiful or 'legitimate' style of singing and playing in jazz,

127

for example, are frequently at odds with the criteria that prevail in 'art music'. The classical operatic voice can be related to instrumental techniques and standards of beauty of tone production within that style. Jazz has its own range of associated vocal techniques, many of which are not found in classical music – scatting, growling, and smearing or bending notes – and can also be related to instrumental techniques within that style (for example, the use of a plunger mute to create a growling sound on trumpet or trombone). The existence of distinct musical style codes in the nineteenth century is made evident in the incompatibility of Beethoven's Viennese style with the Scottish airs he arranged.

An even more distinct style code, *piobaireachd* – a unique kind of bagpipe music that originated among the Gaelic communities of the Scottish Highlands and Islands – may be used to illustrate the way meaning depends on socio-cultural context rather than on universally valid musical devices. The interval of the tritone (that between fah and te in tonic sol-fa) conveyed emotional anguish to seventeenth-century Venetians, as we know from their madrigals and operas; yet, it evidently did not carry this meaning to seventeenth-century Scottish Highlanders. There is an old *piobaireachd* of uncertain date bearing the title 'Praise of Marion' (*Guileagag Moraig*) which, in one variation alone, contains twenty-nine tritones within thirty-two bars.

A final example of how style codes have their own conventions and construct their own meanings is revealed by comparing Richard Strauss's 'Dance of the Seven Veils' (from his opera *Salome*) with David Rose's 'The Stripper'. In the latter, one notes the quasi-vocal slides on trombone and the wailing tremolando on a 'blue' seventh followed by 'jungle' drums: these were among the devices developed originally by Ellington at the Cotton Club to signify the wild and the primitive for his white patrons, and which soon became associated with wild, predatory female sexuality. The eroticism of the Strauss, on the other hand, is encoded in the sensual richness (timbral and textural) of a huge orchestra, the quasi-Oriental (that is, exotic) embellishment of melody, and the devices of crescendo and quickening pace. However, it is surely no coincidence that, despite the anachronism, the Viennese waltz with its connotations of *fin de siècle* decadence lies just below the surface of the Strauss, as the foxtrot lies below that of the Rose. There is no sense, of course, in which one of these pieces of music is really sexier than the other; each encodes eroticism in a different way and for a different function. It would be just as ludicrous to imagine Strauss's 'Dance of the Seven Veils' in a seedy strip club as to imagine Rose's 'The Stripper' incorporated into *Salome*.

MEANING AS AN EFFECT OF DISCOURSE

Seeing seven colours in a rainbow is an effect of Newtonian **discourse**, Newton having added the colour indigo in his determination that a rainbow should have seven colours. Similarly, hearing an octave divided into twelve semitones is an effect of a particular Western musical discourse, that of equal temperament tuning. An empiricist would argue that a human subject acquires knowledge by observing or listening, but other cultures see five or six colours in a rainbow and divide an octave into intervals that differ from the Western classical norm. If a discourse divides the spectrum into certain named coloured segments, then those are the ones that are seen. If a musical discourse – that is, a domain of musical practice or a musical style – divides an octave into quarter tones, these may be perceived in another cultural context as out-of-tune notes or 'corrected' by the ear to the nearest acceptable pitch.

EMPHASIS ON RECEPTION AND SUBJECT POSITION

It has become important to ask who the implied audience might be for a piece of music. Whom do Nanci Griffith, Shirley Bassey and Kiri Te Kanawa think they are singing to? The way the music sounds may indicate that it is intended, for example, for a salon, a concert hall, or outdoors. If so, this may have affected the composition in terms of form and instrumentation. Beethoven's folk-song arrangements for piano, violin and cello suggest he has a salon concert in mind. Certain ensembles carry greater status than others: for example, a string quartet would be regarded in some circles as more refined and 'elevated' than a saxophone quartet no matter what music was played. Some of the Edinburgh bourgeoisie may well have found Beethoven's Scottish folk-song arrangements convincing, since they sought a 'refined' or 'improved' version of their musical heritage. The subject position one occupies can radically affect reception: until the 1980s, few critics in the West recognized the extent of Shostakovitch's use of **irony** in his music.

THE DISAPPEARING 'REAL', THE SIMULACRUM AND PROBLEMS OF AUTHENTICITY

With poststructuralism, notions of an 'inner essence' and a 'real' disappear. 'Authenticity' can be seen to be constructed as one more style: values of truth and authenticity will be set up in the dress codes and styles of singing of performers (folk singers do not wear pin-stripe suits), perhaps in the instruments they play (for example, acoustic instruments tend to signify such values better than electronic instruments). A performer who can be pinned down to a particular image, such as Bruce Springsteen, will communicate a deeper impression of authenticity than a performer who plays multiple roles, such as David Bowie. Yet karaoke singers can pour their hearts out in a quick succession of styles, being Sinatra for one song and Elvis for the next.

In some areas of music there are examples of **Baudrillard**'s **simulacra**, where there is not even an attempt to be real, or where reality has been appropriated by a fiction. The 'jungle music' created by Ellington's band for the Cotton Club, or Hollywood 'cowboy songs' are ready examples. A more complex matter is **Orientalist** music. In spite of the differences that developed over the years in

Western **representations** of the East in music, successive Orientalist styles tended to relate to previous Orientalist styles more closely than they did to Eastern ethnic practices. It is not surprising, because Orientalist music is not a poor imitation of another cultural practice: its purpose is not to imitate but to represent. Representations, however, rely upon culturally learned recognition, which may have much to do with a person's existing knowledge of Western signifiers of the East and little to do with the objective conditions of non-Western musical practices. Indeed, something new may be brought into being, displacing and standing in for the Orient. This can happen whenever music is taken from its home culture into another. Some of the Native American chants on the popular album *Sacred Spirit* of 1995 are given ambient or 'chill out' arrangements, while others are 'housed up' with looped patterns and other features that lend them the character of late twentieth-century dance electronica.

The emphasis on **hybridity** in **postcolonial** studies (much indebted to the arguments of Homi **Bhabha**) demands that musical traditions be examined as mixtures and fusions of styles rather than being analysed in search of 'authentic' features, unadulterated by the impact of **globalization** or a former colonizing presence. Although this enables a reconsideration of, say, South African choralism or Bollywood film music, a problem remains in the term 'hybridity', since it can itself imply the existence of pure strains – as every gardener who has grown F1 hybrids knows.

Musicology has also had to take on board the lessons of **Derrida**'s **deconstruction**, which is concerned with demonstrating the privileging of one term over another in metaphysical oppositions. There is no longer a case to be made for supposedly 'pure' music. Even the music of a composer like Bruckner can be deconstructed to expose ideological assumptions behind what may seem to be abstract musico-logical choices. In his music, meaning is created by differing and deferring (Derrida's *différance*): minor is governed by major and therefore the minor opening of the Third Symphony is not mistaken for the dominant term; we know major will triumph. Minor is *always* the antithesis – but not a true antithesis, because Bruckner privileges major over minor.

DEATH OF THE COMPOSER AS ORIGINATING GENIUS

Music technology, especially sampling, which allows existing sounds to be recorded and reused or manipulated at will has had a major impact on ideas of originality, creativity and ownership. So has the wide availability of pre-programmed features on sound modules, synthesizers, drum machines and keyboards. The producers and DJs in Hip-Hop, House, Techno and Underground Dance, who select parts of records, add sounds, blend features, combine tracks, restructure or remix, eat away at notions of **authorship**. We must also recognize that postmodernist theory, **poststructuralism** and deconstruction have strongly challenged notions of organic unity and the composer's expressive **presence** within his or her music. The use of sampling technology shifts the focus from new *creation* to new *use* of material. In her own person, Madonna has reused existing images and taken on multiple identities in contrast to the stable identity of earlier stars (and of some of her contemporaries, like Bruce Springsteen). Pop music revels in **intertextuality** and the circulation of meanings (for example, through merchandizing). Music is one among its many attributes and not always its most important one, since dance routines, fashion, image, persona creation, special effects, the performance event and its context may each take precedence at one time or another.

POSTMODERN MUSICOLOGY

The rise since the 1990s of 'feminist musicology', 'critical musicology', and 'gay and lesbian musicology' prompts the idea that, instead of there being alternative musicologies, we may be witnessing the disintegration of musicology as a discipline. Perhaps the unitary concept of a discipline is part of a now discredited paradigm for musicological thought. The alternative is to view musicology no longer as an autonomous field of academic inquiry but, in the French psychoanalyst and **semiotician** Julia **Kristeva**'s terms, a field of transpositions of various signifying systems. Critical musicology has revealed what it means to regard musicology as an *intertextual field*, and why this, rather than the notion of a *discipline*, offers a more productive framework for research.

In the late 1980s, a New Musicology developed in the USA amid concerns about the presumption in much historical and systematic musicology that music could be studied autonomously, rather than in a historical and cultural context. In the UK, a Critical Musicology Group was founded (1993) to discuss the importance of critique, including the critique of musicology itself. Critical and New Musicologists wished to explore the socially constituted values of music. In doing so, a variety of methodologies and analytic tools are brought into play: these range from Marxist-influenced cultural sociology to semiotic, post-structuralist and postmodernist theories, Derrida's deconstructive manoeuvres, the discourse analysis of Michel Foucault, and the psychoanalytic insights of Sigmund Freud, Jacques **Lacan** and Julia Kristeva.

Postmodern musicology refuses to be restricted to analysing the formal workings of music and compiling data on the influences of one composer on another; it is keen to address questions of extrinsic meaning in music. There are those who focus on individual works, teasing out their wordy meanings, while others reject close readings, seeking, instead, a radical contextualization of musical production and a deeper understanding of how music is experienced by performers and listeners. The most recent disagreements are between those who look to the way music interacts with everyday life, and those who strive to reveal ideological meanings embedded in the music – often the former return to the empirical models of research that poststructuralism rejected (empiricism being 'the matrix of all faults menacing a discourse' for Derrida).

One of the biggest problems facing current musicology is the disintegration of high and low as aesthetic values, something that has, of course, had an impact already in other subject areas: consider how far **cultural studies** has encroached upon English as an academic discipline. What musicology needs now is a new theoretical model capable of embracing all music. A brief outline of what this might look like is given below.

- A concern with social and cultural processes, informed by arguments that musical practices, values and meanings relate to particular historical, political and cultural contexts.

- A concern with critical theory and with developing a musical hermeneutics for the analysis of the values and meanings of musical practices and musical texts.

- A concern to avoid teleological assumptions of historical narrative (e.g. the 'inevitability' of atonality). Causal narration in musical historiography has been found problematic: **genealogical** lines connecting one composer (or musical style) with another are forever being redrawn or erased, and new musical styles are occasionally presented as if they sprang up fully formed (for example, jazz in New Orleans).

- A readiness to engage with, rather than marginalize, issues of class, generation, gender, sexuality and ethnicity in music, and to address matters such as production, reception and subject position, while questioning notions of genius, canons, universality, aesthetic autonomy and **textual** immanence (the idea, for example, that a 'spirit of the times' exists within the musical composition).

- A readiness to study different cultures with regard to their own specific cultural values, so that a cultural arbitrary is not misrecognized as an objective truth, but also to recognize the necessity of extending the terms of such study beyond explicit cultural self-evaluation.

- A readiness to consider that meanings are intertextual, and that it may be necessary to examine a broad range of discourses in order to explain music, its contexts and the way it functions within them. For example, questions of music and sexuality cannot be considered in isolation from political, biological, psychological, psychoanalytical and aesthetic discourses. There may be no intention, however, to document each area comprehensively.

- A readiness to respond to the multiplicity of music's contemporary functions and meanings (for example, the fusions of practices variously described as 'time-based arts' and 'multimedia arts'). This may be achieved by adopting the epistemological position and methodology outlined above (one requiring intertextual study and the blurring of discipline boundaries); it contrasts with a narrow discipline-based study of music as performance art or as composition (typically represented by the printed score).

14

POSTMODERNISM AND POPULAR CULTURE

JOHN STOREY

Most contributions to the debate on **postmodernism** agree that whatever else it is or might be, postmodernism has something to do with the development of popular culture in the late twentieth century in the advanced capitalist democracies of the West. That is, whether postmodernism is seen as a new historical moment, a new sensibility or a new cultural style, popular culture is cited as a terrain on which these changes can be most readily found.

It is in the late 1950s and early 1960s that we see the beginnings of what is now understood as postmodernism. In the work of the American cultural critic, Susan Sontag (*Against Interpretation* (1966)), we encounter the celebration of what she calls a 'new sensibility'. As she explains: 'One important consequence of the new sensibility [is] that the distinction between "high" and "low" culture seems less and less meaningful.'

The postmodern 'new sensibility' rejected the cultural elitism of **modernism**. Although it often 'quoted' popular culture, modernism was marked by a deep suspicion of all things popular. Its entry into the museum and the academy as official culture was undoubtedly made easier (despite its declared antagonism to 'bourgeois philistinism') by its appeal to, and homologous relationship with, the elitism of class society. The response of the postmodern 'new sensibility' to modernism's canonization was a re-evaluation of popular culture. The postmodernism of the late 1950s and early 1960s was therefore in part a populist attack on the elitism of modernism. It signalled a refusal of what Andreas Huyssen in *After the Great Divide* (1986) calls 'the great divide . . . [a] **discourse** which insists on the categorical distinction between high art and mass culture'. Moreover, according to Huyssen, 'To a large extent, it is by the distance we have travelled from this "great divide" between mass culture and modernism that we can measure our own cultural **postmodernity**.' The American and British pop art movement of the 1950s and the 1960s, with its rejection of the distinction between popular and high culture, is postmodernism's first cultural flowering. As pop art's first theorist Lawrence Alloway explains:

> The area of contact was mass produced urban culture: movies, advertising, science fiction, pop music. We felt none of the dislike of commercial culture standard among most intellectuals, but accepted it as a fact, discussed it in detail, and consumed it enthusiastically. One result of our discussions was to take pop culture out of the realm of 'escapism', 'sheer entertainment', 'relaxation', and to treat it with the seriousness of art.
>
> (quoted in John Storey, ed., *Cultural Theory and Popular Culture* (2001))

Seen from this perspective, postmodernism first emerges out of a generational refusal of the categorical certainties of high modernism. The insistence on an absolute distinction between high and popular culture came to be regarded as the 'unhip' assumption of an older generation. One sign of this collapse can be seen in the merging of art and pop music. For example, Peter Blake designed the cover of the Beatles' 'Sergeant Pepper's Lonely Hearts Club Band'; Richard Hamilton designed the cover of their 'white album'; Andy Warhol designed the cover of the Rolling Stones' album 'Sticky Fingers'.

By the mid-1980s, the postmodern 'new sensibility' had become a condition and for many a reason to despair. According to Jean-François **Lyotard** the postmodern condition is marked by a crisis in the status of knowledge in Western societies. This is expressed as incredulity towards '**metanarratives**', such as God, **Marxism**, scientific progress. Steven Connor (*Postmodernist Culture* (1989)) suggests that Lyotard's analysis may be read 'as a disguised allegory of the condition of academic knowledge and institutions in the contemporary world'. Lyotard's 'diagnosis of the postmodern condition is, in one sense, the diagnosis of the final futility of the intellectual'. Lyotard is himself aware of what he calls the contemporary intellectual's 'negative heroism'. Intellectuals have, he argues, been losing their authority since 'the violence and critique mounted against the academy during the sixties'. Iain Chambers (*Popular Culture* (1988)) makes much the same point but from a different perspective. He argues that the debate over postmodernism can in part be understood as

> the symptom of the disruptive ingression of popular culture, its aesthetics and intimate possibilities, into a previously privileged domain. Theory and academic discourses are confronted by the wider, unsystemized, popular networks of cultural production and knowledge. The intellectual's privilege to explain and distribute knowledge is threatened.

Like Chambers, Angela McRobbie (*Postmodernism and Popular Culture* (1994)) welcomes postmodernism, seeing it as 'the coming into being of those whose voices were historically drowned out by the (modernist) metanarratives of mastery, which were in turn both patriarchal and imperialist'. Postmodernism, she argues, has enfranchised a new body of intellectuals: voices from the margins speaking from positions of **difference** – ethnic, gender, class, sexual preference; those whom she refers to as 'the new generation of intellectuals (often black, female, or working class)'. Kobena Mercer (*Welcome to the Jungle* (1994)) makes a similar point, seeing postmodernism as in part an unacknowledged response to 'the emerging voices, practices and identities of dispersed African, Caribbean and Asian peoples [who have] crept in from the margins of post-imperial Britain to dislocate commonplace certainties and consensual "truths" and thus open up new ways of seeing, and understanding'.

For Jean **Baudrillard** (*Simulations* (1983)), **hyperrealism** is the characteristic mode of postmodernity. In the realm of the hyperreal, the 'real' and the imaginary continually implode into each other. The result is that reality and what Baudrillard calls '**simulations**' are experienced as without difference – operating along a roller-coaster continuum. Simulations can often be experienced as more real than the real itself – 'even better than the real thing', in the words of the U2 song. The evidence for hyperrealism is said to be everywhere. For example, we in the West live in a world in which people write letters addressed to characters in soap operas, making them offers of marriage, sympathizing with their current difficulties, offering them new accommodation, or just writing to ask how they are coping with life. Television villains are regularly confronted in the street and warned about the possible future consequences of not altering their behaviour. Television doctors, television lawyers and television detectives regularly receive requests for advice and help. Baudrillard calls this 'the dissolution of TV into life, the dissolution of life into TV'.

John Fiske claims in *Media Matters* (1994) that postmodern media no longer provide 'secondary **representations** of reality; they affect and produce the reality that they mediate'. Moreover, in our postmodern world, all events that 'matter' are media events. He cites the example of the arrest of O. J. Simpson:

> Local people watching the chase on TV went to O. J.'s house to be there at the showdown, but took their portable TVs with them in the knowledge that the live event was not a substitute for the mediated one but a complement to it. On seeing themselves on their own TVs, they waved to themselves, for postmodern people have no problem in being simultaneously and indistinguishably livepeople and mediapeople.

These people knew implicitly that the media do not simply report or circulate the news, they produce it. Therefore, in order to be part of the news of O. J. Simpson's arrest, it was not enough to be there, one had to be there on television. In the hyperreal world of the postmodern, there is no longer a clear distinction between a 'real' event and its media representation. In the same way, O. J. Simpson's trial cannot be neatly separated into a 'real' event that television then represented as a media event. Anyone who watched the proceedings unfold on TV knows that the trial was conducted at least as much for the television audience as it was for those present in the court. Without the presence of the cameras this would have been a very different event indeed.

Fredric **Jameson** is an American Marxist cultural critic who has written a number of very influential essays on postmodernism. According to his account postmodernism is a culture of pastiche, disfigured by the 'complacent play of historical allusion'. Postmodern culture is 'a world in which stylistic innovation is no longer possible, all that is left is to imitate dead styles, to speak through the masks and with the voices of the styles in the imaginary museum'. Rather than a culture of pristine creativity, postmodern culture is a culture of quotations. Instead of 'original' cultural production, we have cultural production born out of other cultural production. It is a culture 'of flatness or depthlessness, a new kind of superficiality in the most literal sense'. A culture of images and surfaces, without 'latent' possibilities, it derives its hermeneutic force from other images, other surfaces. Jameson acknowledges that modernism itself often 'quoted' from other cultures and other historical moments, but he insists that there is a fundamental difference – postmodern cultural texts do not just quote other cultures, other historical moments, they randomly cannibalize them to the point where any sense of critical or historical distance ceases to exist – there is only pastiche.

Perhaps Jameson's best-known example of the postmodern culture of pastiche is what he calls the 'nostalgia film'. The category could include a number of films from the 1980s and 1990s: *Back to the Future I* and *II*, *Peggy Sue Got Married*, *Rumble Fish*, *Angel Heart*, *Blue Velvet*. He argues that the nostalgia film sets out to recapture the atmosphere and stylistic peculiarities of America in the 1950s. But the nostalgia film is not just another name for the historical film. This is clearly demonstrated by the fact that Jameson's own list includes the *Star Wars* films. Now it might seem strange to suggest that films about the future can be nostalgic for the past, but as Jameson explains in 'Postmodernism and Consumer Society' (H. Foster, ed., *Postmodern Culture* (1985)), *Star Wars* 'does not reinvent a picture of the past in its lived totality; rather, [it reinvents] the feel and shape of characteristic art objects of an older period'.

Films such as *Raiders of the Lost Ark*, *Independence Day*, *Robin Hood, Prince of Thieves*, the *Lord of the Rings* trilogy, and *Pirates of the Caribbean*, operate in a similar way to evoke a sense of the **narrative** certainties of the past. In this way, according to Jameson, the nostalgia film either recaptures and represents the atmosphere and stylistic features of the past and/or recaptures and represents certain styles of viewing of the past. What is of absolute significance for Jameson ('Postmodernism, or the Cultural Logic of Late Capitalism', *New Left Review* (1984)) is that such films do not attempt to recapture or represent the 'real' past, but always make do with certain cultural myths and stereotypes about the past. They offer what he calls 'false realism': films about other films, representations of other representations (what Baudrillard calls simulations). In this way, history is effaced by 'historicism . . . the random cannibalization of all the styles of the past, the play of random stylistic allusion'.

Austin Powers: The Spy Who Shagged Me could be cited as an example of the random cannibalization of the past. As Mike Myers (the film's writer, producer and principal star) himself explains, 'I'm a police composite of every comedian I've ever liked, Peter Sellers, Alec Guinness, Dan Aykroyd, John Belushi, Woody Allen, *Monty Python*, *The Goodies*, the British TV show *Some Mothers Do 'Ave 'Em*, *On the Buses*, the *Carry On* films'. Moreover, Myers' account of the origins of *Austin Powers* could also be cited as evidence of Jameson's argument about the random cannibalization of the past,

I just love the conventions of James Bond and sixties movies. *Wayne's World* is everything I was, growing up in the suburbs of Toronto in the mid-seventies, *Austin Powers* is everything I watched [on TV in the late sixties]. My parents were from

Liverpool, and there's no one more English than an Englishman who no longer lives there. Every molecule of British culture that came across the Atlantic was tasted and worshipped.

Around 1994, I was driving and listening to Burt Bacharach's 'The Look of Love', which is so sixties. And it made me think of all those cult TV shows. I went back home and I wrote the original *Austin Powers* script in just three weeks. . . . I mean, this stuff is coming direct from my childhood.

(Quoted in John Storey, 'The Sixties in the Nineties',
in Bill Ogersby and Anna Gough-Yates, eds, *Action TV* (2001))

Similarly, Quentin **Tarantino** describes *Kill Bill* as 'a combination of kung fu movies, Japanese pop samurai cinema, Chinese wuxia films, spaghetti westerns, female blaxploitation flicks, along with revenge movies in general'.

Popular culture (television, pop music, cinema, fashion, etc.) has always recycled its own history (remakes, revivals, cover versions, comebacks, etc.). Rapid advances in technology (for example, the technologies of 'sampling', the introduction of cable, satellite and digital television, the film-on-video/DVD market) have in recent years rapidly expanded and accelerated this process. But are the textual results of this process best understood using the term pastiche? 'Sampling' is a favourite example of what Jameson (and those who share his perspective) understand as postmodern pastiche. But, as Andrew Goodwin ('Popular Music and Postmodern Theory', *Cultural Studies*, 5:2 (1991)) points out, with particular reference to pop music, what is often missed in such claims is the way in which sampling is used:

these critical strategies miss both the historicizing function of sampling tech-nologies in contemporary pop and the ways in which textual incorporation cannot be adequately understood as 'blank parody'. We need categories to add to pastiche, which demonstrate how contemporary pop opposes, celebrates and promotes the texts it steals from.

Goodwin insists that sampling is often 'used to invoke history and authenticity' and that 'it has often been overlooked that the "quoting" of sounds and styles acts to historicize contemporary culture'. In the main, pop music still tends to operate with an aesthetic which drifts between Romanticism's tortured genius and modernism's avant-garde artist. Because of this, sampling is rarely, if ever, done as a form of pastiche (or even parody); samples are incorporated into the 'organic whole' in much the same way as occurs in T. S. Eliot's classic monument to modernist poetic practice *The Waste Land* (1922).

There is a sense in which what is being claimed as postmodern about popular culture is really only an acceleration and intensification of what has been happening in the traditions of popular entertainment since at least the nineteenth century. In other words, what Jameson (and others like him) identify as post-modern culture has always been a feature of modern popular culture. As David Chaney observes, the privileged qualities of postmodernism – parody/pastiche, depthlessness, allegory, spectacular show, and an **ironic** celebration of artifice – have all been central to the submerged traditions of popular culture. One has only to think of the traditions of music and vaudeville, the fair-ground, the circus and pantomime, the melodramatic theatre and the literatures of crime and romance to find all these qualities clearly displayed.

(The Cultural Turn (1994))

Elizabeth Wilson makes a similar point with regard to fashion: 'some of the themes and hallmarks of what is today termed postmodernism have been around for a long, long time' ('Fashion and Postmodernism', in J. Storey, ed., *Cultural Theory and Popular Culture: A Reader* (1998)). She maintains that 'Fashion [which she describes 'as the most popular aesthetic practice of all'] . . . has relied on pastiche and the recycling of styles throughout the industrial period.' More generally, she contends,

This evidence [especially Hollywood film from the 1920s onwards] from the past that pastiche and nostalgia have been pervasive in popular culture throughout the twentieth century and indeed earlier appears to contradict Jameson's belief that 'nostalgia mode' is peculiarly a feature of his postmodern era.

The play of, and playing with, **intertextuality**, a feature shared by both the **texts** of the postmodern and the traditions of popular entertainment, is not, therefore, something which can be understood using only the concepts of pastiche or nostalgic recycling. As Chaney observes,

Popular entertainment may be structured by the reiteration of certain formulas and genres which provide staple narrative forms, and there may be endless nostalgic regression in re-cycling previous eras and styles, but even so there will be an overwhelming need for novelty in performance, styles and manners. The history of popular music since the development of cheap recordings as a medium of mass entertainment specifically targeted at youth audiences has shown this clearly.

(The Cultural Turn)

The intertextual understood as a form of borrowing from what already exists is always also (at least potentially) a making new from combinations of what is old. In this way, popular culture is, and has always been, about more than a pastiche or a nostalgic recycling of what has been before. I quoted earlier, in a discussion of Jameson's notion of pastiche, Mike Myers' account of the origins of *Austin Powers*. Other things he has to say about how he came to write the two films point to something more complex than pastiche – a certain kind of parody, not of the sixties but of a particular way of understanding the sixties. As Myers explains,

The movie isn't about the 60s. If anything it's about straight culture's view of the 60s. It's like Matt Helm [secret agent played by Dean Martin in *The Silencers* (1965), *Murderer's Row* (1966), *The Ambushers* (1967), and *The Wrecking Crew*

(1969)]. Dean Martin was a man of the 40s and 50s thrust into the context of the 60s and having to deal with all these liberated young people. That was his response to it, it wasn't pot it was booze. It's something I noticed with my dad. He had mutton chops and dyed hair and he put in a bar downstairs at our house. He was like, 'Hey, I'm still a swinger.' It's the whole world of straight culture going, 'I'm with it. Like the kids, you know?' That's what the whole *Austin Powers* thing is about . . . *Austin Powers* is like a huge in-joke that I never thought anyone else would get.

(Quoted in Storey, 'The Sixties in the Nineties')

There may, therefore, be a certain (postmodern) irony in Jameson's complaint about nostalgia effacing history, given that his own critique is structured by a profound nostalgia for modernist 'certainty', promoted, as it is, at the expense of detailed historical understanding of the traditions of popular entertainment.

According to Jim Collins ('Genericity in the Nineties', in Jim Collins *et al.*, eds, *Film Theory Goes to the Movies* (1993)), part of what is postmodern about Western societies is the fact that the old is not simply replaced by the new, but is recycled for circulation together with the new. As he explains, 'The ever-expanding number of texts and technologies is both a reflection of and a significant contribution to the "array" – the perpetual circulation and recirculation of **signs** that forms the fabric of postmodern cultural life.' He argues that 'This foregrounded, hyperconscious intertextuality reflects changes in terms of audience competence and narrative technique, as well as a fundamental shift in what constitutes both entertainment and cultural literacy in [postmodern culture].' As a consequence of this, 'Narrative action now operates at two levels simultaneously – in reference to character adventure and in reference to a text's adventures in the array of contemporary cultural production.'

Collins argues that the appeal of films which self-consciously make reference to and borrow from different genres of film is that they appeal to (and help constitute) an audience of knowing bricoleurs, who take pleasure from this and other forms of **bricolage**. Similarly, Brooker and Brooker (*Postmodern After-Images* (1997)), following Collins, see the development of 'a new historical sense . . . the shared pleasure of intertextual recognition, the critical effect of play with narrative conventions, character and cultural stereotypes, and the **power** rather than passivity of nostalgia'.

Brooker and Brooker argue that Quentin Tarantino's films, for example,

can be seen as reactivating jaded conventions and audience alike, enabling a more active nostalgia and intertextual exploration than a term such as 'pastiche', which has nowhere to go but deeper into the recycling factory, implies. Instead of 'pastiche', we might think of 're-writing' or 're-viewing' and, in terms of the spectator's experience, of the 're-activation' and 're-configuration' of a given generational 'structure of feeling' within a more dynamic and varied set of histories.

They point to the ways in which Tarantino's work presents an 'aesthetic of recycling . . . an affirmative "bringing back to life", a "making new"'.

The widespread eclecticism of postmodern culture is encouraging and helping to produce what Collins calls the 'sophisticated bricoleur' of postmodern culture. For example, a television series like *Twin Peaks*, both constitutes an audience as bricoleurs and in turn is watched by an audience who celebrate its bricolage.

> Postmodernist eclecticism might only occasionally be a preconceived design choice in individual programs, but it is built into the technologies of media sophisticated societies. Thus television, like the postmodern **subject**, must be conceived as a site – an intersection of multiple, conflicting cultural messages. Only by recognizing this interdependency of bricolage and eclecticism can we come to appreciate the profound changes in the relationship of reception and production in postmodern cultures. Not only has reception become another form of meaning production, but production has increasingly become a form of reception as it rearticulates antecedent and competing forms of representation.
>
> (*Film Theory Goes to the Movies*)

In a similar way, Umberto **Eco**, drawing on Charles **Jencks**' notion of '**double coding**', identifies a postmodern sensibility exhibited in an awareness of what he calls the 'already said'. He gives the example of a man who cannot tell his lover 'I love you madly', out of fear that it might produce only ridicule, and so says instead: 'As Barbara Cartland would put it, I love you madly' (Umberto Eco, *Reflections on 'The Name of the Rose'* (1984)). Given that we now live in an increasingly media-saturated world, the 'already said' is, as Collins observes, 'still being said'; for example, in the way television (in a effort to fill the space opened up by the growth in satellite and cable channels) recycles its own accumulated past, and that of cinema, and broadcasts these alongside what is new in both media. But how the past is articulated in the present is always as much to do with the present as the past. Collins provides this example of different strategies of articulation:

> The Christian Broadcasting Network and Nickelodeon both broadcast series from the late fifties and early sixties, but whereas the former presents these series as a model for family entertainment the way it used to be, the latter offers them as fun for the contemporary family, 'camped up' with parodic voice-overs, super-graphics, re-editing designed to deride their quaint vision of American family life, which we all know never really existed even 'back then'.
>
> (*Film Theory Goes to the Movies*)

There can be little doubt that similar things are happening in, for example, music, television, advertising, fashion, and in the different lived cultures of everyday life. It is not a sign that there has been a general collapse of the distinctions people make between, say, high culture/low culture, past/present, history/nostalgia, fiction/reality; but it is a sign that such distinctions (first noticed in the late 1950s and early 1960s, and gradually more so ever since) are becoming increasingly less important, less obvious, less taken for granted. But this does not of course mean that such distinctions cannot be, and are not being, articulated and mobilized for particular strategies of social distinction. The presence of the past in the present is the result of many different articulations, and we should not take any of these at face value; we must always be alert to the what, why and for whom something is being articulated, and how it can always be articulated differently, in other contexts.

Postmodernism has disturbed many of the old certainties surrounding questions of cultural value. It has become somewhat of a commonplace to demonstrate how canons of value form and re-form in response to the social and political concerns of those with cultural power. To the less watchful eye, the changes often seem insignificant – changes at the perimeters, relative stability at the core – but even when the canonical texts remain the same, how and why they are valued certainly changes. So much so that they are hardly the same texts from one historical moment to the next. As the Four Tops put it, in a slightly different context: 'It's the same old song / But with a different meaning since you've been gone.' Or to put it in a less danceable discourse, the cultural text under the sign of the postmodern is not the source of value, but a site where the construction of value – variable values – can take place.

Perhaps the most significant thing about postmodernism for the student of popular culture is the recognition that there is no absolute categorical difference between high and popular culture. This is not to say that one text or practice might not be 'better' (for what/for whom, etc., must always be decided and made clear) than another text or practice. But it is to say that there are no longer any easy reference points that will automatically preselect for us the good from the bad. Some might regard such a situation (or even the description of such a situation) with horror – the end of standards. On the contrary, without easy recourse to fixed categories of value, it calls for rigorous, if always contingent, standards, if our task is to separate the good from the bad, the usable from the obsolete, the progressive from the reactionary. As John Fekete points out in *Life after Postmodernism* (1987):

> The prospect of learning to be at ease with limited warranties, and with the responsibility for issuing them, without the false security of inherited guarantees, is promising for a livelier, more colourful, more alert, and, one hopes, more tolerant culture that draws enjoyment from the dappled relations between meaning and value.

Fekete's point is not significantly different from the argument made by Susan Sontag in *Against Interpretation* at the birth of the postmodern 'new sensibility'. As she explains:

> From the vantage point of this new sensibility, the beauty of a machine or of the solution to a mathematical problem, of a painting by Jasper Johns, of a film by Jean-Luc Godard, and of the personalities and music of the Beatles is equally accessible.

Postmodernism has certainly changed the theoretical and the cultural basis on which to think about popular culture. In fact, the collapse of the distinction (if this is the case) between high and popular culture may signify that at last it may be possible to use the term popular culture and mean nothing more than culture liked by many people.

15

POSTMODERNISM, MODERNITY AND THE TRADITION OF DISSENT

LLOYD SPENCER

It is perhaps characteristic of our age – the age of designer labels, when almost every aspect of culture and identity seems amenable to 'packaging' – that there should be such a fearsome fuss over the label '**postmodern**'. As the novelist and critic, Gilbert Adair notes in *The Postmodernist always Rings Twice* (1992), few 'isms' have provoked as much perplexity and suspicion as postmodernism.

The very term 'postmodern' is a paradox and a provocation. **Modernity**, in the sense of the 'now' which surrounds us, is not something we can be 'post'. But the modernity referred to is not the 'now' of the thoroughly modern. Modernity is more usefully thought of as a long epoch of historical change, fuelled by scientific and technological development and dominated by the spread – *extensively* across the world and *intensively* into every nook and cranny of the soul – of the capitalist market economy. Throughout the modern era, cultural, philosophical and political debates have marked out an intellectual space between the declining authority of the church on the one hand and, on the other, the economic and technical imperatives forcing the pace of change.

Modernity, even in this sense of a centuries-old tradition of change and debate about change, can hardly be said to have come to an end. In the industrial West the declining role of religion and the pace of economic and technological change are factors which will shape the future as decisively as they have shaped our past. But something has changed in the very nature of tradition and in the way that we relate to the past. Every aspect of the past is made accessible, available. But it is *made* available, mediated, packaged, presented and re-presented. Postmodernism could be described as that variant of **modernism** which has given up hope of freeing itself from the ravages of modernity or of mastering the forces unleashed by modernity.

Modernity – however it is conceived – had a history several centuries old before it came to be formulated under the label of 'modernity'. Modernism in art was echoed in the debates that arose in philosophy and social theory. But it should not be forgotten that there were reactionary modernisms as well as progressive, and that most forms of modernism were a compound of quite disparate, ill-assorted, even contradictory, ideas. If modernism implies enthusiasm about some aspects of modernity, it was usually accomplished – in the same writers, in the same works – by despair at other aspects of modernity. Modernism is as much an antidote to modernity as it is its party programme.

If we choose to call these times we live in 'postmodern' then we have to recognize as 'postmodern' intellectuals of an equally wide variety of cultural and political orientations. That at least should be clear from the variety of positions and postures, beliefs and commitments evidenced in this volume. If 'postmodernity' is a way of describing the times in which we live, then we may justly characterize as 'postmodernism' a diverse range of responses to those times. We use labels such as 'modernity' and 'modernism' to refer to historical epochs and trends which we feel constrained to grasp *in their complexity*. The 'postmodernity' of our own time demands similarly to be viewed in its complexity.

Our own postmodern age is extraordinarily self-conscious. It subjects itself to the most glaring scrutiny and to endless commentary. Writers, theologians and artists have their part in this process, as do academics and other intellectuals. So far the cast-list of these scrutinizers and commentators is a familiar one. What has changed is the role of these agents in the age of the mass media. The postmodern era is one in which cultural activity is dominated by media industries capable of appealing directly to a public (itself the beneficiary of 'mass education') over the heads of any cultural elite.

Mass media and the culture industries, informatics and cybernetics, **virtual reality** and an obsession with 'image' – the changes in the increasingly synthetic fabric of social life is mapped by postmodernists and their detractors in remarkably similar ways. Postmodernists present postmodernism as the set of critical tools needed to grasp and criticize new and changing circumstances. For critics of postmodernism the very 'appropriateness' of postmodernist ideas is the ground for suspicion. Some postmodernists (**Baudrillard** is the obvious example) write in a style that is ostentatiously 'postmodern' when they write about postmodernism. The close fit between the tools of criticism and the circumstances criticized opens postmodernists to the accusation – which has been often repeated – that their thinking is itself symptomatic of the ills which need to be diagnosed.

Postmodernism, like modernism before it, has produced a profusion of definitions and redefinitions. Readers who come to this volume in search of clear and stable definitions may begin to feel a sense of vertigo as they explore the entries. Not only does what counts as 'postmodern' change from writer to writer, but what is 'meant' by most other terms depends on who is doing the 'meaning', and what they mean by 'meaning'.

One of the symptoms of the 'postmodern condition' is a hypersensitivity to the ways in which words are strategically defined and polemically deployed. In the early years of the twentieth century, the poets of high modernism seemed each to produce their own virtual thesaurus of the language. Now, towards the end of the century, sociologists and other theorists have been made aware of the constraints imposed by language and engage in related processes of linguistic gymnastics (or linguistic mud-wrestling).

Not only are 'postmodernism', 'postmodernity' and 'the postmodern' difficult to define, but like their ('modern') counterparts, they refer to processes of definition and redefinition. At the heart of debates concerning modernism/postmodernism lies the question of 'meaning' itself (or of *The Meaning of 'Meaning'*) and a host of heated arguments over the meanings of particular key terms (including the various cognates of 'the modern' and 'the postmodern'). The result is that in many contemporary debates these labels (and their cognates) obscure more than they clarify. Inherently vague, ambiguous and slippery, these terms are continually used in conflicting and even contradictory ways. Even when this confusion is acknowledged, there seems to be no simple way out of the maze – and no route back to a simpler clear view of the intellectual landscape.

Dissenting from postmodernity is difficult for at least three, interrelated reasons. First, postmodernity is still so amorphous. Although it is all but ubiquitous it remains ill-defined. Second, the 'postmodern' emerges into fierce debates about the role of language and almost all commentators self-consciously deploy their terms and definitions with strategic, often combative intention. On all sides, agreeing the terms of the debate is less important than acting politically on and in the domain of language itself. The result is a multiplicity of competing definitions of postmodernity. Third, dissent from postmodernism is especially difficult because postmodernism – the awkward label announces this at very least – is itself so thoroughly imbued with the spirit of dissent. By constantly striking an attitude of dissent, postmodernism both declares its **difference** from a previous tradition of dissent – modernism – and at the same time accentuates the attitude which it shares with its predecessor. Postmodernism is always having it both ways: it is both the definitive end and overcoming of modernism and, at the same time, modernism under new management.

Although it has become established in cultural and intellectual discussion over recent decades, the term 'postmodernity' has never gained any precise or clear definition; it has gained currency instead as a vague and all-embracing notion referring to a wide variety of ways in which we have succeeded to the ambiguous legacy of modernity and of its late apologists, the modernists. Postmodernism is much less a programme or intellectual framework than it is a mood or *Stimmung* – the Zeitgeist, a 'feeling in the air'.

If postmodernism can be most accurately described as a certain mood or *Stimmung*, then it is one characterized by ambivalence and uncertainty, or what Lyotard calls a 'slackening'. Postmodernism did not announce itself bravely and proudly but seems to have slunk onto the horizon. Postmodernism has been characterized by dissent and disillusionment in equal measure. Although some of the products or manifestations which are grouped under the heading of postmodernism are playful or joyous, 'postmodernism' always seems to revert to an attitude more often associated with that of an awkward and petulant teenager, continually wavering between anger and revolt on the one hand and sullen reproach and refusal on the other. Postmodernism presents itself as a 'historical

145

complex' – complete with its neuroses and obsessions. And legions of therapists and counsellors are constantly at work on the personality disorders of the Zeitgeist.

Throughout its long history 'modernity', in all its guises, has been characterized by the tension between impulses which were critical or sceptical – destructive or negative impulses – and other impulses which were more positive and affirmative – impulses of hope and longing. The dynamic of modernity stems from the intertwining of these constructive and **deconstructive** tendencies.

Postmodernism can be seen as an extension of the critical, sceptical, dissenting – even nihilistic – impulse of modernity. It is treated in this way by many of its critics. And for many critics of postmodernity this is exactly the problem. Under the 'postmodern condition' dissent becomes generalized: it can seem to involve 'dissent in principle' or even 'dissent from everything possible'.

At the same time, postmodernism is sometimes claimed to be a new form of realism. Postmodernism also includes the call for a return to common sense, for pragmatism in the face of the wilder utopian visions indulged in by modernism. As such it is reproached by its critics, especially **Marxist** ones, as leading to easy assimilation or accommodation with the status quo. Listen to this attack on Baudrillard:

> Baudrillard is still read and received as a political radical, and those who are becoming increasingly attracted to his thought generally perceive themselves as 'radicals' of some sort . . . Baudrillard is the latest example of critical criticism which criticizes everything, but rarely affirms anything of much danger to the status quo . . . A court jester of the society he mocks, he safely simulates criticism, advertises his wares and proceeds to enjoy the follies of the consumer and media society.
>
> (Douglas Kellner, *Jean Baudrillard: From Marxism to Postmodernism and Beyond* (1989))

Postmodernity = 'dissent' minus 'danger'?

It is a recurrent gesture of the 'postmodern' moment to be 'critical' – of Western rationality, **logocentricism**, humanism, the legacy of the **Enlightenment**, the centred **subject**, etc. The most frequent refrain among dissenters from postmodernism is 'critique in the name of what?' Richard J. Bernstein offers one of the most eloquent explorations of this quandary: '[T]he very "grammar" of critique requires some standard, some measure, some basis for critique. Otherwise there is – as **Habermas** claims – the danger of the critical impulse consuming itself' (*The New Constellation* (1990)). And he goes on to cite Jacques **Derrida**, so often claimed by friends and foes as a prototypical postmodernist: 'I cannot conceive of a radical critique which would not be ultimately motivated by some sort of affirmation, acknowledged or not' ('Dialogue with Jacques Derrida', in Richard Kearney, ed., *Dialogues with Contemporary Continental Thinkers* (1984)).

Nihilistic, subjectivist, amoral, fragmentary, arbitrary, defeatist, wilful: the terms sound familiar. They constitute some of the core vocabulary used in the criticism of postmodernism. It is worth pausing to reflect that these terms are not only in wide circulation today – they have much justification – but that they have a surprisingly long and respectable pedigree.

In the first half of this century disapproving critics, such as György Lukács, deplored the tendencies (nihilism, **irony**, fragmentation) of *modernist* literature (Dostoevsky, Kafka, Musil) in just these terms. In doing so they – intentionally – echoed the warnings issued a hundred years earlier by **Hegel** against the subjectivism of his Romantic contemporaries (Novalis, the brothers Schlegel, Schleiermacher and Fries).

The fact that postmodernism – or at least the nihilistic tendency it contains – has such a long tradition is fully recognized by leading postmodernists. Jonathan Arac long ago put forward the hypothesis that postmodernism has always been in search of tradition while pretending to innovation. In diagnosing what he called *The Postmodern Condition* (1979), Jean-François **Lyotard** presented this condition as one that occurs again and again throughout history: 'What, then is the postmodern? . . . It is undoubtedly a part of the modern . . . A work can become modern only if it is first postmodern. Postmodernism thus understood is not modernism at its end but in the nascent state, and this state is constant.'

Lyotard has unearthed many worthy precursors of the postmodern. In considering the criticisms levelled at postmodernism it might be worthwhile to follow his example and to examine an important precedent.

Denis Diderot (1713–84) gave twenty years of his life to editing the great French *Encyclopédie*, and was at the centre of French Enlightenment circles. In *Rameau's Nephew* (1761) Diderot drew a portrait of the new man. Rameau's nephew is a *philosophe* like himself and like his former friend, Jean-Jacques Rousseau. He is an assertive, self-conscious and self-ironizing citizen of the republic of letters. Rameau's nephew has absorbed all of the ('**anti-foundational**') arguments against traditional forms of moral authority: the church, the state. The result is that Rameau's nephew declares himself to be utterly amoral, absolutely self-seeking and nihilistic.

Rameau's nephew is the classical prototype of the nihilist tendencies which have drawn fire from the critics of postmodernism. But Diderot's tale gives the devil the best tunes and offers no effective antidote to the dangerous amoralism and subjectivism so successfully evoked. So the tale itself could be claimed for the very postmodernism it attacks.

Diderot himself felt the tale so dangerous that he left it unpublished. Diderot's most personal reflections show how very much he wanted to be a good man, a moral person. But they show, too, Diderot's awareness that if moral codes were not handed down from above then moral awareness will inevitably involve uncertainty, ambiguity and doubt.

That a moral impulse can and must survive in the postmodernist landscape is a message repeated in book after book by Zygmunt **Bauman**. Bauman's postmodern ethics – which include the notion that we must not attempt to eradicate ambiguity but instead must learn to face it and to live with it – would be well understood by his Enlightenment precursor, Diderot.

When postmodernism is advanced in a thoughtful, non-polemical form – such as in the various recent writings of Bauman – it demands a new asceticism and modesty. It demands that we be scrupulously responsible not only about our actions but even about our hopes and dreams. To dissent from the prevailing postmodern disenchantment with all previous theoretical frameworks, programmes and social movements appears to make one guilty of wanting to resuscitate worn-out illusions, to re-enchant one's world, or at least one's outlook on it.

One way of drawing the line between postmodernism and its critics is to focus on postmodernism's refusal of the utopian, dream-like elements which have accompanied the constant change of modernity. Modernisms, including Marxism, dreamt of a better world. Legislating for this world on the basis of this dream of a better one is seen as the cardinal sin of that modernism which postmodernism seeks to go beyond.

The antagonism between many postmodernists and many neo-Marxists revolves around this fraught issue. Postmodernists treat the authoritarianism of communist regimes as a result of having tried to realize an unrealizable dream, or having tried to lay hands on utopia and to engineer it in actually existing societies.

Marx himself criticized what he ridiculed as the 'utopian' socialists, always respecting the Jewish prohibition on investigating the future. But, for Marx, his refusal to speculate on a future communist society was an aspect of the 'scientific' nature of his socialist social science.

It could not be clearer that, for Marx, capitalism – the unique object of Marx's historical materialism – is a *moral* issue. Throughout his life, Marx's thinking expressed his fierce political commitment. And the question of the relation of theory to practice has always been a crucial one within the Marxist tradition. For seventy years after Lenin's victory in Russia this question increasingly became an entangled and intransigent one for Western Marxist intellectuals. Although many Western Communist Parties and trade unions developed authoritarian forms of organization, the totalitarian form of communism established in Soviet Russia attracted relatively few supporters among leading Western Marxist intellectuals. On the other hand, Chinese communism, and especially the 'Cultural Revolution' initiated by Mao, was viewed with some enthusiasm by many during the student protests of the late 1960s.

Many of the leading figures associated with French postmodernism, including Lyotard and Baudrillard, emerged from Marxist and '**post-Marxist**' groupings. Reaction against totalitarianism within the Soviet Union had its parallels in reaction against the closed minds and authoritarian practices within the French left. By the late twentieth century both Marxism and modernism had become easy targets for the dissenting impulse within postmodernism. Both had been institutionalized and associated with an 'establishment' – even where this was the 'establishment' of oppositional groups, trade unions, party organizations and academic faculties.

Today the very notion of Marxist political practice has a paradoxical ring to it. On the other hand, Marx's theoretical insights and achievements are now so widely accepted that they have long since ceased to be the property of any particular political orientation or grouping. Whoever seeks to understand society today in sociological and historical terms will find themselves borrowing, correcting and extending Marx's ideas.

Not surprisingly much of the fiercest criticism of postmodernist trends has come from writers who feel that they continue to work within the Marxist tradition in one way or another: Alex Callinicos, for example, is a Marxist who stresses that the nature of exploitation remains fundamentally unchanged. In order to understand the changes taking place in society it is essential to begin by analysing the mechanisms whereby surplus-value is extracted. Fredric **Jameson** has developed a Lukácsian or Hegelian-Marxist perspective on historical development and treats postmodernism as expressing the 'logic of late capitalism'. In other words, postmodernism is treated as symptomatic of the capitalist system at a particular phase in its development. In order to develop a critical perspective appropriate to our consumerist cyber-society Douglas Kellner has argued that the **critical theory** tradition of the **Frankfurt School** has more to offer than currently fashionable French theory:

> I am not sure that we have now transcended and left behind modernity, class politics, labour and production, imperialism, fascism and the phenomena described by classical and neo-Marxism, as well as by other political and social theories which Baudrillard rejects out of hand.
>
> *(Jean Baudrillard)*

Kellner, like Jameson, has conducted a very serious engagement with postmodern thought and shows in his own analyses of contemporary society that he has drawn a great deal from the postmodernists. Nevertheless, he insists, French postmodernists have been over-hasty in their dismissal of the neo-Marxist tradition of cultural analysis:

> New French Theorists like Baudrillard, Lyotard and **Foucault** have made a serious theoretical and political mistake in severing their work from the Marxian critique of capitalism precisely at a point when the logic of capital has been playing an increasingly important role in structuring the new stage of society which I conceptualize as a new stage of capitalism – capitalism as techno-capital.
>
> *(Jean Baudrillard)*

For the postmodernists, Lyotard represents the view that in all the advanced societies '[socialist] struggles and their instruments have been transformed into regulators of the system' (*The Postmodern Condition*). Against the postmodernists, neo-Marxist critics allege that postmodernist criticism is always already complicit in the system which it criticizes.

Postmodernism is a label one can attach to cultural manifestations across the entire globe. Postmodernism in philosophy and cultural theory, however, has had a distinct French accent. Leading cultural theorists such as Baudrillard and Lyotard developed away from variants of Marxism with which they were familiar in Paris. Unfortunately there has been no sustained attempt on the part of French intellectuals to engage seriously with the way in which the Marxian tradition was developed in the German-speaking realm. It has largely been left to English-speaking writers such as Jameson, Kellner and Bernstein to bring the two traditions into critical engagement with one another.

The one notable exception to this generalization would seem to be the way in which Lyotard's French theory has defined itself in opposition to the thinking of the German social theorist, Jürgen **Habermas**. In *The Postmodern Condition*, Lyotard developed his most often quoted definitions of postmodernism (as a suspicion of **metanarratives**) as an explicit critique of Habermas's ambitious intellectual project. Habermas was singled out for this unique distinction because his aims remain unashamedly synthetic and constructive (rather than analytical and de-constructive). Habermas acknowledges ideals (albeit highly abstract ones) which he claims as universal, and his social theory is continually related to accounts of human evolution (including the phases of history). Particular diffi-culty has surrounded Habermas's notion of an 'interest in consensus', which occupies a crucial role at the heart of his extensive theorization of communi-cation and **discourse**. Habermas, for whom the concept of modernity is central, is frequently taken to be the boldest defender of the unfinished project of modernity, a forceful champion of the Enlightenment legacy.

Habermas presented an early response to postmodernism in social theory in an essay entitled 'Modernity versus Postmodernity' (*New German Critique* (1981)) in which he drew comparisons between postmodern theory and neo-conservatism. A more sustained and substantial treatment of what Habermas sees as the flaws and dangers of postmodernism was presented in his twelve lectures on *The Philosophical Discourse of Modernity* (1985). But here, too, the engagement is anything but direct. Habermas speaks of Foucault and Derrida as well as the antecedents of postmodern thinking in **Nietzsche**, **Heidegger** and the surrealist Georges Bataille. But he is more concerned to trace what he sees as a more promising basis for understanding modernity (and postmodernity) through the insights of Hegel and the theorization of late capitalism (and late modernism) by **Horkheimer** and **Adorno**. Richard **Rorty** gives a succinct summary of the way in which Habermas and Lyotard talk past one another:

> Anything that Habermas will count as retaining a 'theoretical approach' will be counted by an incredulous Lyotard as a 'meta-narrative'. Anything that abandons such an approach will be counted by Habermas as 'neoconservative', because it

drops the notions which have been used to justify the various reforms which have marked the history of the Western democracies since the Enlightenment, and which are still being used to criticize the socio-economic institutions of both the Free and the Communist worlds. Abandoning a standpoint which is, if not transcendental, at least 'universalistic', seems to Habermas to betray the social hopes which have been central to liberal politics. So we find French critics of Habermas ready to abandon liberal politics in order to avoid universalistic philosophy, and Habermas trying to hang on to universalistic philosophy, with all its problems in order to support liberal politics.

('Habermas and Lyotard on Postmodernity', in Richard J. Bernstein, ed., *Habermas and Modernity* (1985)).

As Richard J. Bernstein has reminded us in *The New Constellation*, the 'most fundamental, powerful – and perhaps seductive – theme in Hegel's philosophy is the promise and fulfillment of reconciliation (*Versöhnung*)'. Habermas's treatment of communication and discourse partakes of this spirit and on this basis seeks to transcend 'systematically distorted communication': 'The "postmodern" celebration of contingency, fragmentation, fissures, singularity, plurality, and ruptures (that defy reconciliation) are profoundly anti-Hegelian gestures.' From Hegel to Habermas (and beyond in many other traditions still active) there persists the hope of reconciliation not only among the living but also reconciliation with the dead. The postmodernist attitude of citing, parodying, pastiching, using and reusing the past is surely a significant symptom of our times. The postmodernist intellectual metropolis is one without a cemetery – there is no 'dead centre' to its town.

At the start of the eighteenth century a great debate raged between the 'ancients' and the 'moderns'. The 'ancients' held that the classical civilizations of Greece and Rome were the source of all standards and all literary ideals. The 'moderns' contended that new times required new standards and new forms of expression. What we should remember in this context is that this was a debate between men raised on Greek and Latin. Even those who belonged to the 'modern' camp, from whom emerged the leading figures of the Enlightenment, were steeped in the classics. All the participants to the debate were on familiar terms with Aristotle and Aristophanes, with Tacitus and Cicero.

Our 'modern' sense of feeling superior to, and hence cut off from, all of our ancestors is an extraordinarily disorienting and alienating experience. We have always felt the need to acknowledge the authority of at least some of the ancients. Throughout modernity the canon of 'classics' has been continually recreated. But, until fairly recently, the search always led back to the huge variety of prototypes and precedents played out in the ancient world. From this stems both the universalism and the elitism which characterizes various forms of modernism, from the reforming zeal of the Enlightenment *philosophes* to the aesthetic experiments of the twentieth-century avant-garde.

The evolution of mass education is one of the key factors in shaping the social history of the twentieth century. Education is the one 'great hope' which we have not entirely given up. One precondition (and effect) of universal education was a dramatically reduced role for Latin, Greek and 'classics'. For the first half of the twentieth century, modernism operated in an intellectual landscape in which the 'classics' still represented an active, if ambivalent, legacy. 'Classics' came more and more to be the cornerstone of a privileged education, allowing access to the heritage of the past. At the same time among disaffected, yet almost always 'well-educated', intellectuals, the perennial subversiveness of classical authors and classical themes (myths and mythemes) fuelled the radical universalism of modernism.

Meanwhile the demands of the market turn yesterday's fashions into something already ancient, utterly out-of-date – into something ripe for revival as 'classic'. The cycles of history are driven by the mandarins of a commercial culture, in order that they, and others, might turn a profit. Among all of the culture industries, it is the heritage industry which experiences the most sustained boom.

The radical avant-garde wish was to overcome the gulf between art and society or between art and everyday life. The aestheticized world prophesied by a modernist avant-garde in the earlier half of the twentieth century has, in our own time, become all too real: it has become the *hyperreal*. And this state of hyperreality has been achieved not by the artistic avant-garde but by commodities and the countless creative workers who sustain our consumer culture. No new aesthetic movements of collective importance, operative across more than one art form, emerged either, after surrealism. As Douglas Kellner has pointed out, post-modernism is continually parodying the revolutionary gestures of the avant-garde earlier in the twentieth-century. This is true at least of one brand of postmodernism which, when it came on the market, announced itself with shrill insistence as something utterly new:

> [A]lmost every discussion of Baudrillard in English seems to presuppose that he is right, that we are in something like a postmodern condition, that we have left modernity behind and are in a qualitatively new society where the old categories and old distinctions no longer hold. Such a vision rests, I believe, partly on wishful thinking.
>
> (*Jean Baudrillard*)

We have lately learnt to be more modest in our modernity, more cautious in our hopes, more sceptical of the promise of the future. We cannot any longer take the project of modernity simply on trust. Even this postmodern tentativeness is no longer new. Postmodernity is ready to enter dictionaries and encyclopaedias as it has already entered into countless textbooks. Debates over the traditions of modernity, late modernity, postmodernity will continue, and will continue to generate sober reflection on where we have come from and where we are going.

Part II
NAMES AND TERMS

A

ABJECTION A term coined by the French psychoanalytical theorist and **semiotician** Julia **Kristeva**. In 1982 she published *Powers of Horror: An Essay on Abjection*, in which she argued that the 'abject' constitutes anything that is excluded from the symbolic order, the site of the social and unambiguous subjectivity. In order to take up a position within such an order, the **subject** must repress that which reminds it of its own material nature by categorizing it as unclean or disgusting. This attempt at exclusion can only ever be partially successful, and thus the abject preserves an ability to render the subject's inclusion in the symbolic order problematic. At moments when the subject is forced to recognize this, the resultant reaction is one of extreme repulsion – what Kristeva terms an 'act of abjection'. [SG]

ACKER, KATHY: NOVELIST (1948–97) Acker began publishing a string of **texts** in the mid-1970s with small underground presses. Her move to London in the mid-1980s coincided with her reaching a larger audience when a major publisher brought out *Blood and Guts in High School* (1984). Her work draws upon Sade, Bataille, postwar French fiction and, most clearly, the 'cut-up' and collage techniques of William Burroughs. Often depicting the global adventures of a young girl, beginning with a sado-masochistic sexual relationship with a patriarchal figure (usually her father) in various confined spaces (harems, family homes), her work is marked by a complete absence of the usual features (and pleasures) of fiction – consistent characterization, plot and psychological motivation.

It is notorious for its extremely graphic descriptions of sex and violence, though the reader has some difficulty deciding which is the more unpleasant. Examples in this manner are *Blood and Guts in High School, Empire of the Senseless* (1988) and *Don Quixote* (1986). 'I wanted to stick a knife, a little one, up the ass of the novel', she has said.

In many ways her books are textbook examples of what **postmodern** fiction can be in its most avant-garde form; here we find sexual transgression, passages of lyricism, occupations of the space of '**Otherness**', the use of different genres (romance, science fiction, pornography, adventure), the plagiarizing of high and popular cultural works (Dickens, Cervantes, William **Gibson**), the representation of fluid subjectivities and the questioning of notions of originality and realism. The hilarious *Hello, I'm Erica Jong* (1984) is a send-up of the consciousness-raising, sexually liberated feminist fiction of the 1970s, of which Jong's *Fear of Flying* (1973) is a prime example. It plays with Jong's realist aesthetics and links sex and death in ways the relentlessly upbeat Jong would never do. It is also a skit on the '**death of the author**' and concludes with a drawing of a tombstone which bears the legend 'RIP E. J.' *I Dreamt I Was a Nymphomaniac* (1975) is, Acker says, 'an experiment with the word "I"', while *Kathy Goes to Haiti* (1978) alternates chapters of seeming autobiography with material lifted from pornographic sources. Using *Treasure Island* as her starting point, *Pussy, King of the Pirates* (1996) relates once more the adventures of a young girl through a landscape that doubles for the female body. These 'belated', highly mediated texts reflect Acker's belief that 'our reality now, which occurs so much through the media, is other texts'.

Needless to say, her work has been controversial; to some it is merely 'porno-babble'. For others it represents in fiction the possibility of a kind of **Deleuzian** 'flow'. At its best it gives the reader a glimpse of the possibilities of contemporary fiction. It offers us the disturbing suggestion, as Jonathan **Dollimore** has put it, that **power** and pleasure are not mutually exclusive but reinforce one another and this, finally, may prove to be the most unpalatable aspect of her work. [PD]

ACKROYD, PETER: NOVELIST, BIOGRAPHER (1949–) A prolific writer, Ackroyd has produced many critically acclaimed novels. *Chatterton* (1987), *First Light* (1989), *English Music* (1991), *The House of Doctor Dee* (1993), *Dan Leno and the Limehouse Golem* (1995), and *The Clerkenwell Tales* (2003) are all, in one way or another, historical fictions which involve the attempt to solve some kind of mystery. Ackroyd has also written successful biographies of T. S. Eliot, Charles Dickens, William Blake and Sir Thomas More (1984, 1990, 1995, 1998). These biographies, as well as the majority of his novels, are, in a sense, about London – where Ackroyd was born and lives. *London: A Biography* (2000) is the logical continuation of this abiding interest.

Ackroyd's third novel was the gruesome (and gruesomely funny) *Hawksmoor* (1985), which made his name and which exemplified what were to be his recurring themes: the presence of the past, occult knowledge and the irrational. The novel tells the tale, in alternating chapters, of a series of parallel murders – one group in the eighteenth century, the other in the twentieth – and the ways in which they might be linked.

While Ackroyd's self-conscious historical pastiches can be seen as **postmodern** in style, they are profoundly anti-**modern** in sentiment; *Hawksmoor* uses the figure of the architect-scientist Sir Christopher Wren to send up the **Enlightenment**'s belief in human progress and human perfectibility. In doing so, his stylistically exhilarating, philosophically conservative and deeply pessimistic fiction questions the intellectual and ethical foundations of modernity. [PD]

ADAMS, JOHN: COMPOSER (1947–) Adams has played a crucial role in the development of the **minimalist** tradition, building upon the foundations laid down by composers his senior, such as Steve **Reich** and Philip **Glass**. Adams was thoroughly schooled in the **modernist** approach to composition (i.e. the European post-war avant-garde – Boulez, Stockhausen, etc.) which he felt was not only going against his instincts but against the natural forces of music. It was only after graduating and moving to San Francisco that Adams was exposed to the minimalist music of Reich, **Riley** and Glass. This music, with its rich polyrhythmic textures and defiantly static harmony, was to be hugely inspirational to Adams, offering an alternative to the modernist musical language.

Minimalism, at least in its early days, rejected self-expression and any form of sentimentality in favour of processes, gradual change and a kind of objective detachment from the music. Adams, along with other composers, was to adopt many of the minimalist techniques but to adapt them to his own more expressive, more climactic and often more dissonant musical language. The tag 'post-minimalism' has often been employed to describe this music. One of Adams' early pieces *Shaker Loops* (1978) employs the familiar minimalist techniques of steady pulse, repetitive structures, tonal stability and polyrhythm, yet develops an emotional and dramatic **narrative**.

Adams has composed two operas. The first, *Nixon in China* (1987), takes as its subject matter the historic meeting in 1972 between Richard Nixon and the Chinese leader Mao Zedong. This full-length three-act work, being described by some as 'realist' and by others as 'surrealist', makes no overt political statements and resists political satire. His second opera *The Death of Klinghoffer* (1990) is inspired by the 1985 Palestinian hijacking of the cruise ship *Achille Lauro* and offers a reflective look at the continuing conflict between the Arab and Jewish people. Leaving the world of opera for five years, Adams concentrated on orchestral works – *El Dorado* (1991), the Chamber Symphony (1992) and the Violin Concerto (1993) – which allowed him to develop a more complex, contrapuntal and dissonant musical style. Returning to the world of music theatre in 1995 he composed the piece 'I was Looking at the Ceiling then I saw the Sky'. This collaboration with the director Peter Sellars and poet June Jordon was not only scaled down and more compact than his operas but also allowed him to return to a simpler, more accessible compositional style. It is clear that not only has Adams developed and expanded the genre of minimalism but also that he has gained for it a sense of respectability with the 'classical' music establishment. [AB]

ADORNO, THEODOR WIESENGRUND: PHILOSOPHER (1903–69) Along with Max **Horkheimer** and Herbert **Marcuse**, Adorno is the major representative of the 'critical thought' developed by the members of the Institute of Social Research, or **Frankfurt School**. At university in Frankfurt Adorno studied philosophy, sociology, psychology and music. Then, in 1925, he studied musical composition with Alban Berg in Vienna and gained a deep appreciation of the atonality of the 'new music' being developed by Arnold Schoenberg. As well as writing numerous musical compositions,

Adorno wrote copiously on music. In this and in other areas of aesthetics Adorno remained a committed advocate of the radical, critical impulses within **modernism**. In philosophy, however, Adorno's work can be read as equally close to modernism (if one concentrates on certain ideas or pronouncements) or **postmodernism** (if one allows for the performative element, the reflexive dramatization of movement of critical thinking – 'thinking against thought' – itself).

Adorno's most important philosophical debt is to **Hegel**. Like Hegel, Adorno's own thinking constantly circles around the dialectical tension between individual and society, between the particular and the universal. On the other hand, Adorno – like **Marx** – regards Hegel's fundamental claim (to have effected the reconciliation of these dialectical poles) as condemning him to illusory forms of idealism. Adorno regards all fantasies of 'organic wholeness', including the Hegelian, as in some ways regressive. The **'negative dialectics'** proposed by Adorno aim at constantly undermining and defeating any final synthesis.

When the Institute for Social Research was forced into exile from Nazi Germany, Adorno went through a profound engagement with mass culture in its commercial American forms. The result was an analysis of the culture and social organization of late capitalism which stressed its propensity to become an integrated, closed, or 'total', system. Adorno contributed many studies of the manipulation of consciousness by what he called the 'culture industries'. These became the cornerstone of a damning portrait of what Adorno saw as an increasingly 'administered world'.

Against an increasingly irrational and intractable world, Adorno seeks to mobilize all the powers of philosophical reason. ('We are wholly convinced . . . that social freedom is inseparable from enlightened thought.') Yet, for Adorno, reason, in the form of scientific rationality and means-end calculations, is itself part of the problem. In *Dialectic of Enlightenment* (1947), Adorno collaborated with Max Horkheimer to diagnose the dark side of the development of reason. According to the allegory of the voyage of Odysseus, which Adorno constructs within the book, the repressive potential of reason does not arise with the eighteenth-century **Enlightenment** conception of reason (which Adorno labels 'identity logic' or 'the philosophy of identity') but has its origins in the very beginnings of Western culture. The rationality bound to identity has always felt compelled to deny, repress and violate singularity, **difference** and **Otherness**. Its extraordinary success in offering mankind domination over nature leads inexorably to domination of men over men (and over women).

In the face of the darkness of this vision, Adorno self-consciously affirms the wildest utopian dream of the Enlightenment of all: an end to *human suffering*. 'The only philosophy which can be responsibly practiced in the face of despair is the attempt to contemplate all things as they would present themselves from the standpoint of redemption . . . Perspectives must be fashioned that displace and estrange the world, reveal it to be, with its rifts and crevices, as indigent and distorted as it will appear one day in the messianic light.' [LS]

ALTERITY 'Alterity' is often used interchangeably in **poststructuralist discourse** with '**Other**'. The 'Other' in the work of Michel **Foucault**, for instance, consists of those who are excluded from positions of **power**, and are often victimized within a predominantly liberal humanist view of the **subject**. Much of Foucault's work is therefore dedicated to retrieving for history and philosophy those who have been excluded from intellectual consideration, and have consequently had their political rights either ignored or erased. The 'Other' in this context are homosexuals, women, the clinically insane, non-whites and prisoners. These figures, collectively and individually, are seen by poststructural and **postmodern** thinkers to exist on the margins of Western society, and are often the negative opposition in **deconstructive** discourse. [DW]

AMIS, MARTIN: NOVELIST (1949–) Amis's blackly satirical novels show a technical virtuosity and verbal brilliance unmatched by his contemporaries. He has displayed all of the formal trickery expected of the **postmodern** novelist: unreliable narrators (two of them in *Success*), bizarre authorial interventions (he plays chess with the main character, John Self, in *Money*) and temporal manipulation (most spectacularly in *Time's Arrow*, which plays the life of a concentration camp doctor backwards).

Amis's first two novels, *The Rachel Papers* (1973) and *Dead Babies* (1975), portray the selfish pursuit of pleasure by the young in a world without traditional moral values. His following two novels, *Success* (1978) and *Other People: A Mystery Story* (1981), show an increasingly adventurous experimentation with form: in the latter the world is seen through the defamiliarizing, innocent gaze of an amnesiac. *Money: A Suicide Note* (1984) and *London Fields* (1989) show Amis at his best, integrating complex formal structures with devastating moral satire. In the former the greed and decadence of the Reagan–Thatcher years and in the latter the seedy moral depravity of the criminal underclass are caught by Amis's brilliant phrasemaking. *The Information* (1995) exposes the fear and loathing running through London's literary elites. More recently, in the highly personal non-fictional work *Koba the Dread: Laughter and the Twenty Million* (2003), Amis has turned his satire on those Western intellectuals (his father briefly included) who supported twentieth-century Soviet communism.

The postmodernist aesthetic that shows in Amis's familiar technical flourishes is matched by a carefully considered post-modernist ethic. Amis is well aware of the critique of **Enlightenment** values, of the crumbling concept of the self and of the coupling together of **power** and knowledge. [AM]

ANDERSON, LAURIE: PERFORMANCE ARTIST, COMPOSER (1947–) Laurie Anderson is **postmodern** in her defiance of categorization. Throughout her work, Anderson has destabilized barriers such as those between art, music and performance, craft and technology, avant-garde and commercial. In her performances she challenges traditional limits of gender and technology while making use of assumptions about them. The forty-five-minute piece *For Instants* (1976) incorporated explanations of the technical difficulties in making the work and postmodern distinctions between 'what happened' and 'what I said and wrote about what happened'. She performed on her viophonograph – a turntable on a violin with a needle mounted onto a bow – playing a recording of her own voice and accompanying it with live singing.

In a later piece she replaced the bow's horsehair with recording tape, playing pre-recorded words on an audio head mounted onto the violin. Effects were designed so that incompleteness could make new meanings, as in Lenin's 'Ethics is the aesthetics of the future', which became *Ethics is the Aesthetics of the Few(ture)* (her title). In *Songs for Lines/Songs for Waves* (1977) she reversed recorded words, exposing the arbitrariness of signifiers.

The 1980s multimedia *United States* used her famous vocoder, tape loops and synthesizers to create a robotic chant which unsettled gender expectations. 'O Superman' condemned the excesses of technological and media control while making use of them. *Language is a Virus* (from William Burroughs' 'Language is a virus from outer space') subverts 'natural' expression, combining media images and computer graphics with Anderson's voice, staccato phrasing and mechanical gestures. The **ironic** distancing produced by decoding her voice and incorporating other sounds stresses the mediation involved in communication. In the 1990s Anderson consolidated her reputation for using innovative technology in the arts with several world tours. [SD]

ANTI-ESSENTIALISM Postmodernist thinkers invariably describe themselves as anti-essentialist, meaning that they reject the notion of there being any essence to phenomena such as truth, meaning, self or identity. Traditional philosophy is taken to be essentialist in believing that there is such a thing as absolute truth underpinned by logical formulae such as the law of identity ($A = A$, or a thing equals itself). This law has been challenged by postmodernists, who claim that it does not always hold (a thing might not equal itself if it is in a continuous process of change over time, for example). Traditional philosophy also tends to posit an essential self (as in the case of Descartes, where the mind is the essence of selfhood: 'I think therefore I am'), which postmodernism has similarly called into question. Self is in fact seen to be a very fluid entity in postmodernist thought, particularly in feminist circles, where the notion of an essentialist self is regarded as part of patriarchal oppression. [SS]

ANTI-FOUNDATIONALISM To challenge the grounds of someone's system of belief, or thought, is to be anti-foundationalist. **Post-structuralist** and **postmodernist** thinkers tend to be self-consciously anti-foundational in outlook. **Derrida**, as a case in point, has challenged the validity of the law of identity (that a thing equals itself, $A = A$), arguably *the* foundation to thought and argument in the West. The basic problem is that any system of thought, indeed any system aspiring to make value judgements of any kind (true or false, good or evil, etc.), requires a starting point, or initial assumption (say, that A = A) that is self-evidently true and beyond all possible doubt. Anti-foundationalists point out that the starting point itself requires a prior assumption. Poststructuralism and post-modernism are merely more extreme versions of positions that have been out-lined earlier in the history of Western philosophy. Sceptics in general, such as the eighteenth-century philosopher David Hume, are anti-foundationally inclined in that they are less concerned with what their opponents say than their ground of authority for making any kind of value judgement at all. Anti-foundationalism in recent times has argued that foundation-alism is authoritarian in intent, and it has become a rallying cry for an attack on the status quo and the establishment. [SS]

APORIA From the Greek, meaning, literally, 'the absence of a passage', and hence a perplexing difficulty or state of being at a loss, aporia denotes in rhetoric a figure in which the speaker or writer expresses doubt about how or where to begin a **discourse**, or how to overcome a particular problem or obstacle. For **deconstructive** criticism, it is precisely around such moments of doubt or apparently unresolv-able problems that reading orients itself. For **Derrida**, as for the criticism of Paul **de Man**, it is these **textual** gaps or stumbling-blocks to which we must pay attention.

The term is also an apt one to describe the kind of 'impossibility' of judgement which **Lyotard** identifies in the aesthetics of the **sublime** and the avant-garde, with which he identifies the **postmodern**. For Lyotard, the moment at which political judgement takes place is an aporetic one, analogous with the disjunction between the faculties of reason and imagination in the sublime, and with the avant-garde injunc-tion to create, but in the absence of any rules for the production of art. [BD]

APPROPRIATION ART A term used to describe works by Sherrie Levine, Barbara Kruger, Cindy **Sherman,** Richard Prince and those artists for whom the real has become coterminous with the image world of contemporary social life. Levine, Sherman and Prince were represented at the seminal *Pictures* exhibition, held at the Artists' Space gallery in Lower Manhattan in 1977. The influential art critic Douglas Crimp, writing in the catalogue, waxes lyrical about artists for whom 'skill' is defined in terms of **simulation** rather than emulation, repetition rather than origin-ality, and confiscation rather than creation. [CT]

ARCHAEOLOGY Archaeology, the scientific study of the remains of the past, is a potent metaphor for excavations of a more sub-jective nature. **Freud** famously used the image of a city to picture the relation between the conscious and the uncon-scious. Like the city of Rome, the thinking **subject** is composed of many different layers of awareness and susceptibility. Destructive drives and **desires** may emanate from buried parts of the self, and the analyst must help the analysand to dig deep and expose repressed memories and fears to the light of waking day. Michel **Foucault** uses a similar concept to describe the investi-gation into the unconscious of the **episteme**, which is shorthand for the ·epistemological field' of assumptions, expectations, values and beliefs of a society at a particular historical moment. *The Order of Things: An Archaeology of the Human Sciences* (1966), for example, seeks to uncover the forma-tional rules and systematic shaping factors which are common to scientific **represen-tations** of the classical period. The **text** is an 'open site', another archaeological metaphor which refers to the necessary in-completeness of the project. So Foucault's speculations should not be read as if they were by a historian of science, but with a **postmodern** provisionality. [BL]

ARTIFICIAL INTELLIGENCE On the one hand, artificial intelligence (AI) forms a powerfully attractive motor for the artificial evolution of human reality into science fiction; on the other, it is a research programme attracting funds from military and corporate sponsors that seeks, for the first time, to place a new created or manufactured species of intelligent life on the Earth. If this still sounds somewhat intoxicated, we need only remember AI guru Marvin Minsky discussing the possibility of real artificial intelligences: 'Of course they're possible; that's not the problem. The real problem is that the first hundred or so are going to be clinically insane.' As contemporary phenomena such as **cyberpunk** demonstrate, AI, along with **artificial life**, forms a haunting cultural threshold beyond which Frankenstein's monster already has us in his virtual grasp.

As Minsky does, however, it is also necessary to insist that these virtual monsters are also real. In AI research proper, then, there are two basic models: the first, top-down, approach seeks to develop software that can capture the core cognitive functions that define human intelligence, and thereafter to upload them into a single central processor that stands in for the human brain. Broadly speaking, this is the model pursued in the production of 'expert systems' and the chess computers against which so many humans have pitted their wits and failed. The other, bottom-up, approach seeks to create machines that learn. Variously called 'parallel distributed processing', 'neural nets', or 'connectionism', this model allows many processors to interact in order to develop a collective response to random phenomena. Over time, such parallel machines establish pathways and **fuzzy** rules for connections in exactly the same way, it is argued, as organic, human brains do: rather than being given a set of rules and parameters as a program that an expert system then applies, neural nets select the best from many options, so that the rules the system learns 'emerge' from its functioning.

While the top-down approach is by now all but redundant, the success enjoyed by neural nets has generated new approaches to the philosophy of mind, generally called 'connectionist' theories. Like the model of the neural net, connectivity and interaction become more important tools for the development of human intelligence than the centralized idea of the mind-brain as a whole. Perhaps, if this trend continues, the question as to which intelligence is derived from the other will be harder to pose than it currently seems, in a world that, temporarily at least, is devoid of artificial intelligences. [IHG]

ARTIFICIAL LIFE Along with **artificial intelligence**, one of the two contemporary sciences of the artificial, artificial life (AL), is a truly bizarre confluence of technology, science and **simulacra**. Generating 'organisms' from algorithms, AL researchers seek not so much to model 'real-life' evolutionary processes, as to extend them into the artificial environment of computer memory. Thomas S. Ray, at the Fourth International Conference on Artificial Life in 1994, suggested that his Tierra, a program that, like a digital simulation of our own primal soup, 'evolves' independent life-forms in a computer, be released onto the **Internet** to 'breed' new species all over the (virtual) world. While Tierra is an example of AL software, AL researchers also investigate hardware – the construction of artificial life-forms such as robots, aiming eventually at the ideal of realizing the self-replicating but abstract 'von Neumann machine' in material form – and wetware – the attempt to create artificial life in a test tube. AL software involves writing programs that perpetually feed back the information they produce into the production of further information, creating an informational complexity from which, it is hoped, artificial life-forms will emerge. Key to the process, therefore, is its 'bottom-up' strategy rather than the 'top-down' approach initially adopted by artificial intelligence research, meaning that more emerges from AL's new, silicon-based evolutionary ecosystems than was programmed in at the start. [IHG]

ASHBERY, JOHN: POET, CRITIC (1927–) Ashbery is regarded as the most prominent poet in English in the last thirty years, whose work has influenced a generation of American avant-garde poets. An art critic for many years, Ashbery's own work is marked by a painterly eye and, early on, by the frequent use of collage techniques. He began publishing in the mid-1950s and rejected the then-fashionable 'confessional' mode made popular by Robert Lowell and Sylvia Plath. Ashbery's often baffling poetry is both grievously abstract and laden with particularity. Readers find it hard to see any causal connection between individual lines, let alone stanzas, and critics have had to make the largest of inferences to extract some thematic sense from the poetry. An Ashbery poem can at times seem like an oddly banal summary of an interesting idea, but his ludic, interrogative verse has had a liberating effect on contemporary poetry.

Many critics see him as pursuing the **modernist** project of representing (in exhaustive, solipsistic detail) consciousness in the act of experiencing reality. Most of his work, from his first volume *Some Trees* (1956) through *The Vermont Notebook* (1975) and the more lyrical *Chinese Whispers* (2002), seems to be taken up with doing just this. Such is the philosophical torque applied by Ashbery, however, that these important, largely epistemological questions finally spin off, leaving a typically **postmodern** 'onto-logical' concern with the medium for the experience: poetic **discourse**. Emblematic of this enormously self-conscious style is Parmigianino's sixteenth-century mannerist painting which inspired the title-poem in Ashbery's best-known volume, *Self-Portrait in a Convex Mirror* (1975). Rather than the 'depth' model of the modernist human **subject** and its **representation** in the artwork, in the poem 'everything is surface', an effect of the very medium in which it is produced: for Parmigianino paint, and for Ashbery language itself. [PD]

AURA A term associated with the German cultural critic Walter **Benjamin**. In an important essay entitled 'The Work of Art in the Age of Mechanical Reproduction' (1936), Benjamin argues that, prior to mechanization, art had a non-reproductive quality which conferred upon it a unique status, or 'aura'. This aura, which signified the artwork's autonomy, had been destroyed in modern times by soulless automation. For Benjamin, the mysticism that he associates with the unique work of art has been 'withered' as a result of the machine age, and art and its artefacts have become divorced from tradition, leading to a 'liquidization of the cultural heritage'. [DW]

AUSTER, PAUL: NOVELIST (1947–) Auster, considered one of the foremost American novelists now writing, made his reputation with a series of three novels, collectively known as *The New York Trilogy* (1987). These are anti-detective fictions influenced by Beckett, French post-war experimental fiction and **postmodern** theory. All three have as their plot some kind of writer in pursuit of another, and in the second and third books, *Ghosts* (1986) and *The Locked Room* (1986), another who is an eerie double of the protagonist. The first, *City of Glass* (1985), alludes to Poe and Walter **Benjamin** in its figuring of a fragmenting self in the city. The city of glass suggests the detective's mastery of the complexity of **signs**, but presents us with the abysmal possibility that, rather than reading the city, it is a mirror-glass that merely reflects

Quinn's own concerns back at him. The novels seem to be psychological studies but the fragmentation at the end of *City of Glass*, for instance, is not psychological (as it would be in many modernist novels) but **textual**: Quinn disappears when his notebook finishes.

Ghosts is the most formal of the trilogy; Blue is employed by White to follow Black. Taking notes, Blue sits in his room and watches Black writing in the building across the road. Black may be writing about him. Black may in fact be White. Again we have a tale of someone who drops out of routine existence and lets social ties fall away in pursuit of an obsession. *The Locked Room* is the most fleshed-out of the early novels and escapes the main criticism made of these works: while admiring the stylistic control, and plenitude of stories within stories, some have found these novels finally exercises in postmodern style, though getting to that 'finally' is gripping.

Auster left the self-confessed influence of Beckett, and after his dystopian *In the Country of Last Things* (1987) he published in some ways his most remarkable novel, *Moon Palace,* which, in the story of Marco Stanley Fogg, continues the quest theme of his first work. *The Music of Chance* (1990) begins as a road novel and ends as a parable about free will and, as in all his fiction, it is saturated with references to American and European literature which are part of a literary technique that teases away at the surface realism of these later novels. *Leviathan* (1992) is concerned with the political implications of public writing, and echoes some of the themes of Don **DeLillo**'s *Mao II* (1990). *Mr Vertigo* (1994) uses the old American form of the tall tale to narrate the story of a boy who can fly. *The Book of Illusions* (2003) and *Oracle Night* (2004) maintain Auster's admirable **desire** to avoid repeating himself, while exemplifying his continuing theme of fluid selves held together (or not) by the ability to narrate, to textualize their lives. [PD]

AUTHOR From **structuralism** through to **postmodernism**, there has been a downgrading of the author's reputation in **continental philosophical** thought, particularly in France. Roland **Barthes**' 'death of the author' notion announced the end of the author as an authority figure responsible for the meaning of his or her work, and shifted the balance of **power** towards the reader. Authority figures are generally frowned upon in postmodernism, and the notion of the author as cultural icon has accordingly been challenged. There is little support among postmodernist theorists for the idea that any one individual should (or in any practical way can) exert control over what a **text** means; hence it is held to be pointless to seek out an author's 'intentions' (see also **death of the author**). [SS]

B

BAKER, NICHOLSON: NOVELIST (1957–)
Many **postmodernist** novels disrupt linear
narrative by burdening the **discourse**
with inordinate description. The books of
Nicholson Baker are classic examples of
this. In *The Mezzanine* (1990), a man's
shoelace snaps during lunch-hour in a local
office complex. While musing on why this
should happen at this particular time, his
thoughts go off on many tangents: how to
open a wing-flap spout on a carton without
splattering the milk, why 'pre-bunching' is
an inefficient way of putting on socks, and
other mysteries of minutiae.

Baker's next book, *Room Temperature*
(1990), also takes place at mealtime. It is
3.15 on a Wednesday afternoon, and Mike,
the narrator, is feeding his six-month-old
baby, the Bug, while his wife Patty is out at
work. As he does so, he reflects idly on
matters as diverse as nose-picking, drawing
the inside of a pillow, sucking the tops of
Bic pens, and the history of the comma. *Vox*
(1992) takes the form of a four-hour erotic
telephone conversation in which a man and
a woman exchange their most intimate
fantasies at obscene length. *The Fermata*
(1994), also descends into pornography
when the central character, Arno Strine,
finds himself blessed with the ability to
freeze time and fondle the females of his
choice. *The Everlasting Story of Nory* (1998)
records the observations of a nine-year-old
American girl as she settles with her family
in a small English town. In *A Box of
Matches* (2003), Emmett, the middle-aged
protagonist, lights a daily fire and cogitates
on the small things of life. [BL]

BANVILLE, JOHN: NOVELIST (1945–)
Considered by many the foremost living
Irish novelist, Banville's work illuminates
in a critical way a series of issues and
concepts that have become central to the
criticism of contemporary writing: **post-
colonialism** and **postmodernism**, history as
textuality, the relationship of ethics to
aesthetics, and the nature of fiction itself.
Writing consciously from the western edge
of modern Europe, his work has overlapping areas of concern. There are the
novels which explore the myth of the
Protestant ruling class's 'big house'. In
Birchwood (1973), *The Newton Letter*
(1981), *Mefisto* (1986), *The Book of
Evidence* (1989) and *Ghosts* (1993), these
colonial houses signify moral and
psychological decay, political oppression
and isolation. There are a series of **metafictional** history novels dealing with the
aesthetics of knowledge: *Doctor Copernicus*
(1976), *Kepler* (1981), *Mefisto* and *The
Newton Letter* draw upon Thomas **Kuhn**'s
concept of scientific revolutions in an
attempt to shift the boundaries of the
history novel itself. The grand theme of
these fictions is nothing less than science's
invention of **modern** reality. *The Book of
Evidence*, *Ghosts* and *Athena* (1995) use
the relationship between a casual murder
and a stolen painting to explore issues of
judgement: artistic, critical and legal.

Finding that 'truth' may be a human
construct chimes in with much postmodern
philosophy, but in Banville there is no
simple celebration of the fact. His fictions
are despairing language games over the

abyss. While *The Untouchable* (1997) and the acclaimed *Shroud* (2002) deal with the forms of betrayal – political, personal and artistic – familiar from his first novel, *Nightspawn* (1971), the latter ends: 'I love words and I hate death. Beyond this, nothing.' [PD]

BARTH, JOHN: NOVELIST (1930–) In 'The Literature of Exhaustion', an essay first published in 1967, John Barth made three points which now read like a manifesto for **postmodernist** fiction. The first was that traditional forms, particularly the classic bourgeois novel, were 'used-up', stale and outmoded. The second, related, point was that writers must strive to create new forms, acquiring a self-consciousness about the nature of literary language and artistic structure. His third point was that the writer still has an obligation to amuse and move the reader, speaking 'eloquently and memorably to our still-human hearts'. In his fiction from *The Floating Opera* (1956) to *The Last Voyage of Somebody the Sailor* (1991), Barth has certainly produced fiction of extreme structural complexity and formal invention. Critics are more divided about his success in moving, or even engaging, the reader.

The Floating Opera, and Barth's second novel, *The End of the Road* (1958), both feature alienated protagonists for whom life has not only lost meaning, but simply stopped making sense. A certain glum existentialism shows the influence of Camus, but the combination of narrative trickery and occasional scatological humour points to Barth's later fiction.

The Sot-Weed Factor (1960) is Barth's masterpiece, an enormous (over 800 pages in its first edition) historical novel about the foundation of the Maryland colony. Its hero, Ebenezer Cooke, a resolutely virginal poet, and his tutor, the pansexual, protean Henry Burlingame, undergo endless picaresque adventures on the way to transcendental union with the animal and

vegetable world. The story is told in a rich, part-fictive, part-authentic seventeenth-century English. Barth jumbles dense philosophical debate with swearing contests, snatches of journals and recipes for aphrodisiacs, without ever losing his grip on what must be the most intricate plot in English literature.

Giles Goat Boy (1966) is an equally huge and intricate work, but it lacks the vitality and humour of *The Sot-Weed Factor*. All of Barth's novels contain their **narratives** within elaborate framing devices, but *Giles* beats them all. No fewer than four stages come between the narrator, a young man brought up among goats and destined to the life of a mythic hero, and the reader. He dictates *The Revised New Syllabus of George Giles, Our Great Tutor* to the West Campus Automatic Computer. The computer then edits and prints the text. The hero's son further edits the computer tapes before giving them to a struggling writer, 'J. B.'. J. B. adds his amendments and then sends it to his publisher. Finally, the publisher appends a 'Disclaimer'. The central conceit is that the university becomes the universe, and the theme, like that of *The Sot-Weed Factor*, is the quest for a unifying vision, a dialectical reconciliation of the intimate and the absolute. *Lost in the Funhouse* (1968) takes experimentation a step further. A series of fourteen short 'fictions' for print, live voice and tape, it became, like *Giles* before it, a surprise best-seller. The stories continue Barth's themes – the grotesque comedy of sex and the difficulties of the storyteller in the modern age.

The three linked novellas in *Chimera* (1972) continue the investigation of myth instigated in *Giles,* dealing with the stories of Scheherazade, Perseus and Bellerophon – although each from an unusual angle; and there is a new theme, an overt feminism absent from his earlier works. The epistolary novel *Letters* (1979) again shows Barth's formal daring. Characters from earlier novels are reborn as correspondents in a tale of the usual architectonic complexity. *Sabbatical* (1982), *The Tidewater Tales* (1984) and *The Last Voyage of Somebody the Sailor* are metaphysical yarns, embodying Barth's love of sailing and, as in much of his fiction, Barth the author appears, more or less disguised.

Barth's star has fallen in recent years. His formal experiments no longer seem so interesting, and his increasing focus on the writer, and the act of creation, seems a shrinking away from his earlier grand themes. Nevertheless he remains one of the central figures in the history of postmodern fiction. [AM]

BARTHELME, DONALD: AUTHOR (1931–89) Barthelme is primarily known for his collections of short stories: *Come Back, Dr Caligari* (1964), *Unspeakable Practices, Unnatural Acts* (1968), *City Life* (1970), *Sadness* (1972), *Amateurs* (1976), *Great Days* (1979) and *Overnight to Many Distant Cities* (1983). However, he also wrote four novels: *Snow White* (1967), *The Dead Father* (1975), *Paradise* (1976) and *The King* (1989).

Barthelme's fictions display many of the features associated with **postmodernist** writing. He once admitted: 'As soon as I hear a proposition I immediately consider its opposite. A double-minded man – makes for mixtures.' This double-mindedness assumes many guises. For instance, his tales delight in surreal incongruities of context. In 'Me and Miss Mandible', a thirty-five-year-old claims adjuster for an insurance company suddenly finds himself back at elementary school. His diary entries record the contrast between his cynicism and the open-eyed fun and games of the eleven-year-olds. 'The Temptation of St Anthony' is posited around a similar reversal. The saint is somehow marooned in suburbia, and faced with the temptation of living an ordinary life. Many of Barthelme's stories operate on the principle of contradiction, with literary forms at variance with their contents. 'Paraguay' mimics the tone of an old-fashioned travel book, but the para-Paraguay it describes owes more to science fiction than any Baedeker guide. There are potted summaries of the country's imports and exports (silence is sold as if it were cement), its citizens (who shed their skins and share the same fingerprints), and its unusual physics (the temperature controls the inhabitants' walking speed). Other stories extrapolate from a ridiculous opening situation and exaggerate it beyond all proportion. In 'The Falling Dog', a Welsh sculptor is knocked to the ground by an Irish setter that jumps from an upper-storey window. The accident gives him ideas for new works based upon the image of the Falling Dog: plywood falling dogs like aircraft models, Styrofoam falling dogs, falling dogs the size of hummingbirds. The tale is the shaggiest of dog stories. A balloon appears over New York City in 'The Balloon'. It covers forty-five blocks from north to south, and an indeterminate area from east to west. City officials are upset about the arrival of this unwelcome object on the skyline, but the citizens soon accept it. Adults scrawl on it, and children bounce on it. Some people speculate about its meaning, as if it were a work of art. So the balloon rapidly inflates from a concrete particular to something vague and abstract and full of hot air.

Barthelme's louche fictions turn their withering gaze onto the shallow indices of designer taste. Yet many of his short stories were published in *The New Yorker*, alongside advertisements for the very furnishings and fashions they satirize. As Barthelme mused on one occasion: 'People read the fiction with after-images of Rolls-Royces and Rolexes still sizzling in their eyes': another instance of postmodern double-mindedness. [BL]

BARTHES, ROLAND: CULTURAL CRITIC (1915–80) In the successive phases in his career

Roland Barthes appears before us as the **Marxist** literary critic, elegantly slaying the bourgeois dragon; as a **semiologist**, carefully revealing the meanings latent in the artefacts of popular culture; as a **structuralist**, intent on a 'scientific' analysis of human society; and as a playful **poststructuralist**, celebrating the quasi-sexual pleasures of the **text**.

The most important work in Barthes' early period, and still perhaps his most influential, is the series of reflections on contemporary French culture, originally written for the magazine *Les lettres nouvelles* between 1954 and 1956, and published, along with a long theoretical essay in 1957 as *Mythologies*. In these essays, Barthes shows how racism, sexism and colonialism lurk behind the apparently natural and innocent. Barthes was among the first theorists to take a serious interest in popular culture, and the influence of *Mythologies* can still be seen whenever car advertisements, sport or soap operas are given the sort of critical attention more traditionally reserved for 'great' novels or the theatre.

Mythologies is an exercise in semiology, the 'science of **signs**' initiated by Ferdinand de Saussure. Semiology was one of the main strands in the great structuralist movement which dominated French intellectual life in the 1950s and 1960s, and which attempted to identify the structures which frame and govern meaningful human activities. Barthes' most sustained attempt at a full-blown structural analysis is *The Fashion System* (1967). Selecting as his field the captions accompanying the photographs in fashion magazines, Barthes constructs a 'grammar' of fashion and demonstrates the different levels at which meanings are generated.

The scientific structuralism of *The Fashion System* was itself out of fashion by the time it appeared. The poststructuralism of Jacques **Derrida** and Julia **Kristeva** carried Saussure's insight into the arbitrariness of

the sign to its extreme, undermining any attempt to discover ultimate meaning in the infinite play of signifiers. Barthes took these criticisms of his own methodology very much to heart, and his texts of the later 1960s and 1970s show an abrupt awakening from what he termed his 'dream of scientificity'.

The most impressive of these later works is *S/Z* (1970), an extraordinary analysis of a short story by Balzac. Barthes demonstrates that even those texts which aspire to 'realism' are always woven from other texts, representing not a picture of reality, but a patchwork of cultural commonplaces, and second- and third-hand observations. Barthes contrasts the classic *lisible*, or readable work, typified by the great bourgeois novels of the nineteenth century, in which the reader is a passive consumer, to the *scriptible* or 'writable' text, in which the reader becomes an active producer.

In *The Pleasure of the Text*, published in 1973, Barthes develops an 'erotics of reading'. The contrast between the ***writerly*** and ***readerly*** encountered in *S/Z* is translated into the two types of sensation experienced by the reader: *plaisir* and *jouissance*. The text of pleasure offers the traditional joys of the classic novel: intelligence, **irony**, delicacy, euphoria, mastery and security. *Jouissance*, or ecstasy, is the shock of the unexpected, where the reader's comfort is destroyed, where language is fissured. Barthes holds out the tantalizing prospect of a text combining *plaisir* and *jouissance*, an ideal of a classic work rent by a disorienting erotic thrill, or a **modern**, avant-garde text made readable as well as shocking.

The final three texts that Barthes published in his lifetime are all profoundly personal. *Roland Barthes by Roland Barthes* (1975) is a whimsical autobiography, in which the author gently mocks his previous intellectual incarnations. *A Lover's Discourse* (1977) picks apart the language of love with an almost novelistic intensity and focus. *Camera Lucida* (1980), is both a theoretical work – a phenomenology of photography – and a very personal exploration of his relationship with his mother. In *Camera Lucida* Barthes suggests that photography gives us access to the 'real' world in a way that language cannot. We are offered a meaning beyond language, and, more than a meaning, the truth. This seems a complete turnaround for Barthes, who had always denied the idea of a unitary truth or a fixed meaning.

Apart from *Mythologies*, Barthes is best known for his notorious 1968 essay, '**The Death of the Author**'. Barthes argues that the concept of an **author** as someone having privileged access to the meaning of a text, a meaning determined by the will of the author, has passed its usefulness. Texts are a 'fabric of quotations, resulting from a thousand sources of culture', and acknowledging the death of the author allows us to turn our attention to the reader, who is reborn as the creator of meanings. [AM]

BAUDRILLARD, JEAN: SOCIOLOGIST (1929–) Baudrillard was initially associated with the revolutionary left, and his work was a neo-**Marxian** critique of late-capitalist societies. In his early publications, *Le système des objets* (1968), *La société de consommation* (1970), and *For a Critique of a Political Economy of the Sign* (1972), he began to study the part played by consumerism in the maintenance of capitalism, arguing the existence of a system of objects, which undergo a process of commodification in order to re-emerge as **signs**. These 'sign-values' are absorbed into a process of mass production and replication which not only fulfils the needs of a consumer society, but creates the very perception of need in the first place.

With the publication of *The Mirror of Production* in 1973, however, Baudrillard began to move away from a Marxist position, arguing that Marxism has failed to conduct a sufficiently radical critique of capitalism and thus has been absorbed into the very bourgeois order it attempts to set itself against. In *Symbolic Exchange and Death* (1976), Baudrillard himself attempts to make that definitive break, in the process developing his self-appointed role as the prophet of 'the end': of economy, production and history itself. Proposing 'a "science of imaginary solutions"; that is, a sciencefiction of the system's reversal against itself at the extreme level of **simulation**, a reversible simulation in a hyperlogic of death and destruction', Baudrillard envisages a **postmodern** society bound up entirely in social reproduction, or 'simulation', in which all sense of origin is lost in the play of endlessly replicating sign systems.

Baudrillard's ideas regarding simulation arise from a fascination with technology and technological processes, dating from his 1967 review of Marshall **McLuhan**'s *Understanding Media*. For Baudrillard, technology is a paradigm for postmodern society in its entirety, where, as he says in *The Ecstasy of Communication* (1983), 'the scene and the mirror have given way to the screen and the network'.

Such concepts reach their apotheosis in *America* (1988), an audacious piece of postmodern theorization which, in its combination of tourist-style photographs with Baudrillard's meditation on the 'meaning' of America, is half travelogue, half cultural analysis. He presents America as a model of a '**hyperreal**' future, where reality has entirely disappeared beneath the glossy, seductive, surfaces of simulation: 'You should not begin with the city and move inwards to the screen; you should begin with the screen and move outwards to the city.' However, in the end it is the desert, not the city, that comes to stand in this book as the ultimate symbol of the postmodern condition, 'because you are delivered from all depths there – a brilliant, mobile, superficial neutrality, a challenge to meaning and profundity, a challenge to nature and culture, an outer hyperspace, with no origin, no reference points'.

America thus also stands as an apposite example of the deliberately provocative **irony** with which Baudrillard presents his ideas. In his self-appointed role as 'intellectual terrorist' the avant-garde nature of many of his proclamations make it difficult to take them entirely seriously – although according to Baudrillard's own definition of the postmodern context, it is of course impossible to establish the 'truth' of any of the theorist's assertions, since his ideas are themselves implicated in the endless self-referential game of simulation. It is not surprising, therefore, that reactions to Baudrillard vary between claiming him as a guru for radical **postmodernity** and castigating him for sloppy and inaccurate thinking.

Baudrillard's penchant for deliberate provocation and half-veiled irony is nowhere more apparent than in *Seduction* (1989), in which he takes issue with feminism's project to increase women's access to the sphere of the social and the political. Seduction, which is neither 'simple appearance, nor a pure absence, but the eclipse of **presence**', is equated with the feminine principle, which is in danger of being destroyed when women attempt to enter the masculine **discourse** of production. Baudrillard's conception of women thus appears to expose him as a male philosopher who conflates his own simplistic notions of femininity with a definition of the 'real' nature of women. Again, however, it is impossible to tell how much of this argument is intended as a genuine attack on feminism, and how much yet another postmodernist game with meaning. [SG]

BAUMAN, ZYGMUNT: SOCIOLOGIST (1925–) Zygmunt Bauman is one of the most articulate and theoretically sophisticated interpreters of modern – that is, **postmodern** – life. Before his expulsion from Poland after the Russian invasion of Czechoslovakia in 1968, Bauman was already a leading Polish sociologist. Active since 1971 at the University of Leeds, Bauman has written major studies of the post-1945 transformation of the English working class. He has also been a key interpreter of the hermeneutic tradition within sociology, the critical tradition of 'Western' or **Hegelian Marxism** and the utopian dimension of the socialist ideal.

In recent years, in a series of books concerned with the problems of **modernism** and postmodernism, Bauman has turned the spotlight on the many confusions and crises which make up the fabric of our lives towards the end of this century. A prolific writer, Bauman offers his analyses in prose that is always lucid and accessible. *Thinking Sociologically* (1990) is a clear unfussy demonstration of what is involved in any discipline attempting to think seriously about our lives in society. It owes much of its richness and accessibility to Bauman's unparalleled grasp of the realities of contemporary life as we actually experience it. Although his learning is prodigious, even in his most far-reaching works Bauman is constantly interpreting facets of everyday life and experiences common to all, rather than simply indulging in the exegesis of theoretical **texts**. Bauman's compellingly readable books can genuinely serve as a 'guide to the perplexed'.

Bauman's stance is that of an interpreter of modern life, not an intellectual seeking to legislate or prescribe. Bauman's most succinct formulation of the **difference** between modernism and postmodernism is captured in the title of one of his shorter books: *Legislators and Interpreters: On Modernity, Postmodernity and Intellectuals* (1987). Ever since the first stirrings of modernity – in the seventeenth and eighteenth centuries – intellectuals have been tempted to identify themselves with social and political programmes which would usher in a completely new social order. Instead of grasping their flights of fancy and their critical insights as the products of a utopian imagination they have been seduced into seeing themselves as the architects of concrete, realizable utopias (a contradiction in terms). Bauman sees the chief weakness of the modernist impulse as being its refusal to live with the problems, the messiness of history. The dream of purifying history (what Marx called the leap from history into the realm of freedom) has led to appalling programmes of social engineering – under fascism in the name of purity of race and under communism in the name of purity of class.

In *Modernity and the Holocaust* (1989), Bauman has given us a compelling interpretation of the ways in which the policies of racial murder pursued by the National Socialists in Germany expressed and exploited the achievements of **modernity** and cannot simply be treated as a irrational aberration. He traces the ways in which modernity made it possible for cruel things to 'be done by non-cruel people'.

Bauman has analysed specifically postmodern forms of violence – arising from the 'privatization, deregulation and decentralization of the identity problem' – and is an acute critic of what he terms 'neo-tribal' tendencies in contemporary society.

Bauman endorses that reading of the postmodern condition which insists that we need to learn to live with the problems – and risks – of modernity. But he remains a critical spirit, committed to opposing evil and exploitation, and his books contain a catalogue of the insanities and obscenities of our contemporary life. In Bauman's terms: 'Postmodernity is the moral person's bane and chance at the same time . . . which of the two faces of the postmodern condition will turn out to be its lasting likeness, is itself a moral question.'

One of the many significant features of (post)modern life of which he is acutely critical is a process he terms 'adiaphorization'

– a process that reflects the increasing distance between our morality and our deeds, and removes certain events and relationships from the domain of moral scrutiny. The term is taken from medieval scholastic debates where ideas were declared to be orthodox or heretical, or adiaphorized – declared neutral from the point of view of religious and moral dogma. Bauman traces this process in detail in *Modernity and the Holocaust* and in *Modernity and Ambivalence* (1991), and shows how the process has been exacerbated by the development of technology.

The strong concern with morality and ethics which has been developed in works such as *Postmodern Ethics* (1993), *Life in Fragments* (1995), and *Postmodernity and its Discontents* (1997) shows that a utopian impulse persists, not as a social or even theoretical programme, but as a guiding or regulative idea which keeps Bauman's unique sociological imagination constantly reflexive and critical. [LS]

BELL, DANIEL: SOCIOLOGIST (1919–) Bell is best known as one of the theorists of '**post-industrialism**', a notion that has had a considerable impact within **postmodern** thought. Bell's best-known works are *The End of Ideology* (1960) and *The Coming of Post-Industrial Society* (1973). *The End of Ideology* has been a seminal text in the development of what has been called '**endism**': the notion that history and ideology have come to an end thanks to the twin triumphs of Western democratic politics and the economic system underpinning it, capitalism. Thinkers like Francis **Fukuyama** have been particularly influenced by Bell's work on 'endism', a theory that has enjoyed a surge of popularity in the last couple of decades with the collapse of the Soviet Union and its client states in Eastern Europe. Bell himself in his later career has become somewhat worried by the rightwing slant of much 'endist' theory, although it is worth pointing out that in its day *The*

End of Ideology was vigorously attacked by left-wing critics, who claimed that it ignored the reality of life in the third world and helped to maintain the political status quo. For such critics, endism was merely another ideology, that of Western political liberalism, whose concern was to discourage the view that any opposition was possible.

The Coming of Post-Industrial Society, subtitled *A Venture in Social Forecasting*, suggested that we were on the brink of a new kind of information-led, service-oriented society that would replace the industrial-based model that had been dominant in the West in the nineteenth and twentieth centuries. A post-industrial society has for Bell three main components: 'a shift from manufacturing to services'; 'the centrality of the new science-based industries'; and 'the rise of new technical elites and the advent of a new principle of stratification'. Since *The Coming of Post-Industrial Society* was published, much of what Bell has forecast has indeed come to pass in the 'mass consumption' societies of the West, although, as many critics would be quick to point out, not without considerable social cost in terms of unemployment and job insecurity. Bell has, however, clearly foreseen the direction Western culture is taking, and his work now looks to prefigure much postmodern thought, which has similarly emphasized the socially transforming **power** of information technology (see, for example, Jean-François **Lyotard**'s *The Postmodern Condition*). The need to break with the outdated narrative of **modernism**, which included within it an uncritical belief in industrial progress and exploitation of the material world, has come to be widely recognized, and most of the advanced Western economies could be described as post-industrial to at least some degree. Certainly, service industries, knowledge production, and information technology form an increasingly important part of Western life, particularly as regards

wealth creation. Whether they agree with Bell's particular vision or not, the kind of ideal society envisaged by most postmodernists is unmistakably post-industrial. [SS]

BENJAMIN, WALTER: CULTURAL CRITIC (1892–1940) Walter Benjamin was born into a prosperous Jewish family in Berlin. Having failed to secure an academic position, he became a literary journalist. He was influenced by Ernst Bloch and György Lukács, and became a friend of Bertolt Brecht, whose work he championed. Following the coming to **power** of the Nazis, he left Germany for France in 1933. In Paris he worked on a project called the 'Passagenwerke' (Arcades Project), which he considered his greatest work but which he never finished. A close friend of – and important influence on – Theodor **Adorno**, his writings stand in an uneasy relation to those of the **Frankfurt School**, with which he was periodically associated (particularly while writing his study of Baudelaire, since published as *Charles Baudelaire: A Lyric Poet in the Era of High Capitalism*). Only two of Benjamin's books were published during his lifetime: *The Origin of German Tragic Drama* and *The Concept of Art Criticism in German Romanticism.* In 1940 – fleeing the Nazis – he left Paris for the Spanish border, where he committed suicide at the age of 48.

Benjamin's 1936 essay 'The Work of Art in the Age of Mechanical Reproduction' (in the collection *Illuminations*) proposes a distinction between, on the one hand, the work of art as an object with a ritual or cult value, a value gained from a specific place in space and time, and, on the other hand, mechanically reproduced work, which can have no such value. In the age of mechanical reproduction, says Benjamin, the work of art has lost its '**aura**': the perceived authenticity that comes from its being an *original*. With **modern** forms of technological representation, such as photography and cinema, not only is the work endlessly reproducible, but it makes no sense to speak of an original in the first place. This state of affairs is open to exploitation in reactionary or progressive ways, leading either to the aestheticization of politics (fascism) or the politicization of aesthetics (communism). Benjamin's ambivalence over the consequences of the new technologies for political and aesthetic **representation** has made this text a crucial one for later **postmodern** explorations of the relations between aesthetics, politics and technology.

A further ambivalence characterizes Benjamin's work as a whole: his writings oscillate between (and do not appear to reconcile) the poles of dialectical materialism and an enigmatic form of Jewish mysticism. Most evidently connected in the late essay 'Theses on the History of Philosophy', the twin allegiances of his intellectual position have in common for Benjamin the attempt to rescue a certain conception of the now, of the *Jetztzeit* ('now-time'), which is obliterated by thinking of history in terms of a progressive linear continuum. For Benjamin, the task of the historian or the critic is to see the historical moment not 'as it really was' (the project of historicism) but *blasted out of the continuum of history*, in its full potential as a moment of crisis or danger. In this he anticipates the postmodern concern with rethinking temporality and historicity. [BD]

BERLIN, ISAIAH: PHILOSOPHER (1906–97) Many people believe that where ideas or beliefs come into conflict there must be some way of either reconciling those differences or deciding between them – some higher court of appeal or overarching system. **Postmodernists** such as **Lyotard** and **Baudrillard** reject this yearning for **metanarratives** that can bring about this great reconciliation. In the place of these unifying systems, postmodernism advocates **pluralism** and celebrates **difference**. This view was given its most coherent and powerful expression not by any of the more exotic postmodernist theorists but by the rather staid, old-fashioned figure of Isaiah Berlin, the great historian of ideas and defender of political liberalism.

For Berlin, the central fact of human existence is that we all want different things; our aims, aspirations, needs and **desires** can never be made to coincide. Berlin's 'liberalism' is based on the acceptance that society must be plural, and that we cannot argue or rationalize our way out of the confusion of human values into a simpler world. To be human is to differ. Berlin's pluralism follows from his rejection of the idea that there is a single human nature. People, for Berlin, are products of the enormously complex web of influences specific to particular cultures and times, and he has always championed those thinkers, such as Vico and Herder, who have recognized this specificity. Giambattista Vico (1668–1744) was among the first to realize the imaginative leap needed to enter the minds of those living in earlier historical periods. Johann Gottfried von Herder carried Vico's insights further, emphasizing the particularity of different contemporary cultures, moulded by their separate geographies, histories, languages and myths. Berlin, although temperamentally a man of the **Enlightenment**, felt that these figures of the 'counter-Enlightenment' were a necessary corrective to the rationalist belief in the unity of mankind and the inevitability of progress.

Although, for Berlin, we are the products of our times, he retains a place for a (limited) freedom of choice for the human **subject**. In his essay 'Historical Inevitability' (in *Four Essays on Liberty* (1969)) he argues that without this freedom our concept of morality, our legal system and our view of history would have no meaning. Introducing an element of free choice means abandoning historicist, deterministic accounts of human history –

there are times when the actions of great leaders have changed history, and those actions were, at least partially, the result of free choices. History therefore can have no master plan, no fixed pattern.

Isaiah Berlin has been one of the most influential theorists of liberalism since the Second World War. It is an influence, however, felt more in the wider world of cultural **discourse** than among professional philosophers. His liberalism is both more humane and conceptually much richer than such neo-liberals as Friedman, Hayek and Nozick, but for that reason it came to seem a little dated in the 1970s and 1980s. However, Berlin's belief in the **incommensurability** of values, and his denial of the possibility of achieving the Enlightenment goal of perfect, transcultural rationality, did put him in the vanguard of contemporary ideas. [AM]

BEUYS, JOSEPH: ARTIST (1921–86) Beuys, a prominent member of the Fluxus group in the early 1960s, was always outside the official spaces of high **modernism**, which, in its rigorous opposition of art and life, endorsed the very **difference** Beuys wished to overcome. His practice, a mixture of performance art, dada and psycho-drama, demonstrated his belief that the aesthetic reveals dynamic processes of bodily energy. Accordingly, the duty of the artist is to factor an alternative public culture from the common materials of existence. Beuys defined himself as an activist, a curator of spaces and experiences that he defines as artworks by making them into gifts for the audience, his collaborators in the process of cultural and social growth. These ideas formed the basis of his teaching. Having spent eleven years as Professor of Sculpture at the Kunstacademie in Dusseldorf, a period in which he became increasingly associated with an anti-modernist radicalism, he was dismissed from his post in 1972 for encouraging a programme of open admission to the academy.

Beuys's conception of art as a non-**discursive** force, a conception that tended to push it in the direction of the mythic and the archetypal, was developed by his star pupil, Anselm **Kiefer**, one of the key figures in the European form of **postmodernism** known as the **trans-avant-garde**. Like Beuys, Kiefer's art offers a double identity marked by the simultaneous sanctification and obliteration of objects. [CT]

BHABHA, HOMI K.: CRITIC, CULTURAL THEORIST (1949–) Homi Bhabha's analyses of the **postcolonial** condition have contributed much to the current critical and theoretical debate. His main works include *Nation and Narration* (ed., 1990) and *The Location of Culture* (1994).

Anti-essentialist in his approach, Bhabha questions the notion of a 'unitary identity' with his concept of '**hybridity**', an anti-monolithic model of cultural exchange which negates the polarity of binary models of culture with elements that are 'neither the One, nor the **Other** but something else besides which contrasts the terms and territories of both'. The alternative, according to Bhabha, is essentialized national stereotypes, constantly driven by a nostalgia for pure origins in an 'attempt to hark back to a "true" national past, which is often represented in the reified forms of realism and stereotype'. He also incisively notes in *Of Mimicry and Man: The Ambivalence of Colonial Discourse* that one of the distinguishing features of a colonial relationship is what he calls 'colonial mimicry' induced in the subject race taught to imitate the dominant race. Thus the colonized is in the position of being 'almost the same' as the colonizer without being actually granted the freedoms that come with sovereignty, dominion and citizenship. Bhabha argues further for a 'discursive conception of ideology' in which ideology is multi-accentual and 'reality' is seen as *produced* by **texts** as opposed to something that is fixed or a given. In this his work reflects

Marxist theorists such as Althusser, **Eagleton** and Macherey; however, Bhabha's critique of contemporary Marxist theory problematizes notions of 'mimeticism' and 'teleology' borrowing from **Freudian** and **Lacanian** psychoanalysis. The colonized is associated with excess and fantasy: 'a site for dreams, images, fantasies, myths, obsessions and requirements'; a discursive repository that is a function of the repression of the colonizer. Thus there is a systematic ambivalence on the part of the colonizer towards 'that otherness that is at once an object of derision and **desire**'.

Bhabha's contribution to the current theoretical debate lies in his interest in the construction of identity and **subjectivity** from the point of view of the colonized. His critiques of **Said**, **Derrida** and **Lyotard** highlight the ways in which the colonized Other has been marginalized by contemporary **critical theory**. He further challenges the notion of the absolute **hegemony** of the colonizing **power** by highlighting the way in which encounters with the colonized destabilize and interrogate notions of cultural identity. Fundamentally against rigid or reductive **binary oppositions**, Bhabha's later work challenges the rigid boundaries between colonizer and colonized using a theoretical methodology that is **pluralist** and diverse, avoiding critical and theoretical exclusivity in the spirit of **postmodernism**. [AY]

BINARY OPPOSITIONS The use of binary oppositions in analysing phenomena is highly characteristic of **structuralism**, and one of the aspects of its methodology that is most vigorously attacked by **poststructuralist** critics. Thus, in **Lévi-Strauss**, 'nature' and 'culture' are set in opposition to each other as mutually exclusive categories, such that given examples of human behaviour must belong to one or other category – but not both. Lévi-Strauss proceeds to run into problems with the incest taboo, which he is forced to admit

does seem to belong to both categories. For **Derrida**, this is an admission that calls into question the whole structuralist project, the methodology of which is seen to be faulty. Poststructuralists like Derrida also consider that the principle of binary opposition (*either* one thing *or* its opposite number) depends on a notion of fixed identity that is no longer tenable; as far as they are concerned, identity is a much more fluid phenomenon than structuralists would like to believe. [SS]

BLACK CRITICISM With its emphasis on tradition, and on experience, often authenticated through the autobiographical voice, black writing seems inimical to a good deal of **postmodern** theory with its talk of the **death of the author**, the fluidity of **subjectivity** and of the end of history. Yet some of the most familiar critical concepts in the postmodern lexicon – marginality, **difference**, **Otherness** – have given a powerful impetus to the exploration of black **texts**, though not without controversy among black scholars themselves. Black American writing is a good example of the tensions between the demands of political and aesthetic expression. Black criticism sees race as a fundamental category of cultural analysis. The publication of self-authored narratives by ex-slaves in the antebellum period was a profoundly political as well as aesthetic act. While many displayed an exuberant 'literariness', they were written as part of the propaganda war against slavery since, as a number of critics have pointed out, literacy was the principal sign of reason, a faculty that white supremacists denied black people possessed. Art would be put in the service of politics from the Harlem renaissance of the 1920s, when critics called for a literature that would show the black race at its best, in the 1940s and 1950s by communist fellow travellers arguing for reform and integration, and in the 1960s by black nationalists in such books as Addison Gayle's *The Black Aesthetic*

(1972), which called for revolution and a cross-class alliance of black Americans. In the 1970s Gayle's essentialism and chauvinism were challenged by growing numbers of black feminist critics and by the emergence of **poststructuralist** analysis. In the postmodern world, critics still value concepts of blackness and tradition, though they are no longer identified by authorial skin colour, but through the very language of the texts themselves. [PD]

BLACK HOLES Despite their being entirely hypothetical or theoretical entities, black holes remain powerfully attractive to cosmologists and astrophysicists such as Stephen **Hawking** and Roger Penrose. For all astrophysics based (as in fact it all is) on general relativity, light is the limit velocity of the universe; nothing, in other words, travels faster than light. The first theoretical account of black holes stems from J. R. Oppenheimer and H. Snyder's application in 1939 of the principles of general relativity to the life cycles of stars. A black hole is a collapsing star of such mass that the velocity required to escape its gravitational field exceeds the velocity of light – which, by the principles of general relativity, is impossible. A black hole is therefore black because it emits no light, and a hole because within it all matter, and even space-time, is destroyed. Black holes are 'expected' to arise when the mass of a neutron star (not all stars will attain the violent end of the neutron star; our Sun, for example, will not) reaches a density so high as to create a gravitational field so strong that even the matter-energy of which the star consists will collapse under its own gravity. Many properties stem from this. One is the notion of the 'event horizon' of a black hole: the limit point of the black hole's gravitational field. As this event horizon is approached, since light is unable to escape it, time slows until within it nothing happens: neither matter nor even space-time survives the event horizon of a black hole.

Some cosmologists have hypothesized that the isolated space-time of black holes turns them, to all intents and purposes, into separate universes, each competing with others, through intense gravitation, for resources in order to realize the 'best of all possible worlds' on the evolutionary basis suggested by the fact that stars have life cycles. It is both tempting and appropriate to suggest that the theoretical physics of black holes, a multiverse composed of timeless and spaceless dematerialized yet physical absences, separated by unbridgeable event horizons the one from the other, provides a genuinely physical instantiation of the **postmodern** condition. [IHG]

BLOOM, HAROLD: CRITIC, THEORIST (1930–) Bloom is one of the most prolific of contemporary critics. His works include *A Map of Misreading* (1975), *Kabbalah and Criticism* (1975), *Poetry and Repression* (1976), *Agon* (1952), *The Book of J* (1991), *The Western Canon* (1994), and *Shakespeare: The Invention of the Human* (1998). In *The Anxiety of Influence* (1973), his most widely read monograph, Bloom argues that every poet is engaged in an agonistic struggle against his literary forebears. In **Freudian** psychoanalysis, the analysand must come to terms with the **Oedipal** love–hate relationship of son to father. Similarly, the poet must try to escape the gravitational pull exerted by his precursors. During this struggle, primary sources are misread and reconfigured by the later poet.

This idea is especially applicable to the production of **postmodernist** texts. Authors as diverse as Kathy **Acker**, John **Barth**, Italo **Calvino** and Umberto **Eco** are only too well aware that everything has already been written before them. Indeed, Barth coined the term 'literature of exhaustion' to denote the condition of 'used-upness'. Faced with this belatedness, the postmodernist novel typically misreads a previous novel or novels. Acker's *Great*

Expectations (1978), Barth's *Sot-Weed Factor* (1960), Calvino's *Invisible Cities* (1972) and Eco's *The Name of the Rose* (1984) can all be usefully studied in terms of their relation to prior texts.

Bloom's emphasis on misreading was congenial to members of the **Yale School** of **deconstruction**, such as Jacques **Derrida**, Geoffrey Hartman and J. Hillis Miller, as it helped displace certain assumptions that once underpinned the study of literature. He himself, however, has little sympathy with deconstructive reading practices, and believes them to be inimical to the upholding of aesthetic value. Bloom's greatest scorn is reserved for what he calls the 'School of Resentment': those feminists, **Marxists**, **Lacanians** and **new historicists** who treat **texts** as pulpits for preaching their own sermons on social inequality.

Since 1990 Bloom has concentrated on addressing a readership outside of what he sees as a decadent academia, and on reasserting the primacy of literary tradition. In *The Western Canon* he focuses on twenty-six of the most prominent European and American authors (Dante, Chaucer, Shakespeare, Dickens, for example). *Shakespeare: The Invention of the Human* exalts the Bard to such an extent that he is credited with creating the concept of personality itself. *How to Read and Why* (2000) does exactly what it says on the tin. These late books constitute a didactic, and often persuasive, counter-attack against the decentralizing tendencies of postmodernism. [BL]

BODY WITHOUT ORGANS A term used by **Deleuze** and **Guattari** to describe all those forces that hinder the free expression of **desire** and **libidinal** energy. For the authors, the body without organs (which they also refer to as 'the body without an image') is sterile and unproductive, and they identify it with the forces of repression in society. Capital, for example, is to be regarded as the body without organs of the capitalist, which appropriates the production of individual **desiring-machines** (in this case wage labourers) for its own ends. Production (a term encompassing the expression of desire and libidinal energy) is a positive force for Deleuze and Guattari, and bodies without organs are to be resisted because they restrict its range while channelling what is left into their own projects (the creation of profits for themselves, for example). [SS]

BOFILL, RICARDO: ARCHITECT (1939–) Claiming the title of the 'Jimi Hendrix of architecture' early in his career, Bofill has more in common with psychedelic fantasy album cover art. His idiosyncratic architecture is a strange overgrown classical encrustation – Corinthian columns pumped full of steroids. It is an aesthetic that is grotesque and surreal – monumental facades decorated with massively overscaled columns concealing **modern** apartment complexes. Recalling a European tradition of fascist architecture and grandeur associated with Napoleon, Hitler and Franco, and an affinity with the conscientious 'mad genius' of fellow Catalans Gaudi and Dali, Bofill found admirers among French property developers. His heroic and triumphalist containers of luxury apartments encrusted with concrete baroque ornament appealed to the imagination of the French homeowners in a way that modernist equivalents failed to. His scheme for the Espaces d'Abraxas, in suburban Paris, invents itself as a ten-storey circular theatre, enclosing an area of public space, while internally fluted one-way mirror columns rise up the facade. Les Arcades du Lac, another Parisian housing scheme, features strange interpretations of Doric columns which house new programmes such as stairways or bathroom blocks.

Bofill's free-wheeling use of classical iconography is made all the more weird by its lack of **irony**. These are buildings that fail to engage with their own absurdity.

Though full of contradictions and complexities, it is an architecture completely engrossed in and enamoured with its own grandeur. [SJ]

BOURDIEU, PIERRE: SOCIOLOGIST (1930–) One of the key claims in the debate over **postmodernism** is the assertion that the distinction between high and low culture is becoming increasingly blurred. This collapse in cultural certainty has brought about a rethinking of traditional ideas of cultural value. The turn to questions of value has witnessed a growing interest in the work of the French sociologist Pierre Bourdieu. He argues that distinctions of 'culture' (whether understood as **text**, practice or way of living) are a significant aspect in the struggle between dominant and subordinate classes in society. He shows how arbitrary tastes and arbitrary ways of living are continually transmuted into **legitimate** taste and the only legitimate way of life. The 'illusion of "natural distinction" is ultimately based on the power of the dominant to impose, by their very existence, a definition of excellence which [is] nothing other than their own way of existing'. For Bourdieu, 'taste classifies, and it classifies the classifier'. We are classified by our classifications and classify others by theirs. While such strategies of classification do not in themselves produce social inequalities, the making, marking and maintaining of them functions to legitimate such inequalities. Taste is a profoundly ideological **discourse**; it functions as a marker of 'class' (using the term in the double sense to mean both socioeconomic category and a particular level of quality). The consumption of culture is, ultimately, he claims, 'predisposed . . . to fulfil a social function of legitimating social **difference**'.

Bourdieu's work on culture is underpinned by his view of education. He argues that the education system fulfils a quite specific function: to legitimate social inequalities which exist before its operations. The cultural tastes of dominant classes are given institutional form and then, with deft ideological sleight of hand, their taste for this institutionalized culture (i.e. their own) is held up as evidence of their cultural, and ultimately social, superiority. Distinction is generated by learned patterns of cultural consumption which are internalized as 'natural' cultural preferences, and interpreted and mobilized as evidence of 'natural' cultural competences, which are ultimately used to justify forms of class domination. To understand this fully we need to understand how Bourdieu distinguishes between three types of capital: economic, social and cultural. In capitalist societies economic capital in the form of money, property, etc. is able to buy access to cultural and social capital. Hierarchies openly based on the accumulation of economic capital are vulnerable to challenge. Cultural and social capital is able to conceal and legitimate economic domination by reproducing it in the form of cultural and social hierarchies.

Bourdieu's purpose is not to prove the self-evident, that different classes have different lifestyles and different tastes in culture, but to identify and interrogate the processes by which the making of cultural distinctions secures and legitimates forms of power and control rooted ultimately in economic inequalities. He is interested not so much in the actual differences, but in how these differences are used by dominant classes as a means of social reproduction. His project is to (re)locate 'value' in the world of everyday experience, to suggest that similar things are happening when I 'value' a holiday destination or a particular mode of dress, as are happening when I 'value' a poem by T. S. Eliot or a song by Oasis or a photograph by Cindy **Sherman** or a piece of music by Philip **Glass**. Such evaluations are never a simple matter of individual taste; cultural value operates both to identify and to maintain social difference and sustain social deference. From this perspective, the much heralded postmodern collapse of standards may be nothing more than a perceived sense that the opportunities to use culture to make, mark and maintain social distinction are becoming more and more difficult to find, as Pavarotti tops the charts and Premier League football becomes, in many instances, as expensive as ballet or opera. [JS]

BRAIDOTTI, ROSI: FEMINIST PHILOSOPHER, CULTURAL THEORIST (1954–) Born in Italy, Braidotti was raised in Australia, and wrote her doctoral dissertation in French at the Sorbonne. Her first book, *Patterns of Dissonance* (1991), was written in French, translated, then extensively rewritten in English, becoming 'a translation without originals'. This self-description as a '**subject** in transit', a thinker with 'no mother tongue, only a succession of translations, of displacements', is crucial in Braidotti's articulation of a **postmodern** feminism.

Patterns of Dissonance analyses the relationship between philosophy and feminist theory, arguing that postmodern French philosophers such as **Foucault**, **Derrida** and **Deleuze** have responded to the contemporary 'crisis' of the rational subject by embracing 'the feminine'. This metaphorical embrace, however, goes hand in hand with a renewed exclusion of women from philosophical **discourse**. Against this, Braidotti sets feminist critiques of rationality and its relation to sexual **difference**. Feminist theory, she argues, insists on the embodied and therefore sexually differentiated nature of subjectivity. The feminist theorist *speaks* as a woman, so that theorizing is reconnected to its roots in the body and in **desire**, and incorporates both an ethics and a politics. Embodiment does not, however, mean 'essentialism'. Braidotti's embodied female subject is not a fixed and monolithic essence, but the site of multiple, complex and potentially contradictory sets of experiences. Her knowledge is situated and partial, her identity simply a map of where she has already been. She is therefore '**nomadic**', a concept developed in *Nomadic Subjects* (1994). The nomad is both situated (hence interconnected) and in movement, with a critical consciousness which resists incorporation. As such, she becomes a metaphor for Braidotti's vision of a postmodern feminism, which can counter the pessimism of postmodern philosophy by embracing its emphasis on the fragmentary nature of identity, while retaining a politics, and an ethics, of sexual difference. [ST]

BRICOLAGE In *The Savage Mind* (1966) **Lévi-Strauss** differentiated between primitive and advanced thought, by describing the former as less structured and theoretically sophisticated than the latter. Just as a *bricoleur* (handyman) might improvise with whatever materials were available to him if mending a broken object or appliance, so the world-view of primitive tribes was constructed out of recycled ideas and beliefs rearranged as needed. The scientist or technologist, on the other hand, approached problems in a highly theoretical manner, and if necessary could invent new tools or methods in search of solutions. Bricolage thus stands in opposition to **modern** thought patterns, being ad hoc in character instead of rigorously systematic.

The sense of improvisation that bricolage carries appeals to the **postmodern** theorist, since it suggests an arbitrary, undetermined quality to creative activity in which the end is not specified in advance. Where a modern thinker might see lack of order or method, his postmodern counterpart would see a welcome exercise of spontaneity. The postmodern enthusiasm for pastiche, whereby creative artists ransack the past for inspiration, underlines this commitment to bricolage as an aesthetic ideal. Most postmodern theorists would also want to argue that there is far more bricolage going on in scientific thought than is generally acknowledged. [SS]

BRYARS, GAVIN: COMPOSER (1943–) While studying philosophy, Bryars played jazz double bass in his spare time, exploring free improvisation. As well as gaining a considerable reputation as a jazz performer, he was a founder member of the Portsmouth Sinfonia. This experimental ensemble that undertook anarchic reinterpretations of standard orchestral concert pieces, consisted mainly of amateurs and gained a certain cult status.

Early pieces such as *Jesus' Blood Never Failed Me Yet* show an indebtedness to the repetitive **minimalist** techniques of American composers such as **Reich** and **Glass**. Bryars has written for a variety of instrumental forces. He has composed orchestral pieces (such as *The Green Ray* (1991)), choral works (*On Photography* (1983)) and many pieces for his own ensemble (such as *The Cross Channel Ferry* (1979) and *Viennese Dance No. 1* (1985). This ensemble was formed in 1979 and tours extensively.

The first of his three operas, *Medea,* a five-act work that was directed and designed by Robert Wilson, was first performed by the Opéra de Lyon in 1984. Bryars' music has also been used by choreographers. *Sub Rosa* (1986) was used by William Forsythe for the Frankfurt Ballet's 'Slingerland' and *Four Elements* (1990) was commissioned by the Rambert Dance Company for a ballet by Lucinda Childs. [AB]

BUTLER, JUDITH: FEMINIST SOCIOLOGIST, PHILOSOPHER (1956–) Butler's work centres primarily around the interrogation of gender identity. In her most widely read publication, *Gender Trouble: Feminism and the Subversion of Identity* (1990), she maintains that feminist theory and politics build their agendas upon an unquestioned assumption that women, purely because of their shared femaleness, share a common identity which cuts through **differences** of race, class and sexual preference. However, Butler, far from regarding gender identity as 'natural', redefines it as a **discourse** which is both constructed and maintained by society.

Butler also argues that feminist theorists such as Luce **Irigaray** are misled in their attempt to posit the existence of a female sexuality which exists independently of the phallocentric order, for 'if sexuality is culturally constructed within existing **power** relations, then the postulation of a normative sexuality that is "before", "outside" or "beyond" power is a cultural impossibility and a politically impractical dream'.

For Butler, any consideration of identity cannot be carried out independently of the interrogation of gender, since gender is the foundation upon which the concept of identity itself is based. In other words, **subjects** only become intelligible when defined in relation to accepted categories of gender. She uses the term 'compulsory heterosexuality' to describe the institution which maintains the coherence of gender identity through persistent reference to the fixed opposition male/female, in which each category is defined through its difference to the **Other**, a distinction which is consolidated through heterosexual practice.

The system, therefore, conceals its own status as construction by presenting the heterosexual dualism as 'normal', 'natural' and 'right'. Nevertheless, however convincing it might be, the construct is not seamless, and its maintenance is far from effortless. Instead, Butler defines gender constructions as 'performances' or 'fabrications', perpetuated by the repeated inscription of gendered 'acts, gestures and enactments' upon the surface of the body. The illusion has to be constantly maintained, however, in order to conceal the fact that it 'has no ontological status apart from the various acts which constitute its reality'.

This performative aspect of gender becomes, for Butler, the means by which its claims to be expressive of 'true' identity can be questioned. While it may be impossible to construct a notion of sexual identity outside this framework, it is possible to find opportunities to expose the regulatory aims within the apparatus of 'gender' from within its margins, by looking at gender identities which do not conform to the heterosexual norm. Homosexual, lesbian or bisexual practices all pose an implicit challenge to the fixed male/female opposition by demonstrating a multiplicity of different ways in which that dualism can be reconfigured.

In *Bodies That Matter: On the Discursive Limits of 'Sex'* (1993) Butler turns to the body of the drag queen as a particularly fruitful source for such subversive readings of gender. Although it can certainly be used in the service of the norm, the parodic nature of the drag act – which ostentatiously appropriates the paraphernalia of femininity or masculinity, then inscribes it upon the 'wrong' body – has the potential to initiate a 'reverse' reading of gender codes, exposing 'the understated, taken-for-granted quality of heterosexual performativity'. [SG]

C

CAGE, JOHN: COMPOSER (1912–92) Cage remains one of the most enigmatic figures of twentieth-century music, with his notorious piano 'work' *4'33* (1952) still capable of generating heated debate amongst critics and the general public alike. Since *4'33* consists of 4 minutes 33 seconds of silence (divided into three 'movements', as the score informs us), or more precisely 4 minutes 33 seconds of whatever incidental noise occurs in the concert hall where it is being 'performed', there is more than a certain degree of **irony** to be noted about this response. Cage made extensive use of chance principles in his compositions, as well as experimenting with electronic music, and generally challenged existing conceptions of what musical composition was about. The famous German composer and musical theorist Arnold Schoenberg, with whom Cage studied briefly, even argued that Cage was an inventor rather than a composer (although he also praised his pupil's 'genius'). Cage was heavily influenced by Zen philosophy, and its effect on his thought can be gauged by the following lines of poetry: 'I have nothing to say / and I am saying it / and that is poetry / as I needed it'.

Cage has usually been regarded as part of the **modernist** tradition, as someone pushing back the boundaries of his art by experiments with form – almost a model of the twentieth-century avant-garde creative artist in this respect. But the extent of his challenge to Western musical traditions suggests that he might be considered a forerunner of **postmodernism**. There is a sense in which he seems to be undermining the entire **metanarrative** of Western art music, and the conventions of performance which have grown up around it. Cage also had a long-term association with Merce **Cunningham**, one of the leading figures in postmodern dance, who not only used Cage's music but adapted many of his ideas into his choreographic practice.

There has been something of a resurgence of interest in Cage's work of late, with a festival in London in 2004 leading to a broadcast 'performance' of *4'33* on BBC national radio (Radio 3). At the very least, Cage continues to intrigue the musical world of the twenty-first century. [SS]

CALVINO, ITALO: NOVELIST (1923–87) Calvino fought for the resistance movement during the Second World War, and his early fictions were coloured by his left-wing politics and neo-realist aesthetic. His first novel, *The Path to the Nest of Spiders* (1947), for instance, is an adventure story in which fourteen-year-old Pin mingles with the partisans during the war. Many of the short stories in *Adam, One Afternoon and Other Stories* (1949) are realistic too, although elements of fantasy are also prominent in this collection. Calvino will be remembered most, however, for his experimentation and bold storytelling gifts. In *If on a Winter's Night a Traveller* (1979), for instance, he adopts the second-person **narrative** viewpoint. To complicate matters further, the addressee is a Reader engaged in the process of reading. Initially the Reader is reading Calvino's book. The Reader soon discovers, however, that his book is faulty and repeats the first chapter several times. So the Reader returns the book, only to discover that the new copy presents a different narrative altogether. In the bookshop, the Reader comes into contact with the Other Reader, Ludmilla, the female counterpart of the male 'you'. The narrative then alternates between two distinct levels: one concerning the relationship between the two Readers, the other revolving around a variety of first chapters – each in a different style – which the first Reader 'reads' in his replacement book.

This subtle and sinuous text is Calvino's masterpiece, and crystallizes many of the techniques and themes that made him into one of the consummate **postmodernist** writers. First, there is the interest in the permutation of plot and content. Other works that play games of combination include *The Castle of Crossed Destinies* (1969), which is based on a set of tarot cards, and *Invisible Cities* (1972), in which Marco Polo describes to Kubla Khan the various cities he has visited within his empire. Second, there are the experiments with generic conventions. His early novels *The Cloven Viscount* (1952), *The Baron in the Trees* (1957) and *The Non-Existent Knight* (1959) merge fantasy and romance deftly. Science fiction is explored in *Cosmicomics* (1965), in which the origins of the universe are observed by a life principle called Qfwfq, and *t zero* (1967), where abstract **binary oppositions** such as chaos and order are personified. Many of Calvino's short stories are based on motifs from folk-tales and fables. Third, despite his bent for philosophical and theoretical speculation, each of Calvino's fictions is grounded in a commitment to the enrichment of human values and the redemptive power of love. John **Barth** once compared writing to lovemaking: passion without virtuosity is clumsy, while virtuosity without passion is cold and clinical. Calvino's triumph is that he demonstrated both passion *and* virtuosity in his work. [BL]

CARTER, ANGELA: AUTHOR (1947–92) Angela Carter is now widely accepted as one of the most innovative writers of recent times. Along with Salman **Rushdie**, she is often classified as an English exponent of **magic realism**. Although she is best known for her novels and short-story collections, in the course of a prolific career she also established herself as a journalist, reviewer, playwright and cultural commentator.

Carter wrote her first novel, *Shadow Dance*, while studying for a degree in English at the University of Bristol. Published in 1966, a year after her graduation, it immediately established the salient characteristics of her work. Written in an elaborate, ornate, prose style, the novel recasts the world of provincial 1960s bohemia as Gothic narrative, and its fascination with costume, theatrics and insane states and situations follows **postmodernism** in asserting the fluidity and malleability of the **subject**, which is not born so much as constructed. It was closely followed by *The Magic Toyshop* (1967), for which Carter won the John Llewellyn Rhys Memorial Prize, *Several Perceptions*, which gained her the Somerset Maugham Award for 1968, *Heroes and Villains* (1969) and *Love* (1971).

Carter used the money from the Somerset Maugham Award to travel to Japan, where she lived until 1972. She earned her living by writing articles for the periodical *New Society*, many of which chronicle her experience of cultural alienation. During her time in Japan she also wrote the short stories collected in *Fireworks* (1974), as well as the novel *The Infernal Desire Machines of Doctor Hoffman* (1972), a piece of macabre fantasy which was heavily influenced by surrealism.

Later, Carter also credited Japan with inspiring her conversion to feminism, although it was characteristic that on her return to England she immediately began work on a controversial study of the work of Marquis de Sade. *The Sadeian Woman*, which was eventually published in 1979, has been condemned by some feminist critics, Andrea Dworkin among them, as an inexcusable defence of pornography. Carter's next novel, *The Passion of New Eve* (1977), written while she was still researching de Sade, exploits the tension that arises from the attempt to combine a feminist analysis of oppression with a continued fascination with the extremities of **desire**.

However, it was Carter's collection of rewritten fairy-tales, *The Bloody Chamber* (1979), which aimed to uncover the latent subversive potential of familiar nursery stories, that was primarily responsible for bringing her work to the attention of a wider audience. As well as the book itself, her version of the tale of Little Red Riding Hood, 'The Company of Wolves', was rewritten by Carter herself as a radio play (1980) and also as a screenplay for a film directed by Neil Jordan (1984).

In the final years of her life she produced her two great novels, *Nights at the Circus* (1984), whose central character is a winged trapeze artist, and *Wise Children* (1991), which is not only a carnivalesque romp through a medley of Shakespearean allusions, but also – given that Carter died less than a year after its publication – an uncannily prescient contemplation of the inevitability of ageing and death. A collection of Carter's criticism, *Expletives Deleted*, was published posthumously in 1992, and a final collection of short stories, *American Ghosts and Old World Wonders*, appeared in 1993. [SG]

CATASTROPHE THEORY Apocalyptic similarities with **chaos theory** notwithstanding, catastrophe theory shares little with the latter beyond both implying, through their names, that mathematics by our day has become a technical code devoted to the analysis of some glamorously crash-and-burn apocalypse. Invented by mathematical 'sorcerer' René **Thom** in *Structural Stability and Morphogenesis* (1972) there is in fact little catastrophic about the theory. Instead, the overt strategy of catastrophe theory is to demonstrate a formal, mathematizable continuity between states in a dynamical system despite gross apparent discontinuities between those states. An ice age, for example, does not appear to be part of the mesh of interconnected systems of life on a temperate Earth, but rather its end. Catastrophe theory seeks to demonstrate that what appear to be catastrophes that change everything are, at the level of mathematical form – *morphogenetically* – profoundly continuous. A catastrophe is not the end of a system, but an inherent, predictable and mathematizable component of it.

So stated, emphasizing continuity over discontinuity, catastrophe theory seems anything but **postmodern**; it is paradoxical, then, that Jean-François **Lyotard** derives some of the more celebrated theses of *The Postmodern Condition* (1979) from this body of theory. Just as, for example, Lyotard famously insists that '**postmodernity** is incredulity towards **metanarratives**', so Thom declares that 'the era of grand cosmic synthesis is at an end' and that science can no longer be characterized as the investigation of the ultimate nature of reality. Accordingly, catastrophe theory recognizes the impossibility of the quantitative global model aspired to by Euclidean geometry, and frames its analyses within the local parameters of the dynamical system under study. Catastrophe theory's emphasis on formal continuity is therefore both local and abstract, the sequence of models amounting to nothing more than 'the play of pure forms' – morphogenesis. Following this abstract line, catastrophe theory thus broaches territories long since barred to mathematics, including sociology, linguistics and **semiotics**, so that it feeds directly into the arenas where postmodernism is currently contested. [IHG]

CHAOS THEORY A chaotic system is one that shows a sensitive dependence on initial conditions. If chaos theory can be said to have a beginning, it was the discovery by Edward Lorenz in 1960 that tiny errors in equations he was using to model weather systems resulted in enormous and apparently unpredictable variations in the outcome of the equations. The consequences of this seemed fatal to any attempt to make long-term weather forecasts – minute differences in the initial conditions could mean the **difference** between flood and drought. This has become known as the butterfly effect – the flapping of a butterfly's wings in China could create a causal chain, the final outcome of which is a hurricane in Indonesia.

Postmodernists have embraced chaos as a counter to the expansive truth-claims of science. Chaos seems, superficially, to throw an element of uncertainty into the activity of the material world: it has been argued that it would require a computer bigger than the universe itself to predict the behaviour of all the chaotic systems it contains.

This is, however, to ignore the constructive side of chaos theory. When data from chaotic systems are plotted, complex but recognizable patterns emerge – the consequence of what are known as strange attractors. These patterns in chaotic behaviour make it possible to make short-term predictions and to predict general trends. The quest to find order in chaos has led to the creation of another new field – the science of **complexity**.

Chaos theory has been used to help explain the baffling orbits of certain satellites, to understand fluctuations in animal populations, to track the movement of the market and to model the beating of the human heart. There are, however, those who claim that there has been precious little real achievement to justify the hype. [AM]

CHORA In Plato's *Timaeus*, chora is the unnameable, unstable receptacle existing prior to the nameable form of the One. Generally, in **postmodern** usage, chora designates a site of undifferentiated being, connoting the experience of continuity with the maternal body as an infinite space. Specifically in Julia **Kristeva**'s work, chora specifies the presignifying traces which underlie and at times break through the order of signification. Hence the shared bodily space of mother and child resists **representation**, yet is experienced as **desire**, the uncanny or the mystical. The chora as maternal desire threatens to destabilize the finite unity and autonomous identity of the **modern** 'man'. [PSA]

CIXOUS, HÉLÈNE: AUTHOR, CULTURAL THEORIST (1937–) Cixous is one of the leading figures in recent French feminist thought, and is usually identified, along with such people as Luce **Irigaray**, with what has come to be known as **difference feminism** (although she herself rejects the description of 'feminist', and is not as radical in her concept of difference as Irigaray proves to be). Within France itself Cixous is also well known as the author of experimental fiction, including works for the theatre.

Cixous is a strong advocate of women's writing (*l'écriture feminine*), arguing that 'Woman must write her self: must write about women and bring women to writing', on the grounds of a perceived sexual **difference**. For Cixous, 'a woman's instinctual economy cannot be identified by a man or referred to a masculine economy': a claim that has led to her being accused by some critics of biological essentialism. However, she has been careful to make it clear that *l'écriture feminine* is not to be identified with women alone. It is to be seen instead as a form of writing that challenges existing linguistic conventions (which are the product of a particular kind of patriarchal society), with the ultimate aim of breaking down repressive cultural structures. Thus Cixous can cite Jean Genet as an example of the *écriture feminine* approach. Given the heavily patriarchal nature of the society in which we live, however, it is likely that most practitioners of *l'écriture feminine* will in fact turn out to be women, although it should be regarded overall as an essentially tactical exercise designed to correct certain social wrongs, rather than a marker of difference between the sexes.

Cixous provides further arguments against biological essentialism when she writes in *The Newly Born Woman* (co-written with Catherine Clement, 1975) that it is at least possible to imagine a radical change in cultural organization, such that 'what today appears to be "feminine" or "masculine" would no longer amount to the same thing'. She speculates that such a change could then lead to existing notions of gender difference being replaced by 'a bunch of new differences'; although exactly what those might be it is extremely difficult to say from our current cultural vantage point. [SS]

COMPLEXITY THEORY The world is full of complex systems, from the internal structure of single-celled organisms to the working of the stock exchange. Complexity theory has attempted to define these 'self-organizing' systems, and then to find the general principles that underlie them, with the goal of producing a unified law of complexity. Although the search for a unified law betrays a deep-seated reductionist bias, there is also a counterbalancing holism in that the behaviour of complex systems cannot be simply deduced from their constituent parts. Complexity therefore calls for new principles, new modes of analysis.

Although there is no consensus among researchers, the nearest thing to a common definition of complexity involves the '**edge of chaos**' hypothesis. The distinguishing feature of complexity, in this view, is high informational content, and informational content is maximized in systems that exist at the border between highly stable states (crystalline structures, regular planetary orbits) and chaos.

Complexity theorists typically spend their time producing computer models of natural behaviours. Shapes squirm and wriggle across computer screens in **simulations** of bacteria or antelope, struggling for survival, competing for resources in harsh environments, evolving, dying. This '**artificial life**' research attempts to find the simple laws that generate both the complexity and the emergent order. Researchers argue that if you can create complex behaviour in a computer from a small number of simple rules, the corresponding behaviours in the 'real' world must equally be the product of a small number of simple rules. If it is countered that there is a fundamental **difference** between real-world organisms and the blips on a computer screen, complexity theorists tend to suggest that the parallels are so close that the 'virtual' organisms should be granted the same status as their flesh and blood cousins. This blurring of real and virtual worlds is, of course, very **postmodern**. [AM]

CONTINENTAL PHILOSOPHY Philosophy in Europe (particularly in France and Germany) has been felt by many to have developed in a radically different way in modern times from that in the English-speaking world, and the term 'continental philosophy' has increasingly come to be applied as a way of differentiating it from what is taken to be the philosophical mainstream. Many would date continental philosophy back to **Kant** (in particular to his *Critique of Judgement* and its theory of the **sublime**), but in a more recent sense it refers to movements such as phenomenology, existentialism, **structuralism, poststructuralism, postmodernism** and **difference feminism. Husserl** and **Heidegger**'s phenomenology is one of the critical influences on later twentieth-century continental philosophy (nearly every major poststructuralist and postmodernist thinker acknowledges their influence), which has also drawn freely on such intellectual traditions as **Marxism** and **Freudianism**, and such maverick philosophical figures as **Nietzsche**.

The English philosopher David Cooper has usefully defined continental philosophy as having the following major concerns: (1) cultural critique; (2) concern with the background conditions of enquiry; (3) 'the fall of the self' (that is, a loss of belief in the notion of a unified personal identity or **subject**). Although such concerns can also be found in the work of English-speaking philosophers, they hardly ever dominate debate the way they do on the continent, where they recur obsessively in the work of such recent figures as **Foucault**, **Derrida**, **Deleuze** and **Lyotard**.

Although it is identified with French and German thought, it is nevertheless possible to be defined as a continental philosopher outside those traditions – the American philosopher Richard **Rorty** being one such example. Continental philosophy is to be regarded as a particular 'style' or 'mood' of philosophical discourse rather than a specific cultural or national tradition as such. [SS]

COOVER, ROBERT: AUTHOR (1932–) Robert Coover has published several short-story collections, including *Pricksongs and Descants* (1969), *In Bed One Night and Other Brief Encounters* (1983) and *A Night at the Movies* (1987). His novels include: *The Origin of the Brunists* (1966), *The Universal Baseball Association* (1968), *The Public Burning* (1977), *Gerald's Party* (1986), *Pinocchio in Venice* (1991), *John's Wife* (1996) and *Ghost Town* (1998). His works are influenced by Latin American **magic realism**. He produces what Salman **Rushdie** calls 'matter of fact descriptions of the outré and bizarre, and their reverse, namely heightened, stylised versions of the everyday'.

In *The Universal Baseball Association*, J. Henry Waugh, a lonely accountant, devotes most of his spare time to a fantasy table-top baseball game. The Association is regulated by dice, and trouble looms when his star player Damon Rutherford is killed by a wild pitch. Waugh is warped by feelings of revenge. He alters the dice in a later game and 'murders' the pitcher, Jock Casey. In the last chapter of the book the baseball world breaks completely free of its creator (whose initials, J. H. W., suggest some obvious biblical parallels with Jahweh).

In a similar manner, Coover demythologizes two religious episodes in the short stories 'The Brother' and 'J's Marriage' from *Pricksongs and Descants*. In the first story, Noah is mocked by his brother for building an ark to save the animals from the flood. The narrator's slack punctuation and **modern** American idioms sink the pomposity of Noah's mission. Even so, his boat stays afloat. In 'J's Marriage', a couple undergo several rites of passage (courtship, matrimony, the birth of their first child): nothing startling in that, perhaps. The husband, however, is no ordinary Joe: he is the carpenter Joseph, his wife is the Virgin Mary and his child Jesus Christ. The immaculate conception and nativity are unfamiliar when framed through the perspective of a husband who knows that his marriage has not been consummated.

The literary form most persistently mimicked by Coover is that of the fairy-tale or fable. The opening story of *Pricksongs and Descants*, 'The Door: A Prologue of Sorts', injects a heady fix of sex and violence into the stories of Little Red Riding Hood and Jack and the Beanstalk. This is Grimm revised by **Freud**. In 'The Magic Poker', a caretaker's son spies upon two sisters as they visit a remote island. The girls find a wrought-iron poker in the grass, a primal scene returned to many times. In some action replays it is Karen who finds the poker, in others it is her sister. When the poker is kissed, it sometimes turns into a handsome man, and sometimes remains its rusty self.

Like Zeuxis in the Greek myth, who painted grapes so lifelike that birds pecked at them, Coover is fascinated by the interface between art and reality. And like Parrhasius, whose curtain on a canvas fooled Zeuxis into thinking it was an actual cloth cover, Coover loves nothing better than to play games with frames. His most recent experiments involve **hypertextual narrative** forms. [BL]

COUPLAND, DOUGLAS: NOVELIST, JOURNALIST (1961–) In 1988, after training as a sculptor and in business management, Coupland wrote an article for a Vancouver magazine on a group of young, disaffected, over-educated and under-achieving twenty-somethings he called 'Generation X'. The following year a publisher asked him to expand this into a sociological guidebook. However, Coupland wrote a novel instead, the extremely successful *Generation X* (1991). It became one of the most influential books of the year and gave birth to thousands of newspaper articles debating Coupland's chapter titles ('Dead at Thirty, Buried at Seventy') and discussing the coinages and definitions which peppered the margins of his book ('A "McJob": a low pay, low status, no future job in the service sector'). The depressing statistics that form the final chapter give empirical support to the characters' reading of the world around them – while everyone now may own a TV set, this post-boomer generation are the first Americans since the Second World War to be worse off than their parents.

Generation X, Shampoo Planet (1992) and especially the short stories in *Life After God* (1994) echo Thoreau in looking to nature to invest the world with meaning, while *Hey Nostradamus!* (2003) examines forms of religious **fundamentalism**. Even in the more upbeat *Microserfs* (1995) Coupland's characters live in a belated, **postmodern** world which has seen the arrival of **Fukuyama**'s 'end of history' – the empty triumph of capitalist democracy in

which his characters keep banality at bay only through a shoulder-shrugging **irony**. [PD]

CRITICAL THEORY Critical theory is a methodology most closely associated with the **Frankfurt School** of social and political thinkers. The term itself does not designate a uniform or unified approach to social and political phenomena, and has been variously deployed by its leading practitioners. Nevertheless, underneath the **differences** that exist in the thought of **Adorno**, **Horkheimer**, **Marcuse** and, most recently, Jürgen **Habermas**, critical theory is most closely associated with **Marxist** philosophy. Critical theorists apply their method to the dominance of capitalism in advanced industrialized societies in Western Europe and the United States, and to the development of Marxism in the former Soviet Union and the Eastern bloc. The philosophical base of critical theory is neo-**Hegelian** and can be found in the works of the Hungarian Marxist György Lukács. Lukács' debate with Adorno and Brecht in this period regarding the nature of **modernism** demonstrates the diversity of opinion in the Marxist tradition regarding the role of aesthetics in modern life. Critical theorists such as Adorno recognize that culture is an industry, though some aspects of art are autonomous.

The historical high point in the work of critical theorists is the period between 1950 and 1970, when the critique of positivism (a particularly strong form of empiricism associated with Auguste Comte) led by Adorno and Horkheimer concluded that positivism does not lead to a realistic interpretation of social events. In this respect critical theorists recognize that economic determinism and historical materialism do not provide a convincing total critique, and stress instead the relationship between structure and agency, with the objective and subjective reflected in social conditions. [DW]

CULTURAL MATERIALISM Cultural materialism is the term used by critics Jonathan **Dollimore** and Alan **Sinfield** to describe their work (and that of like-minded critics). They argue that culture is inseparable from its conditions of production and reception in history. The term was originally coined by Raymond Williams in the early 1980s to describe 'the analysis of all forms of signification . . . within the actual means and conditions of their production'. Cultural materialism's 'key axiom', as Sinfield calls it, is 'culture is political'. For Dollimore 'there is no cultural practice without political significance'. Their method of analysis takes the form of politically engaged and theoretically informed close readings of, for example, Shakespeare's plays, which would take issue with more conservative readings that make the dramas vessels of universal, timeless values. In this respect cultural materialism is akin to American **new historicism**, though this is a more pessimistic method of analysis that looks to **Foucault** rather than to **Marx**, and suggests, as many postmodern critics do, that 'subversion' in Renaissance drama is finally contained and may have been a ruse of **power** to consolidate itself all along. Dollimore finds this work 'salutary', but argues that to contain a threat by rehearsing it at least gives it a voice. [PD]

CULTURAL RELATIVISM Perhaps the first explicit statement of the concept of cultural relativism occurs in Book III of *The Histories* when Herodotus observes that we all follow the customs of the society into which we are born, and that, as a consequence, all such customs should be respected. The following two thousand years saw that principle sadly neglected. While it might be acknowledged that other cultures operated with different value systems, it remained the orthodox view in Western culture from late antiquity to the nineteenth century that alien cultures (African, Oriental, Native American) could be judged from the vantage point of Western 'rationality'.

A fully developed theory of cultural relativism had to wait until the rise of **modern** anthropology in the early twentieth century. A number of American anthropologists began to attempt to understand non-Western cultures 'from the inside'. The proper investigation of other cultures came to involve a complete immersion in the values, traditions and beliefs of those cultures. Other societies came to be seen as self-contained, self-validating 'organic' forms. The corollary of this was a thoroughgoing moral relativism: what is right or wrong is defined within each culture, and there is no objective position from which two different cultural/moral systems might be assessed. [AM]

CULTURAL STUDIES Cultural studies works with an inclusive definition of culture. That is, it is a 'democratic' project in the sense that rather than study only what Matthew Arnold called 'the best which has been thought and said' (*Culture and Anarchy*), cultural studies is committed to examining *all* that has been thought or said. To put it simply, culture is how we live nature (including our own biology): it is the shared meanings we make and encounter in our everyday lives. Culture is not something essential, embodied in particular 'texts' (that is, any commodity, object or event that can be made to signify), it is the practices and processes of making meanings with and from the '**texts**' we encounter in our everyday lives. In this way, then, cultures are made from the production, circulation and consumption of meanings. To share a culture, therefore, is to interpret the world – make it meaningful – in recognizably similar ways.

To see culture as the practices and processes of making shared meanings does not mean that cultural studies believes that cultures are harmonious, organic wholes. On the contrary, cultural studies maintains that the world and all the things in it can be made to have meaning in many different ways. Given this, conflict over making the world mean – insisting on the 'right' meaning(s) – is almost inevitable. It is this conflict – the relations between culture and **power** – which is the core interest of cultural studies.

If meaning is not something fixed and guaranteed in nature, but is the result of particular ways of expressing nature in culture, then the meaning of something can never be fixed, final or true; its meaning will only ever be contextual and contingent and, moreover, always open to the changing relations of power. This is not to deny that the world exists in all its materiality but to insist that it is only made meaningful in culture. Moreover, dominant ways of knowing the world – making it meaningful – produced by those with the power to make their ways of knowing circulate **discursively** in the world, generate ways of seeing, thinking and acting, which may come to assume authority over the ways in which we see, think and act; that is, provide us with 'scripts' from which meanings can be made and actions carried out. This makes practices and processes of signification a key concern in cultural studies' focus on the relations between culture and power. [JS]

Cunningham, Merce: dancer, choreographer (1919–) A featured soloist in Martha Graham's company in the 1940s and 1950s (one of the most influential organizations in the development of **modern** dance), Cunningham has gone on to become one of the foremost practitioners of what has been called '**postmodern** dance'. Over the course of his long career he has collaborated with many leading twentieth-century artists and musicians, including Andy Warhol, Robert Rauschenberg, Jasper Johns and John **Cage**.

Cunningham's main interest is in movement, and he deliberately plays down the metaphorical side of dance as an art form: as he put it, 'I don't work through images or ideas – I work through the body . . . When I dance it means: this is what I am doing'. It is in this rejection of metaphor that Cunningham's postmodern credentials lie. For some commentators this gives his choreography a **deconstructive** aspect, in that the link between signifier and signified is broken: Cunningham's dance works do not refer outside themselves, and in traditional terms do not as such 'mean' anything other than their presentation of movement itself. Dance movement becomes a floating signifier: in Cunningham's uncompromising words, 'I don't even want a dancer to start thinking that a movement means something.'

Cunningham has made extensive use of chance elements in his work to disrupt any build-up of **narrative** 'line' that would encourage metaphorical interpretation (a toss of a coin might decide how a piece unfolds, for example), and has experimented with film, video and computer programs in his choreography. His dancers are also taught to steer clear of anything resembling characterization in performance. In a series of works such as *Suite by Chance, Symphonie pour un homme seul, Theater Piece No. 1* (an early example of multimedia work) and *Events*, Cunningham has succeeded in challenging the conventions of both classical and modern dance. [SS]

Cyberpunk Cyberpunk is a term loosely applied to a variety of recent science fiction. It was first used by critics to describe William **Gibson**'s influential science-fiction novel *Neuromancer* (1984) and then such writers as Bruce Sterling, John Shirley, Pat Cadogan and Elizabeth Vonarburg, who present a grimly commodified dystopian future. Stylistically, cyberpunk is an eclectic collage of influences, among them *Blade Runner*, William Burroughs, Thomas **Pynchon**, Raymond Chandler, *film noir* and the 'psychological' science fiction of late 1960s counter-culture: J. G. Ballard, Philip K. Dick and Samuel Delany. 'Cyber' comes from control and communications systems and 'punk' from the relative youth of the writers and their indebtedness to popular music and TV.

Cyberpunk is interested primarily in the interface (a favourite word) between humans and new technologies such as '**virtual reality**', cloning and in the psychological and philosophical consequences of the blurring of such distinctions as human/machine and illusion/reality. Seen as quintessentially **postmodern** by many critics, the world of cyberpunk is a bleak **Baudrillardian** one of **simulation**, where image and reality have imploded. However, many women writers have been drawn to the genre to explore, through the virtual disembodiment of **cyberspace**, different constructions of gender and gender relations. [PD]

CYBERSPACE Take the mouse on your computer. Remove a document from a file and throw it away. Once upon a time you would have typed DOS (disk operating system) instructions to do this. The graphic user interface (GUI) which spatializes the process is a version of cyberspace, a virtual space that exists nowhere and is made of millions of pieces of information. It is where your money is. What if you could put on a certain kind of headset and could dissolve the distinction between you and your computer, entering the information site through your mind? And what if more than one of you could enter the (non-)space and could interact? This is the premise of *Neuromancer* (1984), William **Gibson**'s hugely influential **cyberpunk** novel. Gibson invented the term 'cyberspace' in the novel and describes it as 'a consensual hallucination experienced daily by billions of legitimate operators in every nation. A graphic representation of data extracted

from the banks of every computer in the human system. Unthinkable complexity.' Cyberspace is a non-space that is everywhere and yet nowhere. This space exists: it is called the **Internet**, the decentralized and global network of networks. We do have interaction: it is called a multi-user domain (MUD). We can make porous the human/machine interface: it is called **virtual reality**. All that makes Gibson's book science fiction is the nature of the interface, which is of an interactive complexity we have not yet achieved. Cyberspace is a world of **postmodern simulation**, where image and reality, human and machine implode, become porous.

While for some cyberspace throws up profound epistemological and ontological problems, for many the democracy of the Internet is a potential liberation, not least from the sexual, racial and bodily identities they live with in the corporeal world. [PD]

CYBORG The term cyborg was first coined in 1960 by Manfred Clynes, a research space scientist. A combination of 'cybernetic' and 'organism', it is used to describe a hybrid being who is half human, half machine. Cyborgs have been a staple motif in science fiction since the 1920s. However, they have gained a new position in the popular imagination since the success of such cult films as *Terminator* (1984). Beneath its playing out of familiar macho fantasies, *Terminator* also communicates the anxiety inherent in the concept of the cyborg, whose technological modifications, combined with the emotionlessness of a machine, make him an invincible instrument of destruction. In its iconic role, therefore, the cyborg acts as a symbol of the fear that humanity itself is in danger of becoming entirely absorbed into a wholly technological future within which the machine becomes the paradigm by which the organic itself functions.

On a more mundane plane, however,

cyborgs already exist, for mechanical body parts are now routinely used as a replacement for human organs, joints and limbs. For **postmodernist** techno-theorists such as Donna **Haraway**, it is these less dramatic manifestations of the cyborg that demonstrate that a future in which the boundaries between the organic and the technological are being transgressed every day is one we already, inescapably, inhabit. [SG]

D

DEATH OF THE AUTHOR Roland **Barthes'** notion of the death of the author is one of the rallying cries for **poststructuralism** in its insistence that the author is not to be regarded as the final arbiter of a **text**'s meaning. In Barthes' view, **authors** had come to be considered as authority figures, thus placing the reader in an inferior position. He called for the death of the author (more precisely, the death of a certain conception of the author, the author as authority figure) in order to free the reader to be creative. Reading was no longer to be considered a passive process, but instead an active one in which the reader was fully engaged in the production of textual meaning. The birth of the reader, as Barthes put it, was to be achieved at the expense of the author.

The major thrust of Barthes' attack is against the **modern** tendency to treat authors as cultural icons (the Author rather than the author, with the capital 'A' signalling the importance accorded this figure), rather than authorship as such, and the death of the author is an implicitly anti-traditional notion much in keeping with the liberationist tenor of the 1960s when it was devised. [SS]

DEATH OF MAN (DEATH OF THE SUBJECT) Michel **Foucault** is somewhat notorious for proclaiming the death of man (for which we are to read the death of a particular conception of man), and this politically charged idea is certainly prevalent in **poststructuralist** and **postmodernist** thought. (Another way of putting this is to speak of the death of the 'subject'.) In Foucault's view, man is a recent, and not particularly noteworthy, invention that will be erased by the passage of time. His target is the humanist conception of man (the dominant one in the West for the last few centuries), where the individual is regarded as the focal point of the cultural process.

Earlier versions of the notion can be found in **structuralist** thought, with Claude **Lévi-Strauss** providing one of the best-known examples: for Lévi-Strauss it is the system, not the individual, that is of importance. Structural **Marxism** too, with its emphasis on the critical role played by institutional structures in determining the ideology of Western society, assumes the death of man as a starting point for its cultural analyses, which it openly declares to be anti-humanist. Critics of this movement have spoken of it as giving us 'history without a subject'. [SS]

DEBORD, GUY: CULTURAL AND POLITICAL THEORIST (1931–94) Debord was one of the leading theorists of the **Situationist** movement, active in the 1950s and 1960s particularly, whose ideas continued to exert an influence in French thought into the **postmodern** era, through figures such as **Baudrillard**. Debord argued that we lived in a 'Society of the Spectacle' (the title of his best-known book (1967)), in which the media were beginning to dominate our existence. To counter the all-pervasiveness of the spectacle, which turned us into passive spectators, Debord and his Situationist colleagues devised several strategies, most notably *détournement*, that is, 'diversion' or 'subversion'. In artistic terms, this involved painting over existing images to subvert their original intention (often with explicitly political messages): a method which had a significant impact on the popular culture of the time. The idea of subverting culture from within has influenced many post-modernist thinkers, particularly Baudrillard and **Lyotard**. The former's concept of **hyper-reality** clearly owes a debt to Situationist thought. [SS]

DECONSTRUCTION Deconstruction is a term coined by the French philosopher Jacques **Derrida** in the late 1960s to offer a mode of reading which is attentive to a **text**'s multiple meanings. Rather than attempting to find a true meaning, a consistent point of view or unified message in a given work, a deconstructive reading *carefully teases out*, to use Barbara Johnson's words, 'the warring forces of signification' at play and waiting to be read in what might be called the textual unconscious. As a mode of reading, then, which exposes a text's internal differences and attends to its repressed contradictions or inherent vulnerabilities, its strategy is also interventionist, and as such, despite many a claim to the contrary, deconstruction is political. This is not only because of the ways in which a deconstructive reading can turn a text's logic against itself by showing how the logic of its language can differ from and play against the logic of its **author**'s stated claims, but also because deconstructors tend to seize on the inconsistencies, inequalities or hierarchies which are expounded or glossed over either by a text, by a whole **discourse**, or even by an entire system of beliefs. For instance, the structure of hierarchy which Derrida sees as implicit in the kinds of '**binary oppositions**' which have traditionally informed, organized and ranked Western thinking, and have therefore led us to value a concept such as 'order' more highly than its opposite, '**chaos**', makes it imperative for Derrida to re-examine other such binary couplets. What the privileging of one term over and above the other (such as good over evil, light over dark, reason over emotion, male over female, master over slave, model over copy, original over reproduction, literature over criticism, high culture over popular culture, etc.) reveals is that the preference for one term always works at the expense or exclusion of the, subordinated, term. **Difference feminists** have drawn on this kind of analysis to question not only the position of women vis-à-vis men, or the **subaltern** vis-à-vis the Westerner, but moreover to deconstruct the very system of conceptual opposition which has enabled, and still perpetuates, such metaphysical and ideological values in Western society.

Deconstruction then is the very means, Derrida suggests, by which to expose, reverse and dismantle binary oppositions with their hierarchies of value; that is, to render untenable the logic which, while pitching one term against the other, fails to recognize that each term both *differs* from and *defers* to the other term (Derrida's '**différance**' captures both senses of this movement simultaneously), and thus also fails to acknowledge that even though 'good', for example, is distinct from 'evil', as the privileged term 'good' also depends for its meaning on its association with its subordinate opposite, 'evil'. This suggests not only a degree of contamination between opposite terms, 'each' a kind of **trace** of the other, but concomitantly also indicates the impossibility of ever maintaining a clear-cut division in the form of an opposition, hence pointing up once more the unstable nature of meaning. [KL]

DELEUZE, GILLES: PHILOSOPHER (1925–95) Michel **Foucault**'s extravagant claim, in a review of two of Deleuze's driest and most complex books, that 'one day this century will be known as Deleuzian' sits ill at ease with the relative infrequency, when compared to thinkers such as Foucault himself, with which Deleuze's name is currently heard in discussions of our '**post-modern** condition'; but there are perhaps reasons to think that his reviewer's prognosis will be borne out in the twenty-first century. In part this is due to the incredible range of Deleuzian thinking, adopting literature (writing extensively on, for example, Proust, Beckett, Melville and Lovecraft) and cinema as ways of thinking rather than objects for philosophical or theoretical study, while practically reinventing the history of philosophy according to its heretics and outcasts, rehabilitating Lucretius, Hume, Spinoza, **Nietzsche** and Bergson against the post-war French canon of **Hegel**, **Husserl** and **Heidegger**.

Ultimately, however, Deleuze's principal contribution is perhaps his consistent experimentation with re-engineering new concepts to propel philosophy beyond the human frame, a concern he carried through from *Difference and Repetition* (1968) to *What is Philosophy?* (1991). Thus time becomes 'deep' or geological, rather than lived or phenomenological, and the species barriers that perpetuate anthropocentric thinking about mineral, animal and – crucially – *machinic* life inevitably break down as the thought augments its scale and reorients its detail towards the vast mineral and chemical vortex of life in geological time. The figure of man is not so much a sketch in sand washed away by incoming tides as it is a minuscule tyrant bearing down upon the 'image of thought'. While this scale might tempt us to think of the individual **subject**, following terms invented in Deleuze and **Guattari**'s two-volume *Capitalism and Schizophrenia: Anti-Oedipus* (1972) and *A Thousand Plateaus* (1980), as 'molecular', the real problem is derived from its 'molar' form. Molecularity has nothing to do with scale, but, as in chemistry, with the gravity or force of molecular bonds that keep them in orbit around a stable centre, just as thought revolves around the human. Molecular thought thus follows the unstable and eccentric or '**deterritorializing**' trajectories of minor particles or flows, much as

Deleuze treats the history of philosophy. The infamous '**desiring-machines**', claimed in *Anti-Oedipus* to be 'real machines, not imaginary ones', that industrialize the psychoanalytic category of the unconscious, to make it into a machine that produces reality rather than merely dream or fantasy, thus conjoin the molecular flows of money in advanced capitalism with the flows of desire in schizophrenia. Both flows, at their most eccentric, 'deterritorialize' the terrains in which they invest: capital has no love of institutions, just as schizophrenia refuses to understand delirium as a bad representation of reality, but as reality intensified.

While machines already take centre stage in Deleuze's 'theatre of philosophy' in the early 1970s, machinic thinking assumes greater complexity in *A Thousand Plateaus*. In particular, the idea of the 'machinic phylum' allows technology to be viewed from the evolutionary perspective of, as Manuel de Landa put it, a 'robot historian contemplating how it got there'. In effect, Deleuze challenges biology, the 'logic of the living', as to the strange prejudice it maintains for carbon- over silicon-based life. It is a further confirmation of the far-sightedness of his wildest work that such issues come into sharper focus as we witness the innumerable scientific, philosophical and cultural shifts attendant upon our fascination with the chaotic nature of technological advance. [IHG]

DELILLO, DON: NOVELIST, PLAYWRIGHT (1936–) If you met the Pope, how would you recognize him? From his image on the TV screen. In DeLillo's fictional biography of Lee Harvey Oswald, *Libra* (1988), the crowd gathers at Love Field in 1963 to see the arrival of John F. Kennedy. They are gratified that the president 'looked like himself'. In other words, for them his authenticity is guaranteed and confirmed by his image in the media. We are at the moment, as DeLillo writes in *The Names* (1983), 'when the image has seeped into the texture of the world'. For Oswald, Kennedy's image is a vision of plenitude and he tries to hollow out an identity for himself in relation to that seductive image. Oswald's assassination attempt is planned imagining how his own death will play in the media. In *White Noise* (1985) the simulation of events takes precedence over the events themselves. In DeLillo's thirteen novels, from *Americana* (1971) to *Cosmopolis* (2003) we enter the **postmodern** realm of **simulation** and **hyperreality**, a fallen world in which reality is profoundly mediated by electronic information systems. When did this fate befall us? DeLillo's first novel, *Americana*, concludes in Dealey Plaza, where JFK was shot. Kennedy's assassination gave DeLillo his theme: the assassination was not the moment when America lost its political innocence and darkness triumphed over light (as it is in Oliver Stone's film *JFK* or in the work of Arthur Schlesinger Jr, where the Kennedy era was a kind of modern Camelot), it was the moment when it became clear that **representation** had been divorced from reality.

The only extant filmic evidence of the Kennedy shooting is the famous Zapruder footage. But, like a dream-text, this amateur film is profoundly 'over-determined' by the number of interpretations it has produced. It will not yield up a singular meaning; rather it provides evidence for a wide range of readings. Its relationship to reality is disturbingly problematic. For DeLillo, this was the significance of the assassination of the first 'TV president'. As *Libra* has it, the Zapruder film signifies 'an aberration in the heartland of the real', the symbolic moment when it appeared that reality and its representation became somehow divorced. In his essay 'American Blood' (*Rolling Stone* (1983)), DeLillo writes of the assassination that 'we seem from that moment to have entered a world of randomness and ambiguity . . . the physical evidence contradicts itself, the eyewitness accounts do not begin to coincide'. The Zapruder film is our 'major emblem of uncertainty and chaos', and with this goes 'the public's growing belief in the secret manipulation of history'. In DeLillo's paradoxical world of both conspiracies and chaos, his characters feel both manipulated by larger forces and appalled by life's lack of pattern and meaning. Like Oswald, they attempt to create meaning from whatever materials they have. For the reader, what redeems the bleakness of the fiction is the immense energy of the plotting and the line-by-line brilliance of the writing itself. [PD]

DE MAN, PAUL: CRITIC (1919–83) Originally from Belgium, de Man was an occupant, together with Harold **Bloom**, Geoffrey Hartman and J. Hillis Miller, of what Frank Lentricchia has called the 'critical house of ill-fame', or what is otherwise referred to as the **Yale School** of criticism. Perhaps its most rigorous **deconstructionist**, and certainly its most notorious personality, given the revelation after his death of his collaborationist and anti-semitic wartime journalism during the Nazi occupation of Belgium, de Man is best known for his work on the relation between literature and philosophy, with his insistence in *Allegories of Reading* (1979) that philosophy might well be 'an endless reflection on its own destruction at the hands of literature'. Since rhetoricity characterizes all language, philosophical writings are also marked by a literariness, and thus not exempt (although their **authors** would seem to deny this or are simply blind to it) from the disruptions, ambiguities and indeterminacies of meaning that literary texts are in the business of playing on. Undermining the claim therefore that philosophical or critical works, unlike literary texts, can reliably transfer a meaningful content and are able to transmit knowledge coherently and truthfully, de Man illustrates that tropes and metaphors, precisely because they are operative in all writing, put an insurmountable obstacle in the way of readers, not only highlighting the limits to intelligibility but also making understanding an error-prone enterprise.

For de Man, the paradigm case of such compound errors as, he claims, inevitably occur in reading and in literature, he calls **aporia**, which literally means 'lack of means'. Language lacks the means to say anything univocally: a text will always say something other than what it seems to, creating an unresolvable undecidability, hence aporia, between conflicting or contradictory readings. This is why rhetoric perpetually presents the threat of mis-reading, and why de Man warns us that the impossibility of reading, an 'unreadability' that is not a product of the reading, but inheres in the text itself, should not be taken too lightly.

De Man's own method of reading thus seeks out those instances in a text that resist understanding, and which have, he demonstrates in *Blindness and Insight* (1983), resisted other critics' understanding, despite their misguided efforts to the contrary, as such frustrating their attempts to master, or gain a total insight into, a given text. Even **Derrida**, de Man illustrates, in his attempt not so much to master Rousseau, but to outwit the master with deconstruction, falls victim to de Man's analyses of Rousseau's text, which shows that the master had already deconstructed himself, long before the upstart Derrida came on the scene of writing. Derrida's blindness to Rousseau's auto-deconstructing text proves to be his greatest insight, proving de Man's point that great works, whether literary as Miller also claims, or philosophical as here, *deconstruct themselves.* What follows from de Man's insights, then, is that the whole history of criticism is nothing other than a history of its own errors and blindnesses. [KL]

DERRIDA, JACQUES: PHILOSOPHER (1930–2004) Derrida is best known for his work on the relation between thought and language with its playful interrogation of the borders between philosophical and literary writing. His most influential books, published between 1967 and 1972, reread major figures of the **continental** tradition of philosophy from Plato to **Heidegger**, to expose what he calls their **logocentrism**. As a system of thought which continually strives to go back to origins, find centres, fix points of reference, certify truths, verify an **author**'s intentions, or locate a **text**'s core of meaning, it is perhaps best encapsulated in the biblical phrase 'in the beginning was the Word [the *logos*]', with its concomitant faith in God, the Self, and the Order of the Universe, and its tendency to privilege the singular and definitive over the multiple and indeterminate. What Derrida seeks to undermine in common with other **post-modernists** is the metaphysical certainty not only that a unique 'I' behind any utterance guarantees a consistent, totally conscious, and rational point of view, or that a unified meaning might be traced back to an originary intention, but also that graphic modes of **representation**, be they in words or images, directly refer to a pre-existent reality. Precisely because concepts such as reality, consciousness, intentionality and purpose are so deeply embedded in Western thinking, as well as in language, and yet go unacknowledged, it is imperative, he contends, to question the assumption that word and world coincide, or that word and deed are one.

By paying attention to the ways in which philosophers use language, seizing for instance on their use of metaphor, Derrida illustrates that figurative devices are operative in all writing, be they literary or philosophical, and that pure thought furthermore, despite philosophers' claims to the contrary, is never independent of its mode of expression. Thus language can give away either an underlying belief system that remains unconscious to the writer's intention (not unlike the **Freudian** slip), or show up a hitherto unrecognized rupture in a text's logic; which is why linguistic ambiguity, once exposed, does not merely highlight that meaning cannot be determined, but can uncover a whole nest of contradictions in the reasoning of those who profess themselves to rely on such concepts as reason and unitary meaning for the coherency of their argument. The Greek term *pharmakon,* for instance, which means both 'cure' and 'poison', and is used by Plato in its latter sense as a metaphor to describe writing, is such a case in point for Derrida in *Dissemination* (1972; English translation 1982). Plato distrusts writing because he sees it as a mode of communication which is always open to reinterpretation and hence distortion in the absence of the originary speaker, leading him to rank it as inferior to living speech, which he sees as potentially able to disclose true meaning, im*mediately* and un*mediated* by the dead weight of the written word. Consequently, Plato associates the written word with 'poison', and merely deems it as a 'cure' in the sense that in recording speech it can act as a remedy for the potential weakness of memory. Despite carefully contextualizing the term as to its specific sense whenever it is used in the *Phaedrus* to avoid possible confusion or ambiguity, Plato's aspiration to the purity of philosophical **discourse** is continually spoilt by the resonances that the word's multiple and contradictory meanings have in his text. What Derrida does then is to prompt Plato's text to refute its own logic, less by pointing to lapses in its author's argumentation or thinking, than by unravelling how the text's language actually works against its stated intentions.

Derrida's close readings therefore attend to those processes *always already* operative in a text, which unknit its ideal unity. The movement by which such processes are brought into play is what Derrida calls **deconstruction**. Working only with the resources presented to it by the text under study, a deconstructive reading displays just how much textuality is always a network of unfinished meanings, with 'each' text differing from itself, for which he coins the term '**différance**', and 'each' text a **trace** of, and endlessly referring to, other texts, which invokes **Barthes**' term **intertextuality**. While arguing that a text is 'no longer a finished corpus of writing, some content enclosed in a book or its margins', Derrida's writing also, however, performs what it states. The arguments in *Of Grammatology* (1967; English translation 1976), perhaps his major book to date and also one of his more 'analytic' works to generalize deconstruction's principles, are brought into a more productive frame in a later more 'synthetic' work such as *Glas* (1974; English translation 1986), which, by knitting together commentary and citation from **Hegel**'s and **Genet**'s writings not only blurs the boundaries between philosophy and literature, but also creates a new kind of textuality. As if anticipating **hypertext,** *Glas*'s typography undoes the linearity of writing, transgresses the borders of text and puts into question the very form of the book. [KL]

DESIRE In **postmodern** thought, desire represents all those libidinal drives in the individual that subvert the **power** of reason. The conception derives from **Freud**, whose studies had emphasized the hidden part of human nature in the subconscious, of whose workings we were at best only dimly aware, but which were often able to override our conscious, rational intentions.

For most postmodern thinkers, desire is what Western culture has been concerned to suppress for the last few centuries on the grounds that it represents a threat to social order and institutional structures. Thus for **Deleuze** and **Guattari** modern psychoanalysis was an exercise in social control, the objective of which was to curb desire and to make individuals conform to an authoritarian social system. The schizophrenic, who frustrated the attentions of the psychoanalyst, turned into an ideal type for them as a result. **Foucault** argued that sexual desire in the modern world had been restricted to one socially acceptable, and also heavily policed, type, that of heterosexuality within marriage – a cultural trend that marginalized, and in some cases criminalized, most other forms of sexual expression. Once again the goal was control of the individual's actions at a basic level. **Lyotard** attacked rationalist-oriented theories such as **Marxism**, which allowed no scope for desire, or '**libidinal economy**' as he dubbed it. In each case, to champion the cause of desire was to criticize the culture in which we live, given that this culture was, in general, concerned to limit the free expression of desire in the name of authoritarian norms of conduct.

The general turn away from reason in postmodern thought has involved a corresponding commitment to desire, which has become a key strategy in the subversion of **modernity** and its allegedly authoritarian systems. Desire represents an implicitly anti-authoritarian force for the postmodern movement. [SS]

DESIRING-MACHINE Individuals constitute desiring-machines in **Deleuze** and **Guattari**'s terminology. In *Anti-Oedipus* (1972) they argue that we have transcended such traditional categories as man and nature, and are now in a society that consists of various kinds of 'machines' – for example, desiring-machines, producing-machines and schizophrenic-machines. It is the point of modern psychoanalysis (summed up under the blanket heading of **Oedipus**) to repress desiring-machines and, indeed, the expression of **desire** in general. The desiring-machine is driven by **libidinal** energy rather than reason, and lacks the unity normally associated with individual identity in Western culture. It is therefore seen by

the ruling authorities as a threat to social order. [SS]

DIFFÉRANCE Différance, a term coined by Jacques **Derrida**, both signals how language works and is also another term for the manoeuvres and movements of **deconstruction**. As a descriptive term, Derrida uses it to illustrate, following the Swiss linguist Ferdinand de Saussure, how any word always depends for its meaning not on its natural bond with the real, as if it were its stand-in, but on its association with other words along a whole chain of significations, to which it refers but also from which it is different, thus indicating perpetual movements as well as potential slippages of meaning in language. As a neologism, created from the French verb *différer* which means both 'to differ' and 'to defer', différance, referring to both senses simultaneously and therefore deliberately ambiguous, demonstrates that language is always indeterminate, and that meaning is always undecidable and thus endlessly deferred. As such, différance not only describes linguistic functions, it also performs them. As an interchangeable term for deconstruction it also, however, fulfils another function. While undermining any sense of unity, it can never just simply be conceived as its opposite; for, to conceive of différance in op*position* to another term, such as unity, would be to fix it in a certain *position* and thus curtail what characterizes it: suspension, movement, deferral. Thus, as its very operations illustrate, it is an alternative term for both unity *and* **difference**. [KL]

DIFFERENCE Difference, as a term in **deconstruction** and **poststructuralism**, signals that a **text** is not an ideal unity, but always subject to indeterminacies inherent in language, which resist interpretive closure of meaning, thus illustrating that although there is a difference between texts, there is also difference within 'one' text. While

postmodernism tends to celebrate difference, schools of thought following **Hegel** seek to overcome it. Thus for Hegel difference is something to be mediated, which results in the dialectical synthesis between two terms in an opposition, to produce an altogether new and different third term. For **Derrida**, on the other hand, to overcome difference is to subsume two opposing terms in one fusion and reduce them from two into one, without preserving their radical **alterity** from, or difference from, each other, and without respecting each 'one' in its 'many-ness'. For this reason, Derrida suggests, as a third term, the notion of **différance**, which as an alternative to both unity and difference is always marked by an excess, resisting the pull to be unified, to be assimilated into one. Derrida's suspicions in *Altérités* (1986) of the Hegelian tendency to gather and fuse that which is dispersed is a reaction to, as he sees it, the dangerous willingness of thinkers such as **Habermas** either to find or to impose unity or consensus, respectively. In common with **Lyotard**, he believes that to force agreement where there is disagreement, to will consensus where there is dissent, is also to level difference, to efface **Otherness**, and to eliminate multiplicity. [KL]

DIFFERENCE FEMINISM A highly contentious concern with **difference** is one of the contemporary characteristics of **postmodern** thought. A similar concern also emerged in the 1970s from the practical domain of an emergent feminist politics. Within the second wave of feminism, difference came to signify all the theoretical complexities arising from the sociological observation that women do not possess a uniform social identity. Postmodern thought and difference feminism come together in a fragile alliance: both recognize the practical and epistemological significance of women being variously situated, like men, in a network of many dimensions of identity and **power**.

However, in the context of feminist psychoanalytic theory, 'difference' is used in a narrower sense: it signifies specifically male–female sexual difference. Unlike a feminist psychoanalytic ethics of sexual difference, difference feminism represents a decisive split within feminism itself over the exclusionary dominance of a white, middle-class perspective. Yet this split raises the hope that a new sort of feminist politics will strive for solidarity without doing violence to the intricacies of social identity, the goal being a transformation of the politics of gender in becoming aware of various relations of oppression.

Difference here is not a description of the attributes of a group, but a function of the relations between groups, intending emancipation rather than exclusion. A positive sense of group difference is emancipatory insofar as it is a creation, and not an assertion, of a singular identity given with certainty by experience. The group 'women' has overlapping experiences with such group differences as race, class, religion and ethnicity. To preserve difference without creating new entrenched forms of identity, difference feminists articulate a politics in which the meaning of difference itself becomes a terrain of political struggle. [PSA]

DIFFEREND To Jean-François **Lyotard**, a differend is a dispute that arises when each party is employing a form of language (or discourse) **incommensurable** with the other. Thus an employee being exploited by an unscrupulous employer cannot find redress from that employer in a court set up according to the laws of a society which specifically sanctions economic exploitation of employees by employers. The dispute is irresolvable, except in the sense that one party can use its greater **power** to enforce its will on the other (as happens, for example, in colonial situations). Differends are, therefore, normally suppressed by means of brute power, but Lyotard wants them to be acknowledged, and not taken advantage of by the stronger party. It is the duty of philosophers to help the weaker parties to disputes to find the language (or 'phrase-regime', as Lyotard refers to it) in which their grievance can be framed.

In a geopolitical sense, recognizing the differend would mean acknowledging the rights of exploited peoples and minority groups to be heard (acknowledging the claims to landownership of the native peoples in North America or Australia, for example), and in general backing away from 'solutions' to political problems based on the mere exercise of power. [SS]

DISCOURSE In **Foucault**'s writings, discourse refers to self-contained systems of thought, belief, or social or political practices, governed by internally accepted regulations and procedures. Foucault pointed out how medicine, for example. became a discourse in modern times, but we can also speak of politics or art – or even sexuality – as discourses, with particular concerns and conventions in given periods. From that point of view **Marxism** is a discourse, as is **modernism** in the arts (and then various subbranches within modernism itself, such as cubism). The sum of all the discourses in a historical period, say the **Enlightenment**, constitutes what Foucault calls an **episteme**.

It is a critical point about discourses that they can come and go; they contain no universal truths that hold over time. They are based on **power** relations, and these can alter. Thus, for Foucault, humanism is merely another discourse, which will one day pass away, 'like a face drawn in sand at the edge of the sea', as he put it at the close of *The Order of Things* (1966). In Foucault's scheme, most discourses are repressive and deserve to be challenged, as he himself challenged the discourse of compulsory heterosexuality in Western culture in his monumental trilogy *The History of Sexuality* (1976–84). [SS]

DISSEMINATION As outlined in the book of the same name by Jacques **Derrida** (1972), dissemination is a method of reading involving the **deconstruction** of certain highly influential **texts** in the Western philosophical tradition – such as Plato's *Phaedrus.* The concern, as so often in Derrida's work, is with challenging the view that speech is privileged over writing, the latter being a standard assumption of **discourse** in the West. The *Phaedrus* takes the customary Platonic form of a dialogue, in which Socrates listens to a speech written by Lysias which is in the possession of Phaedrus. In his response to Phaedrus, Socrates relates the story of Theuth, the inventor of writing. Much of Derrida's discussion turns on the term 'pharmakon', which Plato uses to refer to writing, and which has been variously translated as both poison and remedy. Derrida points to the deeply ambivalent nature of the term, and from this demonstrates that in his condemnation of writing Socrates borrows from the very tools he disparages, thus undermining his arguments. [DW]

DOLLIMORE, JONATHAN: CRITIC (1948–) Through his own publications and through his editorial work with Alan **Sinfield**, Jonathan Dollimore is one of the leading exponents of '**cultural materialism**', the most significant development in Renaissance studies in the 1980s. The term is taken from the work of cultural critic Raymond Williams and means, very broadly, a politically engaged, materialist analysis of culture. Dollimore is an acute commentator on new developments in the field, where his sympathy to (but political difference from) **postmodern** theory can be seen most clearly. He has also been influential in the theorization of lesbian and gay studies. Dollimore's early research, which appeared as *Radical Tragedy* (1984), was an exploration of the relationship between subjectivity, power and ideology in the early modern period. As a materialist,

Dollimore takes the view that there is no essential, irreducible self that exists before entering social relations. The human self is a construct. 'Idealist' criticism, which believes in transhistorical truth, elides or erases cultural, racial and sexual **difference**, the very subjects of Dollimore's attention.

For Dollimore, objectivity in cultural analysis is a chimera; all cultural practice has a political dimension. **Texts** do not simply reflect reality; they play a part in the making of meaning. Using insights from postmodern **continental** theory and the close-reading techniques of ideological critique, Dollimore sees texts as sites of political and ideological struggle where the critic should attempt to locate the text's 'internal dissonance': what Pierre Macherey describes as the text's difference from itself. Dollimore makes the suggestive point that often the culturally peripheral turns out to be symbolically central and this has led him to examine the way such groups are represented in texts. He uses this insight as a way of exploring, for instance, the role of the prostitute in Shakespeare's *Measure for Measure*. While his politically committed interest in 'the subordinate, the marginal, the excluded and displaced' chimes in with the interests of radical postmodernist critics, 'marginal' figures are not simply celebrated. Not for Dollimore 'the too convenient appropriation' of them in an ahistorical way nor 'the identification with the process of victimization rather than the victims'. In Jacobean drama the prostitute, the 'sodomite', and the transvestite are not postmodernists *avant la lettre*, as they appear in some recent radical criticism. Dollimore finds in Jacobean tragedy 'not a vision of political freedom so much as a subversive knowledge of political domination'. Dollimore's work avoids the politically empty valorization of 'subversion'; 'nothing is intrinsically subversive independent of its articulation and context'. In *Sexual Dissidence* (1991),

Dollimore takes as his title a technique for the gender-related unsettling of such oppositions as dominant and subordinate which has similarities to the work of Eve Kosofsky Sedgwick, whose work, along with Dollimore's, has had a shaping influence on recent '**queer theory**'. [PD]

DOT.COMS Dot.coms refer to **Internet**-based companies, taking advantage of the new technology to create a new type of company trading exclusively over the Internet, with largely service-based rather than product-based businesses. The move from production to service – post-Fordism as it is called – is characteristically **postmodernist** in ethos. Although many dot.coms have been and continue to be successful, they have not in general lived up to the expectations they aroused in investment circles in the 1990s. Then, a dot.com bubble occurred, with many companies drawing in massive investment through the stock market way in excess of their actual value. This was thought to be the future for business, with investors seemingly unperturbed by the initial losses of most dot.coms, treating them as worthwhile longer-term bets that would overtake conventional business structures. Many dot.coms soon crashed, however, carrying a huge amount of investment capital with them. Others, such as the on-line bookseller Amazon, managed to survive, but few have delivered the profit margins that investors were hoping for. [SS]

DOUBLE CODING Double coding, according to Charles **Jencks**, describes a defining characteristic of **postmodern** architecture. In *The Language of Post-Modern Architecture* (1977) he describes double-coding as 'the combination of **modern** techniques with something else (usually traditional building)'. Among the many examples Jencks uses is British architect James **Stirling**'s addition to the Staatsgalerie in Stuttgart. While obviously a contemporary building, it echoes and plays with past art and architecture, including classical and pop art. Jencks sees this kind of post-modernist building as a way of opening up the minimalist language of modernism to history, context and **difference**.

During the 1980s, Jencks expanded his theory of double coding into other areas of culture. In art, Jencks sees the return of **representational** painting, self-conscious allegory, eclecticism and **hybridity** as signs of ubiquitous postmodern double coding. In fiction, Jencks admires writers who neither repudiate nor slavishly imitate the experimental modernist writers of the early years of the century, but who, like John **Barth** and Umberto **Eco** for instance, give us the traditional pleasures of plot and work on a number of other levels too. Theories of postmodern fiction such as Linda Hutcheon's 'historiographical **meta-fiction**' have put Jencks' concept to interesting use. [PD]

DUCHAMP, MARCEL: ARTIST (1887–1968) Regarded as one of the most avant-garde of **modernists** in his lifetime (being identified with movements such as dada, surrealism, cubism and futurism), Duchamp is now widely held to be a forerunner of the **postmodern** aesthetic, and has been cited as an influence by many postmodern artists (Jeff **Koons**, for example). His works were invariably controversial, none more than so than the infamous *Fountain*, exhibited in New York in 1917, which turned out to be a urinal, playfully signed 'R. Mutt' by the artist. Such 'ready-mades' offered a radical challenge to standard conceptions of art and the artist's role (as well as of the artist's responsibility to his audience). Other large-scale constructions such as *Nude Descending a Staircase* (1911, 1912) and *The Bride Stripped Bare by her Bachelors, Even* (1915–1923), with their elaborate and eccentric machinery, appeared to be designed to test the limits of art as a meaningful **discourse**. Some critics have described Duchamp's work as 'anti-art', and it is precisely that aspect which exerts an appeal on the postmodern sensibility. Works like *Fountain* seem to be mocking the entire tradition of 'high art' in Western culture.

The implications of Duchamp's anti-art for the postmodern aesthetic were spelled out by Jean-François **Lyotard**, whose book *Duchamp's Trans/Formers* (1977; English edition, 1990) praised the 'pointlessness' of much of Duchamp's works, which actively resisted interpretation. *The Bride Stripped Bare by her Bachelors, Even*, as a case in point, fitted into no scheme and furthered the cause of no political ideology or **grand narrative**. Whereas critics normally set out to explain what artworks meant in terms of their artistic or socio-political context, Duchamp's pieces demanded instead that the critic 'try not to understand and to show that you haven't understood'. By escaping classification, Duchamp's oeuvre demonstrated the futility of any unifying philosophy, and thus for Lyotard struck an authentically postmodern note. [SS]

E

EAGLETON, TERRY: AUTHOR, CRITIC
(1943–) A dramatist and novelist,
Eagleton is best known as the leading
Marxist literary critic writing in Britain.
His work is marked by a critical engagement with continental **critical theory** and
he has produced popularizing works from
Marxism and Literary Criticism (1976) to
Literary Theory (2nd edn 1996), detailed
studies of canonical authors such as
Shakespeare in *Shakespeare and Society*
(1967) and Samuel Richardson in *The
Rape of Clarissa* (1982), as well as a Marxist
reading of the history of aesthetics, the
remarkable *Ideology of the Aesthetic* (1990).
One of its most cogent critics from the left,
he has argued against most aspects of
postmodernism, from his 1985 essay in
New Left Review, 'Capitalism, **Modernism**,
Postmodernism', to his most fully worked-
out response, *The Illusions of Postmodernism* (1996). Here he examines a series of
oppositional pairings familiar to postmodern thinking, such as identity/**difference**
and nature/culture, which Eagleton sees in
the light of the debate over universals and
particulars. Eagleton acknowledges that
postmodernism has allowed us to re-
evaluate our conception of the relations
between **power**, **desire**, identity and
political practice and, at its most militant,
has lent a voice to the humiliated and
reviled. In doing so it has threatened to
shake the imperious self-identity of dominant political systems to their core. It has
produced, in the same breath, an invigor-
ating but paralysing scepticism that valor-
izes a whole series of concepts ('difference',
'culture', 'subversion', 'marginality') in a
formalistic and ahistorical way, lining them
up against such scare-words as 'identity',
'nature' and 'universality'. His main charge
is that postmodern art and thought
acquiesces 'with the appalling mess that is
the contemporary world'.

First, identity/difference: using the postmodern concept of 'difference', a large
number of marginalized groups have found
a political voice. For Eagleton, socialism
goes further and wants to see the emancipation of difference at the level of human
mutuality and reciprocity. This raises the
much discussed topic of subjectivity and its
decentring or destabilizing in postmodern
thought. While the questioning of the self-
identical **subject** of Western thought is
valuable, it is not postmodernism that has
most effectively destabilized the humanist
subject, but advanced capitalism. The most
anti-elitist force in contemporary society is
the marketplace itself, which buries all
distinctions and gradations beneath the
abstract quality of exchange value. Furthermore, the **deconstructed** subject of postmodern discourse is capable of various
subversions of the dominant social values,
but is incapable of the emancipatory goal
of transforming society in any meaningful
way. Rebellion could not succeed if human
agents were not provisionally self-
affirmative and self-identical enough to
carry it through. For Eagleton, you need an
idea of a human subject unified enough to
take significantly transformative action.
He suggests that a reasonably secure identity, as opposed to a paranoiacally cohesive
one, is a necessary condition of human
well-being and it is morally irresponsible
of some postmodernists to deny this.
Difference cannot flourish under forms of

exploitation; to combat those effectively requires a notion of humanity which is necessarily universal.

Second, universality/particularity and nature/culture: **Enlightenment** philosophers argued a radical, universalist case for equal rights. Everyone is entitled to freedom, autonomy, justice and political equality because we are equally individuals and share a common human nature. While postmodernism, sceptical of overarching, universalizing theories of history and the human self, sees not nature here, but culture, Eagleton sees postmodernism as a form of 'culturalism' because it refuses to recognize that what different ethnic groups have in common socially and politically is more important to their emancipation than their cultural differences, which postmodernism drastically underestimates. There are no 'non-cultural' human beings, not because culture is all there is to us, but because culture belongs to our nature. Postmodernism's glamorization of the 'marginal' and suspicion of centres of power and authority forbid it conceiving of a majority political movement, such as Solidarity in Poland or the African National Congress. Finally, postmodern thinking overlooks the fact that capitalism is formidably resourceful and also spectacularly unsuccessful in providing adequate resources for the majority of the world's population. Postmodernism and **post-Marxism** are responses, paradoxically, to a power structure more 'total' than ever. This 'total' system, however, is not homogeneous. Eagleton argues that postmodernists suffer from 'holophobia', a fear of totality; and not looking for totality is code for their main mistake: not looking for capitalism, the very thing that stands in the way of human freedom. [PD]

ECO, UMBERTO: AUTHOR, CULTURAL THEORIST (1932–) An intriguing feature of **postmodernism** is the **desire** for theorists to practise what they preach, and for artists to preach what they practise. It is this blurring of the boundaries between distinct discursive zones that makes Umberto Eco such a pivotal figure on the contemporary scene. He is a writer at ease in low or high culture. He has written extensively for Italian newspapers and magazines, including *La Stampa* and *La Repubblica*. The best of these pieces are collected in *Misreadings* (1993), *How to Travel with a Salmon* (1994), and *Kant and the Platypus* (1997). He has published as an academic a formidable array of volumes on literature and linguistics, including *The Role of the Reader* (1981), *Faith in Fakes* (1984), *The Limits of Interpretation* (1990), *The Search for the Perfect Language* (1993) and *Experiences in Translation* (2001).

Eco's doctoral dissertation at the University of Turin was on theologian Thomas Aquinas, and he has pursued his interest in medieval matters throughout his career. This is not surprising, as there are many parallels that link the Middle Ages with the postmodern moment. Both are periods of in-betweenness: interim states defined in terms of the historical eras they succeed and anticipate. Both are fascinated with the stacking of layers of meaning and the interpenetration of different worlds of meaning.

Such parallels are probed with great dexterity in Eco's worldwide best-selling novel *The Name of the Rose* (1984), which is simultaneously a murder mystery and a **semiotic** mystery. The murder plot concerns a Benedictine monastery in northern Italy, where an important meeting is scheduled in 1327 between two rival factions of the Franciscan order who espouse or oppose the vow of poverty. Against this rich historical backdrop (created by many lucid and learned passages of exposition by Eco), several murders take place, beginning with a young monk who is found at the bottom of a cliff. William of Baskerville investigates these crimes with a novice called Adso, who plays Watson to William's

Holmes. The semiotic plot centres around the monastery library, which seems to provide the vital clue for the murderer's motive. The library is also a labyrinth, and Eco acknowledges his debt to the post-modernist Argentinian writer Borges for this image of hermeneutic intricacy through the character of the blind librarian, Jorge. The solution to the crimes involves Aristotle's famous lost book on comedy, which threatens the **power** of the church by advocating humour as a corrective to tragic self-importance.

Eco's working title for *The Name of the Rose* was *The Abbey of the Crime*, an altogether inferior title, as it directs the reader to a very particular detective-fiction mindset. The actual title, on the other hand, suggests many possible interpretations based upon the complex symbology of the rose. The contrast between these two titles is therefore a good illustration of Eco's distinction between closed and open **texts**, which he makes in *The Open Work* (1989).

If *The Name of the Rose* is destined to be remembered as the quintessential post-modernist novel, Eco's subsequent fictions – *Foucault's Pendulum* (1989) and *The Island of the Day Before* (1995) – did not quite attain the same dizzying heights of academic and popular acceptance. He returned to his beloved medieval period for his comic fable *Baudolino* (2000). There is at least one of Eco's non-fictional statements which has already achieved canonical status as a definition of post-modernism itself. Here it is, quoted in full, from *Reflections on 'The Name of the Rose'* (1984):

I think of the postmodern attitude as that of a man who loves a very cultivated woman and knows that he cannot say to her, 'I love you madly', because he knows that she knows (and that she knows that he knows) that these words have already been written by Barbara Cartland. Still, there is a solution. He can say, 'As Barbara Cartland would put it, I love you madly.' At this point, having avoided false innocence, having said clearly that it is no longer possible to speak innocently, he will neverthe-less have said what he wanted to say to the woman: that he loves her, but he loves her in an age of lost innocence. If the woman goes along with this, she will have received a declaration of love all the same.

This passage summarizes many of the key attributes of postmodernism: its knowing **irony**, its penchant for quotation, its flirta-tion with popular culture and its playful **polysemy** or **plurality** of sense. [BL]

EDGE OF CHAOS Chaos theory posits a world in which randomness and determin-ism can co-exist simultaneously within the same system. The tension between the two phenomena is most keenly felt at what has been dubbed the edge of chaos: the state in which the system is only just preventing itself from lapsing into chaos. For many commentators, this is the optimum con-dition for systems to be in, since it encourages innovation and ingenuity to keep chaos at bay. Without that tension, systems (such as species or societies) stagnate, and eventually die out. [SS]

EISENMAN, PETER: ARCHITECT (1932–) Eisenman produces a brand of dry expres-sionist architecture, a version of **decon-structivism** that perversely refuses to enjoy its formal gymnastics. His is an architecture that stresses the alienation that archi-tecture forces on its occupiers. Many of his obsessions are revealed in his early House series (1–9), where incidents occur within the formalism such as the splitting of the marital bed into two, with a thin gap that separates the two halves, a void above the living space, or a structural column grid that is engineered such that one column does not quite meet the ground. He seems to revel in the difficult, the obscure and the pointless – things that architecture has consistently tried to ignore and exclude – banality and unfriendliness. His own (well-publicized) psychoanalysis has helped him produce an architecture that is both self-obsessed and self-loathing. His buildings attempt to undermine themselves, twisting logics of structure, geometry and order. They are exercises intended to problematize architectural practice – marking out the unresolvable complexities inherent in the contemporary making of buildings. It is the constant formal manipulations of the sparse and abstract language of high **modernism** rather than its contamination with other codes that provides the ground for his work. Whether aligning the axis of the Wexner Arts Centre with the flightpath into Columbus, Ohio Airport, or aligning the Social Housing IBA five degrees off the city grid, his points of reference are deliberately placed beyond the grasp of the buildings' users. [SJ]

ELLIS, BRET EASTON: NOVELIST (1964–)
On the publication of his first novel in 1985 the twenty-one-year-old American author, like Lord Byron before him, awoke to find himself famous. While his four novels, *Less Than Zero* (1985), *The Rules of Attraction* (1987), *American Psycho* (1991) and *Glamorama* (1999), are not **postmodern** in form, they, along with his book of linked stories *The Informers* (1994), detail the lives of the young affluent whites who consume postmodern culture: those whom Jean-François **Lyotard** describes as 'wear-[ing] Paris perfume in Tokyo and "retro" clothes in Hong Kong; knowledge is a matter for TV games'. *Less Than Zero* describes an eighteen-year-old's round of parties, visits to friends, drink and drug abuse, but also ambitiously uses the 'blank generation' as a metaphor for a philosophical emptiness registered in the book's title.

The anger many felt at Ellis's non-judgemental tone turned incandescent on the publication of his black comedy *American Psycho,* the self-narrated tale of the ultimate consumer; a cannibalistic Wall Street yuppie serial killer. The narrator, however, is an extremely unreliable fantasist. We are never offered any psychological explanation of the narrator's actions, so the novel's exhaustive and exhausting catalogues of consumer goods, sexual positions and torture become indices of a whole social layer's alienation and commodity fetishism. *Less Than Zero* begins: 'People are afraid to merge on the highways in Los Angeles', echoing E. M. Forster's liberal plea 'only connect'. Here, though, in Ellis's affectless, postmodern world, there is little hope that such connections can be made. [PD]

ENDISM Endism refers to the various theories circulating in the last few decades proclaiming the end of phenomena such as history. Francis **Fukuyama** is somewhat notorious for arguing that the collapse of communism signals the end of history in the sense that liberal capitalism has now won the global political struggle, and that henceforth it is the only viable political system. Daniel **Bell** had earlier proclaimed that we had moved beyond industrialization to what he called a '**post-industrial**' culture, an idea that influenced thinkers like Fukuyama. Jean **Baudrillard** fits into this developing tradition of endist thought, being happy to abolish history, because, as one of his typically provocative arguments puts it, if we are only alienated in history, then the end *of* history must constitute the end of our alienation.

Postmodernism in general is somewhat ambivalent about endism. On the one hand, postmodernist thinkers are fond of claiming that we have passed over a watershed to a new kind of cultural formation; on the other, postmodernism is often a self-conscious dialogue with the past, in the sense of a recovery of older artistic forms (novelistic realism, figurative painting, premodernist architecture, etc.) or ideas (the 'sublime', for example). [SS]

ENLIGHTENMENT PROJECT Historians use the term 'the Enlightenment' to refer to the 'long' eighteenth century which stretches from England's 'Glorious Revolution' (1688) to the outbreak of the French Revolution (1789). But the Enlightenment was not only a historical period; it was also an intellectual project brought into focus by the group of French intellectuals – the *philosophes* – involved in the publication of the *Encyclopédie*, edited by Denis Diderot over a period of twenty years from 1751. The ideals of this group were increasingly shared by educated men and women across the globe.

To understand the relevance of what is repeatedly referred to in **postmodernism** as the 'Enlightenment project', it is vital to distinguish between a critical, often polemical, element and its more progressive, constructive and sometimes prescriptive developments.

Enlightenment was defined as the project of dispelling darkness, fear and superstition; of removing all the shackles from free enquiry and debate. It opposed the traditional powers and beliefs of the church (branded as 'superstition') and raised questions of political **legitimacy**. All received or traditional notions, and social relations, were to be made subject to the scrutiny of the public, and therefore, collective – or intersubjective – use of 'reason'. The comparatively liberal social arrangements which characterized politics and commerce in eighteenth-century England were one important model or inspiration for Enlightenment thinkers. The other was the fantastic achievements of science and technology, in the wake of Newton's scientific revolution. This was the epoch which first came to terms with extensive and tangible improvements in many areas of life affected by the application of science, giving rise to the dream of a world radically improved, ordered, engineered, mastered. The idea of the improvement of the human race, and of 'moral progress', was born. The desire to master nature developed into the dream of mastering society and history. The dark, nightmarish side of this dream was analysed by **Adorno** and **Horkheimer** in *Dialectic of Enlightenment* (1947), whose opening reads: '[T]he Enlightenment has always aimed at liberating men from fear and establishing their sovereignty. Yet the fully enlightened earth radiates disaster triumphant.'

One shorthand way to define postmodernism is as the end of the Enlightenment dream of mastery and a definitive improvement to human society through knowledge and technology. In recent years the eighteenth century has become the focus of intensive historical research. The results, recorded in fascinating biographies and penetrating monographs, could go a long way to correcting the caricature of the Enlightenment which the 'postmodernism' debates have tended to circulate. The eighteenth century saw traditional certainties dissolve. Even the most optimistic thinkers were plagued by doubt and even despair. It was a time of constant experimentation, not of complacent self-confidence. [LS]

EPISTEME For Michel **Foucault**, episteme stands for a historical period and all the cultural beliefs and practices it contains. Those beliefs and practices are expressed within various **discourses** (the law, politics, the arts, for example), and the sum total of all those historically-bound discourses constitutes an episteme. All those discourses stand in relation to the dominant ideology of the time, which has the **power** to decide what will count as knowledge, or acceptable practice, within the culture in question. For the **postmodern** historian or cultural critic, it is the power relations within an episteme that are of overriding interest; any analysis of a given period will home in on these, as Foucault himself did in works like *The Birth of the Clinic* (1963) and *Madness and Civilization* (1964). [SS]

ERASURE Erasure is a **deconstructionist** technique whereby a word or term is used, but what it commits one to (its meaning, as well as the theory of meaning lying behind it) is denied, or, as Jacques **Derrida** puts it, placed 'under erasure' (*sous rature*). This enables Derrida to claim that he can use the language of Western philosophy without that use committing him to a belief in its concepts or any of its principles. The practice is derived from Martin **Heidegger**, who in *Zur Seinsfrage* used the word 'being' with a line drawn through it, in order to signal that he did not want to be drawn into debates about the concept, since that would imply his acceptance of Western philosophy's metaphysical assumptions about being. Erasure is one of the ways Derrida attempts to answer what has become a standard criticism of his work: that he relies on language to put his arguments across, while simultaneously claiming that language is unstable and meaning indeterminate. Critics have pointed out that Derrida's critique of language could not be understood unless language and meaning were at least relatively stable. Seen from that latter perspective, the technique of erasure is something of a confidence trick. [SS]

ÉVÉNEMENTS In May 1968, the *événements* (the '**events**') shattered the banal peace of urban Paris. While they may not have achieved the overthrow of de Gaulle's government – although, but for the intervention of the unions, they might well have done so – they *practised* the revolution of everyday life according to the theoretical forecasts and personal dreams of many unorthodox Communist Party members and Marxist theoreticians. Following the arrest of the activist leaders of the National Committee for Vietnam, students at the University of Paris formed the 22nd March Movement and, under the emerging leadership of Daniel Cohn-Bendit, occupied its Nanterre campus and vociferously condemned the education regime as a factory for turning out the bureaucrats of everyday life. Similar occupations and demonstrations followed all over France. Meanwhile, union unrest was also growing, with the major unions rejecting government pay policy and sparking protest marches and strikes throughout the country. The unions themselves, however, began to condemn the activist tendencies of both the workers and the students, opening up the rift between the protesters and their union representatives that would eventually see these populist movements caught in a government–union axis. The spark came when, on 3 May 1968, the Paris riot police, the CRS, surrounded and sealed Nanterre before bombarding the campus with tear gas and invading it. The French Communist Party (PCF), meanwhile, condemned the student occupations, prompting a final break between the students and the left-wing political parties. This break is decisive for the widespread sense of the failure of the **Marxist** project, since its PCF vanguard effectively colluded with the government and the unions to bring an end to the *événements*, rather than supporting their revolutionary aims. For the first time, decisively for the politics of **postmodernism** in France, Marxism was revealed as a bureaucratic machine for the suppression rather than the advancement of revolution.

Following a massively successful general strike, the workers, students and the angry and the dissident intellectuals of the **Situationist** International took over the streets of Paris. After a month of barricades and immediate revolution, the government forces eventually put down the insurgents while the trade unions swiftly negotiated a return to work. The *événements* nevertheless mark the closest a modern first world state has come to complete dissolution at the hands of popular revolution. [IHG]

EVENT Jean-François **Lyotard** refers to an 'event' as the change in perspective that takes place after a particularly significant cultural occurrence. The most frequently cited example of this in Lyotard is Auschwitz, which he argues irrevocably altered our perception of human nature and the world in which we live (Theodor **Adorno** had also spoken of the impossibility of writing poetry after the facts of Auschwitz had become known). The 1968 *événements* in Paris are another example of an event which irrevocably altered the world-view of a specific social group, in this case a whole generation of French intellectuals. What was shattered was that generation's belief in the moral supremacy of **Marxism**, as enshrined in the French Communist Party (PCF). The collusion of the latter with the forces of the state in bringing down the alliance of workers and students that had briefly challenged the state's authority was felt by many French left-wing intellectuals, including Lyotard, to have compromised Marxism to the point where it had lost all credibility. Lyotard speaks of the need to be 'open' to the event, meaning to be able to approach new experiences without bringing with us the prejudices of outmoded theories such as Marxism. [SS]

F

FEDERMAN, RAYMOND: NOVELIST (1928–)
Raymond Federman was born in France.
In 1940 virtually his entire family were sent
to concentration camps. He himself only
narrowly escaped because his mother
bundled him into a closet before the Nazis
came. After the war he emigrated to the
United States, and established himself as a
postmodernist writer in the 1970s. His
startling works *Double Or Nothing* (1971)
and *Take It Or Leave It* (1976) are examples
of 'concrete prose': novels whose typographical appearance is as important as
what they say.

Double Or Nothing uses many iconic
designs, where the words on the page are
arranged into a shape imitative of what
they describe. So the word PLUNGING
falls down the page; the word ROLLS is
spaced out like a bread bun; and a ship is
welded out of the words THE CALL OF
THE OCEAN and ATLANTICPACIFIC.
Federman also uses abstract shapes, in
which there is no necessary relation
between the design and the words that
compose it. Entire pages are typed as an
hourglass, a zigzag or an L-configuration.
Federman's 'spatial displacement of words'
continues in *Take It Or Leave It*. These
language games force a split between
sound and sense, **text** and subtext, the
materiality of the book and its meaning. At
the heart of these books, and others such as
The Voice in the Closet (1979), *To Whom it
May Concern* (1990), and *Aunt Rachel's Fur*
(2001) is a silence: the untellable story of
his own personal Holocaust experiences.

Federman has also theorized his literary
practice, and in 1991 he (cheekily) announced the death of postmodernism. [BL]

**FEYERABEND, PAUL: PHILOSOPHER OF
SCIENCE** (1924–94) Paul Feyerabend was,
along with Karl Popper and Thomas **Kuhn**,
one of the twentieth century's most important philosophers of science. Although he
did not call himself a **postmodernist**, and
indeed the dialogue in which he took part
began not with **Lyotard**, **Foucault** and
Baudrillard, but with the pre-Socratic
Greek philosophers of the fifth century BC,
both Feyerabend's relativism and his
irreverent, gadfly style of discourse set up a
profound resonance with postmodernism.
In his three major works, *Against Method*
(1975), *Science in a Free Society* (1978) and
A Farewell to Reason (1987), Feyerabend
battles against two related ideas: first, that
there are objective truths, scientific, political or moral, 'out there' in the world, and
second, that there is one method for
discovering those truths.

Feyerabend was influenced by Thomas
Kuhn's historicist approach to science and,
later, by Michel Foucault's '**archaeology** of
knowledge'. Underlying his view is a
passionate commitment to relativism: to
the argument that truth is always truth for
someone. Different groups, separated by
history, geography or ideology see the
world in very different ways. Often those
world-views will have little or nothing in
common. For an objectivist there must be a
way of either reconciling **differences** or
deciding between them. For Feyerabend,
on the other hand, 'we should simply accept
different world-views as **incommensurable**'. This has led Feyerabend into some
rather strange company. He has argued
that as there is simply no common ground
between the Creationist and Darwinian

views of the origins of humankind they should be taught in schools on an equal basis.

Much of Feyerabend's work can be seen as an answer to the enormously influential philosophy of science of Karl Popper. In his major work, *The Logic of Scientific Discovery*, Popper argued that a scientific hypothesis could never be proven to be absolutely true. We might observe a thousand white swans but that can never prove beyond doubt the theory that all swans are white. On the other hand, the first black swan observed conclusively 'falsifies' the theory. From this basic insight, Popper argued that scientists should spend their time concocting new and radical theories which they then endeavour to disprove. Science progresses, on this model, through a series of conjectures and refutations, driven by imaginative leaps made by great scientists. Although positive truth remains illusive in Popper's theory, he nevertheless retains a realist, objectivist position: there is a real world out there, and the scientist's job is to reveal it.

In *Against Method* (1974) Feyerabend rejects the realism and objectivism of Popper's falsificationism, as he rejects all other positivist and empiricist views of science. Feyerabend argues that scientists have, at different times, made use of many different methodologies, often importing concepts and approaches from other, non-rational, spheres. Without this heterogeneity there would have been no 'progress'. All too often a marginal theory, rejected by the scientific establishment, has proved to be more successful than its more popular rivals. In consequence, science needs **pluralism**, not the exclusiveness inherent in the falsificationist approach. As he puts it: 'There is no single rule, however plausible, and however firmly grounded in epistemology, that is not violated at some time or other.' Rigid definitions of what scientists *should* do simply do not fit what real scientists actually do.

Feyerabend rejects the 'big' science of massive, government-funded schemes (nuclear power, space programmes, the Human Genome Project). Following Foucault, he interprets these as simply a matter of **power,** exerted by elites in order to regulate and control. In its place, he suggests that science should be a way of solving local problems, or of promoting the wealth and well-being of the general community.

Feyerabend's radical politics, brilliant lecturing style and accessible writing always made him more popular with students than with professional philosophers, who tended to regard anyone who took voodoo as seriously as **quantum mechanics** as, at best, irresponsible. [AM]

FOUCAULT, MICHEL: PHILOSOPHER, HISTORIAN, CULTURAL CRITIC (1926–84) Michel Foucault was perhaps the single most influential theorist to have emerged from the transformation of the great post-war **structuralist** programme into the **postmodern** theoretical world. More even than his contemporaries Roland **Barthes** and Jacques **Derrida**, Foucault has inspired whole schools of thought, moulding philosophers of science, literary critics, sociologists and cultural historians to his own distinctive form of **discourse** analysis. Whenever the term 'discourse' is mentioned, whenever a reference is made to 'the body' as an object of control or coercion, we find Foucault's ghostly presence.

Foucault's oeuvre consists of a series of historical investigations into particular institutions, or 'discourses'. A discourse, for Foucault, is the matrix of **texts**, the specialized languages and the networks of **power** relations operating in and defining a given field. He always returns to the relationship between power and knowledge which, for Foucault, amount to very much the same thing.

The first of Foucault's major studies, *Madness and Civilization* (1961), examines the treatment of the insane from the end of the Middle Ages, a period of relative freedom, through the 'great confinement' of the Age of Reason, to the superficially more enlightened policies adopted towards those who were now considered mentally ill after the French Revolution. *The Birth of the Clinic* (1963) is a similar '**archaeological**' project, focusing on the new type of observation, or 'gaze', that began with the first modern teaching hospitals, attended by the bedside physician, the eyes through which the state monitored its **subjects**' health. *The Order of Things* (1966), which established Foucault's critical reputation, and became a best-seller in France, is a more general study of how, from the seventeenth century, the disciplines of psychiatry, medicine, biology, linguistics and economics came to define their 'proper' subjects, carving the world into ordered, controllable units, fixing each into a rigid structure.

Foucault defined the methodology governing these early works in *The Archaeology of Knowledge* (1969). In distancing his approach from that of conventional historians Foucault leans heavily on the concept of discontinuity. For the traditional historian, discontinuity was both 'the given and the unthinkable': the past is made up of innumerable instances – 'decisions, accidents, initiatives, discoveries' – which the historian must annihilate by moulding them into a continuous **narrative**. In contrast Foucault stresses the fact that certain forms of knowledge (about the human mind and body, about biology, politics or language), after periods of stability in which the fundamental processes of a discourse remain largely unquestioned, undergo rapid transformations. During these transformations (which sound uncannily like Thomas **Kuhn**'s '**paradigm shifts**') there is not only a change in the content of a discourse, but also a fundamental change in what might count as knowledge itself.

The most radical and unnerving of Foucault's claims is that the very concept 'man' was the creation of a unique set of historical contingencies, a consequence of certain relationships of power, a figment of discourse. By 'man' Foucault means the (by his account) relatively modern idea of man as a self-contained rational agent: that knowing subject assumed by rationalists, and triumphant in the French Revolution. And if, as he claims, we can trace the moment that 'man' came into existence, so we can predict his end. And with the **death of man**, so might perish the urge to classify, dominate, exclude and exploit that derives from that idea, and which has caused such havoc in our modern age.

In *Discipline and Punish: The Birth of the Prison* (1975), Foucault describes the transformation from the brutal treatment of criminals under feudal regimes to the more diffuse, and yet more effective, forms of social control in modern society. Jeremy Bentham's 'Panopticon' (a design for a penal institution in which prison cells were arranged around a central watchtower) becomes a metaphor for these insidious forms of policing. Never knowing for certain at any time whether or not they were subject to the penetrating gaze of the guard, the prisoners come to regulate their own behaviour.

Foucault's last great project, unfinished at his death, was *The History of Sexuality*. In the first of the three published volumes he seeks to undermine the 'repressive hypothesis': the commonly held belief that the freedom of discussion about sex in the modern age represents a radical and positive departure from the Victorian world of repression and silence. Foucault argues that, on the contrary, the Victorian age saw an acceleration in the multiplication of discourses aimed at delineating, explaining and ultimately controlling sexual behaviour. The modern 'sciences of sex', including psychoanalysis, are simply the continuation of the will to power in the form of the demand to know. The second and third volumes, *The Use of Pleasure* and *The Care of the Self* (both published in

1984), present a series of fascinating case studies showing how sexual behaviour developed from the classical obsession with boy love to the early Christian concern with marriage and heterosexual relations. If he does little to advance the argument of the first volume, Foucault at least gives ample evidence to demonstrate his case against the view that there is anything inherently 'natural' about any particular form of sexual intercourse; sexual relations are always governed by complex codes: strict rules about what can and cannot be done.

Foucault's brand of political activism was closely allied to his intellectual position. After an early flirtation with orthodox **Marxism**, he came to believe that the grand causes and class-based politics advocated by the traditional left in France were as oppressive as the bourgeois establishment they wished to overturn. In places of these meta-issues, Foucault advocated a local, small-scale but tenacious resistance to power. Perhaps the spirit of Foucault's politics is best caught by today's eco-warriors, rejecting as they do traditional forms of political debate, relying rather on causing disruption, challenging the power of the state and big business, and getting stoned. [AM]

FRACTALS Fractal geometry, a field invented by Benoit **Mandelbrot**, builds on work begun but discontinued at the turn of last century by the French mathematicians Henri Poincaré, Pierre Fatou and Gaston Julia. Both Mandelbrot and Julia have fractal sets named after them: sets that have served as a cultural icon of **chaos**. There are three basic types of fractal: linear self-similar (or 'self-repeating'), random self-similar, and fractal or 'chaotic' attractors. The first is best illustrated by a phenomenon known as a 'Sierpinski gasket': take a triangle and subdivide its area into smaller triangles. Following this first subdivision, repeat or 'reiterate' the

operation on these smaller triangles, and so on ad infinitum. Such a figure is linearly self-similar because each part of the object is exactly like the whole from which it is derived.

Random fractals are found in natural phenomena such as coastlines, mountains and clouds. One of Mandelbrot's earliest explorations of what he then called 'fractional dimension' was entitled 'How Long is the Coastline of Britain?' (1967). His paradoxical thesis in that paper is that since a coastline is not a pure curve but a random series of indents and excrescences, the coastline does not have a line that can be measured, but an infinite series of fractional dimensions that cannot be finally measured. If we regard a coastline from the air, it appears jagged and random. From ground level, a different dimension of randomness is revealed. Microscopically, the randomness is different again, and so on. Hence the various dimensions of randomness revealed by studying coastlines, clouds and mountains are randomly self-similar, since each dimension repeats randomness, but repeats it differently.

Third, chaotic fractals, such as the Mandelbrot set itself, model the behaviour of complex systems. Such systems are really chaotic rather than self-similar since each iteration reacts upon the previous one to produce endless bifurcations. The figure produced by the Mandelbrot set, the most familiar image of chaos, consists of a series of 'blobs' each of which repeats the core blob from which the set starts. With each fractal iteration of the blob, however, a new fractal dimension is produced that does not resemble the whole. This system is therefore complex, both linearly self-similar and random, depending upon which fractal dimension of this nonlinear, dynamical system is studied. [IHG]

FRAMPTON, KENNETH: ARCHITECTURAL THEORIST, CRITIC, HISTORIAN (1930–) Frampton is undoubtedly one of the foremost architectural commentators of his generation. The author of countless introductions to architectural monographs, he is best known for two publications: *Modern Architecture, a Critical History* (1980), is probably the most widely read primer for architectural students in print; and the essay 'Critical Regionalism', first published in *The Anti Aesthetic* (ed. Hal Foster (1983)) and reprinted in later editions of *Modern Architecture*, is perhaps his most influential contribution to architectural theory.

Frampton's sympathies are essentially **modernist**. However, his support for 'the unfinished modernist project' is inflected with a critique of the postivist mainstream of architectural modernism derived from the existentialist phenomenological schools of **Heidegger** and Ricoeur. This is most clearly expressed in his promotion of architectural tectonics – that is, the palpable display of the poetics of actual construction – as the primary means of disclosure of authentic architectural meaning. It is also made manifest in his rejection of the universal culture implied by utopian **modernism** which forms the basis of his theory of critical regionalism – a doctrine which, while supporting modernist aesthetics, seeks to resist the homogenization inherent in late-capitalist culture via recourse to the development of local traditions. As such, he is firmly opposed to the architectural manifestations of mainstream **postmodernism** which, by giving precedence to imageability via engagement with **semiology** and other forms of secondary signification, stand in opposition to the primary tectonic architectural culture that Frampton propagates. [SGr]

FRANKFURT SCHOOL The Frankfurt School of Social Research, founded by Max **Horkheimer** at the University of Frankfurt, comprised such well-known figures as Theodor **Adorno** and Herbert **Marcuse**, as well as Horkheimer himself, and, on the fringes of the School, the cultural critic Walter **Benjamin**. The School relocated to America after the Nazi takeover in 1933 had caused its members, basically Marxist in orientation, to leave Germany. While Adorno returned to Germany after the Second World War, Marcuse remained in America, where he became an inspiration to the student protest movement that grew up in the 1960s.

The School is famous for developing the method of analysis called '**critical theory**', which until the rise of **structural Marxism** in the 1950s and 1960s was arguably the dominant form of critique in what has come to be known as Western Marxism. Western Marxism, as borne out by the work of the members of the Frankfurt School, tended to be more interested in philosophical and aesthetic matters than economic ones, the latter being the province of Soviet theorists. Critical theory seeks to uncover the underlying **power** relations within cultural phenomena. Thus in works like *Dialectic of Enlightenment* (1947), Adorno and Horkheimer argue that the so-called '**Enlightenment project**' (the commitment to the liberation of mankind from material deprivation and political oppression) has become a myth that sustains the cultural status quo, leading to the subjugation of the individual within a repressive mass culture.

Adorno's later work, with its stress on '**negative dialectics**' (the insistence that dialectical processes never resolve themselves into a final synthesis where problems are completely overcome), is often seen to prefigure **deconstruction** as well as **post-Marxism**. Marcuse, too, ultimately moved away from the tenets of classical Marxism in his later career, when he became a champion of the new social movements that sprang up in the 1960s. [SS]

FREUD, SIGMUND, PSYCHOANALYST (1856–1939) Sigmund Freud was born in Freiburg to a Jewish family. When he was three the family moved to Vienna where Freud spent most of the rest of his life. Fleeing Vienna in 1938, he died not long afterwards in London. Initially as a neurologist but ultimately as a psychologist Freud studied human motivation. His psychoanalytic writings apply not only to neurotic behaviour but to all human endeavours. Changes in Freud's views constituted a complex catalyst for the reception of his various ideas, allowing the Freudian legacy of concepts to be developed in a variety of ways by modern and **postmodern** theorists. Freud's most central concept of the unconscious changed with the metapsychology – i.e. the theory about the structure of psychic reality. At any one time Freudian metapsychology determined the models – or 'topographies' – used for describing and interpreting the unconscious.

Freud's concept of the unconscious distinguishes psychoanalysis from other psychologies. The unconscious has an energy, logic and ethics of its own, radically incongruent with the contents of consciousness. It is rooted in unavowable and unavowed **desires** which have undergone repression such that their content remains cut off from consciousness. Consciousness expends energy to bar knowledge and memory of such desires from itself. The full complexity of Freud's concept becomes manifest in a first and second topography. These topographies constitute descriptive models for locating the unconscious and repression in terms of spatial and temporal divisions. A division which appears in both topographies is that between, on the one hand, consciousness and what it is permitted to know and, on the other hand, the unconscious.

In 1895 Freud developed a first topography which contained three systems: the conscious, the preconscious and the unconscious. A censorship exists between the unconscious and the preconscious and conscious. This censorship prevents ideas of one system from moving to another or

both others. In 1923 Freud introduced a second topography as the model of intra-subjective relations which function within the psychic apparatus: the ego, the id and the superego enter into relations with each other. The superego becomes the forces of repression; the id becomes the place of repressed desires; the ego balances the demands of the other two, while remaining responsible to external reality.

Both topographies are marked by the censorship which constitutes the barrier to the unconscious. An initial censorship – or repression – of the child's incestuous desires has the crucial role of constituting the unconscious. This original repression has as its object the **Oedipus** complex; and derivative repressions are in some sense based upon the images and desires of the initial censorship, explaining the infantile nature of the unconscious. The repressed remains an idea that is charged with a certain amount of energy; the act of repression cuts the energy off from the idea.

Freud's first topography also employs an interpretative model called 'the energetics' as opposed to 'the hermeneutics' of the second topography. The energetics names Freud's use of an anatomical, quantitative model, while his later hermeneutics is built upon a symbolic, qualitative model of interpretation. Giving Freud's project its scientific distinctiveness, the energetics employs a naturalistic language of energies or organic forces. In contrast the second topography uses hermeneutics to read a symbolic language of double meanings. So Freud's accounts of desire and sexuality treat language in both naturalistic and symbolic terms. If the former terms are used, then expressions of sexual desire should be read as directly referring to psychic forces. If the latter terms are employed, then the analysand's statements conceal unconscious meanings which the analyst must interpret as symbols representing the duplicity of desire. These different models of interpretation imply that the unconscious cannot be merely equated with the latent meaning of consciousness.

Freud does not replace his energetics with hermeneutics. Instead, alongside his interpretation of the double meanings of symbols, Freud continues to discuss affects – of rage, envy, love, hate – in terms of the energies which are organized as a natural science like physics. These energies are simply on a separate level of psychic organization from the symbols of desire. The continuing relevance of an energetics means that psychic reality remains linked with the material reality of energies and forces.

Although no agreement exists on any Freudian discovery, Freud's influence is immeasurable. His impact upon contemporary theory is part of the larger climate of postmodern uncertainty and ambivalence, while the disagreement concerning his ideas is compatible with the general environment of postmodern fragmentation. Notwithstanding disagreements, Freud's theories about the unconscious have had a fundamental influence upon postmodern theorizing, especially theories of desire. [PSA]

FRIEDMAN, KINKY: NOVELIST, SINGER (1944–) Friedman is the **author** of a series of detective novels which manage to be not just witty and entertaining, but to engage with some of the most thought-provoking aspects of **postmodern** aesthetics. An ex-Country and Western singer himself (his band, the Texas Jewboys, performed mainly parodies of the style, in songs such as 'They Don't Make Jews Like Jesus Anymore'), he has invented a fictional character called 'Kinky Friedman', an ex-Country and Western singer now resident in New York, and working somewhat fitfully as an amateurish private detective. His adventures are chronicled in novels such as *Greenwich Killing Time* (1987), *Elvis, Jesus and Coca-Cola* (1993), *The*

Love Song of J. Edgar Hoover (1996), and *Steppin' on a Rainbow* (2001). Friedman involves his real-life circle of acquaintances in his fiction (subjecting them to various indignities like kidnapping along the way), and succeeds admirably in blurring the line between fiction and reality.

The novels are full of self-conscious references to earlier detective fiction (the Sherlock Holmes series, for example, with Friedman's 'Village Irregulars' echoing Conan Doyle's 'Baker Street Irregulars'), but display a largely irreverent attitude to the whole business of crime-solving: Friedman wisecracks his way through his cases in a decidedly unprofessional manner. Friedman is an excellent example of **double coding** at work, having contrived to introduce quite complex issues about personal and authorial identity into a popular literary form. [SS]

FUKUYAMA, FRANCIS: POLITICAL THEORIST (1952–) Fukuyama was propelled into prominence by the controversy with which his book, *The End of History and the Last Man* (1992), was greeted. This presented one of the first philosophically ambitious interpretations of the collapse of Soviet-style communism in 1989. Unfortunately Fukuyama's philosophical capacities were no match for these ambitions. Commentators were astounded by the audacity of Fukuyama's thesis: that with the fall of the Berlin Wall the logic of history had finally been worked out; that history had come to its logical conclusion in the triumph of the twin principles of liberal democracy and the market economy.

Fukuyama studied in Paris with Jacques **Derrida** before becoming an official in a remote corner of the US administration. His book is a rather trite and superficial treatment of the (Hegelian) notion that there are principles or ideas at work in history. In **Hegel**'s attempt to sketch a world history of *Geist* (spirit or intellect), a key dynamic is the struggle to reconcile the principles of freedom and recognition. In a series of lectures in Paris in the 1930s, Alexandre Kojève provided a radical reading of Hegel's *Phenomenology of Mind* based around a passage in which Hegel details the dialectic of master and slave. Fukuyama's 1992 book was thus recycling Kojève's deduction of the idea that the logic of history had, in principle, come to an end. Although Fukuyama has half a century's worth of further examples and historical development to draw on (and to explain), his is a depressingly superficial treatment of history. But the timing of his book made his notoriety inevitable. The crisis in one superpower (what was the USSR) allowed Fukuyama to construct a historical perspective entirely circumscribed by the perspective of the other. Inevitably Fukuyama was read, by friend and foe, as giving a Hegelian, post-facto justification to the USA–Western Europe axis. In countless interviews and commentaries Fukuyama had to explain that his account applied not to the real, painful historical conflicts going on around the world but only to the logic of the ideas which have *so far* played a crucial role in the history of the advanced or industrial world. Yet neither the experience of 9/11 nor the rise of Islamic **fundamentalism** has shaken Fukuyama's faith in the rightness of his thesis.

Fukuyama's major subsequent publication, *Trust*, is a contribution to an important contemporary theme, but, lacking the overwhelming topicality of *The End of History*, it has had little resonance. [LS]

FUNDAMENTALISM Postmodernist philosophers may argue that **grand narratives** are in decline, but the growing popularity of religious fundamentalism around the world suggests this may be an over-optimistic assessment. Most of the major world religions have fundamentalist movements: Christianity and Islam are the most prominent, but Hinduism and Judaism have their committed activists as well. Fundamentalism was coined as a term to describe radical Protestant evangelism in early twentieth-century America. Christianity was reduced to a set of fundamental beliefs (such as the virgin birth of Christ) that could not be questioned by adherents. Central to this outlook was the Bible, which in the more militant forms of fundamentalist thought is taken to be literally true. There are similar attitudes in Islam with regard to the Q'ran.

Fundamentalism is to some extent a reaction to postmodern scepticism towards authority, and has been described as an 'authority-minded' movement. Whatever the complexities of the relationship between these two cultural movements, it is clear there is a larger market for traditional systems of belief, and the security they can provide for individual believers, than postmodernist theorists have been claiming. [SS]

FUZZY LOGICS Otherwise known as 'vague' or 'multivalent' (many-valued), fuzzy logics have been developed since the 1920s, when Jan Lukasiewicz, a Polish logician, formalized a continuum of possible states. Lukasiewicz's impetus came from Werner Heisenberg's uncertainty principle, which postulated that no observer can measure both the position and the velocity of a given electron. In other words, the more precisely the electron's velocity is delineated, the more vague its position becomes. **Quantum mechanics** therefore demanded a more flexible mathematical model, not in order to resolve the uncertainty, but, on the contrary, to account for it.

More recently, fuzzy logics have found a niche in **artificial intelligence** research, where neural nets 'grow' fuzzy rules from fuzzy data, rather than computers getting it wrong with unerring precision. Fuzzy logics allow computers to learn rather than simply to act upon pre-programmed instruction, exactly in the way that humans learn within a context of real-world fuzziness: humans do not act in accordance with formal rules so much as by approximation and adjustment. Thus Bart Kosko's *Fuzzy Thinking* contrasts the fuzziness of everyday life with the artificial, black-and-white, 1 or 0, binary world long championed by science and philosophy, and even goes so far as to suggest that fuzziness has a history repressed by the avatars of precision that, since Aristotle, have acquired an unshakeable prestige under Western science. The logical basis of such models of scientific certainty ('true or false', but not both) was formulated by Aristotle in the fourth century BC as the law of the excluded middle, which states that a thing cannot be both x and not-x at the same time. In reality, of course, things are frequently x and not-x: a half-eaten apple. At what precise point, for example, does a half-eaten apple cease to be an apple; at what point does the apple cease to be red and become not-red? Fuzzy logics therefore replace the two-value abstractions (black or white, x or not-x) of the law of the excluded middle with a multivalent, 'fuzzy' principle of '*both x and not-x*'. What this means in practice is that precise, quantitative points are replaced by qualitative shifts, a phenomenon that, according to many mathematicians, aligns fuzziness with, for example, the new mathematics of **fractal** objects. [IHG]

G

GATES, HENRY LOUIS, JR.: CRITIC, EDITOR
(1950–) Gates is, along with Houston
Baker Jr., the most prominent male theorist
of African-American literature of his
generation. He was one of the first critics to
use the insights of **continental** theory to
examine black **texts**. Gates has argued, in
such books as *Figures in Black* (1987) and
especially in *The Signifying Monkey* (1988),
that black American writing deserves to be,
and allows its most distinctive forms to
show when, examined through close
readings that are alive to their structural,
rhetorical and deeply figural nature. Gates
is also an influential editor and cultural
commentator; he has overseen the publication of the mammoth, path-breaking
*Norton Anthology of African American
Literature* (1997) and is general editor of
an important series of reprints, *The
Schomburg Library of Black Women Writers*
(1988 onwards). In *Loose Canons* (1992),
he eloquently defends the concept of multiculturalism. He has recently reflected on
his own relationship to his past in a highly
praised autobiography, *Colored People*
(1994).

Gates's work is meditation, not just on
what **postmodern** theory can have to say
about black writing but, crucially, on what
these texts already know about the nature
of signification. Furthermore, he asks
whether it is legitimate to translate theories
drawn from a literary tradition that has
often represented blacks as barely human.
The sceptical **anti-essentialism** of much of
postmodern theory with its destabilizing of
authorship and subjectivity would seem
to be unpalatable to the black American
tradition of unearthing the repressed black

voice in the face of slavery and its historical
consequence: racism. Gates has a number
of responses to these questions. First he
argues that '*any* tool that enables the critic
to explain the language of a text is an
appropriate tool, for it is language, the
black language of the black text that
expresses the distinctive quality of our
tradition'. Second, he would say that celebrating the discovery of hitherto forgotten
black writers does not mean that these
authors in any way determine the meanings
that may be read into their work.

In fact the creative rereading of the
black tradition is at the heart of Gates's
own theory of African-American literature
worked out at length in *The Signifying
Monkey*. The kernel of this theory can be
found in his 1983 essay 'The Blackness of
Blackness'. Gates suggests that one of the
distinguishing features of black American
writing is 'saying one thing and meaning
something quite other', a technique of
survival developed by black slaves. Gates's
term for this is 'signifyin(g)', which refers
both to the African-American tradition and
to the influential Swiss linguist Saussure.
'Signifyin(g)' is a term that has been in the
black vernacular for more than 200 years
and refers to the ability to parody, reverse
and revise another's language. Gates
pursues the concept from Africa and the
Caribbean through to contemporary black
writing. A number of critics, especially
black feminists, feel that Gates dispenses
too quickly with the notion of black identity
(which for postmodernists is a social construct) and find his theory of the black text
too narrow. However this may be, Gates
does not want to read off a benighted black

text using a postmodern template; he wishes to explicate black writing in a way that 'changes both the received theory and received ideas about the text'. [PD]

GEERTZ, CLIFFORD: ANTHROPOLOGIST (1926–) A distinguished American academic, Geertz's work has helped to found the discipline of 'cultural anthropology'. Cultural anthropology rejects the ethnocentrist assumptions built into much anthropological enquiry, and attempts to reach an understanding of a culture (as in the case of Geertz's fieldwork studies in Indonesia and North Africa) rather than just provide a description of it.

Geertz is concerned to interpret cultures through a study of the contexts in which human actions occur, such that they become endowed with meaning. This is his so-called 'thick description', as outlined in his highly influential book *The Interpretation of Cultures* (1973), in particular in the essay 'Thick Description: Towards an Interpretive Theory of Culture'. 'Thin description', on the other hand, fails to provide any real interpretation of the culture in question, but contents itself with cataloguing its objective features. The **structuralist** anthropology of Claude **Lévi-Strauss**, with its desire to find common objective features across cultures, would be an example of the latter type.

Geertz is anti-ethnocentrist, believing that anthropological enquiry all too often involves an implicit assumption of the superiority of the anthropologist's own culture, or at the very least uses his/her own culture as a reference point to explain how other cultures operate. This anti-ethnocentrism, with its insistence that no one culture should be privileged in terms of interpretation, aligns Geertz with **postmodernism** and its commitment to **pluralism**, as does his conception of culture as a series of texts whose semantics need to be unravelled before we can understand how their meanings are created.

The postmodern tendency to regard culture as a series of **narratives**, none of which should be considered to have a privileged claim on our attention, and which need to be understood in terms of their rhetorical strategies, has obvious similarities to the approach of Geertz. In *Local Knowledge* (1983) Geertz has reiterated his opposition to 'grand theories', as well as his commitment to pluralism, thus bringing him into the general orbit of postmodern thought where grand theories (or '**grand narratives**' as Jean-François **Lyotard** calls them) are viewed with scepticism and even outright hostility because of their authoritarian pretensions. The impact of cultural anthropology has been felt across the human sciences, with interpretive theories such as **new historicism** drawing inspiration from Geertz's methods, as in the case of Stephen **Greenblatt**'s analyses of Renaissance literary culture. [SS]

GENEALOGY Genealogy denotes the tracings of the origin of a phenomenon, and is associated principally with **Nietzsche**. Whereas **Kant** had looked for the conditions of knowledge, and asked 'how is x possible?', Nietzsche wished to add a second question to this, namely, 'why is x necessary?' Genealogy is therefore an investigation into the combined possibilities and necessities of a form of life. Nietzsche's most sustained exploration into origins is *Toward a Genealogy of Morals* (1887). Here he tracks the formation of notions of 'good' and 'bad', and 'good' and 'evil', and the corresponding states of responsibility, guilt and bad conscience which usually accompany those terms. Nietzsche's project is not primarily etymological. Rather, he is careful to stress that the evolution of a thing is not directed towards a single purpose, but is subject to changing pressures and circumstances.

More recently, **Foucault** has engaged extensively with the work of genealogy. In *Discipline and Punish* (1975), he presents a history of how Western society has dealt with crime. He illustrates a shift from practices involving bodily mutilation and public humiliation, common at the time of Shakespeare, to punishments since the eighteenth century involving incarceration or financial reparation. Again it is the non-continuities and complex transactions between institutions and their **discursive power** that are highlighted. [BL]

GENERATION X Asked by a publisher to write a guide to the twenty-something generation, Douglas **Coupland** turned in a novel, the phenomenally successful *Generation X* (1991), noted for capturing the mindset and language of privileged young 1990s Californians. A good deal of the novel's energy comes from the marginalia – a whole series of Zeitgeist-defining neologisms, asides and summaries which generalize the main characters' experience. Generation X-ers are young, well-educated, under-employed post-babyboomers who despise the corporate ideology of the 1980s, but have little to put in its place. In this vacuum, they affect a postmodern superficiality, an all-pervasive 'knee-jerk **irony**', spending their time practising an ironic form of cultural snobbery by one-upping each other with knowledge of TV trivia ('obscurism') when not doing low-paid, low-esteem, no-future, service-sector work ('McJobs'). They get by through personally tailored but wildly uninformed philosophico-religious beliefs ('Me-ism') and settle for 'lessness' – reconciling themselves to diminishing expectations. If, for some, these modes of living disguise a romantic longing for a form of authentic experience often associated in classic American literature with nature, then other X-ers might say (if they would admit to reading him): 'Nature? How *Ralph Waldo Emerson*.' [PD]

GIBSON, WILLIAM: NOVELIST (1948–) After publishing a number of distinguished short stories in the early 1980s, Gibson made the most spectacular debut in recent science-fiction history with *Neuromancer* (1984), winning the two major science fiction awards. What made it different from other science fiction was its style, an eclectic pastiche of influences, among them *Blade Runner,* William Burroughs, Thomas **Pynchon**, Raymond Chandler, *film noir* and the 'psychological' science fiction of late 1960s counter-culture, J. G. Ballard, Philip K. Dick and Samuel Delany. The self-consciously 'pulp' plot and the glittering, allusive surface of the prose led to it being called '**cyberpunk**'. 'Cyber' comes from control and communications systems and 'punk' from the relative youth of the author and his indebtedness to the sensibility found in the music of the Velvet Underground and garage punk bands. *Neuromancer* is a classic 'caper' novel which assembles a group of experts to break through the defences of a big business information system. It is concerned primarily with the interface between humans and new technologies such as **virtual reality** and cloning, and in the psychological and philosophical consequences of the blurring of such distinctions as human/machine and illusion/reality. Seen as quintessentially **postmodern** by many critics, the world of cyberpunk is a bleak **Baudrillardian** one of **simulation** and the **hyperreal**, where image and reality have imploded.

For Gibson (who invented the term) **cyberspace** is 'a consensual hallucination experienced daily by billions of legitimate operators in every nation. A graphic representation of data extracted from the banks of every computer in the human system. Unthinkable complexity.' Cyberspace is a non-space that is everywhere and yet nowhere. Night city, where most of the action takes place, is memorably described as 'a deranged experiment in social Darwinism, designed by a bored researcher who kept one thumb permanently on the fast-forward button'. Gibson develops this theme in more detail in the two novels that follow, *Count Zero* (1986) and *Mona Lisa Overdrive* (1988). 'Simstim', 'meat puppet', 'prosthetic limbs', 'cranial sockets', 'mimetic polycarbon'; the three novels are obsessed with the porous nature of the human body/technology interface and the ways the body can be both extended and transformed. *The Difference Engine* (1990), written with Bruce Sterling, is a remarkable alternative history involving Babbage's invention of an early computer. Arguably his best work, the melancholy *Virtual Light* (1993) is a tale set in the near future concerned with the inhabitants of a shanty town under the Golden Gate Bridge and is a much more downbeat, socially concerned piece. *Idoru* (Japanese for 'Idol', pronounced in English: 'I adore you') (1997) involves a 'female personality construct'. Its Japanese setting returns Gibson to his most popular landscape. After more than twenty years of publication in a field that often sees careers go by the wayside after initial critical and commercial success, Gibson's fiction is still among the most original and influential science fiction around. [PD]

GIDDENS, ANTHONY: SOCIOLOGIST (1938–) Giddens is probably the best-known British sociologist. Throughout an academic career that began in the early 1960s, Giddens has consistently struggled with some of the central theoretical concerns of sociology. In his early work he made an extensive contribution to the interpretation of the classical sociological texts including books on Weber, Durkheim, social class and a three-volume critique of historical materialism.

He is perhaps best known for his concept of *structuration*, which is an attempt to resolve one of the basic dilemmas of social theory. Sociology has classically been divided between those who are closer to a macro perspective and those who are closer to a micro one. To put this another way, writers have provided social explanations which either give greatest emphasis to the importance of active individuals and human agency (*action theories*) or to constraining social structures and institutions (*structural theories*). Giddens suggests that it is essential to bridge this simplistic duality and argues that human beings always have the capacity to change their social circumstances, even if these are limited by specific social contexts. He has been applauded for the detailed and meticulous way in which he has analysed preceding theories and synthesized these to support his ideas. This is in contrast to the work of more radical writers who have rejected all that has gone before and filled the resulting vacuum which they have created, with a new, but ungrounded orthodoxy. Giddens is a theorist of the middle ground and in his most recent works he has tried to come to terms with the challenge of **postmodern** theory. In doing this he has continued to try to hold the same theoretical space.

In advocating the case for the decline of **metanarratives** and describing a world in which our identities essentially reside in our capacity to shop, postmodern theorists have variously claimed the end of history, of sociology and of all certainty. Critics of postmodern perspectives have pointed to their inherent theoretical helplessness and nihilism. While some of these writers simply wish to see a return to the old ideas, Giddens characteristically holds the middle ground. He incorporates concepts from both sides of this divide, calling the contemporary epoch 'late' or 'high' **modernity**.

He agrees with the theorists of postmodernity that massive changes have occurred in the late twentieth century which have led to a restructuring of social experience, identity and knowledge. However, he does not agree that these changes constitute a complete break with modernity.

Giddens develops the concept of reflexivity beyond its previous usage. He suggests that contemporary life is characterized for the individual by more than a simple capacity to reflect upon the self. Instead he argues that in late modernity it is the process of reflection itself which has become the topic for reflection. This fits with the self-consciousness and **irony** of postmodernism and illustrates the extent to which the self has also become a reflexive project. It also builds a link for Giddens back to his earlier concerns with the connections between social identity and social structure. This provides us with the paradox that the only security that we can find in contemporary life is the certainty that everything is uncertain.

Giddens explores the idea of the self further when he considers the basis of intimacy in contemporary life and attempts to describe and explain the shifting patterns of marriage and personal relationships. He argues that human relations are *unhooked*, lacking traditional linkages with the rules and patterns of family, community and reproduction. Interaction is person-centred and based upon the fulfilment of individual need. We therefore feel that we are at liberty to move on when those needs are no longer adequately met. There are echoes here of the spirit of postmodern consumption applied to love and marriage.

Giddens has maintained a constant set of interests throughout his writing. His latest work attempts a synthesis of some of the central issues of contemporary experience. He continues to explore the interdependence of the individual and social structure by emphasizing the twin themes of security and danger and of risk and trust. He agrees that life in the late twentieth century is precarious, but leaves space for the individual to be rather more than a mere fashion victim. Even if we do choose to collude with the imperatives of corporate capitalism, at least we can also reflect upon them. The central aim of the self in high modernity is to escape the trap of becoming fixed. We have to keep moving. [NW]

GILBERT AND GEORGE: ARTISTS (1943– , 1942–) Tradition, custom and ceremony are entangled in Gilbert and George's monumental art, which first came to prominence in the late 1960s in the form of 'The Singing Sculpture'. Combining pre-war popular culture with performance art, the work comprised Gilbert and George dressed in anonymous business suits singing Flanagan and Allen's 1932 song 'Underneath the Arches'. In these all-day performances, which were enacted in Europe, Australia and the USA between 1969 and 1973, the robotic nature of the 'act' would be reinforced by their machine-like movements. In 1971, the art critic Robert Rosenblum claimed that this **Duchampian** fascination with repetition, at once '**ironic** or nostalgic' and '**postmodernist**', was an unclassifiable combination of the 'ephemeral and permanent, the human and the mechanical'. The era of the postmodern vaudevillian **cyborg** had begun.

Throughout the 1970s other commentators identified these practices as postmodern because they signalled the emptiness of late **modernist** (minimalist) sculpture and deflated the 'virile' rhetoric of much performance art. Confronted by the blankness of the 'singing sculptures' it was possible to assert that modernist creativity had been replaced by mass-produced anonymity: instead of carving, building and making things, Gilbert and George parodied the endless inertia of late modernist art by becoming metallic mannequins; and in the rigidity of their performances could be found confirmation of the 'lifelessness' of late-modernist sculpture.

This knowing combination of avant-garde technique and antiquated subject matter has been a feature of all their subsequent photo-based productions, the

223

most recent of which are organized around dramatic polarities of light and dark, vitality and stasis, alienation and **desire**, security and danger. Using the devices of commercial photography, Gilbert and George have produced a 'brand' art in the format of the observational series which refuses to observe the convention of displaying developmental structures or **events**. Instead, *Crusade* (1982), *Modern Faith* (1983), *The Believing World* (1984), *New Moral Works* (1985) and *The Cosmological Pictures* (1989) contain echoes of pop art, sacred art, Soviet socialist realism and advertising, all of which are played out in compositions where the artists, resembling middle-class versions of Morecambe and Wise, preside over 'heraldic' landscapes festooned with melancholic or taciturn teenage boys. If this camp cornucopia rejects the visionary or utopian aspects of modernism, it still embraces the aesthetics of redemption: in place of the artist as the existential outsider creating 'dense' or 'difficult' art, these fluid and flexible *flâneurs*, entrepreneurs of sensation and sensibility, collaborate in restating the world as a magical kingdom of consumption, a postmodern religion of the self.

In *The Cosmological Pictures* a kind of kitsch fecundity replaces the filmic bleakness of their early black and white imagery; and by deploying the constructed and collaged style associated with American postmodernism, formal repetition is organized by confusions of scale and the juxtaposition of natural forms, many of which glow with vivid, vibrant, over-saturated colours. These exercises in Technicolor are augmented by the domination of the frontal plane, where figures loom in the manner of the incandescent designs found in the stained-glass windows of medieval churches. However, unlike these iconographic sources, Gilbert and George make their figures theatrical amalgamations of the allegorical and the naturalistic; absurdly demotic and **libidinal**, these bodies threaten to destabilize their symbolic status by 'falling' into the space of the viewer, or by ascending to a Whitmanesque heaven of homoerotic love. Even when posture indicates the visual language of devotion, submission and reverence, the mesmeric banality of their witless figures carry with them the imprimatur of mass culture, the mechanisation of experience and the reduction of ceremonial action to formulaic display. Accordingly, organic processes – the endless kineticism of standing, reclining, crouching or kneeling figures – are locked into a bodily rhetoric that generates the meaningless logic of the structures that animate them.

This is art apart: we find the mannerisms and morphologies associated with Michelangelo, Blake and Munch, but in place of content is installed a ritualized inventory of frozen experiences involving the **sublime**, the kitsch and the uncanny. Moreover, in these compositions viewers are caught between observation and participation. It would seem, then, that this is a form of postmodernism where the transcendental verities of modernism have been replaced by a contradictory art that is hermetic and popular, private and public, ironic and serious, animated and blank. [CT]

GLASS, PHILIP: COMPOSER (1937–) Glass has played a key role in the development of **minimalist** music. He received a rigorous formal education in music but was inspired by non-Western musics as well as other composers of minimalist music (such as his one-time colleague, Steve **Reich**). His career has been characterized by collaboration both with a diverse selection of musicians and with people from other artistic fields. He took private composition lessons with a number of composers in America before moving to Paris to study with the renowned teacher Nadia Boulanger. Here he was fortunate enough to meet and work with the world-famous Indian sitar player Ravi Shankar. Thus began a lifelong interest in and study of the music and aesthetic principles of other cultures. Following a period of research in India, North Africa and Tibet, Glass moved back to New York to begin synthesizing his influences into his own unique musical voice.

Serialism – the technique of treating each of the twelve notes of the chromatic scale with equal weighting and thus ensuring that the music never settles into any one key – had become the norm in serious concert music. Glass, while being trained in the serial technique of composition, was quick to reject it, claiming it was elitist, academic and old-fashioned. His work as a performer with Steve Reich's ensemble, coupled with his knowledge of non-Western forms, inspired him to develop his own techniques of composition. His early works, such as *Two Pages* (1968) and *Music in Fifths* (1969), could stay not only in the same key but on the same chord for long periods, drawing their interest from the dimensions of rhythm and structure. His music used structuring principles (such as additive process – whereby notes are systematically added to a repeated motif increasing its length and altering the underlying metre of the music – and cyclical structure) which were derived from Eastern musics, while the surface level utilized the more familiar Western scales and arpeggios.

In addition to setting up his own ensemble (which he did in 1968) Glass, who has always had a love of the theatre, has written a number of collaborative music-theatre works, the first three of which, *Einstein on the Beach* (1976), *Satyagraha* (1980) and *Akhnaton* (1984), form a trilogy.

Glass, perhaps more than any other twentieth-century composer, has continually worked to break down the barriers that rigidly separate 'high' and 'low' art. Many of his collaborations have been with artists from rock, popular and non-Western traditions. In *Songs from Liquid Days* (1986) he worked with a number of popular songwriters including Paul Simon, David Byrne and Suzanne Vega. The songwriter provided the lyrics, which Glass then arranged and set to music. In the late 1980s Glass collaborated with the African composer Foday Musa Suso to produce the music for Jean Genet's stage work *The Screens*. Although Glass had been deeply inspired by the music of Ravi Shankar while working with him in the 1960s, it was not until 1990 that the two were able to collaborate again. The project, which produced a CD recording entitled *Passages*, involved each composer writing a piece based on a theme supplied by the other. Another notable collaboration has been that of Glass's hugely successful *Low Symphony* (1992). This three-movement work for full orchestra was inspired by the David Bowie and Brian Eno album, *Low*, of 1977 which, being a collection of songs and instrumental pieces, provided Glass with the themes on which to construct the symphony. The *Heroes Symphony* (1997) again draws on a Bowie and Eno album of the 1970s.

Like that of his contemporary Steve Reich, Philip Glass's work has been largely shunned by the (essentially **modernist**) music establishment. Again, like Steve Reich, he solved this problem in the early days by writing a large proportion of his material for his own ensemble and forging a new audience away from the traditional concert halls. Glass has been hugely inspirational, not only to many younger composers of 'classical' concert music, but also to the producers of ambient, house and dance music. [AB]

GLOBALIZATION Globalization strives to create a worldwide economic market in which the nation state has an increasingly peripheral role. It is possible to see globalization either as an aspect of, or a threat to, **postmodern** ideals. The **power** of the nation state has certainly been weakened by the ability of multinationals to outsource their production to the lowest bidder: few of the products consumed in the West are actually manufactured there any more. Reducing the power of the nation state is a long-running objective of libertarians, who feel this will increase individual freedom. But if power passes to the multinationals instead, the individual is in many cases left worse off – multinationals, after all, do not have to answer to the voters in elections. The anti-globalization movement has bitterly opposed this shift in power, arguing that it simply reduces the living standards of workers worldwide, even in the third world, where most of the production is transferred. Globalization tends to favour **market fundamentalism** (unregulated capitalism) as its method of operation, which many see as a threat to the ideals of postmodernism. [SS]

GRAMMATOLOGY The term 'grammatology' first came to prominence with the publication of Jacques **Derrida**'s *Of Grammatology* in 1967, and describes a science of writing that puts into question the inherent value of the linguistic **sign**. Derrida's use of the term is part of a critique of Western philosophy for giving precedence to speech over writing. Western philosophical discourse is held to be committed to phonetic writing: the kind of writing that attempts fully to represent speech. Grammatology as a science of writing is part of a general tendency in Derrida's work to redress this balance. Central to this process is the refutation of the **structuralist** notion that signifier and signified form an organic unity. Speech is regarded as an original **presence** in structuralist linguistics and writing an invasion of purity. **Logocentric** writing (the reproduction of the phoneme or the voice), is distinguished by the grammatologist from *écriture*, or grammatological writing, which is concerned with characterizing those actions that create

language. Following Derrida, the grammatologist argues that 'there is nothing outside the **text**', and that language is open to myriad interpretations that continually defer meaning. This involves a rejection of the possibility of an absolute truth fixed by a transcendental signifier. Such a position has affinities with the **postmodern** dismissal of **grand narratives**. [DW]

GRAND NARRATIVE Jean-François **Lyotard** described as grand narratives theories which claim to provide universal explanations and trade on the authority this gives them. An example would be **Marxism**, which processes all human history and social behaviour through its theory of dialectical materialism. According to dialectical materialism all human history has been the history of class struggle, and it denies the validity of all other explanations, laying sole claim to the truth. The ultimate goal of human history is the 'dictatorship of the proletariat', where class struggle has been eliminated for the common good and individuals are no longer exploited. Most religions offer a similarly all-embracing explanation of human history to fit their particular schemes. Lyotard's contention is that such schemes are implicitly authoritarian, and that by the late twentieth century they had lost all claim to authority over individual behaviour. It is part of living in a **postmodern** world that we can no longer rely on such grand narratives (or '**metanarratives**'), but must construct more tactically oriented '**little narratives**' instead if we wish to stand up against authoritarianism. In Lyotard's view, we have now seen through grand narratives and realized that their claims to authority are false and unsustainable. [SS]

GREENAWAY, PETER: FILM DIRECTOR (1942–) Greenaway is best known for an oeuvre of over thirty films that display a unity of art and literature. These films are characterized by rich cinematography and experimental structure providing 'opportunities to play with images, to play with words, to play with their interactions'. Since 1978 the **minimalist** composer Michael **Nyman** has been a regular collaborator, writing scores for many of Greenaway's films.

Greenaway's early works reflect a sustained interest in system and structures. *Windows* (1976), *A Walk Through H* (1978) and *H is for House* (1978), show a preference for a formalist application of letter or number frameworks that self-consciously reference the process of making films. From the 1980s his work is increasingly underscored by a concern with **intertextuality** and eclecticism in both the structure of his films and the characterization of their leading players. *The Draughtsman's Contract* (1982) appropriates the seventeenth century, *The Belly of an Architect* (1987) draws upon another's history, the French eighteenth-century architect Boullée, to provide a cross-temporal search for self in the main character. Greenaway forgoes psychological characterization, however, for a **postmodern** revival of allegory, speaking of his characters as 'ciphers . . . to hold a weight of allegorical and personifying meaning'.

Greenaway's concern to extend the boundaries of cinema in parallel with such developments in art and literature gave his early films an exclusively art-house audience. However the spectacle and excess of films such as *The Cook, the Thief, his Wife and her Lover* (1989), and the attraction of leading actors such as Sir John Gielgud in *Prospero's Books* (1991) and Ewan McGregor in *The Pillow Book* (1996), have gained him a more mainstream audience without compromising on style. (EO)

GREENBLATT, STEPHEN: CRITIC (1937–) Greenblatt is the central figure in American **'new historicism'**, a term which he coined in 1982. New historicism is rooted in a conviction that the American theoretical orthodoxies of the 1970s, notably **deconstruction**, were as ahistorical in their methodologies as the critical schools – new criticism and myth criticism – which they challenged and replaced. Greenblatt rejects criticism which addresses an artwork as a self-sufficient object divorced from its historical contexts and cultural antecedents. However, addressing literature in its historical context is nothing new; what distinguishes Greenblatt from more traditional historicist criticism is his problematizing of its division between literary foreground and political background. In addition, Greenblatt borrows from sources alien to traditional historical criticism: anthropology (notably **Geertz**), **Lacanian** neo-**Freudianism**, and, in particular, **Foucault**. Greenblatt, following Foucault, foregrounds the concept that 'history' is itself **textually** mediated, and problematizes the mimetic model of previous historicist criticism which viewed a text as simply reflecting the history around – and thus still outside – it. **Representations** are not simply the products of an age; they are themselves productive, engaging with and often subsequently altering the forces that brought them into being. Nor is history the stable and incontrovertible backdrop to the work of literature assumed by monological historical scholarship. Non-literary texts are not simply neutral transcriptions of reality; instead, historical fact and experience are available to us only in 'textual **traces**', with all the concomitant rhetorical strategies which characterize textuality.

Renaissance Self-Fashioning (1980) takes issue with the presuppositions of new criticism's close-reading techniques. Art cannot pretend to autonomy, and textual traces are 'selfconsciously embedded in specific communities, life situations, structures of **power**'. Simultaneously, Greenblatt rejects reductive generalizations about his **authors'** relationship to their culture. Shakespeare's plays, for instance, do not offer a 'single timeless affirmation or denial of **legitimate** authority'. Renaissance society was not homogeneous and its literature enacts its ideological struggles. Renaissance literary works are not 'a stable set of reflections of the historical facts that lie beyond them'; they are 'places of dissension'. Despite the repudiation of the ahistorical orientation of much **postmodern** thought, Greenblatt's work owes much to deconstruction, borrowing some of its terminology ('origins', 'rupture', 'inscription', and so on) and arguing that there is no grand originating consciousness available in literary works, which have no 'central, unwavering authorial presence'. *Renaissance Self-Fashioning* addresses the concept of the construction of identity, and its ideas are often heavily influenced by deconstructive notions of human subjectivity. For instance, Othello's self-fashioning is seen as **discursive**, produced by external rhetoric; his innermost self is dependent upon 'a language that is always necessarily given from without and upon representation before an audience'.

Shakespearean Negotiations (1990) employs Foucault's **genealogical** methodology, refusing to privilege canonical Renaissance literature and dwelling upon what Greenblatt calls writings from the 'borders'. This strategy raises issues of canonicity, politicizes major/minor literary argument and, in particular, problematizes orthodox historiography. Greenblatt, like Foucault, is unafraid of connecting supposedly non-literary historical texts with the literary artefact – a legitimate strategy if history is available to us only in the form of **narrative**. For instance, 'Fiction and Friction' uses an anecdote about transvestism in the 1580s to initiate a reading of *Twelfth Night*. Such juxtapositions have become mannerisms in new-historicist writing, but form an 'anecdotal historiography' which repudiates, to use **Lyotard**'s term, the **grand narratives** of orthodox historiography. *Shakespearean Negotiations* is

also Foucauldian in its concern with **power**, especially in its close attention to the concepts of subversion and containment. Greenblatt examines how ideologies 'co-opt' subversive discourses, thereby assimilating or neutralizing them. The gloomy message for the radical is that subversive voices are 'produced by and within the affirmations of order; they are powerfully registered, but they do not undermine that order'.

Marvellous Possessions (1992) examines how selfhood is frequently constructed by the identification of an (often demonic) **Other**. Addressing encounters between Europeans and the inhabitants of the New World, Greenblatt discerns an initial sense of 'wonder'. This leads to a crisis of representation; how does one address the absolutely Other? Colonialists rename, transform and appropriate in a strategy of terroristic estrangement. The Other is made an alien object, a thing that can be either destroyed or subtly incorporated and contained through linguistic colonialism.

Greenblatt's work has set the tone for the new-historical strand within contemporary literary theory. He has been highly influential as a propagandist for Foucault in American academe, and his work is central to the new brand of Renaissance studies which began to reclaim the critical high ground from Romanticism during the 1980s. [JStr]

GREENS (GREEN MOVEMENT) The increasing threat to the environment posed by modern industrial and technological processes (resulting in, for example, the creation of holes in the ozone layer) has led to the formation of pressure groups to resist, and, if possible, arrest this cultural trend. Collectively, such groups have been dubbed the 'Greens', and have had a significant impact on Western culture. It is not just the processes that the Greens have called into question, however, but also the socio-economic and political systems they derive from, with their seemingly insatiable demand for technological progress and ever higher levels of consumption.

Although they have enjoyed a certain amount of success in local and national elections across Western Europe, the Greens function most effectively as a pressure group. In this latter guise they have managed to make most of the continent's major political parties and public institutions pay at least lip-service to Green principles, such as the need to protect the environment by restricting car usage and controlling the disposal of industrial waste. The Green movement can be regarded as **postmodern** in its generally sceptical attitude towards progress, as well as in the way that it cuts across existing political party lines to challenge the prevailing **power** structures in Western society. [SS]

GUATTARI, FÉLIX: PSYCHIATRIST, PHILO-SOPHER, POLITICAL ACTIVIST (1930–92) A psychiatrist at La Borde clinic and rebellious student of **Lacan**, Guattari presaged much of what was to become, in the 1960s, the anti-psychiatry movement most closely associated, in the English-speaking world, with R. D. Laing. Guattari is best known, however, as a prolific philosophical writer and political activist, collaborating with Antonio Negri and the Italian autonomia movement and, more famously, Gilles **Deleuze**, in whose company he wrote *Capitalism and Schizophrenia*, vol. 1: *Anti-Oedipus* (1972), which defined the philosophical terrain of **post-Marxist** French intellectual life following the *événements* of May 1968. His later work, taking its lead from the second volume of *Capitalism and Schizophrenia: A Thousand Plateaus* (1980), turned increasingly towards the sciences – especially molecular chemistry, physics and geology – in works such as *Chaosmosis* (1992), and he established *Chimères*, a journal to which philosophers and social theorists such as Deleuze and Paul **Virilio**, as well as scientist-philosophers such as Ilya Prigogine and Francesco Varela, contributed.

What Guattari drew from this rich, **hybrid** background, however, in line with his long-term political commitments, were ways to remodel political and real-life selves according to self-organizing, 'minoritarian' clusters that emerge, as it were, from the 'ground up' to create new political trajectories. Avoiding – and indeed, regularly attacking – the strait-jacketing dogmas of political movements left and right that impose and reinforce 'top down' or 'molar' subjectivities through mechanisms of internal policing or 'self-criticism', Guattari therefore attempted, with Antonio Negri in *Communists Like Us* (1990), to rehabilitate a form of communism that emphasized the immediacy of the production of **subjectivity** from actions, rather than, as **Marx** did, emphasizing the destruction of a pre-existing 'natural' subjectivity under capitalism. While viciously critical of 'the **postmodern** dead-end', Guattari has perhaps contributed to some of its major themes, but has brought a political edge to them that many refuse to recognize. [IHG]

H

HABERMAS, JÜRGEN: PHILOSOPHER, SOCIO-LOGIST (1929–) Habermas is one of most important figures in German intellectual life today. Many consider him the most important sociologist or social theorist since Max Weber. Between 1956 and 1959 he worked as assistant to Theodor W. **Adorno**, although it is only since the 1980s that Habermas has offered any systematic account of the relationship (which is anything but straightforward) of his own work to that of the earlier generation of '**critical theorists**' (see entry on '**Frankfurt School**'). Habermas has been a key figure in directing and co-ordinating various research programmes and has influenced a wide range of empirical and historical studies.

Habermas's own writings have included a whole series of painstaking critiques and reconstructions of the classics of sociology and philosophy. His early work was placed under the heading of a 'reconstruction of historical materialism'. In it Habermas sought to mobilize all the intellectual resources of the twentieth century in order to redeem the nineteenth-century project of a science of society. In *Knowledge and Human Interests* (1968), Habermas addresses the insight that interests inevitably play a role in determining the nature and shape of sociological (and indeed other scientific) investigation. He sets out to combat the relativist implications of this notion by establishing the constructive, guiding role of 'knowledge-constitutive interests'. As Habermas's enormously ambitious programme of synthesis and criticism has taken shape, communication and discourse are the themes that have come to occupy the foreground. Habermas has drawn widely on empirical studies in sociology, anthropology, linguistics and psychology, but always with the aim of providing a modern, up-to-date version of 'human nature' as the basis for the progressive development and evolution of society. Habermas's work is justly claimed – by friend and foe – to be in direct continuity with traditions in social philosophy that stretch back to the beginnings of the **Enlightenment**.

When **Lyotard** wrote *The Postmodern Condition: A Report on Knowledge* (1979) Habermas was made its main target. Throughout the work, Habermas's ambitious theoretical constructs are taken to be one more (rather abstract and general) **grand narrative**. Lyotard objected in particular to Habermas's adherence to the need to 'unmask' ideology and his insistence on evaluating social relations in terms of their contribution to some future better state of society.

Habermas's immensely elaborate theoretical constructions offer a highly nuanced treatment of levels of **discourse** and of the interrelations between the various structures and behaviour patterns that make up society. But Habermas is condemned by his **postmodern** critics for maintaining a connection – however mediated – between questions of **legitimation** in science and the issue of legitimacy for political institutions. For Habermas the question of 'in the name of what?' retains its primacy when reflecting on how and why social relations become criticizable. Habermas's answer involves the notion of a potential (or ideal) consensus. Serious engagement with Habermas's work involves being very precise about the methodological or epistemological status he assigns to such very abstract notions. But in contemporary academic polemics such subtleties often go unobserved.

Habermas's whole theoretical project is rejected by Lyotard as the unacceptable remnant of a 'totalizing' philosophical tradition and as the valorization of conformist, when not 'terrorist', ideals of consensus. Being singled out for special treatment by postmodernism, Habermas has returned the compliment and offered a sustained critical engagement with his critics and with what he sees as the irrationalist, nihilist and neo-conservative tendencies within postmodernism. Habermas has been consistently sceptical of its inflated claims and deeply suspicious of its extreme scepticism. Habermas's most sustained and substantial treatment of what he sees as the flaws and dangers of postmodernism is presented in his twelve lectures on *The Philosophical Discourse of Modernity* (1985).

Habermas's mentor, Adorno, had held that there was a fundamental flaw in the logic of modernity and that its ineluctable destiny was to give rise to domination. For Habermas there is no historical necessity involved in domination in the modern world of specific forms of *Zweckrationalität* (instrumental reason). He maintains the conviction that a humane collective life depends on the vulnerable forms of innovation-bearing, reciprocal and unforcedly egalitarian everyday communication. Habermas's constant reformulations of his basic inspiration have made clearer his affinity to central themes of American pragmatist tradition. Like C. S. Peirce, Habermas's immense theoretical efforts live off the vision that society is a self-corrective critical community of enquirers without any absolute beginning or finality. [LS]

HALLEY, PETER: ARTIST (1953–) Emerging as an important player in **postmodernist** critical practice in the early 1980s, Halley was the most significant force in the New York neo-geo or **simulationist** movement, reading the formal qualities of **modernism** through his understanding of the theories of **Foucault** and **Baudrillard**.

In place of the serene symmetry or asymmetric purity of classic modernist abstraction, throughout the 1980s Halley imprisons his geometry in unhomely and bleak compositions. There is nothing lyrical, elegant or luminous about such paintings. If he deploys some of the trademarks of transcendental abstract expressionism – the sense of limitless space, the dramatic fields of colour and a compositional register that suggests the **sublime** – there are no traces of the metaphysical in his work. Exhilaration has been replaced by alienation in Halley's anonymous abstract simulations. 'Notes on Painting', an influential essay from 1983, explains his strategy:

> Even though my work is geometric in appearance, its meaning is intended as antithetical to that of previous geometric art. I have tried to employ the codes of minimalism, Colour Field painting and Constructivism to reveal the sociological basis of their origins. Informed by Foucault, I see in the square a prison; behind the mythologies of contemporary society, a veiled network of cells and conduits.

Halley finds in the pictorial logic of geometric art the spatial order of the Panopticon, the nineteenth-century prison model organized around an all-seeing centre from which radiate cells and chambers. Following Foucault, Halley finds in the Panopticon a new geometry of **power** in which vision becomes a regime of control, a form of authority that is applied to a multiplicity of institutional and bureaucratic spaces. From this he goes on to assert that, at all levels of articulation, geometric structures are entangled in the disciplinary and organizational logics of a social system based on surveillance, visibility and spatial order.

Arguing that modern art has been entirely assimilated into the workings of a global technocratic culture, Halley's neo-geo or simulationist works are not so much paintings as models of paintings: they register the flows of power, knowledge and information in postmodern economies; they affirm that experience of the world is produced by simulations and duplications of life. Baudrillard, disinclined to support any attempt to use his ideas by producing an 'iconography' of simulation, denounced Halley's project. However, as can be gathered from his interest in surveillance, Halley has always been more interested in the writings of Foucault. Leaving aside Baudrillard's justifiable claim that it is impossible to represent simulation, we might add that, even if this were possible, why does Halley believe that such **representation** would be 'critical' of simulation? Halley would argue that although it may be impossible to produce a comprehensive knowledge of a rapidly changing complex of institutional processes, we must continue to map the significant structures, practices and spaces of our social systems because the function of art is to register interactions of power and knowledge.

Recent works, such as *Forced Exposure* (1999) and *Escapism* (1999), with their bright but unrelated colours, and confusions of space and scale, can be seen as visual equivalents to Foucault's notion of heterotopia, the place in which other sites are 'simultaneously represented, contested and inverted'. [CT]

HARAWAY, DONNA: CULTURAL SCIENTIST, PHILOSOPHER (1944–) Donna Haraway has led the way in formulating a feminist approach to nature and techno-science. Her work forms a cornerstone of the increasingly popular field of techno-theory, which seeks to analyse the impact of technological development on both the **subject** and society.

As a feminist, Haraway is concerned with challenging the traditional postulation of nature as the site of origin and identity: female identity, in particular. Instead, she attempts to portray female subjectivity as contingent upon the influence of class, race and politics, and thus, like nature, a product of society and of history rather than an incontestable 'given'. She also attempts to undermine the **binary** division that makes nature technology's oppositional **Other**, with the intention of 'dislocating each term in order to open up new possibilities'.

However, although Haraway 'dislocates' this dualism, she does not do away with it altogether, proceeding instead to envisage it in ironic and disturbing ways. While she may not believe in the 'naturalness' of nature, she nevertheless asserts its importance as a powerful **discourse** which can be used as a site which forms common ground between diverse peoples and points of view. Because such links are always partial and contradictory, they thus disrupt techno-science's tendency to act as a totalizing force which eradicates difference.

In this context, Haraway's notion of a multiple, refracted subjectivity linked to others by the play of similarities and **difference** seeks to contest techno-science's schematic conception of the human organism, whose systems, like those of a machine, can be mapped, repaired, and replicated through technological intervention. The most popular aspect of Haraway's thought is that which proffers a notion of identity that transcends the polarities of the nature/technology opposition. To exist between such dualisms, suspended between rejection and appropriation, is what Haraway has most famously defined as a '**cyborg**' subject position. Her essay 'A Cyborg Manifesto' was originally published in 1985, but remains her best-known piece of writing. For Haraway, the cyborg, who is neither wholly natural nor artefactual, becomes the embodiment of the **postmodern** condition, where the positioning of the boundaries dividing nature from techno-culture is an increasingly problematic issue.

Haraway's notion of the cyborg operates on both a literal and metaphorical level. In the here and now we are all inescapably subject to the operations of a highly technological society, and are therefore all cyborgs. However, the cyborg also functions as a powerful imaginary concept, which, in a 'science-fictional move', can act as the means by which new possibilities and orders of being can be envisaged. As a metaphor, it stands for **ironic** and partial meaning, the contradictory self, radical fusions between oppositional concepts, and the impossibility of escaping historical processes.

Although increasingly popular, Haraway's ideas have been attacked by some feminists, who see her as operating on the high ground of postmodern theory, and therefore lacking a theory of ideology grounded in a socio-political awareness of feminist struggle. In response, Haraway argues for the 'corporeality' of theory, which 'is not about matters distant from the lived body; quite the opposite. Theory *is anything* but disembodied.' [SG]

HASSAN, IHAB: CRITIC, THEORIST (1925–) Ihab Hassan was one of the prime movers in placing **postmodernism** on the literary-critical agenda throughout the 1960s and 1970s. *The Literature of Silence: Henry Miller and Samuel Beckett* (1968) introduced Hassan's project of a poetics of anti-literature for which silence was a constituent concept. He aligned Miller with the symbolist Stéphane Mallarmé, and Beckett with Arthur Rimbaud, thus creating a polar opposition between writers confronting the void by trying to say everything, and writers aspiring to nothingness.

Similar metaphors of alienation, silence and the void are unravelled in Hassan's most effective monograph, *The Dismemberment of Orpheus: Toward a Postmodern Literature* (1971). The decapitated head of Orpheus, still singing as it floats down the River Hebrus, serves as the emblem of anti-literature. As the subtitle indicates, Hassan outlines a family tree of five writers who act as precursors to the postmodern. First is the Marquis de Sade, whose transgressive works embrace destructiveness ('wide-eyed and bodiless, Orpheus glares at the sun, waiting eternally for night'). Second is Ernest Hemingway, whose pared-down style attempts to purify the language of the tribe and show courage in the face of nothingness ('Naked, Orpheus enters the great, empty spaces of violence'). Third is Franz Kafka, the seminal figure for postmodernist writing ('We may even learn to enter, through his words, into an Orphic trance, looking onto the enormous calm of existence'). Fourth is Jean Genet, whose works seek to destroy reason itself ('meanwhile, Orpheus and Narcissus embrace in a black pool'). Fifth is Samuel Beckett, patron saint of the mute and the paralysed ('Such silence – Orpheus of the severed head – speaks not only of vanishing things: it must also sing, on pain of universal stillness, of a new kind of love').

In *Paracriticisms: Seven Speculations of the Times* (1975) Hassan emphasizes the constructedness of the concept of postmodernism by printing it as follows: POSTmodernISM. The capitalization of the prefix and suffix draws our attention to two important points. First, the 'ism' indicates that postmodernism comes after **modernism** itself, rather than simply after the 'modern'. Second, the 'post' suggests not just a historical belatedness, but an agonistic relationship to that earlier movement.

Hassan's works of the 1990s struck a retrospective, almost valedictory note.

Rumors of Change: Essays of Five Decades (1995) harvests the fruit of his thinking on such diverse issues as the anti-hero, literary **representations** of the city, and the ideological implications of postmodernism. *Between the Eagle and the Sun: Traces of Japan* (1996) mixes memoir, cultural comment and travel writing. Hassan contemplates his own **hybrid** background and reflects upon the history of Japan. [BL]

HAWKING, STEPHEN: SCIENTIST (1942–)
There are at least two Stephen Hawkings. The first is an important and respected theoretical physicist whose research has helped to form the way in which other scientists think about **black holes**, the origins of the universe and the relationship between space and time. The other Stephen Hawking is the extraordinary media phenomenon, the figure in an electric wheelchair, the author of the biggest-selling scientific book in history, *A Brief History of Time* (1988), who has appeared along with Isaac Newton and Einstein in an episode of *Star Trek* and who has overtaken Einstein in the popular mind as the embodiment of scientific genius. It is this second figure, with its eerie, disembodied, computer-generated voice uttering apparent profundities about knowing the mind of God, that is of particular interest to the student of **postmodernism**.

Since 1979 Hawking has held the post of Lucasian Professor of Mathematics, a position once held by Isaac Newton. Hawking's doctoral research employed Roger Penrose's mathematical work on topology to support the big bang theory of the origin of the universe against the rival 'steady state' theory. Hawking argued that the universe began with 'singularity', predicted but not itself penetrated by general relativity, in which the laws of physics held no sway. Time and space came into existence only with the big bang, making it senseless to talk about anything

happening before the big bang because the very concept of 'before' did not exist.

Hawking's next major work was on black holes. The existence of black holes had been predicted by J. Robert Oppenheimer in 1939. When a star runs out of fuel one of three things will happen to it, depending on its size. If it is relatively small with a mass less than 1.4 times that of our own Sun, it will become a white dwarf; a little larger (between 1.4 and 3 times the Sun's mass) and it forms a neutron star. If it began as a very large body (more than 3 times the Sun's mass) its collapse creates a body with a gravitational field so strong that nothing, not even light, can escape from it.

As nothing can travel more quickly than light it seemed impossible that anything at all could be emitted from a black hole. Hawking employed **quantum mechanics**, which he combined with general relativity in a startlingly original way to demonstrate that black holes must emit thermal radiation. Hawking reimagined black holes as physical objects, rather than some form of intensified vacuum – objects which obey the laws of thermodynamics.

We can deduce much about the highly theoretical nature of Hawking's brand of cosmology from the fact that the very existence of 'Hawking radiation' remains a convincing, but unverifiable hypothesis: no one has claimed that the tiny amounts of radiation emitted will ever be measurable. Hawking's hypothesis was based not on any observation, or careful measurement – what we tend to think of as the nuts and bolts of astronomy – but rather was the consequence of a working through of the logic of quantum mechanics and general relativity.

For Hawking the creation of a black hole was much like the creation of the universe in reverse. The former showed a massive body collapsing into a state of singularity, the latter singularity exploding into the discrete and organized matter of the universe. His later work has returned to those first moments of creation. Hawking's second major contribution to cosmology, the no-boundary principle, posits that there is no definite boundary between space and time, and that they exist together as four dimensions. Our universe is a finite sphere of space and time without edges. This theory predicts an origin to the universe in which an initial rapid but organized period of expansion, or 'inflation', preceded the 'hot' big bang. The inflation stage has left its signature on the universe in the form of ripples in space, which, in a convincing verification of Hawking's hypothesis, were detected by the Cosmic Background Explorer Satellite (COBE) project in 1992.

Despite his worthy contributions to theoretical physics and cosmology, however, it is as a cultural icon, as a signifier for the incomprehensible complexities of science, that Hawking attains his true importance. He reminds us that science is a human undertaking, while retaining its mystique. [AM]

HEGEL, GEORG WILHELM FRIEDRICH: PHILOSOPHER (1770–1831) Hegel's reputation has waxed and waned over the course of the twentieth century. The founder of modern dialectical philosophy and a critical influence on the work of Karl **Marx**, Hegel's philosophical standing has rarely been very high in the English-speaking world, but in the continental tradition it has been a different matter. From the 1930s onwards in France, for example, he exerted considerable influence, and along with **Husserl** and **Heidegger** helped to set the agenda for French philosophy up until the advent of **poststructuralism** and **postmodernism**. Within the Marxist tradition in general, Hegel has continued to be a subject of debate.

The Hegelian dialectic operates on the triad of thesis–antithesis–synthesis, where the conflict of the thesis and the antithesis it generates resolves itself into a new state, or synthesis – and then on to a new cycle.

Hegel saw this as a method working through history, with successive stages of historical development working towards the ultimate realization of what he called the 'world spirit' (see *The Philosophy of History*, for example). The theory as a whole is highly abstract and, for many, deterministic in nature. Marx found it to be over-idealistic, and proceeded to 'turn' the Hegelian dialectic 'on its head' – that is, to relate it to specific developments in the material world, such as the class struggle.

The Marxist tradition has had a love–hate relationship with Hegel, although there has been a recognizably Hegelian strain within modern Marxist thought (most notably seen, perhaps, in the work of the Hungarian philosopher and literary critic György Lukács). In more recent times there has been a tendency to turn to Hegel in an effort to reconstruct Marxist philosophy, or to register dissatisfaction at the direction Marxism was felt to be taking. Poststructuralist and postmodernist theorists have an even more ambiguous relationship to Hegel. While Jacques **Derrida** can argue that 'We will never be finished with the reading or rereading of Hegel' (he says the same thing of Marx, by the way), others such as Gilles **Deleuze** have been more critical, arguing that Hegelian philosophy's totalizing imperative runs directly counter to what they believe a postmodern philosophy should be. Much of recent French philosophy can be regarded as a reaction against Hegel's previous dominance in French intellectual life. There is no denying that all attempts to provide a 'philosophy of everything' (Marx's no less than Hegel's) are largely out of favour in a postmodern world, which finds such system-building enterprises to be authoritarian – although that has not stopped Hegel from remaining an important presence on the **continental philosophical** landscape. [SS]

HEGEMONY The concept of hegemony was most notably used by the Italian **Marxist**

theorist Antonio Gramsci as a way of explaining how the ruling class in a capitalist society managed to impose its ideology on the mass of the population – most of the time without recourse to force. Thus the belief system of bourgeois capitalism could be communicated through the arts and the media, which could present the principles of that ideology as ideals to be aspired to by the general population – or, more simply, as the 'natural' order of things (it is 'natural' for human beings to compete, etc.).

The **structural** Marxist theorist Louis Althusser later built on Gramsci's ideas to suggest that Western societies consisted of various 'Ideological State Apparatuses' (ISAs), and a 'Repressive State Apparatus' (RSA). It was the role of the ISAs (the educational system, the arts and the media, for example) to disseminate the ideological principles of the ruling class, such that they became part of everyday life for the bulk of the population to the point where the population no longer even recognized that it was being indoctrinated. The RSA (the government, police and army) was there to impose order by violent means if the ISAs failed in their objective.

In **postmodernist** thought, the concept of hegemony has been revised by **Laclau** and **Mouffe**, who in *Hegemony and Socialist Strategy* (1985) emphasized its *contingent* nature, pointing out that it had been devised to explain away (in somewhat ad hoc fashion) some apparent failings of Marxist theory. Historical necessity, one of the cornerstones of classical Marxist thought, dictated that the working class eventually *ought* to have risen up against its exploiters; hegemony explained why it generally did not, but in so doing cast doubt on the validity of the classical Marxist conception of historical necessity itself. Neither did Laclau and Mouffe believe in the working class as a homogeneous 'totality' in the manner of classical Marxism, but instead as liable to fragmentation. They

concluded that what hegemony demonstrated was the need to develop a **pluralist** Marxism, which would involve the many new social movements that had arisen in the later twentieth century (the **Greens**, for example, as well as various ethnic and sexual minorities). [SS]

HEIDEGGER, MARTIN: PHILOSOPHER (1889–1975) Heidegger was born and died in Messkirch. Travelling rarely beyond the Black Forest of southern Germany, he was rooted to one place like the modern philosopher Immanuel **Kant**. Yet Heidegger also became a pivotal, however controversial, figure for modern philosophy: he marked the beginning of its end. Positively, Heidegger alerted philosophers to the danger of an era that had lost the ability to question deeply and pointed to the possibility of a new beginning. Negatively, Heidegger was caught up in a reflexive circle: in attempting to give up metaphysics, he remained embedded in the categories of Being, truth and language which defined Western metaphysics. **Postmodern** philosophers argue that, although Heidegger developed a number of strategies by which he endeavoured to escape from the era of **modernity**, he could never finally extricate himself from his own age.

Heidegger's project begins with his hermeneutics of *Being and Time* (1927) and culminates in his reversal of time and Being. Some say that Heidegger devoted his life to one philosophical topic: Being, or the being of Being and the Being of beings. However this topic is not so simple, since he systematically exposes the inscrutability of Being as that which eludes our modes of thought. At the very least, Heidegger's relentless attempts to undo the conceptual knots in the history of the philosophy of Being began the destruction of metaphysics which was to be taken up by **deconstruction** and other postmodern strategies.

Initially, Heidegger uses the two concepts,

'Being' and 'time', to establish what metaphysics is. But he finds that the attempt to give them a non-metaphysical meaning is no easy task: how can Being be thought of other than as that which never changes? And how can time be thought of other than as the perishable, constantly changing realm of existence? Heidegger demonstrates that Being has been thought of in traditional philosophy as a kind of '**presence**'. Roughly stated, the true nature of Being is distorted in the history of Western philosophy because it is always represented as present, rather than being situated in terms of a past out of which it emerges and a future towards which it tends. The traditional emphasis on presence conceals the very question of the meaning of Being.

Heidegger describes the method of his early work as hermeneutical – it interprets one's own understanding and the **texts** of the history of that understanding. The central problem of hermeneutics arises with the recognition that all understanding involves some prejudice. Here one of Heidegger's means to excavate the philosophical tradition is etymology. In seeking the original meaning of a word, he may give the impression of discovering its true sense. Yet this is one of his strategies to escape the tradition of presence: to extricate oneself from the vacuousness of contemporary thought by exposing words which have lost their meaning. So instead of producing a correct account of the meaning of a term, Heidegger unsettles assumptions of meaning.

The word 'Being' itself becomes a problem for Heidegger. Eventually he develops a strategy of crossing out this word in order to make clear that it does not refer to an object with a unitary character. He gradually abandons 'Being' altogether, replacing it with concepts such as 'appropriation' (*das Ereignis*). In the later Heidegger, Being takes on the sense of appropriation which is supposed to express a being's own way of occurring, i.e. the event of 'the being

it itself is' (so not in the sense of 'to be present'). Yet the meaning of such an event virtually coalesces with time, but without simply collapsing into an indifferent sameness. This relation of appropriation and time can be thought of reciprocally: time is the way in which appropriation occurs, while appropriation can be either simply what is or what is given at any moment.

Thus the later Heidegger attempts to leave modern philosophy behind in moving away from his theory of time in *Being and Time*. In his lectures 'Time and Being' (1962) and 'The End of Philosophy and the Task of Thinking' (1963), Heidegger no longer structures time in terms of a present moment such as the Aristotelian 'now'. Neither is time a series of discrete 'nows'. Instead it is a dimension relating the present back into the past and forward into the future. In Heidegger time becomes a relational structure of difference, and so heralds postmodern debates about language as a **differential** system of **signs** which are 'present' only insofar as they relate to another element that is not itself present. [PSA]

HIRST, DAMIEN: ARTIST (1965–) Fascinated by the realms of advertising, business, medicine, funfairs, art galleries and consumption, Hirst's work comes in two brands: the 'grotesque' or 'freak-show' world of sliced cows, pigs preserved in formaldehyde-filled cases, and flayed figures twenty feet tall; and the 'whimsical' world of billboards with rotating slats which display cucumbers paired with Vaseline jars, hammers conjoined with peaches, above which we find the logo-like inscription: 'The trouble with relationships'. In addition to weaving together the violated and the kitsch, the common theme running through his art is the concern with the power of juxtaposition and the authority of framing or classifying objects. Hirst sees the gallery as the home of an ordering system he will 'turn' through his 'fabulous' transgressions.

Hirst aligns himself with a **post-modernist** aesthetic (or rhetoric) when he asserts that his exhibitions seek to deny the idea of artistic coherency or continuity. His 1996 *Flash Art* interview contains this statement about *No Sense of Absolute Corruption*:

> I wanted to make a show where every piece somehow undermined every other piece, but not in a negative way. It became a kind of celebration. It looks more like a group show, with the individual artists being aspects of myself, like an exploded view of an artist.

The exhibition, which toured Britain and the USA, confirmed his status as a media star.

Hirst's heroes are Warhol and **Koons**, both of whom are linked to the capacity to create micro-worlds of artificial but common experience. Hirst is, like them, a belated follower of Marcel **Duchamp** and his readymades; and his formaldehyde-filled cases of sharks, sheep and pigs repeat the gesture made in 1917 when Duchamp's *Fountain*, an upside-down urinal mounted on a pedestal, was displayed as an artwork at the Salon of the New York Independents group. Like his predecessor, Hirst's art questions the assumption that the art object should be unique or original; like many figures associated with the historical avant-garde he wants to believe in the critical or radical nature of art, although such radicalism seems to be somewhat theatrical: 'I like the idea of rich people buying my burned-out fag-ends', he said of his fag-end pastiche of Claes Oldenburg's giant fag-end and ashtray pop-art sculpture of the early 1960s.

It may well be the case that Hirst's work corresponds to Charles **Jencks**' characterization of postmodernism as a fluid, flexible and eclectic 'referencing' of the past: in his cows and sheep we find echoes of Rembrandt, Ford Madox Brown, William Holman Hunt and Chaim Soutine; in his spot and dot paintings we find traces of Lichtenstein, Op-Art, Daniel Buren, Niele Toroni and Phillip Taaffe; in the spin paintings we find the ghostly traces of Duchamp's rotoreliefs; in the medicinal cabinets the assimilation of the sweet shop displays by Peter Blake; in the shiny metallic cases the mirrors of minimalist serialism. This entrepreneurial activity, in which the artist transforms himself into a one-man museum, laboratory or work-station, has kept his profile high, as has his involvement in pop music and the continued patronage of Charles Saatchi, whose gallery of modern art opened in London in 2002 with over thirty works by Hirst on display. By 2003 it was estimated that Hirst, the archetypal 'post-statist, artist', according to Philip Dodd, the Director of the ICA, was worth more than £35 million. [CT]

HOOKS, BELL: CRITIC (1952–) Gloria Watkins, whose pseudonym bell hooks is taken from her maternal great-grandmother, is a prolific **author** and a leading black female cultural critic and commentator. Her first book, *Ain't I a Woman* (1981), made her reputation and she has produced many volumes since, often in the form of collections of essays dealing with fiction, film, feminism and cultural theory. Most prominent among her works are *Feminist Theory* (1984), *Talking Back* (1989), *Yearning* (1990), *Black Looks* (1992) and *Outlaw Culture* (1994). She has published an auto-biography, *Bone Black* (1997), and indeed an autobiographical speculation is often her chosen method of beginning a critical essay. She is one of the few African-American women theorists not only to engage with, but to advocate the use of, **postmodern** theories of **subjectivity** as an enabling **discourse** for talking about blackness in non-essentialist ways. *Ain't I a*

Woman, a book that grew out of hooks' own working-class experience, introduced one of her most enduring themes: the marginalization of black women in feminism. The title of the work comes from a famous 1850 speech by the ex-slave Sojourner Truth, where she lays claim to an identity, and in many ways *Ain't I a Woman* itself is an act of historical recovery.

hooks is a socialist and her feminism is part of a more general struggle against oppression, not just to end male chauvinism and deliver equal rights for women, but also to eradicate 'the ideology of domination that permeates Western culture'; she is unyielding, therefore, in her criticism of feminists, such as Betty Friedan and Naomi **Wolf**, who leave to one side issues of race and class and take their own (usually affluent white) experience for that of all women. Both embrace the opportunities capitalism offers successful women. These two, along with Camille **Paglia** and Katie Roiphe, are subjected to a withering critique for their exclusion or patronizing of black women. Indeed, the 'exclusionary use' of the term 'feminism' by white middle-class women leads hooks to shift from using the phrase 'I am a feminist' to saying 'I advocate feminism', for it serves 'as a way women who are concerned about feminism as well as other political movements could express their support while avoiding linguistic structures that give primacy to one particular group'.

In recent years, African-American cultural critics have heatedly debated the value and appropriateness of postmodern theory for black culture. Most prominent in the negative camp has been Barbara Christian in her influential essay 'The Race for Theory' (1987). In *Yearning*, hooks has argued forcibly the other way, but notes white critics' neglect of black contributions to postmodern culture. Though critical of postmodern critics' obsession with 'discourse' and '**difference**' at the expense of the fight against imperialism, racism and sexism, and their use of '**Otherness**' in a very abstract way, hooks argues for a postmodernism which abandons essentialist and restrictive definitions of 'blackness', allows for a multiplicity of black identities and for the construction of selves 'that are oppositional and liberatory'. It is clear that hooks' postmodernism, against the grain of a large amount of theorizing under that name, both is harnessed to and enlivens her emancipatory politics. [DR]

HORKHEIMER, MAX: PHILOSOPHER, CULTURAL COMMENTATOR (1895–1973) Together with Theodor **Adorno** and Herbert **Marcuse**, Horkheimer was the foremost representative of the '**critical theory**' associated with the Institute of Social Research (or **Frankfurt School**). Horkheimer became director of the Institute in 1930, organized its move into exile from Nazi Germany and supervised the return of the Institute to Frankfurt in 1949.

Horkheimer's programmatic essay on 'Traditional and Critical Theory' (1937) enshrined the ambitions of the Institute. It described the necessity of integrating philosophy and social science, and of developing a relationship of integrity between critical theory and political practice. In later years Horkheimer's vision became increasingly dark and gloomy. His later writings evidence the difficulty – even the impossibility – of fulfilling the original ambition and programme of the Frankfurt School. The result is an increasingly sharp critique of 'enlightened' reason and Western rationality. The *Dialectic of Enlightenment* (1947), written in collaboration with Theodor W. Adorno, was the first and most powerful – if fragmentary – statement of this theme.

After the war Horkheimer's politics became more liberal, but his view of society more pessimistic (his debt to Schopenhauer became clearer and clearer). Whereas the *Dialectic of Enlightenment* had shown up the problematic, darker side of the **Enlightenment project**, Horkheimer felt more and more constrained to defend the legacy of the Enlightenment against its erosion under late capitalism. The critical impulse which forms a crucial element in the Enlightenment conception of reason had been eroded. Rationality had been reduced to instrumental reason, wholly devoted to the calculation of relating means to (usually unquestioned) ends. Positivism and society's uncritical approval of scientific rationality was one symptom of what Horkheimer and Adorno referred to as 'identity thinking'. The triumph of commercialism and the resulting domination of concrete use values by (abstract) exchange values was another. Both led to the suppression of **difference** and particularity.

Consistent in Horkheimer's lifework is the attempt to sustain a critique of reason conducted in acknowledgement of suffering: a critique in the name of the entirely '**Other**', acknowledging everything dominated and suppressed by the regimes of identity thinking. [LS]

HUSSERL, EDMUND: PHILOSOPHER (1859–1938) Husserl's importance to **postmodern** thought lies in his role as founder of the philosophical movement known as phenomenology, a movement that has had a considerable influence on the development of **continental philosophy** in particular. The most detailed exposition is to be found in his book *Ideas: General Introduction to Pure Phenomenology* (1913).

Husserlian phenomenology is particularly concerned with the structures of consciousness, and also with the need to find an unproblematical starting point, or foundation, for philosophical **discours**e – one without any metaphysical presuppositions (or assumptions) that could be challenged by other philosophers. Given such a foundation, one could proceed to construct a theory of knowledge.

The desired starting point for a 'presuppositionless analysis' is found by going back to consciousness and phenomenal experience (taken to be things that cannot be doubted), by means of what Husserl called the *epoche*, or 'phenomenological reduction'. This latter is a technique whereby the world and its preoccupations are temporarily suspended, or 'bracketed', thus avoiding all the standard philosophical challenges to one's theories. Critics, however, have tended to treat the *epoche* as the equivalent of a philosophical cheat, arguing that it makes debate all but impossible.

Poststructuralist philosophers have been just as keen as Husserl to find a form of 'presuppositionless analysis', but have queried whether Husserl really provides them with one. Jacques **Derrida**, for example, has criticized Husserlian phenomenology for being in its turn underpinned by metaphysical presuppositions – such as that a theory of knowledge is even possible. To Derrida the whole idea of a theory of knowledge is based on questionable metaphysical assumptions that go back to the very earliest days of Western philosophy in classical Greece. In general, poststructuralist and postmodernist theorists have been more influenced by the radical phenomenological doctrines of a follower of Husserl, Martin **Heidegger**. [SS]

HYBRIDITY The concept of hybridity is central to the **discourses** of **postcolonial** theory and **cultural studies**. Hybridity refers to the ambivalent conceptual 'space' between adversarial, polarized perspectives and/or ideologies. Challenging the notion that any political ideology can claim transcendent or metaphysical authority for itself, the discourse of hybridity counters notions of the **metaphysics of presence**, and facile **binary oppositions**, by foregrounding the interstices or fault lines where identities are performed and contested.

Theorists such as Homi **Bhabha**, Paul Gilroy, Stuart Hall and Gayatri **Spivak** have written on the concept. Bhabha in particular has developed the idea in relation to the identity of the colonised **Other**. In *Signs Taken for Wonders* he argues that: 'The display of hybridity – its peculiar "replication" – terrorizes authority with the ruse of recognition, its mimicry, its mockery'. He locates the 'hybrid moment' in the interstitial 'third space' wherein meaning is always in between, in process, contestatory and resistant to closure. Critical of essentialist notions of identity with their connotations of fixity and repression, hybridity, for Bhabha, captures the liberatory potential of resistant cultures, by subverting dualistic categories and initiating 'mutual and mutable' identity formations 'in between' the static binarisms of colonizer and colonized. [AY]

HYPERREALITY The term hyperreality is used by Jean **Baudrillard** to indicate the 'loss of the real', where distinctions between surface and depth, the real and the imaginary no longer exist. The world of the hyperreal is where image and reality implode. Baudrillard suggests that we no longer need models of analysis such as **Marxism** with its language of surface and depth, for there are no depths. Marxism, which sees the market *behind* everything, must give way to the idea that the market is *in* everything but *behind* nothing. In a famous example, Baudrillard chooses Disneyland as an illustration of a third-order image, a magical space which masks the absence of the real. He argues that, just as prisons exist to mask the fact that society *itself is* one, 'Disneyland is presented as imaginary in order to make us believe that the rest is real, when in fact all of Los Angeles and the America surrounding it are no longer real, but of the order of the hyperreal'.

While Baudrillard's concept may be criticized in any number of ways, it seems to capture something of the flavour of the commodified and mediated nature of contemporary life. [PD]

HYPERTEXT Hypertext is electronic text that provides links between key elements, allowing the reader to move through information non-sequentially. Now the key technology of the worldwide web, the idea of hypertext can be traced back to an article published in 1945 by Franklin D. Roosevelt's wartime science adviser, Vannevar Bush. Bush envisaged mechanically linked machines for the storage and retrieval of information, allowing scholars, researchers and others access to large amounts of information without having to deal with the cumbersome storage and classification methods of traditional archives and libraries. Bush proposed a device called the Memex, with translucent screens, levers and motors, which would allow the user to annotate and link information on microfilm.

The term itself was coined by Theodore H. Nelson in 1965: 'By "hypertext", I mean non-sequential writing – **text** that branches out and allows choices to the reader, best read at an interactive screen.' Nelson envisaged hypertext in utopian fashion as an encyclopaedic gathering together of all printed texts in a global hypertext publishing system called 'Xanadu'.

For some critics and theorists, the non-linearity, linkage and decentredness of hypertext appear to demonstrate empirically the insights regarding reading and textuality advanced by such thinkers as **Derrida**, **Barthes** and **Foucault**. George P. Landow in his book *Hypertext: The Convergence of Contemporary Critical Theory and Technology* (1992), claims that '**critical theory** promises to theorize hypertext and hypertext promises to embody and thereby test aspects of theory, particularly those concerning textuality, **narrative** and the roles or functions of reader and writer'. At the same time, critics like Landow and J. David Bolter claim that hypertext encourages a more 'natural' and associative way of reading. The inherent utopianism of much hypertext theory has recently come under attack: while the *analogies* between hypertext and the works of Derrida, for example, are clear, it is unclear what the 'realization' or 'fulfilment' of a philosophy like **deconstruction** (not a *project* in any traditional sense) could mean. [BD]

INCOMMENSURABILITY Many **postmodern-ists** hold to a version of the 'Sapir-Whorf hypothesis'. In its strongest form it is the claim that linguistic structures condition thought patterns and *determine* our percep-tion of the world. This could be taken to mean that speakers of different languages in a sense inhabit different worlds. Incommensurability is a term taken from mathematical theory where it refers to two qualities or magnitudes which have no common measure. The notion has been loosely transferred to debates about the role of language. Two languages are incom-mensurable if their structures make exact translation between them difficult or impos-sible. The term 'incommensurability' has gained currency together with a view (or speculative hypothesis) that all languages are incommensurable one with another.

The most precise formulation of this view is presented by the philosopher Willard van Orman Quine as part of a more general scepticism about the very idea of meaning. Quine dramatized what he termed 'the indeterminacy of translation'. This is not the same as the platitude that there are shades of meaning which might be lost in the process of translation; instead, it implies that the very notion of shades of meaning which are uncaptured is pointless. Each language posits a different set of objects, and maps the world in a different way. Thomas **Kuhn**'s work deals with scientific paradigms. At its most basic, a paradigm is simply an exemplary model. But in the context of scientific theories it is also taken to refer to the interrelationships between a whole system of concepts. There are many postmodern writers on the philosophy of science who suggest that competing scientific paradigms are in principle incommensurable.

The notion of incommensurability reappears in **Lyotard**'s concept of the '**differend**'. The differend is incommen-surability politicized. Each party inhabits not simply their own language, and thus their own world; they inhabit a 'phrase regime', embodying interests and object-ives. One phrase regime exerts dominance over another. Incommensurability cap-tured the idea of opacity between lang-uages. The differend suggests an opacity, and a deformation, created by the action of one language – or phrase regime – on another. [LS]

INSTALLATION ART Associated with Marcel Broodthaers, Hans Haacke, Daniel Buren and Michael Asher, 'installation art' was the term applied to a set of critical practices which emerged in the late 1960s. Con-cerned with the conditions in which art is displayed, these artists explored the spatial, social and political networks which comprised the art world. Buren's work, which often took the form of structural/architectural elaborations of the spaces where they were displayed, drew attention to the framing systems of the gallery as a cultural space. Haacke's image-and-**text** work, by contrast, continues to be con-cerned with mapping the boundaries of art and ideology by revealing the political interests of gallery sponsors, museum trustees and corporate patrons. [CT]

INTERNET An electronic space that **cyber-punk** author William **Gibson** has called a 'consensual hallucination', in many ways the Internet, combining a technological reality with immense politically hallucinatory potential, is *the* exemplary **postmodern** object, and arguably even the architecture of postmodern culture. Its technological roots lie in a system developed by the American Advanced Research Projects Agency to link their computers into a network, forming ARPAnet, which went online towards the end of 1969. Since then it has grown geometrically, and has been championed as the source and – although geography is a problem in **cyberspace** – the site of a new, utopian, political order, marking the rise of what Howard Rheingold has famously called 'virtual communities' where information flows without property relations and where anyone can have access to anyone else.

In consequence many of the political conflicts associated with postmodernism, and even the posts one ought to inhabit within postmodern and **post-industrial** societies, are now being contested on the Net. For example, Jean-François **Lyotard**'s call, as *The Postmodern Condition* (1979) draws to an end, for the public to be given access to all databases stems from his thesis that, in a computerized society, information is **power**. Lyotard's pronouncement echoes the Internet ideologues' credo 'information wants to be free'; meanwhile, however, corporate concerns have set about the commercialization of the Internet, ensuring that the days of democratized information flow are running out.

This is not, however, a change of direction following the origins of the Internet; rather, the whole purpose of the ARPAnet was to find a means whereby, in the event of a nuclear strike, no single node or post in the network would be responsible for the continuing functioning of the entire net. In other words, the absence of central control on the Net, championed as its chief political virtue by Internet activists, derives from the military necessity that the defence

grid remain functional even if some of the nodes in the Net are taken out. To this extent, the democratic impetus of Lyotard's proposals, the anarcho-syndicalism of virtual communities and the ideological sloganizing of the informational libertarians seem, in the long run, doomed to lose their political naivety. The Internet is not beyond war and capital; rather, their territories and markets have been uploaded into cyberspace. [IHG]

INTERTEXTUALITY Many classic literary texts, from Rabelais' *Gargantua* and *Pantagruel,* through Robert Burton's *Anatomy of Melancholy* and on to Sterne's *Tristram Shandy,* are woven from other texts: references, citations and quotations tumbling together in disorienting superabundance. However it was only with Julia **Kristeva**'s *Semiotike* (1969) that it was claimed that '*every* text takes shape as a mosaic of citations, every text is the absorption and transformation of other texts'.

The concept of intertextuality derived from the **poststructuralist** claim that signifiers refer always and only to other signifiers: that language can be transformed, translated, transferred, but never transcended. Words gain their meaning not by referring to some object present to the mind of the language user but from the never-ending play of signification. To use the word 'love' is not to refer to some extra-linguistic biological or psychological object but, consciously or unconsciously, to join in a conversation that takes in the lays of the troubadours, Shakespearean tragedy, romantic lyrics and the songs of the Beatles.

Postmodernism embraces an extreme notion of intertextuality, in which the play of meaning is infinite, in which anything goes. The limits of interpretation are set only by the boundaries of the imagination. [AM]

IRIGARAY, LUCE: PHILOSOPHER, PSYCHO-ANALYST (1932–) Formerly a member of

Jacques **Lacan**'s École Freudienne de Paris, Irigaray was expelled as a result of her feminist critique of psychoanalysis and since then has been one of its most vocal critics, seeking, as she does, to liberate the feminine from masculine philosophical thought. Irigaray's work is challenging and varied, ranging in methodology from the densely psychoanalytic to **deconstructive** to the visionary, lyrical and expressive. *Speculum of the Other Woman* (1974), her first major piece of feminist writing, offers a critique of **Freudian** psychoanalysis and Western philosophy from Plato onwards. Here, Irigaray argues that woman as **subject** is excluded from Western philosophy, and that this mode of thought allows full subjectivity to only one sex: the male. Stemming from the primacy accorded the phallus, woman is characterized by absence, lack, negativity. Cast merely as the mirror in which man sees himself reflected, we are only allowed to know woman as man sees her. With this book, Irigaray began a series of publications on language and sexual **difference**, including *This Sex Which is Not One* (1977), *Ethics of Sexual Difference* (1984) and *Sexes and Genealogies* (1987), which continue her quest for the feminine voice and a feminine symbolic order and emphasize the **plurality** of the female sex.

This Sex Which is Not One contains what have become three of Irigaray's most significant essays: 'When our Lips Speak Together', 'Commodities Among Themselves' and the title essay. The volume, and in particular these essays, demonstrate Irigaray's diverse application of her feminist project. The last two focus particularly upon the economics of patriarchy, in which woman is cast as an object endowed only with use value for exchanges between men: exchanges which, Irigaray controversially argues, are testimony to the male homosexual nature of patriarchy. In this system of exchange, woman has no agency, and female **desire** is misrepresented and misconstructed by patriarchal language. However, the title essay of the collection explores Irigaray's own construction and **representation** of female desire through the medium of strikingly lyrical prose. In this collection of essays, Irigaray employs what has become her most memorable metaphor, that of the two lips which symbolize the fluidity, plurality and ambiguity of female sexuality: the pun of the sex which is not (even) one in Western philosophical **discourse** upon the sex which is not (only) one in Irigaray's new method of cultural representation.

While arguing against and critiquing Western philosophy in general, and Freud and Lacan in particular, ultimately Irigaray views the non-subjectivity of women in psychoanalysis and in Western philosophical discourse as an opportunity which women should seize in order to construct their own subjectivity on their own terms. While the feminine is ignored and suppressed in the masculine symbolic order, it is available for women to liberate and reconstruct it in their own symbolic order, argues Irigaray, thereby demonstrating her advocacy of *l'écriture féminine* or female writing.

Luce Irigaray's work has itself been the subject of much critical attention, most notably from Ann Rosalind Jones, Toril Moi, Margaret Whitford and Elizabeth Grosz. She is often grouped together with Julia **Kristeva** and Hélène **Cixous**, although there are considerable theoretical differences between them. The main source of negative criticism is that her writing is too essentialist, too focused upon the physical being of woman, without taking into account the ethnic, economic and political forces which divide the experience of the world's female population. However, her essentialist position is regaining its value as feminists seek to prevent issues of femininity and female sexual difference being obliterated by the postmodern insistence upon the **anti-essentialist** subject. As she says in 'Women: Equal or Different' (Jackson *et al.*, eds, *Women's Studies: A Reader* (1993)): 'Trying to suppress sexual difference is to invite a genocide more radical than any destruction that has ever existed in history.' [SH-W]

IRONY We are all familiar with irony as a figure of speech in which the intended meaning is the opposite of that expressed by the words used. In the form of sarcasm or ridicule, irony can express a degree of hostility. It is common in jokes which sometimes separate 'insiders' (who share the joke) from those being laughed at (who do not 'get it' – that is, do not see the irony). Irony is always connected with a requirement not to take things (including our-selves) too seriously, or at least not to take things at face value. Nothing is so charac-teristic of the current **postmodern** 'mood' as its ironic, detached, self-consciousness. Umberto **Eco** has characterized post-modernism as an attitude in which we cannot give up our cherished hopes and beliefs, but at the same time can no longer embrace them with unqualified or whole-hearted adherence. In *Contingency, Irony, and Solidarity* (1989) Richard **Rorty** sketches and recommends the figure of the 'liberal ironist'. 'Ironists' face up to the contingency of their beliefs; 'liberal ironists' are aware that among these lie such things as 'their own hope that suffering will be diminished'. [LS]

J

JAMESON, FREDRIC: CULTURAL CRITIC
(1934–) Fredric Jameson is the best known
and most influential **Marxist** literary and
cultural critic writing in English. As such,
he has offered one of the most compelling
historical analyses of the general climate
of **postmodernism** as 'the logic of late
capitalism'.

Jameson was a student of Erich Auer-
bach and an early and enduring influence
on his work has been the example of
György Lukács. During the 1920s, and
after his turn to Marxism, Lukács played a
crucial role in the reappropriation of
Hegelian philosophy and the inauguration
of a tradition of 'critical' Marxism.

The most influential part of Jameson's
own early work concentrated on the
serious theoretical treatment of figures
from this tradition of Hegelian, or 'critical',
Marxism. *Sartre: The Origins of a Style*
(1961) already focuses on one of Jameson's
central themes: the question of **narrative**.
His book *Marxism and Form* (1971) introduced a new generation to the work of
Lukács, Bloch, **Benjamin**, **Adorno**, **Marcuse**
and Sartre.

Jameson's appropriation of a critical
(Hegelian) tradition in Marxism has been
complemented by a sustained engagement
with French and other **continental** thinking. In *The Prison-house of Language* (1972),
Jameson summarized the key concepts and
motifs of **structuralist** and **poststructuralist** linguistics and at the same time provided a forceful critique directed against
the more pessimistic conclusions that some
have derived from such theorizing. In his
most ambitious work, *The Political Unconscious* (1981), Jameson developed his own

programme for an interpretive framework
that was political and historical but which
could enrich itself by adopting or adapting
the insights of the structural traditions in
linguistics.

Jameson's magisterial command of a
panorama of theoretical traditions meant
that he was well placed to launch a polemic
against the depoliticizing, relativist or
reactionary tendencies of the age. That
polemic was pointedly formulated in the
article 'Postmodernism, or the Cultural
Logic of Late Capitalism' published in *New
Left Review* (1984). This was expanded into
a sizeable book with the same title (1991)
which is one of the crucial documents in the
debate over postmodernism. Jameson
interprets postmodernism in historical and
political terms. He leans on Ernest Mandel's *Late Capitalism*, which attempted to
adapt and update Marx's economic
analyses to explain the workings of global
capitalism in the post-war information age.
The main aim of Jameson's analysis is the
crisis of historicity in the advanced- or late-
capitalist countries.

In *The Postmodern Condition* (1979)
(whose English-language edition carries a
critical foreword by Jameson), **Lyotard**
had affirmed the prevailing scepticism
towards **metanarratives**. Jameson was
uniquely qualified to instruct the postmodernists about the social relations underlying the symptoms of the 'postmodern
condition'. Jameson's own work returns
again and again to the question announced
in his study of Sartre: 'The question of
narrative, or more exactly . . . the [question
of the] relationship between narrative
and narrative closure, the possibility of

storytelling, and the kinds of experience – social and existential – structurally available in a given social formation.'

'Always historicize!' Jameson calls this 'the one absolute and . . . "transhistorical" imperative of all dialectical thought'. Jameson's thought aims unashamedly at 'totalizing' in a sense elaborated by Sartre (although Jameson's use of commitment in this area connects him also to Lukács and to Adorno).

In the minds of postmodernism's less critical acolytes, the mere invocation of 'totality' is enough to convict Jameson of an outdated/harmful point of view. But Jameson has consistently rejected the idea of a 'total system'. In fact, in Jameson the attempt to think through the category of 'totality' is part of a defence against totalitarian tendencies in thought. In *Late Marxism: Adorno, or the Persistence of the Dialectic* (1990), Jameson seeks to update Adorno's analysis of the tendencies of late capitalism to function as a negative 'totality'. In the face of drastic changes in the relationship between the individual and the social system, Jameson proposes the writings of Adorno, especially Adorno's difficult late works *Negative Dialectics* and *Aesthetic Theory*, as the model of the kind of reflexive dialectic needed in our day.

Lukács' early literary work was inspired by the utopian and metaphysical impulses of the early German Romantics. Jameson's work has remained true to this inspiration in a consistent and courageous fidelity to the utopian impulse. He remains one of the most sure-footed guides to the origins of our present predicament. [LS]

JENCKS, CHARLES: ARCHITECTURAL HISTORIAN, THEORIST (1939–) A prolific author, Jencks has written and edited over twenty-five books, including influential studies of twentieth-century architecture. He is best known as the author of a number of books on **postmodern** architecture, most notably for *The Language of Post-Modern Architecture* (1977). The regular updating of this book and his other writings on postmodernism are part of an ongoing project of definition and redefinition that makes his work both a starting point for many discussions of the forms of postmodernism and an important element of the debate he initially sought to analyse.

The field of architecture has been a useful focus for debates on postmodernism for three main reasons: first because the failure of **modernist** architecture has been so spectacular and so visible. Since the early 1960s, urban critics (Jane Jacobs in *The Death and Life of Great American Cities* (1961)) and architects (Robert **Venturi** in *Complexity and Contradiction in Architecture* (1966)) had been critical of the urban destruction resulting from the complacent, brutal aesthetics and social sterility of high-rise modernism. Second, and as a consequence of this failure, the difference between modern and postmodern architecture has been so stylistically marked. Finally, leading theorists of postmodernism (including **Jameson** and **Lyotard**) have used architecture as an index of 'the postmodern condition'.

Originally a historian of modernist architectural theory and practice, Jencks's work charts his growing disenchantment with it. He was one of the first architectural critics to introduce **semiotic** analysis into architectural criticism. Using rhetorical, grammatical and linguistic categories, Jencks 'read' buildings as forms of communication, and he began to see the modernist 'international style' as a very narrow, homogeneous language, 'as if Esperanto had been enforced everywhere'. By the mid-1970s and especially in his most influential work, *The Language of Post-Modern Architecture*, Jencks argued that postmodern architecture was a number of hybrid departures from modernism, using styles from the past as well as the modernist technique in which at that time all architects were trained. If, as Virginia Woolf declared, literary modernism began in December 1910, then Jencks is most famous for precisely dating its architectural and ideological demise; it 'died in St Louis, Missouri, on July 15th, 1972, at 3.32pm (or thereabouts)', when part of the vandalized and crumbling (and award-winning) Pruitt-Igoe housing project was blown up.

If in 1977, then, 'postmodernism' for Jencks had been 'largely a negative term, its very vagueness appealing', by the second edition of *The Language of Post-Modern Architecture* (1978) he felt able to offer a positive definition, his much-quoted concept of '**double coding**': 'the combination of modern techniques with something else (usually traditional building) in order for architecture to communicate with the public and a concerned minority, usually other architects'. This was not a mere revival of old styles nor a simple anti-modernism, as postmodernism has, for Jencks, 'the essential double meaning; the continuation of modernism and its transcendence'. Among the many examples Jencks uses is the British architect James **Stirling**'s addition to the state gallery in Stuttgart. While obviously a contemporary building, it echoes and plays with past art and architecture, including classical and pop art. Jencks sees this kind of post-modernist building as a way of opening up the minimalist language of modernism to history, context and **difference**; he describes and advocates a **pluralist** approach to cultural communication generally.

During the 1980s, Jencks began to expand his theory of postmodernism as double coding into other areas of culture. 'Double coding' explains the 'postmodern turn' in other arts, for postmodernism has become both 'cultural movement and historical epoch'. His *What is Post-modernism?* (1986) covers fiction and art as well as architecture. This concise little book is a useful guide to Jencks' thought. In art, Jencks sees the return of **representational** painting, self-conscious allegory, eclecticism and **hybridity** as signs of ubiquitous postmodern double coding. In fiction, Jencks admires writers who neither repudiate nor slavishly imitate the experimental writers of the early years of the century, but who, like John **Barth** and Umberto **Eco** for instance, give us the traditional pleasures of plot and work on a number of other levels too. Jencks' case is less convincing when he strays outside architecture and his obsessive periodizing and categorizing runs against the spirit of postmodern thought as it is generally perceived. He celebrates his humanist version of postmodernism, which has little in common with the **poststructuralist** anti-humanist postmodernism of Lyotard and others. [PD]

JOUISSANCE No adequate translation exists for the French term *jouissance*. *Jouir de* implies the ability to profit from pleasure; *jouissance* connotes the bliss of sexual orgasm. In **postmodern discourse** this psychoanalytic term gains significance from its opposite, the lack accompanying **desire**. Julia **Kristeva** suggests the existence of a feminine *jouissance* that exceeds the bounds of patriarchal language, remaining within woman's vision but beyond articulation; this pleasurable experience is associated with the child's joyful continuity with the maternal. Luce **Irigaray** defines a 'hysterical' *jouissance* that would not be 'paternal', but would be unrepresentable – remaining for ever a lack within patriarchy. [PSA]

K

KANT, IMMANUEL: PHILOSOPHER (1724–1804) Kant lived all his life in Königsberg, where he was made professor of logic and metaphysics in 1770. In 1781 he published the *Critique of Pure Reason*. Within ten years this immensely complex and difficult book was being discussed all over Germany. Over the next decades responses to what was called the critical philosophy played a vital role in the extraordinary richness of German philosophy as developed in the writings of Fichte and the Romantics, Schelling, **Hegel**, Fries and Schopenhauer.

The *Critique of Pure Reason* argues that the world as we know it and experience it, the world as studied by scientists, is structured by our modes, or categories, of cognition. Our sense experience is structured and organized by categorical determinants such as space and time. Other categories, such as cause, substance, relation and totality, are involved in our attempts to think any 'thing' at all. Thus, for Kant, in order to be an object, as opposed to a mere subjective impression, means to be subject to the categories. Objectivity is thus based on the mental apparatus of the **subject**. Because he was able to appeal to categories which he believed to be universal (part of human nature) Kant believed that he had definitively defended the possibility of objective knowledge. Many attempts to rescue and secure Kant's achievements by updating his terms have been made by a succession of post-Kantians, including **Husserl** and the phenomenologists as well as many philosophers in the Anglo-Saxon analytical tradition.

Kant's 'critical philosophy' had thrust the concept of *critique* into the foreground of philosophy. During our own century, the tradition of the 'critique' has become the dominant motif in philosophy. But a constant preoccupation with language has undermined Kant's hopes of providing a 'foundation' for objective knowledge.

From a **postmodernist** perspective, what was once presented as 'critical philosophy' seems compromised by its ambition to provide a foundation for knowledge and by its systematic pretensions. Each of Kant's three major works was indeed published under the title of *Critique*, but in each Kant attempted by means of analysis not only to establish the limits of, but also to provide a *foundation* for, a particular domain of human knowledge.

In the *Critique of Pure Reason* Kant set out an analysis of the basis of theoretical or scientific knowledge of the external world; in the *Critique of Practical Reason* the basis of our moral understanding; and in the *Critique of Judgement* the basis of aesthetics. The first two *Critiques* are concerned with the principles presupposed in our *objective* judgements as to what is the case (pure reason), and what *ought to be* the case (practical reason). The *Critique of Judgement* seeks to uncover the *subjective* principles which underlie (a) the systematic impulse and (b) our apprehension of beauty.

Kant deduced as the fundamental basis of all morality – what he called the 'categorical imperative' – the idea that one should always act in such a way that one's behaviour could become the basis of a universal law. Thus the will to universality – rather than any fixed set of precepts – is seen as the foundation of morality. Kant was attempting to reformulate in philosophical language Jesus of Nazareth's precept: 'Do unto others as you would have them do unto you.' [LS]

KIEFER, ANSELM: ARTIST (1945–) Like his teacher and mentor, Joseph **Beuys**, Kiefer's practice is informed by a romantic aesthetic which affirms the mystical unity of art and the world through the mediating agency of the artist. Kiefer follows Beuys in his presentation of art as a form of magical fertility, a fecund force generated by the **powers** embedded in cultural tradition. In a sense, then, individual creative power is imagined as a form of bardic incantation: the artist remembers national histories and myths by refiguring the canvas as an organic latticework of drips, inscriptions, **erasures** and blockages. Hovering between **representation** and abstraction, the troubled, violent and raw surfaces of Kiefer's paintings mark the space where paint becomes a **nomadic**, viscose and bleeding presence. Associating his work with transmutation and transcendence, critics have found in Kiefer's compositions a form of alchemy in which painting makes manifest the truths buried within ancient myths and symbols.

By the early 1980s this interest in the mythological and religious roots of cultural expression could be seen as part of a return to traditional modes of artistic practice. The Italian critic Achillo Bonito Oliva identified Kiefer as one of the most important figures in what he termed the **trans-avant-garde**, although, unlike Clemente and Baselitz, Kiefer's work is characterized by its 'expansive' technique: oil, acrylic, emulsion, crayon, shellac, photographs, ferns, straw, lead, steel and glass are found in *Niger* (1984), *Iron Path* (1986) and *Saturn Time* (1986). [CT]

KOOLHAAS, REM: ARCHITECT, THEORIST, AUTHOR (1944–) Very much the current darling of the architectural scene, Koolhaas, founder of the Office of Metropolitan Architecture (OMA), came to architecture late in life having spent numerous years as a scriptwriter in Hollywood, a vocation that has clearly influenced his attitude to architecture. A product of the Architectural Association in London during the school's most vibrant years, Koolhaas came to prominence on the back of an illustrated book, *Delirious New York*, which paid homage to Coney Island and celebrated 'the culture of congestion' and 'supra rationality' of Manhattanism. The lyrical exuberance of the **text**, which captured the essential character of the American (as opposed to the European) city, is complemented by a series of eclectic and surreal architectural drawings. Koolhaas is transfixed by the **irony** that the dream of the most radical of architectural **modernists** – the suprematist city – is actually realized in New York under the auspices of real-estate development rather than the social programming which was at the heart of radical modernism. He also revels in the fact that the immediate architectural manifestation of this tendency – the 'typical' open plan of the office block – is the one that allows the constant shifting and accommodation of multiple architectural programmes that was also the dream of the Russian avant-garde. For Koolhaas, this plan also marks the end of the idea of European architecture and its dominant trait – the plan as the generator.

These ideas have informed his conception of a 'retroactive' architecture – one which reactivates past avant-garde tendencies, but which capitalizes on the unexpected ways in which they have been used. This idea drove OMA's winning competition entry for the Parc de la Villette which is conceived as a horizontal skyscraper, and is structured around a series of strips containing disparate functions which correspond to the floors of a highrise building. This project led to Koolhaas's inclusion in the infamous exhibition,

Deconstructivist Architecture at the Museum of Modern Art, New York, where the essentially postmodern aesthetic of extremely stylized or 'stretched' modernism, a style which has since become de rigueur among architectural students worldwide, was made manifest in the OMA drawings.

Since catapulting to fame, Koolhaas has realized many projects including the Kunsthal in Rotterdam, the National Dance Theatre in The Hague and the canonical Villa Dal'ava on the outskirts of Paris. Despite his interest in the real-estate-inspired metropolis, Koolhaas has recently become interested in gigantic planning projects, and has realized the master planning of Euro Lille. Koolhaas enjoys the contamination of his projects by other architects (although all seem to work in the stylized modernist idiom) and by commercial processes, and takes his cue from Wallace Harrison, the commercial architect whose contribution supposedly contaminated the purity of Le Corbusier's vision for the UN in New York. His continuing interest in enormous projects is reflected in the publication of *Small, Medium, Large, Extra Large (SMLXL)* (1996), a 1,400-page novel about architecture which juxtaposes his writings and projects in the aforementioned categories. [SGr]

KOONS, JEFF: ARTIST (1955–) Koons came to prominence in the mid-1980s when he exhibited with **Halley**, Steinbach, Taaffe, Bleckner and Levine. During this period it was widely believed that his work was part of a **postmodern** engagement with the role of culture within **post-industrial** society, an economic order where leisure and consumption become processes of great symbolic and material importance. Like Steinbach's work of this period, Koons positioned domestic and leisure objects within gallery spaces in such a way as to draw attention to their almost totemic significance. His *New Shelton Wet/Dry*

Double Decker (1981) consists of two vacuum cleaners within Plexiglas boxes. The product, ubiquitous yet elusive, imprisoned yet powerful, seems to be displayed in order to register the **aura**, magic and potency associated with the experience of consumption. A similar process of encapsulating the serene inertia of a frozen micro-world of commodities characterizes his *2 Ball Total Equilibrium Tank* (1985), where the water-filled glass container carrying two basketballs both invites and frustrates a sense of intimacy through its cold, oceanic materialism.

This monumental isolation addresses the interplay between possession and **power**, consumption and knowledge, **desire** and control, purity and utility. These hollowed-out icons attracted the interest of writers searching for signs of postmodernism in artistic spaces other than painting, photography and **appropriation**-based practice. In the important *Endgame* exhibition, held at Boston's Institute of Arts in 1987, which established a critical overview of post-modernist practice, Koons' 'mediated sculpture' was identified as an example of **simulation** art. In making his art register the power of leisure commodities, Koons revivified the language of **Duchamp**'s readymades, which, seventy years earlier, had seen mass-produced industrial products displayed as aesthetic objects. Koons, like Duchamp, wanted to 'demystify' the art realm. Moreover, in confronting the spectral quality of the commodity, Koons had, it was believed, cleverly informed us that it is the ordinary object of consumption rather than the **modernist** artefact that retains some mysterious property or principle.

The end of the 1980s saw Koons' work move away from the **sublime** void of the commodity as he began to assemble a vast army of kitsch objects, all of which demonstrated the disappearance of high art beneath the detritus of mass culture. Where his earlier 'mediated sculpture' bodied forth a vast frozen landscape of endless repetitive inertia, *Rabbit* (1986), *Louis XIV* (1986), *Fisherman Golfer* (1986) and *Bear and Policeman* (1988) were informed by a welcoming hyper-vitality, a tacky duplication of luxury. In place of the obsessional clarity and eternal cleanliness of the early objects, the spectator is propelled into a fabulous realm of non-identity, populated by impossible things and creatures. Welcome, then, to the realm of mass-produced memorabilia, where the delirium of False Memory Syndrome mutates into media-inflected nostalgia. In a similar fashion, the landscape of leisure is retraced by the frenzied, deranged 'charm' of tourism: now we are confronted with an endless parade of souvenirs, micro-emanations of community, love and longing in the guise of stainless-steel trolls, 'plastic' rococo figurines, camp-Catholic porcelain busts, wooden Yorkshire terriers and other items derived from 'bingo-prize' culture. Where the earlier work suggested that as commodities were more interesting than traditional objects the art gallery had become a department store, these later objects appeared to belong to tourist culture, confirming that the art gallery had become assimilated into the kitsch culture of the souvenir shop. [CT]

KRISTEVA, JULIA: FEMINIST PSYCHOANALYST, LINGUIST, THEORIST (1941–) Together with Hélène **Cixous** and Luce **Irigaray**, Julia Kristeva is one of the most famous proponents of French feminist theory (*l'écriture féminine*). Born in Bulgaria, Kristeva moved to Paris in 1966, where her work quickly became associated with the group of **structuralists** and **poststructuralists** attached to the radical journal *Tel Quel*. Kristeva's earliest major work was *Revolution in Poetic Language*, published in 1974, in which she set out her basic theories concerning language and its role in the construction of identity. She differs from **Freud** and **Lacan** in siting the origin of language in the pre-**Oedipal** phase, where the relationship between mother and child is still intact. In what Kristeva terms the '**semiotic**', the child has no sense of itself as possessing an identity separate from its mother, and therefore perceives no need for a means of communication between self and **Other**. However, its existence is regulated by physical drives, pulsations and impulses which the child gradually learns to order and control, and it is this which forms the ground for the practice of signification.

The Oedipal crisis signals the intervention of the father in the dyadic relationship between mother and child, and initiates the child's movement into language. Within the symbolic order, the child becomes an independent **subject**, and so depends upon language both to define the content of the world around it and to communicate with other independent subjects. However, the symbolic does not supersede the semiotic: instead, the two 'modalities' combine in order to form a **discourse**.

For Kristeva, therefore, language is not a fixed system, but an ongoing process, since meaning is generated out of the dynamic interplay between semiotic and symbolic, whereby each modality regulates the other. The energies of the semiotic allow for a flexible and creative use of language to produce new meanings, but without the ordering abilities of the symbolic it becomes incomprehensible 'psychotic' babbling. In contrast, the symbolic attempts to create an exact correspondence between word and object, but without the compensating presence of the symbolic, which deteriorates into a totalitarian urge to control what is 'Other' by maintaining an absolute distinction between it and the self.

Different modes of discourse are formed out of the vacillating relationship between symbolic and semiotic. In scientific language, for example, the semiotic is almost entirely repressed, since it allows for very little slippage between the word and the thing described. However, in poetic language, the dominance of semiotics is manifested through rhythm, syntactic irregularities and linguistic distortions such as metaphor, metonymy and musicality.

However, in spite of the fact that the semiotic is identified with the mother, its use is not gender-linked, for Kristeva differs from Cixous and Irigaray in arguing against the kind of linguistic essentialism which claims that men and women have a different relationship to language. By this token, poetic, rhythmic or expressive language is not the especial province of women, any more than scientific discourse is necessarily 'masculine'. Indeed, the writers Kristeva most frequently cites as creative exponents of the semiotic impulse, such as Mallarmé and James Joyce, are male.

Kristeva has kept a consistent distance between herself and the wider feminist movement, claiming that she objects to an agenda that seeks political **power** within existing bourgeois frameworks. She argues that it is in danger of becoming another 'master discourse' which, rather than posing a fundamental challenge to the hierarchical distinction between centre and margins, will do no more than reverse the familiar powerful/powerless opposition. As she states in her essay 'Women's Time' (1979), 'The very logic of counter-power and of counter-society necessarily generates, by its very structure, its essence as a **simulacrum** of the combated society or of power.'

In this essay, Kristeva identifies two stages in the history of feminism. Before 1968, the feminist demand was for an equal place *within* history and the order of linear time. After 1968, feminism's second generation emphasized women's essential **difference** from men, and their right to remain *outside* the historical and political realm. Both positions, however, have their disadvantages. While the first generation surrendered the semiotic power of the maternal, the second runs the risk of being completely identified with it, to the extent that any ability to relate to the symbolic may be lost. The challenge for feminism, as Kristeva sees it, is to reconcile maternal time, or motherhood, with the historical and political order of linear time, in order to institute a third option: a fluid discourse which, allowing for multiplicity and difference, abolishes the distinction between centre and margins altogether. [SG]

KUHN, THOMAS: PHILOSOPHER AND HISTORIAN OF SCIENCE (1922–) Originally trained as a physicist, Kuhn soon moved into the philosophy and history of science, and his work there, particularly on scientific method, has had reverberations well outside his chosen fields. The author of several important books, Kuhn is best known for *The Structure of Scientific Revolutions* (1962), where he outlined his controversial concept of 'paradigm' (basically meaning 'framework of thought'): a concept which has come to be widely adopted in critical debate across a range of intellectual disciplines.

Kuhn adopted a much more radical view of the history of science than most of his peers, for whom it was in general to be seen as a steady process of accumulation of knowledge that led, fairly inexorably, to our current state of technical and theoretical sophistication. For Kuhn, on the other hand, the history of science was a much more exciting and even chaotic affair, where revolutions of thought periodically occurred and new theories swept away older ones. Scientific revolutions were, therefore, the norm, and each successful revolution brought with it a new paradigm which, crucially, was incompatible with the old. Thus the change from Ptolemaic to Copernican astronomy (the Earth as the centre of the universe to the Sun as the centre), involved two contrasting worldviews which could not be reconciled: one had to believe either one or the other.

Kuhn explored just this topic in *The Copernican Revolution* (1957). A similar **paradigm shift** had accompanied the work of Albert Einstein on relativity (which directly challenged the principles of Newtonian physics), and in recent years such shifts have tended to occur with, as far as the general public is concerned, somewhat bewildering regularity.

Once a paradigm established itself, what Kuhn called 'normal science' took over. Normal science consisted of applying the current set of theories to phenomena in the world around us, and trying to plug as many of the gaps in our knowledge as possible: 'puzzle solving' in Kuhn's terminology. Most scientists' careers consisted, in fact, of just such puzzle solving, conducted according to the principles of the current paradigm. The dominant theory would be persevered with even if it left some problems unanswered, and, if necessary, ad hoc adjustments would be made to try and save its authority. Problems that persistently resisted solution (such as the precise path of the planets in Ptolemaic astronomy) would eventually, however, call the dominant scientific theory into question, ushering in a period of instability, and featuring various competing theories, which would finally be resolved by the institution of a new paradigm able to explain previous anomalies. Thus Copernican astronomy could predict the positions of the planets with far greater accuracy than the Ptolemaic system could, and without the host of ad hoc adjustments that Ptolemaic astronomy had latterly required.

The degree of **incommensurability** in world-view between an old and new paradigm meant that believers in the old paradigm could not always be converted to the cause of the new, and it was often the case, as Kuhn pointed out, that the new paradigm did not become completely dominant until the older generation of scientists opposing it had died out. For Kuhn, scientific revolution is a necessary and vital part of scientific history, and he sees many parallels with political history in this regard. In both cases the goal is to change institutions which have become set in their ways, and more concerned with maintaining their privileges and aura of authority than admitting the value, indeed the necessity, of new ideas and methods.

Kuhn's importance for **postmodernism** lies in the notion that one paradigm is not necessarily better than another, but simply constitutes another way of looking at things. In postmodern terms of reference, paradigms are effectively '**narratives**', some more believable than others no doubt, but none of which can claim to be in possession of the absolute truth. Each constitutes a world-view which could be supplanted by other worldviews. Kuhn's ideas have been highly controversial and, particularly in philosophy-of-science circles, the notion of paradigm has been attacked as both vague and too neat an explanation of historical process. Sir Karl Popper was a vociferous critic of Kuhn's views, and the debate conducted between the two men and their supporters dominated the philosophy of science for much of the 1960s and 1970s. Outside the philosophy of science, the notion of paradigm has had a considerable vogue, particularly in the context of debates about cultural change. [SS]

L

LACAN, JACQUES: PSYCHOANALYST (1901–81) Along with Claude **Lévi-Strauss**, Michel **Foucault** and Roland **Barthes**, the psychoanalyst and philosopher Jacques Lacan was one of the central figures of French 'high' **structuralism**. Like Foucault and Barthes, his work has proved adaptable and fertile enough to continue to influence **poststructuralist** and **postmodernist** thought. Indeed Lacan is one of the founding fathers of postmodernism – his dense, difficult and convoluted prose, cut with puns, heavy with allusion; his giddying flights of fancy; his often apocalyptic style, have all influenced postmodernist **discourse**. Lacan became something of a celebrity with the publication of a collection of articles and other pieces, *Écrits*, in 1965. Transcriptions of his weekly seminars, held for the training of psychoanalysts, continue to appear.

Although Lacan's work could be seen as an extended debate with Sigmund **Freud**, it is a debate illuminated by Lacan's plundering of **Hegel**, surrealism, structuralist linguistics and the anthropology of Lévi-Strauss. Lévi-Strauss had shown how Saussure's structuralist method could be used to understand kinship relationships and primitive myths, and Lacan, from the early 1950s until his death in 1981, attempted to employ the same methods to map the underlying structure of the human psyche.

Like the other great structuralists, Lacan begins with language. In many ways his work is the extension of Saussure's insights into language to the operation of the mind. Perhaps his most famous statement is the claim that the unconscious is structured like a language. This means that the unconscious works with the same tools as language, and that it only comes into existence *because of* language. Saussure had argued that it is the overall structure of a language, the system of **differences**, that gives language the ability to *mean*. For Saussure the link between a word (the signifier) and the idea it conveys (the signified) is purely arbitrary; nevertheless, he argues that there is a certain stability in the relationship. Lacan, like Jacques **Derrida**, challenges that cosy relationship. For Lacan words always refer to other words: signifiers form a chain along which we slip without ever reaching a fixed or definite meaning. A sentence can always be added to, and that addition can completely reverse its meaning. Metaphor and metonymy, both of which involve the substitution of one signifier for another, further disrupt the links between signifier and signified.

Lacan's emphasis on language is part of his reaction against the reductionist, biological reading of Freud prevalent among Freud's American followers. Lacan's 'return to Freud' is in reality a return to the earlier works of the master, such as *The Interpretation of Dreams* and the *Psychopathology of Everyday Life*, in which the biological origins of our thoughts, emotions and behaviour are de-emphasized in favour of social or cultural factors. Lacan extends the reach of these non-biological forces, interpreting, for example, the **Oedipus** complex as a linguistic transaction: the incest taboo is a cultural phenomenon, reliant on the linguistic categories of 'father' and 'mother', quite independent of any biological instinct or need.

Indeed, for Lacan, the biological concept of need is largely displaced by the concept of **desire**. A need can be gratified, but desire is irrepressible. A child has a need for its mother's milk, which can be gratified, but it desires its mother's love and that desire for love can never be satisfied.

Lacan's model of development involves three interlinked 'orders' – the imaginary, the symbolic and the real. The imaginary phase comes with the child's recognition of itself in the mirror, when it sees itself for the first time as a coherent entity, rather than some fragmented, ill-assorted jumble of fleshy odds and ends. But this unity is illusory, an ideal of integration. From the imaginary, the child emerges into the symbolic – the world of culture, of language, and in particular the world of signifiers. It is the realm of culture in which the human subject comes into existence, a world ruled over by the symbolic 'name of the Father', which acts as an enforcer of stability, the word of the law. The real is not in any sense the 'real world' but is that which evades images and symbols, a threatening absence lurking behind the symptoms of neurosis.

Lacan has had a great influence on literary studies and, in particular, feminist theory. Feminists have valued Lacan's emphasis on the cultural/linguistic origins of gender differentiation, which seems to offer an escape from brutalist biological theories of sexual difference. Feminists are, however, sharply critical of the patriarchal assumptions deeply embedded in Lacan's discourse. [AM]

LACLAU, ERNESTO: POLITICAL THEORIST (1935–) Laclau is one of the major names in the field of **post-Marxism**, especially in terms of his collaborative work with the political philosopher Chantal **Mouffe** (although he has also published widely under his own name). Laclau and Mouffe's major collaborative work, *Hegemony and Socialist Strategy* (1985) is now regarded as one of the most important contributions to the development of post-Marxism as a distinctive theoretical position in its own right.

As a theoretical movement post-Marxism might best be described as an uneasy coalition between those who have rejected Marxist beliefs altogether, and those who wish to synthesize **Marxism** with more recent cultural and philosophical theories such as **deconstruction**, feminism and **postmodernism**. In the former camp we would place figures such as Jean-François **Lyotard**, Michel **Foucault** and Jean **Baudrillard**, all of whom have, in their own way, turned their backs on Marxism in their later careers; in the latter we would place Laclau and Mouffe, who see their goal as a revitalization of the Marxist tradition to take account of rapidly changing cultural circumstances. Post-Marxism is, therefore, as much as anything a matter of the attitude adopted towards Marxism's heritage. *Hegemony and Socialist Strategy* is a bold plea for Marxism to be revised, such that it sheds some of its authoritarian image and makes itself attractive to a new audience sceptical of the notion of universally applicable theories.

Laclau and Mouffe identify a crisis in Marxist thought, arguing that the cultural climate has changed so radically over the course of the twentieth century that most of what were taken to be the 'evident truths' of classical Marxism, such as a belief in homogeneous social classes (the working class, for example), or the historical inevitability of socialism, can no longer stand up to close scrutiny. Put bluntly, Marxism must now reorient itself or go into terminal decline. The authors float the idea of a 'radical democratic politics' that would encompass both Marxism and the various new social movements (such as feminism, the **Greens**, or ethnic and sexual minorities) that have sprung up in recent times, as well as new developments in the field of theory. They describe their approach as broadly deconstructive in that they are trying to point out instabilities and paradoxes in Marxist thought, thus undermining its claims to authority. In effect, they are arguing that Marxism is in danger of becoming irrelevant and has to be brought up to date, meaning that it must embrace political **pluralism** and dispense with the dogmatism of classical Marxist thought, which saw itself as the theory to end all theories and could only regard any commitment to pluralism as heresy. Laclau and Mouffe therefore call for a 'democratic revolution' where the left consciously establishes as many links as it can with the new social movements, rather than, as was the more usual practice, trying to impose its own ideology on all political struggles in an authoritarian manner. It is precisely that authoritarianism that Laclau and Mouffe wish to see eradicated.

Laclau and Mouffe's ideas have given rise to considerable controversy, with traditionally oriented Marxists dismissing the notion that Marxism is in any need of 'improvement' or has anything of note to learn from theories such as deconstruction. To go beyond Marxism is, for such an audience, to betray its heritage, not to revitalize it. Laclau and Mouffe have replied in robust fashion to their critics, reiterating their belief in the necessity of reformulating the socialist project such that it is more receptive to new ideas, although for many on the left the new ideas are incompatible with socialism. Their Marxism can seem no more than residual, although there is no doubting the sincerity of their motives.

From a postmodernist standpoint, Laclau and Mouffe are to be seen as representative of the decline of Marxism as a '**grand narrative**' (they are certainly unwilling to defend its claim to be a universal theory in possession of absolute truth), and part of the new wave of pluralism that has taken the place of the grand narrative tradition in general. Where they differ from post-Marxists such as Lyotard, Foucault and Baudrillard is in their desire to retain something of the spirit of Marxism, even if they are no longer prepared to adhere strictly to the letter. [SS]

LATOUR, BRUNO: SOCIOLOGIST (1947–) Latour has been critical of the projects of both **modernity** and **postmodernity**, arguing of the latter that it is a symptom of, rather than any effective solution to, cultural crisis. As the title of his best-known book has it, Latour believes *We Have Never Been Modern* (1991); therefore it makes no sense at all to claim to be postmodern: you cannot be 'after' what has not yet occurred. He rejects the notion, popularised by **modernists**, that there has been a definitive break with the past from the period of the **Enlightenment** onwards. Latour tends instead to emphasize cultural continuity rather than rupture, describing himself as being 'non-modern' (or 'amodern'). To be non-modern is to refuse to accept the separation of nature and culture encouraged by modern thought, with science and politics inhabiting different realms. For Latour, nature and culture, science and politics, are inextricably mixed up, and we stop being modern when we recognize this. We are confronted by '**hybrids**' of nature and culture, such as the debate on the ozone layer, that demand a rethinking of our socio-political institutions. Neither modernity nor postmodernity offers the means to do this, in Latour's opinion, and he posits instead a 'Middle Kingdom' where the distinction between nature and culture will be erased, and hybrids become the focus of attention. In his projected 'Non-modern Constitution', freedom becomes redefined as the capacity to choose culturally beneficial hybrids, and democracy as the state where such hybrids are nurtured.

Latour has written extensively on the sociology of science. His co-**authored** book (with Steve Woolgar) *Laboratory Life: Social Construction of Scientific Facts* (1979), is an example of what has become known as the 'constructionist' view of science, in which scientific facts (in this case, the discovery of a particular hormone in the human brain) are held to be as much the product of research imperatives and funding mechanisms as any scientific 'truth'. The supposed objective of scientific method is called into question by such studies. For all his criticism of the postmodern movement, Latour's work in this area seems very close to its concerns. [SS]

LEGITIMATION To speak of the legitimation of a theory or political system is to speak of what gives it authority. Thus **Marxism** regards itself as based on scientific principles, as opposed to mere ideologies which set out to excuse the domination of one part of society by another: what legitimates Marxism is its status as a 'science of society', rigorous in execution and free of sectional interest. Similarly, Western liberal democracy takes its authority from a particular conception of the individual human being as the possessor of certain inalienable rights (right to equality before the law, to own property, to sell one's labour on the open market, etc.); the political system of Western societies is legitimated by its protection of those rights.

Thinkers like **Lyotard** consider that there is a crisis of legitimation in the **postmodern** world, in that theories such as Marxism (**grand narratives** or **metanarratives** in Lyotard's terminology) have had their authority called into question to the point where there is open incredulity towards them. We can no longer rely on grand narratives to solve all our socio-political problems; rather, we have to realize that they are the *source* of most of these problems, by arousing hopes that they cannot fulfil. Marxism also demands uncritical acceptance of certain key principles (the desirability of the dictatorship of the proletariat, etc.), and for Lyotard this is authoritarian and a suppression of individual creativity. Generally speaking, postmodernist thinkers are suspicious of most means of legitimation in the twentieth century, tending to find authoritarianism lurking behind the scenes in some guise or another. [SS]

LÉVI-STRAUSS, CLAUDE: ANTHROPOLOGIST, CULTURAL THEORIST (1908–) Lévi-Strauss originally studied law and philosophy, but eventually turned to anthropology to become one of the subject's leading voices in the twentieth century. He has also been one of the most prominent figures in the **structuralist** movement, and his various anthropological studies are considered classics of the structuralist approach. Given his eminent status in this regard, Lévi-Strauss has been a prime target of the **poststructuralist** movement, which has been highly critical of the methodology lying behind his structural anthropology, in particular its system-building bias.

Lévi-Strauss's overriding concern has been to identify the underlying deep structures of cultural phenomena, and his research tends to concentrate on finding patterns and common features within those phenomena, which are taken to be structured on the model of language. In one of his most famous pieces of analysis in *The Raw and the Cooked* (1964), a group of apparently disparate South American tribal myths are argued to be variations on a theme, having a similar underlying structure and narrative elements which undergo subtle modifications (or 'transformations') from tale to tale.

Like all structuralist theorists, Lévi-Strauss makes extensive use of **binary oppositions**, with the nature/culture distinction being one of his main ways of classifying human behaviour. The theory is that all instances of human behaviour must belong to one or other of these mutually exclusive categories, but Lévi-Strauss himself is forced to admit that the incest taboo seems to fall into both. **Derrida** has been particularly critical of

Lévi-Strauss on this issue, arguing that his admission casts doubt on structuralist methodology in general and the principle of binary opposition in particular. Lévi-Strauss becomes for Derrida symbolic of the structuralist desire to make everything fit into pre-arranged, ordered systems – a tendency he regards as authoritarian. [SS]

LEVINAS, EMMANUEL: PHILOSOPHER (1905–95) Born in Lithuania to a Jewish family, Levinas subsequently studied philosophy in France. In 1928 he travelled to Freiburg to study phenomenology with Edmund **Husserl**, and was introduced to the work of Martin **Heidegger**. Later, after gaining French citizenship, it was largely Levinas who introduced German phenomenology to France. Levinas became associated with the French existential branch of phenomenology, influencing Jean-Paul Sartre, Simone de Beauvoir, Gabriel Marcel, Jean Wahl, Maurice Merleau-Ponty and Maurice Blanchot. But the first major publication of his own original philosophy appeared in 1961 with *Totalité et infinité*. This work combined a radical critique of Western philosophy with a retrieval of the pre-Platonic tradition of Hebrew thought, bringing Levinas's formative ideas to the attention of the **postmodern** world.

The roots of Levinas's philosophy lie in both his Jewish background and his original work deriving from German phenomenology. But these roots alone do not explain the enormous impact which Levinas's works written after he turned fifty-five had upon the subsequent generation of philosophers. Jacques **Derrida**'s critical essay of 1964, 'Violence et métaphysique: Essai sur la pensée d'Emmanuel Levinas', greatly influenced the reception of Levinas internationally by postmodern thinkers. Derrida contributes to Levinas's reputation with respect for and criticism of his efforts to move beyond Western metaphysics. Publication of Levinas's second major work *Autrement qu'être ou Au delà de l'essence* (*Otherwise Than Being or Beyond Essence*) in 1974 represented a new stage in his thinking. Here he endeavours to renew and revise more thoroughly the methods of philosophy after Heidegger. The revisionary core of Levinas has been approached from many perspectives as part of the climate of postmodern thought. But these perspectives converge on Levinas's account of the relation between the **Other** and oneself, elaborating his concern with the external authority that relates the Other to the same without, however, uniting them.

Levinas writes movingly of the meeting with the Other as an encounter with 'the human in the total nudity of its eyes'. The Other is not a potential threat, but a demand that 'Thou shalt not kill'. Levinas's whole oeuvre demonstrates the wisdom of an exhausting love for the Other (*philia*) rather than the contemplation of the wisdom that has dominated the history of Western philosophy. The phrase that both encapsulates the wisdom of *philia* and echoes the postmodern claim to the end of Western metaphysics is Levinas's 'ethics as first philosophy'. Here ethics points to something radical and originary. Instead of seeing the theory of the good as the ultimate level of human perfection, Levinas insists that the practice of the good transcends contemplation. Such practice reveals the birthplace of all theoretical relationships as prior to any ontological origin, in one's ethical relation to the Other: that is, in 'one's being-for-the-Other'. To illustrate this, Levinas uses the face of the Other. There is an authority in the face which commands me not to leave this mortal Other to dwell alone. This imperative is not a universal command but a particular responsibility of mine for the Other.

However, debate continues in feminist circles over Levinas's implicit form of patriarchy. Notwithstanding his highly influential account of Otherness, the contention is that Levinas ultimately subordinates the feminine to the masculine. In his 1947 text, *Le temps et l'autre* (*Time and the Other*), the figure of the feminine serves as the paradigm in Levinas's account of the absolutely Other, in his discussion of eros. But even in this early work he exhibits a certain suspicion of femininity. Next in his 1961 text, and later in *Otherwise Than Being* the feminine Other is gradually reduced to the role of mother. As Levinas becomes increasingly concerned with the ethical relation between self and Other, his early interest in eros and so in the feminine Other decreases. Instead he turns to paternity and the face-to-face relation between father and son. The erotic falls short of an ethical relation because it involves a return to self. Levinas defines the Other in terms of the paternal God's relation to his son, while leaving the feminine Other without her own specific face.

Ultimately for Levinas ethics in its feminine achievement means to be a mother, nothing else, and so the meaning of the Other as a passive body and a failure of virility can be learned from the mother. Yet perhaps the feminine can also achieve the disruption of being with goodness beyond maternity in a utopian identity for the other. [PSA]

LIBIDINAL ECONOMY Libidinal economy is Jean-François **Lyotard**'s term for the various drives within human beings that resist the workings of logic and reason. These are to be seen as analogous to the subconscious drives identified by psychoanalytical theorists such as **Freud**, although Lyotard is perhaps more openly in favour of their free expression than most psychoanalytical theorists, and more prone to celebrate their anarchic, socially disordering effect. One of Lyotard's major objections to **Marxism** is that it fails to allow any place for these drives within its theories, seeing them as irrational and unpredictable, and therefore to be resisted. For Lyotard, however, the denial of libidinal

drives in this way is an authoritarian act, and one that ultimately can only be unsuccessful: the drives will always find some means of expression and cannot be suppressed indefinitely. He goes so far as to suggest that the working class in the nineteenth century identified with industrialization as a massive outburst of libidinal energy, and that where Marxists saw simply exploitation the workers instead saw excitement, variety and change.

Libidinal economy is therefore to be regarded as a direct attack on Marxism as both a philosophy and a cultural project. In a more general sense it also constitutes a rejection of philosophy's rationalist heritage, to the extent that it has been dubbed a post- and even anti-philosophical notion. The context of the theory is important to note: Lyotard's book *Libidinal Economy* was published in 1974; that is, in the aftermath of the 1968 *événements* when many French left-wing intellectuals had become severely disenchanted by Marxism, largely as a result of the failure of the French Communist Party to support the anti-state cause. *Libidinal Economy* represents one of the most vicious attacks on Marxist thought of the period, and charts a sea change in Lyotard's own career. [SS]

LITTLE NARRATIVE In the **grand narratives** of Jean-François **Lyotard** (all-embracing explanatory theories such as **Marxism** or **Hegelian** dialectics) individuals are oppressed and find themselves being sacrificed to the objectives of those controlling the grand narrative. Thus Marxism in its Soviet model demanded that all individuals follow the Communist Party line, since the Party was assumed to be the repository of all truth. Lyotard points out how this destroys individual initiative, leading to a totalitarian society where dissent is ruthlessly repressed and creativity stifled. The failings of grand narratives had, however, been well recognized by the late twentieth century (thus the collapse of the

Soviet Union and its client states), and what we should now be supporting is little narratives. These are tactical groupings (or coalitions of interest) which seek to oppose specific social ills. Little narratives, of which the worker–student collaboration in the 1968 *événements* in Paris remains an outstanding example for Lyotard, are not designed to last, but merely to achieve limited, short-term objectives. One might regard the individual as the ultimate little narrative seeking to resist the **power** of authoritarian grand narratives, such as the state or multinational corporations. [SS]

LOGOCENTRICITY Logocentricity is the assumption that words can unproblematically communicate meanings present in individual's minds such that the listener, or reader, receives them in the same way as the speaker/hearer intended. Words and meanings are therefore considered to have an internal stability. This is a standard assumption of **discourse** in Western culture, but one that has come under attack from the **deconstructionist** movement. Jacques **Derrida** in particular regards this as an unsustainable position to adopt, on the basis that words always carry **traces** of previous meanings, as well as suggesting other words which sound similar to the one being used. [SS]

LYNCH, DAVID: FILM DIRECTOR (1946–) Lynch's work foregrounds the painterly and non-**narrative** in films of subversive disquiet. His first major film, *Eraserhead*, was completed in 1976, establishing his taste for surrealist juxtaposition and exploration of psyche, through an unsettling use of the absurd and banal. This was followed by *The Elephant Man* of 1980, his most conventional film but equally concerned with the bizarre and monstrous in its account of the deformed John Merrick. *Dune* (1984), a science-fiction thriller, was a much publicized failure, but Lynch recovered to move into mainstream Hollywood cinema with

his most popular films *Blue Velvet* (1986) and the Cannes Film Festival Palme d'Or winner *Wild at Heart* (1990). In 1990–1 he embraced the most popular of screen forms, the TV soap serial, becoming a household name with the unprecedented success of *Twin Peaks*, co-written with Mark Frost. This transferred to the big screen as *Twin Peaks: Fire Walk With Me* (1992).

Critics have felt that Lynch's work sits uneasily in commercial Hollywood cinema. It is considered to tread too fine a line between elitist art house and mainstream popular appeal, resulting in a series of shocking images lacking substance. Not least Lynch's disregard for traditional narrative and plot, transgressing all the conventions of Hollywood film, identify him as an anomaly within mainstream cinema. Lynch's achievement, however, could be said to rest with the very translation of such qualities into commercial success. The mainstay of his style draws upon the staples of **postmodern** aesthetics: a love of parody and cliché; an eclectic use of film genre, from high art *film noir* and surrealism to horror to pornography; an interrogation of surface image and employment of psychoanalysis to probe that surface and reveal the hidden and **abject** where least expected.

Lynch's territory is small-town America, his point of crisis the American dream, whose wholesome quality becomes exaggerated to parody and in turn unease. The overstated colour of the suburban lawn and picket fence in the opening scene of *Blue Velvet* is the facade for a darker, more transgressive existence. Reinforcing this transgression, our entry into this dangerous but compelling world is in voyeuristic glimpses. In *Blue Velvet* we first see the horror of Dorothy's world through the innocent eyes of Jeffrey secreted in her wardrobe; in *Eraserhead* Henry spies on his seductress through the keyhole of his apartment; and in *Twin Peaks* Audrey witnesses her father's illicit deals through a peephole in his office.

Reflecting postmodern notions of artifice as the reality of contemporary experience, Lynch's world is one of cliché and pastiche with images that exist for themselves rather than for any inherent meaning or interpretation. Trained as a painter, Lynch excels in the purely visual; but criticism of his work as devoid of characterization ignores his iconographic and self-conscious use of motif. The recurring velvet curtain, for example, suggests surface and the intrigue of what surface conceals, providing an anticipation of revelation but not necessarily establishing meaning. Seductive but artificial, it is utilized to aid psychopath Frank's masturbation fantasies in *Blue Velvet*, while in *Twin Peaks* it is the fabric of the ambiguous red room containing the unspeakable truth of Laura's death. Lynch's work revolves around the surfacing of what is hidden. In this he remains true to his surrealist beginnings, although his mature style suggests the transformation of these sources through postmodern experience.

Mulholland Drive (2001), a film derived from a rejected TV series, demonstrates that Lynch has lost none of his ability to tease and intrigue his audience through eccentric storylines, parody and pastiche. [EO]

LYOTARD, JEAN-FRANÇOIS: PHILOSOPHER (1928–99) A prolific and protean writer, Lyotard himself described his wildly divergent paths through philosophy, politics and art as 'promiscuous'. In the English-speaking world he is chiefly renowned for *The Postmodern Condition* (1979), a work which has been regarded as unrepresentative of his oeuvre, but in which many of his earlier interests are drawn together, as can be seen from his extended conversations with Jean-Loup Thébaud, concerning that text and his previous works, and published as *Just Gaming* (1979), and from his summative statement of 1988, *Peregrinations*.

In many ways, Lyotard's work never left the paradigms with which it began: principally, the synthesis of **Freud** and **Marx** which so troubled French intellectuals, from Althusser to Deleuze, in the early 1970s. Although most evident in *Libidinal Economy* (1974), traces of these concerns remain evident in *The Differend* (1984) and in the 1993 re-publication of a collection of essays from 1973 on matters libidinal, political, **postmodern** and aesthetic, *Des dispositifs pulsionnels* (*The Drives and their Apparatuses*).

Like other aspects of his thought, Lyotard's political theory polarizes around **events**: the Algerian war of independence provided his earliest foray into political terrain, during which time he was teaching in Algeria and monitoring the situation for the radical Trotskyite group, Socialisme ou Barbarie. During this time, Lyotard professed a faith in the central tenets of Marxism, although this commitment excommunicated him from his comrades in the former group in 1966, when he joined Workers' Power. But his political articles of faith were to disappear altogether with the *événements* of May 1968, where a popular revolt nearly brought down the Gaullist government, despite accusations of 'childishness' directed at the broad coalition of activists by the largely uninvolved official left and fringe left intellectuals. Far from following the French Communist Party in carping about the theoretical and practical inadequacies of the events, Lyotard condemned the Marxists for failing to follow the initiative seized in the streets, and split definitively with them, the bitterest fruit of which can still be sampled in *Libidinal Economy*.

The collapse of this particular **grand narrative** is what provoked Lyotard to adopt the analysis of the 'end of ideology' proffered by the politically right-of-centre theorist of post-industrial society, Daniel **Bell**. But it also led him to proclaim the dawn of a **postmodernity** in politics: a consistent and extended rewriting of politics, its goals, its methods and its ideals, that has resulted in his own philosophical turn to 'Kant after Marx' and Freud, and in his rejection of the hegemony of political – and libidinal – economy in favour of analyses of the potentialities for thought and action offered by the raw materials of the social bond found in exchanges of sentences. This philosophical 'back to basics' campaign, reaching its fullest philosophical statement in *The Differend*, may seem to reduce the scope of Lyotard's focus from politics, aesthetics and philosophy to another, very **modern** 'linguistic turn' paralleling the later philosophy of Ludwig Wittgenstein, on whose concept of a society linguistically *and therefore* conceptually and practically composed of 'language games' Lyotard drew in *The Postmodern Condition.* However, far from flattening out the field of postmodern **events** and enclosing them within the enfranchisable horizons of linguistic possibilities, linguistic events come to form the 'particles in Brownian motion' that unpredictably coalesce into extremely heterogeneous series of social, political, aesthetic, scientific and technological phenomena, allowing Lyotard's philosophy to explore everything from the minutiae of the **narrative** organization of modern philosophies to the fate of thinking after the death of our system's Sun.

The question, however, that continues to hang over this body of thought, and to which Lyotard constantly returned, concerns the political bite of his analyses. His famously weak response to the crises of limited information flow in computerized societies, that the public ought to be given free access to the data banks, perhaps suggests that nothing has yet replaced the power of modernity's Marxist narrative in terms of its critical and imaginative power, at the same time as, perhaps **ironically**, the reasons behind Lyotard's often vicious rejection of that programme are more compelling still. This dichotomy lies at the core of Lyotardian postmodernity: our modern programmes are refuted, yet there are no successors. Postmodernity is therefore a period without a programme, working over the accumulated debits against one modernity while experimenting with its roots to invent another. It is in this sense that postmodernity comes not at the end, but at the beginning of modernity. [IHG]

McLuhan, Marshall: cultural theorist
(1911–80) Marshall McLuhan makes a
cameo appearance in Woody Allen's film
Annie Hall (1977). He pops up in a cinema
queue to support an opinion expressed by
the central character, who is trying to
impress a girlfriend. McLuhan's fame,
however, extends far beyond these fifteen
seconds. As founder and director of the
University of Toronto's Centre for Culture
and Technology in the 1960s and 1970s he
invented the subject of media and communication studies virtually single-handed.

McLuhan's first book, *The Mechanical
Bride* (1951) consists of fifty-nine short
pieces which scrutinize adverts, comic strips
and the front pages of newspapers for
evidence of what he calls the 'replaceable
parts' dynamics of Western society. His
central thesis is that to industrial man
everything is mechanizable, even – especially – sex (the book's title comes from a
hosiery ad in which two detached female
legs are displayed on a pedestal). McLuhan
has a lynx's eye for the absurd heterogeneous yokings of popular culture, such as
the newspaper headline 'Scientists Await
Cow's Death to Solve Mathematics
Problem'.

The Gutenberg Galaxy (1962) abandons
the detached, fixed perspective of the
scholarly study and adopts instead a
'mosaic or field approach'. So the book
presents 310 short meditations on the consequences of the invention of the printing
press and the advent of 'Typographic Man'.
Each section is preceded by a provocative
gloss: 'The new electronic interdependence recreates the world in the image of a
global village' and 'Heidegger surf-boards

along on the electronic wave as triumph-
antly as Descartes rode the mechanical
wave' are two examples. In both statements
– one brilliant, the other banal – we find
foreshadowings of **postmodernist** culture.
The **Internet** has indeed created a global
village, and at least forty million people
worldwide surf its electronic waves on a
regular basis.

In *Understanding Media* (1964), McLuhan
looks at the threats to the mechanized,
print-oriented regime posed by the new
electronic media. Separate chapters on
telephones, the phonograph and television
demonstrate how each development
extends the capacities of the human nervous
system, and alters our perceptual 'sense-
ratio'. Again, many of McLuhan's comments prefigure postmodernist obsessions
with machines and distortions of the
body, particularly in the work of Jean
Baudrillard and Paul **Virilio**. After the
publication of this book, McLuhan's own
life became an exemplification of his ideas.
His fame was fed by the very media he
flattered. Within a short period of time he
was not only the subject of some intense
intellectual debate (with contributions by
Raymond Williams, Susan Sontag, George
Steiner *et al.*), but he became a kind of guru
to the tuned-in and the turned-on. He has
some claim to being called the first genuine
television talking head.

He has had his critics. Dwight Macdonald
moaned about McLuhan's lack of interest
in cultural standards, and Christopher Ricks
castigated McLuhan's style as a 'viscous
fog, through which loom stumbling metaphors'. In many ways, however, it was
his catholicness (though not, perhaps, his

Catholicness) which led the general public to take him seriously. Like Andy Warhol and the Beatles in their own respective fields, he championed the breakdown of distinctions between high and low culture which theorists such as Fredric **Jameson** see as symptomatic of the postmodern.

McLuhan's *The Medium is the Message* (1967), *War and Peace in the Global Village* (1968) and *Counterblast* (1969) are visual jamborees, collages of photographs, cartoons, slogans and jokes. Pick any page and you will find an iconic image and an oracular aphorism. One chosen at random from *The Medium is the Message* shows a shadowy profile of Bob Dylan, captioned with lines from one of his lyrics: 'Because something is happening / But you don't know what it is / Do you, Mister Jones?' The same book closes with a 1966 cartoon from the *New Yorker* in which a bemused, besuited gentleman (Mr Jones?) is sitting in his study, while his check-shirted, guitar-toting son explains to him:

> You see, Dad, Professor McLuhan says the environment that man creates becomes his medium for defining his role in it. The invention of type created linear, or sequential, thought, separating thought from action. Now, with TV and folk singing, thought and action are closer and social involvement is greater. We again live in a village. Get it?

By the look on his face, Mr Jones *didn't* get it. Something was happening and he did not know what it was. McLuhan *did* get it, and he did know what it was: it was nothing other than the 'brand-new world of allatonceness', aka postmodernism. [BL]

MAGIC REALISM As the term itself suggests, magic realism is a form founded on the juxtaposition of two modes of **representation** which normally exist in opposition: realism and the fantastic. Although the term is now almost exclusively associated with literature, it was originally coined by Franz Roh in 1925 to describe a form of art that portrayed scenes of fantasy and imagination through the use of clear-cut, 'documentary' painting techniques. It is, however, primarily identified with the writing of Latin America, where authors such as Gabriel Garcia Marquez, Carlos Fuentes and Octavio Paz create **narratives** in which the realistic elements of the **text** are continually being undercut by the intrusion of impossible or inexplicable events. In this context, magic realism is also a politicized term, since it charts the contradictory responses of a **postcolonial** culture that is engaged in the process of recovering a lost past, while remaining unable completely to escape the lingering influence of its more recent colonial history.

Since the 1970s, however, magic realism has become a fashionable label for any writing that subverts realistic expectations, and has been particularly associated with the work of writers such as Salman **Rushdie**, Angela **Carter** and Jeanette **Winterson**, all of whom exploit the disruptive potential of fantasy in order to pose a challenge to cultural perceptions of 'normality'. [SG]

MANDELBROT, BENOIT: MATHEMATICIAN, SCIENTIST (1924–) Working both outside the academy, for IBM, and in a variety of academic fields, including pure and applied mathematics, physiology and economics, Mandelbrot found his intellectual feet by inventing what, in 1963, he modestly entitled 'the new scientific discipline' of **fractal** geometry. Fractal geometry studies the form of what traditional Euclidean geometry expelled from its ideal world of straight lines and perfect curves: the 'pathological' forms of mountains, the exact measurement of coastlines, clouds and so on. Mandelbrot's researches, presented in detail in *The Fractal Geometry of Nature* (1977), turn this redundant paradigm's idealist prejudice into a realist error, insofar as they reveal that it is fractals that are the norm in nature, and that perfect curves are, on the contrary, inestimably rare.

It is for this 'revolution' in geometry that **Lyotard** singles out Mandelbrot as an exemplar of **postmodern science**, and, by extension, as providing a model of post-modern practice: if the aim of postmodern science is no longer to seek the known, as Lyotard says, but rather the unknown, then fractal geometry fits the bill insofar as it both inverts the principles of traditional geometry and creates new regions of ignorance where, it was thought, things had been well and truly settled. So successfully does fractal geometry model the geometries of phenomena such as coastlines, however, that paradoxically, while the scientific community found them initially unacceptably pathological for theoretical reasons, fractals found a niche in the generation of realistic computer images of unknown planets, such as the Genesis planet in *Star Trek II*, or even the damaged death-star in *Return of the Jedi*.

Like René **Thom**, then, Mandelbrot is interested in topology, the mathematics of form. While Thom remains defiantly abstractive, however, extrapolating from the local events his **catastrophe theory** is intended to analyse, Mandelbrot insists on natural forms as the core of his earthbound geometry. Fractal dimension, however, is not only analytic, but also generative. Thus the other objects of fractal geometry are the dynamical systems that exhibit deterministic **chaos**, and **ironically**, given his commitment to a geometry of natural form, it is in connection with this field that Mandelbrot's work is best known, whether within the academic fields of economics, physiology and mathematics, or through the ubiquitous images of Mandelbrot sets associated with rave culture, beyond them. Far from disparaging this, Mandelbrot tends to celebrate it as an 'aesthetic' of chaos, tempering the cold formalism of mathematics with the 'pure, plastic beauty' generated by fractals. [IHG]

MARCUSE, HERBERT: PHILOSOPHER (1898–1979) Marcuse emerged as a philosopher and scholar within Weimar Germany. After participating in the attempted social democratic revolution in Berlin in 1917 and becoming familiar with the works of **Marx** he went to study with **Heidegger** at Freiburg University in 1928. Marcuse's hopes for a radical new beginning for philosophy (and a synthesis between existentialism and Marxism) led him back to Hegel. In 1932 he published a major study of Hegel and in 1933 he published the first major review of Marx's rediscovered 1844 manuscripts. In 1934 he fled Nazism and emigrated to the USA, where he lived for the rest of his life.

Reason and Revolution (1941) provided a study of the genesis of Hegel's thought and drew Hegel and Marx closer together as social philosophers responding to revolutionary possibilities (and social movements) in the society of their time. Marcuse's thinking was closely related to the Hegelian Marxism – or '**critical theory**' – developed by the members of the **Frankfurt School** (the Institute for Social Research) under the guidance of **Horkheimer** and **Adorno**. *Eros and Civilization* (1955) presented a reading of **Freud** influenced by Marcuse's own existentialist form of Marxism. In it he upheld the view that the liberation of society would need to overcome, or at least transform, that repression which Freud had regarded as constitutive of ego formation and therefore as a constant in civilization. In 1958 Marcuse published *Soviet Marxism*, a study that was critical of developments in the Eastern bloc. *One-Dimensional Man* (1964) traced similarities between the industrialized and bureaucratized societies under advanced capitalism and under Soviet communism. It argued that technology and bureaucracy have taken on a life of their own, imposing their own forms of institutional domination, buttressed by an unreflective scientific (or scientistic) rationality. Despite the pessimism of his main thesis – that the potential for revolution was being drained from **modern**, complex, administered societies – Marcuse became the darling of the New Left during the student protests of the 1960s. In an essay often quoted on the left, 'Repressive Tolerance', Marcuse **deconstructed** the liberal toleration of dissent which appeared to characterize advanced Western societies (in contradistinction to the tyranny of the Soviet state). In the atmosphere of **postmodernist** relativism and disorientation, Marcuse's demonstration of the repressive function of liberal tolerance retains its polemical edge.

One of Marcuse's most influential essays challenged 'The Affirmative Character of Culture' (1937), by which he meant that tendency to see culture as 'a world essentially different from the factual world of the daily struggle for existence, yet realizable by every individual for himself "from within", without any transformation of the state of fact'. Marcuse promoted the idea of the 'great refusal' and never ceased to challenge the ruses of 'affirmative culture' which aimed to 'contain' the human need for freedom and happiness within the strict limits of a repressive consumer culture and manipulative mass media. Nevertheless, against the tendencies of our 'one-dimensional' society, Marcuse maintained a lifelong faith in what his last work entitled *The Aesthetic Dimension* (1977). In it he defends art's 'distance from actuality' and invokes Stendhal's definition of beauty as the *'promise* of happiness', rather than its immediate possession. 'The basic thesis that art must be a factor in changing the world can easily turn into its opposite if the tension between art and radical praxis is flattened out so that art loses its own dimension for change.' [LS]

MARKET FUNDAMENTALISM The term coined by the financier George Soros to describe the unregulated capitalism favoured by institutions such as the World Bank and the International Monetary Fund (IMF). As several commentators have pointed out, market fundamentalism involves the same kind of closed mind and unquestioning commitment to basic principles that are to be found in religious **fundamentalism**. For market fundamentalists, the market has an almost divine status: its will is law and it must be left to its own devices, with the so-called 'invisible hand' providing a self-correcting mechanism. Government intervention is strongly resisted, and national economies are expected to find their own level in competition with all others. Market fundamentalism wants to reduce the public sector to a bare minimum, and feels that the private sector is not just more efficient but morally superior.

The application of such principles in debtor countries, as a price for receipt of IMF and World Bank aid, has often had disastrous consequences, as witness the plight of Argentina in the late 1990s, when the currency and banking system collapsed, plunging the nation into political anarchy. In its belief in the authority of the market, market fundamentalism runs counter to the **postmodern** scepticism towards authority, although some postmodernist thinkers would see the market as a way of undermining traditional social and political values. [SS]

MARX, KARL HEINRICH: PHILOSOPHER, CULTURAL THEORIST (1818–83) What Marx shares with so many **modernists** is his detestation of history. His life was dedicated to the search for political and intellectual means to get a handle on history, to bring history in the form it had always existed – which, according to Marx, has hitherto been a history of ceaseless class struggle – to an end. In the classless (and stateless) society that he campaigned to bring about, history would no longer be a demonic force. Instead, social arrangements would make possible the empowerment, the many-sided flowering, of each individual.

Throughout his life Marx poured scorn on what he termed 'utopian' socialists who focused their energies on developing elaborate visions of a better society while neglecting both the analysis of actual states of affairs and the political struggle to change them. After a century and a half of 'Marxism' it is clear that despite this taboo on imagining the future, Marx's own thought is utopian through and through.

Marx studied law and philosophy in Bonn and Berlin where he was engaged in the fierce debates over the legacy of **Hegel**. In 1843 he began a lifelong friendship and collaboration with Friedrich Engels. In 1847 Marx and Engels helped found the Communist League, for which they wrote the *Communist Manifesto*. After the failure of the revolutionary upheavals of 1848, Marx went into exile in London.

Living in poverty in London, Marx devoted himself to the task of providing a systematic theory of capitalism. The result was *Das Kapital* (the first volume was published in 1867, with subsequent volumes after his death). The International Working Men's Association (1864–72), in which for a while Marx was the moving spirit, promoted communist-inspired opposition to capitalism.

In order to provide the political struggle of the working classes with a sound theoretical framework, Marx had set out to effect a radical transformation of the discipline of political economy. He took over wholesale many aspects of the economic theories of Adam Smith and David Ricardo, but completely recast them so as to reveal the exploitative relation which lay at the heart of the capitalist accumulation of profit.

Marx aimed to provide not only economic analyses but what he regarded as a complete 'science' of society and of history. What he termed the materialist view of history involves both a view of the fundamental role of economic factors in shaping the forms of all social relations and also a periodization of the whole course of human history. It is this that constitutes the basis of the Marxist **grand narrative** repudiated by postmodernists such as **Lyotard**.

One of the most far-reaching implications of Marx's ideas is the development of the critique of ideology. Marx's belief that ideas and ideologies can be traced back to their origin in the material basis of human life has made him – together with **Nietzsche** and **Freud** – a pioneer of what Ricoeur termed the 'hermeneutics of suspicion': the tendency to read all ideas and statements in terms of the interests (economic, political, sexual) they reveal (or conceal).

For over a hundred years after his death Marx's ideas have fed into both trade union organization and the thinking of revolutionary groups in the capitalist countries of Western Europe. During all of the twentieth century almost every serious social theorist – friend or foe – was influenced by the challenge of Marx. The legacy of Marx's ideas is so immense and complex that we cannot even begin to draw up a balance-sheet. But for many intellectuals the collapse of Soviet-style communism and the triumph of consumer capitalism as a global system mean that Marx's inspiration is more relevant than ever. Jacques **Derrida**'s *Specters of Marx* (1994) is an impassioned (but philosophically nuanced) plea: in order truly to come to terms with the significance of the events of our time we need to think carefully, responsibly, about Marx's tangled and ambivalent legacy. [LS]

METAFICTION Postmodern literature is often described as metafictional, meaning that it has a self-conscious, self-referential quality that blurs – or at the very least explores – the distinction between the fictional world and reality. The **author** may choose to disrupt the **narrative** in a variety of ways to draw attention to its fictive status, self-consciously playing games with the reader in the process. The act of writing itself is foregrounded, with the author insisting that we recognize the artifice involved in constructing a narrative.

Although used widely of postmodernist fiction (as in the case of novelists such as **Barth**, **Barthelme**, **Pynchon** and **Vonnegut**) the term can also be read back onto literary history, with Laurence Sterne's *Tristram Shandy* (published 1759–67), for example, often being cited by critics as a metafictional **text**. [SS]

METANARRATIVE Jean-François **Lyotard**'s term (used interchangeably with **grand narrative**) for any theory claiming to provide universal explanations and to be universally valid. **Marxism** is probably the outstanding example of the phenomenon. Lyotard is resolutely opposed to metanarrative, considering it to be authoritarian and restrictive to individual creativity (see also **grand narrative**). [SS]

METAPHYSICS OF PRESENCE The **deconstructionist** Jacques **Derrida** considers that the history of Western philosophy, and by implication the history of all **discourse** in the West, is marked by a commitment to what he calls '**presence**'. This is the assumption we make that we can grasp meaning in its entirety, and that when we hear a word or phrase it is totally 'present' to us in our minds. Presence is therefore an unacknowledged metaphysical assumption that we make when we engage in communication with others. Behind the metaphysics of presence lies a belief in the stability of words and meanings, which, to a **poststructuralist** thinker like Derrida, invites attack. Derrida's point is that language is much more slippery than believers in

presence care to admit, and that, in effect, any given word has a cluster of associations around it that undermine its supposed purity. What language features, to Derrida, is instability and indeterminacy of meaning: never any moment of full presence. Part of the reason for this inability of words to achieve full presence can be found in the nature of time. Derrida makes great play of the fact that time rolls remorselessly on, and that words are constantly being exposed to new states of affairs. There can never be any moment at which full presence, or for that matter full identity, is possible.

Full presence and full identity are two of the main assumptions on which discourse in the West is based, and by his critique of the metaphysics of presence Derrida is calling into question an entire intellectual tradition, which in his opinion is built on an illusion. In the absence of the metaphysics of presence communication appears a much more erratic and anarchic activity than we are normally led to believe, although for the deconstructionist it is also a more creative affair. [SS]

MINIMALIST MUSIC The movement towards minimalism in music began in the early 1960s in America. This movement, which was pioneered by Terry **Riley**, Steve **Reich** and Philip **Glass**, soon spread to Europe where it was further developed by composers such as Michael **Nyman**.

Minimalism can be seen as a reaction against the **modernist** aesthetics of the post-war avant-garde which came to be the norm within 'serious' concert music of the 1960s and 1970s. The minimalists rejected modernist music on the following grounds: (a) it was often complex for the sake of complexity and lacked an accessible surface level (thus modernist composers, in alienating their audiences, often harboured elitist attitudes, showing nothing but contempt for the average listener); (b) it maintained the division between 'high' and 'low' art and relegated the role of popular, jazz or folk musics to that of mindless entertainment; (c) the emphasis on dissonance, atonality and loss of regular pulse contradicted the fundamental axioms of music and, again, alienated audiences.

Minimalist music was, for the most part, ignored or vilified by the 'classical' music establishment who often labelled it 'banal', 'retrogressive' or 'not worthy of serious consideration'. Even today, a significant number of European university music departments do not include it in their undergraduate modules, regarding minimalist music as unworthy of serious academic study.

The genre has been diversifying and developing over the past four decades (the term post-minimalism often being employed to describe more recent works), but the original features of the music were: *repetition* (often, small musical fragments, maybe only one or two bars long, would be repeated (and developed) over long periods of time); *static harmony* (a sense of stasis was achieved by remaining not just within one key or mode but often on one chord for long periods of time); *rhythmic complexity* (the simplicity of the harmony was often contrasted with complex polyrhythmic and polymetric structures); *process and impersonality* (the composers deliberately avoided self-expression and emotionalism, and maintained a detachment from the music by setting up processes which then generated the flow and structure of the music – this is most evident in the 1960s music of Steve Reich); and *cultural eclecticism* (the composers, not content to draw solely on the art tradition, often made studies of jazz, rock and non-Western musics which then informed their own work). [AB]

MISE-EN-ABYME Originally a heraldic term denoting an escutcheon bearing in its centre a miniature replica of itself, *mise-en-abyme* was used by André Gide to describe the same technique in literary **narratives**. In contemporary criticism, it has been used since the 1950s in a more general sense to describe self-reflexivity or self-consciousness in fiction. The term first gained currency in descriptions of the *nouveau roman*, particularly in the criticism of Lucian Dallenbach and Jean Ricardou.

A good example of the technique is provided by John **Barth**'s collection *Lost in the Funhouse* (1968), which includes a story entitled 'Lost in the Funhouse', in which the narrator, Ambrose, describes the difficulty of writing a story called 'Lost in the Funhouse', about a character called Ambrose who is lost in the funhouse. Other examples are the novels described in Nabokov's *The Real Life of Sebastian Knight* (1941), the novels-within-novels of Flann O'Brien's *At Swim-Two-Birds* (1939) and Italo **Calvino**'s If *on a Winter's Night a Traveller* (1979). The technique is not only to be found in twentieth-century fiction: Cervantes and Sterne contain early novelistic uses of the *mise-en-abyme*. It has become important for **postmodernism** as a way of denoting the self-reflexive nature of **representation** in general, as this is taken – accurately or otherwise – to be a central tenet of **deconstruction** and postmodern philosophy. [BD]

MODERNISM Modernism usually refers to a constellation of intellectual and, especially, artistic movements which emerged around the middle of the nineteenth century. Baudelaire provided early but clear and far-reaching formulations of the doctrines of modernism. **Marx**'s dream of the global abolition of capitalism by means of a proletarian revolution is, in a sense, a modernist vision. Modernist movements included impressionism, symbolism, cubism, futurism, art nouveau, imagism and so on. By the beginning of this century, modernist doctrines came to dominate and define the whole of the literary and artistic landscape.

More specifically – if more intangibly – modernism refers to an impulse within artistic and literary circles. For modernism, one's response to the challenge of the 'modern' has become a fundamental issue. Confusions in our terminology result from the fact that modernism is a relatively late development in the history of **modernity**. By the middle of the nineteenth century, modernity had so thoroughly established itself that the sense of scandal and challenge which it once suggested has to some extent been displaced by a belief in progress and evolution. Modernism is a response to these developments which keeps alive an awareness of the conflict, upheaval, and even destruction involved in modernity and modernization. With the emergence of modernism, modernity entered a new, conflict-ridden and self-conscious phase. Modernism and **postmodernism** are intimately interrelated responses to the crises of modernity. In most of its forms, modernism has been characterized by the (often desperate) hope of solving the problems of modernity, by a heightened, more radical (more absolute, more utopian) form of the 'modern'. All too often modernism has been seduced by the vision of a 'final solution' to the problems of history, and of modernity. Postmodernism's even more final solution is to give up the hope of finality. It is thus both a strict and logical continuation of modernist thought and its thoroughgoing revision or reversal. [LS]

MODERNITY Postmodernism is inevitably confused in its definition by being counterpoised to a whole series of impulses and ambitions which have emerged during the last, say, 500 years. Postmodernism, **postmodernity**, the postmodern: these are often treated as synonymous. Their 'modern' counterparts cannot be. Historians commonly refer to the 'early modern' as that broad period in history which encompasses the rise of capitalism, science and technology. Each new expression of these forces represented a challenge to traditional and relatively settled ways of life. In addition they brought with them challenges to the traditional authority of the Christian church and to the **legitimacy** of political power. Modernity in this sense is the precondition of the emergence of comparatively liberal regimes as well as of political theories of liberalism.

Equally characteristic of modernity, however, is the emergence of the modern state, and with it the more efficient, and sometimes more ruthless, exercise of political power. During the seventeenth century, Protestant countries, such as England and The Netherlands, suffered political upheavals and religious wars, but also succeeded in capitalist and imperial expansion and put themselves in the vanguard of modernity. During the **Enlightenment**, modernity became an explicit and central theme of almost all significant thinkers. Modernity, in other words, came to consciousness of itself. It should be remembered that the Enlightenment, the great cultural project of the eighteenth century, was constantly defined in opposition to the continuities of traditional ways of life. It set itself against the arbitrary personal authority of political rulers and the church's dogmatic (and sometimes violent) defence of superstitious and mysterious rituals. A vision opened up of nature and eventually society (and history) being brought under human control. The Enlightenment proposed one – secular and liberal – route to modernization. Another form of modernization was represented by the absolutism of the French kings, Louis XIV, XV and XVI.

By the nineteenth century, change, transformation and periodic upheaval were increasingly seen as the norm. Doctrines of progress and evolution were and are confronted by revolutionary visionaries and the theorists of crisis and convulsion. Industrial capitalism, and subsequently (and in total opposition) communism, can both be seen to represent the historical movement of modernity. Even until very recently the 'modern' (in the form of new technology, new scientific discoveries, new patterns of behaviour) has generally been the source of enormously inflated hopes. In recent years – at least from the 1974 oil crisis – we have become much more aware of the costs and the burdens associated with modernity. Postmodernity in this sense could be characterized as the growing awareness that the 'modern' is something to which we are condemned. [LS]

MORRIS, MEAGHAN: FEMINIST, CULTURAL CRITIC (1950–) Meaghan Morris is Australia's best-known feminist cultural critic. The focus of her writing is feminist cultural politics. She has made an enormous contribution to the ongoing international development of the post-disciplinary field of **cultural studies**, publishing work on, for example, intellectuals, **Marxism**, photography, popular cinema, the **postmodern** analysis of Jean **Baudrillard**, David Harvey, Fredric **Jameson** and Jean-François **Lyotard**, **power**, shopping centres and tourism.

In many ways a reluctant postmodernist, it is Morris's commitment to feminism that has led her into debates on postmodernism. Although she is critical of the reductive sweep of much postmodern analysis, she recognizes that postmodernism is the location where contemporary debates on culture and politics are now taking place. Moreover, she knows that postmodernism has changed the terrain of debate, making previous modes of cultural politics completely ineffective. Therefore, although she does not herself define her work as postmodern, it is certainly defined by others as belonging to the debate that is postmodernism.

Her principal contribution to this debate is her focus on the connection between feminism and postmodernism. She is critical of a paradoxical mode of thought which claims on the one hand that the debate on postmodernism would be

unthinkable without the impact of feminist cultural politics, yet on the other that there has been little or no feminist input into this debate. She wonders if the best response is to 'adopt a complacent paranoia, and assume that the male pantheon of postmodernism is merely a twilight of the gods – the last ruse of the patriarchal university trying for power to fix the meaning and contain the damage, of its own decline'. But with less complacency, paranoid or otherwise, she wonders if women still have to ask whether men are reading their work. [JS]

MOUFFE, CHANTAL: POLITICAL PHILOSOPHER (1943–) Although she has published widely under her own name, Mouffe is best known for her collaborative work with her fellow political philosopher Ernesto **Laclau**, and as such is one of the leading voices in the post-**Marxist** movement. Post-Marxism became an increasingly important theoretical movement in the later decades of the twentieth century (sparked at least in part by the collapse of communism as a political force in the Western world), and encompasses both theorists who have rejected their **Marxist** past as well as those who, like Laclau and Mouffe, wish to see Marxism reformulated in terms of new cultural and theoretical developments.

On her own Mouffe has written on subjects such as the Italian Marxist theorist Antonio Gramsci, but her reputation rests mainly on *Hegemony and Socialist Strategy* (1985), the book she wrote jointly with Laclau. This call for a more open Marxism in sympathetic dialogue with the various new social movements that had been springing up (especially since the 1960s), is considered to be one of the most significant works of post-Marxist theory, and has been the source of much heated debate on the left. While their detractors have claimed that the book represents a betrayal of the Marxist heritage, Laclau and Mouffe have spiritedly defended their contention that Marxism must change with the times or die.

In *The Democratic Paradox* (2000) Mouffe puts the case for 'agonistic **pluralism**', the condition where political dissent is actively encouraged and the various conflicting viewpoints that arise in any culture are allowed to flourish. We have to learn to live with the paradox that no society will ever resolve such conflicts, and that it is to our advantage for that tension to be maintained. [SS]

N

NARRATIVE Roland **Barthes** was one of the first to recognize just how narrative-based our culture had become, remarking in his essay 'Introduction to the Structural Analysis of Narratives' (1966) that 'the narratives of the world are numberless' (the list could even include stained-glass windows for Barthes). It was through narrative that we made sense of our world. **Lyotard** has also made a strong case for the central cultural role of narrative, arguing in *The Postmodern Condition* (1979) that it enables traditional societies to evolve methods of value judgement without having to resort to any overarching **grand narrative** as a method of validation. Lyotard distinguishes between **little narratives** and grand ones, recommending that our culture should be based on the former rather than the latter, since, unlike grand narratives, they do not attempt to exert control over others.

The Postmodern Condition claims that grand narratives are in decline, but the dramatic growth of religious **fundamentalism** around the globe, especially since Lyotard made his pronouncement in the late 1970s (not to mention **market fundamentalism**), casts more than a little doubt on this assessment. Preventing narratives from being turned into grand narrative remains, however, one of the major tasks of **postmodern** philosophy and cultural critique. [SS]

NEGATIVE DIALECTICS *Negative Dialectics* (1966) was the title given by **Adorno** to his philosophical magnum opus. The huge ambitions of the work include both a summation and **deconstruction** of the legacy of what Adorno regards as the tradition of Western philosophy – stretching from classical Greece up to **Hegel** and **Marx**. In particular, negative dialectics presupposes and incorporates the achievements of Hegel's dialectical philosophy. At the same time, Adorno seeks to hold Hegel's thought at a distance, and indeed to subject it to a painstaking deconstruction. Hegel's philosophy is historical through and through. It constitutes itself through a historical recapitulation of the ideas and principles which have constituted the whole history of the world as reflected by philosophy. Hegel's thought is dialectical in that it effects a 'reconciliation' of the whole and the part, of unity and **difference**, of individual and society, of particularity and totality. Adorno affirms the need to think in these Hegelian terms because, under late capitalism, the world tends to take on the characteristics of an integrated totality. On the other hand, Adorno asserts the need for dialectics to be thoroughly 'negative' in the sense that it should be alive to the extent of (social) oppression and (individual) repression in the integration of the 'administered world'.

Negative dialectics are needed to allow thought to think the relationships which make up the totality without itself succumbing to the totalitarian tendencies within thought itself. Adorno reverses many of Hegel's dictums. Where Hegel believed only the whole to be true, Adorno (basing himself on the state of the world as he saw it) declared, 'The whole is untrue.' In restoring the critical tension to Hegelian thinking, Adorno believed he was able to represent the perspective of suffering.

Hegel's philosophy depends on a logic which proposes 'the identity of identity and non-identity'. Negative dialectics seeks to remain true to the 'non-identical', or to that which is subjugated by thought. [LS]

NEO-MODERNISM Jürgen **Habermas** has argued that **modernity** is an 'unfinished' project, and there are many thinkers and artists who would agree with this claim and consider themselves as carrying forward that project's ideals. Any attempt to do so, however, has to contend with the challenge of **postmodernism**, which calls into question the ideals of modernity and **modernism** – ideals such as cultural progress and the cult of originality and formal experimentation in the arts. The term 'neo-modernism' has been applied to this trend, which tends to be deeply suspicious of the postmodern ethos, regarding it as lazy and lacking in creative inspiration. For Habermas, this is enough to dismiss postmodernism as neo-conservative. [SS]

NEW HISTORICISM The new historicism that emerged during the 1980s insists upon the necessity of studying literature within its historical and social contexts. Centring around the figure of Stephen **Greenblatt** and his journal *Representations*, new historicism's critical heartland is early **modern** culture. Prominent in new-historicist accounts of Renaissance literature are Greenblatt himself, Jonathan Goldberg and Louis Montrose. New-historicist strands are also to be found in Romantic studies (notably in the work of J. J. McGann, Marjorie Levinson and Alan Liu) and criticism of American literature (most notably Walter Benn Michaels). A transatlantic cousin of American new historicism is the '**cultural materialism**' of British critics Jonathan **Dollimore** and Alan **Sinfield**.

New historicism repudiates new criticism's formalist tendency to address a work of art as a self-sufficient object divorced from its cultural setting. Simultaneously, new historicists argue that the American theoretical orthodoxies of the 1970s, notably **poststructuralism** and **deconstruction**, were as ahistorical in their methodologies as the critical schools – new criticism and myth criticism – which they challenged and replaced. What distinguishes the new historicism from more traditional historical criticism is its problematizing of the division between literary foreground and political background. Following **Foucault**, it foregrounds the concept that 'history' is itself textually mediated, and problematizes the mimetic model of previous historicist criticism which viewed a text as simply reflecting the history around (and thus still outside) it. To use Montrose's phrase, new historicism insists upon the 'the historicity of **texts** and the textuality of history'.

For Greenblatt, literary works are not 'a stable set of reflections of the historical facts that lie beyond them'; they are 'places of dissension'. From this premise is developed a number of readings of Renaissance literature, many of which address issues of **power**. For some such writings offer a subversive riposte to the dominant structures of authority, while for others their dissident potential is contained by the power of the state. Renaissance new historicism, though it quarrels with the ahistorical aspects of **postmodernist** theory, borrows heavily from some of its techniques. Greenblatt's founding document, *Renaissance Self-Fashioning* (1980) is heavily dependent upon deconstructionist terminology ('origins', 'rupture', 'inscription', etc.). The new historicism is an attempt to fuse the supposedly dissonant tendencies of postmodern thought with literary historical enquiry. Equally important is the adaptation of critical sources hitherto neglected in historicist writing, notably the work of Foucault, **Lacanian** neo-**Freudianism**, and the anthropological theory of Clifford **Geertz**. For new historicism of the Romantic period, the French structural **Marxism** of Althusser and Macherey is also an important influence. However, there is no systematic theoretical methodology evident in new-historicist writing: Greenblatt has argued, against two of the major figures in postmodern thought, that the 'historical relation between art and society . . . does not lend itself to a single, theoretically satisfactory answer of the kind that **Jameson** and **Lyotard** are trying to provide'. Nonetheless, one can discern certain key preoccupations within this body of writing: structures of authority, the subversion/containment debate, the tendency to use anecdotes to initiate a wider cultural **narrative**, the inscription of the body within **discourse** and the social construction of identity; and, throughout all, the devotion to Jameson's injunction: 'Always historicize!' [JStr]

NIETZSCHE, FRIEDRICH: PHILOSOPHER (1844–1900) Nietzsche is undoubtedly the most important nineteenth-century thinker in relation to **postmodernism**. Among the people he has influenced by his **anti-foundationalist** ideas are **Derrida**, **Baudrillard** and **Lyotard**. His aphoristic style of writing has impressed Mann, Kafka and Wittgenstein. 'God is dead', the famous assertion made in *Thus Spake Zarathustra* (1886), has passed into common currency.

The essay 'The Philosopher: Reflections on the Struggle between Art and Knowledge' (1872) outlined clearly the interests which lie behind Nietzsche's critique of the notion of truth. He shows how culture suffers if the demand for truth and certainty is allowed to override the pragmatic implications for knowledge. Lyotard's *The Postmodern Condition* (1979) echoes many of Nietzsche's conclusions. Another essay, 'On Truth and Lies in an Extra-Moral Sense' (1873), distinguishes between two kinds of truths. The first is those truths that fall under the general rubric of illusions, lies and interpretations (i.e. the various

world-views of metaphysics). The second is those truths that make the world habitable (i.e. scientific insights which yield practical knowledge of the environment). Both are the expression of the general will-to-truth which seeks to appropriate life according to its needs. The **difference** between them is that the first kind of truth flaunts its reliance upon a particular perspective, while the second seeks to deny its subjective construction. At heart, though, all truth is figurative. As Nietzsche puts it, answering Pilate: 'What, then, is truth? A mobile host of metaphors, metonymies and anthropomorphisms . . . Truths are illusions which we have forgotten are illusions.'

Nietzsche continued to undermine the foundational pretensions of truth throughout the remainder of his philosophical **texts**, in a manner which was to inspire **Foucault** and others. *The Gay Science* (1882) explores the idea of a science which is aware of its own presuppositions and biases of perspective. The knowledge-drive is to be assessed in terms of its cultural benefits, and not according to its correspondence to an ideal. In *The Genealogy of Morals* (1887), the will-to-truth is traced back to its roots. Behind every system of morality lurks a philosopher seeking to justify his own ethical prejudices. This is why the 'will-to-system is a lack of integrity'.

The Twilight of the Idols (1888) is a series of essays on the theme of the transvaluation of all values, where truth is to be understood as 'true for us' and not 'true to a noumenal world'.

How, though, are we to function in a world of such radical relativism? If all truth is contextual and situational, how can we make sense of the flux of experience? This is one of the most frequently voiced anxieties within postmodern thought. Nietzsche's answer is: through art. He argued that in a healthy culture, aesthetics should replace metaphysics or epistemology as the primary philosophical discipline.

As he stated in *The Birth of Tragedy* (1872): 'Only as an aesthetic phenomenon can the world be justified to all eternity.' The supreme artistic discipline for Nietzsche is music, precisely because its content is inseparable from its structure. Music is a process, and is irreducible to any kind of causal account. Its 'truth' is not a product of communicative intent and emotive response, or a correlation with a hidden order of things, but a complex interaction of the personal, social and historical. Such views led Nietzsche to champion Wagner as a modern Aeschylus who could unify the German state through his mythological opera (an allegiance he later regretted).

Another area in which Nietzsche prefigures many concerns of the postmodern is that of identity. Psychology and common sense encourage us to think of the self as something solid and deep. Nietzsche, however, celebrates the surfaces of the self and compares it with a melody or leitmotif. Its end is not its goal, but nevertheless as long as '[it] has not reached its end, it also has not reached its goal', as he states gnomically in *The Wanderer and his Shadow* (1879). It is our very shallowness that is our most profound aspect. *The Genealogy of Morals* goes further and posits that '*the doer is* merely a fiction added to the deed – the deed is everything'. In other words, we are what we do. This opens the door for a very fluid conception of the self, one which is not based on being and substance, but on the process of 'becoming' and the imposition of style. (When Nietzsche went insane towards the end of his life, he began signing his letters 'Dionysus' and 'The Crucified'. Whether this uncertainty of being was connected in some subterranean way with his earlier speculations is impossible to determine.) [BL]

NOMADISM In *Anti-Oedipus* (1972) and *A Thousand Plateaus* (1980) **Deleuze** and **Guattari** put forward nomadic existence as a socio-political ideal. Nomads inhabit no fixed territory (they are '**deterritorialized**'), thus lack all the social and political structures that traditionally go along with the nation state: structures that Deleuze and Guattari consider to be repressive. Nomadism is as much an intellectual as a physical condition for these **authors**, representing a refusal to commit oneself to an authoritarian system of belief. It can thus be considered something of a **postmodern** ideal, and has functioned that way for many other thinkers, such as the feminist theorist Rosi **Braidotti**. [SS]

NORRIS, CHRISTOPHER: CRITIC, PHILOSOPHER (1947–) Christopher Norris's earlier writings include work on the application of **poststructuralist** theory to English literature, on **Derrida** and on music, politics and culture. More recently, his has become a noticeable, some would say strident, voice in the debates about **postmodernity** and **postmodernism.** Norris has launched a series of attacks on what he sees as the principal ideas of postmodernism, and on some of the most prominent postmodern thinkers (notably, Jean **Baudrillard** and Jean-François **Lyotard**). Three of his books – *What's Wrong With Postmodernism* (1990), *The Truth About Postmodernism* (1993) and *Uncritical Theory: Postmodernism, Intellectuals and the Gulf War* (1992) – have advanced the broad claim that postmodernism is a form of groundless relativism which has not just rejected the *rationalism* of **Enlightenment** thinking, but has in fact abandoned rational and critical thinking entirely, leaving behind in the process the Enlightenment project of emancipation. For Norris, postmodernism is essentially a form of nihilism and political quietism which can provide no basis for an emancipatory politics, and which sees the Enlightenment conception of human liberation as simply part of a broader rationalistic and ultimately totalitarian system of thought. The rejection of rational Enlightenment values takes the form primarily, says

Norris, of an aestheticization of politics. It is on these grounds that he launches his attacks on Baudrillard and Lyotard.

Norris's reading of Baudrillard – most fully worked out in *What's Wrong With Postmodernism* – takes the latter's position with regard to the real – what Norris calls 'extreme referential agnosticism' – to be one which plays into the hands of the forces of global capitalism and imperialism. While he concedes that Baudrillard is 'a first-rate diagnostician of the postmodern scene', Norris claims that the fundamental mistake Baudrillard makes is to assume that because we live in an age of illusion and misinformation, it therefore no longer makes sense to speak of reference, reality and truth. For Norris, it is precisely because of Baudrillard's first claim that we must resist the second. Accordingly, much of Norris's recent work has aimed at the reclamation of a notion of truth in the face of the perceived abandonment of the concept in postmodernism.

The position Norris adopts with regard to Lyotard is equally dismissive of the latter's claim that it is no longer possible to attach credence to the **grand narratives** of **modernity**, the overarching discourses of truth, Enlightenment and progress. When Lyotard proposes a state of affairs in which there are only competing 'phrase regimens' which are not reducible to the terms of any one political or philosophical **discourse** (such a reduction is for Lyotard a definition of injustice), he is, according to Norris, rejecting not only the totalizing impulses of modernity, but also disallowing the possibility of radical political action on the basis of critical judgement. Lyotard's thought, then, is for Norris indistinguishable from the quietistic pragmatism of Richard **Rorty** and Stanley Fish. In opposition to the relativism and scepticism of postmodernism, Norris proposes a return to the concept of truth and a notion of rational communication close to that offered by Jürgen **Habermas**. [BD]

NYMAN, MICHAEL: CRITIC, MUSICOLOGIST, COMPOSER (1944–) Nyman is most famous for his film music (particularly in collaboration with Peter **Greenaway**) but, as he is always quick to point out, he is also a successful composer of concert music. He undertook a formal music education at the Royal Academy of Music and King's College London, graduating in 1964. For the following twelve years he wrote little or no music but worked as a music critic for, among other publications, *The Listener*, *The New Statesman* and *The Spectator*. As a musicologist, he worked during this period both on a Ph.D. thesis (a study of sixteenth- and seventeenth-century English repetitive and systems music, i.e. rounds, canons and catches) and on his book *Experimental Music – Cage and Beyond* (1974). Many of these techniques studied in his thesis were inspirational to Nyman when he began composing in the late 1970s, whereas *Experimental Music – Cage and Beyond* documents the composers who have, through the influence of John **Cage**'s work, explored alternative compositional aesthetics to the **modernist** mainstream.

It was almost by accident that Nyman took up composition when, in 1976, he was asked to arrange some eighteenth-century Venetian popular songs for a production of Goldoni's *Il Campiello* at the National Theatre. In trying to recreate the sound of a Venetian street orchestra, an ensemble, using a combination of medieval instruments (rebecs, sackbuts and shawms) and more conventional ones, was put together. The production finished but the ensemble wished to stay together and so Nyman took to composing music for them to play. Soon, however, the ensemble redirected itself away from the medieval timbres, employing instead a collection of amplified but conventional strings, wind and pianos. Nyman was then working in a similar fashion to his American counterparts **Reich** and **Glass** in that his music was repetitive and highly diatonic (in contrast to the extreme chromaticism of much twentieth-century music) and he had his own ensemble as a vehicle for his ideas. There are, however, a number of sharp contrasts between Nyman and the American **minimalists**. Unlike Reich and Glass, who drew greatly on non-Western traditions, Nyman found his inspiration in earlier composers from the Western 'classical' tradition.

Music for the Greenaway film *The Draughtsman's Contract* (1982) drew heavily on the music of the English baroque composer Henry Purcell. All the pieces written for this film could be described as chaconnes. This is when the music revolves around a repeated bass line (a ground bass), often with implied harmony, while melodic material is then layered on top in the upper parts. For this project, Nyman took all his ground basses from the works of Purcell. The music for *Drowning by Numbers* (1987), another Peter Greenaway film, draws exclusively on Mozart's Sinfonia Concertante for Violin and Viola (KV364). For the music to the Jane Campion film, *The Piano* (1992), Nyman used, as his source material, nineteenth-century Scottish folk songs and popular piano pieces. The music, while maintaining a melodic lyricism and an emotional intensity, also adopts the repetition and polyrhythmic complexities of minimalist music.

Besides numerous film scores, Nyman has also written many orchestral, chamber and choral pieces for the concert hall. His style, which could be described as a kind of 'English minimalism', is often far more evocative and expressive than that of original minimalism and he has been successful in achieving a sense of tragedy in his music. He has, like Reich and Glass in America, done much to subvert the modernist dialectic of 'high' and 'low' music. [AB]

O

OEDIPUS Deleuze and **Guattari**'s term for the body of theories, processes and institutional structures by which modern psychoanalysis sets about repressing **desire** (or **desiring-machines**, as they refer to individual human beings). The Oedipus complex itself (with its source in classical myth) is only one aspect of this repressive mechanism, which attempts to force individuals into socially conformist behaviour such that they are more easily controlled by the political authorities. Psychoanalysis in this reading is an ideologically motivated activity, and Oedipus becomes symbolic of the authoritarianism (and even fascism) felt by the authors to be endemic to **modern** social existence. [SS]

ORIENTALISM Edward **Said**'s pathbreaking work, *Orientalism* (1978), leans on **Foucault**'s discussion of knowledge/**power** as well as Jacques **Derrida**'s insistence that we should '**deconstruct**' certain privileged **binary oppositions**. The words for 'Orient' and 'Occident' derive simply from Latin words for sun rising (*oriens*) and sun setting (*occidens*). Orient and occident are thus by nature entirely relative to the positioning of the observer (for inhabitants of Tokyo the sun rises in the east over Hawaii). However, as Said explains, a huge and ancient historical regime has taken this necessarily mobile and relational positioning and reduced it to a fixity, specifying, for example, the 'Near', 'Middle' and 'Far East' posed in opposition to a supposedly originary point in Europe.

Placed at this imaginary centre, Europe claims to be a **subject** able to know the 'Orient', the entire non-Western world, as an object, so exercising power over it (in his epigraph to the book, Said cites **Marx**: 'They cannot represent themselves; they must be represented'). By bracketing the question of what may or may not be true about 'the Orient', Said opens for interrogation an extraordinary range of writing – 'not only scholarly works but also works of literature, political tracts, journalistic **texts**, travel books, religious and philological studies'.

This manoeuvre for categorizing and denigrating the Orient secures a particular notion of identity for the West: 'European culture gained in strength and identity by setting itself off against the Orient as a sort of surrogate and even underground self.' If Westerners are, as Said says, 'rational, peaceful, liberal, logical, capable of holding real values, without natural suspicion', then what he terms 'Arab-Orientals' are 'none of these things'; and of course if the Oriental is classified as none of these things this ensures that the Western subject is 'rational, peaceful, liberal', etc.

Thus the West established a good image for itself by disavowing irrational feelings which are then projected on to an Oriental **Other**. But the repressed returns: for the West the Orient becomes the place of the unconscious itself – it must, as Said points out, open on to 'terrors, pleasures, **desires**', an Other which is both seductive and terrible.

Said must risk the accusation of functionalism, for in his account orientalism works only too well, perfectly hailing subjects into fixed positions (as Western or Eastern) which they are forced to take up. Homi **Bhabha** asserts that 'there is always,

281

in Said, the suggestion that colonial **power** and **discourse** is possessed entirely by the coloniser' and in response he looks for resistance to the power of orientalism. Bhabha draws on psychoanalysis to propose that orientalizing is a struggle always liable to fail since the colonial subject is constructed in 'a repertoire of conflictual positions'; these render him or her 'the site of both fixity and fantasy' in a process which cannot but be uneven, divided, incomplete (Bhabha details mechanisms through which orientalism always threatens to undo itself).

Said's analysis has been extended as a way to understand how any cultural, ethical or racial group may be 'known' and so dominated by a more powerful bloc. For example, his argument that no generalization (about 'races, types, colours, mentalities') remains a neutral description because it always makes an 'an evaluative interpretation' has been foundational for multiculturalism in the United States. [AE]

OTHER (see **alterity**)

P

PAGANISM Jean-François **Lyotard** terms the state where we make judgements without criteria as paganism. In effect, this describes the **postmodern** condition, since in that condition we no longer have any universal theories to fall back on in order to validate our criteria. Without such universal theories (whether they be theories of truth or politics) we are reduced to making judgements on a case-by-case basis, which for Lyotard is the only honest way to proceed. Lyotard finds a precedent for this method of making judgements in the work of Aristotle, whom he considers to be a particularly pragmatic thinker. Lyotard wishes to introduce this kind of pragmatism into our public life in a more general way, since it moves us away from an uncritical and slavish reliance on universal theories (**grand narratives**). In his reading of recent history, it has been this uncritical reliance which has been the source of most of our socio-political problems, in that it has sanctioned such horrors as Auschwitz, and the many inhuman things done in the name of theories such as **Marxism**, communism and socialism. A 'pagan' society would reject such authorities and examine each demand for political action on its own merits, the assumption being that this would result in a more just society than one based on rigid rules and regulations. Judgement without preconceived criteria thus becomes one of the defining characteristics of a postmodern society. [SS]

PAGLIA, CAMILLE: CULTURAL THEORIST (1947–) Self-styled 'Amazon of letters', Camille Paglia's notoriety springs more from her headline-grabbing contentiousness than her intellectual achievements. She is a vocal opponent of French theoreticians such as **Lacan**, **Derrida** and **Foucault**, whom she believes to have overrun humanist disciplines with their 'rigid foreign ideology', and is also notable for her hostile relationship with mainstream feminism, whose best-known figures she insults with frequency and enthusiasm. Probably her most famous opponent in this respect is Gloria Steinem, whom she accused in an interview in *Vanity Fair* of becoming 'the Stalin of our time, addicted to the high life and choking off feminist dialogue'. According to Paglia, feminists are 'desensualized, desexualized, neurotic women, who, displacing their personal problems with sex on to society, purvey an appalling diet of cant, drivel and malarkey'. Although not always consistent on this point, she appears to consider herself as a kind of **post-feminist**, who had passed beyond the central tenets of mainstream feminism by the time she began her university education.

Paglia first came to public attention in 1990, when her monumental work *Sexual Personae: Art and Decadence from Nefertiti to Emily Dickinson* was published. Over 700 pages long, it is characteristically audacious in its ambition and eclecticism, and is an early example of Paglia's provocative talent for mingling the canonical with the popular and the sacred with the profane. Edmund Spenser, for example, is approached as an early precursor of the Marquis de Sade, with whom he shares an ability to see 'the daemonism in sex and nature'. Paglia's ultimate intention in this study is to *reclaim* the essentialist notion of the fundamental

difference between men and women, arguing for the necessity of abandoning 'the pretense of sexual sameness and admit the terrible duality of gender'. In the universe according to Paglia, the female body, subject to the cycles of menstruation and gestation, is irrevocably tied to the rhythms of nature; while male physiology, symbolized by genitals which point out and away from the body, is identified with culture, which is perpetually attempting to dominate and contain natural processes.

Although, to give her her due, Paglia attempts to portray nature as a powerful, elemental force which persistently evades masculine categorization and control, the dangers of this train of thought are perfectly illustrated by the furore that has sprung up around her apparent defence of 'date rape', a theme that dominates her collection of essays published in 1994, *Sex, Art and American Culture*. Date rape, pronounces Paglia, is the inevitable consequence of woolly liberal feminist thinking, which teaches young women that the sexes are the same, and are in possession of the same rights. She argues that such a notion is fundamentally flawed, since it ignores the way in which aggression and eroticism are ineradicably entwined in the male psyche. Women should therefore be aware of the risks they run in being alone with a man, and either be prepared to defend themselves against his inevitable advances, or submit. Although that does not absolve the rapist from punishment, it is an event for which the woman should take her fair share of the blame. Although ostensibly still portraying rape as a criminal act, Paglia has at times slipped perilously close to upholding an 'all women want it really' stance, claiming, for example, in an interview reproduced in *Sex, Art and American Culture*, that 'most women want to be seduced and lured'.

The outrageousness of such pronouncements, which often seems to originate more from an addiction to self-publicity than genuine belief or intellectual endeavour, does Paglia few favours. *Sex, Art and American Culture*, for example, is characteristic in not only containing a selection of her essays and interviews, but also an appendix which chronicles her rise to fame. As a consequence, Paglia's repudiation of mainstream feminism and theory can easily be interpreted as pique against more famous or more respected academic competitors. Moreover, her openly displayed ambition and aggressive outspokenness, as well as her public espousal of bisexuality, threatens to act as a repudiation of the very ideas she is promoting, for she certainly does not conform to the notions of 'natural' femaleness she endorses for other women. Nevertheless, beneath the inflammatory rhetoric and endless self-dramatization is work that deserves attention precisely because of its relentless interrogation of academic and ideological orthodoxies. [SG]

PARADIGM SHIFT In the work of Thomas **Kuhn**, a paradigm is a framework of thought within which scientific enquiry takes place in any given era. Thus scientists are constrained by institutional and peer pressure to conduct enquiry within the guidelines laid down by currently accepted theories and their prescribed models of practice. This is what Kuhn refers to as 'normal science'. It is in the nature of scientific experiment, however, to generate anomalies that cannot always be explained away by current theories, and when such instances become frequent enough, science finds itself in a state of crisis that can only be resolved by the creation of a new paradigm. The new paradigm is usually **incommensurable** with the old, and we then speak of a paradigm shift, or radical change in perspective. The shift from Ptolemaic to Copernican astronomy (from the Earth as the centre of the universe to the Sun as the centre) is presented by Kuhn as a classic instance of paradigm shift, where one can believe in one theory or the other, but not both.

Kuhn's theory can be applied outside the sciences, and the notion of cultural paradigm shifts is now widely accepted. One such shift might be from **modernity** to **postmodernity**, although it is also part of the postmodern outlook constantly to challenge the authoritarianism felt to be encoded within almost *any* paradigm. Postmodern thinkers are, as a rule, more concerned with contesting the validity of frameworks of thought in general than upholding their authority. [SS]

PHILLIPS, TOM: ARTIST (1937–) After visiting France as a small boy, Tom Phillips returned with some old bones. This presaged his interest in death and dissolution, themes permeating his output as a painter, printmaker, composer and film maker. 'Benches', for instance, is a series of 'treated' postcards which feature the ordinary park bench as an emblem of mortality. The images were collected haphazardly – chance is another of his obsessions. In the mid-1960s, he read an interview with William Burroughs about the 'cut-up' technique, whereby words are plucked from a **text**, shuffled together, and placed in unusual juxtapositions. Enthused, Phillips searched for some randomly chosen source material, and decided that 'the first (coherent) book that I could find for threepence . . . would serve'. This is how W. H. Mallock's *A Human Document* (1892), a neglected three-decker novel, became his Bible. Phillips began painting over the text, isolating certain phrases to extract unusual meanings, and published a completed version of this project as *A Humument* in 1980.

The musical opera *Irma* was also composed using this method, and released on Brian Eno's Obscure Records label in 1975. Irma is the robust heroine of Mallock's book, but in the hands of Phillips becomes a shadowy, blurry figure – a **postmodern** equivalent of Wordsworth's Lucy. She is the platonic love-object for Bill Toge, a character who crops up whenever the words 'together' or 'altogether' appear in Mallock's text. *Irma* and *A Humument* deserve to be far better known than the rather ponderous *A TV Dante*, which Phillips co-directed with Peter **Greenaway** in 1990. [BL]

PLANT, SADIE: AUTHOR, FEMINIST (1964–) Sadie Plant is a proponent of 'cybernetic feminism', which she defines as 'an insurrection on the part of the goods and materials of the patriarchal emergence composed of links between women, women and computers, computers and communications links, connections and connectionist nets'. As this quotation indicates, Plant challenges the notion that technology is antithetical to female concerns. On the contrary, she argues that technological progress and women's liberation have always advanced in tandem, and that in the late twentieth century we have arrived at a situation where an alliance between women and machines is threatening the entire history of patriarchal dominance.

In publications such as *Zeroes and Ones: Digital Women and the New Technologies* (1997), Plant traces this association on two levels. One aspect of her concern is sociological, and in a process that is comparable to Elaine Showalter's search for a hidden tradition of female **authorship**, she uncovers a forgotten history of female involvement with the advance of information technology. Figures who are central to this project are Ada Lovelace, who assisted Charles Babbage in the development of the world's first programmable machine, the Analytical Engine, in the 1840s, and Captain Grace Murray Hopper, who was the chief programmer of the Analytical Engine's successor, Mark 1, developed by the United States during the Second World War.

On a more theoretical level, however, Plant sees a more profound connection between women and technology. The Analytical Engine was programmed by a series of punched cards, which was a process taken from the operation of the mechanized Jacquard loom, and Plant makes much of the fact that weaving is a traditionally female art. She persistently returns to, and dramatically reverses, the **Freudian** argument that the activity of weaving stands in a metonymic relationship to the criss-crossing of pubic hair which conceals women's genital 'lack'. In her scenario, which itself weaves together Freudian and feminist theory, history and science fiction, the computers created to serve patriarchal interests have now far exceeded man's control. Information systems like the **Internet**, which are dispersed and non-hierarchical, cannot be contained by an authority imposed from above. According to Plant, therefore, **cyberspace** is not a disembodied space, but one that is closely identified with the female body and female forms. What Freud saw as a hole, a vacancy that must be decently concealed, Plant reads as a zero, which is the very basis of binary machine code. [SG]

PLURALISM It has become all but an article of faith in **postmodernism** to argue against absolute notions of truth or authority, and to encourage plural interpretations of **texts** and situations instead. Thus for Jean-François **Lyotard** there is no overriding **grand narrative** (or universal explanatory theory) in the political domain any more, but rather a plurality of **little narratives** seeking to achieve limited objectives. Roland **Barthes** argues in *S/Z* that texts are no longer to be seen as having central meanings that critics should be striving to reveal, but instead as sources of plural interpretations. **Poststructuralism** in general has encouraged that view. The idea that there can be any unquestionable central authority (whether in the political or intellectual domain) has been vigorously

resisted by poststructuralists and postmodernists alike. Even truth is seen as plural: that is, not reducible to one central meaning that excludes all others, but as relative to the interpreter and situation at hand. **Nietzsche** provides much of the inspiration for this view in his insistence that truth is simply an army of metaphors, available to be wielded on behalf of a specific cause. For poststructuralists and postmodernists there is no one privileged interpretation of any situation, but rather a plurality of possible interpretations. [SS]

POLYSEMY Polysemy initially referred to a single word with two or more meanings, e.g. 'pen' which, according to context, can mean either 'a writing instrument' or 'a small enclosure for domestic animals'. More recently, literary theorists have extended the term to include larger units of sense, such as an entire fictional work. The classic demonstration of this is *S/Z* (1975) by Roland **Barthes**. In this study, Barthes dissects the text of Balzac's short story 'Sarrasine' into 512 fragments, or lexias. He then shows how five arbitrary codes (hermeneutic, proairetic, semic, cultural and symbolic) multiply meaning in each fragment. [BL]

POSTCOLONIALISM 'Colonialism' is the conquest and direct control of another people's land, a phase in the history of imperialism, which in turn is the **globalization** of the capitalist mode of production from the sixteenth century onwards. In the context of cultural production, 'postcolonialism' is 'writing after empire': the analysis of both colonial **discourse** and the writings of the ex-colonized. In relation to British imperialism, this work would have once been called 'Commonwealth literature', but the field has been transformed by the use of a variety of **postmodern** theories concerning language, gender, **subjectivity** and race. The proliferation of full-length studies, readers and conferences on the subject testifies to its importance over a range of **cultural studies**.

The two most important dates in postcolonial studies are 1947, which marks the beginning of a massive decolonization of the British Empire, and 1978, when the founding text of postcolonial studies was published: Edward **Said**'s *Orientalism*. Drawing upon the work of **Foucault** and others, Said examines the **representation** of the Orient in Western discourse and finds there 'Europe's deepest and most recurring image of the **Other** . . . a Western style for dominating, restructuring and having authority over the Orient'. Though much criticized, this book gave an impetus to the study of the culture of post-independent states, from Africa and the Caribbean to South and South-East Asia. It ushered in a period in which the literature of colonial struggle and nationalism, most importantly the writings of Frantz Fanon, was reread from various post-modernist perspectives.

More recently, 'postcolonial' has come to mean something other than 'post-independent', and includes writing that resists colonialism in all its forms. This allows postcolonial critics to examine the work of influential anti-colonialists such as Fanon and the huge body of culture affected by the imperial process from the moment of colonization to the present day. [PD]

POST-FEMINISM   Post-feminism has appeared as a result of contemporary manoeuvres to discredit feminism as passé and bad. The post-feminist contention is that the dangers and damage of feminism 'prove' women are wrong to seek equality with men in a man's world. In particular, the mass media both pronounce the official equality of women and catalogue the ills that this equality brings. Post-feminist doctrine in the media encourages women to blame feminism for their exhaustion and disillusionment with equality. For instance, women's magazines make post-feminist assertions such as the following: feminism spoiled women's right to be sexually attractive, to flirt, to enjoy domestic bliss; it damaged the family, leaving young children to grow up without correct moral standards; it resulted in violence against women and by women. However, acceptance of such messages reveals the public's failure to recognize a political structure that profits, literally, from the inequalities it promotes.

Post-feminism may claim to promote 'the new', e.g. the new femininity or the new monogamy. But the reality is the opposite. It claims that feminism as anti-family stance has destroyed what most people see as the essential foundation of a healthy and just society, while supporting a return to traditional values. Portraying feminism as the disease of 'the terminally single woman', and women's liberation as the source of an endless catalogue of contemporary personal, social and economic evils, post-feminism creates a backlash. It defends men against blame for the oppression of women, and so produces reversals of freedom and justice: the movement for women's liberation is made to appear tyrannical and unrepresentative of the demands of women. If there is any lesson to be learnt from post-feminism, it is that the openness and celebration of **postmodern** relativism can be co-opted into its opposite: an uncritical and absolutist stance. [PSA]

POSTHUMANISM   One of the implications of **postmodern** thought is that we are now deemed to live in a posthumanist age as well. Humanism is identified with the discredited **Enlightenment project**, and in particular with its concentration on the cultural importance of the individual. The individual **subject** was held to be a being with a unique essence, whose goal was self-realization. It was regarded as one of the primary objectives of culture to provide the basis for such self-realization, by guaranteeing the freedom of the individual through the establishment of appropriate institutional structures (governmental, legal, educational, etc.). Various French theorists such as Claude **Lévi-Strauss,** Roland **Barthes** and Michel **Foucault** have argued against this conception of the subject, and can be seen to contribute in their own particular way to the dismantling of the humanist ideal. The **structuralist Marxist** philosopher Louis Althusser gave a particular boost to the development of a post-humanist consciousness by openly declaring himself to be an anti-humanist – that is, to be in opposition to the Enlightenment vision of mankind as the centre of the universe.

More recent **poststructuralist** and postmodernist thinkers such as **Lyotard,** **Deleuze** and **Guattari** have also consciously distanced themselves from the humanist tradition of thought, which they see as an integral component of **modernity;** as do **difference feminists,** for whom humanism is part of the patriarchal ideology they are actively seeking to shake off. [SS]

POST-INDUSTRIALISM A post-industrial society relies on service industries, knowledge production, and information technology to create wealth, rather than, as in most Western societies from the time of the Industrial Revolution onwards, heavy industrial manufacture. Post-industrialism can be identified with the **postmodern,** in much the same way that industrialism, with its commitment to exploitation of the environment in the name of social progress, can with **modernism.** A concern with knowledge production is in fact now seen as one of the hallmarks of a postmodern society.

One of the great proponents of the notion of post-industrialism is the American sociologist Daniel **Bell,** whose highly influential study *The Coming of Post-Industrial Society* (1973) outlined the likely characteristics involved. Bell envisaged a society where there was a dramatic shift away from manufacturing to services; science-based industries took on a central role; and new elites based on services and science-based industries arose, thus altering the balance of power in that society. Most of the advanced economies in the West can now be described as post-industrial in some sense, in that they have moved significantly towards a position where services, knowledge and information have become the most valuable commodities for trading purposes. [SS]

POST-MARXISM The term 'post-Marxist' can be applied in two specific ways: to those who have rejected **Marxist** beliefs, and to those who have attempted to open up Marxism to more recent theoretical developments such as **poststructuralism,** **postmodernism,** feminism and the various new social movements (such as the **Greens**) that rose to prominence in the later decades of the twentieth century. In the terminology of Ernesto **Laclau** and Chantal **Mouffe,** arguably the leading theorists of post-Marxism, this would equate to being either *post*-Marxist or post-*Marxist*.

In both its main senses, post-Marxism has become an increasingly important theoretical position from the later twentieth century onwards, with such key events as the 1968 *événements* and the collapse of the Soviet bloc in the 1980s serving as catalysts for its development. A whole generation of French intellectuals, including such high-profile figures as Jean-François **Lyotard,** Gilles **Deleuze** and Michel **Foucault,** took a post-Marxist turn in the aftermath of the former event, and proceeded to argue vigorously against what had hitherto been one of the major paradigms of post-war French thought. Lyotard, in *Libidinal Economy* (1974) unleashed a vicious attack on Marxist doctrine, which in many ways sounded the death-knell of the theory as a major factor in French intellectual life.

Deleuze and **Guattari**'s *Anti-Oedipus* (1972) also represented a highly symbolic move away from uncritical acceptance of Marxist doctrine in the period. Laclau and Mouffe's *Hegemony and Socialist Strategy* (1985), with its call for a new kind of politics structured around the objectives of the new social movements, as well as rejection of many key Marxist principles as outmoded, created considerable controversy in Marxist circles when it was published. The Marxist establishment has tended to argue that to incorporate ideas from other sources is to compromise the integrity and authority of Marxism itself. [SS]

POSTMODERN SCIENCE In Jean-François **Lyotard**'s terms of reference, **postmodern** science is that form of science which seeks to discover the unknown rather the known, and is less interested in solving problems than revealing uncharted territories. Prime examples of this kind of scientific practice would be **catastrophe theory** (which Lyotard relies on heavily in his most famous work *The Postmodern Condition* (1979)), **chaos theory** and **complexity theory**. Such theories feature a host of mysterious entities (strange attractors, dark matter, **black holes**, etc.) that seem to defy any possibility of rational explanation, although of course we cannot prove that they will always do so. [SS]

POSTMODERNISM Postmodernism is a wide-ranging cultural movement which adopts a sceptical attitude to many of the principles and assumptions that have underpinned Western thought and social life for the last few centuries. These assumptions, which constitute the core of what we call **modernism**, include a belief in the inevitability of progress in all areas of human endeavour, and in the power of reason, as well as a commitment to originality in both thought and artistic expression.

As a cultural ethos, modernism is uncompromisingly forward-looking and, at least implicitly, makes the assumption that present civilization is to be considered superior to that of the past in the extent of its knowledge and the sophistication of its techniques. As an aesthetic, modernism promotes the view that originality is the highest state of artistic endeavour, and that this can best be achieved by experimentation with form. Postmodernism has turned such ideas on their head, by calling into question modernism's commitment to progress, as well as the ideology underpinning it, and encouraging a dialogue between past and present in thought and the arts. Postmodernism has therefore involved a rejection of the modernist commitment to experiment and originality, and a return to the use of older styles and artistic methods – even if this is done in an **ironic** manner. The characteristic postmodernist style is pastiche, with **authors** returning to a realist style of novel-writing, artists moving away from abstraction and back to figurative painting, and architects freely mixing old and new styles in building. Charles **Jencks** has spoken of the latter practice as '**double coding**', and regards it as a way of overcoming the alienating effect of much modern architecture, which was geared towards professional practitioners rather than the public. Jean-François **Lyotard** has encouraged us to see postmodernism as a rejection of all-encompassing cultural theories (such as **Marxism**), and has argued for a much more pragmatic attitude to political life and artistic expression that simply ignores the oppressive rules laid down by **grand narrative**. Postmodernism is therefore as much an attitude of mind as a specific theoretical position in its own right.

In general, postmodernism can be regarded as part of a longer-running philosophical tradition of scepticism, which is intrinsically anti-authoritarian in outlook and negative in tone: more concerned with undermining the pretensions of other theories than putting anything positive in their place. Lyotard himself sees postmodernism and modernism as cyclical movements which alternate throughout the course of history. [SS]

POSTMODERNITY Postmodernity describes the cultural situation we are now assumed to inhabit, in the wake of **modernity**'s collapse as a cultural ethos. Modernity represented a culmination of several trends in Western culture, including the belief in economic and social improvement and, in a general sense, the inevitability of progress in human affairs (each generation having greater knowledge and techno-logical sophistication than its predecessor). A commitment to progress was built into the politics of modernity, whether this took a capitalist or socialist form, the assump-tion being that the quality of life could indefinitely be improved, and that science and technology could be utilized to guarantee this. There was in effect an ideology (or **grand narrative**) of progress accepted by most nations, including those in the impoverished third world.

Postmodernity, on the other hand, is the state where scepticism is expressed about notions like the inevitable march of pro-gress, or the necessity to continue exploiting the environment around us irrespective of the long-term effect (from that point of view the **Green Movement** can be seen as a postmodernist phenomenon). It is one of the characteristics of postmodernity that there is a decline in belief in universal theories, and a greater commitment to pragmatism in political affairs. This is accompanied by a generalized suspicion of authority and its grand narratives, and a concern to encourage diversity and cultural **difference**. Against that, it could be argued that grand narratives are still very much with us in the postmodern world in the form of religious **fundamentalism**.

How long postmodernity will last is an open question: as far as theorists like Jean-François **Lyotard** are concerned, the modern and the postmodern alternate over time, in which case our current phase of postmodernity may be no more than a temporary respite before another outbreak of modernity. [SS]

POST-PHILOSOPHY Reflection upon the future direction of philosophy has been a fundamental of philosophical discourse since the time of Socrates. But an unusually menacing aura accompanied the repeated announcements of the end of philosophy from **Nietzsche** to **Heidegger** and **Lyotard**, ultimately rendering problematic the very possibility of **postmodern** philosophical **discourse**. At the least, post-philosophy means after philosophy conceived accord-ing to the ideals of autonomous rationality, historical progress and metaphysical truth. Post-philosophy designates the postmodern situation in which these **Enlightenment** ideals have come under criticism. But different responses can be given to this situation. The post-philosopher queries: has philosophy come to an end or a trans-formation? The alternative answers offer both strong and weak versions of what comes after philosophy.

Those who seek to transform philosophy admit that an autonomous, fully trans-parent **subject** of rationality is no longer beyond critique, that the hoped-for progress of history under the guidance of Enlighten-ment philosophy has resulted in its own failure, and that a grand truth as the out-come of metaphysical reflection is wisely replaced with the 'local' character of truth. Yet these same metaphysical ideals were already being questioned by Enlighten-ment philosophers such as **Kant**. For this reason, Kant's critiques offer a useful frame-work for many in the post-philosophy debates.

Those who make the stronger claim to a decisive end of philosophy find support in a radical critique of the necessity that characterizes Kantian reason. These post-philosophers insist upon the contingency of the rules, criteria and results of what counts as rational thought and action at any given time and place. They give priority to the empirical and fallible over the a priori and certain, to heterogeneity over unity, to the fragmentary over the total and to the irreducible **plurality** of **incommensurable** language games over the universality of philosophical discourse. [PSA]

POST-POSTMODERNISM Whether such an entity as post-postmodernism actually exists is open to debate, but some cultural theorists have taken to using the term to argue that we have passed beyond **postmodernism**, which in this reading becomes an essentially late twentieth-century phenomenon that has run its course. **Lyotard** saw **modernism** and postmodernism as much more general terms, describing cultural movements which continually replaced each other over time in serial fashion. From that perspective, post-postmodernism might be simply modernism in a new guise. More worryingly, however, given the rise of religious **fundamentalism**, post-postmodernism might instead be a regression to a much more dogmatic society of the type that modernity replaced. [SS]

POSTSTRUCTURALISM Poststructuralism is a generic term used to refer to all those theories that came to reject the principles of **structuralism**, which, from the 1950s through to the 1970s, constituted the major paradigm of French intellectual enquiry. Among the theories that came to challenge the stranglehold of the structuralist paradigm were **deconstruction**, feminism and **postmodernism**, all of which can be considered as poststructuralist in that they challenged the assumptions on which structuralism was based. Structuralists had held that underlying all phenomena were deep structures that dictated how those phenomena developed (we might think of deep structure as being something in the nature of a genetic programme), and that the world was organized into a series of interlocking systems, each with its own 'grammar' of operation. All systems were amenable to structuralist analysis, given that their grammars were seen to operate in similar ways, and structuralism became an exercise in classification whose goal was the comprehensive mapping of all systems. In principle, at least, the world was completely knowable through the analysis of its systems and their grammars.

For poststructuralists this was at once too neat and also oppressive, since it seemed to allow little room for either human agency – individuals being assumed to be mere channels through which deep structure operated – or the workings of chance (an increasingly important factor in scientific enquiry in the later twentieth century). Against this essentially orderly picture of the world, deconstructionists offered a far more anarchic alternative, where **difference** rather than similarity was the defining characteristic, and where there were assumed to be many gaps and paradoxes in the workings of systems, which were not as predictable as structuralists would have had us believe. Jacques **Derrida** spoke of the 'innocence of becoming' rather than the predetermined working out of deep structural patterns, meaning that the future was always to be considered open and unknown. From a deconstructionist perspective structuralism was to be considered authoritarian, since the theory prescribed exactly how systems had to operate. Postmodernists, too, have reacted against the rigidity and apparent authoritarianism of the structuralist model, and have expressed similar sentiments to the deconstructionists – that is, a commitment to the open-endedness of cultural processes, and to the notion of the 'innocence of becoming'. Once again the thrust of the argument is against theories that claim to offer universal explanations of phenomena, and this dislike of totalizing theory has been a constant feature of the poststructuralist outlook. [SS]

POWER For most **postmodernist** theorists, politics is a question of power rather than morality, and their cultural analyses are often geared to revealing how the former tries to masquerade as the latter in order to present a more acceptable face to the general public. **Foucault**'s work is centrally concerned with this issue, and how the dominant group in **modern** societies has created a series of institutions – asylums, hospitals, the prison service, for example – to maintain its control over the mass of the populace. The **discourses** that resulted were based on power relations rather than any moral considerations. Political **grand narratives** (liberal democracy, **Marxism**, etc.) may present themselves as a set of ideals that we all share, but in reality they are a means of keeping certain groups in power. Postmodern politics is dedicated to disrupting the power relations that had become entrenched within modernity as a cultural movement. [SS]

PRESENCE Jacques **Derrida** argues that Western thought in general is based on the notion of presence: that is, that the full meaning of words (or concepts) is 'present' to us in our minds when we think them, and that there is no 'slippage' between word and meaning. For Derrida, this is a metaphysical assumption that we are unjustified in making (see also **metaphysics of presence**). [SS]

PYNCHON, THOMAS: NOVELIST (1937–) Pynchon studied physics and then English at Cornell University between 1953 and 1955, and then served in the United States Navy in the 1950s as part of the Signals Corps. He also worked as an editorial writer for Boeing Aircraft in Seattle between 1960 and 1962. Little more is known about his private life or public activities. Since his early short stories – collected in *Slow Learner* (1984) – were published in the early 1960s, he has seldom given interviews or attended book-signing

sessions. This reclusiveness became his most saleable asset when his later novels *Vineland* (1990) and *Mason & Dixon* (1997) were promoted.

The reputation created by his previous three novels – *V.* (1963), *The Crying of Lot 49* (1966) and *Gravity's Rainbow* (1973) – fuelled further media interest. These works are based on complex metaphors which, instead of acting as anchors of sense, scatter meaning across a wide terrain. Exhaustive in scope, they include references to electronics, the history of the US postal system, information theory, ballistics, the second law of thermodynamics and many other weighty topics. Despite this encyclopaedism, Pynchon mocks the urge to construct a **grand narrative** out of these disparate materials.

In *V.*, for instance, Herbert Stencil looks back into moments of European history for evidence of a mercurial woman, possibly his mother, whose nickname, 'V', is the only clue to her identity. But, as his search proceeds, the dark lady recedes. These episodes betray Stencil's Rorschach-like projection of meaning into random data and his pulsating paranoia. 'V' becomes a 'remarkably scattered concept', encompassing the V-Note jazz club, the Via dei Vecchietti, and the sewers where the rat Veronica lives. Then there are the various incarnations of V herself: the Lady V. of Paris, Vera Meroving in South-West Africa, and others.

Gravity's Rainbow (1973) is sometimes called the **postmodern** Ulysses, and with good reason. It follows a similar pattern of quest and excess. Tyrone Slothrop, an American lieutenant in Europe after VE Day, is programmed by behaviourist Ned Pointsman to find the advanced V-2 rockets launched by the Germans towards the end of the Second World War. He travels around the Zone (a demilitarized space in Central Europe swarming with bootleggers, conmen and migrants) to seek out a crack group of African rocketeers, called the Schwarzkommando. However, the rocket is elusive, and allusive too. Like the letter V, the rocket has to be many things – too many things. Slothrop eventually crumbles under the weight of this information overload. He forgoes his search in favour of the 'mindless pleasures' (the novel's working title) of sex and drugs.

Mason & Dixon follows the fortunes of Charles Mason and Jeremiah Dixon as they plot their famous line to divide Maryland and Pennsylvania in the 1760s. They are like Rosencrantz and Guildenstern, unaware of the larger implications of their actions, especially the significance their work will have one hundred years later in the American Civil War. [BL]

Q

QUANTUM MECHANICS Quantum mechanics grew out of increasing anomalies generated by classical physics and Einstein's modifications of it. Composed of the three spatial dimensions plus one of time, the world of classical physics is the one of large-scale, observable structures and events that we live in. Ironically, Niels Bohr, one of the originators of quantum physics, did not intend to demonstrate the physical limits of classical laws at the scale of subatomic particles, but to patch up the fraying fabric of classical reality. Having entered this quantum world, however, Bohr and others have found that it cannot even be comprehended within a classical frame. Thus a key problem in quantum mechanics, famously described by Heisenberg's uncertainty principle, has it that since all our measurements are macroscopic and classical rather than microscopic and quantum, how can events at the subatomic level be measured by macroscopic means? If we take one classical parameter – position – and measure a subatomic particle accordingly, we not only sacrifice measurement of similarly classical parameters, such as velocity, but actually alter the behaviour of those particles. If we do not measure particles in this way, however, quantum events become undecidable catalogues of classically incompatible possibilities: quantum cats, for example, classically either alive or dead, become superpositions of live cats and dead cats. When an observer physically intervenes, the cat reverts to one or the other classical state, but at the same time all information about its quantum states is instantaneously dispersed. [IHG]

QUEER THEORY In the early 1990s, there were a number of articles, conferences and special issues of journals that dealt with lesbian and gay culture by embracing the stigmatized term 'queer'. This was both to remind the reader of homophobic prejudice and to suggest a form of criticism that uses a pejorative signifier of transgressive **desire** and sexual instability as a metaphor to describe a category that goes beyond categories. Heavily marked by **deconstruction**, queer readings use a variety of **postmodern** theories 'to destabilize the entire system of sex regulation, that undoes **binary oppositions** such as gay/straight', as Judith **Butler** has argued. Identity, rather than being the essence of our being, is a '**simulation**', a contingent, provisional performance.

Queer theory produces a disturbing, profoundly philosophical kind of criticism that argues not for alternative forms of identity, but for identity's confounding. For Butler and other influential theorists of queer reading such as Eve Kosofsky Sedgwick and D. A. Miller, identity, and in particular sexual identity, is non-essentialist and formed in a material reality that is mediated through **discourse**. Some critics have argued that this formidable body of criticism plays down sexual **difference** and that its sceptical stance forbids it producing any useful or emancipatory knowledge. [PD]

R

READERLY TEXTS Roland **Barthes** in his later, **poststructuralist,** phase (roughly from the publication of *S/Z* in 1970 onwards) distinguished between readerly and **writerly texts**. The former were taken to impose a meaning on the reader, whereas the latter invited the reader to engage in the production of textual meaning. Barthes argued in *S/Z* that readerly texts encouraged passive consumption, being designed to constrain the exercise of the reader's imagination. In such cases the **author** was exerting **power** over the reader, and readerly texts therefore played a part in maintaining the cultural status quo. It is difficult to be precise as to what constitutes a readerly text, but nineteenth-century realist novels, with their carefully worked-out plots, omniscient narrators and overt moral purpose, are probably good candidates. In these cases, as Barthes sees it, the reader is forced to respond in a predetermined way and to accept the author's world-view as expressed through the **narrative**. Reading becomes passive consumption, but passive consumption in the service of a particular socio-political structure. To argue in favour of writerly texts (where the reader is assumed to be actively involved in the production of textual meaning) is therefore to take a stance against the prevailing political and intellectual order. [SS]

REED, ISHMAEL: NOVELIST, POET, PLAYWRIGHT (1938–) From the mid-1960s when he began to publish his work, Reed has developed his own style and critical terminology. It was left to others to label it **postmodernism**. His own aesthetic principles, which he calls 'neo-HooDoo', derive from Egyptian myth and Voodoo religious symbolism found in Caribbean and African folklore. These are 'syncretic', taking from other religions what they need, as Reed's fiction does. His novels, from the first, *The Freelance Pallbearers* (1967), to *Japanese By Spring* (1993), are **intertextual** carnivals: **hybrid** fictions that draw on an enormous range of **discourses**. As a character in *Yellow Back Radio Broke-Down* (1970) remarks, 'no one says a novel has to be one thing'.

A good example of Reed's approach *is Mumbo Jumbo* (1972). Here we find footnotes, cartoons, photographs, illustrations and a bibliography. Reed, always a disputatious writer, often uses his fiction to settle scores with his critics. He has an implacable hatred of white supremacism, but also both black nationalism for its largely essentialist notions of blackness and its prescriptive aesthetic principles, and feminism for its collusion with white racists in denigrating black men. Very schematically, the black narrative tradition has two major modes: at one pole would be testamentary and confessional writing from slave **narratives** to tales of self-discovery, while at the other would be the parodic and 'signifying' tradition represented by the likes of Ralph Ellison, Clarence Major and, most exuberantly but unevenly, by Reed himself. [PD]

REICH, STEVE: COMPOSER (1936–) A pioneer of **minimalist music**, Reich's musical language owes a lot to non-Western musics (such as West African drumming and Balinese gamelan), medieval music, jazz and earlier twentieth-century styles. He came from a musical family, and his early musical training included piano lessons and studying Western percussion and drumming. Reich also studied with the composers Darius Milhaud and Luciano Berio.

Following his formal education in composition he was quick to reject the **modernist** aesthetics and techniques such as serialism and atonality, which had come to dominate the art tradition of music in the twentieth century. He felt that the so-called avant-garde composers had not only lost touch with the essential ingredients of music (e.g. pulse, rhythm and tonal direction) but had alienated their audiences with music that was mathematical, over-intellectual and preoccupied with structure. His early works were concerned with process, repetition and gradual changes, and utilized the technique of 'gradual phase shifting'. This was achieved by playing two identical tape loops on tape recorders, one machine playing fractionally faster than the other, so that they were gradually shifted out of phase with one another. This process was later realized using live musicians.

Reich, who had had a growing interest in traditional African music since the early 1960s, travelled to Ghana in the summer of 1970 to study with a master drummer of the Ewe tribe. He later studied gamelan (in 1973) with a Balinese musician-in-residence at the University of Washington in Seattle. His compositions of the 1970s and 1980s show a marked influence from these two non-Western genres in that the music was complex in its rhythmic aspects but remained, harmonically, relatively simple. Compositions such as *Six Pianos* (1973) and *Music for Eighteen Musicians* (1976), both being written for his own ensemble (formed in 1966), exhibit an intensity and complexity of rhythm coupled with harmony which remains static for long periods. Counterpoint – the technique of layering and intertwining a number of independent melodic lines – was also

emerging, in this period, as one of his fundamental techniques. *Different Trains* (1987), *The Cave* (1993) and *City Life* (1995) contain a strong narrative drive and make use of speech samples to generate the fabric of the music. This contrasts sharply with his earlier works which abstained from the dialectics of **narratives** or self-expression.

Reich's music has until quite recently been ignored by academia, and for the most part been rejected by the modernist music establishment. During the 1960s and 1970s his music, which was almost entirely written for his own ensemble, was often performed (away from the established concert halls) in galleries and lofts attracting an audience who might have been more at home in a theatre, art gallery or rock concert than at a 'classical' recital. Reich is, however, one of the most influential composers of the late twentieth and early twenty-first centuries and has not only inspired, but also paved the way for a host of younger composers such as John **Adams** and Michael **Nyman**. [AB]

REPRESENTATION Postmodern theories of representation take many forms. In painting, for instance, the 1970s and 1980s are said to have witnessed the reintroduction of representation accompanied by **irony**, illusion and disbelief, where content rather than form was deemed to be of central importance. These are ideas primarily associated with American theorists of painting, such as Donald Kuspit and Lawrence Alloway. In continental Europe, however, representation is figured in very different terms by philosophers of the **poststructuralist** school, with **Lyotard** and **Derrida**, for example, pointing to the impossibility of representing reality. In their denial of 'reality' as such, works such as Lyotard's *The Postmodern Condition* (1979) and *The Differend* (1983) emphasize that the 'unpresentable' (or the **sublime**) exists. Attempts to represent the unpresentable are considered to be the defining characteristic of the avant-garde artist.

Following Derrida, **deconstructionists** concentrate on the slippery and ambivalent nature of language, and are similarly negative about the possibility of representing reality. Deconstructionist analyses of representation are **anti-foundationalist** in intent, and attack the idea that the Western philosophical tradition provides a transcendental set of beliefs which are 'truthful'. **Foucault**, on the other hand, draws attention to the pervasiveness of **power** inside representation, particularly as it relates to institutions, and the manner in which certain representations of power are favoured at the expense of others. Consequently, a Foucauldian analysis of representation engages in a more direct fashion with questions of gender, race and class. Postmodern theorists on the left – **Baudrillard** and **Jameson**, for example – argue that representation in the arts has been made impossible by the cultural **hegemony** of capitalism. [AE]

RETRO As part of its campaign against **modernism** and **modernity**, and their cult of the new and original, **postmodernism** has encouraged dialogue with the past. Perhaps most famously, this change of attitude towards the past can be found in Charles **Jencks'** notion of **double coding**, where a deliberate attempt is made to appeal to both specialists and the general public by mixing together old and new architectural styles in one building. Such reappropriation and recontextualization of older forms and styles, often referred to as retro, has become a hallmark of the postmodern aesthetic and features prominently in areas such as art, music and fashion. In keeping with the postmodern ethos, retro often involves an **ironic** attitude towards the earlier style, and is not a simple act of homage or mere imitation – more a case of a critical comment on the cult of originality for originality's sake. [SS]

RHIZOME In *A Thousand Plateaus* (1980), Gilles **Deleuze** and Félix **Guattari** put forward the notion of the rhizome as a model for how systems should work in a **postmodern** world. Prime examples of rhizomes in the natural world would be tubers or mosses, and it is characteristic of a rhizomatic system that, as Deleuze and Guattari put it, any point on it can be connected up to any other (as in the intertwining of mosses). Rhizomes are contrasted to trees and roots, which, in Deleuze and Guattari's opinion, 'fix an order', and are thus implicitly restrictive and authoritarian. The implication is that since rhizomes do not feature the linear development pattern of trees and roots, they are more democratic and creative, thus forming a better basis for systems in a postmodern world than the tree-like hierarchies most Western societies tend to favour.

In common with their poststructuralist and **postmodernist** peers, Deleuze and Guattari are firmly opposed to hierarchy and authority, and concerned to find alternative methods of constructing networks. Something like the rhizome idea can be found in the **Internet**, which similarly allows for connections to be established between any two points of the system, as well as having no clearly identifiable 'centre', or central authority. [SS]

RICHTER, GERHARD: ARTIST (1932–) Although Richter has been a major figure in German art from the 1960s, his international reputation was made in the late 1970s, when Benjamin Buchloh and other exponents of **postmodernist** art criticism began to take an interest in his work. Richter's artistic industry and heterogeneity – his productions include site-specific objects, sculpture, paintings, photography and painting – is striking. What continues to fascinate commentators, however, are his so-called photo-paintings, which he began in the 1960s. These have been discussed in terms of postmodern culture for their capacity to operate as **hybrid** objects, eroding the **difference** between the operational needs of cultural practice and visual information.

Critics have seen in his photo-paintings meditations on the nature of visual knowledge analogous to the writings of **Debord** and **Baudrillard**. That is, Richter's works are taken as evidence of a fascination with a new order of visuality in which the visual **sign** is generated by a technological order where everything begins with reproduction. Thus *Woman Descending the Staircase* (1965), *Motor Boat* (1965), *Toilet Paper* (1965) and *Cathedral Square* (1968) become evidence of a process in which to represent the real is to acknowledge that visual experience is organized by *systems* of vision. This interest in the mechanization of perception can be related to a broader range of postmodern concerns with the development of optical technology and the governmental logic of media systems and circuits.

In addition to an interest in the mechanization of vision, Richter went on to produce a body of work which seemed to combine an engagement with techniques of visual experience with technologies of **power**. In *18 October 1977* (1988), a series devoted to the activities and demise of the Baader-Meinhof group, we find an inexplicable and arbitrary cluster of fragments of experience – blurred or grainy figures lost in inky chambers, fuzzy and indeterminate objects and forms, inaccessible and poorly defined spaces, featureless, fluid or insubstantial surfaces. Painting becomes a monument to failure, a record of degraded vision, and the **erasure**, or dissolution, of the conditions in which meaning is comprehended.

Confrontation 1 is a good example of how the series reduces knowledge to the shadowland of an undefined perceptual agency. We seem to be in a prison cell looking at whom we assume to be Ulrike Meinhof. Yet the spacing of the photo-painting is disorientating. Are we in the cell with this **subject**, or does our presence indicate that we are interrogating her? Richter eschews the rhetoric associated with **representations** of this kind; he makes this subject illegible; we cannot read the expression on her face, which might be a smile, a sign of fear, or panic. Here, as in many of his other works, he announces a major theme of postmodernism: we exist in an uncertain world where material evidence contradicts itself. [CT]

RILEY, TERRY: COMPOSER (1935–) An early pioneer of **minimalist music**, Riley was one of the first to use techniques which became central to the minimalist aesthetic, such as repetition, tonality and the building up of a collage of sound from just a few musical cells or motifs. While studying composition at the San Francisco State College and, later, piano at the San Francisco Conservatoire, he supported himself by working as a ragtime pianist. He also studied Indian classical music with his friend and mentor, Pandit Pran Nath.

While Riley's early works were influenced by **modernist** composers such as Stockhausen, it was in the 1960s that he began to experiment with repetition, layering and the superimposition of small rhythmic cells. He used tape loops and tape delays to achieve this, producing works such as *The Five Legged Stool* (1961) and *Dorian Reeds*. Being an accomplished pianist he, more than the other minimalists, gave greater weight to improvisation and also wrote many solo piano pieces. The *Keyboard Studies*, intended for solo performance, were often not written down, or were notated in the briefest possible way.

Perhaps his most famous piece, often regarded as the first minimalist piece ever, is *In C* (1964). The piece, for any number of performers playing any suitable instruments, consists of fifty-three short musical figures. While a steady pulse is established by the continuous repetition of a high C note, the performers are left to repeat each motif as many times as they wish before moving on to the next one. Thus a complex, overlapping, polyrhythmic web is created from just a few short motifs.

Riley's music has been hugely inspirational to both **Reich** and **Glass** who further developed the minimalist techniques and aesthetics. [AB]

RORTY, RICHARD: PHILOSOPHER (1931–) Rorty has been among the foremost American champions of recent **continental philosophy (Derrida, deconstruction, post-structuralism**, etc.), and also an important voice in what has come to be known as **post-philosophy**.

In his early career Rorty is self-consciously the heir of the American pragmatist school of philosophy, and in particular of the work of John Dewey and C. S. Peirce. Rorty put the case for pragmatism most famously in *Philosophy and the Mirror of Nature* (1980) and *Consequences of Pragmatism* (1982), both of which challenged Western philosophy's commitment to absolute notions of, for example, truth or goodness. For Rorty, such notions were chimerical, and all the apparent problems surrounding them were in reality non-problems. He saw pragmatism's role as the dissolution of such issues as the nature of truth, arguing that a pragmatist was uninterested in taking sides or weighing up the pros and cons of the argument, but instead merely wanted 'to change the subject' to something more interesting.

Philosophy and the Mirror of Nature discusses the various theories of mind and knowledge put forward over the course of philosophical history, only in order to demonstrate that the problems they deal with are non-existent – the product of a particular world-view and set of historical imperatives that can be changed if we so wish. In this case, what Rorty wishes to call into question is Western philosophy's long-running obsession with the notion of the mind as a mirror of reality, and he is highly critical of the belief that there can be any such thing as an 'accurate **representation** of reality'.

Consequences of Pragmatism argues that truth is not something we should expect to have philosophically interesting theories about, since such theories tell us very little about our world. Any world they do tell us something about is, in Rorty's view, 'a world well lost'. Rorty feels that theories ought to be judged in terms of their usefulness to us rather than their truthfulness anyway, truth being merely, as another American pragmatist philosopher William James had put it, 'what it is better for us to believe'. Seen from this perspective it makes more sense to ask if a theory makes us happy than whether it is true.

Ultimately, Rorty's major concern is to ensure that debate and discussion continue rather than that one theory is allowed to dominate proceedings (politically he describes himself as a liberal). His model for such debate has been academic common-room conversation (and he does tend to regard philosophy as little more than a form of conversation), which he contends is less interested in reaching final conclusions – such as the *real* nature of truth or mind – than in examining a subject from as many angles as possible. This, rather than the fruitless search for watertight theories, becomes Rorty's ideal. He distinguishes between what he calls 'systematic' and 'edifying' philosophy, with the latter being described as the form of philosophical enquiry that enables us to break free from outmoded **discourses** – such as debates on the nature of truth or mind. It is a kind of philosophy that we can find in the work of the American pragmatists, or in Martin **Heidegger** or Ludwig Wittgenstein. Systematic philosophy, the search for watertight theories, is, on the other hand, what Rorty feels we should be trying to avoid at all costs.

In his later work, such as *Contingency, Irony and Solidarity* (1989), Rorty has espoused what can only be called a post-philosophical position, arguing that philosophy is something like a bad habit we should be striving to overcome (there are intimations of this view in the earlier writings too, where he queries whether philosophy even has the right to call itself a professional field of enquiry). For the later Rorty, subjects such as literature or social theory are of much more value to us, as a guide to our behaviour and personal development, than philosophy ever can be, and he often sounds as if he wishes to turn his back on philosophy altogether.

In his disenchantment with the standard **narrative** of Western philosophy Rorty strikes an authentically **postmodern** note. Certainly, there is no commitment to absolutes or universal theories to be found in his writings, which see no privileged position for philosophy as the supposed arbiter of all other intellectual discourses. Rorty's suggestion that **irony** (or 'liberal ironism' as he dubs it) is the appropriate attitude to adopt towards life, is authentically postmodern too. [SS]

RUSHDIE, SALMAN: NOVELIST (1947–) Salman Rushdie was born into a Muslim family living in Bombay a matter of months before two of his most famous characters: Saleem Sinai, the narrator of Rushdie's finest novel *Midnight's Children* (1980), and the state of India. *Midnight's Children* tells the story of modern India through the eyes and other senses of Sinai, an unreliable if entrancing narrator. Rushdie has a political message, but that message never comes between the reader and the joy of the endlessly intricate plot and the moving, comic, tragic characters. As in all of his fiction, Rushdie wears his **postmodernism** a little heavily: 'reality' is a sham, or rather a construct – the true reality is the story, the **narrative** through which and for which we live. *Midnight's*

Children made Rushdie's career. It became a best-seller, and won the Booker Prize in 1981.

Rushdie's third novel, *Shame* (1983), has some of the same elements that made *Midnight's Children* – the extraordinary and the ordinary rubbing shoulders in the East (this time the Pakistan of the 1950s to the 1970s), the same narrative tricks and the same florid prose. The story is a transparent retelling of the Bhutto-Zia feud in which it is difficult to work out who comes out best, the decadent Bhutto or the malevolent Zia. The openly scornful treatment of **fundamentalist** Islam in *Shame* became a scabrous, scatological attack on the very foundations of the Muslim world in *The Satanic Verses* (1989), a sort of alternative life of the Prophet, in which Mohammed is portrayed as all too human. Like all Rushdie's fiction, the book blurs the boundaries between fact and fantasy, and, in true postmodernist style, the everyday reality of the modern world becomes crazily mixed up with the fantastic and the supernatural.

The publication of *The Satanic Verses* changed Rushdie's life for ever, after a fatwa was issued against him by the Ayatollah Khomeni. The incident, which saw massive demonstrations in Iran, India and the United Kingdom, showed both the gulf in understanding between the West and the Islamic world, and how, for all the postmodernists' **irony** and detachment, literature can have a deadly impact in the 'real' world.

The Moor's Last Sigh (1995), tells the story of Moraes Zogoiby. Another of Rushdie's bizarre narrators, Zogoiby, who is condemned to age at twice the normal rate, tells the stories of his family, particularly of his artist mother, a Christian, possibly descended from Vasco da Gama, married to a Jew. The model for this cascade of stories is that perennial favourite of postmodernist authors, *The Thousand and One Nights*.

Not all of Rushdie's critics have been raging clerics. Some secular commentators in India have criticized what they see as Rushdie's patronizing, Western-influenced liberalism (he has subsequently attacked both Hindu and Muslim **fundamentalism**). His portraits of Indians have been condemned as Western stereotypes and his own rendering of Anglo-Indian speech idioms has been ridiculed. Many Eastern and Western critics have described his post-*Midnight's Children* work as boring and unreadable. [AM]

S

SAID, EDWARD, W.: CRITIC, CULTURAL THEORIST (1935–2003) Said was born in Jerusalem and educated in Egypt and America. His publications include *Beginnings: Intention and Method* (1975), *Orientalism* (1978), *The World, the Text and the Critic* (1983) and *Culture and Imperialism* (1993).

In an afterword to the 1995 edition of *Orientalism*, Said distinguishes 'two broad currents: **postcolonialism** and **postmodernism**'. He argues that the prefix 'post' suggests not so much a 'sense of going beyond but rather continuities and discontinuities'. His contribution to the current theoretical debate has been in his analyses of seminal postmodernist thinkers such as **Barthes**, **Deleuze**, **Derrida** and **Foucault** in *Beginnings*. Indeed, *Orientalism*, which Said describes as 'an antecedent of postmodernism and postcolonialism', appears to draw upon Foucault's notion of the relationship between knowledge and **power**. The first of what can be viewed as a trilogy of studies examining the relationship between East and West, Orient and Occident, *Orientalism* is arguably Said's most influential work. It resists notions of a natural and stable human identity and undermines the belief in the certain positivity and unchanging historicity of a culture, a self or a national identity. The Orient and the Occident correspond to no stable 'reality' that exists as a natural fact. The apparatus of orientalism manufactures the 'Orient' and thus helps to regulate colonialist relations. Thus Said draws on Vico's observation that human history is made by human beings, while adhering to the **poststructuralist** idea that there are only **representations** in texts. This is highlighted in the second and third works of this 'trilogy': *The Question of Palestine* (1979) and *Covering Islam* (1981). Both of these texts are concerned with the representation of the Arab world by the Western press.

Culture and Imperialism (1993) focuses, in the early chapters, on canonical writers such as Jane Austen and Rudyard Kipling. The focus then shifts to 'national' writers and colonized intellectuals with readings of W. B. Yeats and Ranajit Guha. A later reading of Yeats (*Field Day Pamphlet 15*) takes up the question of nationalism and the dangers inherent in it, while pointing to the crucial role of literature in the re-establishment of a national cultural heritage, and in the reimagining and refiguring of local histories, geographies and communities. The danger lies in the concept of an imagined community resulting in a nativist impasse. Liberation (not nationalism) involves a transformation of social consciousness beyond national consciousness.

The impact of Said's work, in particular his theory propounded in *Orientalism*, has been considerable in the field of postcolonial studies. His attempts to dismantle naturalized assumptions about language and textuality, and his preoccupation with the importance of ideological construction in socio-textual relations, align him with the poststructuralist movement, while the accessibility of his works make him a widely read and influential figure in contemporary literary and cultural theory. Described by the poet Tom Paulin as the 'Archangel Michael – who stood out against power and injustice to build through his writings, his lectures and broadcasts and ceaseless passionate communicativeness what Milton called "the great palace *now* of light'", Said will be remembered as a consummate intellectual and a champion of human dignity and freedom. [AY]

Schizoanalysis A form of anti-psychoanalysis devised by Gilles **Deleuze** and Félix **Guattari** in their controversial study *Anti-Oedipus* (1972), based on the experience of the schizophrenic. The theory is that the schizophrenic provides a better model for resisting authority (as embedded in the procedures of psychoanalysis, for example), than such types as the neurotic – and resisting authority is all but an article of faith for **postmodernists** such as Deleuze and Guattari. Schizophrenics, with their multiple identities, are seen to defeat the efforts of the psychoanalyst to make them conform (that being the point of psycho-analysis, as far as Deleuze and Guattari are concerned), whereas neurotics are more likely to be induced to co-operate, thus help-ing to perpetuate an authoritarian system.

Psychoanalysis is regarded by the authors as a form of politically inspired social control, and the ability of schizophrenics to frustrate the process turns them into post-modernist role models. Loss of ego amounts to a politically subversive act in this respect. (See also **Oedipus**.) [SS]

Semanalysis A synthesis of **semiotics**, **Marxism**, and **Freudianism** put together by Julia **Kristeva** in her first major work of theory, *Semiotike: Recherches pour une semanalyse* (1968). Kristeva's contention was that **semiotics** was both a critical science in its own right and a critique of science itself. She coined the term semanalysis to describe semiotics in this new critical-political role that she had designed for it, and saw her project as being very close in spirit to the structural **Marxism** of Louis Althusser and his disciples, with its concern to turn Marxism into a hard-edged 'science of society'. The inspiration behind the development of semanalysis, designed to provide a scientific basis for the study of all **sign** systems, came from such formal sciences as mathematics and logic. [SS]

Semiotics Semiotics (or semiology) is for a **structuralist** the science of **signs**, but for a **postmodernist** merely the study of them. Ferdinand de Saussure first broke from the study of language through its history (philology) to investigate language as a structure (linguistics). For Saussure, and all subsequent semioticians, a word is made up of a material component, such as a sound, or a mark on a page, which he terms the *signifier,* and a mental component, the concept or idea represented by the signi-fier: the *signified.* The signifier and the signified together form a *sign*. Saussurean linguistics became the model for the investigation of all patterned human com-munication. If a semiotician gives her boyfriend a bunch of roses she knows that it is a sign that can be broken down into the matter of the roses, their petals and leaves – the signifier – and the message they convey: 'I love you' – the signified.

After Saussure, semiologists have con-centrated on showing the influence of signs, their **power** and ubiquity. One classic illus-tration of the semiotic method is Roland **Barthes**' *Mythologies* (1957). Barthes takes various aspects of French popular culture – car adverts, wrestling, soap-powders – and analyses them to reveal the subtle mean-ings they convey – often sinister, conserva-tive and repressive.

The emergence of **poststructuralism** towards the end of the 1960s meant a shift in emphasis from the signified to the signi-fier. In the work of Jacques **Derrida** and Julia **Kristeva**, the links between signifier and signified are broken, replaced by the **intertextual** free interplay of signifiers. Struc-turalists had sought to find *the* meaning of **texts**; poststructuralists revel in multiple meanings, none of which can be allowed priority.

Postmodernism takes this process one stage further. For Jean **Baudrillard**, present-day society is so saturated with signs pumped out by the media that it is no longer possible to distinguish between signs and reality. [AM]

SHERMAN, CINDY: ARTIST (1954–) Sherman became famous with her *Untitled Film Stills* (1977–80), a series of black-and-white photographs in which she played out a multiplicity of filmic conventions concerned with feminine identity. Initially, these images were celebrated for their apparent concern with the 'mythology' of originality. In 1979, Sherman stated: 'Some people have told me they remember the movie that one of my images is derived from, but in fact I had no film in mind at all.' Early versions of **postmodernist** art criticism, which concentrated on cultural artefacts opposed to the **simulated** nature of contemporary experience, paid homage to an artist committed to illuminating and disrupting the way in which everyday life was orientated, regulated and encoded by the materials of the mass media.

Throughout the *Untitled Film Stills* Sherman positions herself as both 'actress' and 'director', recalling, through the use of lighting, depth of field, camera angle, clothing, decor and topography, a range of filmic conventions in which femininity is conventionalized. This sense of inhabiting cultural identities in order to 'foreground' their ideological or **discursive** nature was linked to the postmodernist strategies of Peter **Halley** and Sherrie Levine, both of whom defined art as a technology of **power** rather than as a neutral aesthetic form. Thus critics like Douglas Crimp and Lisa Phillips applauded work that concentrated on the media construction of reality and the concomitant 'elimination' of the artistic self. It could be affirmed that not only was Sherman revealing the mythic or fictive nature of feminine stereotypes, but her use of photography demonstrated its

complicity in the process of identity formation. Therefore her critique was construed as double-fold: it was feminist, in that it illuminated the devices by which women were subordinate to the 'instrumentalized' norms of Hollywood; it was postmodern, in that it confirmed the illusionary nature of originality, authenticity and individuality.

By the early 1980s, it was no longer possible to see in Sherman's work a fascination with unravelling the matrix of filmic conventions associated with articulations of female subjectivity. However, *Fashion* (1983–4), *Disasters* and *Fairy Tales* (1985–9), *Civil War* (1991) and *Sex Pictures* (1992) were still identified as exemplars of postmodernist art. Here she began to use new compositional formats, **subjects** and truncated plastic mannequins. These incomplete or 'aberrant' commodities, purchased from medical suppliers, were immediately integrated into a new 'somatic' postmodernist discourse that emerged from an engagement with the psychoanalytical writings of Julia **Kristeva**. Laura Mulvey, writing in the *New Left Review* (1991), claimed that Sherman's 'bulimic' images confront the construction of female identity through a re-evaluation of the relationship between interior and exterior spaces. She saw in Sherman's new bodily landscape of 'disgust' an engagement with the experience of the fear, anxiety and shame of having a body that is always 'unhomely' or unfinished. Anxiety replaces alienation in these deliquescent, decomposing images where the human being becomes a viscose web of grotesque forms, part biological, part **cyborg**. In this amorphous zone Mulvey discovered the appearance of what Kristeva calls '**abjection**': the confrontation with the primal 'unspeakable abyss' of 'liquidity' and 'decay' that precedes our division between the clean and the unclean, the pure and the impure.

Sherman's career has coincided with the mutation of postmodernist art from a concern with the codes, techniques and **narratives** in which subjectivity is produced, to an engagement with the processes of **representation** – a confrontation with the chaotic formlessness from which bodies and matter are made readable, legible and intelligible. Since the mid-1990s, however, she has attempted to fuse these interests by documenting the layering of 'absurd' identities – such as the clown – that are made janus-like in their combination of the blubbery joyfulness of their bodies and the menacing qualities of their expressions. [CT]

SIGN In Saussurean linguistics, the sign is constituted by the union between a signifier (word) and signified (concept). This union takes place in the individual's mind, and its end product is a recognition of the meaning of the word in question. This meaning is held to be a more or less stable entity, which does not change arbitrarily or at any given individual's whim. It is shared, therefore, by all the members of a given linguistic community at a particular historical moment, although it can change over time. Saussure regarded language as a sign system, which elicited common responses from individuals, and his linguistic theories went on to form the basis for **structuralism**. Structuralist theorists took Saussurean linguistics as the model for the study of all other sign systems, demonstrating how, for example, literary genres were made up of signs (or **narrative** conventions) that signalled to readers to respond in a particular manner.

Poststructuralist theorists such as Jacques **Derrida** have taken a very different view of the sign, regarding it as a fractured entity which can never capture the 'full' meaning of words. One commentator on Derrida, Gayatri Chakravorty **Spivak**, has spoken of the sign as being 'half not there, and half not that', and as such being open to a wide range of interpretations by individuals. The sign is therefore an *unstable* entity in post-structuralist thought, and meaning shot through with ambiguity. [SS]

SIMULACRA, SIMULATION **Baudrillard**'s theories relating to simulation stem from his early work on **sign** systems in the 1970s, where he argued that commodity and sign had combined in order to form a self-referential loop within a closed 'object system'. While the collective imagination may be deceived into thinking that such signs refer to something real and solid outside the system, this is an illusion. What is being generated is a 'simulacrum', which, although the product of the system, also acts as the external referent by which it justifies its function.

In *Symbolic Exchange and Death* (1976), Baudrillard organized the history of the production of simulacra into three parts. In the 'classical' era (from the Renaissance to the Industrial Revolution), simulation takes the form of counterfeiting. This is followed by the 'industrial' era, in which techniques of mass production allow an order of infinitely reproducible objects. Finally, in our contemporary **postmodern** order, new cybernetics and communications technologies have absorbed human **subjectivity** itself into a network of busily self-replicating digital systems.

In *Simulations* (1983), Baudrillard sums up the status of the 'real' in the postmodern world. Transformed into the '**hyperreal**', which bears no relation to any reality whatsoever, it has disappeared entirely into the process of simulation, and become 'its own pure simulacrum'. [SG]

SIMULATIONISM A development from the mass-media appropriators of the late 1970s, simulationism emerged in New York in the shape of Peter **Halley**, Sherrie Levine, Phillip Taaffe, Ross Bleckner, Jeff **Koons** and Ashley Bickerton, most of whom were part of a critical network where the writings of **Foucault, Baudrillard** and **Debord** were well known. Two assumptions characterize this art: the idea that the contemporary social order is structured by the **representations**, **signs** and values embedded in the processes of consumption; and the belief that the scope and **power** of art must be measured through its capacity to demonstrate that reality has been assimilated into a **globalized** image culture.

If Halley, Bleckner, Taaffe and Levine 'copied' the styles of Newman, Stella, Ryman, Mondrian and Malevich, emphasizing the material character of their work, they did so in order to deny the idea that art posits its own formal purity. Copying is not an act of homage but a parody of the idea that art possesses unique powers, an acknowledgement that it is derived from the mechanical and scientific processes it ostensibly rejects. In abstract art, concerned as it is with fundamental orders and optical regimes, could be seen the technocratic geometries of circuits, networks, and other signs of the material logic of the social order. From these conceptual foundations two forms of practice were developed: first, Bickerton's self-styled 'defiant complicity', where the cybernetic **hybridity** of the object-as-platform attempts to assimilate all aspects of the infrastructure of art by referring, as Bickerton put it, 'to every station of its operational life, i.e. storage, shipping, gallery access, rack reproduction, and on the wall'; second, Halley's simulated **sublime**, where the painting, composed of grids, nodes, conduits and cells, confirms the priority of abstract codes and languages within a **postindustrial** social system where reality has become co-extensive to the duplication of signs within the simulated spaces of computer circuitry. [CT]

SINFIELD, ALAN: CRITIC (1941–) In such works as *Literature in Protestant England 1560–1660* (1983), *Literature, Politics and Culture in Post-War Britain* (1989) and *Faultlines* (1992) Sinfield has been an influential exponent of '**cultural materialism**', a version of ideological critique which has absorbed the insights of Michel **Foucault** on the relationship between sexuality and **power**. As an extension of that work, his later books, especially *Cultural Politics – Queer Reading* (1994), are engagements with '**queer theory**' from a cultural materialist perspective. In Sinfield's work we find some of the most familiar themes of **postmodern** criticism – marginality, sexual **difference**, the instability of **subjectivity**, **cultural relativism**, the politics of identity – but these are anchored by a socialist politics that sets itself against what he calls the 'apocalyptic vision' of postmodern **discourse** that 'depoliticizes culture by imagining it as flowing, necessarily with the stream of consumer capitalism'. He began his most original work in the early 1980s.

'Against Appropriation' in *Essays in Criticism* (1981) suggests that literary **texts** will serve us better if we allow them to 'challenge rather than confirm ourselves'; the real relevance of texts from the past resides precisely in their distance from our time, their very '**Otherness**', a quality critics in the more traditional universalizing humanist tradition seek to suppress in their quest for enduring human values. If, for instance, Shakespeare is our great universal poet, then his world-view must in important ways be close to ours. Much of Sinfield's work involves disabusing the complacent reader of this idea. Sinfield suggests that we reverse the principle of relevance; earlier writing illuminates not because it appeals to enduring needs, but because it offers an alternative perspective, a chance to confront our unexamined assumptions. By 1985 and *Political Shakespeare,* Sinfield and his co-editor Jonathan **Dollimore** had worked out a critical approach they called 'cultural materialism': the politically engaged, materialist analysis of culture.

In *Faultlines*, Sinfield describes what he calls 'dissident reading'. He chooses the term 'dissident' over the more glamorous 'transgressive' or 'subversive' because these terms imply that something has already happened; 'dissident' suggests that the dominant culture tells stories in which there are faultlines, and through which dissident readings can be made. A dominant discourse that speaks of subversion can, in the very act of demonizing it, give it a voice. Sinfield shows in *The Wilde Century* (1994) that nineteenth-century discourses on homosexuality made possible new forms of social control, but also enabled a 'reverse discourse' whereby homosexuality began to speak for itself, often using the very terms in which it was subordinated. A recent example would be the adoption of the pejorative term 'queer' by many gay activists and writers, Sinfield among them. For Sinfield, the subculture the term names is a source for possible oppositional selfhoods. [PD]

SINGULARITY In physics, a singularity is a point (described as being of infinite density) from which a series of effects unfold, but which is not itself 'caused' by anything else. The 'big bang' theory of the universe presupposes one such singularity, claiming that it is pointless to ask what caused the big bang, or existed before it, since the big bang *itself* was the beginning of space and time – and thus of causal sequences. Some theorists have speculated that the universe might ultimately collapse back into a singularity again. There are also held to be singularities at the centre of **black holes**.

Singularities have something like the properties traditionally attributed to divinity, in that they transcend physical explanations, such as those of cause and effect (the Christian God similarly creates a universe where there was not one before). The notion of singularity, with its insistence that there are limits to explanation (rather as there are with the **sublime**), appeals to the **postmodern** mind in that it provides one solution to the problem of foundations – although, philosophically

speaking, it could be said to constitute rather too neat a solution to that problem. [SS]

SITE: DESIGN FIRM (1970–) SITE ('Sculpture in the Environment') was founded in New York in 1970 by James Wines and Alison Sky. SITE's buildings have a freshness rarely seen in architecture. They played with the codes and iconographies of ubiquitous contemporary buildings: the supermarket, the highway and the parking lot. Within these recognizably ordinary buildings they made subversive interventions. With gestures located somewhere between the surreal and spectacle, such as the corner of a brick supermarket seemingly collapsing (the Indeterminate Facade showroom), or an undulating section of freeway populated by cars, aeroplanes, and boats (Highway 86 at the Vancouver Expo '86), they made these supposedly unarchitectural conditions special. This process of the transformation of the banal or everyday objects was borrowed from a tradition leading back through the conceptual art of the 1970s via pop to Marcel **Duchamp**. These tactics attempted to open up the restrictive and increasingly irrelevant practice of architecture – proposing a thoroughly contemporary alternative one that embraced the physical and cultural terrains of a highly developed capitalist economy.

SITE's work functions without complex spatial articulation, formal dynamics or esoteric architectural references; rather it engages the building as a means of questioning the nature of architecture – where the building is regarded as a site of communication. Their architecture has a thoroughly American flavour, mixing the **narrative** and iconographic play of Disney with banal suburban conditions. Best Products Company gave SITE numerous opportunities to subvert the generic out-of-town retail unit. This series of buildings demonstrates some of the tactics of what

SITE term 'de-architecture' – inversion, inclusion and indeterminacy, allied with humour and critique. [SJ]

SITUATIONISM Formed in Italy in 1957, the Situationists were a loose grouping of disputatious political activists, writers and artists who played a significant role in the Paris uprisings of May 1968. The most prominent members of the group were Guy **Debord**, political theorist and author of *The Society of the Spectacle* (1967), and the artist Asger Jorn. Debord edited the group's journal, which carried articles on Vietnam, urban geography, and cultural and political issues and was full of examples of the Situationists' distinctive and influential approach to graphic design, using political slogans and doctored images from the popular press and advertising. Debord's **Marxist**-influenced *The Society of the Spectacle* suggests that social relations themselves are mediated through images and that we have become spectators in our own lives, while Jorn's technique of *détournement* ('over-painting' found images with political messages) was used extensively by the late 1960s underground press and by punk bands and fanzines in the 1970s. Situationism both prefigures and inaugurates important elements of **postmodern** thinking; **Baudrillard**'s '**hyperreality**' has similarities to Debord's spectacle, while the Situationists' concept of the *dérive*, a psycho-geographical 'drift' through an urban landscape, becomes the philosophical 'drifting thought' of **Lyotard**. [PD]

SOKAL, ALAN: SCIENTIST, CULTURAL THEORIST (1955–) Alan Sokal created uproar in theoretical circles by managing to get a spoof article, 'Transgressing the Boundaries: Towards a Transformative Hermeneutics of Quantum Gravity', accepted by the prestigious American academic journal *Social Text* in 1996. His intention was to challenge what he considered to be the misuse of recent scientific theory (particularly in the field of physics) by certain **poststructuralist** and **postmodernist** theorists. In conjunction with another practising physicist, the Belgian Jean Bricmont, Sokal went on to mount a sustained critique of the French theoretical establishment in *Intellectual Impostures: Postmodern Philosophers' Abuse of Science* (French edition, 1997; English translation, 1998). The book created a storm of controversy in France with its savage attacks on such figures as **Baudrillard**, **Lyotard** and **Kristeva**, the latter dismissing the book as 'disinformation'. The **authors**' main point was that Baudrillard *et al.* simply misunderstood the scientific concepts, such as **chaos**, that they were deploying so freely in their own theorizing, and that any conclusions they drew were to be treated with deep suspicion. [SS]

SPIVAK, GAYATRI CHAKRAVORTY: CRITIC, FEMINIST, CULTURAL THEORIST (1941–) Variously labelled as feminist, **Marxist**, **deconstructivist** and **postcolonialist**, Gayatri Spivak epitomizes **postmodern subjectivity** in her constant reinvention of herself, her refusal to advocate absolutes and her ability to elude absolute definition. Born in Calcutta, Spivak was educated in India and America, where she was a student of Paul **de Man**. Her main works include *In Other Worlds: Essays in Cultural Politics* (1987), *Can the Subaltern Speak?* (1988), *Poststructuralism, Marginality, Postcoloniality and Value* (1988) and *Outside in the Teaching Machine* (1993).

Spivak's contribution to postmodern thought cannot be overestimated, as she has produced a number of learned disquisitions on a wide range of literary and cultural practices that raise questions about the constitution of identity, challenge the notion of any monolithic, **legitimizing** discourse, and undermine the epistemological status of historical thought within a self/**Other binarism** imposed by both patriarchy and imperialism. Spivak's deconstructive practices develop a strategy for reading that inverts the structures of domination by questioning the forms that constitute and disarticulate 'the **subaltern**' (i.e. women) who has been colonized in both a literal and metaphorical sense. Thus she writes at the intersection of post-colonialism and feminism reinstating the marginalized in place of the dominant with what she describes as 'a strategic use of positive essentialism in a scrupulously visible political interest'. She has insisted on the need for the deconstructive and the political to go hand in hand in order to highlight the material reality of racism/sexism in society, stressing the importance of ideology in forming the ideas of the colonial/female subject.

Deconstruction is the theory underlying Spivak's work, whether she is writing as a feminist, Marxist or postcolonialist. An accomplished philosopher who insists that she is described as a 'literary critic', she translated and prefaced Jacques **Derrida**'s *La Grammatologie* in 1976, which she said was 'a better way of describing what I am trying to do'. Her debt to deconstruction is obvious in her method of questioning the basic assumptions of dominant systems of language and thought in order to unsettle and decentre meaning, yet she is not uncritical of the project, cautioning that the unsettling of meaning per se will not promote a feminist future. For Spivak deconstruction should be a companion to the Marxist project. However, she is sceptical of the notion that deconstruction can be practised either as a theoretical discipline or as an ideological/political practice. In relation to feminism she describes Derrida's work as 'solipsistic' and 'marginal' when he writes from a pro-feminist perspective.

Her works on both feminism and post-colonial theory are attached to the notion of marginality which she describes as 'a buzzword in cultural critique now'. She questions the legitimacy of such terms, suggesting that the centre (patriarchy/neo-colonialism) fabricates its attitudes by proposing a share of the centre, not by rupture but by displacement, by offering disciplinary support for the conviction of 'authentic' marginality by an aspiring elite. Her argument for postcoloniality as a deconstructive case comes from the illogical, but naturalized, values that are coded within the legacy of imperialism: nationhood, constitutionality, citizenship, democracy and culturalism. Thus the supposedly 'authentic' cultural narratives from the 'margins' are written elsewhere, in the centre. Spivak articulates the relationship between feminism, **poststructuralism** and the discourse of postcoloniality, examining a number of persistent Western practices crucial to colonization and imperialism associated with what she calls 'Othering' (the ideological mechanism that excludes persons or groups from the systems of 'normality' as perceived by oneself). The self is represented by traditional patriarchal authority and British colonization in relation to the subaltern Other which is constituted in 'the Self's shadow'. Thus the Other is inextricably linked yet fundamentally embedded in the self.

Spivak's contention that 'there is no place from which the subaltern (sexed) subject can speak' exposes the signifying systems of colonialism and patriarchy as oppressive and silencing. She links post-coloniality and feminism by highlighting the fact that both women and colonized peoples have been forced to articulate their experiences in the language of the oppressor. Further, she has remained at a tangent to Marxist, feminist and post-colonial schools of thought by her constant critiques of them through the lens of deconstructivism, and has highlighted the pitfalls of marginality while resolutely refusing to remain in the margin. [AY]

STIRLING, JAMES: ARCHITECT (1926–92) Some of Stirling's greatest admirers might well object to his inclusion in a dictionary of **postmodernism** and to some extent they may have a point. Stirling's architecture was very much rooted in the traditions of **modernism**. Particular motifs in his work, such as the emphasis on circulation, the use of ramps, the plays on symmetrical and asymmetrical axes, and the privileging of the plan as the generator, owe a lot to Le Corbusier, of whom Stirling was, in his own idiosyncratic way, a follower. However, it is the very idiosyncratic and highly individual nature of his work which equally marks him out as a postmodernist. For Stirling was never a typical modernist. Nor when his work, like archetypal postmodernist architecture of the 1970s and 1980s, began to display overt historical reference, could he be described as a typical postmodernist. Paradoxically, the postmodernist tactics he employed, such as his predilection for in-built jokes, tended to be much more overt and go much further than more mainstream postmodernists.

Stirling was also a highly controversial figure. For some he was unquestionably the greatest British architect of the post-war years, while for others he was little more than incompetent. Early buildings such as the Engineering Block in Leicester (designed with James Gowan), the Cambridge History Faculty Library and the Florey Building in Oxford display a virtuoso control of expressionist neo-constructivist form and a sophisticated grasp of the relationship between form and programme. These buildings constituted an exciting and radical departure from the worthy and sanctimonious brutalism which dominated British architecture at the time. However, for all their formal mastery and the brilliance of their conception, these buildings were to be plagued by technical failures which were to blight Stirling's reputation for years to come.

These problems were a precursor to a barren patch in which Stirling received few commissions but which led to the development of a radical shift in his work. During the 1970s Stirling's work began to display references to historical sources, beginning with the unbuilt project for the Derby Civic Centre. This furrow was increasingly ploughed via a number of competition entries for museum buildings in Germany, which culminated in Stirling being awarded the commission to design the Staatsgalerie in Stuttgart, arguably his masterpiece. The Staatsgalerie is conceived essentially as an architectural promenade which forms a public route through the site. The building itself is anchored around a central open-air drum which forms a court within the complex. The public route circulates around the edge of the drum at high level, knitting the museum into the fabric of the city, creating a theatrical expression of integrated and yet separate public and semi-public circulation systems.

The styling of the building is an overblown monumental classicism broken down by the clash of classical and modernist elements. The building resolves itself into a series of stratified layers with ramps at the front creating an artificial landscape of levels which contradict and infect the monumentality of the building. Hence the building constitutes a highly sophisticated juxtaposition of object against landscape, of route against axis, of public against semi-public space, of monumental classicism against modernist tropes, and of abstraction against representation. The success of the Staatsgalerie led to the completion of several more high-profile projects before Stirling died. These include the Clore Gallery in London and the Fogg Museum in Cambridge, Massachusetts. [SGr]

STRING THEORY Haunted by the incompatibility of general relativity and **quantum mechanics**, twentieth-century physics' most recent 'theory of everything' is string theory. To combine these theories, super-string theorists explain, we need to explore the subatomic world at a much smaller scale, one-thousandth of one-billionth the size of a nucleus. As we descend the scale of subatomic particles, the theory goes, we find that the smallest – quarks – are composed of oscillating strings. Each string vibrates at a particular frequency and assumes a particular tension, like a violin string, producing quarks that will form neutrons, protons, electrons and so on, depending on the string's particular frequency. As we ascend the scale, everything dances to 'the music of the strings'. Apart from its successes in explaining 'high-energy' subatomic physics, advocates of string theory hold that its mathematics also make sense of the 'low-energy' planetary gravity to which Einsteinian relativity applies.

However, in order to explain subatomic particles in terms that make equal sense of cosmic gravity, string theory suggests that at sub-quark scales strings 'unfold' into at least six extra dimensions. Since the energies required to observe real strings in the four dimensions we inhabit would be at least ten million billion times as high as current particle accelerators are capable of, strings remain elegant mathematical fictions that must yet explain how ten 'stringy' dimensions fold up into our apparently four-dimensional world. [IHG]

STRUCTURALISM When, in the early years of the twentieth century, Ferdinand de Saussure began to study language as a system of interlinked units, each of which had a meaning only in relation to the system as a whole, he inaugurated one of the great movements in Western intellectual history. Saussure sought the underlying rules of language, the deep structures that must exist if language is to perform its function. These deep structures are independent of the human agents who

use language, and this displacement of the human **subject** from the focus of interest is one of the characteristics of structuralism.

For Saussure, language was a system of **signs**. A sign was made up of a 'signified' – a mental component (a concept) – and the 'signifier' – a physical component (for example a sound, or a mark on paper). Each took its place in a rigid and relatively stable system of **differences**. The sound 'dog' is only capable of carrying a meaning because it is different from the sound 'dig'. Convention then ties the sound 'dog' to the image of man's best friend.

Structural linguistics became a model for researchers in the humanities who were attempting to make sense of the complex products of human cultures. The anthropologist Claude **Lévi-Strauss** was among the first to realize the potential of the structuralist approach. He analysed the intricate rules determining kinship relationships and, later, the myths of 'primitive' peoples in terms of simple **binary oppositions**. In both cases the linguistic/cultural structures produced by these binary oppositions are a reflection of mental structures: the shape of the social world is determined by the structure of the human mind.

After Lévi-Strauss, Roland **Barthes**, Michel **Foucault** and Jacques **Lacan** applied structuralist modes of analysis to, respectively, literary studies, cultural history and psychoanalysis. In each case, the aim was to find the underlying system of relationships, the structure, within which any individual **event** could come to have a meaning.

By the late 1960s, however, a radical reaction to structuralism's ambitious claims to have explained the world had set in. Jacques **Derrida** and other **poststructuralists** launched a series of devastating critiques of structuralist poetics, anthropology and historiography, focusing on the inability of structuralists to understand the radicalism inherent in their own view of language. Derrida emphasized the fragility of the conventional link between signifier and signified, thus rendering 'meaning' a more elusive and slippery beast than the structuralists had supposed. [AM]

SUBALTERN THEORY *Webster's Dictionary* defines subaltern thus: 'A commissioned officer below the rank of captain / a person holding a subordinate position / particularly with reference to a related universal.' This links subalternity with the notions of *marginality* and **Derrida**'s notion of *presence* as the subaltern **subject** is, owing to either race, class or gender, marginalized and placed in a subordinate position in relation to the determining authority of 'the centre'. In other words, the centre is designated an invariable 'presence'; it is a point of reference or authority from which norms are established. That which is outside the centre or in the margins is designated '**Other**'.

Postcolonial theorists such as Gayatri Chakravorty **Spivak** and the Subaltern Studies Group led by Ranajit Guha examine this process of 'Othering' by examining the way in which the signifying system of the centre, i.e. colonialist discourse, renders the experience of the subaltern, or colonial **subject**, as irrelevant as it is outside the system of normality and convention. Thus the colonial subject is 'muted' owing to its being constructed within a disabling master **discourse**. The alternative to this silencing is espoused by Homi K. **Bhabha** in his notions of 'mimicry' and 'parody' in which the subaltern's voice is characterized by inappropriate imitations of the master discourse of the centre.

Subaltern studies can be viewed as a form of postcolonial historiography which interrogates the centre from the margin using **deconstructive** and **poststructuralist** practices. It focuses attention on the function of the centre as a site of the operation of **power** and thus confers insight on the marginalized or subaltern by exposing the oppressive nature of this discourse. [AY]

SUBJECT **Postmodernism** has rejected the concept of the individual, or 'subject', that has prevailed in Western thought for the last few centuries. For that latter tradition, the subject has been a privileged being right at the very heart of cultural process. Humanism has taught us to regard the individual subject as a unified self, with a central 'core' of identity unique to each individual, motivated primarily by the **power** of reason. **Modernity** encouraged the notion of the entrepreneurial subject exploiting the world of nature and bringing it under his (the pronoun being appropriate in this case, given the patriarchal bias of modernity as a cultural movement) domination. Rights and privileges could be ascribed to that subject, whose development and self-realization came to be regarded as a central objective (if not *the* central objective) of Western culture.

This model of the subject as a rational, unified, powerful and controlling being has come under increasing attack from the days of **structuralism** onwards and, particularly in France, there has been a concerted move on the part of theorists to destabilize this model. Claude **Lévi-Strauss** spoke of the **death of man**, arguing that deep structures worked *through* mankind, using it as a channel; Roland **Barthes** spoke of the **death of the author** as a controller of **textual** meaning (the reader becoming the key element instead); Michel **Foucault** spoke of the modern conception of the subject as something that could be erased quite easily, rather as marks made in the sand could be. For **poststructuralists** and postmodernists, the subject is a fragmented being who has no essential core of identity, and is to be regarded as a process in a continual state of dissolution rather than a fixed identity or self that endures unchanged over time. The old model of the subject is held by such thinkers to inhibit creativity and cultural change; as **Deleuze** and **Guattari** put it, 'there is no fixed subject unless there is repression'. [SS]

SUBLIME As an aesthetic concept the sublime can be traced back to classical times and the work of Longinus, but in its modern manifestation it dates from the eighteenth century and the work of Edmund Burke and Immanuel **Kant**. It has since come into prominence again in **postmodern** theory, particularly in the work of Jean-François **Lyotard**, for whom it has become an increasingly important concept in his later philosophy (much of which is a conscious dialogue with Kant).

In Burke and Kant the sublime represents a force larger than the human, which holds human beings in a state of awe. Essentially, the sublime cannot be comprehended by individuals, who can at best come to recognize the incomprehensibility of its magnitude and **power** (as in the case of the power of nature), and their inferiority before it. For Lyotard the sublime is the 'unpresentable', the element which always militates against the possibility of any complete understanding of the world. **Grand narratives** (or universal theories) always try, ultimately unsuccessfully, to deny the existence of the sublime. Great art, on the other hand, makes us aware of the unpresentable, and Lyotard proceeds to judge works of art in terms of their attitude to the unpresentable. [SS]

SUKENICK, RONALD: NOVELIST (1932–2004) American writer Ronald Sukenick's distinctive brand of **postmodernist** fiction substitutes improvisation for plot, split selves for characters, and explores the fluid **subjectivity** of experience. *Up* (1968) presents what seems to be thinly veiled fictionalizations of his early struggles to make a living as a writer in Brooklyn. But the Ronald Sukenick who authors the novel-within-the-novel is not necessarily co-extensive with the Ronald Sukenick on the jacket cover. In *Out* (1973), too, the author adopts a variety of disguises: (a) Ronald, who describes himself as a shapeless bag of protoplasm; (b) Sukenick, who shoots one of his own characters; and (c) Roland Sycamore, who dissolves into the enigmatic 'R'. The chapter numbers reverse from 9 to 1, a countdown determining the number of lines in each section's short blocks of prose.

98.6 (1975) is also written in fragments, or the 'law of mosaics' as Sukenick puts it. The mosaic patterns are retained in *Long Talking Bad Conditions Blues* (1979), in which conventional forms of punctuation disappear altogether, and in *The Mosaic Man* (1999) 'Ron' searches for his Jewish roots. Sukenick's most extreme gesture towards doing away with the artificial filters of plot, characterization and setting is 'Roast Beef: A Slice of Life' from *The Death of the Novel and Other Stories* (1969). This transcribes a taped conversation between Sukenick and his wife as they prepare a meal in the kitchen. It attempts to make us 'hemidemisemiquaveringly interested' in the complex nuances of reality-in-the-raw, an admirable project for the postmodernist writer. [BL]

SUPPLEMENT In its **poststructuralist** sense, the term originates from **Derrida**'s *Of Grammatology* (1967) and his reading of Rousseau, who is accused of devaluing writing in favour of speech. Rousseau's contention is that writing is a supplement to speech, is inessential and therefore inferior. By this reckoning, writing adds nothing affirmative to speech and is in itself unnatural, creating, according to Rousseau, a distance between those in communication, and distorting intention and meaning. Rousseau's **logocentrist** discourse is then **deconstructed** by Derrida, for whom speech and writing exist as **binary oppositions** in a 'violent' hierarchy, in which positive value is always accorded to the first term.

The French verb *suppléer* (root of *supplément*) has two meanings: in the first instance it means 'to make up' (as in adding to); it can also mean 'to take the place of' or 'to substitute'. The distinction in what seem to be oppositions is, however, difficult to maintain upon close analysis. The supplement appears as a replacement and/or addition for the terms that the deconstructionist herself has 'violently' reversed. In the endless process of deconstructive reading, the instability of the **sign** ensures that as the newly inverted hierarchy begins to take shape it too is subverted by the supplement. Other examples include active/passive and good/evil; the first term is deemed 'natural', but is subverted by the second, which is in turn supplemented by another. [DW]

T

TARANTINO, QUENTIN: FILM DIRECTOR
(1963–) When *Reservoir Dogs* appeared
in 1992 it marked Tarantino's directorial
debut and the announcement of a major
new talent. With its extreme violence and
scrupulous attention to realistic dialogue,
Reservoir Dogs became a landmark in the
genre of the 'heist' film. Tarantino
followed this up with *Pulp Fiction* (1994),
the **postmodern** masterpiece of his films to
date. *Pulp Fiction* is marked by its playful
reverence for the 1950s – the 'Jack Rabbit
Slim' sequence – and its constantly teasing
and often deferential references to other
films. Its other notable feature is the
switchback **narrative** technique in which
Tarantino **deconstructs** any notion of
linear progression and constantly defeats
our expectations of what should logically
happen next. This film was followed by
Jackie Brown (1997), another 'caper'
movie, in which Tarantino flummoxed an
audience expecting the postmodern trick-
siness of *Pulp Fiction*. Instead, he adapted
the Elmore Leonard crime novel *Rum
Punch*, and created a relatively straightforward story with a conventional narrative
timeline.

The devices of pastiche, parody, and
double coding so apparent in *Pulp Fiction*
are once more drawn upon in *Kill Bill*,
released in two parts (2003, 2004). Here
the world of American gangsters and street
life is forsaken in favour of homage to
Hong Kong and Japanese martial arts
films. This is especially the case with the
reference to Sonny Chiba, who made his
name in films concerned with samurai
warriors, and has a minor role in *Kill Bill*. A
further set of **intertextual** references point
to the spaghetti westerns of Sergio Leone,
acknowledged in the revenge theme and
also in the soundtrack, which in part nods
respectfully to Ennio Morricone. *Kill Bill*
also deploys Tarantino's signature narrative techniques of time dislocation, with
liberal use of flashback. To embed the film
further in Far Eastern popular culture,
Kill Bill includes an *anime* (Japanese
animation) scene, that is used not simply
for decorative effect but to advance the
narrative. The overall effect is one of
unsettling the audience. [DW]

TERRITORIALITY In **Deleuze** and **Guattari**'s
A Thousand Plateaus (1980), a territoriality
is any entity or institution that restricts the
free flow of individual **desire**. The family
and the state count as prime examples of
territorialities, and they conspire to produce the modern **subject** – the controlled
and, as Deleuze and Guattari see it,
inhibited subject of liberal humanism and
the **Enlightenment project**; 'there is no
fixed subject unless there is repression',
they insist. They argue that desire needs
to be 'deterritorialized', and they treat
nomadic existence as some kind of ideal of
deterritorialization. [SS]

TEXT In **postmodern** thought, 'text' refers
not only to written materials but also to
painting, architecture, information systems
and to all attempts at **representation**,
whatever form this may take. **Derrida**'s
famous dictum that 'there is nothing outside the text', for instance, has been badly
misrepresented as a call for a kind of super-
formalism. This reading of Derrida's key
works has been advanced by members of

the so-called **Yale School**, such as Geoffrey Hartman, whose work on the use of the pun in literature has been highly influential in the American academy. There is, however, more to postmodern usage of the word 'text' than an endless game of word-play. For postmodernists, it would be more accurate to state that the world is constituted by text. [DW]

THOM, RENÉ: MATHEMATICIAN, SCIENTIST (1923–) Thom, who developed **catastrophe theory** in a work entitled *Structural Stability and Morphogenesis* (1972), is not an easy character to get to grips with, whether his work is approached from the point of view of his native discipline of mathematics; from that of sciences resistant to theoretical modelling in general, and to mathematical treatment in particular (such as biology); or from what looks at first sight like perhaps the most unpromising and certainly uninvitingly tortuous perspective of the social, cultural and philosophical theories of **postmodernism**. Yet Thom's work has had enormous impact on each of these fields, despite infrequent recognition, especially in the latter case.

In mathematics, catastrophe theory (CT) shares the language, now familiar from **chaos theory**, of 'nonlinear dynamics', of 'attractors' and 'bifurcations', so that many theorists are currently seeking, under the provisional rubric of 'bifurcation theory', to synthesize its insights with chaos; if CT is concerned to model catastrophic changes in form, which Thom calls 'morphogenesis', at the formal and abstract level, chaotic systems are found very much embodied at the material level. If CT remains avowedly deterministic, emphasizing predictability, the emergence of chaotic behaviour introduces novelties and casts physical laws, especially the second law of thermodynamics, into question as regards their universal applicability.

In biology, while Thom has waged war on what he claims to be an inappropriate

metaphorics of information, his work has also had some constructive impact. Drawing the term 'morphogenesis' from that discipline, where it refers to the development of organs, Thom has developed it into an abstract mathematical theoretical framework and re-exported it, thus modified, whence it came; and as biologist C. H. Waddington's enthusiastic introduction to Thom's first major work demonstrates, the graft has taken. But morphogenesis does not stop there. Perhaps **ironically**, from the point of view of the history of postmodern thought, Thom extends it – in *Structural Stability*, in the essays collected in the French best-seller, *Mathematical Models of Morphogenesis* (1983) and subsequently in *Semiophysics* (1990) – to the human sciences (linguistics, **semiotics**, sociology and anthropology) whose scientific status Michel Foucault had so rigorously challenged in *The Order of Things*. While the human sciences finally become susceptible of mathematization through CT, the term and the theory of morphogenesis subjects this new-found scientificity to a peculiarly postmodern twist: science itself can no longer be taken to be 'the investigation of the ultimate nature of reality', so that the 'objectivity' associated with that ethos, along with the universalist pretensions of modern science, fall simultaneously. With the demise of the 'era of grand, cosmic synthesis', science becomes postmodernistically local: the analytical tools and the mathematical models remain intact but, as **Lyotard** has it of the postmodern in general, they give rise only to islands of 'local determinism' and 'institutions in patches'.

The proximity of Lyotard's and Thom's formulations is not accidental; Thom is one of the principal references in the characterization of **postmodern science** from which Lyotard would like to draw political lessons. Indeed, if it seems absurdly reductionist to attempt to model politics on science, this is one of the many questions that Thom's work insistently raises: at what degree of abstraction do phenomena of whatever nature, whether scientific or cultural, become susceptible of a single method of modelling? In other words, Thomian speculations with CT invite us to consider to what extent the general applicability of a concept (such as morphogenesis or postmodernism) guarantees a correspondingly global theory; or whether, on the contrary, the generality of a concept is an index, as perhaps **Baudrillard** might say, of its loss of content, the concept thus becoming, in Thom's words, 'a pure play of forms'. Thom's answer, one to which Lyotard lends support, is that only science, with its relentless quantification of phenomena into abstract form, can provide a theory suitably abstract and plastic to chart the profound cultural morphogenetic catastrophe called postmodernism. [IHG]

TRACE As a translation of the French for a track or footprint, 'trace' indicates something that is no longer present, yet has left its mark. Understood as a structure of **difference**, trace marks a relation to what is not present. Following **Levinas** and **Derrida**, the structure of every linguistic sign is determined by the trace of that other which is forever absent. Breaking with the classical sense of an empirical mark standing for an original non-trace, its origin is equally a trace. A lack of nostalgia for what has been lost gives the term its **postmodern** distinctiveness: its differential relation to a non-origin. [PSA]

TRANS-AVANT-GARDE The term trans-avant-garde was invented by the Italian critic Achille Bonito Oliva to distinguish the works of Anselm **Kiefer**, Francesco Clemente, Sandro Chia, Georg Baselitz and Markus Lupertz from their **modernist** predecessors. According to Oliva, who became an important cultural commentator in the 1980s, this group of European painters, eschewing the utopian rhetoric of modernism, had escaped the burden of art history by using it

as a resource base for their elaborations of myth, will and self-expression. In place of the universalism of modernism, the trans-avant-garde would reveal the magical roots of art in the conflation of ego and symbol, thus producing a new generation of shamanic-bohemian and culturally '**nomadic**' artists. [CT]

TSCHUMI, BERNARD: ARCHITECT (1944–) 'To experience architecture', Tschumi proclaims in *Advertisements for Architecture*, 'one might have to commit murder.' His confrontational and provocative work set the tone for much architectural theory in the 1980s. Influenced by the **Situationists**, and initially concerned with **representation**, he argued that the traditional forms of architectural drawing excluded ideas of occupation and **event**. *The Manhattan Transcripts* presented an alternative and inclusive form of spatial representation and notation. Taking the form of film stills and storyboarding, the project outlined a series of events, movements and incidents intertwined with both the drawing style and the space depicted.

Tschumi was soon given the opportunity to speculate by building, winning one of the highest-profile commissions of the 1980s, Le Parc de la Villette, in north-eastern Paris. The ground plan of the park was layered with three organizational systems, based upon different types of spatial occupation – route, encounter and event – which set out an organization of territory which is subsequently programmatically defined.

Tschumi's belief that programme is as much the medium of architecture as iconography has led to a series of propositions that attempt to engage with the experience of the contemporary urban situation. His current work manages to retain the radical ideas of his theory while proposing new architectural scenarios – coining new terminologies such as cross-programming and disprogramming, and opening up fresh possibilities for architectural practice. [SJ]

VATTIMO, GIANNI: PHILOSOPHER (1936–)
Vattimo's first book was *Essere, storia e linguaggio in Heidegger* (*Being, History and Language in Heidegger*), published in 1963, and he has published studies of **Heidegger**, Schleiermacher and **Nietzsche**. In the late 1960s and early 1970s, he played an active role in the politics of the Radical Party. Vattimo is best known for his writings on *il pensiero debole* ('weak thought'); in 1983, he co-edited, with Pier Aldo Rovatti, a collection of essays entitled *Il pensiero debole*. Vattimo conceives of weak thought as a refusal of the **Enlightenment** identification of the intellectual as avant-garde legislator: *il pensiero debole* refuses the strength of will which is assumed by **modernity**.

Vattimo defines the modern as that era in which being modern itself becomes a value. The new becomes a value, for Vattimo, at the end of the fifteenth century with the beginnings of a conception of the artist as creative genius whose work is characterized by *originality*. This is linked, says Vattimo, with the more general perspective from which human history is seen in terms of an emancipation conceived as advancement, progression and refashioning. Such a conception of history is by definition a linear one. This modernity ends, says Vattimo, when it no longer seems possible to regard history as unilinear. Vattimo sees the philosophical challenge to the unilinear model as coming from a project in the nineteenth and twentieth centuries that exposes this view of history as an ideological one. Walter **Benjamin**'s 'Theses on the Philosophy of History', for example, 'maintained that unilinear history is a **representation** of the past constructed by dominant groups and social classes'. It is in relation to the writings of Nietzsche and Heidegger, however, that Vattimo's ideas are most fully developed.

In *The End of Modernity* (1985), Vattimo argues that what he calls 'the scattered and often incoherent theories of **postmodernity**' only begin to make sense when placed in direct contact with Nietzsche's concept of the eternal return and Heidegger's notion of the overcoming of metaphysics. If the works of Nietzsche and Heidegger can be placed in productive relation to those of **postmodernism**, that project involves first of all, for Vattimo, a careful attention to the prefix 'post' in postmodernism. 'Post' signifies for Vattimo the same relation with the past of European thought – with the modern – that is advanced by the two thinkers in question. Both Nietzsche and Heidegger, he claims, recognize the necessity of calling into question the tradition of European metaphysics and of breaking with it in some fundamental sense. At the same time, though, they acknowledge the paradox of claiming to have severed all ties with a tradition which considers itself as a process of constant development or overcoming in the first place: simply to claim to have broken with the modern, then, would be to repeat the logic of the modern. Both Nietzsche and Heidegger recognize in the modern not merely an impulse toward progress or novelty, but also the basis of this drive in a notion of 'origin' or 'foundation', and it is towards this concept that their respective critiques of metaphysics are oriented. According to Vattimo, what is postmodern in Nietzsche and Heidegger is not an abrupt break with metaphysics, but an attempt to *rethink* this origin. Postmodernism is, then, to be seen as a weakening of the relation to an origin, a weakening which takes place philosophically in Nietzsche's 'accomplished nihilism' and the Heideggerian concept of *Andenken* (rethinking). For both thinkers, Vattimo points out, the aesthetic is the site of this weakening, which institutes an altered conception of truth, 'not as an object which can be appropriated and transmitted, but as a horizon and a background upon which we may move with care'.

In later works such as *The Transparent Society* (1992) and *Beyond Interpretation*, Vattimo has extended these arguments while, in the latter volume, warning against any hasty reduction of the thought of modernity to a purely aesthetic phenomenon. Truth, argues Vattimo, in a rejection of what he sees as the groundless relativism of much postmodern thought, requires an act of interpretation, but this does not excuse us from attending to *historicity*. [BD]

VENTURI, ROBERT: ARCHITECT, THEORIST (1925–) Possibly the first architect whose work attracted the label **postmodern**, Venturi revolutionized architectural thinking in the 1960s and 1970s via the design of a number of controversial buildings which reintroduced ornament and historical motif as generators of architectural meaning. This approach amounted to an unprecedented attack on the hitherto unquestioned doctrine of architectural **modernism**. However, while the offending buildings did little more than dent the ubiquitous monolith of modernist practice, two books, *Complexity and Contradiction in Architecture* (1966) and *Learning from Las Vegas* (with Denise Scott Brown and Stephen Izenour, 1972) met with huge popular acclaim and blew a gigantic hole in the dominance of modernism.

Venturi persists in being a controversial and paradoxical figure. While continuing to oppose the mythical 'heroic and original' ambitions of modernism, the phrase 'complexity and contradiction' became itself a heroic slogan for those opposing the sanctimonious and esoteric purity exhibited by the aesthetics of modern architecture. *Complexity and Contradiction* calls for evolutionary rather than revolutionary change and promotes an attitude of 'both/and' rather than 'either/or', in opposition to the singularity and univalence of modernist functionalism. Perhaps the most blasphemous of the book's proposals is the promotion of ornament and historical reference as a means of architectural communication. When placed in the context of slogans such as 'ornament is crime', Venturi's position, in terms of the modernist doctrine of progress, appears conservative but, in respect of the overriding elitism and authoritarianism of modernist humanism, it seems extremely liberating. Venturi takes delight in the parody of modernist slogans. Mies van der Rohe's 'less is more' becomes in Venturi's words, 'less is bore'.

If the first book, with its emphasis on legitimate historical architecture, was just about acceptable to the modernists, *Learning from Las Vegas*, which extended the analysis of ornament to a study of the symbolism of the commercial strip, sent the architectural establishment into apoplexy. The apparent political ambivalence implied by the acceptance of commercial codes has, however, been read by other practitioners, such as the artist Dan Graham, as a complex form of political commentary.

In engaging with commercial signification, Venturi refuses to submit to the modernist myths of rationality and transparency which, in the buildings of modernist masters such as Mies van der Rohe, served as alibi for capitalist bureaucracy and economic imperialism. Recognizing his own contribution to twentieth-century architecture, Venturi is at pains to stress his role as an architect rather than as a writer. However, it is likely that posterity will disappoint him in this matter. This is not because he has not produced buildings of quality and note. The Vanna Venturi House and North Penn Nurses Association Building are highly sophisticated dialogues between the codes of conventional architecture and those of a prevailing modernism. The Benjamin Franklin Museum in Philadelphia manages to incorporate references to popular significations of shelter, pop art and minimalism, and the Sainsbury wing to London's National Gallery, designed in response to a fierce debate between the modernist architectural establishment and the Prince of Wales, managed, in its witty and knowingly paper-thin appropriation of the host building's mediocre classicism, to undermine both the sanctimoniousness of the former and the pomposity of the latter. This, his only excursion into the British architectural scene, serves as a prime example of the complexity and contradiction with which this architect's career and reputation are riddled. [SGr]

VIRILIO, PAUL: CULTURAL THEORIST (1932–) Virilio's thought begins from the idea that **modernity** is characterized less by the control of spatial territory than by the 'government of time'. In *Speed and Politics* (1977) he argues that the city is founded first of all on a temporal phenomenon: the advantage of speed afforded by a vantage point. To see one's enemy from an elevated lookout position is to gain a temporal advantage: a period of time in which crucial tactical decisions can be made. Virilio extends this observation to his examination of the modern city, where, he claims, the technological infrastructure is geared toward the control of time: 'The new capital is no longer a spatial capital like New York, Paris or Moscow, a city located in a specific place, at the intersection of roads, but a city at the intersection of the

practicabilities of time, in other words, of speed.' The crucial political relations in modernity have to do, he says, with speed, which Virilio calls 'the hope of the West'. He takes this to mean that the political must now be thought of in terms of a 'chronopolitics', rather than in the geopolitical or spatial terms we are used to.

Much of Virilio's work is concerned with what he calls the 'logistics of perception'. In a line of argument that is partly indebted to Michel **Foucault**'s theorization of the relations between **power** and vision, Virilio claims that there is an intimate link between modern technologies of vision and the speed of which he wrote in his earlier work. In *War and Cinema* (1984) he outlines the complicated connections between the development of military technology and the optical technology that is now – in cinema, television and video – a part of everyday life. According to Virilio, the logic of this technology – and of the form of the state of which it is part – results from the insight that *that which can be seen can also be destroyed.* This leads Virilio to posit an 'aesthetics of disappearance', in which the dominant relation in modernity turns out not to be (as modern philosophy had conceived it) the relation between appearance and reality, but that obtaining between appearance and disappearance.

While he is sometimes seen as occupying a 'nihilistic' position close to that of Jean **Baudrillard**, Virilio's work exists outside of the terms of recent intellectual movements and debates in **postmodern** thought. He does not expressly couch any of his insights in terms of the postmodern; indeed, it would be impossible to extract from his work any periodizing formulation of a modern/postmodern distinction. Rather, Virilio thinks of the phenomena he describes as various 'flows' or drifts, a notion reflected in his difficult and deceptively seductive writing. Virilio's method takes the form of the piling-up of examples in a kind of flow that both resists any hasty assimilation into rigid 'positions' and appears not to be bound by the limits of any one of his works. It is easy to get the impression when reading Virilio that his work is one long **text** rather than discrete books, an impression which Virilio has himself justified in interviews.

Virilio's later work has seen an inevitable critical engagement with the new technologies of the **Internet**. As with his earlier work on visual technology, he sees here a continuation of the impulse towards speed: it is a question here, though, of an apparently achievable *simultaneity* which will destroy, in what Virilio calls a 'generalized planetary accident', our relations to our bodies, time and space. In the instantaneity of the transfer of information, Virilio sees the end of the possibility of critical distance: his call to resist the 'government of time', which he identifies in this technology, is revealed in works such as *The Vision Machine* (1992), *The Art of the Motor* (1996) and *Open Sky* (1997) as an attempt to rescue a notion of a localized *present* in the face of the generalized instantaneity of technology. The argument has a clear precedent in **Benjamin**'s mystical invocation of *Jetztzeit* or 'now-time'. [BD]

VIRTUAL REALITY The oxymoron 'virtual reality' was coined by Jaron Lanier in 1986 to describe technology that attempts to create computer-generated interactive environments, in which users can immerse themselves by means of 3D goggles and gloves which act as computer-input devices. Initially developed in the late 1960s, virtual reality is now an increasingly common phenomenon in the world of entertainment, art, and scientific and medical research. However, in the popular imagination it still has more than a hint of the science-fictional about it, and it is therefore not surprising that the concept is capable of arousing feverish speculation and paranoia far beyond what its current capabilities would allow.

Virtual reality is certainly a common theme in contemporary science fiction, where it becomes the focus of both horror and celebration. David Cronenberg's film *Videodrome* (1982), for example, led the way in portraying it as an invasive technology which hijacks the human brain, making it incapable of distinguishing between the virtual and the real. *Videodrome* anticipates by two years what is probably the most famous fictional evocation of virtual reality: William **Gibson**'s *Neuromancer*. Gibson's vision of the world within the computer is more equivocal than Cronenberg's, however, for he invests the concept of computer-generated worlds with a sense of vertiginous freedom, in which, free of the body's 'meat', the disembodied mind can traverse the limitless realm of **cyberspace**.

The concept of virtual reality, therefore, is inherently double-edged, offering us a window into a world of imagination and exciting possibility, while also threatening us with its implicit challenge to our assumptions concerning 'authentic' reality. With good enough technology, perhaps no one will be able to tell where the computer **simulation** ends and reality begins. Indeed, who would want to accept the limitations of the 'real', anyway, when one can be and do anything one wants in the world behind the screen – even if it means sacrificing a society of human interaction? It is such speculations that continue to energize the work of science-fiction writers and film makers, and make virtual reality a potent motif through which the increasingly tenuous status of reality within **postmodern** culture can be foregrounded and problematized. [SG]

VONNEGUT, KURT: NOVELIST (1922–) Vonnegut was born in Indianapolis, and his Mid-West birthplace may well explain his fiction's uneasy balance between high art and pulp, gravity and levity. Vonnegut was drafted into the US army in 1943, and his capture during the Battle of the Bulge led to internment in an abattoir in Dresden during the intense Allied fire-bombing in February 1945. His apprentice works – *Player Piano* (1952) and *The Sirens of Titan* (1959) – both explored standard science-fiction themes. The former is a Wellsian view of a mechanistic society and the latter a comic space opera.

It was with his next book, however, that Vonnegut found his **postmodernist** voice. *Mother Night* (1961) is written in a multitude of short chapters with oddball titles. His other novels of the 1960s – including *Cat's Cradle* (1963) and *God Bless You, Mr. Rosewater* (1965) – adopted this fragmented style. So too did several novels of the 1970s and 1980s, including *Breakfast of Champions* (1973), *Slapstick* (1976) and *Deadeye Dick* (1982). Vonnegut explained his organizational preference in this way: 'My books are essentially mosaics made up of a whole bunch of tiny little chips; and each chip is a joke.'

Vonnegut compensates for his extremely fragmented structures through repetition. Every book has its running typographical joke. *Slapstick*, for instance, refers to metric measurements throughout, instead of feet and inches (Vonnegut brags that it was probably the first American book to do so). *Jailbird* (1979) spells out each year instead of using numerals and has a helpful index at the back. In *Galapagos* (1985), an asterisk is placed before the names of those characters who will shortly die.

Several of his books contain recurrent catch-phrases. The refrain of 'So it goes' follows every death (human, animal or otherwise) in *Slaughterhouse-Five*. 'And so on' crops up persistently in *Breakfast of Champions*, which ends with a giant hand-drawn 'ETC'. The equally nonchalant 'Hi ho' peppers *Slapstick*. These phrases migrate from book to book. The same is true of many of Vonnegut's characters. Kilgore Trout appears in at least five works, and Eliot Rosewater plays major roles in several novels. Sometimes characters who make cameo appearances in earlier works are later given star billing: Rabo Karabekian, the Armenian abstract expressionist, appears briefly in *Breakfast of Champions* and is the subject of a full biography in *Bluebeard* (1987). Vonnegut's locations are repeated too. The cities of Ilium and Midland City, and the alien planet of Tralfamadore, are particular favourites.

A Vonnegut text is a 'chrono-synclastic infundibulum', a Tralfamadorian term for a place where all spaces and times merge. He returned to themes of temporal disorder in *Timequake* (1997), where a glitch in time makes everyone live again the exact same lives. [BL]

WHITE, HAYDEN: HISTORIAN (1928–) In his influential book *Metahistory: The Historical Imagination in Nineteenth-Century Europe* (1973) Hayden White introduced a significant element of relativism into history as an academic discipline. He saw history writing as consisting of **narratives** expressing a particular cultural bias, or what White dubbed 'metahistory'. This meant that some narratives were privileged over others: the narrative of the winners over the losers to put it in colloquial terms. White spoke of there being a 'precritically accepted paradigm' at work in such cases (we might call this a **metanarrative**) that disposed an **author** to construct a particular narrative framework around her material. In fact, any historical period was capable of generating a **plurality** of narratives.

White's ideas have been enthusiastically embraced by many younger historians, and there is now a distinctively **postmodern** school of history in the academic world, as found in the work of figures such as James Vernon and Patrick Joyce. By challenging historical narratives, and drawing our attention to the many competing ones, such historians call into question the notion of historical 'truth'. [SS]

WINTERSON, JEANETTE: NOVELIST (1959–) Winterson's fascination with personal identity throughout her fictional output marks her out as an important **postmodern author**. From her debut novel *Oranges Are Not the Only Fruit* (1985) onwards, she has shown a preference for identity as a very fluid phenomenon, particularly where female identity is concerned (*Oranges* is a lesbian rites-of-passage **narrative**). Female identity is invariably more flexible and selfless than male, which tends to be very self-centred and **power**-seeking: Winterson can be something of an essentialist on this issue.

This gender distinction comes out most strongly in *Gut Symmetries* (1997), where the personality of the scientist Jove is very unfavourably compared to that of his wife Stella and his erstwhile lover Alice, who proceed to enter into a lesbian relationship. Drawing on concepts from **quantum mechanics**, such as **string theory** and the wave function, Winterson suggests that female identity has the capability to breach the laws of space and time in a way that the more earthbound male identity cannot aspire to do. Females are more in tune with the natural mysteries and rhythms of the universe than males are. Both identity and sexuality are pictured as similarly fluid in Winterson's other fictions, such as *Sexing the Cherry* (1989) and *The Passion* (1987). [SS]

WOLF, NAOMI: FEMINIST THEORIST (1962–) Wolf's first book, *The Beauty Myth* (1990) begins with a paradox: since the late 1960s, affluent women in the West have had an increasing amount of political and social autonomy; they have entered the workforce in boardrooms and offices, in the main political institutions and on the shop floor. They have gained reproductive rights over their own bodies, and they have more money and **power** than at any other time in human history. Concurrently, however, there has been an exponential rise in women with eating disorders, and cosmetic surgery has become the fastest-growing medical speciality. So, while women have gained both respect and self-respect, in relation to their own bodies women are 'worse off than [their] grandmothers'. Wolf explains this paradox by means of 'the beauty myth', a violent backlash against women that uses images of female beauty as a weapon against female betterment. It is one of the last remaining ways of controlling women. The myth says that the quality called 'beauty', which women need because men want to possess it, is natural and universal. Wolf says that none of this is true; ideals of beauty are **culturally relative**. The oppressive concept of 'beauty' is not about women at all, but about male institutional power. The book has been criticized (most forcefully by bell **hooks**) for its assumption, in keeping with the beauty myth itself, that black women do not exist. *The Beauty Myth* was an international best-seller, though many feminists criticized it for lack of originality.

Wolf's second book, *Fire with Fire* (1993) is a good example of what she calls 'power feminism'. She argues that feminists need to be critical of their own movement; she attacks radical feminism's 'reflexive anti-capitalism' and 'rigid ideology' and argues for a 'flexible feminism to reclaim the majority'. She quickly dismisses the work of Adrienne Rich, Andrea Dworkin, Catherine McKinnon and Audre Lorde as varieties of 'victim feminism': their attitude of blaming men holds back the women's movement. Only women themselves stand in the way of their empowerment. They need to adopt a 'bad girl' persona and leave behind the 'good girl' image internalized from the age of three. Women need to take responsibility for the fact that they can be equally aggressive and violent as men. From this follows the argument that women therefore need to use the same tactics as men to gain political and economic power: 'Whether used to scar or illuminate, whether used by men or women, fire is fire.' While feminists have argued this position

before, Wolf's 'fire' is quite capable of burning other women, despite her rhetoric of sisterhood. From a socialist-feminist perspective, a notion of sisterhood that calls for women to enter the workforce as both workers and bosses is politically confused. Emblematic of this approach is her only example of a power feminist who is black: Madame J. C. Walker. This ex-slave became the richest woman, black or white, in nineteenth-century America by selling hair-straightening products which were, as bell hooks notes, the very sign of white supremacy and black women's oppression until at least the late 1960s. The book therefore reproduces earlier, predominantly middle-class feminists' marginalization of black women.

Promiscuities (1997) and *Misconceptions* (2001) used her own and her friends' experiences to generalize about sexuality and motherhood. Critics argue that this is what Wolf has done in her other work too – taken her own relatively privileged experience as an example of women's in general. [DR]

WRITERLY TEXTS Roland **Barthes** divides **narrative** fiction into two main types in his **poststructuralist** study *S/Z* (1970): writerly and **readerly**. The latter comprises narratives that promote passive consumption on the part of the reader, whereas the former invite the reader to participate in the production of **textual** meaning. **Modernist** texts are good examples of the writerly category, in that the reader frequently has to fill in gaps in the narrative, thus, in Barthes' terms of reference, becoming part of the production of textual meaning. Such texts are to be regarded as 'open' to the exercise of the reader's invention and imagination. Readerly texts, on the other hand, are designed to prevent such invention and imaginative play. A candidate for this category would be the nineteenth-century realist novel, which, with its meticulously structured plot, omniscient narrator, and overt moral agenda, severely constrained the nature of the reader's response.

Readerly texts are therefore in the service of the cultural status quo, whereas writerly ones help to undermine it by calling into question the extent of the **author**'s control over interpretation. Many critics have taken the line, however, that writerly texts are just as manipulative in their way as the readerly texts that Barthes accuses of being ideologically suspect. [SS]

Y

YALE SCHOOL The Yale School comprised a group of literary critics at Yale University who, in the 1970s, came under the sway of the **deconstructionist** Jacques **Derrida**, a visiting professor at Yale during the period. Its members included Harold **Bloom**, Paul **de Man**, Geoffrey Hartman and J. Hillis Miller. They can be considered a 'school' only in the loosest sense, and there were marked differences in the way each critic responded to deconstruction and utilized its techniques. Their best-known collaborative effort (with Derrida) is the book of essays *Deconstruction and Criticism* (ed. Harold Bloom (1979)). [SS]

YOUNG, IRIS MARION: PHILOSOPHER, FEMINIST THEORIST (1949–) Young has written on democratic theory, feminist social theory, female bodily experience and the politics of **difference**. In particular, Young objects to the liberal theory of distributive justice which answers questions such as 'What would be a fair distribution of property?' and 'What rights should individuals have?' with appeals to abstract ideals of formal equality and individual freedom. Young's studies of embodiment led her to formulate an alternative theory which recognizes concrete issues of difference among persons and incorporates substantive content into an account of justice. This means challenging the presumption that justice is a question of distribution. Young's philosophy differs not only from the liberal tradition of J. S. Mill, but from the post-**Enlightenment** tradition of German philosophy in raising fundamental questions about oppression and domination. In response to such questions,

political theories of liberal democracy need to address the problem of an inclusive participatory framework. Young contends that democratic theorists generally assume a conception of the public which excludes people not culturally identified with white European male norms of reason and respectability.

Although deriving her method from German **critical theory**, Young resists any modern commitment to a homogeneous public. Instead she proposes that normative theory and public policy can undermine group-based oppression by affirming rather than suppressing social group difference. Her vision of the good society is the differentiated, culturally plural network of contemporary urban life. Her goal is a principle of group **representation** in democratic publics, along with group differentiated policies. She resists feminist theories of embodiment which retain an ideal of a shared **subjectivity** and unified desires over the basic opacity and asymmetry of subjects and their desires. She fears the suppression of difference and of concrete **Otherness**.

Young's distinctive passion for the **postmodern** finds the desire for community among the members of radical organizations dangerous. Community produces homogeneity; it directs energy away from political goals, creating a clique atmosphere which excludes difference. Instead Young proposes an ideal of urban life, nurturing diversity and co-operation in providing services conceived, distributed and administered justly. Critics worry that Young is against friendship, but arguably she has realistic doubts concerning the transparency and affection of face-to-face relationships. **Ironically**, the problem attributed to Young constitutes her distinctiveness: rejection of identity and community for difference and diversity is criticized as often as it is celebrated. **Modern** feminists are sympathetic with, but ultimately critical of, Young's postmodern account of difference over identity, multiplicity over unity, heterogeneity over homogeneity. Possibly overstating her case, Young objects that the identity of the modern self as a unified centre of **desire** is a mere fiction. Yet Young recognizes that the child must separate from its joyful continuity with the maternal in order to enter language and become a self – the consequence of which is the identity and the difference of individual persons. Simply stated, it is difficult to realize both a social ethic of care (preserving identity and unity) and a politics of difference. [PSA]

ZAPPING. The technique of rapidly cutting between television channels using a remote control device, or 'zapping' as it is colloquially known, can lay claim to being one of the most characteristically **postmodern** acts. The channels themselves are treated like some kind of continuous **narrative** which can be connected together in any order at all, according to the whims of the individual viewer. There are clear similarities in this respect with the way that **hypertext** or the **Internet** work. The effect of zapping is to break up the flow of linear narrative and, arguably, to empower the viewer to a certain extent by giving her control over the sequencing, if not the content, of her viewing. If nothing else, the **grand narratives** of the programme makers, which demand passive viewers who consume what is given to them in a relatively uncritical manner, is challenged by the process of zapping. [SS]

ŽIŽEK, SLAVOJ: PHILOSOPHER, CULTURAL THEORIST (1949–) Žižek trained as a philosopher in Slovenia, part of Yugoslavia until that state broke up in the 1980s. He has become an increasingly influential figure in cultural theory in recent years, with his book *The Sublime Object of Ideology* (1989) in particular attracting considerable attention. Other key works include *Looking Awry: An Introduction to Jacques Lacan Through Popular Culture* (1991), *Enjoy Your Symptom!: Jacques Lacan in Hollywood* (1992), *The Plague of Fantasies* (1997) and *The Fragile Absolute: Or Why the Christian Legacy is Worth Fighting For* (2000). As the book titles

indicate, Žižek is a keen student of the psychoanalyst Jacques **Lacan**, whose theories he applies to both politics and popular culture. He takes over from Lacan the notion of the **subject** as lacking unity; in fact of being structured on this sense of 'lack'. The subject will always be driven by a **desire** that can never be wholly satisfied.

Žižek is one of the most important theorists of **post-Marxism**, particularly in the way that he undermines the key **Marxist** concept of false consciousness (see *The Sublime Object of Ideology*). As far as Žižek is concerned, we are generally complicit in our ideologies, in that even when they fail to deliver what they promise (which is invariably the case) we still delude ourselves into believing they might. Belief in the ideal dies hard even when personal experience fails to back it up: in Žižek's formulation, 'they know that, in their activity, they are following an illusion, but still they are doing it'. The classical Marxist notion of a working class having the true state of their socio-political condition kept hidden from them by a ruling establishment, by various devious means (**hegemony**, as the process has been called), is dismissed as simplistic. In practical terms, the working class 'know that their idea of Freedom is masking a particular form of exploitation, but they still continue to follow this idea of Freedom'. Our lives are structured on what Žižek calls an 'ideological fantasy', with ideology in its ideal state functioning as a 'sublime object' – Lacan's 'impossible-real object of desire'.

Although identified with a post-Marxism which draws heavily on **postmodern** thought for inspiration, Žižek has been ambivalent about postmodernism as a cultural movement, particularly its claims to be moving towards a 'post-ideological' **discourse**. Rather like the American Marxist theorist Fredric **Jameson**, Žižek views this post-ideological turn as being entirely congenial to those in control of 'late capitalism'. In this respect, Žižek retains more of a Marxist bias to his thought than many leading post-Marxists tend to do, regarding with suspicion any attempt (such as is found in the work of **Laclau** and **Mouffe**) to create common ground between the left and the disparate group of 'new social movements' which have grown up in recent decades. For Laclau and Mouffe these represent an opportunity to regenerate Marxism; to Žižek they are more likely to lead to an incoherent political message marked by contradiction (such as when 'the fight for African-American ethnic identity' brings with it a commitment to 'patriarchal and homophobic attitudes' that the left can only reject). Žižek has also been critical of postmodernism's enthusiasm for new technologies, such as virtual reality, again seeing these as serving the cause of late capitalism by shifting the focus away from political action. [SS]

BIBLIOGRAPHY

The following is a bibliography of the texts referred to in the essays and the editor's introduction. The original date of publication is given in square brackets after the title where appropriate.

Ackroyd, Peter, *Hawksmoor* (London: Hamish Hamilton, 1985).

Adair, Gilbert, *The Postmodernist Always Rings Twice: Reflections on Culture in the 90s* (London: Fourth Estate, 1992).

Adam, Ian and Tiffin, Helen, *Past the Last Post: Theorizing Post-Colonialism and Postmodernism* (Calgary, Alberta: Calgary University Press, 1990).

Ahmad, Aijaz, 'Third World Literature in the Age of Multinational Capitalism', *Social Text*, 15 (1986), pp. 65–88.

Ahmad, Aijaz, *In Theory* (London and New York: Verso, 1992).

Aldridge, John W., *The American Novel and the Way We Live Now* (New York: Oxford University Press, 1983).

Anderson, Pamela Sue, *A Feminist Philosophy of Religion: The Rationality and Myths of Religious Belief* (Oxford: Blackwell, 1998).

Anderson, Pamela Sue and Clack, Beverley, eds, *Feminist Philosophy of Religion: Critical Readings* (London: Routledge, 2004).

Ang, Ien, *Living Room Wars: Rethinking Media Audiences for a Postmodern World* (London: Routledge, 1996).

Apple, Max, *The Propheteers* (London: Faber & Faber, 1987).

Armour, Ellen, 'Beyond Belief: Sexual Difference and Religion after Ontotheology', in John Caputo, ed., *The Religious* (Oxford: Blackwell, 2001), pp. 212–16.

Auster, Paul, *The New York Trilogy* (London: Faber & Faber, 1987).

Baker, Nicholson, *The Mezzanine* (London: Granta, 1989).

Barth, John, 'The Literature of Exhaustion' [1967], in Malcolm Bradbury, ed., *The Novel Today: Contemporary Writers on Modern Fiction* (Manchester: Manchester University Press, 1977).

Barth, John, *Letters* (New York: Putnam, 1979).

Barth, John, 'The Literature of Replenishment', *Atlantic Monthly*, 245 (1980), pp. 65–71.

Barthelme, Donald, *Unspeakable Practices. Unnatural Acts* (New York: Farrar, Strauss, 1968).

Baudrillard, Jean, *Seduction* [1979], trans. Brian Singer (Basingstoke and London: Macmillan, 1990).

Baudrillard, Jean, *Simulations*, trans. Paul Foss, Paul Patton and Philip Beitchman (New York: Semiotext(e), 1983).

Baudrillard, Jean, *America* [1986], trans. Chris Turner (London and New York: Verso, 1988).

Bauman, Zygmunt, *Freedom* (Milton Keynes: Open University Press, 1988).

Beauvoir, Simone de, *The Second Sex* [1949], trans. H. M. Pashley (Harmondsworth: Penguin, 1972).

Benjamin, Walter, 'Experience and Poverty' [1933], in *Illuminationen* (Frankfurt-am-Main: Suhrkamp Verlag, 1977).

Berger, Roger, 'Review of Past the Last Post', *Postmodern Culture*, 2:2 (1992).

Bernstein, Richard J., ed., *Habermas and Modernity* (Cambridge: Polity Press, 1985).

Bernstein, Richard J., *The New Constellation: The Ethical-Political Horizons of Modernity/Postmodernity* (Cambridge, Mass.: MIT Press, 1990).

Bhabha, Homi K., *The Location of Culture* (London and New York: Routledge, 1994).

Bordo, Susan, 'Feminism, Postmodernism, and Gender-Scepticism', in L. J. Nicholson, ed., *Feminism/Postmodernism* (London and New York: Routledge, 1990), pp. 133–56.

Bourdieu, Pierre, *Outline of a Theory of Practice*, trans. Richard Nice (Cambridge: Cambridge University Press, 1977).

Boyne, R. and Rattansi, A., eds, *Postmodernism and Society* (London: Macmillan, 1990).

Bradbury, Malcolm, ed., *The Novel Today: Contemporary Writers on Modern Fiction* (Manchester: Manchester University Press, 1977).

Bradbury, Malcolm and Ruland, Richard, *From Puritanism to Postmodernism: A History of American Literature* (London: Routledge, 1991).

Braidotti, Rosi, *Nomadic Subjects: Embodiment and Sexual Difference in Contemporary Feminist Theory* (New York: Columbia University Press, 1994).

Brautigan, Richard, *The Hawkline Monster: A Gothic Western* (New York: Simon & Schuster, 1974).

Brooker, Peter and Brooker, Will, eds, *Postmodern After-Images: A Reader in Film, Television, and Video* (London: Edward Arnold, 1997).

Brooks, Ann, *Post-feminisms: Feminism, Cultural Theory and Cultural Forms* (London: Routledge, 1997).

Brown, David, *Tradition and Imagination: Revelation and Change* (Oxford: Oxford University Press, 1999).

Burroughs, William, *Naked Lunch* (Paris: Olympia, 1959).

Burroughs, William, *Nova Express* (New York: Grove, 1964).

Burroughs, William, *The Soft Machine* (London: Calder & Boyars, 1968).

Burroughs, William, *The Ticket That Exploded* (New York: Grove, 1967).

Burroughs, William, *The Place of Dead Roads* (New York: Holt, Rinehart & Winston, 1983).

Butler, Judith, *Gender Trouble: Feminism and the Subversion of Identity* (London and New York: Routledge, 1990).

Butler, Judith, 'Gender Trouble, Feminist Theory, and Psychoanalytic Discourse', in L. J. Nicholson, ed., *Feminism/Postmodernism* (London and New York: Routledge, 1990), pp. 324–40.

Butler, Judith, 'Imitation and Gender Insubordination', in D. Fuss, ed., *Inside/Out: Lesbian Theories, Gay Theories* (London and New York: Routledge, 1991), pp. 13–31.

Calvino, Italo, *Cosmicomics*, trans. William Weaver (New York: Harcourt Brace Jovanovich, 1965).

Caputo, John D., ed., *The Religious* (Oxford: Blackwell, 2001).

Caputo, John D. and Scanlon, Michael J., eds, *God, The Gift, and Postmodernism* (Bloomington, Ind.: Indiana University Press, 1999).

Chambers, Iain, *Popular Culture: The Metropolitan Experience* (London: Methuen, 1986).

Chaney, David, *The Cultural Turn: Scene-Setting Essays on Contemporary Cultural Theory* (London and New York: Routledge, 1994).

Chodorow, Nancy, *The Reproduction of Mothering: Psychoanalysis and the Sociology of Gender* (Berkeley, Los Angeles and London: University of California Press, 1978).

Clough, Patricia Ticineto, *Feminist Thought: Desire, Power and Academic Discourse* (Oxford: Blackwell, 1994).

Collins, Jim, 'Genericity in the Nineties', in Jim Collins *et al.*, eds, *Film Theory Goes to the Movies* (London and New York: Routledge, 1993).

Collins, Jim, Radner, Hilary and Collins, Ava Preacher, eds, *Film Theory Goes to the Movies* (London and New York: Routledge, 1993).

Collins, Patricia Hill, 'The Social Construction of Black Feminist Thought', in B. Guy-Sheftall, ed., *Words of Fire: An Anthology of African-American Thought* (New York: New Press, 1995), pp. 338–57.

Connor, Steven, *Postmodernist Culture: An Introduction to Theories of the Contemporary* (Oxford and New York: Blackwell, 1989).

Coover, Robert, *Gerald's Party* (London: Paladin, 1986).

Creed, Barbara, 'From Here to Modernity – Feminism and Postmodernism', *Screen*, 28:2 (1987), pp. 47–67.

Crimp, Douglas, 'Pictures', *October*, 8 (1979).

Crowley, H. and Himmelweit, S., eds, *Knowing Women: Feminism and Knowledge* (Cambridge: Polity Press, 1992).

Currie, Mark, *Postmodern Narrative Theory* (London: Macmillan, 1998).

Debord, Guy, *The Society of the Spectacle* [1967] (Detroit, Mich.: Black and Red, 1970).

Deleuze, Gilles and Guattari, Félix, *Anti-Oedipus* [1972], trans. Robert Hurley, Mark Seem and Helen Lane (London: Athlone Press, 1984).

Delmar, Rosalind, 'What is Feminism?', in J. Mitchell and A. Oakley, eds, *What is Feminism?* (Oxford: Blackwell, 1986), pp. 8–33.

Derrida, Jacques, *Of Grammatology* [1967], trans. Gayatri Chakravorty Spivak (Baltimore, Md. and London: Johns Hopkins University Press, 1976).

Derrida, Jacques, *Specters of Marx: The State of the Debt, the Work of Mourning, and the New International* [1993], trans. Peggy Kamuf (London and New York: Routledge, 1994).

Derrida, Jacques, *The Monolingualism of the Other, or, The Prosthesis of Origin*, trans. Patrick Mensah (Stanford, Calif.: Stanford University Press, 1998).

Diderot, Denis, *Rameau's Nephew* [1761], trans. Leonard Tancock (Harmondsworth: Penguin, 1976).

Di Stefano, Christine, 'Dilemmas of Difference: Feminism, Modernity, and Postmodernism', in L. J. Nicholson, ed., *Feminism/Postmodernism* (London and New York: Routledge, 1990), pp. 63–82.

Docherty, Thomas, ed., *Postmodernism: A Reader* (Hemel Hempstead: Harvester, 1993).

Doctorow, E. L., *Ragtime* (London: Macmillan, 1975).

Eco, Umberto, *The Name of the Rose*, trans. William Weaver (New York: Harcourt Brace Jovanovich, 1983).

Eco, Umberto, *Reflections on 'The Name of the Rose'*, trans. William Weaver (London: Secker & Warburg, 1984).

Eco, Umberto, *Foucault's Pendulum*, trans. William Weaver (New York: Harcourt Brace Jovanovich, 1988).

Fekete, John, ed., *Life after Postmodernism: Essays on Value and Culture* (London: Macmillan, 1987).

Federman, Raymond, *Double or Nothing* (Chicago: Swallow, 1971).

Federman, Raymond, ed., *Surfiction: Fiction Now . . . and Tomorrow* (Chicago, Ill.: Swallow, 1975).

Federman, Raymond, *Take It or Leave It* (New York: Fiction Collective, 1976).

Filler, Martin, 'Building in the Past Tense', *The Times Literary Supplement*, 24 March 1989, pp. 295–6.

Firestone, Shulamith, *The Dialectic of Sex: The Case for Feminist Revolution* (London: Women's Press, 1979).

Fiske, John, *Media Matters* (Minneapolis, Minn.: University of Minnesota Press, 1994).

Flax, Jane, 'Gender as a Social Problem: In and for Feminist Theory', *Amerikastudien/ American Studies*, 31 (1986), pp. 193–213.

Flax, Jane, 'Postmodernism and Gender Relations in Feminist Theory', in L. J. Nicholson, ed., *Feminism/Postmodernism* (London and New York: 1990), pp. 39–62.

Forster, E. M., *Howards End* [1910], ed. Oliver Stallybrass (Harmondsworth: Penguin, 1989).

Foster, Hal, ed., *The Anti Aesthetic: Essays on Postmodern Culture* (Port Townsend, Wash.: Bay Press, 1983). Reprinted as *Postmodern Culture* (London and Concord, Mass.: Pluto, 1985).

Foucault, Michel, *The History of Sexuality*, vols I–III. vol. I: *The History of Sexuality: An Introduction* [1976], trans. Robert Hurley (Harmondsworth: Penguin, 1981); vol. II: *The Use of Pleasure* [1984], trans. Robert Hurley (Harmondsworth: Penguin, 1987); vol. III: *The Care of the Self* [1984], trans. Robert Hurley (Harmondsworth: Penguin, 1988).

Fowles, John, *The French Lieutenant's Woman* (London: Jonathan Cape, 1969).

Frampton, Kenneth, 'Towards a Critical Regionalism', in Hal Foster, ed., *Postmodern Culture* (London and Concord, Mass.: Pluto, 1985), pp. 16–30.

Fraser, Nancy and Nicholson, Linda J., 'Social Criticism without Philosophy: An Encounter between Feminism and Postmodernism', in L. J. Nicholson, ed., *Feminism/Postmodernism* (London and New York: Routledge, 1990), pp. 19–38.

Fried, Michael, *Three American Painters* (Cambridge, Mass.: Fogg Museum of Art, 1965).

Frith, S. and Horne, H., *Art into Pop* (London and New York: Methuen, 1987).

Fuss, D., ed., *Inside/Out: Lesbian Theories, Gay Theories* (London: Routledge, 1991).

Gass, William, *Willie Masters' Lonesome Wife* (Evanston, Ill.: Northwestern University Press, 1967).

Gellner, Ernest, *Postmodernism, Reason and Religion* (London: Routledge, 1992).

Giedion, Sigfried, *Buildings in France: Building in Iron, Building in Ferro-Concrete* [1928] (Santa Monica, Calif.: Getty Center, 1995).

Gilligan, Carol, *In a Different Voice: Psychological Theory and Women's Development* (Cambridge, Mass.: Harvard University Press, 1983).

Goodwin, Andrew, 'Popular Music and Postmodern Theory', *Cultural Studies*, 5:2 (1991), pp. 174–203.

Gray, Ann and McGuigan, Jim, eds, *Studying Culture: An Introductory Reader* (London: Edward Arnold, 1993).

Grossberg, Lawrence, 'The In-Difference of Television', *Screen*, 28 (1987), pp. 28–45.

Guha, Ranajit, *Dominance Without Hegemony: History and Power in Colonial India* (Cambridge, Mass. and London: Harvard University Press, 1997).

Guy-Sheftall, B., ed., *Words of Fire: An Anthology of African-American Thought* (New York: New Press, 1995).

Habermas, Jürgen, 'Modernity versus Postmodernity', *New German Critique*, 22 (1981), pp. 3–14.

Habermas, Jürgen, 'Modernity – An Incomplete Project', in H. Foster, ed., *Postmodern Culture* (London and Concord, Mass.: Pluto, 1985), pp. 3–15.

Habermas, Jürgen, *The Philosophical Discourse of Modernity* [1985], trans. Frederick Lawrence (Cambridge: Polity Press, 1987).

Halley, Peter, *Collected Essays 1981–1987* (New York: Sonabend Gallery, 1987).

Haraway, Donna, *Primate Visions: Gender, Race and Nature in the World of Modern Science* (London and New York: Routledge, 1989).

Haraway, Donna, 'A Manifesto for Cyborgs: Science, Technology, and Socialist Feminism in the 1980s', in L. J. Nicholson, ed., *Feminism/Postmodernism* (London and New York: Routledge, 1990), pp. 190–233.

Haraway, Donna, *Simians, Cyborgs, and Women* (London: Free Association Books, 1991).

Harding, Sandra, 'The Instability of the Analytical Categories of Feminist Theory', in H. Crowley and S. Himmelweit, eds, *Knowing Women: Feminism and Knowledge* (Cambridge: Polity Press, 1992), pp. 338–54.

Hartsock, Nancy, 'Foucault on Power: A Theory for Women', in L. J. Nicholson, ed., *Feminism/Postmodernism* (London and New York: Routledge, 1990), pp. 157–75.

Heidegger, Martin, *Poetry, Language, Thought*, trans. Alan Hofstadter (New York: Harper & Row, 1971).

Heller, Joseph, *Catch-22* (London: Jonathan Cape, 1962).

Hitchcock, Henry-Russell and Johnson, Philip, *The International Style*, 2nd edn (New York: W. W. Norton, 1966).

Humm, Maggie, ed., *Feminisms: A Reader* (Hemel Hempstead: Harvester, 1992).

Hutcheon, Linda, *A Poetics of Postmodernism: History, Theory, Fiction* (London and New York: Routledge, 1988).

Hutcheon, Linda, *The Politics of Postmodernism* (London: Routledge, 1989).

Huyssen, Andreas, *After the Great Divide: Modernism, Mass Culture, Postmodernism* (Bloomington, Ind.: Indiana University Press, 1986).

Irigaray, Luce, *This Sex Which is Not One,* trans.Catherine Porter, with Carolyn Burke (Ithaca, N.Y.: Cornell University Press, 1985).

Jameson, Fredric, 'Postmodernism, or, The Cultural Logic of Late Capitalism', *New Left Review*, 146 (1984), pp. 53–92.

Jameson, Fredric, 'Postmodernism and Consumer Society', in H. Foster, ed., *Postmodern Culture* (London and Concord, Mass.: Pluto, 1985).

Jameson, Fredric, *Postmodernism, or, The Cultural Logic of Late Capitalism* (Durham, N.C.: Duke University Press, 1991).

Jardine, Alice, 'The Demise of Experience: Fiction as Stranger than Truth?', in T. Docherty, ed., *Postmodernism: A Reader* (Hemel Hempstead: Harvester, 1993), pp. 433–42.

Jencks, Charles, *The Language of Post-Modern Architecture* [1975], 4th edn (London: Academy Editions, 1984).

Jencks, Charles, *What is Post-modernism?* (London: Art and Design, 1986).

Johnson, B. S., *The Unfortunates* (London: Panther, 1969).

Joyce, James, *A Portrait of the Artist as a Young Man* [1916], ed. Chester G. Anderson (Harmondsworth: Penguin, 1977).

Kaes, Anton, Jay, Martin and Dimendberg, Edward, eds, *The Weimar Republic Sourcebook* (Berkeley, Los Angeles and London: University of California Press, 1994).

Kant, Immanuel, *Critique of Practical Reason* [1788], trans. and ed. Mary McGregor (Cambridge: Cambridge University Press, 1997).

Kaplan, E. Ann, *Rocking Around the Clock: Music, Television, Postmodernism, and Consumer Culture* (London and New York: Routledge, 1987).

Kearney, Richard, ed., *Dialogues with Contemporary Continental Thinkers* (Manchester: Manchester University Press, 1984).

Kellner, Douglas, *Jean Baudrillard: From Marxism to Postmodernism and Beyond* (Cambridge: Polity Press, 1989).

Kesey, Ken, *One Flew Over the Cuckoo's Nest* (New York: Viking, 1962).

Kuhn, Annette, *The Power of the Image: Essays on Representation and Sexuality* (London: Routledge and Kegan Paul, 1985).

Kuhn, Thomas, *The Structure of Scientific Revolutions* (Chicago, Ill. and London: University of Chicago Press, 1962).

Laclau, Ernesto and Mouffe, Chantal, *Hegemony and Socialist Strategy: Towards a Radical Democratic Politics* (London: Verso, 1985).

Le Corbusier, *The Decorative Art of Today* [1925], trans. James I. Dunnett (London: Architectural Press, 1987).

Le Corbusier, *Towards a New Architecture* [1923], trans. Frederick Etchells (Oxford: Butterworth, 1989).

Lem, Stanislaw, *Solaris*, trans. Joanna Kilmartin and Steve Cox (London: Faber & Faber, 1961).

Lovibond, Sabina, 'Feminism and Postmodernism', in T. Docherty, ed., *Postmodernism: A Reader* (Hemel Hempstead: Harvester, 1993), pp. 390–414.

Lyotard, Jean-François, *The Postmodern Condition: A Report on Knowledge* [1979], trans. Geoffrey Bennington and Brian Massumi (Manchester: Manchester University Press, 1984).

Lyotard, Jean-François (with Jean-Loup Thébaud), *Just Gaming* [1979], trans. Wlad Godzich (Manchester: Manchester University Press, 1985).

Lyotard, Jean-François, *The Differend: Phrases in Dispute* [1983], trans. George Van Den Abbeele (Manchester: Manchester University Press, 1988).

Lyotard, Jean-François, *The Inhuman: Reflections on Time* [1988], trans. Geoffrey Bennington and Rachel Bowlby (Oxford: Blackwell, 1991).

Lyotard, Jean-François, *Libidinal Economy* [1974], trans. Iain Hamilton Grant (London: Athlone Press, 1993).

Lyotard, Jean-François, *Lessons on the Analytic of the Sublime*, trans. Elizabeth Rottenberg (Berkeley, Calif.: Stanford University Press, 1994).

McCaffery, Larry, *Postmodern Fiction: A Bio-Biographical Guide* (Westport, Conn.: Greenwood, 1986).

McHale, Brian, *Postmodernist Fiction* (London and New York: Methuen, 1987).

McRobbie, Angela, *Postmodernism and Popular Culture* (London and New York: Routledge, 1994).

Mercer, Kobena, *Welcome to the Jungle* (London: Routledge, 1994).

Milbank, John, Pickstock, Catherine and Ward, Graham, eds, *Radical Orthodoxy: A New Theology* (London: Routledge, 1999).

Millett, Kate, *Sexual Politics* [1970] (London: Virago, 1977).

Mitchell, J. and Oakley, A., eds, *What is Feminism?* (Oxford: Blackwell, 1986).

Modleski, Tania, *Feminism Without Women: Culture and Criticism in a 'Postfeminist' Age* (London and New York: Routledge, 1991).

Morris, Meaghan, *The Pirate's Fiancée: Feminism, Reading, Postmodernism* (London: Verso, 1988).

Moseley, Rachel, 'Makeover Takeover on British Television', *Screen*, 41:3 (2000), pp. 299–314.

Nicholson, L. J., ed., *Feminism/Postmodernism* (London and New York: Routledge, 1990).

O'Brian, John, ed., *Clement Greenberg: The Collected Essays and Criticism*, vols 1 and 3 (Chicago, Ill. and London: Chicago University Press, 1986, 1989).

Ogersby, Bill and Gough-Yates, Anna, eds, *Action TV: Tough Guys, Smooth Operators and Foxy Chicks* (London: Routledge, 2001).

Omnès, Roland, *Quantum Philosophy: Understanding and Interpreting Contemporary Science* (Princeton, N.J.: Princeton University Press, 1999).

Owens, Craig, 'The Discourse of Others: Feminists and Postmodernism', in H. Foster, ed., *Postmodern Culture* [1983] (London and Concord, Mass.: Pluto, 1985), pp. 57–82.

Perec, Georges, *Life: A User's Manual*, trans. David Bellos (London: Collins Harvill, 1978).

Plantinga, Alvin, *Warranted Christian Belief* (New York: Oxford University Press, 2000).

Prigogine, Ilya and Stengers, Isabelle, *Order Out of Chaos: Man's New Dialogue with Nature* (London: Heinemann, 1984).

Pynchon, Thomas, *V.* (London: Jonathan Cape, 1963).

Pynchon, Thomas, *The Crying of Lot 49* (Philadelphia: Lippincott, 1966).

Pynchon, Thomas, *Gravity's Rainbow* (London: Jonathan Cape, 1973).

Pynchon, Thomas, *Vineland* (London: Secker & Warburg, 1990).

Pynchon, Thomas, *Mason & Dixon* (London: Jonathan Cape, 1997).

Rand, Ayn, *The Fountainhead* [1943] (London: HarperCollins, 1971).

Reed, Ishmael, *Yellow Back Radio Broke-Down* (New York: Doubleday, 1969).

Reed, Ishmael, *Flight to Canada* (New York: Random House, 1976).

Rich, Adrienne, *Blood, Bread, and Poetry: Selected Prose 1979–85* (New York: Norton, 1986).

Rorty, Richard, 'Habermas and Lyotard on Postmodernity', in Richard J. Bernstein, ed., *Habermas and Modernity* (Cambridge: Polity Press, 1985), pp. 161–75.

Royle, Nicholas, ed., *Deconstructions: A Users' Guide* (London: Macmillan, 2000).

Saussure, Ferdinand de, *Course in General Linguistics* [1916], ed. C. Bally, A. Sechehaye and A. Reidlinger, trans. Wade Baskin (London: Peter Owen, 1960).

Sim, Stuart, *Fundamentalist World: The New Dark Age of Dogma* (Cambridge: Icon, 2004).

Simon, Herbert, *Sciences of the Artificial*, 3rd edn (Cambridge, Mass.: MIT Press, 1996).

Sontag, Susan, *Against Interpretation, and Other Essays* (New York: Dell, 1966).

Spivak, Gayatri Chakravorty, *The Post-Colonial Critic: Interviews, Strategies, Dialogues*, ed. Sarah Harasym (London and New York: Routledge, 1990).

Stelarc, 'Towards the Post-human: From Psycho-body to Cyber-system', *Architectural Design [Profile 118]*, 65:11–12 (1995), pp. 90–6.

Storey, John, ed., *Cultural Theory and Popular Culture: A Reader*, 2nd edn (Harlow: Prentice Hall, 1998).

Storey, John, ed., *Cultural Theory and Popular Culture: An Introduction*, 3rd edn (Harlow: Prentice Hall, 2001)

Storey, John, 'The Sixties in the Nineties', in Bill Ogersby and Anna Gough-Yates, eds, *Action TV: Tough Guys, Smooth Operators and Foxy Chicks* (London: Routledge, 2001).

Sukenick, Ronald, *The Death of the Novel and Other Stories* (New York: Dial, 1969).

Sukenick, Ronald, *Out* (Chicago, Ill.: Swallow, 1973).

Swift, Graham, *Waterland* (London: William Heinemann, 1983).

Tanner, Tony, *City of Words: American Fiction, 1950–1970* (London: Jonathan Cape, 1971).

Toulmin, Stephen, *The Return to Cosmology: Postmodern Science and the Theology of Nature* (Berkeley, Calif.: University of California Press, 1982).

Toynbee, Arnold, *A Study of History*, vols I–VI, abridged by D. C. Somervell (New York and Oxford: Oxford University Press, 1947).

Vardy, Peter, *Being Human: Fulfilling Genetic and Spiritual Potential* (London: Darton, Longman & Todd, 2003).

Venturi, Robert, *Contradiction and Complexity in Architecture* (New York: Museum of Modern Architecture, 1968).

Venturi, Robert, *Learning from Las Vegas: The Forgotten Symbolism of Architectural Form* [1972] (Cambridge, Mass. and London: MIT Press, 1977).

Vonnegut, Kurt, *Slaughterhouse-Five* (New York: Dial, 1969).

Ward, Graham, *The Postmodern God: A Theological Reader* (Oxford: Blackwell, 1997).

Ward, Graham, *The Blackwell Companion to Postmodern Theology* (Oxford: Blackwell, 2001).

Waugh, Patricia, *Metafiction: The Theory and Practice of Self-Conscious Fiction* (London and New York: Methuen, 1984).

Wilson, Elizabeth, 'Fashion and Postmodernism', in John Storey, ed., *Cultural Theory and Popular Culture: A Reader* (Harlow: Prentice Hall, 1998), pp. 403–13.

Wollstonecraft, Mary, *A Vindication of the Rights of Women* [1792] (Harmondsworth: Penguin, 1992).

Young, Robert, *White Mythologies: Writing History and the West* (London and New York: Routledge, 1990).

Ziman, John, ed., *Technological Innovation as an Evolutionary Process* (Cambridge: Cambridge University Press, 2000).

INDEX

Items in **bold** also have their own entry in Part II, Names and terms; page references in bold indicate where the entry is located.